Beyond the Legacy of Genghis Khan

Beyond the Legacy of Genghis Khan

Edited by

Linda Komaroff

BRILL

LEIDEN • BOSTON
2013

This paperback was originally published in hardback under ISBN 978 90 04 15083 6

"The (LS font name(s)) font(s) used toprint this work is(are) available from Linguist's Software, Inc., P.O. Box 580, Edmonds. WA98020-0580 USA tel (425) 775-1130 www.linguistsoftware .com."

Cover illustration: Enthronement Scene, illustration from the Diez Albums, Iran (possiblyTabriz), early 14th century. Ink, colors, and gold on paper. Staatsbibliothek zu Berlin-Preußischer Kulturbesitz, Orientabteilung (Diez A, fol. 70, S. 22)

The Library of Congress has cataloged the hardcover edition as follows:

Beyond the legacy of Genghis Khan / edited by Linda Komaroff.
p. cm. — (Islamic history and civilization. Studies and texts ; v. 64)
Includes bibliographical references and index.
ISBN-13: 978-90-04-15083-6
ISBN-10: 90-04-15083-8 (hardback : alk. paper) 1. Iran—History—1256-1500—Congresses. 2. Mongols—Iran—History—Congresses. 3. Ilkhanid dynasty—Congresses. I. Komaroff, Linda, 1953- II. Title. III. Series.

DS289.B49 2006
955'.026—dc22

2006049041

ISBN 978-90-04-24340-8 (paperback)
ISBN 978-90-47-41857-3 (e-book)

This book is printed on acid-free paper.

MIX
Paper from responsible sources
FSC® C109576
www.fsc.org

Printed by Printforce, the Netherlands

CONTENTS

Culture and Commerce in the Mongol World Empire

Lifestyles at the Courts of the Ruling Elite

LIST OF ILLUSTRATIONS

Color Plates

Black and White Figures

NOTES ON TRANSLITERATIONS AND DATES

1. The transliteration of Arabic and Persian (excluding place names) is in accordance with the system found in the *International Journal of Middle Eastern Studies*, with some exceptions. For instance, the Persian consonants v and ż have been rendered as w and ḍ.

2. The transliteration of Chinese words and names is generally given according to the Wade-Giles system. In instances where the pinyin system had been used it has been left accordingly.

3. The tolerance of contributors and readers alike is requested with regard to the transliterations of Turkish and Mongolian, which, if nothing else, have hopefully been realized with some degree of consistency. 'Genghis Khan' has at times been given in preference to 'Chinggis Khan,' reflecting the original usage of this name in the title of the exhibition and the symposium that inspired this publication.

4. Dates are given according to the common or Christian era, which for the papers dealing with the Islamic world are preceded by *hijrī*, or Muslim, dates.

LIST OF CONTRIBUTORS

Dr. Sheila S. Blair, Fine Arts Department, Boston College, 140 Commonwealth Avenue, Chestnut Hill, MA 02467, USA

Dr. Jonathan M. Bloom, Fine Arts Department, Boston College, 140 Commonwealth Avenue, Chestnut Hill, MA 02467, USA

Dr. Devin DeWeese, Department of Central Eurasian Studies, Indiana University, Goodbody Hall 157, 1011 East Third Street, Bloomington, IN 47405, USA

Dr. Teresa Fitzherbert, Creswell Photographic Archive, Department of Eastern Art, Ashmolean Museum, Beaumont Street, Oxford OX1 2PH, United Kingdom

Dr. Bert G. Fragner, Institut für Iranistik der Österreichischen Akademie der Wissenschaften, Prinz-Eugen-Str. 8-10, 1. Stock, A-1040 Vienna, Austria

Dr. Robert Hillenbrand, Fine Art Department, Edinburgh University, 19 George Square, Edinburgh EH8 9LD, Scotland, United Kingdom

Dr. Dietrich Huff, Deutsches Archäologisches Institut, Postbox 330014, 14191 Berlin, Germany

Dr. Ralph Kauz, Institut für Iranistik der Österreichischen Akademie der Wissenschaften, Prinz-Eugen-Str. 8-10, 1. Stock, A-1040 Vienna, Austria

Dr. Linda Komaroff, Department of Middle East, Los Angeles County Museum of Art, 5905 Wilshire Boulevard, Los Angeles, CA 90036, USA

Dr. Dickran Kouymjian, Armenian Studies Program, California State University, Fresno, 5245 N. Backer PB4, Fresno, CA 93740, USA

Dr. Mark Kramarovsky, State Hermitage Museum, 34 Dvortsovaya Naberezhnaya, St. Petersburg 190000, Russia

Dr. Donald P. Little, Institute of Islamic Studies, McGill University, 3485, rue McTavish, Suite 319, Montreal H3A 1Y1, Canada

Dr. Charles Melville, Faculty of Oriental Studies, University of Cambridge, Sidgwick Avenue, Cambridge CB3 9DA, United Kingdom

Dr. David Morgan, History Department, University of Wisconsin, Madison, 4113 Humanities, 455 North Park Street, Madison, WI 53706, USA

Dr. Bernard O'Kane, Department of Arabic Studies, The American University in Cairo, 113 Kasr El Aini Street, P.O. Box 2511, Cairo 11511, Egypt

Dr. Judith Pfeiffer, The Oriental Institute, University of Oxford, Pusey Lane, Oxford OX1 2LE, United Kingdom

Dr. George Saliba, Department of Middle East and Asian Languages and Cultures, Columbia University, 604 Kent Hall, New York, NY 10027, USA

Dr. Noriyuki Shiraishi, Faculty of Humanities, Niigata University, 2-8050 Ikarashi, 950–2181 Niigata, Japan

Dr. Marianna Shreve Simpson, 333 Tuscany Road, Baltimore, MD 21210, USA

Dr. Eleanor Sims, 331 Carlisle Mansion, Carlisle Place, London SW1P 1EZ, United Kingdom

Dr. John Masson Smith, Jr., History Department, University of California, Berkeley, 3229 Dwinelle Hall, Berkeley, CA 94720, USA

Mr. Abolala Soudavar, 8403 Westglen Dr., Houston, TX 77063, USA

Dr. Oliver Watson, Department of Eastern Art, Ashmolean Museum, Beaumont Street, Oxford OX1 2PH, United Kingdom

Dr. Elaine Wright, Islamic Collections, The Chester Beatty Library, Dublin Castle, Dublin 2, Ireland

ACKNOWLEDGMENTS

It is usually a pleasure to write the acknowledgments to a publication, not only because it generally signals the end of a lengthy project (in this case one that was nearly a decade in the planning and rendering), but also for the reason that it gives one a chance to count one's blessings, so to speak, and to thank those responsible. First and foremost, I would like to thank each of the contributors to this volume who approached the task of turning their symposium papers into full-fledged articles with great diligence, enormous skill and erudition, and in most cases in a timely manner. For those who were less than timely, I am nonetheless grateful for their genial responses to my relentless harassment. In addition, I would like to acknowledge those who participated in the symposium on which this publication is based but did not contribute to this volume: Stephen Album and Priscilla Soucek, who presented papers, and Stefano Carboni and Morris Rossabi, who served as session chairs.

This publication and the symposium that preceded it would not have been possible without the generous support of the Hagop Kevorkian Fund, as well as Amina and the late Ahmad Adaya and the late Joan Palevsky. In the blessings' department I would certainly have to count the Adaya family, Joan Palevsky, and especially Ralph Minasian and the Kevorkian Fund, who have on multiple occasions supported projects I have proposed. I would also like to express thanks to the National Endowment for the Humanities for its financial support for the exhibition *The Legacy of Genghis Khan* and its related programs, including the symposium that led to this publication. Finally, I am most grateful to the Ancient Art Council at the Los Angeles County Museum of Art for its generous assistance.

At the Los Angeles County Museum of Art, where this volume was edited, I am grateful to the administration for recognizing that endeavors such as this are integral to the intellectual life of the institution, and to the many colleagues here who knowingly or unknowingly eased the burden of this project. Among these I would especially like to thank Jaclynne Kerner, Camilla Chandler Frost Postdoctoral Fellow in Islamic Art (2004–6), for many matters large and small, and in particular for systematizing the substantial bibliography that buttresses this volume. I am also pleased to acknowledge Sara Cody (associate editor at LACMA) for her adroit skills as a copy editor, as well as for her good-humored and unflappable responses to innumerable phone calls and unannounced visits. Thanks, too, to Megan Knox, in Middle East Art, and to Steve Oliver in Photographic Services.

Finally, I would like to express my gratitude to Trudy Kamperveen and her colleagues at Brill, as well as their anonymous reader, for believing that this publication would make a valuable contribution to the study of Islamic history and civilization.

Linda Komaroff

INTRODUCTION

LINDA KOMAROFF

An international symposium was held June 13–15, 2003, at the Los Angeles County Museum of Art in connection with the exhibition *The Legacy of Genghis Khan: Courtly Art and Culture in Western Asia, 1256–1353*, co-organized by LACMA and the Metropolitan Museum of Art. The exhibition was the first to examine the important artistic developments that occurred in the Iranian world as an effect of the Mongol conquests of western and eastern Asia. As a preliminary investigation into a period of extraordinary creativity and momentous cultural achievements, *The Legacy of Genghis Khan* and its associated publication raised or left unanswered many questions, offering symposium participants ample opportunity to move beyond the confines of the exhibition and its catalogue—hence the title of this volume. Although not every paper presented at the symposium could be included here, two of the session chairs contributed papers germane to the topic. Taken as a whole, this collection should provide a good overview of a still-evolving area of scholarship examined from multiple perspectives by means of diverse disciplinary practices.

Through war and conquest, Genghis Khan and the Mongols created the largest land empire in history—stretching at its greatest extent from Hungary to Korea. The types of cultural collisions resulting from the creation of this world empire particularly fascinate in today's global age; most recently, the Mongol invasions have been viewed as an often disquieting parallel to contemporary events in the Middle East (also see David Morgan's contribution to this volume). The opening of *The Legacy of Genghis Khan* in Los Angeles in the spring of 2003 (figs. 1–2), for example, was covered by local media in close relation to the U.S.-led invasion of Iraq. One headline in the *Los Angeles Times* proclaimed: "Beauty from a troubled land. As war threatens Iraq's treasures, LACMA prepares 'Legacy of Genghis Khan'."[1] Eerily, American and British troops entered Baghdad the

[1] Suzanne Muchnic, *Los Angeles Times*, March 28, 2003, Calendar section, 1, 27.

day the exhibition previewed to the press—April 9.[2]

Not all reactions to the exhibition and especially to its title were quite so preoccupied with contemporary events. Instead, for some members of greater Los Angeles's very large Iranian diaspora community, it was the thirteenth century all over again as some feelings ran fairly high against Genghis Khan and the Mongols.[3] Though by no means pervasive, this mindset generally did not allow for the possibility that the Mongol conquerors' promotion of pan-Asian trade, methods of governance, avid taste for luxury goods, and practice of relocating skilled personnel might have resulted in an unprecedented cross-fertilization of cultural ideas throughout Eurasia. Nor was it considered that the so-called 'Pax Mongolica' might have had the effect of energizing Iranian art and infusing it with new meanings and forms that were subsequently spread throughout the Islamic world. Nevertheless, this reaction was a good reminder of the very deep imprint that the Mongol invasions left on the lands they conquered and in the collective memories of their inhabitants and their descendants.

The ultimate irony is that the Ilkhanids in Iran, as well as their Yüan cousins in China, became strong proponents of their adoptive cultural patrimony. In Iran, for instance, the Ilkhanids, under the guidance of their Iranian advisors, co-opted the trappings and symbolism of ancient Persian kingship by building a palace at Takht-i

[2] Again from the *Los Angeles Times*: "As Baghdad fell to American and British forces Wednesday morning, the Los Angeles County Museum of Art was holding a preview of its new exhibition 'The Legacy of Genghis Khan: Courtly Art and Culture in Western Asia, 1256–1353.'...The juxtaposition was vaguely unnerving." (Christopher Knight, *Los Angeles Times* April 12, 2003, Calendar section, 10–11.) According to the less staid *LA Weekly*, "The timing of this exhibit is ridiculous. The show...outlines the artistic record of the Mongol conquest of the Middle East, culminating in the fall of Baghdad in 1258 to the greatest pre-corporate terrestrial empire in history. It opened...as U.S. troops made their anticlimactic advance on the stronghold of Tikrit, having only just liberated Baghdad a few days earlier." (Doug Harvey, "Hordes of Babylon" *LA Weekly*, May 9–15, 2003.)

[3] One member of this community stated (nearly verbatim) that if not for Genghis Khan, Iran would have put a man on the moon. This underscores a commonly held Iranian belief that the Mongol invasions set Iranian civilization back by a century or more—or perhaps even a thousand years if one closely follows Ḥamdallāh Mustawfī Qazwīnī, the late-Ilkhanid geographer and historian, who said that the destruction wrought by the Mongol invasions "will not be repaired in a thousand years, even if no other calamity happens; and the world will not return to the condition in which it was before that event." See Mustawfī (1915–19), vol. 2, 27.

Sulayman (see the paper by Dietrich Huff) specifically because of the site's ritual association with the coronation of the Sasanian king. The palace itself was even decorated with glazed tiles inscribed with verses abridged from the Iranian national epic, the *Shāhnāma*, possibly selected and subtly revised to suggest that they were addressed to the resident, the Ilkhanid ruler.[4] In a now-dispersed illustrated manuscript of the so-called Great Mongol *Shāhnāma* (see the paper by Eleanor Sims)—probably produced for the last Ilkhanid ruler, Abū Saʿīd—Mongol legitimacy is underscored through the paintings, which depict the pre-Islamic kings and heroes of Iran recast in the guise of Mongols. For example, an illustration to the section on the founding of the Sasanian dynasty culminating in Ardashir taking captive Ardavan (the last Parthian ruler) clearly depicts Ardashir and his entourage as Mongol horsemen, who are distinguished by the fabric and design of their clothes (about which more will be said below).[5] The painting recommends that the universal story lies not only in the narrative but also resonates through the details. In the larger view, the picture is far richer and more complicated than sheer destruction,[6] as this collection of papers ably demonstrates.

These papers offer a wide-ranging account of the Mongols in western and eastern Asia in the aftermath of Genghis Khan's disruptive invasions of the early thirteenth century, focusing on the significant cultural, social, religious and political changes that followed in their wake. An important subtext of this volume (and a major theme of the exhibition and the related symposium) is the cultural transmission that occurred in concert with the establishment of a Mongol world empire. One of the main figures in this area of cross-cultural transasiatic research is Thomas Allsen; though he was unable to participate in the symposium, his publications, particularly his *Commodity and Exchange in the Mongol Empire*, were a major source of inspiration and information for *The Legacy of Genghis Khan* exhibition and catalogue.[7]

As Allsen's work indicates, the Mongols placed great emphasis on

[4] See Masuya (2002), also Melikian-Chirvani (1991).

[5] See Komaroff and Carboni, eds. (2002), fig. 163.

[6] For an interesting revisionist view of the early Ilkhanid period characterized as an Iranian renaissance see Lane, G. (2003).

[7] Allsen (1997), also Allsen (2001; his work also informs several of the papers in this volume.

the production and acquisition of luxury textiles—especially so-called cloth of gold, or *nasīj*, a form of portable or wearable wealth. Based on the evidence of the extant textiles, and in relation to other arts of the Ilkhanid period, I have elsewhere proposed that this medium was perhaps the primary carrier of East Asian (mainly Chinese) visual culture to the West.[8] Given the significant role of textiles in cultural transmission and interchange, and considering that this important medium was not touched upon at the symposium, I will insert this subject here by very briefly considering a group of spectacular tent panels in the Museum of Islamic Art, Doha, and a single panel in the David Collection, Copenhagen, that were included in the exhibition (pl. 1a).[9] The tent hangings, which will be the focus of a more extensive study, help to delineate one process by which visual language was altered by external cultural forces.[10]

The group of textiles is comprised of five full panels and a narrow, vertical strip of a sixth (in Doha) and a vertically divided half panel (in Copenhagen). Each of the five full panels is defined by narrow, vertical bands forming slender columns supporting a pair of 'cloud point' arches. When placed side by side (pls. 1a–b), the panels suggest an arcade formed of engaged columns and shallow, arch-like niches of a type that came into common use in Iranian architecture by the eleventh century and continued into the Ilkhanid period and beyond. The intended sequential arrangement of these wall-coverings is indicated by the fact that each panel has only two of the three sets of 'columns' necessary to support the arcade; each is completed by the next panel. Neither the original number of panels nor the size of the structure they once decorated can be conjectured, although it seems likely that were made for an impermanent edifice such as a tent.[11] If so, the group of textiles would represent the earliest surviving tent interior.

[8] Komaroff (2002).

[9] Although the tent panels were included in *The Legacy of Genghis Khan* exhibition, only the David Collection panel was published in the catalogue; see Komaroff and Carboni, eds. (2002), no. 73, fig. 42. For the Doha panels, see Thompson (2004), no. 19, where the computer-generated reconstruction seems to follow the installation of the panels at LACMA.

[10] This has been undertaken in collaboration with Nobuko Kajitani, who has been far more conscientious than I in pursuit of this project; any mistakes contained here are entirely my own. I am grateful to Oliver Watson, formerly Chief Curator at the Museum of Islamic Art, Doha, for permission to publish the tent panels.

[11] On the types of princely and ceremonial tents that can be associated with

Even after they established capital cities and built palatial residences, the Ilkhanid court remained itinerant. Seasonal camps, which could include both permanent and temporary structures, were the location for many important royal events, ranging quite literally from birth to death.[12] The types of princely tentage that were used on ceremonial occasions are described in contemporary historical and traveler's accounts; they were enormous, holding as many as two thousand men, and constructed of costly and elaborately worked textiles.[13] One was portrayed as "that gilded cupola and heaven-like tent," so striking that "the disc of the sun lost its brightness out of jealousy...and the resplendent moon wore a sulky expression."[14] Tents were also depicted in manuscript illustrations of the Ilkhanid period, although none matches contemporary descriptions in terms of either scale or opulence.[15]

Any structure embellished by these panels would have been truly opulent. They were woven from now-faded red silk and gilt thread, of which the latter is of two types—threads wrapped with a paper substrate and threads having an animal-based substrate, a combination that marks a rare technical occurrence.[16] The panels are elaborately decorated (within the previously described architectural framework) by a wealth of motifs reflecting the textiles' hybrid style (pl. 1b). Beneath the 'cloud-point' arch is a group of four large, vertically oriented roundels, each with a pair of confronted roosters with elaborate tail feathers flanking a stylized Tree of Life. The roundels alternate with pairs of smaller lobed medallions bearing a coiled dragon. While the latter is ultimately of East Asian inspiration, the confronted birds with Tree of Life motif has a long history in Islamic art, including pre-Mongol and Mongol-period Iranian textiles.[17] The roundels are framed by interlocking circles, a well-known motif in twelfth- and

---

the Mongols and their kin, see the magisterial work by Peter Andrews (1999).

12 Masuya (2002), 81–84. Also see Allsen (1997), 13–15.

13 Masuya (2002), 78.

14 Juwaynī (1958), vol. 2, 616.

15 Andrews (1999), pls. 95–108.

16 Komaroff and Carboni, eds. (2002), no. 73, based on Kajitani's initial research.

17 Both confronted and affronted birds occur. For pre-Mongol examples, see, for instance, Wiet (1947), pls. 7, 9, 12, and 16. Several Mongol examples are illustrated in Wardwell (1988–89), figs. 12, 13, 36, and 38. On the symbolism of roosters in Persian art and literature see Daneshvari (1986), 56–67.

thirteenth-century Iranian metalwork. Also mixing East and West, the background is filled with a scrolling, arabesque-like peony design and small floral medallions bearing a stylized bird, possibly a phoenix. Across the upper edge of the panels is a pearl border, a type of design found in Iranian textiles dating back to Sasanian times; this was originally surmounted by a pseudo-Kufic inscriptional band of which only a fraction survives on some panels.

As already noted, the architectural frieze depicted by the conjoined panels was already well-known in Iranian architecture and architectural decoration prior to the Mongol invasions, including the use of decorative roundels or medallions, which continue into the Ilkhanid period.[18] With the substitution of the Chinese 'cloud-point' for the Iranian arch in the tent panels, the arcade has been updated to reflect the new, more cosmopolitan and eclectic visual language. Perhaps somewhat ironically, the textile arcade lining the interior of a tent would have imaginatively echoed the form and, to some extent, the decoration of a more permanent domed structure. Even the original placement of the pseudo-Kufic inscription above the tent arcade relates to the placement of monumental inscriptions that encircle the upper walls just beneath the transitional zone of the dome,[19] while medallions bearing confronted and entwined birds occur, for example, within shallow arched niches in a tomb tower at Kharraqan, c. 1067–68.[20]

The particular circumstances that produced the stylistic, iconographic, and technical fusion demonstrated by these panels and by a number of other contemporary textiles are documented by historical evidence.[21] Under both Genghis Khan (d. 1227) and his son and

---

[18] For example, the decorative frieze of trilobed arches in the twelfth-century Masjid-i Jāmiʿ, Qazwin; see Baer (1973–74), fig. 16. For Ilkhanid examples see Wilber (1955), figs. 141 and 200 (both interior views); the latter example, the so-called Imāmzāda of ʿAlī b. Abū Maʿālī of 1359–60, incorporates decorative medallions.

[19] One could even imagine that the open space above the textile arcade was meant to be understood as a dome or even a conical roof, but here we enter the arena of which came first: did tents inspire so-called tomb towers or did the buildings inspire or even invite comparison with tents? (See quote above from Juwaynī.)

[20] I am grateful to Yury Karev for the reference to the painted decoration at Kharraqan. For an interpretation of the possible meaning of this decoration see Daneshvari (1986), 41 ff. On the interrelationship between textiles and architecture see Golombek (1988), 34–36.

[21] For other contemporary textiles see Komaroff and Carboni, eds. (2002), nos. 69–72; 74–76.

successor Ögödei (r. 1229–41), communities of textile workers were established on the southern boundaries of the Mongol homeland by the relocation of captured Iranian artists. The artists were taken primarily from cities in Khurasan (such as Herat, which was renowned for its silk and gold cloth) and in Turkestan. In a different direction, Chinese textile workers were resettled in eastern Central Asia to manufacture fine stuffs for the Mongol overlords there.[22] This transfer of artists and their techniques facilitated a kind of hybrid development in textile art and its technology, which for a time articulated the new visual language of the Mongol world empire.

The tent panels, which were likely made somewhere in eastern Iran or western Central Asia where their architectural form would have been best appreciated, represent a new and short-lived artistic *koiné* expressed primarily through luxury objects, in which the opulence of the material itself, above and even beyond its decoration, conveyed a message of status. It is certainly this quest for status on the part of the Mongols that helped to drive the transmission of textile arts.[23] Although only a few illustrated Persian manuscripts survive from the late thirteenth century, the depictions they contain of the new Mongol rulers and ruling elite convey the conquerors not only by their physiognomies but also quite specifically by the silk and gold fabrics of which their clothes, accoutrements, and even horses' accessories are made.[24] Whether artists included these details based on observation or through coercion is not possible to say, but considering some of the disparaging remarks made about the Mongols' alleged sacerdotal preferences—for example the historian Juwaynī noted that before Genghis Khan the Mongols wore clothing made "of the skins of dogs and mice"—their acquisition of elaborate silk textiles was clearly a notable improvement.[25] The Mongols neither wove the sumptuous cloth of gold that they craved nor is it likely that their personal taste played much of a role in the design of the textiles, but the structures they set in place brokering all manner of cultural exchanges between East and West helped to create, however

[22] Allsen (1997), 38–45; Rossabi (1997), 14–15.

[23] See Allsen (1997), 46–47, on the symbolic value of clothes for the Mongols.

[24] See Komaroff (2002), 173–74.

[25] See Juwaynī (1958), vol. 1, 21.

briefly, a new mode of artistic expression, which in turn laid the foundation for still greater achievements.[26]

As already indicated, this discussion of the tent panels will evolve into a deeper study, but it serves to highlight here the types of issues concerning not only art but governance, diplomacy, commerce, religion, court life, and urban culture in the Mongol world empire as presented at the 2003 symposium and now distilled in this volume. This collection of papers demonstrates both the scope and the depth of Mongol-related studies and that will, I hope, inspire and provoke further research.

---

[26] The mechanism for this is proposed in Komaroff (2002), 184 ff.

CULTURE AND COMMERCE IN THE MONGOL WORLD EMPIRE

CULTURAL TRANSMISSION AND EXCHANGE IN THE MONGOL EMPIRE: NOTES FROM THE BIOGRAPHICAL DICTIONARY OF IBN AL-FUWAṬĪ

DEVIN DEWEESE

Biographical dictionaries have remained relatively poorly utilized for the political, social, and even cultural history of the Mongol era. This is especially true for one of the most remarkable works of the genre, compiled at the beginning of the fourteenth century by Kamāl al-Dīn ʿAbd al-Razzāq b. Aḥmad, known as Ibn al-Fuwaṭī, who was perhaps uniquely well-placed to produce a compendium of biographical data on the scholars, writers, and statesmen of the Muslim world down to his time: through most of his life he had direct and unparalleled access to the major library collections of the western part of the Mongol-ruled world. His biographical work, the *Majmaʿ al-ādāb fī muʿjam al-alqāb* (arranged by *laqab*, the 'honorific' title of the form 'Kamāl al-Dīn,' etc., and then alphabetically by *ism* or common name within each *laqab*) is of tremendous value even though it survives only in abbreviated and fragmentary form—abbreviated because what we have is said to be not from the original work, but from an abbreviation (*Talkhīṣ*) that Ibn al-Fuwaṭī made himself, reducing the original work's fifty volumes to just five, and fragmentary because only a portion of the putative abbreviation survives, namely the sections covering *laqab*s from "Izz al-Dīn' through 'Muwaffaq al-Dīn,' i.e., the letters *ʿayn* through *mīm*.

The surviving portion is preserved in two manuscripts, one in Damascus and the other in Lahore, which were both copied by Ibn al-Fuwaṭī himself (he was known as an excellent scribe); the Damascus volume covers the letters *ʿayn* through *qāf*, the Lahore copy *kāf* through *mīm*. The latter copy was the first to be edited and published, by Muḥammad ʿAbd al-Quddūs al-Qāsimī, in a serialized and handwritten form, appearing in a supplement (from 1939) and in regular volumes (1940–47, volumes 16–23) of the *Oriental College Magazine* from Lahore.[1] The Damascus manuscript was edited and published

[1] This edition was generally difficult to obtain; when I began going through Ibn

by Muṣṭafā Jawād, in Damascus, in three volumes, between 1962 and 1965; this publication has been much better known, and provided the chief access to Ibn al-Fuwaṭī's work for over thirty years.[2] In 1995, finally, the entire surviving section of Ibn al-Fuwaṭī's biographical dictionary was republished (not re-edited from the manuscripts, but newly typeset even for the portion published by Jawād) and issued in five volumes, with a sixth volume for the index; the new edition was prepared by Muḥammad al-Kāẓim in Qum, and was published in Tehran.[3] This latest edition, easy to use, well-indexed, and in several respects superior to the earlier versions, makes the text more widely accessible and manageable.

Ibn al-Fuwaṭī's life is known primarily through comments in the surviving portions of his work and from entries on him in later biographical dictionaries.[4] He was born in Baghdad in 642/1244, and his early education included, beyond memorization of the Qurʾān, close study of *ḥadīth* with the famous traditionist Muḥyī al-Dīn Yūsuf b. al-Jawzī. He was fourteen years old when the Mongols under Hülegü captured his native city, and he was among those enslaved and sent to Azerbaijan. His captivity ended when Naṣīr al-Dīn Ṭūsī took notice of him (perhaps because of his reputation as Ibn al-Jawzī's pupil), secured his release, and, in 660/1261–62, installed him as head of the library assembled for the great observatory established in Maragha by command of Hülegü. Ibn al-Fuwaṭī served in that post for nearly twenty years, even after the death of his mentor Ṭūsī. His time at the observatory library appears to have been the most important in terms of his contacts with scholars from throughout the world (he compiled a special treatise as a record of those who visited the observatory). After Naṣīr al-Dīn Ṭūsī's death, and at the

al-Fuwaṭī's work in 1987, no copy could be found in the United States, and even the British Museum's holdings, of which I obtained copies, were incomplete.

[2] Ibn al-Fuwaṭī (1962–65); the three volumes are labeled as parts 1–3 of vol. 4.

[3] Ibn al-Fuwaṭī (1995).

[4] On the life and works of Ibn al-Fuwaṭī, see the encyclopedia articles of Rosenthal (1971) and Melville (1997b) (and in addition to the sources cited there, see the fifteenth-century work of Ibn Ḥajar al-ʿAsqalānī; al-ʿAsqalānī (1974), 159–161, no. 2414 [tracing Ibn al-Fuwaṭī's paternal genealogy back fifteen generations]). The brief and unfinished article by Mohammad Iqbal (Iqbal, M. [1937]) summarizes his life from later sources and describes the Lahore manuscript of the fifth volume (a continuation of this article was promised, but did not appear).

behest of ʿAṭāʾ Malik Juwaynī, Ibn al-Fuwaṭī moved in 679/1280–81 to become director of the library at the Mustanṣiriyya *madrasa* in his native Baghdad, remaining there, despite considerable travel in Iraq and some extended stays in Azerbaijan, into the reign of Öljeitü; he was evidently removed from his post in 712/1312–13, but continued to live in Baghdad, though with continued travels, until his death in Muharram 723/January 1323.

Ibn al-Fuwaṭī and his biographers refer to several works he wrote, most of which appear to have been based on the biographical material he assembled (e.g., a poetic anthology, 'histories' of a host of cities that were probably—as befits the genre of such city histories—biographical dictionaries of the city's eminent people, and other specialized biographical arrangements); the possible exception is a chronicle covering much of the thirteenth century, known as *al-Ḥawādith al-jāmiʿa*, but the work published under this title as the work of Ibn al-Fuwaṭī, despite its frequent citation as such, is now generally believed not to be his work (its editor, again Muṣṭafā Jawād, himself later argued against Ibn al-Fuwaṭī's authorship). That leaves the extant portions of the *Majmaʿ al-ādāb fī muʿjam al-alqāb* (or of its *Talkhīṣ*) as the only surviving work of Ibn al-Fuwaṭī.

Though it clearly reflects material collected throughout Ibn al-Fuwaṭī's lifetime, the bulk of the *Majmaʿ al-ādāb* appears to have been compiled in its existing form between 1312 and 1316; there are several later dates, however, with a number of entries mentioning meetings or events into the early 720s/1320s. The latest date mentioned is Rabīʿ I 722/March–April 1322, just nine months before Ibn al-Fuwaṭī's death; it was then that he met Ghiyāth al-Dīn ʿAbd al-Laṭīf Simnānī, the *qāḍī* of Simnan, appropriately enough, in the book market in Baghdad. Ever a source as well as seeker of abstruse information, Ibn al-Fuwaṭī writes that this Simnānī "asked me about Ḥizqīl, one of the prophets of the Banū Isrāʾīl," who was said to be buried on a mountain near Simnan.[5]

It is naturally difficult to speak of Ibn al-Fuwaṭī's plan for his work, or of his historical or prosopographical vision, when so much of the *Majmaʿ al-ādāb* has not survived; nevertheless, it appears at least in part to reflect the broader project of the late Ilkhanid period, aimed at integrating the Mongols into the Islamic world. There is none of

---

[5] Ibn al-Fuwaṭī (1995), vol. 2, 443, no. 1776.

the Iranocentric vision noted in the case of some Persian historians of this period, but at the same time there is little evident interest in Mongol lore or traditions as such (of the sort evident in the work of Rashīd al-Dīn, for instance). As a biographical compendium, the work is distinctive among extant works from this era for its organization by *laqab*. Better-known works of this genre from the thirteenth century—those of Yāqūt (d. 626/1229) and Ibn Khallikān (d. 681/1282), for instance, as well as the continuations of the latter's *Wafayāt* by al-Ṣafadī (d. 764/1362–63) and al-Kutubī (d. 764/1363)—are organized by *ism*, as is the compendium of biographies of Ḥanafī jurists compiled by Ibn Wafā' al-Qurashī (d. 775/1373), while the biographical compendium of al-Yāfiʿī (d. 768/1367) is arranged chronologically; the works of al-Dhahabī (d. 748/1347–48), who made extensive use of Ibn al-Fuwaṭī's work, reflect organization by *ism*, *nisba*, and year. The choice of *laqab* as the foundation of Ibn al-Fuwaṭī's work may have facilitated the inclusion of a great many rulers, officials, and cultural figures with Turkic and Mongol names; at the same time, it situated Ibn al-Fuwaṭī's Mongol overlords, among others, within an Arabic-Islamic classificatory system.

Ibn al-Fuwaṭī's access to the library collections assembled for the observatory in Maragha, and in Baghdad, was naturally vital to his literary enterprise, and certainly much of his work's value stems from the sheer volume of written material he consulted and recorded.[6] For present purposes what is often more important, however, is the access to individuals facilitated for him by those collections: serving at these institutions allowed him to meet those who visited the collections, and much of the material in his work reflects their discussions with him. In this regard we are especially fortunate that Ibn al-Fuwaṭī typically pays scrupulous and explicit attention to his sources of information. Within a single biographical entry he will cite books and other written material (above all, lists of teachers and masters) that he inspected personally, including samples of poetry he solicited

[6] As Ibn al-Fuwaṭī himself tells it, his own erudition was such that natives of a particular region who came to see him would often ask *him* about some cultural production of their homeland; for example, a native of Banakat, near Tashkent, who came to Maragha in 671/1272–73 and worked as a copyist, asked Ibn al-Fuwaṭī about "poetry by the learned men of Mawarannahr and Turkistan" (Ibn al-Fuwaṭī [1995], vol. 3, 361, no. 2760 [Quṭb al-Dīn Abū al-Muẓaffar Aḥmad b. Maḥmūd b. Abū Bakr al-Banākatī]).

himself and licensures he requested, as well as accounts transmitted orally; for the latter he will name his source, and will usually tell us when and where the information was passed on. Even when he has already told us that he met a certain individual, he will inevitably add, when indicating that individual's birth date, for example, "I asked him when he was born, and he told me..." It is naturally this sort of material, gathered through such interviews, that is of special value for Ibn al-Fuwaṭī's own era.

Ibn al-Fuwaṭī's attention to his sources thus lends his work an admirable 'self-consciousness' that is evident also in his habit of giving cross-references, mentioning in one entry sources or individuals mentioned elsewhere in the work (and thus preserving a record, if not the content, of many entries now lost); as a result of the latter habit, his work is not simply a blind database, but an internally coherent reference tool whose value is enhanced by comparing and collating entries throughout the work. It is indeed often the case that entries devoted to particular figures are less illuminating than incidental references to them in entries devoted to other figures, making the careful collation of his accounts an essential first task in tracing the activities of many individuals mentioned in his accounts (including those for whom no specific entry has survived).

As noted, Ibn al-Fuwaṭī's biographical dictionary has drawn relatively little attention despite the richness of its first-hand accounts and despite its accessibility, at least in part, for several decades. Aside from the encyclopedia articles of Rosenthal and Melville and the brief article by Mohammad Iqbal, cited above, there has been no general study of Ibn al-Fuwaṭī or his biographical dictionary, nor any survey of his contribution.[7] As for specialized studies based on his work, I have found only a brief article from 1981 by a Soviet historian, the late Ziya Buniiatov, discussing the biographical dictionary's material on Qara-Khanid history, and including an account of Ibn al-Fuwaṭī's life and works and a description of his method of compiling biographical data;[8] a few other scholars have utilized his work's

[7] A study in Arabic from the 1950s discusses the *Majmaʿ al-ādāb*, but is focused on Ibn al-Fuwaṭī's material on the history of Iraq, primarily from the chronicle ascribed to him: al-Shabībī (1950–58). A Chicago Ph.D. dissertation from 1990 is again based primarily on the chronicle: Weissman (1990).

[8] Buniiatov (1981), 5–10 (7–10 on Ibn al-Fuwaṭī). No doubt as a result of the isolation of Soviet scholarship, Buniiatov consulted only Muṣṭafā Jawād's edition

data on particular figures, but without significant discussion of the *Majmaʿ al-ādāb* as a source.[9]

Among historians of the Mongol era, however, and even of Ilkhanid Iran, the work has been strangely neglected, and Ibn al-Fuwaṭī is rarely used or mentioned as a valuable source on the Mongol-ruled Middle East, much less on the broader Mongol empire.[10] To their credit, art historians have proved the only exception to this neglect,[11] inasmuch as Ibn al-Fuwaṭī's reference to witnessing a painter illustrating the *Jāmiʿ al-tawārīkh* of Rashīd al-Dīn has been widely known since Franz Rosenthal drew attention to it,[12] but for all practical purposes the riches of the *Majmaʿ al-ādāb* remain to be mined.

The new edition of Ibn al-Fuwaṭī's work includes 5,291 numbered entries (some include only a name, leaving the total of actual biographical entries less than this); while this may serve as a measure of the work's potential, it will be obvious that only a small fraction of the entries relevant to the Mongol era—each of which offers in effect a vignette of cultural interaction in that period—can be discussed here. Moreover, what the work is especially useful for facilitating is a reconstruction of connections and relationships among figures of diverse origins and social roles, relationships that often lie at the foundation of the larger patterns of cultural exchange and transmis-

of the fourth volume, and appears to have been unaware of the earlier publication of the fifth volume in *Oriental College Magazine*.

[9] Literary scholars have noted Ibn al-Fuwaṭī's data on the famous poet Farīd al-Dīn ʿAṭṭār: see Reinert (1997) (referring to Jawād's edition), and Shafīʿī Kadkanī (1999), 51–52, 67 (citing al-Kāẓim's edition). Ibn al-Fuwaṭī's two accounts of the famous Ḥabash-ʿAmīd, the vizier of Chaghadai, identified as a Turkistani under "ʿAmīd al-Mulk" (Ibn al-Fuwaṭī [1995], vol. 2, 211, no. 1345), but as a Samarqandī under Quṭb al-Dīn (Ibn al-Fuwaṭī [1995], vol. 3, 369, no. 2777), were noted in Iqbāl, ʿA. (1950–55), 493–500.

[10] Though the chronicle ascribed to him is often cited, Ibn al-Fuwaṭī's biographical dictionary does not appear to have been used in recent outstanding studies on the Mongol era, such as Amitai-Preiss (1995), Allsen (1997), or Allsen (2001), or in the contributions to the fine collective volumes, Aigle, ed. (1997) and Amitai-Preiss and Morgan, eds. (1999); it is also not mentioned in Lane, G. (2003). Though the work as a whole is unannotated, the late Jean Aubin's study of Ilkhanid *amīr*s and viziers (Aubin [1995]) offers no indication that Ibn al-Fuwaṭī's work was utilized for it.

[11] See Blair (1995), 62, citing Rosenthal (1971) and Ibn al-Fuwaṭī (1962–65); cf. Blair (1986a) 6–7, 75 (nn. 5–6), 76 (n. 11).

[12] See Rosenthal (1968), 176, n. 1 (giving the correct page reference [Ibn al-Fuwaṭī (1962–65), vol. 4/1, 528], which was transposed to read "258" in his entry on Ibn al-Fuwaṭī in Rosenthal [1971]; see n. 4, above). The entry appears in Ibn al-Fuwaṭī (1995), vol. 1, 478–79, no. 768.

sion under Mongol rule. By collating and piecing together material from biographical entries scattered throughout the work (and not just biographical data as such, but above all the sources and informants cited by Ibn al-Fuwaṭī), we can derive a broad, composite picture of such patterns both within and among particular fields, whether literature or astronomy or jurisprudence or statecraft. While one study along these lines is in preparation—focused on Ibn al-Fuwaṭī's material on Sufi communities in the Mongol era and their relationships with the Mongol elites[13]—space constraints require limiting our discussion here to a handful of those vignettes of cultural interaction. Accordingly, what follows is a brief consideration of a few examples of Ibn al-Fuwaṭī's material on rulers of the Mongol empire, on the process of Islamization, on linguistic interaction, and on literary production—subjects that, while they hardly exhaust the work's riches, are at least somewhat representative of Ibn al-Fuwaṭī's own interests, and hence of the particular value of the *Majmaʿ al-ādāb*.

Amid the jurists, Sufis, poets, and scholars whose biographical entries predominate in Ibn al-Fuwaṭī's work, the extant portions of the *Majmaʿ al-ādāb* include entries on four Mongol rulers,[14] each assigned an appropriate *laqab*; their inclusion in itself signals an interesting assimilation of the Mongols into a world defined and understood in terms of Islamic cultural norms, and neither these nor the many entries on *amīr*s, of diverse origins, in Mongol service convey any sense that Mongol rule had marked any more decisive a rupture with an Islamic past than had the rule of the various Turkic

[13] The *Majmaʿ al-ādāb* is especially valuable for our understanding of Sufi communities in the thirteenth century; in addition to preserving relatively early and in some cases otherwise unknown information on such well-known figures as Ibn ʿArabī and Shams al-Dīn Tabrīzī (as well as on Sufi poets such as Farīd al-Dīn ʿAṭṭār, and Saʿdī, with whom Ibn al-Fuwaṭī corresponded in 660/1262), the work includes the earliest-known biographical account of the remarkable *shaykh* ʿAlāʾ al-Dawla Simnānī (who left the service of Arghun to take up the life of a Sufi), important early references to Simnānī's master Nūr al-Dīn ʿAbd al-Raḥmān Isfarāʾinī, and extensive material on such figures as Majd al-Dīn Baghdādī, Najm al-Dīn Kubrā, and Sayf al-Dīn Bākharzī.

[14] Others, to be sure, are mentioned in the work (Möngke appears several times, most often as Hülegü's brother, while Chaghadai is mentioned three times, and others are named in the lineages included for those accorded separate entries), but the extant portions of the work do not refer to specific entries on these figures that have not survived. So far as I can tell, there is no reference whatsoever to any member of the Jochid house, no doubt reflecting the hostile relations between the Ilkhanate and the Golden Horde.

dynasties whose members are accorded entries as well. There is no reference to the status of some as infidels, and while support for Islamic institutions is mentioned, none are imputed any hostility toward the faith or toward Muslims in particular.

Chinggis (Genghis) Khan himself is accorded an entry, under the *laqab* 'al-Qāhir' ('the Conqueror').[15] In it, Ibn al-Fuwaṭī cites Rashīd al-Dīn as his source on the lineage of the ruler and for the detail about Chinggis holding a blood clot in his hand at his birth, but then cites an otherwise unknown treatise (or letter: *risāla*) by his mentor Naṣīr al-Dīn Ṭūsī, which he says was written already in 661/1262–63 and sent to Baghdad in the hands of *al-ṣadr* Ṣafī al-Dīn ʿAbd al-Muʾmin b. Abū al-Mafākhir. In this short citation, Ṭūsī observes that the state established by Chinggis Khan and his successors had seized control of the entire world from the east to the west "in less than fifty years," and was a state unlike any ever heard of in any historical works or ever described in the past.[16] The remarkable size of the Mongol empire and the speed of its establishment are not new information for us, of course, yet it is nevertheless of interest—for our understanding of Ilkhanid politics, of the very term '*Ilkhan*,' and more generally of the hybrid cultural envisioning of the Mongol state that underlies Ibn al-Fuwaṭī's work—that Ibn al-Fuwaṭī cites Naṣīr al-Dīn Ṭūsī referring to the entire Mongol empire established by Chinggis Khan as "*al-dawla al-qāhira al-īlkhāniya*," and himself identifies the subject of this entry as "al-Qāhir Jinkiz Khān b. Y.n.sūkāy [*sic*] Bahādur b. Abūkāy Bahādur *al-mughūlī al-īlkhān al-aʿẓam*," ruler of the Turkic east and seizer of most of the countries of the inhabited world.

The remaining Mongol rulers accorded individual biographical entries in the surviving portion of Ibn al-Fuwaṭī's work all belong to the Ilkhanid dynasty (into which Chinggis Khan is thus duly incorporated), beginning with Hülegü, who is assigned the *laqab*

[15] Ibn al-Fuwaṭī (1995), vol. 3, 319–20, no. 2697.

[16] Ṭūsī's citation here of a Qurʾānic passage (3:140) alluding to calamitous events—"such days We give out among people" (*wa tilka al-ayyāmu nudāwiluhā bayna al-nās*)—suggests that the text from which Ibn al-Fuwaṭī was citing had something in common with the Persian account of the Mongol seizure of Baghdad attributed to Ṭūsī and attached to some manuscripts of Juwaynī's *Taʾrīkh-i jahān-gushāy* (see Wickens [1962], 23–35, and Boyle [1961]), but unfortunately there is no further correspondence between what Ibn al-Fuwaṭī ascribes to Ṭūsī here and the Persian text linked with his name.

'Malik al-ʿarḍ' ('King of the Earth').[17] His entry is relatively brief and summarizes his progress from the east through Mawarannahr and Khurasan, his 'cleansing' of the Ismāʿīlīs in Quhistan, and his attack on Baghdad and the killing of the caliph; the rest of the entry (nearly half of it) is focused on Hülegü's establishment of the observatory in Maragha where Ibn al-Fuwaṭī worked. None of Hülegü's successors is accorded an entry until Ghazan, the first relatively successful Muslim ruler of the dynasty, under the heading 'al-Maḥmūd,' treated as a *laqab*. Ibn al-Fuwaṭī's account is again dependent upon Rashīd al-Dīn at first, but then notes the ruler's visit in the company of Rashīd al-Dīn to the library of the Mustanṣiriyya *madrasa*, "when he came to Baghdad and performed the Friday prayers there in the sultan's cathedral mosque."[18] The entry on Öljeitü, finally, describes him as the current ruler, with blessings for his continued reign (even though dates well after his death appear elsewhere in Ibn al-Fuwaṭī's work); Öljeitü is included under a 'normal' *laqab* (Ghiyāth al-Dīn), but beyond praise of him as "the ruler of the east and king of the earth," the entry on him includes only the mention of his accession following his brother Ghazan's death, and the date of his birth (12 Dhū al-ḥijja 680/24 March 1282).[19]

A crucial aspect of cultural transmission and exchange during this period is, of course, the process of Islamization; Ibn al-Fuwaṭī on the one hand is silent about the role played in this process by some of the figures typically said to have contributed substantially to the Islamization of the Mongol elite in the Ilkhanate, but on the other hand his accounts may help us expand our understanding of what Islamization involved in this context. In the first regard, for instance, the extant portion of Ibn al-Fuwaṭī's work includes three biographical entries for Kamāl al-Dīn ʿAbd al-Raḥmān (d. 683/1284–85), to whom Ibn al-Fuwaṭī matter-of-factly refers as "the *shaykh* of Sulṭān Aḥmad," i.e., Aḥmad Tegüder, the first royal Ilkhanid convert (whose

[17] Ibn al-Fuwaṭī (1995), vol. 5, 489, no. 5550: 'Malik al-ʿarḍ, Hūlākū b. Tūlī Khān b. Jinkiz Khān.'

[18] Ibn al-Fuwaṭī (1995), vol. 5, 39–40, no. 4589: 'al-Maḥmūd, Abū al-Muẓaffar Ghāzān b. al-Sulṭān Arghūn b. al- Sulṭān Abāqā b. Malik al-ʿarḍ Hūlākū al-Jinkizkhānī, *al-sulṭān al-aʿẓam*.'

[19] Ibn al-Fuwaṭī (1995), vol. 2, 433, no. 1758: 'Ghiyāth al-Dīn Muḥammad Öljeitü b. al-sulṭān Arghūn b. al-sulṭān Abāqā b. al-sulṭān Hūlākū b. Tūlī b. al-Qāhir Jinkiz Khān.'

Mongol name Ibn al-Fuwaṭī consistently writes as "Takūtār");[20] the accounts hint at specific skills (in his case, alchemy and woodworking) that may have made Shaykh ʿAbd al-Raḥmān attractive to the Mongol elite, but there is no mention of his role in Aḥmad Tegüder's adoption of Islam, and if Aḥmad himself was the subject of an entry, it has not survived. Likewise, the entry on the more successful royal convert, Ghazan, notes his role in spreading Islam, supporting its *imāms*, killing the *bakhshiyya*, and destroying idols,[21] but Ibn al-Fuwaṭī never mentions his conversion as such, nor does he provide any basis for ascribing his adoption of Islam to anyone in particular (other than Ghazan himself). This in itself is of some interest, since the conversion of Ghazan is attributed in various sources to quite a few separate figures, mostly Sufis; the extant portions of Ibn al-Fuwaṭī's work support none of the claims, however. It is clear, moreover (from an autobiographical report as well as many other sources), that Ṣadr al-Dīn Ibrāhīm, the son of the Saʿd al-Dīn Ḥammūyī (or Ḥamuwayhī) played a crucial role in Ghazan's conversion; Ibn al-Fuwaṭī was personally acquainted with Ṣadr al-Dīn Ibrāhīm, and even though no specific entry dealing with him has survived, the work includes extensive information on his teachers and connections in Sufism and other religious sciences, yet there is no hint of his relationship with Ghazan in the extant portions of the work.

In the case of Öljeitü, finally, Ibn al-Fuwaṭī provides ample evidence of the honor he showed to *sayyid*s after his accession, but never addresses the issue of his conversion or of his preference for Shīʿism. He does identify a particular Sufi *shaykh*, ʿIzz al-Dīn Abū al-Ḥasan ʿAlī b. Muḥammad, known as al-Khalīlī al-Fīnī, as the master "who put the *khirqa* on the current sultan, Ghiyāth al-Dīn Öljeitü, with his own hand, in Ujan, in 704/1304–5,"[22] but if we seek extended accounts of how or why the Ilkhanid elite adopted Islam, we will not find them in this work.

---

[20] The three entries include two under 'Kamāl al-Dīn' (one identifying him as ʿAbd al-Raḥmān b. Masʿūd [Ibn al-Fuwaṭī (1995), vol. 4, 177–78, no. 3614] and one as ʿAbd al-Raḥmān b. Yaḥyā [Ibn al-Fuwaṭī (1995), vol. 4, 178–79, no. 3616]) and one under 'Quṭb al-aqṭāb' (Quṭb al-aqṭāb, Kamāl al-Dīn ʿAbd al-Raḥmān b. Masʿūd [Ibn al-Fuwaṭī (1995), vol. 3, 395, no. 2832]). On this figure, and the conversion of Aḥmad Tegüder, see the recent dissertation of Judith Pfeiffer (Pfeiffer [2003]); also see Pfeiffer's contribution to this volume.

[21] Ibn al-Fuwaṭī (1995), vol. 5, 39–40, no. 4589.

[22] Ibn al-Fuwaṭī (1995), vol. 1, 270, no. 352.

Nevertheless, if we read carefully, we will find much in Ibn al-Fuwaṭī's work that sheds light on what the complex process we refer to as 'conversion' or 'Islamization' entailed in the Ilkhanid environment, outside the royal context that is often the focus of both our sources and the secondary literature. One entry, for instance, deals with an otherwise unknown *shaykh* (identified as an 'Alid, a preacher, and a descendant of Sufis, who hailed from Mecca but settled in Wasit), who died in 679/1280–81 and whom Ibn al-Fuwaṭī knew personally ("so much occurred to me in his service that this abridgement could not contain it"); this figure, Muḥyī al-Dīn 'Alī b. 'Īsā b. Muḥammad, known as Ibn Hawwārī, had come to Maragha in 667/1268–69 and associated there with Ibn al-Fuwaṭī's mentor, Naṣīr al-Dīn Ṭūsī, and later settled in Baghdad. The account also notes that this Muḥyī al-Dīn "frequented the company of *amīrs* and *khāns*," and that a great many people among the Mongols and Turks adopted Islam at his hand; in this case we are told more precisely what this means: "they repented at his hand, and they began to pay *zakāt* and to perform their prayers diligently."[23]

Elsewhere, moreover, Ibn al-Fuwaṭī affirms that this Muḥyī al-Dīn 'Alī was himself active as a Sufi *shaykh*; he gives an account of 'Alā' al-Dīn 'Alī b. al-Ḥusayn b. 'Abdallāh al-Tabrīzī, *al-ṣūfī*, identifying him also as a descendant of Sufis (*min awlād al-fuqarā' wa al-mashā'ikh*), but specifying that this 'Alā' al-Dīn had "donned the *khirqa*" from the hand of the *shaykh* Muḥyī al-Dīn 'Alī b. al-Hawwārī. Ibn al-Fuwaṭī says further that he himself wrote the certificate of licensure, or *ijāza*, affirming the transmission from Muḥyī al-Dīn to 'Alā' al-Dīn, in the year 670/1271–72.[24] The disciple, in any case, as Ibn al-Fuwaṭī makes clear, was involved in efforts to secure the institutional foundations of his Sufi community: he left his native Tabriz and settled in a village near Maragha, where he established "a *zāwiya* for the *fuqarā'*," as well as "a fine garden" for their support.[25] The example of these

---

[23] Ibn al-Fuwaṭī (1995), vol. 5, 78, no. 4671 (*wa aslama 'alā yadihi khalqun kathīrun min al-mughūl wa al-turk wa tābū 'alā yadihi wa ṣārū yakhrujūna al-zakāt wa yawāẓibūna 'alā al-ṣalawāti*).

[24] This small detail is of further interest as a reminder of Ibn al-Fuwaṭī's own activities and compilative methods: he clearly worked as a scribe, preparing documents on behalf of others, but he also clearly kept a record, or perhaps even a copy, of his work.

[25] Ibn al-Fuwaṭī (1995), vol. 2, 325–26, no. 1559.

two figures reminds us of the intimate connection in this period between the cultivation of the Mongol elites by Sufi leaders (often entailing or accompanied by conversion), on the one hand, and the institutional success of their Sufi communities on the other.

Perhaps of greater importance, however, are other types of accounts that reveal specific encounters of the sort that must have facilitated Islamization, broadly understood. That is, we generally tend to regard 'Islamization' as involving the sort of adoption of Islamic norms alluded to in the case of Ibn Hawwārī; but Islamization also entailed, and in large measure must have depended upon, the development of mutual cultural proficiencies as individuals knowledgeable about and representative of one cultural world entered the other cultural environment with various differentials of power and status and found ways of mediating between separate knowledge systems through classification, commentary, and cultural 'translation.' Thus in one entry we meet a Ḥusayni *sayyid*, whose ʿAlid lineage passed through a line of local rulers of Tabaristan and who is praised by Ibn al-Fuwaṭī for his deep knowledge about his ancestors; Ibn al-Fuwaṭī met this *sayyid* in 716/1316–17 in Sultaniyya, where he was among the intimates in the service of Öljeitü.[26] In another entry we meet a figure of clear Mongol or Turkic lineage, Muʿizz al-Dīn Rukn al-Islām Ésen Qutlugh b. Zangī b. Sibnā b. Ṭārum b. Tughril b. Qilīj b. Sunqūr b. Künjik b. Ṭūsbūqā b. Aktān Khān, whom Ibn al-Fuwaṭī also met personally (in 716/1316); this figure, characterized as a "powerful *amīr*," is praised for his extensive knowledge of "past kings and sultans" and for his excellent writing and research in "the science of history" (we are not told, however, which kings or whose history). Ibn al-Fuwaṭī also stresses his piety and good works, and notes that he had established in Hamadan a *khānqāh*, a *madrasa*, and a hospital (*dār al-shifāʾ*) for the benefit of Sufis; but we are also told that he was "well-versed in political methods (*asbāb al-siyāsa*), in the protocols of leadership (*ādāb al-riyāsa*), and in knowledge of the *yāsa*," referring to the famous (and controversial) 'law-code' of the Mongols.[27] Unfortunately in this case Ibn al-Fuwaṭī gives an apparently shortened

[26] Ibn al-Fuwaṭī (1995), vol. 5, 410–11, no. 5382 (Muʿīn al-Dīn Abū al-Fatḥ Muḥammad b. Jamāl al-Dīn ʿIzz al-Sharaf).

[27] The editor evidently misunderstood the latter term and suggested emending the text to read "*maʿrifa al-kiyāsa*" instead of "*maʿrifa al-yāsa*" (Ibn al-Fuwaṭī [1995], vol. 5, 333–34, no. 5200).

account of this man, whom he says he had discussed earlier in the section on *laqab*s beginning with the letter *rā*, which has not survived; his ability to function in and mediate between two cultural worlds is evident, however, and such individuals were undoubtedly central in making those two worlds into one.

Yet another account is valuable in this regard for reminding us of the variety of skills beyond the mystical discipline, contemplative vigor, or miraculous powers highlighted by later hagiographers that made Sufis attractive to the Mongol elite as transmitters of cultural knowledge and thereby facilitated their role as 'bearers' of Islam. It deals again with a Sufi known personally to Ibn al-Fuwaṭī, Majd al-Dīn Abū Ṭāhir Ibrāhīm b. Muḥammad b. ʿAbdallāh al-Isʿirdī al-Ḥashāʾishī *al-mutaṭabbib*, known as Ibn al-Ḥutaytī, whom he calls further "the physician (*al-ḥakīm*) and Sufi."[28] This figure, who died in Isʿird in 706/1306–7, "was a gnostic *shaykh* and had complete knowledge of herbs and of the places to find them and of their properties and benefits; and he had also a purity of soul and a high aspiration and praiseworthy character." He came to Maragha and established a Sufi hospice (*zāwiya*) in its environs, the account continues, and frequented a mountain nearby which "holds a great many medicinal herbs (*ḥashāʾish al-tiryāq*)." At some unspecified time, "he was summoned to the presence of Sulṭān Ghazan b. Arghun, and the sultan went up the mountain with him; and he taught him the varieties of herbs. The sultan liked him and lavished gifts upon him annually."

The latter account makes no explicit mention of the language in which Ghazan and the *shaykh* conversed, but Ibn al-Fuwaṭī typically pays close attention to the linguistic skills of his subjects, which were naturally a crucial aspect of the cross-cultural interaction of the Mongol era—an aspect, indeed, on which we may do well to remember all others depended. Ibn al-Fuwaṭī himself may have known some Mongol, and was probably familiar with Turkic as well as Persian and Arabic; his entries often highlight his subjects' facility with multiple languages, whether among translators or merchants or state officials, and the preponderance among them of men who were apparently of Muslim Turkic origin and who bore the title *amīr* may suggest the social class in which such linguistic training

[28] Ibn al-Fuwaṭī (1995), vol. 4, 380, no. 4020.

was both useful and accessible. In his entry, for instance, on the famous Maḥmūd Yalavāch—"Fakhr al-Dīn Abū al-Qāsim Maḥmūd b. Muḥammad, known as Yalavāch, al-Khwārazmī, the vizier of the Qān" (i.e., of Chinggis Khan)—we are told not only that he held control over the affairs "of the country of Turkistan and the land of China and Mawarannahr and Khwarazm," and that "under his deft management the Mongols' kingdom was well-ordered," but also that this most eminent Muslim in early Mongol service "wrote in Mongol, Uighur, Turkic, and Persian, and spoke Chinese, 'Hindi,' and Arabic."[29] Similarly, he refers to a certain Muẓaffar al-Dīn Qutlugh Beg b. Ibrāhīm, "*al-turkī al-amīr al-tarjumān*," who served in the *dīwān* as a translator, rendering "Turkic and Uighur and Persian into eloquent Arabic."[30] This figure's name betrays a Turkic origin and *amīr*id status, but we are not told how or when he became proficient in these languages.

A perhaps more intriguing case of likely native knowledge of multiple languages and scripts is a figure whom Ibn al-Fuwaṭī says he met in the army camp of Öljeitü, namely Quṭb al-Dīn Abū al-Fatḥ Muḥammad b. Ḥamd 'Ṭānīkū' al-Khwārazmī. The second part of the father's name here, read thus ('Ṭānīkū') by the editor, clearly conceals the title *Ṭayangu*, borne by high military officials in the state of the Qara-Khitais; the first part of the name, read 'Ḥamd,' suggests some further garbling in this case, but the *nisba* 'Khwārazmī' may well bespeak a family origin among Qara-Khitai officials drawn into the service of the Khwarazmshah as the Qara-Khitai state collapsed on the eve of the Mongol conquest. In any event, Ibn al-Fuwaṭī affirms that this Quṭb al-Dīn Muḥammad was serving the viziers in 705/1305–6, and that he was "a skilled scribe in Uighur and Turkic and Chinese."[31]

In this case it seems clear that the needs of the Mongol state created a market for skills that were especially prevalent among

[29] Ibn al-Fuwaṭī (1995), vol. 3, 197–98, no. 2472 (he wrote "*bi al-mughūlīya wa al-uyghūrīya wa al-turkīya wa al-fārsīya*," and he spoke "*bi al-khiṭā'īya wa al-hindīya wa al-'arabīya*"). It is possible that "*al-khiṭā'īya*" refers to the language of the Qara-Khitais, but on balance it is more likely that Ibn al-Fuwaṭī used the term to refer to Chinese. Also noteworthy is the distinction made between "*al-uyghūrīya*" and "*al-turkīya*."

[30] Ibn al-Fuwaṭī (1995), vol. 5, 287–88, no. 5106.

[31] *kātibun sadīdun bi al-uyghūrīya wa al-turkīya wa al-khiṭā'īya* (Ibn al-Fuwaṭī [1995], vol. 3, 422, no. 2885).

Central Asians; in other cases they created incentives for language-learning among men who entered Mongol service under different circumstances. Ibn al-Fuwaṭī tells us of a good friend of his, Mujāhid al-Dīn Abū al-Faḍā'il Ṣad-mard b. Nuṣrat al-Dīn Baghdī [?] b. Bahā' al-Dīn Arghish [?] al-Baghdādī, the scribe, who he says was from a family of *amīrs* (possibly of more distant Turkic origin) and entered the service of the Mongols when his father was taken captive after the fall of Baghdad; his father was with Amīr Sūghūnjāq (one of Hülegü's commanders), and both he and his son came to Maragha in 663/1264–65. The son, Ibn al-Fuwaṭī continues, "kept company with the learned men of the Uighurs and *bakhshīs*, and learned from them how to write the Uighur script as well as their language."[32] In this case the scribe in question evidently had no knowledge of the Uighur script before he came to Maragha; Mongol captivity, and the patronage of Buddhist monks in Iran, created the circumstances in which it was useful, and possible, to learn it.

Another figure, Ghiyāth al-Dīn Qutlugh Beg b. Tāj al-Dīn Zīrak b. ʿAzīz Khwāja al-Kāshgharī *al-amīr*,[33] is identified as belonging to a family of merchants and as being proficient in "the Persian, Turkic, Mongol, and Chinese languages" (*lughāt al-furs wa al-turk wa al-moghūl wa al-khiṭā*); though his family was evidently of Kashghari origin, this Ghiyāth al-Dīn, we are told, was born and grew up in Bukhara and came to Baghdad in the service of the Mongol *noyon* Arūq[34] when the latter came to Iraq as governor under Arghun (r. 683–90/1284–91) in 683/1284. It was evidently both his commercial success and his knowledge of languages that made him useful to the Mongol governor; beyond the general good character attributed to him in the account, his only other talent mentioned by Ibn al-Fuwaṭī—who affirms that he met him in Maragha through another *amīr* and native of Kashghar—is his talent in reciting the Qur'ān, which he learned in Bukhara. Ibn al-Fuwaṭī was evidently better acquainted, however, with Ghiyāth al-Dīn's brother, ʿImād al-Dīn Masʿūd b. Tāj al-Dīn

---

[32] *wa lāzama ʿulamā' al-uyghūr wa al-bakhshīya wa taʿallama minhum kitābat al-khaṭṭ al-uyghūrī wa lughatahum* (Ibn al-Fuwaṭī [1995], vol. 4, 366–67, no. 3995).

[33] Ibn al-Fuwaṭī (1995), vol. 2, 448, no. 1785.

[34] He is called "*al-nūyan* Arwaq" ("*arūq*" is written; the editor vowels it "*arwaq*"); Arūq was the brother of the more famous Amīr Būqā, who helped engineer Arghun's victory over his uncle Aḥmad Tegüder (both brothers were executed in 688/1289).

Zīrak b. ʿAzīz Khwāja al-Kāshgharī, *al-amīr*, who was evidently a patron of Naṣīr al-Dīn Ṭūsī and spent considerable time with Ibn al-Fuwaṭī in Maragha beginning in 668/1269–70; the account affirms that this ʿImād al-Dīn learned something of science and of poetry, but otherwise mentions only his generosity to the pupils of Mawlānā Naṣīr al-Dīn, with no reference to language skills.[35]

Another aspect of cross-cultural language skills is suggested in the entry about a poet and intellectual who frequented the assemblies of the Mongols early in the Ilkhanid period. The man in question, Kamāl al-Dīn Manṣūr b. Aḥmad, known as Ibn al-Shudīdī, was evidently a native of Kūfa and is praised for his poetry, no doubt in Arabic; Ibn al-Fuwaṭī says that he died in 675/1276. The poignancy of the new cultural circumstances in which this man—who is described by Ibn al-Fuwaṭī as among the great intellectuals (*ẓurafā*) of his age—found himself is underscored by the only detail his biographer preserves for us: Kamāl al-Dīn, Ibn al-Fuwaṭī writes, used to don simple clothes and attend the assemblies of the great lords, where, to the amusement of those present, "he would speak Mongol by pronouncing the words with great emphasis but without understanding them."[36]

The cultural impact of Mongol rule is likewise nicely encapsulated by the clear, if unfortunately general, description of yet another Arab intellectual from a fine family, Kamāl al-Dīn Abū al-ʿAbbās Aḥmad b. Muḥammad b. Muḥammad b. al-Ḍaḥḥāk al-Asadī al-Qurashī al-Nīlī al-Baghdādī, who, Ibn al-Fuwaṭī tells us, was born in 631/1234 and died in 693/1294; this figure, whom Ibn al-Fuwaṭī met personally, came from a noble house and was marked by fine character and excellent handwriting, but he had lost all his property in what Ibn al-Fuwaṭī regularly refers to simply as "the event" (meaning the sack of Baghdad by the Mongols in 656/1258). His motives for this are not explicitly addressed, but in any case the distinctive thing Ibn al-Fuwaṭī tells us about this Kamāl al-Dīn Aḥmad is that "he used to imitate the Mongols in their manners and actions" (*wa kāna yatashabbahu bi al-mughūl fī aḥwālihim wa afʿālihim*); what this entailed in terms of departure from the *sunna* of the Prophet is of course not

[35] Ibn al-Fuwaṭī (1995), vol. 2, 173–174, no. 1275.

[36] *yatakallam bi al-mughūlīya bi-tafakhkhum al-alfāẓ min ghayri maʿrifa bihā wa yutamaskharu fī kilāmihi* (Ibn al-Fuwaṭī [1995], vol. 4, 263, no. 3812).

mentioned, but Ibn al-Fuwaṭī does affirm that he was buried at the shrine of ʿAlī in Najaf.[37]

With such accounts, brief as they may be, Ibn al-Fuwaṭī gives us a feel for the substance, at the individual level, of the cultural encounter entailed by the Mongol conquest.

As a librarian, professional scribe, and avid collector of books, Ibn al-Fuwaṭī gives special attention to writers, scribes, and the production of manuscripts. His mention of the painter he saw illustrating the book of Rashīd al-Dīn was noted above; the account of ʿAfīf al-Dīn Muḥammad al-Qāshī identifies him as a poet in Persian as well as a painter, but what is again most interesting with regard to the cultural encounters of the age is the scene of his meeting with Ibn al-Fuwaṭī: "I saw him in Arran, in the encampment of the sultan [Öljeitü] (*fī mukhayyam al-sulṭān*), and he was painting in the book of my lord, the vizier and physician, Rashīd al-Dīn, in the year 705/1305–6."[38] The artist was thus not working in an urban studio or scriptorium, but was traveling with the ruler in the steppe.

Less well-known, evidently, is Ibn al-Fuwaṭī's account of another scholar from Ardabil who was responsible, he tells us, for the collation (*muqābala*) of Rashīd al-Dīn's work. The scholar, Kamāl al-Dīn Mūsā b. ʿAbdallāh b. Maḥmūd b. Ismāʿīl b. Kākila al-Ardabīlī, belonged to family of physicians and *qāḍīs*, and was the wisest among them; at the time when Ibn al-Fuwaṭī prepared his entry, in 714/1314–15, he was working in the royal *madrasa* established by Ghazan (*al-madrasa al-sulṭānīya al-ghazānīya*), "and in his presence was accomplished the collation of the book *Jāmiʿ al-tawārikh*, which the just master Rashīd al-Dīn composed."[39]

Ibn al-Fuwaṭī's accounts of the illustration and collation of such an important work as the *Jāmiʿ al-tawārikh* are naturally of interest, but of arguably greater value are his excerpts from and references to other works, ranging from multivolume biographical compendia, histories, and anthologies to personal letters, licensures, and notes that have not survived; such references often preserve specific information, but they also give us an idea of the scope and character of cultural

[37] Ibn al-Fuwaṭī (1995), vol. 4, 116–117, no. 3478.

[38] Ibn al-Fuwaṭī (1995), vol. 1, 478–79, no. 768; cf. Blair (1995), 62 (Rosenthal did not note where they met); also see Blair's contribution to this volume [ed.].

[39] Ibn al-Fuwaṭī (1995), vol. 4, 263–64, no. 3814.

production extant in his time. It may be helpful, then, and humbling, to close with a few examples of the sources, known to Ibn al-Fuwaṭī but now lost (or not yet discovered), which we may assume would have contained invaluable material on the Mongol empire.

– He mentions a learned jurist who studied under the famous Muʿtazilī Ḥanafī scholar and transmitter of the works of Zamakhsharī, Burhān al-Dīn Nāṣir al-Muṭarrizī al-Khwārazmī (d. 610/1213–14), and who was in turn the master of another Khwarazmian scholar (Muḥammad b. Maḥmūd b. Muḥammad al-Khwārazmī), who wrote a history of Khwarazm that must date to the first half of the thirteenth century.[40]

– He mentions a jurist of Bukhara who wrote a treatise describing "the circumstances of the countries of Khwarazm and Mawarannahr."[41]

– He mentions a Sufi from Isfahan, an eloquent preacher and literary man who "donned the attire of Sufism," who "wrote an excellent book and called it *Kitāb al-zahr al-muʿniq fī ashʿār ahl al-mashriq*"; evidently Ibn al-Fuwaṭī did not see this one, but only heard that the author had collected in it "the verse of Khwarazm and Mawarannahr and the lands of the Turks."[42]

– He mentions an astronomer of Daylami origin, taken captive by the Mongols during the conquest of Baghdad but later released, whom Ibn al-Fuwaṭī befriended after he moved to Baghdad from Maragha; this figure, he says, was "among the most learned of men in the science of the stars and in the evaluation of astrological charts and calendars," used to compose poetry in Turkic, and wrote, among other books, a comprehensive "history of the kings and sultans and literary figures and astronomers."[43]

– He mentions that a native of Khotan told him about his own teacher, from Kashghar, who had written "a *qaṣīda* in praise of the

[40] Ibn al-Fuwaṭī (1995), vol. 2, 365–66, no. 1643 (ʿAlāʾ al-Dīn Abū Ṭāhir Muḥammad b. Maḥmūd al-Tarjumānī *al-faqīh al-adīb*).

[41] Ibn al-Fuwaṭī (1995), vol. 5, 429, no. 5425 (*muftī al-mulūk* Abū al-Thanāʾ Maḥmūd b. ʿAlī al-Bukhārī *al-faqīh*).

[42] Ibn al-Fuwaṭī (1995), vol. 4, 95, no. 3421 (Kamāl al-Dīn Abū Isḥāq Ibrāhīm b. Abū ʿAlī b. Hājir al-Iṣbahānī *al-ṣūfī*).

[43] Ibn al-Fuwaṭī (1995), vol. 4, 60, no. 3333 (Karz al-Dīn Abū al-Mafākhir Isḥāq b. Jibraʾīl b. Mardshīr al-Daylamī al-Baghdādī *al-munajjim* [b. 608/1211–12, d. 680/1282]).

army of Chinggis Khan."[44]

– He mentions a poet, equally skilled in Arabic and Persian, whom he met personally and who had composed a verse account of the "kings of the Turks" in the fashion of the *Shāhnāma*, and had dedicated it to "the great Sulṭān Ghāzān Maḥmūd b. Sulṭān Arghūn" (this poet, he says, was never heard from again after accompanying the Mongol army that set off for a campaign in Gilan in 706/1306–7, suggesting that part of his job was to compose verse celebrating military exploits).[45]

– He mentions a history written by a court official who died in 694/1295; this writer had been taken captive during the conquest of Baghdad and had traveled to the country of the Turks, dwelling among them for a long time before being released and settling in Damascus.[46]

– He mentions an historian and poet whom he met in Baghdad in 703/1303–4, and who "had written a narrative (*qiṣṣa*) of the great Sulṭān Ghāzān b. Arghūn, and had versified his events and circumstances in fine form; and it is a valuable book."[47]

– And he mentions a certain Nūr al-Dīn ʿAlī b. ʿUthmān, who wrote "a treatise in which he described the stations and cities (*al-manāzil wa al-buldān*) from Mosul to Qaraqorum, the capital (*dār al-mulk*) of *al-sulṭān* Qāʾān."[48]

We can only conjecture how much our knowledge of the Mongol empire might be expanded had some of these works survived; in their absence, Ibn al-Fuwaṭī's rich and still largely untapped work offers a degree of access, if not to the works themselves, then at least to the labors of a diligent researcher who sought them out.

---

44 Ibn al-Fuwaṭī (1995), vol. 3, 431, no. 2904, in the entry on Quṭb al-Dīn Abū al-Faḍl Muḥammad b. Muḥammad b. ʿAbdallāh al-Kāshgharī *al-adīb*, who was "among the most famous of the *ʿulamā* of the East and of China [*al-sharq wa al-ṣīn*]"; his pupil, Ṣadr al-Dīn al-Muʿīnī al-Khutanī, told Ibn al-Fuwaṭī about him, and about his *qaṣīda*, at the observatory in Maragha in Rabīʿ I 671/October 1272.

45 Ibn al-Fuwaṭī (1995), vol. 4, 99, no. 3431 (Kamāl al-Dīn Aḥmad b. Badīʿ al-Dīn Abū Bakr b. ʿAbd al-Ghaffār al-Bakrī al-Zanjānī).

46 Ibn al-Fuwaṭī (1995), vol. 1, 288, no. 298 (ʿIzz al-Dīn Abū Bakr Maḥfūẓ b. Maʿtūq, known as Ibn al-Bazūrī, al-Baghdādī).

47 Ibn al-Fuwaṭī (1995), vol. 4, 328, no. 3932 (Mubāriz al-Dīn Abū al-Fatḥ Malikshāh b. Makkī b. Malikshāh al-Daylamī, *al-ṣadr al-muʾarrikh al-shāʿir*).

48 Ibn al-Fuwaṭī (1995), vol. 5, 238, no. 5000 (in the entry on Mushayyad al-Mulk Abū al-Majd b. al-Wazīr al-Bukhārī, the governor of "Āmūy," who was mentioned in the treatise of Nūr al-Dīn ʿAlī).

DIPLOMATIC MISSIONS AND GIFTS EXCHANGED BY MAMLUKS AND ILKHANS

DONALD P. LITTLE

On 9 Dhū al-qaʿda 700/17 July 1301, a courier named al-Amīr Anaṣ arrived in Cairo from Damascus with news of hostile movements of the army of the Ilkhan Ghazan toward the Euphrates, the dividing line between Mongol and Mamluk territories, and that Ghazan was sending an advance messenger to alert the Egyptian sultan. Such was the Mongol custom, according to the contemporary Mamluk historian, Ibn al-Dawādārī, in the days before peace had been established between the Ilkhans and their main adversaries, the Mamluks of Egypt and Syria. Now, however, Ibn al-Dawādārī says, that at the time he was writing his history, sometime after 723/1323 presumably, when peace prevailed and "the hearts of the Mongols were filled with awe of the [Mamluk] sultan al-Malik al-Nāṣir, Mongol missions come without interruption, arriving in Cairo with beautiful gifts and objets (*ṭuḥaf*), as I will be mentioning," says Ibn al-Dawādārī, "in the history of al-Nāṣir's reign."[1] Al-Amīr Anaṣ's arrival in Cairo had been preceded, apparently, by that of a *mamlūk* of the Viceroy of Aleppo bearing news of the arrival of the Mongol envoys in Aleppo.[2] The advance Mongol party, consisting of a military commander, al-Amīr Nāṣir al-Dīn ʿAlī Khwāja, and a Muslim judge/preacher from Mosul, al-Qāḍī Ḍiyāʾ al-Dīn b. Bahāʾ al-Dīn b. Yūnus al-Shāfiʿī al-Khaṭīb (such being the usual combination for diplomatic missions), reached Damascus on 23 Dhū al-qaʿda/31 July 1301 with an entourage of about twenty persons, and were quartered at the citadel. After a few days the commander and the judge, accompanied by a "Tatar-Turk slave,"[3] having left their heavy baggage and grooms in Damascus, set out for Cairo escorted by al-Amīr Sayf al-Dīn Kurāy al-Silāḥdār and post riders sent for this purpose from the capital in Egypt, and arrived at the

[1] Ibn al-Dawādārī (1960), vol. 9, 51.
[2] Al-ʿAynī (1992), vol. 4, 133.
[3] Anonymous, ms. fragment in Zetterstéen, ed. (1919), 92.

Cairo citadel on 15 Dhū al-ḥijja 700/22 August 1301.[4] Obviously, then, the Mamluks had an elaborate early-warning system in place regarding movement of the Ilkhans into their territory—as well they might since in the previous year the Mamluks had been decisively defeated at the Battle of Wadi al-Khazindar, which had resulted in the Mongols' temporary occupation of Homs and Damascus.

At this point it might well be asked, why indulge in so much detail about a single diplomatic mission? There are several answers. One, my subject is too large for a comprehensive survey of Mongol-Mamluk diplomatic missions, given the wealth of data to be found in the Mamluk—Arabic—sources to which my research is confined; two, the material available in these sources for this particular diplomatic exchange is fuller than for any other embassies exchanged between the two great power blocs of the thirteenth and fourteenth centuries in the Middle East; and three, the historiographical complexity of these particular missions, as reflected in the scholarly apparatus for this article, demonstrates the problematics of such an undertaking. Accordingly, this episode is worth looking at as a case study for what it tells of the Mamluk-Mongol confrontation and exchanges in general, and the role of gifts in these exchanges in particular.

In respect to historiography, it should be noted that one reason for the abundance of information available for this particular mission is the 'fact' that the father—Jamāl al-Dīn ʿAbdallāh al-Dawādārī—of our main contemporary historian, Ibn al-Dawādārī, served in Damascus in an official capacity as *mihmandār*, a protocol officer in charge of hospitality for guests, and dealt with the Mongol party so ably that the chief envoys promised to reward him well upon their return from Cairo. This, despite the fact that Jamāl al-Dīn's appointment, according to his son, dated from 710/1310–11![5] Be that as it may, when informed of this promise, the Mamluk Viceroy of Damascus—the above-mentioned al-Amīr Sayf al-Dīn Kurāy—teased the officer, saying, "don't devour the gift alone but share with us what you have been promised." True to their word, after their return to Damascus from Cairo, the envoys presented Jamāl al-Dīn with two gifts: one consisting of three *ṭawāmīr ʿaẓm* and two rings—*ḥalqatayn ṭ-s-mā*—of some sort.[6]

---

[4] Ibn al-Dawādārī (1960), vol. 9, 52; Zetterstéen, ed. (1919), 92.
[5] Ibn al-Dawādārī (1960), vol. 9, 51.
[6] Ibid., 52.

It would be informative for art historians, of course, if the nature of these objects could be readily and reliably identified, but given the present stage of research, this is not easy. Some of the terms for gifts are indecipherable in the manuscripts that I have used; others, in edited sources, as in the present case, have not been identified by their editors because the terms are not to be found in the standard lexicons. Still, we must try. A *ṭūmār* is known to be a word used for a scroll, often for a register of accounts. But what are bone scrolls or registers? Or, for that matter, what is an iron *ṭūmār* found in a box of arrows that Ibn al-Dawādārī mentions elsewhere as another gift?[7] Until recently I suspected that a *ṭūmār* might be a container of some kind, maybe even a quiver, but that was just a guess. In *Letters in Gold: Ottoman Calligraphy from the Sakip Sabanci Collection, Istanbul,* M. Uğur Derman writes that *ṭūmār* in the Ottoman period refers not only to one of the scripts used for official correspondence but also to the shaft of the pen used to write the script.[8] In all probability, then, if the same terminology applied in the Mamluk period, the Ilkhanid envoy presented Jamāl al-Dīn with three bone pens as a token of his thanks for services rendered. Apparently this gesture was not made lightly, for we are told that the envoys "deliberated for a long time" before they decided upon a suitable gift.[9] The two rings are more problematic, but since Ibn al-Dawādārī's editor was unable to identify the qualifying word—*ṭ-s-mā*—I have no suggestions for them. We will return to the subject of gifts with better results. Besides, Ibn al-Dawādārī's father deemed it prudent to turn over the gifts to the greedy viceroy in exchange for "a complete unicolored silk robe of honor (*khil'a kāmila muṣmat*)."[10] And to complicate the issue even further, we must remember that Ibn al-Dawādārī is reputed to have been a notorious 'fictionalizer' of Mamluk history, especially when his father was involved and to whom he attributed accounts that can be traced to other sources.[11] In any event this anecdote demonstrates that diplomatic gifts were not awarded just

---

[7] Ibid., 372.

[8] Derman (1998), 5: "...*tûmâr* (a very large script, and pen, for use on scrolls), which was standard in [Ottoman] official correspondence."

[9] Ibn al-Dawādārī (1960), vol. 9, 52.

[10] Ibid., 52.

[11] See, with references, Little (1998), 424–25, and, especially, Ibn al-Dawādārī (1971), 11–22.

at the highest levels but could be, and were, distributed at lower levels of the political hierarchy.

As stated above, the envoys reached Cairo in late August, more than a month after the Ilkhans were reported to be on the warpath. In Cairo, the government, headed by the sixteen-year-old al-Nāṣir, went all out to give the envoys a memorable reception. After settling them in the finest of quarters with generous stipends, the sultan ordered the highest ranks of his army—*amīrs*, commanders, officers of the non-slave regiment (*al-ḥalqa*), and his Royal Mamluks—to don their dress uniforms, meaning brocade caps and tunics with gold embroidered inscriptions (*al-kalawtāt al-zarkash wa al-ṭirāz al-dhahab*).[12] Thus attired, these soldiers were stationed in two lines stretching from the gate of the citadel into the interior of the court. To heighten the gravity and awe of the occasion, the envoys' procession through these troops was delayed until after the last prayer so that it could take place by candlelight. As planned, the effect was startling. When the envoys reached the sultan's council chamber, "they were stunned by the dignity and bearing of the spectacle; they saw troops which seemed to embody beauty, awe, and elegance."[13] Suitably impressed, the *qāḍī* envoy delivered an eloquent sermon to the assemblage on the theme of peace between Ilkhans and Mamluks, with appropriate citations of the Qur'ān and *ḥadīth,* as well as prayers for the two rulers. The judge then presented Ghazan's letter to the sultan, who did not deign to open it on that ceremonious occasion. Instead, he waited until the next night, when he had the letter read in the presence of the chiefs of the army, even though it was written in Mongolian. We are told even the size and cut of the paper: "*qaṭ' niṣf al-Baghdādī.*"[14] It had been written in early Ramaḍān of 700/May 1301, at Jibal al-Akrad. I will not dwell on the contents, which are well known.[15] Suffice it to say that it is couched in religious terms, justifying the Mongol occupation of Damascus in the previous year by outrages committed by the Mamluks in the frontier town of Mardin during the sacred month of Muḥarram of the previous year. Thus we have the ironic claim of the recently converted Ghazan to be the defender

---

[12] Ibn al-Dawādārī (1960), vol. 9, 53.
[13] Al-ʿAynī (1992), vol. 4, 132.
[14] Ibn al-Dawādārī (1960), vol. 9, 53.
[15] See the article by Horst (1967), 349–70, for translations of the correspondence between the two rulers along with historiographical data.

of Islam against the impious Mamluks, Muslims of long standing! Nevertheless, Ghazan proclaims that having punished the Mamluks, he is now ready to make peace with them. The letter ends with a reminder that the sultan should accompany his official reply with suitable gifts from Egypt so that "we might know your true intent in regard to peace. And we shall reciprocate appropriately with gifts from our land."[16] Distrustful of Ghazan's true intentions, the sultan and his *amīrs* sought oral reassurances from the *qāḍī* envoy, who swore that to his knowledge the Ilkhans' only purposes were "peace, sparing blood, (free) coming and going of merchants, and the welfare of the subject populations."[17]

Satisfied with this response, on 28 Muḥarram of the following year/3 October 1301, the sultan reassembled the envoys in the presence of all his *amīrs*, on whom he bestowed robes of honor. The envoys "were astonished by the array of the resplendent sultanate and the bearing of the Islamic armies, the like of which they had never seen."[18] The sultan sent them on their way back to the Ilkhan, having given them travel robes of honor (*khilaʿ al-safar*), ten thousand *dīnārs* apiece, fabrics (*taʿābī qumāsh*), etc. (including the pens and rings?), accompanied by his own envoys, al-Amīr Ḥusām al-Dīn Uzdamir al-Mujīrī and al-Qāḍī ʿIzz al-Dīn al-Sukkarī. These envoys bore the sultan's official response in kind, written by ʿAlāʾ al-Dīn b. Muḥyī al-Dīn b. ʿAbd al-Ẓāhir, a scribe of distinguished family in the chancery, depicting the Mamluks as devout, law-abiding Muslims in contrast to the ungodly Ilkhans. Despite the vituperation, al-Nāṣir responded favorably to the peace overtures, inviting Ghazan to send an official empowered to negotiate the terms of peace. In closing his letter, the sultan addressed the issue of gifts raised by the *khān*. Pledging to err on the side of generosity with his presents from Egypt, al-Nāṣir demanded gifts of equal value from Iraq "in order that we might verify the sincerity of the *khān*'s intentions."[19] We shall return to this question of diplomatic gifts.

In the meantime we shall look briefly at the reception given by Ghazan to the Mamluk delegation, headed, as was usual, by a military commander and a judge. In contrast to the pomp and circumstance

[16] Ibn al-Dawādārī (1960), vol. 9, 56; Zetterstéen, ed. (1919), 95.
[17] Ibn al-Dawādārī (1960), vol. 9, 56; Zetterstéen, ed. (1919), 95.
[18] Ibn al-Dawādārī (1960), vol. 9, 66.
[19] Ibn al-Dawādārī (1960), vol. 9, 70; Zetterstéen, ed. (1919), 100–1.

of the Cairo reception, we know nothing of the Ilkhan's ceremonies, if indeed there were any or where, even, they may have been held: Tabriz, Sultaniyya, or in the field. Instead, if Ibn al-Dawādārī's father, a close friend of al-Mujīrī, is to be believed, the *khān* engaged the Mamluk *amīr* in an intimate conversation which reflects the Ilkhans' ignorance of the Mamluk army and society. Ibn al-Dawādārī alleges that al-Mujīrī reproduced this conversation for the author's father some four years later, in 704/1304, when he was finally permitted to return to Egypt. But this attribution may well be a fabrication since the fifteenth-century historian, al-ʿAynī, attributes it to another historian, al-Qāḍī Jamāl al-Dīn b. al-Karīm.[20] Accordingly al-Mujīrī gave Ghazan elementary instruction on the Mamluk military with data on nomenclature, ranks, loyalties, and, most importantly, strength and manpower, obviously designed to impress the *khān* and to deter him from an attack. All this Ghazan regarded with considerable skepticism but managed to maintain his equanimity until he himself brought up, out of the blue, the subject of sexual preferences.

> "How is it," Ghazan asked, "that your men, the *amīrs*, forsake women and make use of young men, i.e., beardless boys?"
>
> Even though I knew that he might kill or injure me [Uzdamir opined], I could not avoid answering, for everything belongs to God.
>
> "God save the *Khān*!" I said. "Our *amīrs* knew nothing of this! It was an innovation in our land brought by Ṭurghāy [a Turco-Mongol immigrant] when he came to us from you. He arrived with Tatar youths, and people applied themselves to them at the expense of women."
>
> Angered and upset, Ghazan turned to the Mongol notables around him and spoke to them in Mongolian. I knew that I was a goner, [Uzdamir thought,] no doubt about it.... But then Ghazan said to his chamberlain, "Tell him what you have to say about our women and yours."
>
> I knew that he only wanted to make sure of my execution, so I silently called upon God as my witness and consecrated my intention to meet God the Exalted and said, "You are King of the East. But it is unseemly for women to be mentioned in this council, for our women show modesty before God the Exalted and the people by veiling their faces. As for your women, you are best informed of their state."[21]

This was too much for Ghazan, who ordered that the Mamluk envoys be shot from catapults, a sentence later commuted to confinement in a *madrasa,* which lasted until 704/1304–5, when Ghazan's brother

---

[20] Al-ʿAynī (1992), vol. 4, 128.

[21] Ibn al-Dawādārī (1960), vol. 9, 74–75; Zetterstéen, ed. (1919), 102–3.

and successor, referred to by Ibn al-Dawādārī as Khudābandā—also known as Kharbandā, Uljaytu, and Öljeitü—released them. Conveniently, Ibn al-Dawādārī also records a conversation between the new *khān* and al-Mujīrī, the tone of which contrasts sharply with the contretemps with Ghazan. Khudābandā obviously did not hold his predecessor in high esteem and, indeed, raised doubts about the sincerity of his conversion to Islam, echoing the motif of suspicion of religious commitment that we have already noted. Al-Mujīrī reports:

> When I came into Khudābandā's presence, he showed me honor and seated me, drawing me near and spoke to me without the presence of a chamberlain. "O Ḥusām al-Dīn," he said, "how do you view God's use of the accursed Ghazan when he was tyrannical and waxed large?"
>
> I rose, kissed the ground, and said, "May God save the *khān* and lengthen his life!"

This prudent answer obviously pleased Khudābandā, who, according to al-Mujīrī,

> bestowed favor upon me and ordered horses, robes of honor and gifts for me and gave me things which no other king of his likes had given to the likes of me. He gave me a letter to all his lands and to the kings under his obedience, commending us to them.[22]

This is also the year, 704/1304–5, when Khudābandā sent his own envoys with a letter to the sultan of Egypt, along with gifts. Curiously, the Mamluk historian, al-ʿAynī, writing in Arabic, characterizes this letter as another peaceful overture, offering "brotherhood (*ukhuwwa*), an end to strife, and peace among the Muslims."[23] *Curiously*, I say, because according to J. A. Boyle, the tone of the letter as preserved by the Persian historian, Waṣṣāf, indicates "that this was not a conciliatory move," and at the same time the *khān* was unsuccessfully seeking the support of Christian monarchs of Europe in mounting a joint campaign against the Mamluks.[24]

Although an alliance did not materialize, Khudābandā did launch an attack against the Mamluks in 712/1312 with the advice of two high-ranking Mamluk defectors, Qarāsunqur and al-Afram. This attack foundered in Rahba (in Iraq); the Mongols retreated across

[22] Ibn al-Dawādārī (1960), vol. 9, 129.
[23] Al-ʿAynī (1992), vol. 4, 345. Cf. al-Nuwayrī (1998), 87.
[24] Boyle (1968), 399.

the Euphrates to Iran, ending Mongol-Mamluk hostilities, which had lasted sixty-plus years, in 713/1313. Thereafter, diplomatic exchanges continued at a rate of at least one a year. In 720/1320 the Ilkhan Abū Saʿīd sued for peace on the basis of seven proposals: (1) the Mamluk sultan was to ban the presence of Ismāʿīlī assassins in his territory; (2) Egyptians present in Ilkhanid territory and Ilkhanid subjects in Egyptian domains were not to be repatriated without their permission; (3) no Arab or Turkman tribesmen would be allowed to raid Ilkhanid territory; (4) the roads between the two domains would be open to merchants and all others; (5) the Ilkhans should be granted a royal Mamluk banner to be borne on their official pilgrimage to Mecca alongside the Mamluk standard; (6) the Mamluk fugitive Qarāsunqur, who had been given asylum with the Ilkhans, should not be sought by the Mamluks; (7) the Mamluks should send a trustworthy envoy with the sultan's oath to observe the conditions of peace, and the *khān* and his chief minister, Jūbān, should swear the same. Once these provisions had been ratified with oaths, "peace between us would prevail, and the two regions would be one."[25] Needless to say, despite protestations of compliance from both sides, these terms remained negotiable so long as the Mamluks continued secretly to send assassins against Qarāsunqur, so that diplomatic exchanges and gifts continued, until in 722/1322 a peace agreement was reaffirmed, with assurances that the required rituals of Islam—including the profession of faith, the Friday sermon, prayers, and pilgrimage—were being performed in Ilkhanid territory. Previously, in 720/1320 Abū Saʿīd had made a great show of destroying the wine stores in his kingdom and prohibiting its sale, and al-Nāṣir, in compliance with Abū Saʿīd's request, had sent a royal yellow silk standard with a gold finial to be borne in the Iraqi pilgrimage procession.[26] By 723/1323 the Mamluks' commercial agent at the Ilkhanid court reported in Cairo that "all the [Mongol] lands were obedient to the [Mamluk] sultan, that Islam had spread there, that the *ʿulamāʾ* had proliferated, that the state of Islam had improved among the Mongols, and that hearts were united in love for the

[25] Badr al-Dīn Maḥmūd ibn Aḥmad al-ʿAynī, *ʿIqd al-jumān fī taʾrīkh ahl al-zamān*, Istanbul, Topkapı Palace Museum Library, ms. Ahmet III 2912/4, fol. 328b, and al-Maqrīzī (1941), vol. 2, 209–10, provide the fullest accounts of these terms.

[26] Al-ʿAynī, ms. Ahmet III 2912/4, fol. 327b; al-Maqrīzī (1943), vol. 2, 211.

sultan and in prayers for him."[27] Despite the harmony, exchanges continued between the two sides on such issues as marriage alliances to cement the political ties. Ironically, while each side requested a royal bride from the royal family of the other, both demurred on one pretext or another, so that no marriage alliances were formed to my knowledge, despite the fact that al-Nāṣir himself was the son of a Mongol woman.[28] Surprisingly enough, another bone of contention was the incarceration in Damascus of the celebrated Ḥanbalī scholar and activist, Ibn Taymiyya. To the *khān*'s attempt to intervene on his behalf in 726/1326, the sultan referred the matter to the four chief judges of Cairo, who refused to reopen the case.[29] But peace was not really established until 728/1328, when Timurtāsh, son of the chief minister, Jūbān, was executed at the Ilkhans' request by the Mamluks, even though they had treacherously granted Timurtāsh asylum in exchange for the Ilkhans' promise to execute the fugitive, Qarāsunqur, at their court. The Ilkhans could not bring themselves to execute Qarāsunqur so he died either from natural causes or, perhaps, from suicide.[30]

At this point I shall turn as promised to the exchange of gifts. I have already indicated that appropriate gifts were essential to both the Ilkhans and the Mamluks as tokens of respect and good faith on the highest level between the two rulers. But this principle also operated on a lower, unofficial level as we have seen with Ibn al-Dawādārī's father. Typically, the Mamluk historians insisted on personalizing the peace process and attributed its success to three individuals who exchanged gifts of their own: (1) the merchant Majd al-Dīn al-Sallāmī, who in 722/1322 was given official recognition as "resident merchant in the Mongol camp (*ordū*), in charge of buying *mamlūks* and slave girls";[31] (2) al-Qāḍī Karīm al-Dīn, a Coptic convert to Islam, who by hook and crook had risen to be keeper of the sultan's privy purse and master of the bureaucracy; and (3) Khwāja ʿAlī Shāh, Abū Saʿīd's vizier. According to al-ʿAynī,

---

[27] Al-ʿAynī, ms. Ahmet III 2912/4, fol. 339b.

[28] On the other hand, in 720/1320, al-Nāṣir did, at his request, marry a princess of the Golden Horde Mongols descended from Genghis Khan, a niece of Uzbek Khan. But the wedding night did not turn out to the sultan's satisfaction so he left Cairo the next morning for a hunting trip. Al-Maqrīzī (1943), vol. 2, 203–4.

[29] Al-ʿAynī, ms. Ahmet III 2912/4, fol. 369b.

[30] Ibid., fol. 380b.

[31] Ibid., fol. 339b.

> there was firm friendship between Majd al-Dīn and Khwāja ʿAlī Shāh.... Majd al-Dīn also wove friendship between the other two, so that Karīm al-Dīn sent to him valuable gifts and objects, as well as money for trading in merchandise. Majd al-Dīn sometimes resided in Tabriz and sometimes in the *ordū*. Everyone in Cairo used to resort to Majd al-Dīn.[32]

In 723/1323, the following year, this claim was confirmed when Jūbān and ʿAlī Shāh sent gifts to Karīm al-Dīn in addition to those conveyed to the sultan, and Karīm al-Dīn reciprocated. Thus,

> the basis of peace between these two kings was Karīm al-Dīn in Egypt and Vizier Khwāja ʿAlī Shāh in the East. The embassies and gifts between the two viziers were uninterrupted, with Majd al-Dīn al-Sallāmī as the ambassador. In this al-Qāḍī Karīm al-Dīn had dazzled ʿAlī Shāh with all sorts of presents and gifts which he used to send to him, until he finally won him over. ʿAlī Shāh, in turn, prevailed with Jūbān, and Jūbān prevailed with Abū Saʿīd and the Mongol chiefs, it being God's desire to unite Islam.[33]

As simplistic as this interpretation may be, it highlights nonetheless the importance assigned to diplomatic gifts both by officers of state and by historians.

Now I shall try to suggest the nature of the gifts that were exchanged in various missions. As far as the Ilkhans are concerned, they could be counted on to send animals, both bipeds and quadrupeds. The bipeds, of course, were slaves, both *mamlūks* and girls; the latter are often characterized as pretty and accomplished in music and dancing, as the sultan was known to be an admirer of pulchritude.[34] Quadrupeds included trains (*qiṭār*) of Bactrian camels, sometimes as many as four trains. (How many camels made up a *qiṭār* I do not know.) Also among the gifts were Anatolian horses (*akādīsh*) known for their stamina and quick gait. Sometimes they were provided with covers of rough red broadcloth (*jūkh*). Cheetahs were also sent, obviously to be used for hunting, a favorite royal pastime, as were the falcons and birds of prey sent on occasion. Aside from animals, the Ilkhans also frequently offered jewels of great price, including big pearls and Balkash rubies, which Abū Saʿīd bought on the cheap, perhaps upon the advice of his vizier Khwāja ʿAlī Shāh, "who was

---

[32] Ibid., fol. 339b.
[33] Ibid., fol. 344a.
[34] Ibid., fol. 391b.

a dealer in jewels and precious stuffs."[35] Similarly, bejeweled golden belts (*ḥiyāṣa, ḥawā'iṣ*) and saddles trimmed in gold were included among the gifts. The Mongols liked to offer weapons: swords of various types, plus maces and arrows. Quantities of fabrics, including clothes, were often presented. Though these are usually unidentified, once a collection of fabrics of native manufacture was specified: "*jumlat qumāsh min ʿamal al-bilād*."[36] But these are examples of ordinary, routine gifts. Infrequently the Mongols must have decided that they should find something for the Mamluk sultan who had everything. Thus, in 720/1320, when peace negotiations began in earnest, Abū Saʿīd sent al-Nāṣir an assortment of special gifts, including a unique steel helmet upon which a complete Qur'ān was engraved in pure gold (*khūdhat fūlādh manqūsh ʿalayhi al-Qur'ān kāmilan jamīʿuhu dhahab ʿayn*).[37] As if this were not enough, Abū Saʿīd also accompanied it with three trains of Bactrian camels, ten slave girls, six *mamlūk*s, and a few pearls. Moreover, this royal mission had been preceded by the merchant of the Mamluks, Majd al-Dīn al-Sallāmī, who bore his own gifts, including a bejeweled pavilion—a *khargāh mujawhar*—and a Siqlāṭ tent (*khayma siqlāṭ*), *siqlāṭ* being a scarlet silk manufactured in Anatolia that became famous throughout Europe.[38] These tents were also accompanied by *mamlūk*s, Turkish slave girls, Bactrian camels, and precious stuffs. In the following year, 721/1321, al-Sallāmī arrived in Cairo with a letter from Abū Saʿīd and a complete copy of the Qur'ān in sixty large parts,[39] reminiscent of the famous Ilkhanid Qur'ān in thirty parts sent earlier by Khudābandā, which ended up in the hands of the Mamluk sometime royal favorite, Baktimur, and is still preserved today.[40] One last Mongol object should be mentioned: a cap sent in 729/1329 by Baghdād Khātūn, intended for her brother Timurtāsh in Cairo but intercepted by Abū Saʿīd. After all, Timurtāsh had no use for it, having been executed, unbeknownst to his sister. The cap was a *qubʿ* of Mongol workmanship, resembling a *jamala*—a turban—adorned with Balkash rubies worth

[35] Boyle (1968), 402.
[36] Ibn al-Dawādārī (1960), vol. 9, 372.
[37] Al-ʿAynī, ms. Ahmet III 2912/4, fol. 328b.
[38] Ibid., fol. 328b.
[39] Al-Nuwayrī (1997), 12. Although Qur'āns divided into sixty sections were not common, they are known. See James (1988), 21.
[40] See Rogers (1972), 388–89. Cf. James (1988), 110–26.

100,000 *dirhams*. It was paired with a gold belt studded with jewels worth five hundred *dīnārs*.[41]

With one exception we do not have as much information about the Egyptian gifts of this period, i.e., the first quarter of the fourteenth century. The favored presents were apparently garments, weapons, and horses, none of which seems to have been on the same scale as the most lavish of the Ilkhans' offerings. As for garments, the sultan more than once sent robes made in Alexandria bearing the *ṭirāz* titles of the Ilkhan Abū Sa'īd and his deputy Jūbān. More specifically, for example, in 1320, in response to the Mongols' peace proposals and gifts, al-Nāṣir sent to Abū Sa'īd a *fawqānī*—an outer garment with *ṭirāz* embroidery and a brocade border made in Bawal,[42] a place said to be famous for its silk—and a Tatarī coat in the latest fashion, apparently meaning it had a reverse diagonal hem across the chest.[43] In addition to court costumes, the sultan also sent military apparel, including mail shirts/brigandines (*qarqalāt*), caparisons (*barkustawarāt*), presumably for horses, and helmets.[44] Robes of honor were distributed routinely to all envoys to the Mamluk court, ranging from satin brocades to those of an Alexandrian fabric called *ṭardwaḥsh* for lesser figures.[45]

But to give a fuller picture of Mamluk gifts I shall have to violate the limits of my paper and revert to an earlier era and a different set of Mongols. In 661/1263, news reached the Mamluk sultan that Berke, *khān* of the Golden Horde Mongols in southern Russia, having converted to Islam, proposed joint action against the Ilkhan Hülegü. To welcome this auspicious Muslim alliance against the Ilkhans, Baybars sent him a shower of lavish gifts. According to Ibn al-Dawādārī the contingent of animals included elephants, giraffes, monkeys (apes?), Arabian stallions, wild spotted asses from Yemen as well as Egyptian asses of some sort, plus white racing camels. In addition, Ibn al-Dawādārī states, Baybars sent a large number of garments, jewelry, brocades, silver-inlaid candlesticks, Abadan mats, China vessels, cloth from Alexandria, fabric manufactured in the Dār al-Ṭirāz (Court Workshop for Fabric Inscriptions), plus sugar

41 Al-'Aynī, ms. Ahmet III 2912/4, fol. 384a–b.
42 Ibid, fol. 328b.
43 See Mayer (1952), 20–21.
44 Al-'Aynī, ms. Ahmet III 2912/4, fol. 328b.
45 Ibid., fol. 344b.

products.[46] Curiously, we have a different, more detailed, list preserved by another historian, Ibn ʿAbd al-Ẓāhir, the sultan's private secretary. In addition to the animals listed by Ibn al-Dawādārī, Ibn ʿAbd al-Ẓāhir mentions noble Arabian racing steeds, rare Nubian camels, and fabulous trained monkeys (*nasāsīs*), along with various types of gear and costumes for these beasts. Human gifts included eunuchs and slave-girl cooks. Among the inanimate gifts, most spectacular was a Qurʾān said to have been written by the third caliph, ʿUthmān, in the mid-seventh century, housed in a red satin brocade cover inside a leather case lined in taffeta, complete with its own stand worked in ivory and ebony filigree with silver clasp and bolt! There were also prayer rugs and mats of various kinds along with Lawātī (Berber?) garments of various colors and many pieces of Venetian stuff. Weapons included double-edged sabers with silver trim, maces with gilded handles, bows of various types, hook-nosed lances, Arab spearheads, finely crafted arrows contained in leather-bound chests, Frankish helmets with silver edges, enameled targes, plated bridles strung with silver ribbon, Khwarazmian saddles of Bulgarian leather, ammunition sacks trimmed in silver, and silver-plated chain armor. Among the domestic items were lamps—silver and otherwise—with Venetian plating, enameled candle holders, silver lanterns with Venetian covers, and cushions and mats.[47]

In conclusion I will say only that diplomatic exchanges obviously provided occasions for cultural exchanges, both on material and non-tangible levels. These, coupled with other types of interaction, such as emigration of Mongols to Mamluk territory, Mamluk purchase of Mongol slaves, Mamluk marriages with Mongol women, and trade, insured opportunities for cultural influences and borrowing, though the evidence for these is problematic. But to end on a realistic note and to draw attention to the fact that relations were by no means always cozy and cordial, I would mention that the most spectacular Mamluk gift of all was the severed head of the Ilkhanid noble and warrior, Timurtāsh, which al-Nāṣir sent unofficially to Abū Saʿīd in 729/1329.

---

[46] Ibn al-Dawādārī (1960), vol. 8, 97.

[47] Ibn ʿAbd al-Ẓāhir (1976), 172–73. For a list probably derived from Ibn ʿAbd al-Ẓāhir, see Baybars al-Manṣūrī (1998), 83. Because of linguistic difficulties mentioned at the beginning of this paper, I have by no means exhausted the possibilities offered by these lists—including Ibn al-Dawādārī's—which deserve further detailed study.

JOCHID LUXURY METALWORK: ISSUES OF GENESIS AND DEVELOPMENT

MARK KRAMAROVSKY

In two recent publications (the exhibition catalogue *Treasures of the Golden Horde*[1] and the book *The Gold of the Chinggisids: The Cultural Legacy of the Golden Horde*[2]) I have analyzed the formation and development of the luxury metalwork associated with the branch of the Mongol dynasty, the descendants of Jochi, son of Chinggis (Genghis) Khan, the *ulus* Jochi, best known as the Golden Horde. Building upon my previous work, in this paper I intend to concentrate on two related topics.

The first is the more complicated issue. It concerns the problem of the genesis of Chinggisid luxury metalwork in general and its relationship to the Golden Horde material in particular. The second issue has to do with the characterization of the main vector in the development of Jochid toreutics, or relief-decorated metalwork. This paper will not address the stylistic quality of single objects or groups of objects, nor will it consider the interpretation of the stylistic and iconographic links between the metalwork and roughly contemporary East and Central Asian textiles. The former has already been discussed by the present author (in the aforementioned publications), while the latter topic has been ably documented by James Watt.[3]

Watt's highly original proposal that masterpieces of Mongol Empire metalwork made prior to 1270 were the work of Chinese craftsmen[4] runs contrary to earlier theories in which certain objects were associated with the workmanship of Jurchens of the Jin State. Central to this revised way of thinking, though apparently unknown to Watt, is the fact that no Chinese belts were actually found with the buried treasure from the Crimea, discovered in the area of the modern

---

[1] Kramarovsky (2000).
[2] Kramarovsky (2001).
[3] See Watt, J. C. Y. (2002).
[4] Ibid., 67.

city of Simferopol.[5] Misinformation regarding a Chinese 'silver' belt previously thought to have come from the Crimea is the double mistake of the English editor of the recent discussion of the belt and its archaeological context.[6] First, the belt is made not of silver but brass. Second, it was found not in the Crimea but in the Volga area at the site Selitrennoe, identified as Saray al-Makhrus—the first capital of the Golden Horde. Third, the belt dates to the fourteenth century and therefore it postdates the tradition of the Chinggisid luxury metalwork of the period before 1270. The artifact in question reflects the contacts between the Golden Horde and China's Yüan dynasty.

The question of the important find from the Gashun-Ust region in the North Caucasus is more complicated. Watt believes that the gold belt from Gashun-Ust, which includes the *tamgha* associated with the house of Batu (r. 1227–55), Jochi's son and founder of the Golden Horde, either belongs to the period of the Jin dynasty in Northern China and was made by a Chinese master and later became a trophy of the Mongols, or the object was produced by a Chinese artisan from Jin state expressly for a member of Batu-Khān's family (pls. 2a–c).[7] In this instance, I can agree with only one of Watt's suppositions, namely, that the belt belonged to the *oglan* or prince of the blood from the 'Batu House.' The small pendant with the *tamgha* testifies to this assumption (pl. 2a). Furthermore, the type of the *tamgha* dates this find to the 1270s.

Before looking further at Watt's findings, let us first pose the following question: why shouldn't the workmanship of the gold belt from Gashun-Ust be linked with Jurchens of the Jin state? Perhaps because of the fact that in the Jin Empire the Jurchens altogether accounted for no more than 10 percent of the total population? Or because only the Chinese (including artists and craftsmen) could have been taken prisoner and forced to work for the Jin? These are certainly not adequate reasons against a Jurchen attribution, and indeed evidence for a Jurchen connection will be cited below.

The belt type from Gashun-Ust is not specifically Chinese. Another (non-Chinese) belt that is very close in style was found in the Tash-

---

[5] Kramarovsky (2001), 114–20.

[6] See Fedorov-Davydov (1991), 153, cat. no. 34; however, on 51, and evidently not consulted by Watt, the correct information is given.

[7] Watt, J. C. Y. (2002), 67.

Bashat cemetery in the Talas valley, Kirghizia.[8] As on the Gashun-Ust example (pls. 2b–c), the main motif in the ornamentation of the belt plaques from Tash-Bashat is again the figure of a deer set against a landscape background. The same theme is likewise found on several unprovenanced gold belt plaques from the Khalili Collection.[9] There is no doubt in my mind that the Khalili belt fittings are not Chinese, yet at the same time these belt fittings share the features of the art of East Asia. Let us try to trace which traditions of East Asian art are reflected in the objects under consideration.

Bronze and iron belt buckles with the decorative motifs in question have been found in the levels of the twelfth to early thirteenth centuries at the Jurchen site at Lazovskoe in extreme far eastern Russia or Russian Primor'ye territory.[10] Similar objects were uncovered at two other sites in the same region: bronze belt plaques with images of deer were found at Shaiginskoe (houses 134, 174),[11] while two other objects decorated with the same decoration were discovered at Ananjinskoe (a leaden belt lap from house 27 and a stone seal from house 11).[12] The finds from Lazovsskoe (two belt buckles and plaques discovered during the excavation of the house) were produced by Khitan craftsmen, according to the excavator.[13] Furthermore, the common occurrence of deer motives in nephrite objects of the Liao and Jin dynasties points to connections with the Khitan and Jurchen traditions. I can cite as examples the unpublished sword plaques (c. 960–1279) in the Gugun Museum, Beijing, and the Jurchen plaque with the scene of an autumn hunt from the collection of the National Palace Museum, Taipei.[14]

Another possible link between the proposed Jurchen workmanship of the belt from Gashun-Ust and its Jochid connection may have to do with the events of the year 1233, when the Mongols under the command of Subedai took the Jin capital of Kaifeng. The combined population of the inhabitants of Kaifeng and the people of the surrounding provinces, numbering some one million, were

[8] Kramarovsky (2001), 45, fig. 20.
[9] Watt, J. C. Y. (2002), 67, fig. 65.
[10] Shavkunov (1990), 140, tab. 41, 1–4.
[11] Ibid., 140.
[12] Ibid., tab. 43, 3, 4, 18.
[13] Khodzevich (1988).
[14] Fong and Watt, J. C. Y. (1996), 60, pl. 23.

spared, perhaps on account of the extreme concentration of such a large number in one city. My observations are similar to those of Watt, but with one difference: the tradition of Jurchen workmanship seems too obvious.

It is difficult to explain the means of transmission of this tradition, for we do not have any textual evidence attesting to the activity of Jurchen craftsmen among the Golden Horde. Perhaps the answer lies in part in the assumption that the volumetric details of the belt would have been made with the use of a matrix or mold. In fact such bronze molds with the image of a reclining deer have been found at sites of Golden Horde cities.[15] One of the molds was recently found in the eastern Crimea in the region of the Golden Horde site of Solkhat, where the expedition of the State Hermitage Museum has an ongoing excavation.[16]

Let us return once more to the problem of the dating of the Gashun-Ust belt ornaments. The reverse sides of the large plaques are decorated with the so-called 'Arabian' lotus.[17] These stylized flowers resemble neither the lotuses on the Tash-Bashat belt cited above, nor the lotus-like decorative elements from the Khalili Collection.[18] One can see an analogy in the decoration of certain of the luster-painted star tiles from the tomb chamber of the Pīr-i Ḥusayn mausoleum and *khānqāh*, Baku, whose inscriptions range in date from 1284 to 1286.[19] The belt's dating to the period 1270–80 provides some basis to consider the find from Gashun-Ust within the framework of Jochid toreutics, maintaining, as I have asserted, Jurchen tradition.

We should also connect the splendid belt of gilt silver, found not far from Voronezh in southern Russia, with Jurchen workmanship.[20] The belt was discovered in a nomad grave among funerary goods that included chain-link armor and a helmet, a cup with a dragon-shaped handle, and a battle axe.[21] I would here like to correct the

---

[15] For example, objects from the Volga region or Istanbul [Constantinople]; see Kramarovsky (2001), 50, fig. 22.

[16] Kramarovsky (2004), tabl. III, 27, 28.

[17] Kramarovsky (2000), 22.

[18] Komaroff and Carboni, eds. (2002), 17, fig. 10.

[19] Krachkovskaia (1946), 101. For a color illustration of the group of tiles now in the Hermitage, see Piotrovsky and Vrieze, eds. (1999), 217. Also see fig. 80 in this volume.

[20] Kramarovsky (2000), 63–66, cat. 20.

[21] Ibid., 68, cat. 22.

mistake that I made in the catalogue,[22] and redate the axe between the twelfth and the turn of the thirteenth centuries. Axes of the same type have been found in Central Europe, for example in Shlenska in Monrovia,[23] where, after the Mongols' victory in Silesia (Lignitza, 9 April 1241), the western Mongol corps of Batu-Khān passed through Bohemia and Monrovia. It is quite possible that the Mongol burial near Voronezh belonged to a veteran of the Central European campaign, completed in 1242. Hence follows the proposed date for the belt with images of panthers dating from the late twelfth to the first half of the thirteenth centuries.

It would be somewhat simplistic to state that such finds bring us to the epoch when the culture of the Mongol Empire was first formed. Rather, it is important to stress that the initial step in the development of Jochi *ulus*, beginning from 1207 and up to the end of European campaign in 1242, coincides with the formative period of a culturally defined Chinggisid Empire. Therefore the gold and silver objects connected with the first generations of Chinggisids both from Central Asian regions and from south Siberia or the Eurasian steppe beyond the Urals are very important for us. We have already considered one such find from the Voronezh area. As already noted, a cup with dragon-like handles was found in that same Mongol burial.[24] Vessels of the same type are known in Siberia,[25] northern Caucasus,[26] and in the Volga and Dnieper regions.[27] The two-handled wine cup related to this group of vessels was found in the excavations of the site of Tsarev (Old Saray).[28] All the vessels from this group are datable to the thirteenth century.

Let us now turn to a group of military belts with dragon images. The heraldry of the 'Emperor' and his 'guards' used the image of the dragon, formed in the brief stretch of time from 1204–6 to 1217. In 1221, Chao Hung observed it during his visit to Yen Jing (Bei-

---

22 Ibid., 218, cat. 22.

23 Paulsen (1956), 170–84, figs. 88, 89a–b, 90a–b, 90a–b, 92.

24 Kramarovsky (2001), 64, fig. 25.

25 Kramarovsky (2000), 213, cat. 12, 214, n. 14; Kramarovsky (2001), 63, fig. 24; 65, fig. 26.

26 Kramarovsky (2000), 213, cat. 13; Kramarovsky (2001), 61–72.

27 Smirnov (1909), pl. CXVIII, n. 300; Kramarovsky (2000), 59, 214, 215, cat. 15.

28 Ibid.

jing), the former Jurchen capital.[29] This chronological framework is likely to be shortened. Up to the present, the finds of soldiers' belts with dragon representations are known only from the archaeological materials from the European steppe zone, where they had already penetrated with the first generation of Jochid riders in the 1220s–40s. The topography of the finds is delineated by the regions of the Dnieper region, the middle Don region, the steppes of the Caucasus foreland, and the middle and lower Volga regions.

There are three finds from the Dnieper region.[30] One is from a destroyed burial near the village of Kargi, a belt (now lost, probably of silver) from a grave on Berezan, an island in the Dnieper estuary, and a belt from a barrow near Novo-Podkiaj village in the middle Priorelie. The best information has survived only for the nomad grave near Novo-Podkiaj village, which produced belt gear with faces decorated with depictions of dragons and decorated on the reverse with scale patterns.

Three other belts of the type in question came from the middle Don region and from the Caucasus foreland[31] (from Vlasov cemetery burial goods, from the barrow near the village of Novoberezanskaya in Krasnodar area and from the cemetery in the Stavropol area).

Among the finds from the lower Volga region, we should consider a belt from a destroyed burial at the site of Krasny Yar,[32] where a fragment of the leather strap has survived (pl. 3). The gilt silver set consists of the buckle, the tip, the sliding girdle, two sword plaques with loops for suspending the scabbard, and twenty-five small lunette-shaped plaques. As the key elements of the belt have been preserved we can estimate that it originally measured 125–150 cm in length, and was formed of as many as sixty-five to seventy separate elements. The composition of the decoration of the obverse plaque of the belt tip has two dragons with complementary inverted fishtails; the back is covered by a scale pattern. The sword plaques are rectangular in shape with large loops. They were produced in the technique of openwork casting. The greater part of the design space is occupied by the image of a three-clawed dragon, while the lower field is filled by the figure of the bird in flight, its large beak

[29] See Meng-Ta Pei-Lu und Hei-Ta Shih Lüeh (1980), 72.
[30] Kramarovsky (2001), 35–40, figs. 14, 1–9; 10–16.
[31] Ibid., 40–41, figs. 14, 17–19.
[32] Ibid., 41–45, fig. 18.

and powerful feathering suggesting that it is a falcon. This type of sword plaque with the loop marked out and the relief representation of three-clawed dragon on the obverse is known in carved nephrite of the Sung dynasty. The belts mentioned above belong to a single cultural tradition.

As already noted, in the circle of the new Chinggisid elite, the figure of the dragon carried the charge of a pan-imperial symbol. There is no representation of the five-clawed dragon of imperial China among the Golden Horde finds. A dragon with three claws is represented on each of the eight gold belt plaques from the grave of the Khitan Princess Chenguo, the niece of Emperor Shengzong, who died in 1018,[33] while four-clawed dragons occur among the tile decoration of the Mongol palace at Takht-i Sulayman in north-western Iran.[34] It is significant to note that the Chinese ambassador to the Mongols attached importance not to the details (the number of dragon's claws), but to the material with which the object had been made.[35] Belts with dragon heraldry seemed to appear among the Mongols virtually overnight. Apparently, they were called into being by the abrupt changes in the level of state-building after the reforms of 1206, when the creation and rapid growth of a number of new branches of the military aristocracy demanded new emblems of authority.

Both groups of belts belonged to the first generation of Jochid military corps that came to the European steppe zone around the middle of the thirteenth century. The typological and stylistic predecessors of these belts originated in Central Asia before the Jochi *ulus* had separated from the Yeke Mongol *ulus*, or Great Mongol State (1211–64). It is precisely in these objects that one can see a part of the Mongol legacy that was brought to Dest-i Kipchak (the lands from the Altai Mountains to the Volga River) by the first generation of invaders and there, on new ground, gave rise to the phenomenon later called Golden Horde culture.

The loss of the norms of Mongol nomadic culture can be seen among the Golden Horde by the time of their conversion to Islam in

[33] Shaanxi Historic Museum (n.d.), 8. See also *Wen Wu* 11 (1987), 22, fig. 39, for two of the eight belt plaques.

[34] On this see also Masuya (2002), 96–97 [Ed.].

[35] Chao (1975), 76.

the middle Jochid period (late thirteenth to mid-fourteenth century). Take, for example, the great variety of objects from the Simferopol hoard, which can be dated to the first half of the fourteenth century. This hoard, which belonged to a Mongol ruler of the Crimea, included three belts.[36] Two of them follow Italian tradition and are perhaps of Venetian and Tuscan workmanship; only one is of the Golden Horde. It is very interesting for our subject that one of the most remarkable things about the composition of the Simferopol hoard is the set of ornaments for a tiny woman's cap.[37] In the tradition of the construction of the central adornment of this headdress several traits can be traced back to Chinese workmanship of the sixth through seventh centuries,[38] yet all the parts of the cap were produced at the same time and place, perhaps at the capital of Golden Horde in the Crimea, the city of Solkhat.

In this paper we have traced the development of several forms of Jochid luxury metalwork beginning with its sources in the early thirteenth century and linked with the cultural formation of the Great Mongol State in the time of Chinggis Khan up to the middle of the fourteenth century. The latter period witnessed the intensive Islamization of the Golden Horde, and in their deviation from the old cultural paradigm of the first generations of nomadic invaders a new paradigm, based on sedentary, urban, and Islamic values, was initiated. As we have already seen, Latin workmanship of Venice and Tuscany exerted a marked influence on the formation of a new artistic tradition in Golden Horde Crimea.[39]

---

[36] Kramarovsky (2000), 83, cat. 527–64; 323, cat. 517–26; Kramarovsky (2001), 140–56.

[37] Kramarovsky (2000), 82, cat. 307–22; Kramarovsky (2004), 69, pl. IV, 1, 2.

[38] Han and Deydier (2001), 112, 274.

[39] For further details about this interesting phenomenon see Kramarovsky (2001), 140–61.

THE MARITIME TRADE OF KISH DURING THE MONGOL PERIOD

RALPH KAUZ

Kish[1] was one of the major emporia in the Persian Gulf in medieval times; it is chronologically and geographically located between the two others, namely Siraf and Hormuz. Siraf, nearby modern Bandar Taheri, served as the main port of the Sasanian dynasty and continued to operate well after the Arab occupation of Iran. At the end of the tenth century an earthquake damaged parts of the city, and the occupation by its rival Kish during the 1060s or 1070s destroyed this former center of trade on the Iranian shores.[2] However, Kish could not keep its undisputed position for long: a new rival grew in the city of Hormuz at the beginning of the thirteenth century. (Old) Hormuz was a town located at the mouth of the Persian Gulf on the mainland, near Minab. Around the year 1300, Hormuz was largely abandoned and most of its inhabitants relocated to the island of Jarun, probably due to raids of Mongol-Turkic bands.[3] This new emporium, also known as Hormuz, would irrevocably substitute for Kish as the major port of the gulf in the 1330s. Thus, one can observe a movement of the Persian Gulf emporia from east to southwest and west, directing to the entry of the gulf. The harbors that laid closer to this entry could naturally block the traffic, and trade was, in fact, frequently accompanied by piracy.[4]

---

[1] For the various spellings of the island's name see Houtsma, ed. (1913–38), vol. 2, 695–97, s.v. '*Kais*.' The entry in the second edition of the *Encyclopaedia of Islam* contains only a few sentences without much relevance; see Gibb et al. (1960–2002), vol. 4, 832, s.v. '*Kays*'; Pelliot (1959), vol. 1, 244–45; Sīstānī (1998–99), 41–50. The main forms are *Kīsh* (Persian) and *Qays* which is also pronounced as *Qīs*; the last form probably derives from the occupation of the island by Qays ibn ʿUmayra; Houtsma, ed. (1913–38), vol. 2, 695.

[2] Whitehouse (1983), 328–34 and 328–29.

[3] The situation in Kirman was principally unstable in this period; thus, there might have been more reasons for the Hormuzian princes to carry out this move (cf. Gibb et al. [1960–2002], vol. 5, 162–63, s.v. '*Kirman*').

[4] See, for example, the story of an act of piracy committed by two Banī Qayṣar in Waṣṣāf; Waṣṣāf (1853), 174 (page citation is to the 1959–60 reprint edition). Besides

Kish constituted the main port during the rule of the Seljuks and their aftermath, and the city's rivalry with (Old) Hormuz had just started when the Mongols campaigned against Iran and finally occupied it. The superiority of one of the two ports alternated during the period of Ilkhanid rule in Iran, but, when this dynasty came to an end, Hormuz was the final winner in the struggle.

This slow shift can be observed through the eyes of some contemporary travelers. The first, Benjamin of Tudela, who traveled through the Middle East in the years 1164 to 1173, mentions Kish as the major port of the Persian Gulf,[5] while one hundred years later Marco Polo traveled directly to Hormuz on his way to China. Upon arrival, he and his elders changed their minds and chose to make the journey overland because they regarded the local vessels as 'wretched affairs' (according to the translation of Yule), but they came back by ship from China to the same city. Marco Polo mentions Kish only briefly, while he describes Hormuz in greater detail.[6] Ibn Baṭṭūṭa, however, during his journeys in the first half of the fourteenth century obviously stayed in Kish for some time, as his notes indicate.[7] At first glance, these few observations apparently show that Kish reached its height before the Mongol occupation of the Middle East, but this paper will show that a dense interaction,

---

his 'Geschichte Waṣṣāfs,' the first chapter of Waṣṣāf's opus, Joseph Hammer-Purgstall also translated the remaining four. This translation shall be published by the Institute of Iranian Studies of the Austrian Academy of Sciences in due course. Karl Jahn ordered a typescript of the original manuscript and made some annotations. I will also quote this translation according to the pagination of this typescript, thus Waṣṣāf (n.d.), 102–3.

[5] Benjamin of Tudela (1966), 62–63; Gabriel (1952), 28–31. Nāṣir-i Khusraw, who traveled in the middle of the eleventh century through the region, mentions Kish only by name besides the other ports Qatif and Makran; Nāṣir-i Khusraw and Rastegar (1993), 97. We hear nothing from him about either Siraf or Hormuz. The following two renowned compilations list the records of the Arab geographers on Kish: 1969 reprint of Schwarz (1896), 88–89 (page citations are to the 1969 reprint edition), and Le Strange (1905), 257 (page citation is to the 1966 reprint edition); see also Wilson (1954), 97–100, and Krawulsky (1978), 192–193.

[6] Polo (1903), vol. 1, 63, 84 (Polo writes here, "Dealers carry their horses to Kisi and Curmosa...," and treats them thus more or less as equivalents); vol. 2, 340, 452; for Hormuz see especially 107–122 (page citations are to the 1991 reprint edition). It should, however, be noted that Rashīd al-Dīn starts his description from the route to China not in Hormuz but in Kish; see Rashīd al-Dīn (1980), 35.

[7] Ibn Baṭṭūṭa (1958–2000), vol. 4, 848; Ibn Baṭṭūṭa also gives a rough description of Kish, which he falsely names Siraf, and its pearl fishing industry (ibid., vol. 2, 407–9, see n. 138 regarding the confusion of the two toponyms).

as well as confrontation, existed between the two emporia and that none of them permanently predominated during the Mongol rule in Iran.

This paper will pursue several aims: (1) outline the geopolitical setting of Kish; (2) elucidate its position in the maritime network of the Indian Ocean; and (3) discuss the interaction and confrontation with Hormuz, as well as Kish's position in the Mongol world.

I

The island of Kish, situated about eleven miles from the mainland, is about ten miles long and four and a half miles wide. It is surrounded by a reef and has no natural harbors, which suggests that larger boats had to anchor outside of the reef or had to be hauled up onto the beach.[8] The main industry until recent days—except trade—has been pearl fishery, whose technique is vividly described by Ibn Baṭṭūṭa.[9] The island was essentially bare of vegetation, but due to cisterns in which rainwater could be collected and a rather high water level at some places, land could be cultivated. As in other places on the shores of the gulf, most travelers complained of the great heat in the summer months, but they described also the wealth and abundance of the island.[10] The city of Kish stood on the northern shores of the island, where its ruins are still visible.[11] Shiraz was for Kish the main commercial and political center on the mainland. A convenient communication with Shiraz, the capital of the province of Fars, was one of the necessities for the emporium because it constituted one of the major regional markets. The description of this route via Khonj to Hozu, the anchorage at the mainland opposite of Kish, is given in the *Nuzhat al-qulūb*.[12] This

---

[8] Adamec, ed. (1989), 595; Stiffe (1896), 645; Whitehouse (1976), 146.

[9] Ibn Baṭṭūṭa (1958–2000), vol. 2, 408–9.

[10] Mustawfī (1915–19), 135 (Eng.), 136 (Per.) (page citations are to the 1993 reprint edition); Adamec, ed. (1989), 595; Wilson (1954), 97–100; on the cisterns and the *qanāt* found on Kish see Stiffe (1896), 644–45.

[11] For short descriptions of these ruins see Whitehouse (1976), 146–47, and Sīstānī (1998–99), 58–60.

[12] Mustawfī (1915–19), 176 (Eng.), 185–86 (Per.) (page citations are to the 1993 reprint edition). Schön (1990), 14–15, states that the route passed Khonj; see also Aubin (1969), 21–37.

route was the most important route on the land; on sea, merchants had already in pre-Islamic times woven a close net with the other ports in the Persian Gulf and beyond.[13] The history of Kish should be seen in the context of these commercial and economic networks, but unfortunately the relevant sources focus on political rather than economic history.

A somewhat rough sketch shall be drawn of the historical development of Kish for two reasons: this paper focuses on Kish's role in international trade, and second, Jean Aubin has already written a detailed study of the political history of the Persian Gulf including Kish during the period that is here of concern, though he put Hormuz at the center of his study.[14]

Waṣṣāf relates that the first rulers of Kish came from Siraf and were sons of a shipmaster named Qayṣar; the name of his eldest son was Qays. They occupied the formerly uninhabited island which was called Kish in 'Iraq-i 'ajam.[15] There is no clue when exactly this occupation took place, but the early Arabic geographers already mention the island itself.[16] Kish successfully repulsed Seljuk attempts to avert its rising political and commercial influence and surpassed Siraf in the course of the eleventh century. The contemporaneous ruler of Kish, Abū al-Qāsim, finally occupied the former hub of the Persian Gulf in the 1060s or 1070s.[17] Under the formal suzerainty of the Seljuks, Kish quickly rose to become the major emporium in the region.[18] An indispensable necessity of this growth was the hindrance of potential competitors. Therefore the rulers of Kish tried in vain to acquire Hormuz from Malik Dīnār, the Ghuzz ruler of Kirman,

---

[13] For the importance of the Sirāfī and other merchants see Piacentini (1992), 167–73.

[14] Aubin (1953), 77–138, for Kish esp. 80–105; see also Piacentini (1975), 69–89.

[15] Waṣṣāf (1853), 170, 174 (page citations are to the 1959–60 reprint edition); Waṣṣāf (n.d.), 90, 101.

[16] Schwarz (1896), 88–89 (page citations are to the 1969 reprint edition); Whitehouse (1976), 146, puts this occupation in the eleventh century.

[17] Whitehouse (1983), 328–29; Ibn al-Balkhī (1921), 136–37; Ḥāfiẓ-i Abrū (1996–2000), vol. 2, 126–27, remarks in his chapter on Siraf that ships from India and China came to Siraf. This is one of the remarks which could incline one to the assumption that Chinese ships came to the western Indian Ocean. This is, nevertheless, rather improbable and Ḥāfiẓ-i Abrū could have judged from his own period or have meant ships traveling to China.

[18] Iqtidārī (1966–67), 160–63.

at the end of the twelfth century.[19] This incident anticipated the rivalry between the two provinces of Kirman (capital Kirman) and Fars (capital Shiraz) concerning their role as mercantile centers in the hinterland of the *entrepôts* of Hormuz and Kish.

But Hormuz did not really threaten the position of Kish in that early period; a more formidable competitor was the famous port of Aden. Walad al-ʿAmīd, ruler of Kish, attacked Aden around 1135, probably only aiming to conquer the seaside fort and not the whole city. The attackers could have been aiming to seize the duties or to prevent Indian merchants embarking at Aden. Be that as it may, the inhabitants of Aden succeeded in repulsing this assault with the assistance of some Indian vessels that reached Aden just in time.[20]

Here we should remember the description of Benjamin of Tudela, who, at the end of the twelfth century, drew a picture of a prosperous port where all sorts of commodities were traded by merchants from Arabia to India.[21] In that period, Kish was still ruled by the Banū Qayṣar, who controlled the major *entrepôt* of the Persian Gulf and acquired, according to Waṣṣāf, considerable fame among the other realms bordering the Indian Ocean.[22]

This almost uncontested status nevertheless changed with the emergence of Hormuz not many decades later. The following century is characterized by a fierce competition between the two emporia. For the sake of brevity, only the more important events of this period shall be mentioned.

The actors were the respective rulers of the two ports, the governors of Fars (first the Salghurids; after their fall in 1286–87, the province came under direct Mongol rule), then with minor significance the governors of Kirman and the Mongols themselves.[23] The capable *atabeg* Abū Bakr (r. 1226–60) himself submitted to the Mongol conquerors and thus saved his own rule and Fars from occupation.[24]

Due to this tactical move, he could act relatively independently in the areas adjoining the Gulf and soon came into conflict with the

[19] Houtsma, ed. (1913–38), vol. 2, 696.

[20] For a study on this incident see Goitein (1954).

[21] Benjamin of Tudela (1966), 62–63.

[22] Waṣṣāf (1853), 174 (page citation is to the 1959–60 reprint edition); Waṣṣāf (n.d.), 104.

[23] For a short history of these provinces see Spuler (1968), 139–55.

[24] Juwaynī (1997), 234.

rulers of Kish who occupied large parts of it. Yet Abū Bakr lacked the necessary naval equipment to attack Kish and consequently permitted Sayf al-Dīn Abā Naṣar, prince of Hormuz, to attack and occupy Kish in return for one third of the realm of Kish. Sayf al-Dīn succeeded in conquering Kish, which had no standing army, killing the ruler Malik Sulṭān and wiping out the members of the Banū Qayṣar clan on 8 May 1229 (12 Jumada II, 626). The most important factor for the triumph of the Hormuzians was probably Abū Bakr's ban on the inhabitants of the coast serving Kish as soldiers.[25] Consequently, the dynasty of the Banū Qayṣars and with them the first period of the history of Kish came to an end; for the next decades, the island was no longer ruled by its own sovereigns.

After his conquest, Sayf al-Dīn decided not to hand over Kish as promised to the *atabeg* of Fars and thus provoked a counterattack from that side. Abū Bakr had to prepare for about a year for the operation because he still lacked the necessary equipment; for the time being, he forbade the other ports to deal with Sayf al-Dīn. Two shipmasters of Kish, who earlier transported warships from Maʿbar (roughly the Coromandel Coast)[26] to Hindustan (i.e., northern India), came to the help of Abū Bakr. After they had sold their merchandise (cloth brought from India) in accordance with Sayf al-Dīn, they changed their minds, went to Shiraz and offered Abū Bakr the goods they had just acquired with their capital in Kish. This treasure probably facilitated Abū Bakr's efforts to organize a naval expedition against Hormuz—he conquered Kish from the Hormuzians and killed Sayf al-Dīn on 12 November 1230 (4 Muḥarram 628). Afterwards, Abū Bakr also occupied the other emporia Bahrayn (modern Bahrain) and Qatif; in the latter he met, however, great resistance—but not Hormuz.[27] The Salghurids of Fars remained the overlords of Kish

---

[25] Waṣṣāf (1853), 176–77 (page citations are to the 1959–60 reprint edition); Waṣṣāf (n.d.), 107–10.

[26] This is one of many hints pointing to the close relation between Maʿbar and Kish (and other ports of the Persian Gulf. Another one is told in a legend incorporated in Rashīd al-Dīn's 'History of India,' where Zanāḥīhir/Jayāpīḍa attacks Kish and Bahrayn, but is taken into captivity. After a shipwreck he strands on the shores of Maʿbar, kills a lion, and can conquer Kish with the help of the king of Maʿbar. See Rashīd al-Dīn (1980), 52–53. More of the relations between Kish and Maʿbar will be told below.

[27] Waṣṣāf (1853), 177–79 (page citations are to the 1959–60 reprint edition); Waṣṣāf (n.d.), 113–22.

until 1272, when the Mongols replaced them with their own governors. Mongol suzerainty over Kish was nevertheless mostly a formal affair, as we shall see shortly.[28]

The initiative of the two shipmasters of Kish gives rise to the suspicion that the merchants of the island had no interest in being ruled by the Hormuzians. Why they preferred the sovereignty of the *atabegs* remains open for debate. Aubin suggests that they could maintain a certain decree of autonomy;[29] perhaps they could also continue their business on a less limited scale than would have been possible under the rule of another emporium.

The history of Kish after the overthrow of the Banū Qayṣar remains somewhat obscure, and one may only guess whether their economy and trade flourished. Though it was closely connected with its mainland rulers, its power seemed to diminish to some extent with the increasing power of its rival Hormuz. The next major event that happened to Kish was the occupation by troops of Maḥmūd Qalhātī, a former governor of Qalhat and later ruler of Hormuz in 1272. Sūghūnjāq, Mongol governor of Fars, would expel the Hormuzians in the spring of 1273 by occupying Kish and Qalhat, on the shore of the Sea of Oman.[30] We might recall that Marco Polo visited Hormuz for the first time only in the year 1272.[31] According to his travelogue he showed no inclination to dock a ship in Kish, though it was under the rule of the Mongols who protected him and his elders, but instead went directly to Hormuz. This indicates that Hormuz must have been the primary choice when traveling to the East, even for foreign voyagers who would have heard about the ports only in hearsay.[32]

The fortunes of the two ports changed at the end of the thirteenth century, when (Old) Hormuz was forced to relocate to Jarun, as noted earlier. Bahā' al-Dīn Ayāz, a Turk who had been in the service of Maḥmūd Qalhātī, had the courage to undertake this move. He was

[28] For a short history of Fars in that period see Spuler (1968), 141–45.

[29] Aubin (1953), 82.

[30] Ḥāfiẓ-i Abrū (1996–2000), vol. 2, 178; Aubin (1953), 84–85; Lane, G. (2003), 135–36; on the geopolitical importance of Qalhat, see, for example, Houtsma, ed. (1913–38), vol. 4, 500–1.

[31] Polo (1903), vol. 1, 107–22 (page citations are to the 1991 reprint edition).

[32] The Polos chose later to travel overland because they doubted the safety of the local ships (ibid., 108), but their prior plan was certainly to leave Hormuz by boat.

at times the ally and at other times the enemy of Shaykh al-Islām Jamāl al-Dīn Ibrāhīm b. Muḥammad al-Ṭībī, the sovereign of Kish from the end of the thirteenth century until 1306. It is always questionable to attribute historical developments to a single person, but Jamāl al-Dīn's role in the history of Kish was certainly crucial, as will be demonstrated.

The establishment of the rule of Jamāl al-Dīn remains somewhat obscure. Waṣṣāf first mentions him in an account of sleeping watchmen in the bazaar of Isfahan under the rule of the governor Bahā' al-Dīn (r. 1265–79), son of Shams al-Dīn Juwaynī. João de Barros gives a slightly later date when he notes that in 1281 the entire gulf was under the control of 'Malec Cáez' (Jamāl al-Dīn).[33] The rise of Jamāl al-Dīn and his family was certainly rather swift. He was one of the major merchants of the Persian Gulf who traded with India and China. He was granted the governorship of Fars in 692/1293 for four years and the Ilkhan Geikhatu (r. 1291–95) bestowed on him the title 'Malik-i Islām.'[34] Jamāl al-Dīn's brother Taqī Allāh (according to Waṣṣāf Taqī al-Dīn) b. 'Abd al-Raḥman b. Muḥammad al-Ṭībī was vizier of the sovereign of Ma'bar in this period,[35] and his son Malik-i Mu'aẓẓam Fakhr al-Dīn Aḥmad al-Ṭībī was for some time the supervisor of the regions along the gulf before Ghazan (r. 1295–1304) sent him as an ambassador to China.[36] These offices of the Ṭībī family indicate that they had close relations with many parts of the Indian Ocean. Here it may be stressed that there was a clear discontinuity between the ruling families of Kish—the Banū Qayṣar and the Ṭībīs—though continuity in transmaritime relations.[37] Before we turn to these relations, the rather intricate history of Kish up to its fall shall be roughly outlined.

Jamāl al-Dīn achieved predominance in the Persian Gulf region in the 1280s and 1290s, at least in part because the successful Maḥmūd Qalhātī had died in 1277–78. He could even interfere in the affairs

[33] Waṣṣāf (1853), 62 (page citation is to the 1959–60 reprint edition); Spuler (1968), 347; Barros (1973), part 2, book 2, chap. 2.

[34] Aubin (1953), 90; Waṣṣāf (1853), 268 (page citation is to the 1959–60 reprint edition).

[35] Rashīd al-Dīn (1980), 37; Waṣṣāf (1853), 302 (page citation is to the 1959–60 reprint edition).

[36] Aubin (1953), 92, 96; Waṣṣāf (1853), 505–7 (page citations are to the 1959–60 reprint edition); Waṣṣāf (n.d.), 1332–37; Karashima (1989), 74.

[37] Cf. Aubin (1953), 90–91.

of Hormuz, as during the struggles after Maḥmūd's death when the aforementioned Ayāz achieved dominance over the feuding sons of the deceased ruler. Jamāl al-Dīn granted Ayāz asylum in Kish and assisted him in regaining Hormuz from his adversary Rukn al-Dīn Masʿūd, son of Maḥmūd Qalhātī, in 1294. Additionally, the government of Kirman interfered in the struggle for control over Hormuz. After his return to Hormuz, Ayāz accordingly acknowledged the supremacy of Jamāl al-Dīn's son Fakhr al-Dīn. However, a conflict soon arose between Ayāz and Fakhr al-Dīn which could presently be settled, probably because Jamāl al-Dīn dwelled in Hormuz at this time and because of Ayāz's obligation towards him, but this conflict was only the beginning of a decades-long struggle between Kish and Hormuz. Ayāz seemed to have been too capable an opponent to let him further develop the position of Hormuz as a major emporium in the gulf. Consequently, with the consent of the Mongol rulers, an army consisting of Mongol and Turkic soldiers was equipped in 1296–97 to attack Hormuz and Masʿūd was made commander, though he had plundered Kish in 1294. Ayāz did not continue to commit himself to Jamāl al-Dīn and prepared for the fight. He proved to be the better nautical tactician, defeated the enemy forces completely, and even plundered Kish itself. Jamāl al-Dīn had to sue for peace, not least because he was expecting the annual boats from Maʿbar, and a settlement was reached with Ayāz, though the enmity continued.[38]

The main reason for this struggle was probably the competition between the two emporia for supremacy in the gulf and we find all possible interested parties participating. The strategies of Kish and Hormuz were completely different. Jamāl al-Dīn proceeded in close collaboration with the Mongols and their forces, while Ayāz relied on his own army, whose strategy proved to be in the end the winning one. Ayāz and also the other sovereigns of Hormuz had an enormous, if not decisive, advantage: they could, especially in cooperation with their sister port Qalhat, block the entrance of the gulf and therefore hinder the maritime traffic to the upper regions.

[38] Waṣṣāf (1853), 296–300 (page citations are to the 1959–60 reprint edition); Waṣṣāf (n.d.), 578–93; al-Qāshānī, Abū al-Qāsim (1969–70), 156–61 (Qāshāni depends for this part of his chronicle largely on Waṣṣāf); Teixeira (1902), 160; Aubin (1953), 85–94; Spuler (1968), 148–50.

However, Jamāl al-Dīn still had a strong position as a close ally of the Mongols and governor of several provinces. Ayāz thus could not seek an uncompromising confrontation. This attitude appeared to be essential when Ayāz had to flee from the mainland on the island of Jarun, which he purchased from Jamāl al-Dīn.[39] However, the former center of the realm, Old Hormuz, remained inhabited, especially because it was important for the food supply and a common retreat during the unbearable summer months.

Once settled on the island, Ayāz and his successors could further improve their position, while that of Jamāl al-Dīn seemed to decline. He had difficulties in paying his annual lease for the governorship of Fars and Iraq, which was therefore not extended in 1298, he had difficulties with the Mongol *dīwān* regarding the lease of Kish in 1303, and in 1304 he even refused the governorship of Fars and Baghdad.[40] Jamāl al-Dīn died in late 1306, after his son Fakhr al-Dīn had died on his return journey from China, not far from the coast of Maʿbar, one year earlier.[41]

The violent conflict between Kish and Hormuz ceased during the last years of Jamāl al-Dīn's life and was not resumed by Ayāz, who lived for five years after the death of his rival. Kurdānshāh, a member of the old ruling house and new ruler of Hormuz, and Malik ʿIzz al-Dīn ʿAbd al-ʿAzīz, the rebellious son and successor of Jamāl al-Dīn, started the feud again. ʿIzz al-Dīn still dominated the upper part of the gulf (including Basra) and was for some time also the governor of Fars. He was therefore still closely affiliated with the Mongol government. The erstwhile luck was at this time on the side of Kish, because ʿIzz al-Dīn captured Kurdānshāh after some battles and forced him to pay regular tribute to Kish. This status lasted until 1317–18 when Kurdānshāh died. During the ensuing struggles for succession, Kish launched an unsuccessful attack on Hormuz. ʿIzz al-Dīn was killed in Tabriz in 1325. After the following upheavals had ceased, two grandsons of Jamāl al-Dīn, sons of Fakhr al-Dīn named Ghiyāth al-Dīn Aḥmad and Fakhr al-Dīn Aḥmad, tried to

[39] For a discussion of this transfer see Aubin (1953), 94–96; also Schwarz (1914), 533–35.

[40] Aubin (1953), 98; this does not necessarily mean that Jamāl al-Dīn had financial problems. The Hormuzians were also not good taxpayers and provoked a Timurid attack in 1394 (Sharaf al-Dīn ʿAlī Yazdī (1957–58), vol. 1, 587–89).

[41] Aubin (1953), 99.

conquer Hormuz again after their succession. However, they were not serious enemies for Quṭb al-Dīn, who occupied Kish while they were absent and killed both of them after he returned to Hormuz (1330 or 1331). The same fate awaited all the other descendants of Jamāl al-Dīn, except for two, Malik Shams al-Dīn and Niẓām al-Dīn, who were not present. Niẓām al-Dīn tried with the help of his uncle Shams al-Dīn to regain the island, but they were hindered by Maḥmūd Shāh Īnjū. Shams al-Dīn died soon afterwards and Niẓām al-Dīn followed him a few years later in Delhi, where he had sought asylum.[42]

II

Hormuz would maintain its position as central *entrepôt* of the Persian Gulf until it was conquered by Afonso de Albuquerque in the beginning of the sixteenth century;[43] after that date it continued to be an important port under the control of the Portuguese. During the Mongol period, however, the positions of Hormuz and Kish were more or less equal as the preceding section showed. It should be stressed again that the main difference between the two ports was their relations with the Mongols. Hormuz remained semi-independent with its own forces, whereas the rulers of Kish had offices within the Mongol dominion from which they also obtained parts of their earnings.

It is almost a cliché that the Mongols encouraged trade and communication with China. This empire was of special importance to the Ilkhanids because they acknowledged the Yüan emperors as their superiors. Due to the enmity with the Chaghatayids, overland traffic was perilous and envoys were in danger of being killed. Traveling by sea therefore often seemed to be the safer option.[44] China was the

---

[42] Ibid., 100–5; for Jamāl al-Dīn and his descendants see the plate there on 138; al-Qāshānī, Abū al-Qāsim (1969–70), 154, 161–63; Zarkūb Shīrāzī, (1931–32), 73–75; Teixeira (1902), 169–73; Shabānkarā'ī (1984), 217–19.

[43] Albuquerque commanded only seven ships and 460 men; according to João de Barros, who probably exaggerated the numbers, Hormuz still had 30,000 troops and sixty larger vessels, which all lay anchored in the harbor, to its disposal, but these forces were of no avail; Barros (1973), part 2, book 2, chaps. 1–3.

[44] Yarshater, ed. (1985 continuing), vol. 5, 434–35, s.v. 'Chinese-Iranian Relations III'; Allsen (1996), 9–10.

terminus of these journeys, which certainly included many stopovers in various ports, but the most important stop during the Mongol period was Maʿbar on the southeast Indian coast.[45]

Before we turn to the position of Kish in the Indian Ocean network it may be useful to have first a look at the Chinese side. I know of only three Chinese sources where Kish is mentioned;[46] two mention the island only by name.

Kish is mentioned in Chen Dazhen's 陳大震 fragmentary *Dade Nanhai zhi* 大德南海志 (1304; preserved in the *Yongle dadian* 永樂大典) as 'Jishi' 記施.[47] The toponym appears among a list of various names of Indian Ocean realms and cities. Hormuz (Kuolimosi 闊里秣思) is listed some places before Kish—a fact that should not be overvalued. Chen Dazhen placed Kish between Bengal (Pengjialuo 鵬茄囉) and Malwa (Maluohua 麻羅華). There is not much to learn from this text, except that around the year 1300, Kish was known in China. The toponyms seem to have been put together at random; Middle Eastern names are mixed with Indian names.

The next text, the Yüan annals,[48] is slightly more interesting. We can find Kish (Qieshi 怯失) in the appendix 'Northwestern territories' of the sixth geographical chapter of these annals. The header of the respective section is named 'Busaiyin' 不賽因, viz. Abū Saʿīd, the last Ilkhanid ruler (r. 1316–35). The first five names of the following list of toponyms were put higher in the lines and are thus, according to Chinese customs, pointed out. The names are in the respective order: Bahrayn (Bahalayin 八哈剌因), Kish, Baghdad (Bajida 八吉打), Sultaniyya (Sundanniya 孫丹尼牙) and Hormuz (Hulimozi 忽里模子).[49] The Yüan annals were written in the Ming period and it is significant to see that the authors considered three ports, which were only partially controlled by the Mongols, as belonging to the five major cities of Abū Saʿīd's dominion. The authors of the annals had almost no direct information about the Persian Gulf at their

---

45 Allsen (2001), 41–42.

46 Cf. Chen Jiarong 陳佳榮, Xie Fang 謝方 and Lu Junling 陸峻嶺 (1986), 970.

47 Chen Dazhen (1986), 38.

48 Song Lian 宋濂 (1976), j. 63, 1571 (page citations are to the 1995 reprint edition); see also Bretschneider (1910), 129–30.

49 A few of the following names on a place below shall be listed: Kazarun (Kezanlong 可咱隆), Shiraz (listed for whatever reasons twice as Shelazi 設剌子 and Xielashi 泄剌失), Kufa (Kufa 苦法), etc.

disposal, but gathered their wisdom from secondary sources. It is thus remarkable that they, according to their data, regarded Hormuz and Kish as equal, when they were in fact under Abū Saʿīd's rule.

The 'Records of all Barbarians' (*Zhufan zhi* 諸蕃志, 1225) dates much earlier than the preceding texts and is thus of only limited concern here.[50] Nevertheless, Zhao Rugua described some habits of the population of Kish and some basics of the economy that should not have been altered noticeably one hundred years later.[51] The products of Kish are of major importance in this regard. Zhao Rugua writes that the country produces pearls and fine horses; Spuler confirms the importance of Kish for horse breeding,[52] though this might have been carried out on the mainland and not on the rather small island. The author of the book is in some respects more accurate than his successors because he clearly distinguished between commodities produced in the country and other ones imported for trade. As in the case of Hormuz, there were not many possibilities in Kish to produce items for trade, and horses and pearls may have been the sole exceptions. Here the list of the commodities carried from 'Arabia' (*Dashi* 大食) translated by Hirth and Rockhill shall be cited to give an impression of the goods bartered in Kish: rosewater, gardenia flowers, quicksilver, white brass, silver bullion, cinnabar, madder, and fine cotton stuffs.[53] These commodities came only from Arabia; nothing is said about regions further away. One can only assume that products listed in the *Zhufan zhi* under the entries of Indian and other ports were also transported to Kish.

One Chinese work exists in which we should expect reference to Kish: the *Daoyi zhilüe* 島夷誌略 of Wang Dayuan (1349).[54] Here a number of toponyms of the Middle East are mentioned, but we can find no allusion to Kish, and even Hormuz is difficult to verify, but

[50] Hirth and Rockhill, eds. (1966), 133–34; Zhao Rugua 趙汝适 (1996), j. shang, 108–9.

[51] Bertold Spuler, for example, could have made use of these data; Spuler (1952), 509, 518.

[52] Spuler (1952), 392.

[53] Hirth and Rockhill, eds. (1966), 134; for a discussion of some of these products see ibid., 202–4, 217–20, 229–30; they translated 'spelter' for *baitong* 白銅 (here white brass); fine cotton stuffs are simply *xibu* 細布; no other names are given.

[54] Wang Dayuan 汪大淵 (1981); the translations of various entries can be found in Rockhill (1914–15), vol. 15 (1914), 419–47, and 16 (1915), 61–159, 236–71, 374–92, 435–67, 604–26.

the entry 'Ganmaili' 甘埋里 should refer to it.[55] Assuming Wang Dayuan made no mistakes when he described the geography of the Persian Gulf, he was well informed about the fact that Kish had ceased to have any significance after 1330/31. Chinese texts thus offer little information about the relations between Kish and China and its role in maritime trade. Waṣṣāf clearly mentions in his history that China had close relations to Kish:

> The island Qays, a major island of Fars and of the world, is mentioned in all languages and at all places. They present commodities of the countries of Hind and Sind and of the farthest [regions] of China (Chin) and Turkestan in this harbor. Wonderful things, rarities, and preciosities from Egypt, Damascus, and the boundaries of Qayrawan sparkle in this market.[56]

However, even this text is no clear indication that Chinese ships called regularly at the harbor of Kish. Waṣṣāf's narrative might just be an exaggeration to show the glory of Kish when recording all famous place names, but one can presume that the products of these countries indeed reached Kish. A journey from the Persian Gulf to China or back was still a dangerous venture as Marco Polo's return journey also proved.[57] Long-distance travels were thus few and one may assume that goods from China reached Kish more likely via different stages.

We may here return to the embassy of Fakhr al-Dīn, son of Jamāl al-Dīn, whom Ghazan sent to Temür Qā'ān in the year 697/1297–98.[58] Waṣṣāf narrates the whole course of the embassy from its departure until the death of Fakhr al-Dīn in Dhū al-ḥijja of the year 704/June–July 1305. Trade was a major aspect for Fakhr al-Dīn

---

[55] The description of Hormuz could without many problems be adopted for Kish, but the name Ganmaili resembles the Ganmei 甘眉 of the *Zhufan zhi*, included in a list of realms that depended on Arabia; Wang Dayuan (1981), 364–69. Kish was also included in this list, thus Ganmei cannot mean Kish; see Zhao Rugua (1966), 90; Hirth and Rockhill, eds. (1966), 170; Kauz and Ptak (2001), 39–46; in a recent Chinese text, the centers of trade in the gulf during the Mongol period are according to the description found in the *Daoyi zhilüe* named Basra and Hormuz; Zhu Jieqin 朱傑勤 (1984), 88.

[56] Waṣṣāf (1853), 169–70 (page citations are to the 1959–60 reprint edition); Waṣṣāf (n.d.), 88.

[57] Polo (1903), vol. 1, 23–24 ('Introductory Notices' by Henry Yule; page citations are to the 1991 reprint edition).

[58] Waṣṣāf (1853), 505–7 (page citations are to the 1959–60 reprint edition); Waṣṣāf (n.d.), 1332–37.

when he accomplished this mission. He took pearls, jewelry, and other goods from his own property and received also some of his father's treasure to barter in China. Even Ghazan Khan entrusted him with ten *tūmān* of gold for trade. After the official part was finished, Fakhr al-Dīn showed considerable concern in commercial enterprises. These seem to have been a success during his four-year sojourn in China. He was dismissed after a final audience during which he was granted a diploma and a wife from the Qā'ān's relatives. The return journey turned out to be very dangerous, with the ship of the ambassador Toqay[59] wrecked, while Fakhr al-Dīn barely escaped on another ship. He met his end, however, shortly thereafter.

There is a slight possibility that Fakhr al-Dīn can be identified with a certain Bohali 孛哈里 who appears in the Korean annals. This Bohali came as a prince from Ma'bar to the Korean court because of his matrimonial relations with a Korean lady. This incident should have taken place in 1297, but Fakhr al-Dīn had just left his home at that time.[60] The ancestors of this Bohali (also spelled Bu'ali 不阿里) came from a place identified with Qalhat by Liu Yingsheng.[61] It seems somewhat difficult to identify this Bohali with Fakhr al-Dīn.

Finally, we may consider the region Ma'bar on the southeast Indian coast. This region has been mentioned several times in this paper, and we may assume that it was a central knot in the net woven by Jamāl al-Dīn and his relatives. Marco Polo was immensely impressed by Ma'bar; he describes it as the finest and noblest province in the world. He continues by saying that merchants from all parts of the western Indian Ocean (including Kish) bring horses and other things to this coast, and in the part on Cail he says: "It is at this city [Cail] that all the ships touch that come from the west, as from Hormos and from Kis and from Aden, and all Arabia..."[62] Rashīd al-Dīn continues this description by relating that ships bring products from China and also from Hind and Sind. According to him Ma'bar is the "key to India."[63] Embassies were regularly sent from Ma'bar

---

[59] I read the name Toqay; Hammer-Purgstall throughout read Nokai (Waṣṣāf [n.d.]).

[60] Karashima (1989), 74.

[61] Liu Yingsheng 劉迎勝 (1985), 90–95; idem (1992), 77–82.

[62] Polo (1903), vol. 2, 331, 340, 370 (page citations are to the 1991 reprint edition).

[63] Rashīd al-Dīn (1980), 37.

to the Mongol court in China from 1284 to 1314. After this year embassies obviously ceased but the reasons are unclear.[64] We may deduce from all these descriptions that Maʿbar played a central role as an emporium in the middle of the trade routes from the West to the east Indian Ocean in the decades before and after 1300.

This was the time when Kish flourished and there existed some major links between Kish and Maʿbar. First, the brother of Jamāl al-Dīn, Taqī al-Dīn, was vizier in Maʿbar. Through this relation the trade between Maʿbar and Kish was closely controlled by the two brothers, who enjoyed a number of privileges if not monopolies in Indian Ocean trade due to their positions.[65]

Most important for the trade with Maʿbar were horses and Jamāl al-Dīn agreed with the rulers of Maʿbar to send horses to them each year. The price of one horse was fixed for 220 golden *dīnārs* each, and the sum was to be paid even if the horse died en route.[66] Marco Polo confirmed the great desire of Maʿbar for horses; he put this down to the maltreatment of them there.[67]

To summarize: Maʿbar must be considered the major link between Kish and China and as an immense market in itself. Ships from Kish anchored there and bartered their goods for local products or for imports from China. Each arrival of the Indian boats in Kish was probably a major event.

III

The ruins of Kish at its zenith (early fourteenth century) are considerably smaller than those of Siraf in the tenth century and Hormuz in the fourteenth and fifteenth centuries.[68] But this does not necessarily suggest that Kish's importance was less than that of its predecessor and successor. After a general decline of trade in the Persian Gulf

[64] Karashima (1989), 72–74.

[65] Waṣṣāf (1853), 302–3 (page citations are to the 1959–60 reprint edition); Waṣṣāf (n.d.), 603–4.

[66] Waṣṣāf (1853), 301–2 (page citations are to the 1959–60 reprint edition); Waṣṣāf (n.d.), 600–1; Rashīd al-Dīn (1980), 37, 38.

[67] Polo (1903), vol. 2, 340 (page citations are to the 1991 reprint edition).

[68] Whitehouse (1983), 333.

in the course of the eleventh century we can observe a new increase in the time of the thirteenth century.[69]

After the overthrow of the Banū Qayṣar in 1229, the history of Kish remains somewhat unclear for the next decades, but we may assume that the merchants of the island still had a fair share of the Indian Ocean trade. One of these families was the Ṭībīs, and with Jamāl al-Dīn as their head they emerged as one of the major mercantile leaders of the Persian Gulf at the end of the thirteenth century. They must have been rooted in the society of Kish, otherwise their swift political rise and their closely woven trade network is hardly explicable.

The fortune of Kish depended on two bases: its close connection with the Maʿbar coast and via that emporium with China proper. Direct travel from the gulf to China seems to have been rarely undertaken. Maʿbar's role in maritime trade during this crucial period can hardly be overestimated. Second, Kish was closely connected with the Ilkhanid rulers; the Ṭībīs were several times governors of neighboring provinces and derived their riches to a certain degree from them.

This last fact was decisive in the fierce competition and dispute with Hormuz. The rulers of Hormuz cared for their own army and seem to have been more orientated to the sea. When Shams al-Dīn Juwaynī had to flee from the Mongol court, he was advised to go to Hormuz and not to Kish due to the relative independence of that emporium from the Mongol rulers.[70] Thus Hormuz could finally defeat Kish and the Ṭībīs and become the center of commerce in the region for the next centuries.

However, times changed again. Today, the island of Hormuz is totally barren and almost uninhabited, while Kish has become a center for (Iranian) tourism and an area of free trade.

---

[69] Wink (1991–97), vol. 2, 18–19.
[70] Rashīd al-Dīn (1941), 63.

ILKHANID RULE AND ITS CONTRIBUTIONS TO IRANIAN POLITICAL CULTURE

BERT G. FRAGNER

Before turning to the announced subject of this paper, some preliminary remarks may serve as a helpful introduction to the theme. According to a widespread and commonly accepted discourse, most of us follow a more or less strict pattern whenever we discuss any general and specific consequences of the Mongol conquests in Eurasia lead by Genghis Khan and his successors in the thirteenth century. We—typical Middle Eastern and Western intellectuals with some interest in world history—adhere more or less uncritically to the following attitude:

We tend to see the civilizations conquered by the Mongols as respectably old and well-established cultural units, relying strongly on their thoroughly developed and deeply rooted, sedentary cultural achievements. It is these achievements which, by virtue of their aggressive, unexpected, and 'new' enemies, seem to have been severely endangered. My point is not whether or not this view is correct and follows historical evidence. Rather, I wonder whether there might be a different vantage point from which to view the Mongol invasions, and if so, how do we begin to construct such a perspective? I invite the reader to follow my thought processes in formulating such an alternate perspective.

In considering the Mongols and other transhumant groups and individuals belonging to the Eurasian steppe cultures, they certainly did not conceive of themselves as 'new' cultural elements within their world—including the territories inhabited by their sedentary neighbors. There is good reason to assume that they perceived of themselves as representatives of a fairly 'old' and traditional way of life preserved within their cultural and natural environment since ancient times. Without a doubt, Chinese sedentary civilization was certainly known to those nomadic or migratory tribes and group formations living for generations beyond the Great Wall, and at least for those living within the Semirechye area (nowadays in Kazakhstan and Kirghizstan) they were probably also familiar with the highly developed sedentary cultures of Transoxiana and Bactria. In spite of this fact, cultural areas like the Indian subcontinent, the central regions of the Abbasid caliphate and even of the entire Islamic world, including Iran, Mesopotamia, and the Near East, and as well as early medieval Russia (the 'Rus of Kiev') and eastern Central Europe might have been rather strange and alien to them! Whilst from the point of view of the recently conquered 'old' sedentary civilizations the main task of the survivors must have been to preserve and maintain as much as possible of their pre-Mongol 'Golden Ages,' for the Mongols there arose a completely different agenda: they had to study the basic cultural structures of their recently acquired territories and regions in order to determine to what extent they could adapt these new cultures and sublimate them to their own cultural agency.

To put it another way, when we argue from the perspective of the conquered sedentary civilizations, we perceive of them—the sedentaries—as the main transmitters and bearers of history and tradition, whilst we are clearly inclined to see the Mongol invaders as rather bare and stripped of any kind of history—barbarians from inside an almost unknown steppe continent. From the Mongol conquerors' vantage point, it was rather the Mongols themselves who possessed history. Their victims were not conquered with the express purpose of taking over their historically mature and valuable (not to say even higher ranking) cultural qualifications; on the contrary, they perceived of the conquered primarily as less valuable than themselves. But they understood very soon that to maintain their freshly acquired power they had to fit themselves within the structures of the subjugated. To explain this pragmatic understanding of what some may call the fascination exacted by the sedentary cultures on the minds of the 'barbarian' Mongols from the steppe indicates quite typically sedentary preoccupations towards nomads and transhumant social entities, and we still seem to be trapped by these kinds of preoccupations.

Let me therefore invite the reader to see things the other way around. Such an approach will offer us immediately a new set of explanatory tools and, at least to a certain extent, we may make greater and more far-reaching strides in understanding historical phenomena so amply preserved up to our own time.

It happened but one generation after the death of Genghis Khan that, in close accordance with the concept of the whole Chinggisid Empire being partitioned into four so-called *ulus*es, quite peculiar forms of Mongol identities came into existence. In the Volga basin, under the rule of the *khāns* of the Golden Horde, 'being Mongol' was closely related to a takeover of Northern Turkic languages and dialects, widely correlated with embracing Islam. Reconstructing the ways and means by which Mongol identity developed throughout the following centuries is nothing more than reconstructing important phases in the genesis of contemporary Northern Turkic ethnicities like Tatars, or Bashkirs, and Kazakhs, as well as others.

There were clearly different features of Mongol self-understanding in the *ulus* of Chaghadai, the eastern part of which (in the territories of today's Xinjiang region in the People's Republic of China) remained almost archaically Mongol for centuries while its western part followed the footprints of the cultural traditions of pre-Mongol Islamic Transoxiana. The appearance of Amīr Tīmūr and, subsequently, the ethnogenesis of the Eastern Turkic-speaking Chaghadai people (Islamized but nevertheless with strong Mongol self-perception and above all, proud of their cultural and courtly refinement in comparison with their disliked brethren from the Golden Horde) seem to be closely related to the particular developments of Mongol identities in the Chaghatayid *ulus*.

What about the Mongols in Iran? For generations we scholars have followed the concept that those Mongols, having established themselves on Iranian soil, soon fell victim to the elaborate and refined Persian culture and eventually dissolved themselves within the historical mainstream of 'Iranianness,' not only linguistically but also in terms of aspects of religion, court life, and urban culture. Even Vladimir Bartol'd had widely accepted this pattern, albeit with limitations, to say nothing of scholars like Vladimir Minorsky, Bertold Spuler, Hans Robert Roemer, Jean Aubin, and others. However, there were also scholars who agreed only reluctantly with this concept, among them Marshall G. Hodgson.

It might be of some interest to apply the Mongols' vantage point and their quest for identity to the Ilkhanid Empire. Allow me a short and, I hope, not too polemic remark. Due to the rising importance of social sciences, and among them social history, during the last fifty years, we have followed a growing inclination toward grassroots perspectives, i.e., preferring the points of view of the lower classes, the oppressed, the subjugated. It should be noted that in cultural sciences since Michel Foucault and particularly following Norbert Elias, the elites were not entirely forgotten. We should bear in mind that power plays an important role in history, past and present, and take into consideration that the oppressed and deprived often react advantageously to the intentions and measures of the oppressor, even in cases of open resistance against oppression! It may therefore happen that mighty powers may take over cultural values and elements from the subjects they rule; it is nevertheless the ruled who, of necessity, take over certain of the cultural modules of the ruler. We ought, therefore, to regard both currents in cultural history, and not omit one or the other.

Let us now turn to the theme implied in the title of this paper, namely, aspects of the political culture of the Mongol rulers of Iran, mainly belonging to the Ilkhanid branch of the descendants of Genghis Khan. In the middle of the thirteenth century, the position of the so-called Great Khan passed from the *ulus* of Ögödei to the *ulus* of Tolui. After a series of political complications, Möngke became successor to the late Great Khan Güyüg. Like Güyüg, Möngke belonged to the second generation of Chinggisids after Genghis Khan himself. He and his brothers Qubilai (who succeeded him as Great Khan and founded the Yüan dynasty in China) and Hülegü (the founder of the Ilkhanid dynasty in Iran) were sons of Tolui. In dynastic terms, the Ilkhans belonged without a doubt to the *ulus* Tolui but, in terms of territory, Iran was clearly an external region to the Toluid lands (originally eastern Mongolia, Manchuria, and Northern China). In any event, the Ilkhans remained most loyal and obedient to the Great Khans in East Asia, with their imperial capital at Beijing, for a very long time. In terms of their location, they had to take into consideration that their lands definitely belonged to Western Asia, or the Middle East as we call it nowadays. Their loyalty to the Toluid line was expressed, among others ways, by their intention to maintain some form of Tantric Buddhism as their official religious confession at least for some decades, in full accordance with the Great Khans in Beijing, but in clear contrast to their immediate Mongol (and also Chinggisid) neighbors who belonged to the *ulus*es of Jochi (the Golden Horde) and Chaghadai (in Transoxiana, southern Semirechye, and in the Tarim Basin) who were Muslims and/or of Shamanist faith, respectively.

The late thirteenth century witnessed a shift of the Great Khans' strategic interest from the all-Mongol concept towards the heartlands of their *ulus*. This shift was expressed by Qubilai Khan's establishment of the Chinese imperial dynasty of Yüan and subsequently his own enthronement as Emperor of China. It should be taken into consideration whether this important political step might have served as an incentive for the Ilkhans to establish themselves in a similar manner, in far-off Iran, as they were gradually more and more isolated from their imperial cousins in China, separated from them by the rather hostile lands of Chaghadai, at least.

Whatever the incentives might have been, the results are obvious. At the end of the thirteenth century, the Ilkhans converted from Buddhism to Islam. This change of religion obviously implied a change in the Ilkhans' perception of their own position within their political mental mapping system. To them it had become gradually more important to define their own place within West Asia than to continue symbolizing their loyal attitude towards the Great Khans in Beijing. It was roughly at the same time that their territory eventually acquired officially a very prestigious denomination, full of almost legendary historical power—Iran, or, according to the proper wording, '*Īrān-zamīn*.'

This important step in historical development warrants a brief glance at the history of the term 'Iran.' With the breakdown of the Sasanian Empire in the middle of the seventh century, the official designation of that empire, 'Iran,' or more precisely 'Eran-shahr' (in Middle Persian), expired as well as an actual appellation of a political territorial entity. The word remained legendarily in the collective memory as the great name of a vanished empire, strongly supported by Iranian literary traditions but also transmitted by ethnic non-Iranians like the Turkic Ghaznavids or the Seljuks. It is therefore fascinating to compare the self-rooting of the Toluid Great Khans in Eastern Asia and their brethren in Western Asia. Those located in the East proclaimed themselves officially as Chinese emperors, thus establishing their own center as the future capital of China—Beijing, or at that time, Khanbaligh. Quite similarly, the Ilkhans proclaimed themselves as the rulers of Iran (*pādishāhān-i Īrān*), converting their own hitherto political and economic center Tabriz into their imperial capital. In the case of the Ilkhans, there was an important difference between themselves and their just recently sinicized cousins in Beijing. While in the East, the Mongols were in the position of taking over a political entity that had existed for more than a thousand years up to Genghis Khan's conquest, i.e., China; in the West, the Ilkhans had to reinvent and reconstruct something that had only survived in the collective consciousness, but not as a political reality, almost throughout the preceding seven hundred years!

Reinventing Iran after an interval of seven centuries did not at all mean a return to Sasanian circumstances or even to what at that time might have been perceived as such. Rather, reinventing Iran under Ilkhanid conditions meant also establishing a new regional power, shaped and modeled first of all along the pattern of the vanished Abbasid caliphate and the Khwarazmshah's empire, both of which were extinguished by Mongol armies in the thirteenth century. I lay some stress on my wording 'regional power.' Presentation and representation of the Ilkhans as a (if not *the*) regional power meant not only their identification with the Mongol Chinggisids, and particularly Toluids, who were closely related to the otherwise rather exotic Great Khans in Beijing, but also their manifestation as a power belonging to the cultural and political area, rather than as an alien authority, by using a well-developed means of communication of political semantics immediately understandable to those whom they ruled and whom they wanted to recognize the Mongol yoke.

When Ghazan Khan embraced Islam and proclaimed himself '*pādishāh-i Īrān wa Islām*' at the end of the thirteenth century, the stage was finally set for this kind of representative political performance. Ghazan's strategic aim was to resist the challenge of the hostile Golden Horde Khans and their close and intimate allies the Mamluks in Egypt (thus following his predecessors). Entering the realm of Islam meant nothing other than entering a contest for supremacy with these two powers, both of whom were Muslim but who also had an intra-Chinggisid, *ulus*-based understanding of themselves. The Mongols along the Volga's banks were by then Islamized for at least two generations, but their allies the Mamluks, rulers on the banks of the Nile, could demonstrate their 'Muslimness' with a very striking and convincing symbol. They hosted shadow caliphs of Abbasid descent in Cairo, thus concentrating in their hands a high degree of Islamic prestige with an influence much more far-reaching than the political boundaries of their empire in Egypt and Syria.

Against this background we get a deeper understanding of what the Mongol Ilkhanid rulers had in mind when they re-established 'Iran.' Presumably the popular glory of old 'Iran' would help them to strengthen the second image they wanted to support, namely for their ruler to be recognized not only as the preserver of ancient Iran but as the actual *pādishāhān-i Islām* as well. The Ilkhanids wanted to be understood as an important (if not as the most important) regional player in the late medieval Middle East. The reconstructed imagined

Ilkhanid Iran was therefore shaped by a large number of diverse modules, all of them being compatible with Islamicate concepts, and not offending them, at first glance, at least. For art historians and specialists in literary history and criticism, the Ilkhans' particular treatment of Firdawsī's great epic poem, the *Shāhnāma*, comes immediately to mind. The most famous redaction of the *Shāhnāma* text was conceived under the auspices of the geographer and administrator Ḥamdallāh Mustawfī Qazwīnī, not to mention the production of the most famous Ilkhanid illuminated manuscript of this marvelous text, the so-called Great Mongol *Shāhnāma*.

Let us look at some of the ways in which the Iranian Mongols intended to present themselves and to create symbols of their political power. The choice of their capital fell rather early on to Tabriz, which was not only the unchallenged urban center of Azerbaijan but also one of the most important metropolitan sites of western Iran, or 'Irāq-i 'ajam (Persian Iraq), as it was known. As for explaining the Mongols' preference for Azerbaijan, many scholars refer to topographic affinities between northwestern Iran and the Mongolian heartlands. The area of Azerbaijan was definitely very fertile and attractive in terms of economics, particularly through the perspective of a shepherds' society. Moreover, there are also aspects of political regionalism that would favor this area by taking into account the Ilkhans' desire to play a major role in Middle Eastern politics. As already mentioned, Azerbaijan belonged to a large region called 'Persian Iraq,' in apposition to Mesopotamia, or 'Arab Iraq,' both of them having been named as a twofold mega-region called 'Irāqayn, i.e., the 'Two Iraqs.' If the Ilkhans intended to present their own capital as a successful rival to the formerly strong site of Baghdad, from their view no other place could have served this purpose better than Tabriz. Presenting Tabriz as the successor of Baghdad meant nothing less than supporting the idea of portraying themselves as the quasi-natural successors to the Abbasid caliphs, thus probably aiming at surpassing the Mamluk Sultans of Egypt and Syria.

There is another thing worth mentioning. During the later Abbasid period, particularly in the eastern lands of the Caliphate, cities were rhetorically decorated by specific titles. Baghdad was without a doubt something like the queen of all cities within the realm of Islam. It was therefore named *Dār al-salām*, the abode of peace or, politically even more precise, *Dār al-khilāfa*—the seat (or center) of the Caliphate. Any other princely residences officially recognized by the caliphs could bear an honorific title that was clearly subordinate to Baghdad, e.g., *Dār al-mulk*, the seat of rulership. Isfahan under the Great Seljuks was *Dār al-mulk*, and similarly late Seljuk Hamadan, and a respectable number of other cities in the region.

In the time of Ghazan Khan, there was no longer a really functioning *Dār al-khilāfa* anywhere in the whole Middle East. By creating a new metropolitan title for a city, the position of the new capital could therefore be presented publicly in a very effective way. Eventually, Tabriz became officially *Dār al-salṭana*, the seat of unconditional rulership! Just as Baghdad had been absolutely unique as *Dār al-khilāfa*, Tabriz should also be uniquely recognized as *Dār al-salṭana*, clearly of a higher value than the former *Dār al-mulk*s, and basically even higher than *Dār al-khilāfa*, with the decisive difference that about the year 1300 *Dār al-salṭana* (Tabriz) still existed and flourished, whilst *Dār al-khilāfa* (Baghdad) seemed to be finished.

We have to take into account that this kind of semiotic symbolism played an important role in premodern political culture and therefore should not be underestimated. Every single individual paying with coins struck at the Tabriz mint or, in the other direction, receiving them, could read the wording *Dār al-salṭana* in immediate connection with the new Ilkhanid metropolis, the undisputed successor of the former *Dār al-khilāfa* Baghdad!

Let us trace the further destiny of this kind of honorific titulature in post-Mongol Iran. Tabriz remained *Dār al-salṭana* until the early twentieth century. However, after the Safavids' conquest of Herat, the former Timurid capital became in the early sixteenth century a second *Dār as-salṭāna*, followed by Qazwin under Shah Tahmasp, and from ʿAbbās the Great onward the most famous *Dār al-salṭana* was Isfahan. Other cities soon followed the custom of bearing titles of similar construction, some of them even prior to the Safavids, others in the Safavid period (1502–1722). Rasht became *Dār al-marz*, Ardabil *Dār al-irshād*, Qum and Astarabad (modern Gurgan) were both *Dār al-mu'minīn*, and so on. There is even some irony in this story; as there were already four *Dār al-salṭana*s at the end of the eighteenth century, the early Qajars decided to stop this tradition by coining a novel title for their new urban center, Tehran. In order to distinguish Tehran from the other, older *Dār al-salṭana*s, Tehran was honored by the revival of the almost forgotten title *Dār al-khilāfa*! In the imagination of semiotic symbolism, nineteenth-century Tehran was understood as some kind of reestablished Abbasid Baghdad—a very strange effect of odd political rhetoric!

Coins and coinage should also be mentioned. Minting coins bearing the name of a caliph or a ruler has been regarded as an important prerequisite of monarchs from early Islam until modern times. There is no surprise in the fact then that the Ilkhans also made use of a new coinage system in order to demonstrate their political self-perception.

The classical regulations of Islamic currency were based on the usage of silver for a coin called *dirham* (inherited from the Sasanians in the East) and of gold for striking the so-called *dīnār* (a carryover from Byzantium). At least according to canonical regulations the values of these two types of currency were interrelated by the gold-silver ratio.

About the year 1300, the Toluid Ilkhans and in particular Ghazan Khan, in spite of all their loyalties toward their cousins in the Far East, established a new system of coinage according to which the traditional Islamic coin names *dīnār* and *dirham* were preserved. However, the Ilkhanid *dīnār* was structurally entirely different from a traditional Islamic *dīnār*. Ghazan Khan's *dīnār* was not a gold coin but was struck in silver. The silver *dīnār* served as the basic unit of the new system of currency, in which the sum of 10,000 *dīnār*s was used as a unit of account in congruence with the Chinese silver *Tael*. This account unit of 10,000 *dīnār*s was called *tūmān*, after *tümen*, the Mongol word for 'ten thousand.' The term *tūmān* has remained in public and popular usage up to the present day in Iran.

According to Ghazan Khan's system of currency reform, there was also a unit of coinage called *dirham*. *Dirhams* were also struck in silver, and an Ilkhanid *dirham* was perceived as the sixth part of a *dīnār*. Calculating by sixth-parts of a given whole resembled a traditional pre-Islamic custom followed since antiquity in Mesopotamia and Iran. Using the terms *dīnār* and *dirham* made it possible to convince ordinary people of the seriousness of the new coinage system, particularly after the failure in the attempt to introduce Chinese-style paper money under Geikhatu. Nevertheless, the arithmetic structure of the new monetary system remained Chinese. Ghazan Khan's mint reform also carried a number of semiotic messages from the Ilkhan leadership: 1) We are reliable Muslim rulers. 2) We follow a publicly accepted tradition by minting *dīnār*s and *dirhams*. 3) While adhering to these values, we nonetheless have introduced a new system to the Islamic

Middle East corroborating the fact that we basically belong to the realm of the Chinggisid Great Khan in Beijing, thus disregarding all the other superficial 'Islamicate' paraphernalia.

The monetary history of the last seven centuries in Iran is an absolutely convincing proof of the new system's success. The performative blending of Islamicate traditions with the distinctive Ilkhanid mode of self-presentation remained in place until the twentieth century, and even the contemporary currency system of Iran, now based on the so-called *rial*, can be described as originating with Ghazan Khan's concept. The modern *rial* is successor to the so-called *qirān*, which came into existence under Fatḥ 'Alī Shāh in the early nineteenth century and was to be defined by a value of 1,000 *dīnārs*. Up to the present day, the popular designations *qirān* and *hazār* (i.e., 'thousand') can be heard everywhere in Iran. And still, the sum of ten *rials* is calculated popularly as one *tūmān*, according to the value of the vanished *qirān*, which resembles the sum of 10,000 old-fashioned *dīnārs*. Thus, the contemporary Iranian monetary system represents a structural continuation of Ghazan Khan's mint reform of 1300!

The last theme to be mentioned is the way in which Ilkhanid administrative chancelleries promulgated their royal decrees, the so-called *farmāns*, or *yarlighs*. As is well known, in Genghis Khan's lifetime, and more so under his immediate successors, the Mongols took over the basic structure of their administrative systems from the bureaucrats and administrators belonging to the so-called Western Liao people, also known as Qara-Khitai. Their leaders had for a while shaped the Liao dynasty in northern China, contemporary with the Sung emperors in southern China, and annihilated by their hostile successors, the Jurchen (another people of southeast Siberian origin, who had established the Chin dynasty of northern Chinese emperors and were eventually extinguished by Genghis Khan). By the time of Genghis Khan and his immediate successors, the Western Liao or Qara-Khitai people, or at least their elites, must already have been culturally sinicized for several generations. They had left their eastern homeland in the vicinity of the Amur River, from where they had been driven away by the rival Jurchen, and had found a new area to live in the west, roughly in today's Xinjiang territories. It was Western Liao specialists and experts in administration who passed to the Mongols basic concepts of bureaucracy and chancellery, all of them originating more or less entirely from traditional Chinese patterns.

If we take this fact into consideration, and in addition the Ilkhans' strong inclination towards Chinese manners and fashions due to their close relationship to the Great Khans in Beijing, we can roughly estimate the importance they paid to Chinese-style measures in their administrative system, though they nevertheless had to rely on the services of Iranian and Islamicate bureaucrats in their West Asian territories. In accordance with the examples already given, it is not surprising that we should again meet with various—*nota bene* successful—attempts to blend East Asian structures with Middle Eastern, Iranian, and Islamicate traditions.

Farmān-writing under the early Ilkhans mainly followed Chinese practice, using the then newly invented Mongol script (or, more precisely, the Uighur script adopted for Mongolian). As this script was then written in vertical fashion, when it came to writing in Persian they had to rotate the prescribed formula of Chinese origin ninety degrees (a quarter of a circle)—and in due course Persian became the main linguistic component of Ilkhanid official documents.

The Mongols in Iran abrogated the already centuries old custom of signing royal decrees with a *tughra*, a kind of a formalized signature of the monarch, whether caliph, sultan, king, or prince. The use of *tughra*-like symbols had characterized the chancellery customs at least of the later Abbasid period, and continued in use under the Mamluks in Egypt, the Muslim dynasties of India, and, above all, under the Ottomans who used the *tughra* until the end of the dynasty in 1924.

Instead of the *tughra*, the Ilkhans followed the again very traditional Chinese pattern according to which, instead of a *tughra*, the imprints of stamp-seals were used. These seals, mostly square in shape, served mainly to corroborate the originality of a document, thus to be stamped at all points where the sheets of paper were glued together and, of course, at the end of the document's text. This function of the seal was clearly separated from the decree's royal titulature by means of which the name of the promulgating ruler was mentioned. If we compare a *tughra*-document with a Chinese-style sealed one, it is apparent that the *tughra* serves as much as an intitulation as it does as means of corroboration, while in the Chinese-style document these two functions are quite separate, with the royal titles being written at the head of the document and the seal primarily used to prevent forgery.

By using Chinese-style seals on documents (written in the Persian language, particularly under the late Ilkhans), Chinggisid rulers of

Iran undertook a further measure to combine elements of two distinct areas of civilization, namely, Islamicate Middle East and China. And, as we already saw in the case of monetary affairs, they were clearly inclined to take over structural aspects from East Asia and to use aesthetic elements associated with the Middle East. The script and stylistic aspects of the texts of Ilkhanid documents apparently followed local Iranian and Islamicate traditions; however, there is another interesting aspect. The Ilkhans' chancelleries tended to use Persian more as a language of administration than was the case during Abbasid times. There had been already a trend to intensify the use of Persian in bureaucratic affairs under the Samanids and the Ghaznavids, but in Mongol times Persian was treated as the main linguistic means of communication for Muslims between Iran and China.

The Ilkhans' official seals were of square shape and initially bore Chinese inscriptions—no wonder because the seals were manufactured in Beijing by supreme order of the Great Khans (or, respectively, the Chinese emperors). These seals were called by the Turkic term *al tamgha*, i.e., 'red stamp,' because they had to be stamped in red ink. It was under the last Ilkhanid ruler, Abū Saʿīd, or possibly earlier, that direct relations between Tabriz and Beijing lost their regular character. As a consequence, the latest Ilkhanid square seals, and those of the succeeding Jalayirid princes as well, were no longer produced in China but by local craftsmen, while they no longer bore Chinese inscriptions but rather Arabic ones. In terms of their content, Islamic pious formulas replaced Chinese moralist devices. But throughout the fourteenth century, down to Tīmūr's conquest, the square seal remained as a typical element of decrees issued in Mongol-Iranian chancelleries. It might have been the prescribed square shape of the seal that gave rise to the increased popularity in the fourteenth century of the famous so-called square-kufic *ductus* of the Arabic script. Under Tīmūr, the square shape of the seals was abandoned but the seal as an element replacing the *tughra* in other Islamicate chancelleries remained in its position in Iran and in Iranian-influenced chancelleries until the twentieth century.

To summarize the observations made in this paper, we find some recurrent patterns in Ilkhanid political semiotics of power. First of all, they aimed clearly to create a realm characterized by peculiar features, combining various aspects of local tradition with structural elements imported from East Asia. The result was Ilkhanid

'Iran'—a very conscious and almost artificial construction of a territorial empire, created from various elements belonging to Islamicate local traditions and composed of structural measures, a good part of which had originated in East Asia. Second, these intentions resulted in manifold distinctive semiotic contrasts between the Ilkhans' realm versus neighboring territories—originally, mainly the Mamluks in Egypt and Syria, and not to forget rival Mongol *ulus*es like the Golden Horde and Chaghadai. For about four or five generations, Ilkhanid loyalty to their Toluid cousins in Beijing—the Great Khans—was an important element of their political thought, and it became decisive in bringing their political culture into reality.

But this political culture of the Ilkhans also turned out to be decisive in the bigger picture of Iranian cultural history, even centuries after the fall of Ilkhanid power. Many aspects of what they had shaped as their particular imperial territory may have been consciously aimed at imitating their powerful Toluid sovereigns in Beijing, which then survived the fall of Mongol power in West Asia. They became integrative modules of what we perceive today as typical aspects of Iranian national political culture. If we retrospectively consider the incredible and cruel destruction the Mongol armies had brought to Iran and its population in the first half of the thirteenth century as an extreme case of 'deconstruction,' Ilkhanid creative 'reconstruction' of what then remained as 'Iran' and continuing to the present day must still be perceived as an important contribution to Iranian cultural history.[1]

[1] The author refers the reader to the following selected references: Aigle (1997); Allsen (1987); Allsen (2001); Amitai-Preiss and Morgan, eds. (1999); Buell (1979); Busse (1961); Fragner (1997); Fragner (1999); Fragner (2001); Franke (2000); Herrmann (2004); Hinz (1991); Hoffmann (1997); Krawulsky (1978); Krawulsky (1989); Melville (1990); Morgan (1986); and Weiers, ed. (1986).

LIFESTYLES AT THE COURTS OF THE RULING ELITE

AVRAGA SITE: THE 'GREAT ORDŪ' OF GENGHIS KHAN

NORIYUKI SHIRAISHI

Introduction

Genghis Khan founded the Mongol empire in 1206 and died in 1227. The Mongol empire (1206–1388) influenced most of the Eurasian continent, set up taxation and transport systems, and succeeded in ruling various nations that held many different religions. In present times, where globalization is very common and disputes are frequent, studying the Mongol empire could be a very significant help to us.

In order to reveal the process through which the Mongol empire was formed, it is necessary to study Genghis Khan, who played a pivotal role in its formation. Furthermore, in order to learn about Genghis Khan, I believe that we must delve into his upbringing and daily life. Although there are many historical documents describing him, most of these, unfortunately, are written in the language of fables, and it is difficult to accept them as historical fact.

In the event that such textual materials cannot be used, archaeological research is available based on physical sources, but the archaeological approach has not achieved a great deal of recognition in the field of research into the Mongol empire. It seems that many historians believe that archaeology is not appropriate for research into nomadic peoples, as indicated by "nomadism is no friend to the archaeologist."[1]

However, this is a mistake. Since 1990, I have conducted archaeological studies of the Mongolian plateau. As a result of this, I have been able to investigate twenty sites containing the remains of settlements and towns from the time of the Mongol empire. In fact, the Mongolian plateau was well-suited to archaeological research. I would like to introduce one such example: the discovery of Genghis

[1] Morgan, D. (1986b), 30.

Khan's main palace and the results of an archaeological study thereof. These have enabled us gradually to gain a clearer picture of Genghis Khan's lifestyle, which had been a mystery until now.

The Seasonal Movements of Genghis Khan and his Palace

According to historical sources, Genghis Khan led a nomadic lifestyle similar to that of the average nomad, shifting the location of his residence in accordance with the change of season. These movements were not haphazard, but involved traveling between fixed seasonal camps within a specific area. I would like to discuss this separately.

According to historical documents, Genghis Khan had three main seasonal palaces.[2] During the winter and spring months, he stayed at the palace that was built in the Kherlen River basin area. During the summer months, he stayed at Sa'ari Ke'er. It is my opinion that this site can be located about 110 kilometers southeast of Ulaan Baatar in the district of Erdene County, Töv Prefecture. In autumn months he stayed at Qara Tün. It is thought that this site is 30 kilometers southwest of Ulaan Baatar. He moved between them throughout the year, a distance of 400 kilometers each year. In the same way, it is clear that Möngke, the fourth emperor of the Mongol empire, moved over a distance of 400 kilometers each year, and a reconstruction of the migration route shows that the emperor had a domain of 14,000 square kilometers.[3]

Of these, I believe that 'Kherlen' Palace was Genghis Khan's main and most important palace. There are two reasons for this, as follows: first of all, the sources *Yüan-Shih*[4] and *Jāmiʿ al-tawārīkh* (Compendium of Chronicles)[5] state that in the spring of 1211, Genghis Khan was living in the Kherlen River basin. From there, he departed for the campaign against Chin, and the *Yüan-Shih* states that in the spring of 1216 he returned to the Kherlen River.[6] These sources tell us the following: firstly, as both the period when he was preparing to depart

---

[2] Shiraishi (2001), 76–78.
[3] Shiraishi (2004), 115.
[4] Song Lian (1976), fasc. 1, 15.
[5] Rashīd al-Dīn (1952), 163.
[6] Song Lian (1976), fasc. 1, 19.

for a long war, and the time following his battle-weary return from that war were spent in the Kherlen River basin, we can see that this was an important stronghold for him. In addition, we know from a passage in the *Yüan-Shih* that he spent the first month of the lunar calendar there.[7] Even though the first month of the calendar would have been in the spring, it would still have been bitterly cold and nomadic peoples usually spent this time of year in their winter camp. Consequently, we can assume that the camp in the Kherlen River basin was Genghis Khan's winter camp. The winter camp would have had fences designed to protect against the cold as well as permanent buildings, such as stables for livestock. Despite the nomads' peripatetic lifestyle, it would have been an important place where they would have spent the longest period of time during the year. If we could pinpoint its location, we might well be able to obtain significant sources that would allow us to gain a clearer image of the real Genghis Khan.

Where was 'Kherlen' Palace?

So let us try to pinpoint the location of 'Kherlen' Palace from historical sources. The *Jāmiʿ al-tawārīkh* states that after Genghis Khan's death, his main palace was left and maintained as it was.[8] This seems to imply that it was in a fixed location. *Jāmiʿ al-tawārīkh* describes it as "the great *ordūs*." The palaces of nomadic dynasties are frequently called *ordū*, but if we narrow our focus to the Mongol empire, there was apparently only one called "the great *ordū*(s)."

We know this from the *Hei ta shih lue*, which was written by the South Sung emissary P'eng Ta-ya, who traveled in the Mongolian plateau in late 1232 and early 1233. At that time, he visited the palace of Ögödei, the second emperor, and he wrote that only that palace was called "the great *ordū*."[9] According to the *Yüan-Shih*, Ögödei was at "Genghis Khan's palace" at that very time, so we know that the one and only 'great *ordū*' was 'Genghis Khan's palace.'[10] Furthermore,

[7] Song Lian (1976), fasc. 1, 15.
[8] Rashīd al-Dīn (1971), 322.
[9] P'eng and Wang (1983), 203.
[10] Song Lian (1976), fasc. 2, 32.

we can also ascertain that this was his winter camp.

So where was the great *ordū*? In 1323, the tenth emperor of the Mongol empire, Yesün Temür, was enthroned at 'the great *ordū*' of Genghis Khan; the *Yüan-Shih* states that its location was beside the Lung chu he River, that is to say, in the Kherlen River basin.[11] In the imperial edict issued concerning the enthronement ceremony, the great *ordū* is also called "*Ta ying p'an*."[12] This means the great headquarters. In Mongolian, it is "*Yeke a'urugh*." *Yeke a'urugh* frequently appears in *The Secret History of the Mongols* (sections 233, 253, and 257) and is a term that is used in each case to denote Genghis Khan's stronghold.[13] This should provide an important clue in searching for this stronghold. Knowing that the place named *a'urugh* existed in the Kherlen River basin, I wasted no time in going there to conduct a study.

The Investigation of the Avraga Site

The term '*a'urugh*' turned into '*Avraga*' in the modern Mongolian language.[14] The site at Avraga is located at 109°09' E and 47°05' N, in the present district of Delgerkhaan in the province of Khentii in eastern Mongolia (fig. 3). The site was long believed to be the site of '*Yeke Ordu*' (the great *ordū*) of Genghis Khan. *Yeke Ordu* means 'main palace' in the medieval Mongolian language. Researchers from Mongolia and East Germany excavated the site in the 1960s. However, conclusive evidence that this was the site of the great *ordū* was not discovered. Since 1992, I have been mapping all of the remains and making detailed surface surveys. As a result, I have been able to confirm that these remains were in use during the period from the end of the twelfth to the fourteenth centuries because the geographical situation of the site agrees with descriptions in the historical document *Hei ta shih lue*, which contains references to the great *ordū*.[15] At the rear, north-facing part of the site, there is a hill, which blocks the seasonal winds of winter (fig. 4). To the south, a

[11] Song Lian (1976), fasc. 29, 638.
[12] Song Lian (1976), fasc. 29, 638.
[13] Kuribayashi and Choijinjiab (2001), 466, 522, 540.
[14] Maidar and Maidar (1972), 151.
[15] P'eng and Wang (1983), 203.

stream winds along. These agree with the description of *Hei ta shih lue*. I consider the Avraga site to be the remains of the great *ordū*.

The site covers an area measuring 1200 meters from east to west, and 500 meters from north to south (fig. 3). Inside this area, there are many square earth mounds of approximately 20 meters per side. These earth mounds are the ruins of building platforms. As we found evidence of iron manufacturing, it is thought that this site was used for manufacturing in addition to being a residential area. In the central part of the site, there is Platform 1. It is the largest set of building remains in the site and is surrounded by double earthen walls.

When Ögödei, the second emperor of the Mongol empire, stayed at Genghis Khan's great *ordū* in the spring of 1233, a Chinese messenger who visited the area wrote in *Hei ta shih liu* that there was a palace in the center of many buildings, and on the south side of the palace was vacant space.[16] This description agrees with the geographical situation of the remains at Platform 1. There is no doubt that Platform 1 is the remains of this palace. We decided to carry out the excavation at Platform 1.

Results of Excavations

During the excavations of 2001 to 2003 at Platform 1, I discovered that there were four cultural levels (I call them 'phases') at the site (figs. 5–6). Results of the excavation were as follows.

1. Phase 1: The platform was built using sandy mud, which was heaped upon the ground. The height was approximately 60 centimeters. The upper surface of the platform was hardened and flat. I believe that this surface was the floor of a building. A column hole without a base stone was found on the floor at the northeast part of the platform (fig. 7). The results of radiocarbon (C-14) dating indicate dates of 1190–1270 and 1155–1220. No ceramic or metal materials were found on the floor. I called this building the 'Lowest Building.' It is difficult to gain a detailed understanding of the structure of the building because the excavation was of an extremely small section of the site. However, judging from the arrangement

[16] P'eng and Wang (1983), 203.

of the holes, it is assumed that the Lowest Building was a tent-like structure with a square plan. In all probability, the length of each side would have been 17.4 meters.

2. Phase 2: This cultural level consisted of a hardened clay floor and column base stones. They were the structure that I called the 'Lower Building.' The floor was built by heaping up sandy mud, 10 centimeters in thickness, on top of the floor of Phase 1. Five column base stones and a column hole were found on the floor. By measuring the interval of base stones, I attempted to determine the measurement scale used at that time. As a result, it became clear that the standard unit of measurement that was used in the construction of this building was equivalent to 31.6 centimeters. I concluded that the standard measurement used was the *ch'ih*, which originated during the Sung or Chin Dynasty; 31.6 centimeters was one *ch'ih* at that time.[17] The entire structure of the building had an east-west width of 19 meters (60 *ch'ih*), and a north-south length of 11 meters (35 *ch'ih*). However, judging from the extent of the floor, I assume the north-south length of the entire building was also 60 *ch'ih*. I was not able to find any roof tiles from this cultural level. A complete image is unclear now, but I assume that the building was a tent-like structure with a square plan.

3. Phase 3: From the detailed investigation of the level of Phase 3, it was discovered that dark-colored soil had accumulated on the floor of the Lower Building (Phase 2). The accumulation was of windborne origin and approximately 5 centimeters in thickness. It signifies that there was no building at that time. The radiocarbon (C-14) dating indicates a date of 1210–70.

4. Phase 4: In this phase, the so-called Upper Building was constructed and came into use. The building was built 40 centimeters above the Lower Building. From the Upper Building, I excavated fragments of earthenware made in the fourteenth century in a *Tz'u chou yao* kiln and fragments of porcelain made in the late fourteenth or early fifteenth century in a *Ching te chen* kiln. The radiocarbon (C-14) dating is 1290–1320 or 1340–90, and 1310–60 or 1385–1410.

[17] Shiraishi (2002), 152–159.

The structure of the Upper building consists of walls made of stone blocks and column base stones. The walls form a 凸 shape with the projection on the north side, and are 80 centimeters wide and 40 centimeters high. The standard unit of measurement that was used in the construction of the Upper Building, the *ch'ih*, was equivalent to 31.6 centimeters. The entire structure has an east-west width of 11.1 meters (35 *ch'ih*), and a north-south length of 7.9 meters (25 *ch'ih*). A structure made of sundried mud bricks fitted into the inside of a projection in the north wall. I assume it to be a chair or an altar. In front of this structure, there was a blackened area covering part of the floor. This area had a diameter of 60 centimeters. In my opinion, this area was used for making fires over a long period of time. There was an entrance in the central part of the south wall. Two circular column bases were situated to the left and right of this entrance. I was not able to discover any roof tiles from this cultural level. An entire structure belonging to the Upper Building became clear after the excavation at the north part of the platform. Column holes were found at the northwest and northeast corners. Judging from the arrangement of columns and walls, it can be assumed that this upper structure of the building was a tent-like dwelling with a square plan. The length of each side would have been 19 meters.

Characteristics of Buildings

As I have already mentioned, the location of Ögödei's palace in the *Hei ta shih liu* agrees with the geographical situation of Platform 1.[18] There is no doubt that Ögödei's palace was located at Platform 1. According to the *Yüan-Shih*, Ögödei, after his enthronement in 1229, rebuilt the palace of Genghis Khan.[19] In 1235, Ögödei planned Qaraqorum as his capital and built a palace called Wan an kung. At Wan an kung Palace, I attempted to determine the design and measurement scale used at that time. I determined that the unit of measurement used in the construction of the building, the *ch'ih*, was

[18] P'eng and Wang (1983), 203.
[19] Song Lian (1976), fasc. 153, 3610.

equivalent to 31.6 centimeters.[20] This unit of measurement is the same as at the Avraga site. The entire structure of the Wan an kung Palace had a north-south length of 37.9 meters (120 *ch'ih*) and an east-west width of 37.9 meters (120 *ch'ih*). The layout of the Wan an kung Palace was square in shape and its area was four times as large as that of the building in Phase 2 at Avraga. Because Wan an kung and the Ögödei palace had a homologous plan, I believe there is an obvious relation between these two buildings. According to the description of the *Yüan-Shih*,[21] the same engineer built those two buildings. His name was Liu Ming. Judging from the above, I feel confident in stating that the building in Phase 2 was the palace rebuilt by Ögödei and the building in Phase 1 was therefore Genghis Khan's palace.

After 1235, this palace site seems to have assumed a religious purpose. For example, from the west brink of the platform, the skull of an ox, which had had both horns cut off, was excavated. A hornless ox appears in a scene from the enthronement of Genghis Khan in *The Secret History of the Mongols* (section 121). A hornless and fallow ox

> lifted up the great shaft under the tent, harnessed it on to himself and pulled it after him. As he proceeded following Temüjin [Genghis Khan] on the wide road, he kept bellowing, "Together Heaven and Earth have agreed: Temüjin shall be lord of the people!"[22]

I assume that this skull was connected with the enthronement of the emperor. Moreover, many bones were excavated from the east brink of the platform. Judging from the stratigraphical condition, the level belongs to the second half of Phase 2 (after the capital of the Mongol empire moved to Qaraqorum in 1235). The level from which the bones were unearthed shared the same stratigraphy as that of the skull of an ox at the west brink. Both belong to the same period. Most of the bones from the east brink were the ribs of horses. The ribs number more than three hundred pieces. According to the historical documents and the ethnographical reports, the sacrifice of the horse was consecrated for the ceremony that worshiped the spirits of the nobles in Mongolia at that time. In particular, it

[20] Shiraishi (2002), 130.
[21] Song Lian (1976), fasc. 153, 3610.
[22] de Rachewiltz, ed. (2004), 48.

was known from the ethnographical investigation that the breasts of horses were used for Genghis Khan's ceremony at Ejen Qoroga in Inner Mongolia.[23] It is clear that the unearthed horse ribs were related to the ceremony. According to a description given in the Persian historical document *Jāmiʿ al-tawārīkh*, Genghis Khan's palace, after his death, became a place to enshrine the souls of successive emperors.[24]

The building in Phase 4 (Upper Building) had a religious purpose. The fragments of an incense lamp for the religious ceremony were found in the building. The structure of this building resembled the tent of a nomad, a yurt (*ger*). The layout, however, was not a circle but a square. Ethnographical reports indicate that the original plan of Genghis Khan's shrine tent at Ejen Qoroga had been a square.[25] According to descriptions from historical materials, the shrine tent moved from the Kherlen River basin of Outer Mongolia to Inner Mongolia in the late fifteenth or early sixteenth century. I hypothesize that the Upper Building of Phase 4 was the earliest model of the shrine tent for Genghis Khan.

Reconstructing Genghis Khan's Court

The complex of ruins could be broadly divided into three districts. These are Platform 1 and the eastern and western building complexes to the left and right of it. Between the southern part of Platform 1 (the main frontage) and the eastern and western building complexes is a large open space with no buildings. In addition, there is a low mound of earth around the outskirts of the ruins, surrounding all the groups of buildings apart from those on the southern side. On the southern side, which has no mound, the Avraga River formed the boundary demarcating the inside and the outside of the palace. The total area of the site is approximately 50 hectares (pl. 4).

Platform 1, that is to say, Genghis Khan's palace, was encircled by an earthen wall that forms a rectangle measuring 150 by 90 meters. In what is more or less the center of this enclosure there is a large

[23] Mostaert (1956), 280–81.
[24] Rashīd al-Dīn (1971), 322.
[25] Andrews (1981), 10.

platform. This was formed by leveling the ground and then stamping down clay on top of that to make a 27 by 22 meters rectangular platform 60 centimeters high. The palace was built on top of this.

I could envisage the palace building to be a square tent measuring 17.4 meters along each side of the base. The pillars were placed in holes dug into the foundation platform, which formed the floor, and were then fixed in place. It was a completely different type of tent from the round, mobile yurt (*ger*) type of tents used by the nomadic peoples of the Mongolian plateau since ancient times, but it is clear that it was used for this palace.

There were many tent-like buildings among the eastern and western building complexes, but I also know that there were some buildings of the *Ssu he yuan* type, a traditional Chinese form of architecture. These Chinese-style buildings had tiled roofs and some of the tiles were painted with a green glaze, while others were white, having had plaster applied to them. Bricks that had been baked in a kiln or dried in the sun were used for the walls of these buildings. Radiocarbon dating of carbides excavated from the ruins showed them to originate from between the latter half of the twelfth century and the first half of the thirteenth century.

Chun yao and *Tz'u chou yao* ceramics, and grey and burnt umber earthenware vessels made in the Avraga ruins were unearthed (figs. 8–9). These all date from between the latter half of the twelfth century and the first half of the thirteenth century. In addition, bronze Chin dynasty coins called *Ta ting t'ung pao* were also found (fig. 10). These were first made in 1179. From this I assume that residential districts and commercial establishments of people who had come from China were located in this area.

Furthermore, at the eastern edge of the eastern building complex and the western edge of the western building complex, I discovered the sites of a number of blacksmiths' workshops in which ironware was made. Radiocarbon dating has ascertained that these workshops were in use at the end of the twelfth century and the beginning of the thirteenth century. A metallurgical examination revealed that the raw materials used to make ironware here had been imported from iron mines in such distant places as Shantung in China. It is apparent that, rather than the iron ore or iron sand being imported as it was, it was smelted at a smelting plant near the iron mine and formed into cast iron bar ingots, before being sent to Avraga. The bar ingots were 5–10 centimeters long and measured 1 centimeter on each side in cross-section; it is thought that their small size meant that not only were they convenient to carry around, but it was also easy to process them in order to manufacture ironware.[26] At the blacksmiths' workshops, these ingots were used to make iron weapons, such as arrowheads and swords. '*A'urugh*,' the word from which the name of the ruins was derived, means 'the rear support base' in Mongolian. It is thought that this precise location functioned as a rear support base for Genghis Khan's army.

Moreover, looking at aerial photographs, I can make out the remains of furrowed arable land spread around the complexes of buildings, particularly along the Avraga River. At this point in time, I cannot state positively that this site is land that was cultivated during the time of Genghis Khan, but given that there was a significant influx of Chinese culture to Mongolia and the fact that Chinese people also seem to have lived here, there is a distinct possibility that crops were produced in the surrounding area for consumption by those who lived in the settlement.

My investigation should eventually clarify conditions on the Mongol plateau during the period of the Mongol empire. Avraga is still only partially excavated, but this study, which is based on archaeological materials, could provide new, positive results that differ from those obtained from the study of historical documents, which include many legendary stories that cannot be verified. Further excavations and research of this area will be effective in unraveling the state structure of the Mongol empire and the background to its prosperity.

[26] Osawa (2005), 52–54.

THE ILKHANID PALACE AT TAKHT-I SULAYMAN: EXCAVATION RESULTS

DIETRICH HUFF

The residence that the Ilkhan Abaqa (1265–1282), the second Mongol ruler of Iran, built on present day Takht-i Sulayman in Azerbaijan, then called Shiz by the Persians and Sughūrlūq (Satūrīq) by the Mongols, is briefly but precisely described by the Persian Ḥamdallāh Mustawfī of Qazwin, a long serving state accountant of the Ilkhanid administration. Mustawfī compiled his *Nuzhat al-qulūb* under the last Ilkhan Abū Saʿīd (r. 1316–35), continuing probably after Abū Saʿīd's death into the 1340s, during the period of the Ilkhanid empire's dissolution.[1] Mustawfī writes:

> In the Anjarud district is a city which the Mongols call Satūrīq; it stands on the summit of a hill and it was originally founded by King Kay Khusraw the Kayanian. In this town there is a great palace, in the court of which a spring gushes forth into a large tank, that is like a small lake for size, and no boatman has been able to plumb its depth. Two main streams of water, each in power sufficient to turn a mill, continually flow away from this tank; but if they be dammed back the water in the tank no wise increases level; and when the stoppage is removed the water again runs as before in being at no season more or less in volume. This is a wonderful fact. This palace was restored by Abaqa Khan the Mongol, and in the neighbourhood there are excellent pasture grounds. Its revenues amount to 25,000 *dīnārs*.[2]

The site lies about 100 kilometers distant as the crow flies southeast of Maragha and northwest of Bijar.[3] It is accessible from the small town of Takab or by a new track from the Zanjan-Bijar road westward via Dandi. Geographically and administratively for most periods it belonged to Azerbaijan, although it has been temporarily ascribed to the province of Jibal.[4] Located at an elevation of over 2100 meters in a wide valley at the foot of a mountain ridge of more

[1] Krawulsky (1978), 18–39.
[2] Mustawfī (1915–19), 69.
[3] Adamec, ed. (1976), 639, map I-21-A.
[4] Le Strange (1905), 223–24 (page citations are to the 1930 reprint edition).

than 3000 meters, crowned by the late Sasanian fortress of Takht-i Bilqis,[5] the site is surrounded by picturesque rock formations and rolling meadows (fig. 11).

In order to understand the choice of a remote place like that for building a palace, one has to recall the political situation of the Ilkhanid empire in its early phase. Under Abaqa's father, Hülegü, the first Ilkhan of Iran, the Mongol armies had advanced through northern Iran—southern Iran had submitted—into eastern Anatolia, the Caucasus, and Mesopotamia. Baghdad was conquered, the Caliphate extinguished, and the armies had advanced into Syria.[6] As the natural hinterland and as the headquarters of the ongoing westward campaign, the northwestern Iranian province of Azerbaijan had become the political center of the Ilkhanid empire. Geographical advantages of the province certainly played a part in this development: the high but gently sloping mountains with lowland plains of mild climate around Lake Urmia and the Mughan steppe nearby offered ideal pasture ground for the flocks of the nomadic Mongol warriors, whose families could easily move their tents and household between *qishlaq* and *yaylaq*, winter and summer camps.

Although the Mongol conquerers, from common warrior up to the Ilkhan, stuck for a while to the traditional tent encampment as their proper residences, at least the nobility began rather quickly to adopt also the settled Persian way of life. The Ilkhans started building palaces in cities as well as at their *ordū*s, their royal encampments.[7] Hülegü's favorite residence was his *ordū* at the lower Zarrina-Rud, a river called Jaghatū by the Mongols, which flows into Lake Urmia, south of Maragha, in the area of Miyandoab. No palace is mentioned there, but Hülegü had built palaces in the *ordū* at Alatagh north of Lake Van, in the cities of Tabriz, Khoi, and Maragha. In Maragha, close to his main *ordū*, he employed alchemists in the futile hope for production of gold, and here he had built an observatory, *raṣadkhāna,* by and for Naṣīr al-Dīn Ṭūsī, the most famous scientist and philosopher of his time and also among Hülegü's foremost political

[5] Naumann, Huff, et al. (1975), 196–204.

[6] For detailed discussion of the subject of the Mongol armies, see the contribution of John Masson Smith, Jr. in the present volume.

[7] Rashīd al-Dīn (1836), 401–2 (page citations are to the 1968 reprint edition); Spuler (1939), 449. See also Melville (1990a); Blair (1993b); O'Kane (1993); Masuya (2002), 84–103.

counselors.[8] There can be no doubt that Hülegü had a predilection for the southeastern surroundings of Lake Urmia. It was in his *ordū* at the Jaghatū that he died on 8 February 1265,[9] and it was here that his eldest son, Abaqa, was proclaimed Ilkhan by the Mongol nobility immediately afterwards. Official confirmation of his election by the Great Khan at Qaraqorum and coronation ceremonies followed later.

Abaqa certainly intended to continue his father's strategies. He obviously felt committed to overcome the defeat the Mongol army had suffered by the Egyptian Mamluks at ʿAyn Jalut near Damascus in 1260, which had halted the Mongols' advance towards Egypt and the Mediterranean coast. Correspondence with the Mamluk Sultan Baybars proves that Abaqa had not given up his original plans to conquer Syria and Egypt.[10] He also had to check repeated intrusions by the rival Mongol Khanate of the Golden Horde into Ilkhanid territory in the Caucasus. The suitable strategic position of the Tabriz–Maragha–Jaghatū headquarters was unchanged and therefore there was no reason to abandon the area as the chief residence of the empire. We may assume that it was during this very first period of Abaqa's reign that he decided to build a summer and hunting palace at Takht-i Sulayman; he might not have done so later on, when he was forced to turn his attention to the northeastern border and fight the increasingly hostile Chaghatayid Khanate.

The new palace was clearly meant to be a summer resort for Maragha and the *ordū* at the lower Jaghatū. It was situated at the very headwaters of the northern tributary of the Jaghatū, the traditional name of which, Saruq, still reminds us of the Mongol name of Sughūrlūq/Satūrīq, and which must have been the name of the surrounding valleys, because it also lives on as the designation of a type of Bijar carpets produced there. In addition to its agreeable summer climate, attributable to its elevation above 2000 meters, and its easy, year-round open access along the rivers, excellent pasture grounds, scenic beauty, the seemingly bottomless lake and especially the still-intact, strong fortification wall with 38 bastions were decisive

[8] Hammer-Purgstall (1842–43), vol. 1, 228 (page citations are to the 1974 reprint edition); Varjavand (1975). See also George Saliba's contribution to this volume.

[9] Rashīd al-Dīn (1836), 417 (page citation is to the 1968 reprint edition); Hammer-Purgstall (1842–43), vol. 1, 229.

[10] Hammer-Purgstall (1842–43), vol. 1, 258; Amitai-Preiss (1994).

in the choice of the ancient site for reuse as a palace (fig. 12).[11] The beginning of the construction of the new palace immediately after Abaqa's accession seems to be also indicated by Mustawfī's original text.[12] Dates inscribed on wall tiles of the palace begin at 1271,[13] which means the raw construction must have been ready by then. Just three years later in 1274 Abaqa's grandson Ghazan was brought there at the age of three to be raised by the Great Lady Bulughan Khātūn, Abaqa's favorite wife,[14] at which date the palace must have been fully functional.

The Sasanian Period

As Ḥamdallāh Mustawfī correctly reports, Abaqa's palace was not built on virgin soil, but on the ruins of the Zoroastrian fire temple of Ādur Gushnasp, the most honored fire of the later Sasanian period. The sanctuary, dating from the second half of the fifth century AD, was laid out around a calcinating thermal spring lake about seventy meters deep on top of a hill around sixty meters in height, which had been created throughout the centuries by the sediments of calcium-rich water flowing over the shores, continuously building them up. There are a number of limestone mounds like this around, showing different sizes and all stages of formation: old, decayed ones; some still having water; others just in process of growth. Most impressive is the volcano-like Zindan-i Sulayman with its now-empty crater, about one hundred meters deep and sixty-five meters in diameter, still releasing sulfuric gases but never having spit magma.[15] This, too, is the result of sedimentation of calcinating water that once filled the total height of the crater. There are rings of fortification around the shoulder of the conical mountain, dated to the first half

[11] For the ideological meaning that was possibly ascribed to the palace, see Melikian-Chirvani (1984), and Melikian-Chirvani (1991).

[12] Schwarz (1896), 1467 (page citation is to the 1969 reprint edition) gives in his German translation of Mustawfī: 'Der Mongolenhan Abakaj ließ sogleich (wohl nach seiner Thronbesteigung) jenes Schloss wieder herstellen.'

[13] Qūchānī (1992), 91; Masuya (1997), 667.

[14] Hammer-Purgstall (1842–43), vol. 2, 5.

[15] Damm (1968), 22–40.

of the first millennium BC.[16] At Takht-i Sulayman the growth of the mountain ended when Iron Age settlers began to canalize the water of the lake for irrigation of their surrounding fields, thus interrupting unregulated overflow. During periods of abandonment of the valley, which was the case in the period after the fourteenth century AD, the water again spilled over the plateau and caused thick layers of sediment around the lake and all over the western and southern areas within the wall of fortification (fig. 12).[17]

It was certainly the enigmatic, seemingly bottomless lake with its warm water at a permanent temperature of 21° C that, after brief Achaemenid and Parthian occupation,[18] attracted the building of the Sasanian fire sanctuary there. According to literary tradition, Ādur Gushnasp was the fire of the warriors and knights, and was highly honored and sponsored by the Sasanian kings.[19] It may be an exaggeration to say that the kings had to make their pilgrimage there after coronation, walking by foot halfway from Ctesiphon; however, their frequent presence at the sanctuary, with audiences, receptions, and other acts of representation taking place during the pilgrimage, is beyond doubt. The excavated Sasanian layout of the site is perfectly suited to such purposes.

The sanctuary was divided into two areas, with the Adūr Gushnasp temple in the middle.[20] Within the oval fortification wall there were two square areas enclosed by an interior circumvallation. The northern square was the sanctuary proper. It also contained the comparatively small public zone for the common pilgrims, extending along the main axis from the exterior northern gate to the rather small *īwān* at the northern side of the temple. The southern square, enclosing the lake, was a zone reserved for the royal court. It had a larger *īwān* at the south side of the temple and at its northwestern corner a palace with a huge *īwān* for audiences, adjoined by smaller side and living rooms. A podium in front of the fire temple and on the axis of the palace obviously served as an open-air throne seat. Access to the royal area was through the exterior south gate, which

[16] Kleiss (1971).

[17] Excavation in these areas is nearly impossible without removing the sediment by pneumatic chisel.

[18] Naumann, Huff, et al. (1975), 138–42, 164.

[19] Cf. Schippmann (1971), 318–25.

[20] Naumann, R. (1977), 34–68; Huff (2000), 103–09; Huff (forthcoming).

was shifted away from the main north-south axis of the whole layout towards the southeast, to the highest ground outside the wall, obviously in order to provide the most comfortable entrance facilities through the gate on a nearly level surface.

The Ilkhanid Palace

When Abaqa Khan chose the site for his summer palace, it was covered by the houses, stables, and workshops of the small peasant town of Shiz,[21] which was evacuated and razed to the ground. Domes and vaults of the Sasanian buildings had mostly fallen into decay before the ruins were occupied by squatters. The square circumvallation of the royal palatial area around the lake, the southern part of which had consisted of mud brick on stone socles, had probably vanished. However, the massive ruins of the old fire temple and the palace, as well as the general direction and axis of the ancient layout, were substantial enough to dictate the plan of the Ilkhanid palace; Ḥamdallāh Mustawfī's description of Abaqa *restoring* the palace therefore is basically correct. The layout of the Sasanian palace area in the south was practically repeated in the Ilkhanid palace, whereas the northern, formerly public area became the backyard of the palace. The Mongol palace, like the Sasanian palace before, was arranged along the four sides of a courtyard of 120 to 145 meters with a *hawz* (tank), the lake in the center, bordered by arcades in front of various buildings, the main buildings opening to the court by symmetrically placed *īwāns*. The most important change was to bring the old plan to geometric perfection by lengthening the old north-south axis throughout the whole site and breaking a new south gate through the fortification wall on this axis.[22] The old Sasanian south gate probably remained in use as a side or domestic gate and as an outlet for the rivulet. As the new south gate no longer met with high ground outside the wall, a ramp had to be constructed, starting from the high ground near the old gate. For this reason, the second bastion to the left of the old gate was removed from the

[21] Schwarz (1896), 1111–20 (page citation is to the 1969 reprint edition).
[22] Probably by miscalculation the new south gate is slightly shifted west of the axis 1.1 meter. See Naumann, Kleiss, et al. (1964), 29.

wall to provide straight and easy access to the gate alongside the wall from the east (fig. 13).

The facade of the Ilkhanid south gate is completely destroyed. The restored plans show two transverse entrance rooms in succession with rather narrow entrance and passage doors.[23] Taking into account the typical design of a representative Persian gate of the time, one might expect instead that the first room was originally a high, wide open *īwān*. In addition, the inexplicable thickness of the wall between the two rooms with a multistepped passage seems to indicate that this was not a simple wall of division, but the back wall of an *īwān* and the entrance proper to the site. Two remarkable, hollow constructions outside the second room may have been buttresses for the vault, which has a span of 7.7 meters. The gate building was followed by two oblong courtyards of different sizes. The first, wider forecourt (23.5 x 30 meters) ended at a monumental facade with niches, framing a central main door of 3.5 meters and lateral doors of 1.8 meters. The second court (14 x 24 meters) seems to have belonged more closely to the inner palace area. It was connected by another tripartite but wider passage with an *īwān* of approximately the same width as the court (14.4 meters) and it is not clear whether this last passage had closing devices.

The *īwān*, with its strong side walls, was a monumental entrance building in the middle axis of the southern arcade of the palace courtyard, with the lake as a natural *hawz*, the obligatory water basin, in the center. The span of its vault was considerably wider than that of the western palace *īwān*, inferior only to the *īwān* of the great throne hall north of the lake. The entrance *īwān* seems to have been an intricate building with more functions than just a shady passageway. There were square winding stairs in both southern corners, accessible neither from inside the *īwān* nor from its southern forecourt, but from the obviously domestic quarters outside the zone of representation. There were, however, lateral doors from the *īwān* to the same domestic quarters. The stairs were certainly not designed for use by the royal entourage or by arriving guests, but more likely for the use of servants. They are also too elaborate to serve merely to access the roof. Instead, they seem to have led to some kind of

[23] Cf. Naumann, Kleiss, et al. (1964), 27–28; Naumann, R. (1977), 74–102, plan 3.

balconies or upper chambers, indicating a type of building like the *īwān* of Pir-i Bakran at Linjan near Isfahan,[24] although there cannot be any similarity of function. Perhaps the *īwān* was designed and used as a *naqqārakhāna* for musicians or for some other special acts of state ceremony.[25]

The main building of royal identity was doubtlessly the rebuilt former fire temple on the northern shore of the lake, opposite the entrance *īwān* (pl. 5). The architecture of the temple was completely altered; as its dark and narrow rooms obviously did not at all fulfill the requirements of a medieval royal audience hall, and as the surface around the lake had been raised up about 1.5 meters during interim occupation, the ruin of the temple was used as a basement and substructure only, and a new hall was erected on the top of its restored dome and vaults.[26] To bridge the difference in height of more than 5 meters, a freestanding straight stair was erected on the axis of the old fire temple *īwān*, which was pulled down and a new *īwān* of double span, nearly 17 meters (instead of 8.4), was built. The rear section of this gigantic *īwān* contained a gallery along its back wall high up at the floor level of the newly constructed hall.[27] The straight main stair, as well as a square, winding service stair behind the left corner, led up to this gallery from which the new hall could be entered through probably three gates; the threshold of the left one is preserved.[28] The gallery was supported by vaultings; the abutments of the central vault are still visible. The lateral constructions are uncertain; fragments of stucco *muqarnas*, found in the debris, may have been associated with them.[29] Under the gallery, behind the central stair, the door of the fire temple was kept accessible, which

[24] Wilber (1955), 121–24, cat. 20.

[25] Lambton (1992), 928.

[26] Cf. Naumann, Kleiss, et al. (1964), 30–34; Naumann, R. (1977), 77–79.

[27] The possibility of a wooden second floor, filling the whole *īwān*, as considered by Naumann, R. (1977), 79, seems rather remote.

[28] Cf. Naumann, Kleiss, et al. (1962), 651–52, fig. 9.

[29] The fragments of *muqarnas* might also have belonged to a higher area of the wall or vault of the *īwān*. They were found together with a vertically collapsed part of a wall with two layers of decoration: stucco niches overlaying an earlier facade of imitated bricks and plugs, carved in stucco. Naumann, Kleiss, et al. (1964), 32–33. Regarding the wide span between the stair and the lateral walls of the *īwān*, one might expect some intermediate supports, but obviously no pillars or walls were observed; wooden posts would be rather unusual in this context.

meant that its rooms were used for domestic purposes; in a corner of the corridors traces of a bathroom were observed.

Interpreting the Remains

When H. C. Rawlinson visited Takht-i Sulayman in 1838, he found the square, central room of the fire temple filled with trash, waste, and debris to half its height, but still covered by a slightly damaged dome, the four squinches intact, and the barrel vaults of the surrounding corridors partly destroyed but recognizable.[30] One hundred years later, when members of the American Institute's expedition under A. U. Pope (1937)[31] and M. B. Smith (1938)[32] saw the ruins, the dome had already collapsed into the square central room as a result of brick-robbing from its supporting corner piers; recent excavators found similar conditions.[33]

Rawlinson had mistaken the black soot on the interior of the dome as produced by the smoke of the sacred fire. He could not have known that the dome was a 'modern' Ilkhanid reconstruction with a framework of reed-reinforced gypsum struts filled in with masonry. But his keen observation of evidence for a second floor or some kind of superstructure, which he again misinterpreted as belonging to the Sasanian temple, is of great importance.[34] What he had seen was obviously the light substructure of small barrel vaults that carried the floor of the Mongol hall above the empty, uneven spaces between the apex of the dome and the vaults of the corridors.[35] That Rawlinson could notice the remainder of the upper floor and its supporting constructions seems to indicate that the upper

---

[30] Rawlinson (1841), 51–52.

[31] Pope et al. (1937), 99–101. Pope's team obviously could not enter under the cupola. The report remains vague and information falls back upon that of Rawlinson.

[32] The photographs of M. B. Smith in the Freer Gallery of Art Archives, Washington, D.C., also show only an inaccessible mound of debris. I am greatly indebted to the staff of the Freer Gallery for making M. B. Smith's excellent photographs accessible to me. I thank also Robert Hillenbrand for informing me of the location of Smith's archive.

[33] Osten, Naumann, et al. (1961), 54.

[34] Pope's team also recognized traces of a second story.

[35] Cf. Naumann, Kleiss, et al. (1961), 31–35, fig. 2.

level was not covered by great quantities of debris of the broken vaults of the Mongol hall. Debris should be expected if the hall was a normal Iranian vaulted construction, more or less repeating the layout of the temple, with a domed central room and barrel-vaulted side rooms, perhaps with small, separate domes at the four corners. The lack of abundant debris covering the floor of the Mongol hall might be seen as evidence for a very different type of building: a hypostyle hall with wooden columns or a Chinese throne hall. Also, the position of the stairs, directed straight towards the entrance, may remind us of Chinese stairs leading to throne halls, whereas Persian palace stairs, at least from Achaemenid to Sasanian times, usually had double flights of steps running parallel to the facade. The very close relationship of the Ilkhans, and especially of Hülegü and Abaqa, to the Great Khans is well-known, and the Chinese court of the Great Khans was in many respects a model for their Iranian dependents. Therefore a Chinese hypostyle hall could have been not only a practical constructive solution in this special case, but also would have been ideologically fitting in the early phase of Ilkhanid rule. Strong Chinese influence on the iconography of the architectural decoration of the palace is undeniable.[36]

The great Sasanian *īwān* building at the northwestern corner of the royal courtyard was rebuilt by Abaqa as a veritable Iranian standard palace, which in some way it had not been before, lacking the upper private rooms around the high audience hall (figs. 14–15).[37] Today only the northern side wall of the *īwān* hall stands upright. But on the outside of this wall, the outlines of upper-level rooms are clearly visible in the rubble stone masonry of the Mongol repair above the Sasanian bricks, testifying to a now-destroyed, multistoried northern wing of the building. A Mongol staircase south of the hall proves the same for the southern wing. The repair replaced the fallen Sasanian brick vault of the *īwān* by a pointed barrel vault of rubble masonry, the span of about 11.5 meters remaining the same, but with more than three meters added to its height. The projecting bricks of the lower corbel zone of the Sasanian vault were chiseled off above a row of vertical bricks, indicating the springing line.[38] As shown by

[36] On the subject of Chinese influence, see also Masuya (2002).
[37] Huff (1993), 50–53; Huff (1999), 149; Huff (2005), 371–95.
[38] Pope et al. (1937), 101, fig. 20.

Pope's photographs from 1937,[39] the graphical restitution of the curvature of the Mongol front arch was still feasible before the collapse of the south wall in about 1940, again after brick robbing.[40] The photographs also attest that the facade had been altered during the palace's lifetime: the lower *muqarnas* niche on either side had been walled up and covered with wall tiles; the mortar beddings seem to indicate a cross and star pattern (fig. 14).[41] In addition, a fragment of an Arabic inscription on the south wall, already mentioned by Rawlinson, was preserved before the collapse.[42]

The most magnificent ensemble of rooms was added to the rear of the *īwān*: a nearly square hall even wider than the *īwān*, probably hypostyle with a wooden roof, and two lateral octagonal pavilions (known as the north and the south octagons), with eight large and deep niches or cabinets surrounding each of the central domed areas. Benches along the walls and wide windows reaching down nearly to the floor indicate that the north octagon in particular was deliberately designed to take advantage of the splendid view down the valley, whereas four secluded chamber-like niches in the south octagon seem to have offered places for inhabitants or guests of the palace to retire. The layout of these rooms anticipates the qualities of the best examples of Safavid architecture and demonstrates an amazingly sophisticated lifestyle of early Ilkhanid upper-class society.

Few other buildings of the palace area exhibit so many and varied traces of luxurious architectural decoration with wall and floor tiles, carved stucco, and wall painting as the *īwān* building (figs. 16–19, pl. 6).[43] We may also assume that the few Ilkhanid capitals, or bases with dragon decoration,[44] and the half dozen small Gothic capitals of Crusader architecture[45] (certainly imported from Syria)

---

[39] Ibid., 100, fig. 18.

[40] Ibid., 133 (photo inverse).

[41] Cf. the photographs in Pope et al. (1937), 100, fig. 18 and in Naumann, R. (1977), 82, fig. 61, where the walled-up masonry had collapsed.

[42] From the photographs of the fragment by M. B. Smith, copies of which were kindly provided by the Freer Gallery of Art, C.-P. Haase of the Museum für Islamische Kunst, Berlin, gave the provisional reading: "...and (they) made populous...at the shadow-giving..."

[43] Naumann, E. and Naumann, R. (1969); Naumann, R. and Naumann, E. (1976), 39–67; Franke, U. (1979); Masuya (1997), 223–561

[44] Naumann, Kleiss, et al. (1961), 58–62, fig. 14.

[45] Naumann, Huff, et al. (1975), 169–72.

were employed here, if not in the throne hall or in its *īwān*. The debris in the south octagon contained fragments of carved plaster and stalactites fallen down from above. They enabled the reconstruction of panels of stucco decoration and, with the help of a *muqarnas* design on a plaster tablet found reused in a house, of variants of the rich *muqarnas* dome of the octagon.[46] Only in the *īwān* building were extensive plaster beddings with the impressions of the former tile revetment preserved, giving at least an idea of the shapes of the tiles that had been applied here (fig. 20). There were very few cases of broken tile fragments stuck in the plaster at corners to indicate the decorative type of tiles.

The fact alone that practically no wall tiles were preserved *in situ* is clear proof that the revetment of decorative tiles had been systematically removed. The procedure of plundering could be partially traced: the tiles must have been hacked off the walls and carried away; the trash was left on the site, later dispersed among the local people, partly stored elsewhere (e.g., in the northern cabinet niche of the southern octagon, which was filled with fragments, or in abandoned *tandurs*, or waste pits of the farmers' houses). The pillage most likely took place during the time when Sughūrlūq had lost its importance after the fall of the Ilkhanid dynasty and before the abandonment of the place, most likely in Timurid times. Complete tiles were always found stowed away in the corner of a house; larger fragments were often used, upside down, to pave storage boxes.[47]

There can be no doubt that the great *īwān* building was the main living area of the palace for the royal inhabitants of Sughūrlūq. Only here do we find the arrangement and variety of halls and rooms (for different social events and for privacy as well) typical of a traditional Persian palace. The additional throne hall, taking over the part of the *īwān* as an audience hall, is befitting of a monarch who was bound to both Iranian and Far Eastern traditions.

---

[46] Naumann, R. (1977), 80–97; Naumann, E. and Naumann, R. (1969), 35–65; Naumann, R. and Naumann, E. (1976), 39–63; Harb (1978), 1–77; Yaghan (2000).

[47] Quantities of wasters and other unused tiles were found in the large Sasanian side room south of the western *īwān*, which had been intact in Mongol times, and was used as a basement and junk room under the southern wing of the *īwān* building, accessible from the large hall added to the rear of the *īwān* from the corner behind the south octagon. These tiles seem to have been left over from construction work.

The interpretation of other structures of the palace area is difficult, although they all may have served as habitation.[48] The incredible variety of rooms and pavilions behind the arcades east and west along the lake, of which only the western series was excavated, gives reason to admire the genius of the architects. The individual layouts of these structures, however, seem to indicate special functions or personal predilections of the users. One might argue that there are two separate groups with a four- or three-*īwān* house each, a plan that seems to have been the normal parlor of upper-middle-class residences. The occurrence of polygonal, nearly round buildings may be regarded as a reminiscence of a Mongol *yurt,* but the Mongols were certainly not the first Central Asian nomads to make this practical structure known in Iran.

The eastern *īwān*, at the northeast corner of the royal courtyard exactly opposite the western *īwān*, was clearly erected in order to establish a well-balanced, symmetrical ensemble.[49] Along the east-west axis, which runs through these two *īwāns*, two four-*īwān* houses stand outside the royal courtyard, one on the eastern fortification wall, the other halfway between the western *īwān* building and the western wall. They were only superficially cleared and surveyed. Based on their axial position, they seem to be kiosks or garden pavilions of the palace.

Of considerable interest is a large four-*īwān* house behind the northwestern arcade of the royal courtyard, between the old fire temple and the great *īwān* building.[50] Its position between the two main buildings of the site and its direct access to the great northern *īwān* or by the winding side stair into the throne hall itself, as well as its obviously exquisite interior decoration of fine stone pavement and

---

[48] Naumann, Kleiss, et al. (1962), 666–70; Naumann, Huff, et al. (1965), 698–703.

[49] Naumann, Huff, et al. (1965), 693–97. Traces of a Sasanian east *īwān* were found here under a thick sediment of limestone.

[50] Naumann, Huff, et al. (1965), 704–11; Naumann, R. (1977), 78–80. Due to the lack of bonding of the walls, an Abbasid date is suggested for the first period of the building, with later Ilkhanid alterations. This however, is rather improbable, based on the stratigraphic situation, and bonding is not always obligatory in Iranian masonry. Roofing of its nearly 10-meter central square is not certain, but the reinforced southern wall construction seems to speak in favor of a dome. The sunken floor is certainly the result of the settling of loose fill around a massive pier of the underlying Sasanian building.

wall tiles, bestow on it special importance. With its apse-like protrusion on the main axis, it bears some similarity to a building at the *raṣadkhāna,* the observatory of Naṣīr al-Dīn Ṭūsī at Maragha, which is interpreted there as a library, though without definitive proof.[51]

Similarly important, yet unexplained, is an isolated building outside the royal courtyard to the west. The simple square structure is distinguished by its decorated doorjambs and its four massive columns with torus bases, all of red sandstone. The jambs of the 3.6 meter-wide entrance were built of huge blocks on which four-lobed flowers set between knotted bands were carved in high relief (fig. 21). The building had once been dated to the Parthian period, chiefly for its ornaments,[52] but these are clearly close to Rum Seljuk art, and stratigraphic research proved an Ilkhanid date.[53] It is doubtful that the four columns carried any kind of dome.[54] Perhaps this impressive hall, comprised of a central square (measuring seven meters in diameter between the columns) was covered by a flat timber roof, forming a traditional *ruzan* construction, bridging the corners and diminishing the square layer by layer for a suitable opening for light and smoke. The remains of windows high up in the better-preserved back wall may indicate up to three windows on each side. The building does not fit into the category of religious architecture of the Buddhist, Christian, or Muslim creeds, and there is obviously no evidence for a funerary purpose. One may only suppose that it served for assemblies of various kinds.[55] It may, however, be noteworthy that it was robbed of its architectural elements after the abandonment of the site by the Ilkhans; the doorjambs were pulled down and some heavy blocks were transported to the north gate and used there for the walls of a small mosque, perhaps as a symbolic act against an especially reviled, non-Muslim monument.

The hall of four columns seems to have stood in a wide enclosure, covering most of the area west of the palace. In the remaining narrow space before the fortification wall, the premises of a well-to-do

---

[51] Varjavand (1987), 224–32, figs. 119–23 (Persian), 12 (French).

[52] Wilber (1931), 389–410.

[53] Naumann, Kleiss, et al. (1961), 55–57.

[54] Naumann, Kleiss, et al. (1961), 53–58; Naumann, R. (1977), 97–102.

[55] Even the function of an arsenal or of a special store house might be taken into consideration. A smaller building with four reused columns north of the throne hall belongs to the post-palace period; cf. Naumann, Huff, et al. (1965), 713–16.

individual (probably in the service of the royal court), which seem to have been built more or less contemporarily with the palace, were excavated (T 8).[56] There were no spoils of Ilkhanid architecture used in the walls, but scraps of red sandstone. The complex was divided into two areas: a four-*īwān* parlor on a level with the preserved top of the fortification wall, and a lower domestic area, the *khāna*, for everyday life. The four-*īwān* house had one corner room equipped with a fireplace in the wall, and in front of it on the edge of the fortification wall was certainly a loggia, from which a masonry stair still leads down to the domestic area. The latter consists of three large rooms, the largest one with two slender octagonal pillars of masonry, all with benches and *tandur*-ovens in the brick-paved floors. In addition, there are small chambers, also equipped with fireplaces, ovens, and benches—obviously the living quarters of servants—as well as stables and storerooms. The complex is a model for an estate, a middle-class residence of the time.

Less spacious living quarters were excavated behind a bazaar-like line of chambers along the northern entranceway into the backyard of the palace, where traces of a *ḥammām* and of the aforementioned post-Ilkhanid mosque were found.[57] The rooms may have housed workmen or servants from the time of construction of the palace, but were enlarged and enriched with spoils of architectural material from the palace when it was abandoned.[58] Comparable to the excavated estate at area T 8, however, is another complex on the northwestern edge of the fortification wall (Kiosk A), which was only surveyed, as well as the remainders of a house on top of the Sasanian structures PC/PD northwest of the throne hall, and the so-called potter's workshop northeast of the throne hall.[59] In all these cases there is a division into a neatly built four-*īwān* space and an obviously domestic area with a number of rectangular rooms.

The four-*īwān* section of the so-called pottery workshop was carefully furnished with brick-paved floors, the sunken central square bordered by bricks standing upright.[60] A corner room housed a *tandur* flanked by masonry shelves. The dadoes of this area were

[56] Huff (1977), 224–29.
[57] Naumann, Huff, et al. (1975), 134–37.
[58] Huff (1977), 223–24.
[59] Naumann, Huff, et al. (1965), 687–93.
[60] Naumann, Huff, et al. (1975), 132–34; Naumann, R. (1977), 102–10.

decorated with mosaics of cut pieces of glazed tiles, turquoise, *lajvard*, and white plaster as a third color (fig. 22). Along the opposite wall was a low bench with two niches beneath, which were filled with mostly unfinished wall tiles, the majority coarse, exterior relief tiles that would have been glazed. From the room, which must have looked like the kitchen of a teahouse, steps led down into two connecting domestic rooms, also paved with brick and with benches, *tandurs*,[61] a fireplace for large cooking cauldrons, and a stone-clad storage basin. Unfortunately, the complex could not be excavated as a whole, but what was uncovered fits well into the typology of a wealthy residence. The wall tiles might have been brought here by chance, as must have been the case with other complete pieces in the other houses. The fact that they are a large and uniform group of a not-especially precious type seems to indicate that they are the unused remainders of a suspended production, which someone in charge had stowed away. Moreover, some 30 meters south are the kilns[62] where, besides green glazed pottery, wall and floor tiles were evidently fired and where the Sasanian room O had been used as a large refuse pit for potter's equipment and wasters when construction work was finished.[63] The areas east of the Sasanian fire temple or the Mongol throne hall and behind the northeastern arcades of the royal courtyard, in fact, seem to have comprised an area of workshops during the time of the palace's construction, and later, during periods of rebuilding; the house neighboring this area in the north may have belonged to someone involved in tile production. The workshops proper, like the upper parts of the kilns, certainly disintegrated through disuse, and there was no later occupation by houses here. Instead, a graveyard spread from a small mausoleum[64] that was built outside against the eastern wall of the Mongol *īwān* of the throne hall.

[61] Most *tandurs* do not belong to the original phase of the room but were dug down from higher, later levels. Cf. Naumann, Huff, et al. (1975), 133, fig. 26 b.

[62] Naumann, R. (1971), 173–87; Naumann, R. (1977), 103–11; Naumann, R. and Naumann, E. (1976), 64–67.

[63] Naumann, Kleiss, et al. (1961), 660–65; Naumann, R. (1963), 301–7. A bronze cauldron, probably for preparing glaze colors, was also found here.

[64] Naumann, Kleiss, et al. (1964), 42–50.

Later History

The town of Sughūrlūq seems to have been abandoned in the fifteenth century, based on the lack of later pottery or small finds. The whole area must have been depopulated, perhaps as a consequence of the Timurid wars and the subsequent influx of nomadic tribes; it was during the following centuries that the massive layer of sediment was built up on the site by the unregulated flow of water. The name of Sughūrlūq lived on as a geographical eponym, and, as mentioned above, Shiz and Ādur Gushnasp were remembered only in literature. The name of Takht-i Sulayman appeared in the early Safavid period in connection with princely *yaylaq*s or summer quarters for hunting and pleasure.[65] These, however, must have been tent encampments; it is doubtful that the palace could still have been used at that time. The culturally heterogeneous groups of Kurdish and Azari-Turkish inhabitants who later set up new villages around Takht-i Sulayman had no knowledge of the history of the site.[66] They identified the ruins and the surrounding localities with the mythological ensemble of Takht-, Zindan-, and Tawilah-i Sulayman, Throne, Prison, and Stable of Solomon and Takht-i Bilqis, the throne of the queen of Sheba, his consort.

---

[65] Cf. Masuya (1997), 103–12.

[66] A number of small ruins in the area, however, are remembered as *kilisa*s, or churches.

HÜLEGÜ MOVES WEST: HIGH LIVING AND HEARTBREAK ON THE ROAD TO BAGHDAD

JOHN MASSON SMITH, JR.

Hülegü traveled to the Middle East at the command of his elder brother Möngke, the newly elected *khān* of the Mongol empire, who decided in 1253 to take care of unfinished business there. Mongol armies had established pastoral bases in Azerbaijan starting in 1229 on the orders of Ögödei, and subjugated many smaller potentates of northern Iran as well as the Cilician Armenians and Rum (Anatolian) Seljuks. But they had failed to overawe or defeat the caliphal state in Iraq, or the Ismāʿīlī 'Assassins' in their strongholds scattered across northern Iran. The Caliphate, although no longer the Islamic empire it had once been, still possessed fertile Mesopotamia, a strong army and a great, fortified capital city at Baghdad. The Mongols attacked Baghdad in the 1230s and c. 1242, but were repulsed.[1] The Assassins relied, and had for over a century, on their inaccessible mountain castles and the suicidal murderers whom they dispatched against enemy leaders.[2] Möngke, wanting to deal with persistent 'rebels' against his empire, now sent Hülegü to the Middle East and their brother Qubilai ('Kubla Khan') against Sung China, the other great holdout against Mongol supremacy.

Möngke authorized both Hülegü and Qubilai to form an army by taking two men in every ten of the imperial forces, which, by this time, were extremely numerous. They included the current descendants of Chinggis's (Genghis's) original army—call this the 'Army of Mongolia'—which numbered 145,000 at the time of Chinggis's death. Chinggis's will apportioned this force among his close relatives. One hundred and one regiments (*hazaras*, thousands) were based in Mongolia (and to some extent in north China), and commanded at first by Tolui, Chinggis's youngest son by his first wife, Börte. An

[1] Jūzjānī (1881), vol. 2, 1117–18; Rashīd al-Dīn (1998), vol. 2, 397.

[2] Since 1090, according to 'Alā' al-Dīn 'Aṭā Malik Juwaynī; Juwaynī (1958), vol. 2, 670.

additional 28,000 men went to other members of the imperial family; each of Tolui's older brothers, Jochi, Chaghadai, and Ögödei, received four regiments. During Chinggis's lifetime, these brothers had been assigned territories as well, west of Mongolia: Jochi's west from roughly Lake Balkash to the Volga (this came to include not only most of Kazakhstan, but Russia, Ukraine, etc.: the realm of the so-called Golden Horde); Ögödei's *ulus* (realm) centered on the valleys of the Emil and Qobaq rivers, east of the Ala Kul (Lake) and included the area beyond (north of) the Tarbagatai range; and Chaghadai held the Ili valley, Almalyk, and Transoxiana.[3] Thus, some 133,000 troops of the Army of Mongolia were stationed in Mongolia or to its east and south and only 12,000 from Mongolia west to Anatolia and Ukraine.

These westerly realms, like Mongolia, supported large nomad populations, predominantly Turkic but otherwise quite like the Mongols; many of them were conscripted into the imperial army, complementing the brothers' four original regiments. Rashīd al-Dīn says that in his own time (the early fourteenth century), the army of the *ulus* Jochi (the Golden Horde) consisted of descendants of these four thousand Mongols, plus Russians, Qipchaq Turks, Circassians, and Magyars. It probably numbered some fifteen (nomad) *tümens* (divisions of ten thousand); each region seems to have been limited to a regular nomad army of fifteen *tümens*, even if more manpower was available, so as not to outnumber the forces of Mongolia proper.[4] Ögödei and Chaghadai surely enlarged their followings in the same way.

Hülegü also had to raise most of his army outside Mongolia. Few Mongolian troops could be spared him because Möngke intended to use most of them against China in a campaign engaging ninety *tümens*—a nominal 900,000 men. Of these, some considerable part was non-Mongolian: 'Ja'uqut'—Chinese, Tangqut, Manchurian Jurchens, and Koreans. Since twenty-four Mongol commanders are named (including Möngke and Qubilai), I assume that the ninety *tümens* included twenty-four Mongol (cavalry) units and sixty-six of Ja'uqut

[3] Juwaynī (1958), vol. 1, 42–43.

[4] When Möngke assigned "two men in ten" from the imperial armies to Hülegü, the Golden Horde sent him three *tümens* (3 x 5 = 15): Juwaynī (1958), vol. 2, 607–8.

(mostly infantry).[5] This suggests a doubling—or more: some forces remained in Mongolia—of the Mongolian population in about fifty years, an increase not implausible in light of Fredrik Barth's study of a nomad tribe that grew by a factor of three per generation.[6] Rashīd al-Dīn says that the 101,000 men bequeathed by Chinggis to Tolui, and those assigned his other children, "have multiplied and become many times the number they were originally."[7] Population increase could more than account for the Mongol force used in China. But with so many from the army of Mongolia involved in this campaign, it seems unlikely that it could have spared a fifth ("two in ten") for Hülegü.

The Journey

Möngke sent Hülegü back to his own *ordū* in February of 1253, the Ox Year, to prepare for the campaign. In autumn of 1254, the Leopard Year, Hülegü led out his army on a journey that was to cover about five thousand miles.[8] He left his *a'urughs* behind (more on these below).

The long journey took what might seem a very long time. The army reached Baghdad only on 22 January 1258, about three years and three months (some 1200 days) after it had set out, thus moving at an average pace of only about four miles per day (mpd). Compare the progress of the Mongol army sent against West Inner Asia, Russia, and Eastern Europe starting in 1236. That army reached Bulghar on the Volga from Mongolia by autumn 1236, about three

---

[5] Rashīd al-Dīn (1998), vol. 2, 414–15, mentions that Taghachar, commander of the Left Wing for a time during this campaign, led "100,000 horsemen"; these would be the soldiery commanded by the eleven Mongols named by Rashīd al-Dīn as commanders in the Left Wing.

[6] Barth (1964), 115. Plus, perhaps, nomads from Inner Mongolia and Manchuria.

[7] Rashīd al-Dīn (1998), vol. 2, 282; see also 279–80: the *hazara* (nominally a thousand) of Müge Noyan had four thousand even in Chinggis's (Genghis's) time, and had further "multiplied and increased" by Rashīd al-Dīn's day.

[8] The date usually given for the start of Hülegü's march is 1253. This is consistent both with Juwaynī's information (Juwaynī [1958], vol. 2, 611): 19 October 1253, and Rashīd al-Dīn's statement (Rashīd al-Dīn [1998], vol. 2, 413: Ox Year). But as Rashīd al-Dīn returns to the story (ibid., 479) when taking up Hülegü's history, the departure is restated as autumn of the Leopard (*bars*) Year, that is, 1254.

thousand miles in six months (assuming a start in spring) at 16.7 mpd. This would have been about top speed for a Mongol force: ponies should only travel for about four hours per day to leave time for grazing, and should walk (4 mph) to avoid overexertion.[9] Chinggis required his cavalry to travel with their cruppers (which help secure the saddle) and bridles removed, so that they could not 'horse around' and exhaust their mounts.[10] Let us examine the route and timetable, and discuss factors that slowed Hülegü's march.

Assuming that Hülegü started in autumn, probably October as Juwaynī wrote (despite Juwaynī's mistake about the year[11]), I suggest that his army made its way from somewhere near Qaraqorum, across (Outer) Mongolia, through passes of the Altai, and along river valleys leading to Lake Zaysan. These suggestions, and others below, are based on some guesswork, often guided by convenience. The sources seldom specify or clearly indicate the route taken, but do name significant way stations: Almalyk, Samarqand, the Oxus River, Shiburgan, etc. I have connected these points by routes that are more or less measurable: more when detailed in guide books, and less when measured by me on a map. This procedure shows about 824 miles (1327 km) from Qaraqorum (I assume Hülegü's *ordū* was in central Mongolia) to the western Mongolian border at the Bulgan Nature Preserve.[12] From there, a plausible route, with pasture and water, of some 224 miles (approx. 360 km) leads to Lake Zaysan.[13] Next, on to the modern town of Ayagoz, about 202 miles (c. 325 km) from Zaysan; thereafter to Aktogay, roughly another 75 miles (c. 120 km); then, Ayagoz to Alma-Ata/Almaty, 350 miles (565 km).[14] Almaty is fairly near ancient Almalyk, where Hülegü and his force

[9] The campaign of Samuqa in northern China (1216–17) covered 14 mpd; Ghazan's in Syria (1299–1300) moved at 15.1 mpd: Martin, H. D. (1950), 191, and map of 'Chingis Khan's Campaigns in China, 1209–1227'; Smith, J. M. (1984), 307–45, esp. 335–37.

[10] Cleaves, trans. (1982), section 199.

[11] Juwaynī (1958), vol. 2, 611, has 24 Shaʿbān, which, for 1254 instead of 1253, would have been 10 October.

[12] Robert Storey, *Lonely Planet: Mongolia* (Hawthorn, Vic., Australia: Lonely Planet, 1997), 108, 174, 237.

[13] I considered sending Hülegü to the upper Irtysh region, where Chinggis Khan assembled his army in preparation for the Khwarazmian campaign, but my sources give no distances for this route, and I have tried to rely as little as possible on map-and-ruler estimates (which I qualify as 'approximately,' 'about,' or label 'c.').

[14] Mayhew, Plunkett, and Richmond (1996), 216.

arrived in 1255, presumably in spring, since he spent that summer in the mountain pastures of the region.[15] This estimate yields a journey of about six months, October to 'spring'—say April. The total distance is around 1675 miles (c. 2697 km). The pace of march, according to these data and assumptions, was 9.3 mpd.

This part of the journey took place in winter, as often on Mongol campaigns. The steppe climate is fairly dry and snow accumulations usually slight, so the larger animals, like ponies, can dig through to grass. Winter even aided the armies, as in Russia, where the cold froze rivers that otherwise would have presented obstacles, or in the Middle East, where the winter temperatures are safer for horses and the rains provide them better pasture and more water. And the army could keep warm, even on the frigid steppes: each soldier had several ponies, and the animals and men, traveling together in close formation, generated heat enough for comfort.[16]

Hülegü and the army summered in 1255 on the mountain pastures around Almalyk where the expedition's ponies could fatten up; the Mongols took great care of their mounts, indeed of all their livestock.[17] In late summer, Hülegü left his *a'urughs* (again, see below) at Almalyk and proceeded on to Samarqand, 772 miles (1243 km), arriving in Shaʿbān 653/1255 (5 September–4 October).[18] The rate of march cannot be ascertained; there is no clear start date. They should have left by the end of July to reach Samarqand in Shaʿbān at a likely pace.

Hülegü, after spending "nearly forty days," moved on from Samarqand, sometime after 3 November 1255.[19] He stopped briefly at Kish (now Shahr-i Sabz, later the birthplace of Tīmūr), then proceeded to the Oxus/Amu Darya River and crossed into what is now Afghanistan on 1 January 1256.[20] The distance covered is about two hundred

---

[15] Rashīd al-Dīn (1998), vol. 2, 480 (the date should be 653); Juwaynī (1958), vol. 2, 612 (he is also mistaken about the date, which should be 653/1255).

[16] Collins (1975), 265.

[17] Rashīd al-Dīn (1998), vol. 2, 480; Juwaynī (1958), vol. 2, 612. According to the Armenian prince Haithon, who had campaigned with the Mongols, "The Tartars have much more consideration for their horses than for themselves." See Dulaurier (1858), 172.

[18] Juwaynī, (1958), vol. 2, 612. D. Streatfield-James, *Silk Road by Rail* (Hindhead, Surrey: Trailblazer, 1993), 279, 281.

[19] Juwaynī (1958), vol. 2, 612; Rashīd al-Dīn (1998), vol. 2, 480.

[20] Rashīd al-Dīn (1998), vol. 2, 480.

miles (322 km), the pace 2.4–3.8 mpd, depending on the start date. The army then proceeded to Shiburghan (perhaps 70 miles in ten days), where heavy snow and hailstorms shortly set in and compelled it, contrary to plan, to camp for the winter.[21]

Leaving this involuntary *qishlaq* in spring, Hülegü led his force to Tun in the region of eastern Iran called Quhistan, where followers of the Assassins held many strongholds. He besieged Tun on 4 May 1256, and took it on 16 May.[22] Ketbugha had left Mongolia before Hülegü to pacify Quhistan in advance of Hülegü's passage, but had not finished the job.[23] Quhistan later became a favorite Mongol *qishlaq*.[24] From Shiburghan to Tun is c. 530 miles (some 853 km); no date is given for the departure from Shiburghan.

From Tun, the army traveled via Tus (near Mashhad), Radkan, and Khabushan (modern Quchan) to reach Bistam on 2 September 1256. The distance covered was about 697 miles (1123 km), as measured along modern highways and railroads.[25] If the army left Tun on 20 May, the average pace was 6.6 mpd.[26] Along the way, the army lingered at Tus for a few days, and at Radkan for "some time," to obtain supplies and fodder for the animals, among other things, from Merv, Yazir, and Dihistan, districts north of the mountains separating Iran from Turkmenistan.[27] Then they spent a month at Ustuva beyond Khabushan until the grazing was exhausted.[28] Discounting the time at Ustuva, the army moved at 9.3 mpd.

From Bistam the army, now dividing into several corps traveling separately but to a fixed timetable, approached the Assassins, setting out on 2 September 1256. Hülegü reached Maymun Diz, the Assassin Master's castle, on 7 November 1256.[29] The march from Bistam had taken sixty-seven days, covering about 400 miles (c. 644 km) at a pace of about 6 mpd. The other corps arrived almost

---

[21] Rashīd al-Dīn (1998), vol. 2, 480.

[22] Rashīd al-Dīn (1998), vol. 2, 482. Juwaynī (1958), vol. 2, 615, has Hülegü take Tun "at the beginning of Rabīʿ I," which was 29 March.

[23] Rashīd al-Dīn (1998), vol. 2, 481.

[24] Smith, J. M. (1999), 53–54.

[25] Boulanger, ed. (1956), 774 (Gurgan–Bistam), 871–72 (Tun–Mashhad), 896 (Mashhad–Gurgan).

[26] For the likely date, see Rashīd al-Dīn (1998), vol. 2, 482.

[27] Juwaynī (1958), vol. 2, 616–17; Rashīd al-Dīn (1998), vol. 2, 482.

[28] Juwaynī (1958), vol. 2, 616–18.

[29] Juwaynī (1958), vol. 2, 717.

simultaneously; the routes taken by the Right and Left were about the same length as those of the Center; forces from the Golden Horde coming via the Caucasus joined too, probably by prearrangement at the *quriltai* of 1253.[30] The army surrounded the castle; the Master was summoned to yield, and refused (his officers claimed he was not there). On 13 November the Mongol attack began, and on 19 November the Assassin Master, weakened by Mongol cajolery and catapults, finally surrendered.[31] He and all his people came to a bad end. The Assassins were finished in Iran and historically, although some survived in Syria, tolerated and used for a while by the Mamluks and later restrained by them after an agreement with the Mongols.[32] After his victory, Hülegü camped for the winter of 1256–57 near Qazwin and Lammassar.[33]

Hülegü started for Baghdad from Qazwin in March 1257.[34] The direct distance is 511 miles (823 km).[35] The journey was complicated, however, by diversions. Hülegü reached Dinavar on 26 April, and then decided to go to Tabriz. He came back to Hamadan on 26 July, and returned to Tabriz. He next reached Hamadan on 21 September, and finally set out for Baghdad.[36] Subtracting the time spent traveling back and forth to Tabriz, Hülegü's 603-mile journey from Qazwin to Baghdad may be divided into two parts, an estimate for the Qazwin–Dinavar part—say 254 miles (409 km) covered between sometime in March and 26 April; if in thirty days, then 8.5 mpd (but adjust to please)—and a fairly precise measure for Hamadan–Baghdad: 349 miles (563 km) in seventy-three days (10 November–22 January) at 4.8 mpd.[37]

The distance covered between central Mongolia and Baghdad,

---

[30] The commanders who led these forces through the Caucasus, Balagai and Tutar, had been with Hülegü in Mongolia and had set out, presumably for home and with instructions from Hülegü, at the time of Hülegü's departure. See Juwaynī (1958), vol. 2, 612.

[31] Juwaynī (1958), vol. 2, 630–34.

[32] The low-keyed survival of what might be called 'post-Assassin' Nizarī Isma'ilism in the regions around Alamut and in Quhistan after Hülegü's campaign is treated by Shafique N. Virani; Virani (2003).

[33] Juwaynī (1958), vol. 2, 721–22.

[34] Rashīd al-Dīn (1998), vol. 2, 486.

[35] Boulanger, ed. (1956), 711.

[36] Rashīd al-Dīn (1998), vol. 2, 488.

[37] Rashīd al-Dīn (1998), vol. 2, 493 and n. 4; Boulanger, ed. (1956), 705 (Dinavar), 706 (Hamadan).

adding up the figures given above, was 4947 miles (7966 km). The parts of the journey for which reasonable estimates of the pace may be estimated are: Qaraqorum–Almalyk, 7–8 mpd; Samarqand–Oxus, 2.4–3.8 mpd; Tun–Bistam, 7.2 mpd; Bistam–Maymun Diz, 6 mpd; Hamadan–Baghdad, about 5 mpd. (Low) average mpd: 5.5.

This time-and-motion study shows that, while the journey from Mongolia to Baghdad proceeded at an average speed of about 4 mpd, the movement involved was not continuous, but interrupted by a number of halts of some duration. When in motion, the army proceeded at a pace that averaged 5–6 mpd, where this can be calculated. This was far slower than usual for campaigning Mongols, who could, as noted at the beginning, average 15–16 mpd. At the other extreme, an ordinary Inner Asian nomadic migration, with its full panoply of livestock, sheep, goats, cattle, horses (ponies), and camels, averages only 2–3 mpd.[38] Why did Hülegü move at the pace he did?

Logistics

Sieges were awkward for the Mongol cavalry. They required positional warfare instead of the campaigns of movement most congenial to cavalry, especially nomad cavalry operating on steppe with grazing at the end of each march. Möngke had reserved pastures for Hülegü, but during the siege of Maymun Diz, some generals complained that "the horses are lean. Fodder has to be transported from [the regions] from Armenia to Kirman."[39] Accessible grazing had clearly been used up. One might speculate that, to reduce reliance on pasture, Hülegü took fewer mounts than the five per soldier usual for a Mongol army; the Crimean Tatars (descendants of the Golden Horde), for instance, took only three.[40] Fewer mounts meant more work for each, and care had to be taken not to overwork them. Steppe-raised, grazing-dependent equines do not grow very

[38] For example, 200 km in one and a half months: 2.8 mpd, for the modern Yoruk in southern Turkey. Bates (1973), 5, 7.

[39] Rashīd al-Dīn (1998), vol. 2, 484.

[40] Collins (1975), 261; but cf. 267: some Tatars changed horses five times a day, and one Tatar force moved at 20 mpd; both items imply five horses per soldier, the Mongol standard.

large;[41] the average Mongol pony weighs around 600 pounds (cf. modern, fodder-fed riding horses at 1000–1500 pounds) and cannot therefore bear heavy burdens for long. An appropriate burden for a 600-pound pony is 102 pounds, 17 percent of its bodyweight; Mongol riders overburden their ponies, but only for a day at a time, and then give them several days off and ride others (hence the five ponies per soldier).[42] If a day's march for troops with five ponies each was 16 miles (at 4 mph; then eight hours of grazing and eight of sleeping), then the length of march appropriate with three each might be around nine miles, reducing the workload and burden on pasture, while increasing grazing time. This might help explain the slowness of the journey.

Another explanation involves the pace of ox-wagons. Hülegü expected to conduct sieges, and brought along Chinese artillerists—one thousand 'families' of them—probably by wagon. They might have walked, given the army's pace, but if their 'families' were in fact whole 'military households' with three adult males (one a soldier, the others supporting him) and their wives and children, they would have needed wagons.[43] Two oxen could draw a cart carrying seven persons, who, if mounted, would have needed three to five ponies per person. Cavalry needed ponies to function, artillerists did not.[44]

The artillerists did need equipment requiring wagons. They used large engines to project a variety of heavy missiles over considerable distances. Although they constructed some of these weapons on the

---

[41] A pony measures less than 14 'hands' (56 inches) at the withers, the high point of the back.

[42] John of Plano Carpini (1955), 47 on rotation; on loads: Epstein (1969), 100; Engels (1978), 128. Also, Smith, J. M. (1997), esp. 250–51.

[43] Hsiao (1978), 18–19. The Mongols counted on one soldier per nomad family, but knowing sedentary families tended to be more than nuclear, and needed more subsistence labor, conscripted only one man from Chinese three-man families. Since Hülegü's forces were intended as a permanent garrison for the Middle East, the one thousand 'families' of Chinese artillerists, et al., might have been whole extended families.

[44] The artillerists included "catapult men, naphtha throwers, and crossbow men": Rashīd al-Dīn (1998), vol. 2, 478. The naphtha throwers, I believe, would have prepared incendiary missiles for use with the catapults and crossbows, which latter would have been the large 'ox's bows' mentioned by Juwaynī (1958), vol. 2, 631, rather than weapons for individual soldiers, since the Mongols' conventional archery was more than sufficient: faster shooting and accurate to greater range.

spot, using trees growing around Maymun Diz to build catapults, they had to bring along, for instance, saws, adzes, hammers, pulleys, ropes, javelins, and even some of the major weapon-components: naphtha for incendiaries, and the oversized bow component of the 'ox's bow' engine would have required manufacture involving special woods given special treatment long in advance to give them the 'cupid's bow' shape their name suggests.[45] All this artillery gear required transportation by wagon. It could, in theory, have been broken down into camel-loads, but, at 300 pounds per camel-load, as against 1000–1500 pounds on a two-ox cart, or 3000 pounds on a three-camel wagon, wheeled vehicles were the obvious choice to reduce the numbers of animals.[46] And ox-wagons would have slowed the army: without relays of oxen, they would have made no more than 10 mpd.[47]

Because the army was possibly not taking the usual complement of ponies for riding and, if so, probably none for eating, and since (as we shall see) it did not bring along the sheep, goats, and cattle that provide subsistence in normal nomadism, Möngke made other arrangements.

> In advance of the army envoys were sent to reserve all the meadows and grasslands from Qaraqorum to the banks of the Oxus that had been calculated as lying in the path of [Hülegü's] army and to build strong bridges across deep canals and rivers. ... From all lands for every individual one *taghar* of flour and one skin of wine as troop provisions were to be made ready.[48]

[45] Juwaynī (1958), vol. 2, 631.

[46] Engels (1978), 14 and n. 11 for oxen and pack-camels. Pegolotti's fourteenth-century commercial manual states that three-camel wagons traveled between Urgench and Otrar (c. 650 miles) in 35–40 days (16–18 mpd; probably with relays of camels) drawing 3000 pounds; his text on Silk Road trade in the Mongol period in Pegolotti (1936) is translated in Lopez and Raymond (1955), 355–58.

[47] Draft oxen move at 2 mph and work a five-hour day, according to Engels (1978), 15 (but cf. Epstein (1969), 3: 30 km per day). Using relays of animals, ox-wagons delivering supplies to Outer Mongolia under a program initiated by Ögödei averaged 12.5 mpd; Western traders traveling to China in the fourteenth century averaged 17 mpd, using horses and camels for the most part instead of oxen. See Smith, J. M. (2000), 41 and Hsiao (1978), 59–60.

[48] Rashīd al-Dīn (1998), vol. 2, 478. See also Juwaynī (1958), vol. 2, 609–10. Ibn Baṭṭūṭa traveled with the entourage of Bayalun Qatun, the Byzantine wife of Özbek, the Golden Horde ruler, as she journeyed to Constantinople, and "At every halting-place in this land there was brought to the khātūn a hospitality-gift of horses, sheep, cattle, *dugi*, *qumizz*, and cows' and sheep's milk." See Ibn Baṭṭūṭa (1958–2000), vol. 2, 498–99.

This was not to be a conventional, self-sufficient nomad campaign.

Business and Pleasure

The army made many stops on its way west that afforded opportunities, among other things, for lavish partying, which the Mongols loved.[49] While the army rested at Almalyk, Orqina Khātūn, the regent of the *ulus* Chaghadai, treated Hülegü and his establishment to a series of banquets.[50] At Samarqand, Hülegü and his entourage enjoyed some proper high living. The local administrator of Turkestan and Transoxiana for the Mongols, Masʿūd Beg, had summoned all the commanders (*amīrs*) of those regions, and erected a tent of gold brocade with a white felt exterior in which Hülegü received them. The assembly engaged in "constant merrymaking and revelry" (Juwaynī) and "constant drinking" (Rashīd al-Dīn) for the nearly forty days they stayed there.[51] Möngke had admonished Hülegü, as they parted, to "be awake and sober in all situations," but no source indicates that he departed from Mongol norms either by abstemiousness or excessive drunkenness.[52]

Somewhat later, after crossing the Oxus River, Hülegü and some of his men enjoyed a different entertainment. While out for a ride by the river, Hülegü noticed tigers (or lions: *shīr* can mean either) in the woods nearby, and sent his guards to encircle them in the usual Mongol fashion (the circle was called *nerge* and was used in battle as well as hunting). Their ponies sensibly refused to face the tigers, so the soldiers mounted camels and managed to kill ten.[53]

While snowbound at Shiburghan, Hülegü and his entourage "constantly engaged in pleasure and enjoyment."[54] In spring, Arghun Aqa produced an enormous tent, made of embroidered "gold-on-gold" cloth and held up by a thousand tent-pegs. All the princes, officers, administrators, grandees, and regional rulers gathered in it to per-

---

[49] Smith, J. M. (2000), 35–52.
[50] Rashīd al-Dīn (1998), vol. 2, 480; Juwaynī (1958), vol. 2, 612.
[51] Rashīd al-Dīn (1998), vol. 2, 480; Juwaynī (1958), vol. 2, 612.
[52] Rashīd al-Dīn (1998), vol. 2, 479.
[53] Rashīd al-Dīn (1998), vol. 2, 480; Juwaynī (1958), vol. 2, 613–14.
[54] Rashīd al-Dīn (1998), vol. 2, 480; see also Juwaynī (1958), vol. 2, 614.

form rituals and banquet on food and drink served on and in gold and silver plates and cups embellished with gems.[55]

Near Tus, Arghun Aqa pitched yet another fine tent for Hülegü. "For a few days they feasted and revelled" there.[56] Then they moved on to Radkan, stopping "for a while in order to enjoy the scenery," and wine imported from Merv, Yazir, and Dihistan (along with fodder for the animals).[57] Further on, at Ustuva by Khabushan, the army's animals received their feast, spending a month grazing until "mountain and plain had been denuded of grass" and the army moved on.[58]

The army now had no rest until Maymun Diz had surrendered. Then, on the way to Alamut—which, like several other Assassin castles, still held out—Hülegü halted at Shahrak nine days for a victory feast.[59] After that, having visited Alamut, which shortly yielded, and Lammasar, which did not, Hülegü camped for the winter of 1256–57 near Lammasar and then, from 13 January 1257, near Qazwin, where he celebrated the (Mongolian) New Year with a week of banqueting.[60] In March of 1257, Hülegü started for Baghdad.[61] No more banquets are reported for the rest of the campaign. Hülegü fell sick on the way back from Baghdad to Hamadan, and had earlier been ill while proceeding to Tun; he may have felt disinclined to engage in the copious drinking obligatory at such events.[62]

But banquets were not just for hard drinking and heavy eating. Some were also business meetings. Samarqand saw working parties. Amīr Masʿūd Beg, 'the [Mongol-appointed] lord of Turkistan and Transoxiana,' and the region's *amīrs* (commanders) had joined Hülegü. Möngke had ordered them—and all authorities along Hülegü's intended route—to prepare supplies for the army, and to get ready to accompany Hülegü to Iran with their forces.[63] Hülegü had come to collect.

Samarqand lay in the *ulus* Chaghadai. To get there, as we have

[55] Rashīd al-Dīn (1998), vol. 2, 480–81.
[56] Juwaynī (1958), vol. 2, 616.
[57] Rashīd al-Dīn (1998), vol. 2, 482. Juwaynī (1958), vol. 2, 616–17.
[58] Juwaynī (1958), vol. 2, 617.
[59] Juwaynī (1958), vol. 2, 718.
[60] Rashīd al-Dīn (1998), vol. 2, 485; Juwaynī (1958), vol. 2, 718–19.
[61] Rashīd al-Dīn (1998), vol. 2, 486.
[62] Rashīd al-Dīn (1998), vol. 2, (Tun): 482; (Hamadan): 500.
[63] Rashīd al-Dīn (1998), vol. 2, 479

seen, Hülegü had proceeded through the Zaysan region, belonging to the (former) *ulus* Ögödei, and along the way, in both *ulus*es, he would have encountered in their winter quarters (*qishlaq*s) and with their families, so that they could not escape, the nomads who lived in those regions (and summered in the adjacent highlands). Hülegü conscripted large numbers of them (more on this below).

At Kish, Hülegü stopped for a month and did more business. Arghun Aqa, the Mongols' administrator for Iran, joined Hülegü, along with "the grandees and nobles of Khurasan."[64] They ordered the Mongols' vassal "monarchs and sultans of Iran" to mobilize soldiers and supply weaponry and provisions for the campaign against the Assassins. Local rulers from Anatolia, Fars, Persia, Khurasan, Azerbaijan, Arran, Shirvan, and Georgia obeyed.[65] Many of them joined Hülegü and his entourage at Shiburghan to banquet and perform rituals in Arghun Aqa's thousand-peg tent.[66] They also must have taken care of business, as the next stages of the journey would bring the army into Iran, where the men and supplies summoned up from Kish would be awaiting further orders, which they would receive at Bistam.

We can see the growth of Hülegü's forces in the increasing number of commanders named as the army proceeds west. For example, Ketbugha, with Köke Ilgei, started off from Mongolia ahead of Hülegü with twelve thousand men; Ketbugha was in charge, probably commanding a *tümen*, while Köke Ilgei led two *hazara*s which were to serve as cadre for future conscripts filling out a *tümen*.[67] Hülegü followed with, presumably, a *tümen* (it is mentioned later). Thus, the army apparently consisted of two *tümen*s and two *hazara*s at the outset. By the time the army arrived at Bistam in Iran, it had five *tümen*s, with two more unit commanders named: Tegüder Oghul and Buqa Tīmūr.[68] And more were coming.

After taking Maymun Diz and wintering near Qazwin, Hülegü proceeded to Hamadan in March 1257, and "began outfitting the

---

[64] Rashīd al-Dīn (1998), vol. 2, 480. Mongol Khurasan included not only the modern province, but also parts of Turkmenistan and much of Afghanistan. See Smith, J. M. (1999), 53, map 3.

[65] Rashīd al-Dīn (1998), vol. 2, 480.

[66] Rashīd al-Dīn (1998), vol. 2, 480–81.

[67] Rashīd al-Dīn (1998), vol. 2, 481.

[68] Rashīd al-Dīn (1998), vol. 2, 483; Juwaynī (1958), vol. 2, 618.

army," which was apparently completed by mid-April, as he had moved on to Dinawar by 26 April on his way to Baghdad.[69]

Besides the play-and-work stops, some delays were forced by bad weather: by the blizzard at Shiburghan, and by the dangerous (especially for ponies) summer heat at Baghdad, which Hülegü apparently discovered as he neared Iraq and which caused him to meander during the summer (26 April [hot weather arrives early in Mesopotamia]–21 September 1257) between Dinawar, Tabriz, Hamadan, Tabriz, and Hamadan before resuming his march on Baghdad. The moves, besides acquainting Hülegü with the principal urban center of Azerbaijan, would have enabled him to survey, and his accompanying troops to use, some of the *yaylaqs*: Siyahkuh, Sughurluq, and Qonqur Öleng, which were to become major bases for Mongol divisions.[70]

Finally, all these play-and-work stops helped the diverse elements of the army become familiar with one another, and their leaders to learn to work together, as they did so well when the time came.

Weaponry, Strategy, and Tactics

Military operations also slowed Hülegü's march. Since his mission targeted mountain strongholds (the Assassins' lairs) and a fortress-city (Baghdad), he had prepared for siege warfare. By this time, the Mongols had conducted many sieges during their campaigns in northern China, Central Asia, Russia, and Hungary. Their Mongol (and Turkic) soldiery, all archers, could outshoot the cities' defenders (few of them skilled in archery), while Chinese, Manchurian, and other conscripts provided engineers and artillerists, laborers, and 'arrow-fodder' for storming fortifications—and, in the worst case, for besieging them until the defenders yielded.[71] Hülegü started off with only a few of these troops, about two *tümens* of Mongols, and

[69] Rashīd al-Dīn (1998), vol. 2, 487–88.

[70] Smith, J. M. (1999), 45–47.

[71] On Mongol archery, see Smith, J. M. (1984), 315–16. Worst case: After the fall of Maymun Diz, the Mongols besieged Assassins in Girdkuh for *fifteen years* (Rashīd al-Dīn [1998], vol. 3, 535–36). Mongols were also prepared to participate in sieges: every Mongol soldier's equipment included "ropes for hauling [shooting] engines of war," John of Plano Carpini (1955), 33.

the one thousand 'families' of Chinese soldiers discussed above. He found more manpower *en route*.

The Chinese soldiers with Hülegü employed state-of-the-art siege engines. One was a catapult of the sort called *trebuchet* or *mangonel* in Europe, *manjanīq* or *'arrāda* by the Muslims, *pao* in China, and *orbu'ur* by the Mongols.[72] By the beginning of the thirteenth century, two types of these had been developed in China. Both had a long pole pivoting on an axle set on a scaffold; the axle divided the pole into a short and a long section; the long section terminated with a sling holding a missile, the short attached to a power source that turned the pole on its axle and impelled the sling and its shot. The first, older 'traction' type was powered by teams of men pulling on ropes tied to the short end. It was labor-intensive, none too powerful, and dangerous to use. A team of 250 men could propel a stone of only 90 pounds for only 33 yards; the enemy's archers could shoot accurately and pierce armor at 50 yards. The other type, the 'counterweighted' catapult, resembled the traction variety, except that a weight replaced the ropes at the short end of the pole, and gravity, not muscle, impelled the missile. A crew of only 10–15 men could shoot such a catapult 167 yards; other ranged to 180 and 233 yards, at the limit or beyond of useful archery.[73] No crew sizes are given for the latter, and although no missile weights are given, later Chinese records, contemporary illustrations, and modern replicas show that they could reach 250 pounds.[74] These weapons could thus operate in safety and hurl an irresistible missile.

---

[72] See Allsen (2002a), 265–93, esp. 267–69.

[73] Franke, H. (1974), 167–69.

[74] Needham, vol. 5, part 6 (1995), 217. Also *Secrets of Lost Empires II: Medieval Siege*, Nova (for PBS), Boston: WGBH, 2000, videocassette. Modern craftsmen, using medieval techniques, built two large catapults (one very like the Mongol catapult depicted in Rice, D. T. [1976], 52–53, 146–47, 156–57; also Komaroff and Carboni, eds. [2002], 36, fig. 33, cat. no. 24), both of which, from 200 yards, hit and broke a wall copied from a Welsh fortress of Edward I. The counterweights, one fixed and one—the Mongol type—pivoting, weighed 6 and 6.5 tons. Construction took forty craftsmen about two weeks (Hülegü's larger workforce worked much faster) after obtaining the materials, including poles fashioned from single tree trunks (weighing one ton on the fixed-counterweight engine). The poles of the Mongol catapults depicted in Rice, D. T. (1976), 52–53 and Komaroff and Carboni, eds. (2002), fig. 33, unlike the replicas', were composites of several shafts bound together, simplifying procurement and fabrication.

The Mongols probably acquired this Chinese counterweighted catapult during their conquest of north China.[75] The defenders of Lo-Yang had used them against the Mongols in 1232.[76] Earlier, Chinggis had taken a whole *tümen* of artillerists to Central Asia in 1219–23—and they had failed to take Ashiyar castle in Gharchistan,[77] probably because they still used the old-style high-manpower, short-ranged, light-missile traction catapults, no more than 40 of them if 250-man teams were drawn from the 10,000-man unit. Hülegü's siege train included only a thousand families, but they produced better results at Maymun Diz and Baghdad, probably because they could man some 65 of the low-manpower, long-ranged, heavy-missile counterweighted catapults.

Besides catapults, Chinese artillery also included oversized crossbows, mounted on a stand or cart (which the Romans called *arcuballista*).[78] Hülegü had some: "a *kāmān-i-gāw* ["ox's bow"], which had been constructed by Khitayan craftsmen and had a range of 2,500 [*gām*], was brought to bear on those fools [the Assassins in Maymun Diz]...and...many soldiers were burnt by those meteoric shafts."[79] Boyle, Juwaynī's translator, gives "pace" for "*gām*," which can also

[75] The common impression that the Mongols adopted the counterweighted catapult in the Middle East (see Allsen [2002], 265–93, esp. 267–69; also Needham [1995], 218–20) derives from Qubilai's importation in the 1270s of Arab engineers to design catapults for his Sung China campaigns (Marco Polo falsely claimed the credit). The Arabs' contribution was most likely the metal bushings and axles used in Iranian Mongol catapults; see Rice, D. T. (1976), 52–53. In Chinese catapults, wooden axles turned in sockets or notches in the supporting wooden scaffold. The bearings of the Iranian catapults would have turned more smoothly and suffered less wear from the tremendous forces exerted upon them (by a counterweight of perhaps 6.5 tons to swing a beam of perhaps a ton) and would therefore have shot more reliably, more consistently, more accurately, and farther than their Chinese counterparts.

[76] Needham (1995), 218. Clearly a counterweighted catapult from its small crew, but still short-ranged.

[77] Jūzjānī (1881), vol. 2, 1074-77. Ashiyar eventually fell to starvation.

[78] Franke, H. (1974), 166–67. Their effective range, according to Franke, is about 200 yards, similar to that of the counterweighted catapult, and about twice that of a hand-drawn war bow.

[79] Juwaynī (1958), vol. 2, 631. Boyle translates *gām* as "pace." For the name "ox's bow," compare the limbs of a multiple 'composite crossbow' illustrated in Franke, H. (1974), 162, with the bows of ox-harnesses depicted in the fourteenth-century paintings of *Eighteen Songs of a Nomad Flute: The Story of Lady Wen-chi* (Rorex et al. [1974], scenes 16–18). The working of the 'composite crossbow' is explained in Needham (1995), 194–95, figs. 63–64.

mean foot, cubit, or step.[80] But the only remotely plausible of these measures is the foot; a *gām* of twelve inches would make the range of the 'ox's bow' 833 yards, about half a mile (.47).

No such performance is recorded. Franke documents a Chinese *arcuballista* with an effective range of 300 *pu*/paces, which he converts at two feet to the *pu*/pace into "something like 200 yards."[81] Needham lists a "large winch-armed" crossbow (which he appears to think was an *arcuballista*) as shooting 1,160 yards, a distance he acknowledges "seems credible only with difficulty."[82] More likely, incredible. Compare a European winched crossbow with a 1,200-pound draw and range of (only) 460 yards.[83] And consider Needham's "arm-drawn" crossbow with a range of 500 yards (300 *pu*) in light of the difficulty of drawing (i.e., cocking) by hand a crossbow drawing more than 150 pounds.[84] The discrepancies arise from different conversions of the Chinese measure *pu*. Franke has it as a pace of two feet, and Needham as a "double-pace" of five feet. Using a two-foot *pu*, Needham's arm-drawn crossbow had a range of 200 yards, and (getting back to the main matter) his large, winch-armed weapon's range was about 460 yards. But with the double-pace dismissed and the *gām* reduced from pace to foot, the ox's bow still shoots nearly twice as far as any recorded *arcuballista*.

Juwaynī's 2,500-*gām* shot may have been powered by hyperbole, but rocket assistance should also be considered. The thirteenth century saw the development in China of weapons using the propulsive effect of lowgrade gunpowder: 'ground rats,' a bamboo tube containing powder which escaped through an aperture on combustion and propelled the tube along or about on or above the ground, originally as an entertainment, eventually to frighten or injure men and horses; and 'fire lances,' flamethrowers best visualized as reversed rockets attached to a lance and projecting flaming gas toward the enemy.[85]

---

[80] Steingass et al. (1957), 1072.

[81] Franke, H. (1974), 166.

[82] Needham (1995), 176, 177.

[83] Paterson (1990), 31.

[84] Needham (1995), 176, 217; Paterson (1990), 40. Increasing draw weight does not translate directly into greater range: much of the added power goes into moving the heavier limbs of the bow rather than the impulsion of the projectile.

[85] Needham, vol. 5, part 7 (1987), ground rats, 135; fire lance, 222–25, and figs. 44–45.

The next step, according to Needham, was taken between 1150 and 1350 when this explosive force was applied to propel arrows and javelins independently of bows or crossbows.[86] I imagine an intermediate step, the addition of rockets to the conventional fire-missiles shot from *arcuballistas* (not from handheld bows or crossbows because of the rockets' fiery blowback). Winch-cocked siege crossbows and *arcuballistae* shot about 460 yards, and wholly rocket-powered Chinese missiles by the late sixteenth century flew for 400–467 yards.[87] These combined powers should account for the 833-yard range of the missiles of Hülegü's ox's bow. After Maymun Diz, no more is heard of the ox's bow, perhaps because premodern rocketry performed unreliably, and any inconsistency would have produced inaccuracy in the long shots at Maymun Diz. At Baghdad, on level terrain, the range of the unassisted missiles of the *arcuballistae* sufficed.

As for strategy, Hülegü's plan for the defeat of the Assassins—and of the caliph—was a standard Mongol method: surround the target, immobilize (and demoralize) the enemy, and employ all weapons and as much manpower as possible.[88]

At Bistam, Hülegü arranged the attack on Maymun Diz, the Assassins' headquarters, arraying the army in the conventional Mongol order of battle: Left Wing, Center, and Right Wing. Hülegü's *tümen* (here explicitly mentioned) constituted the Center; the Left included forces—probably *tümens*, as also in the Right—under Ketbugha and Tegüder Oghul, a Chaghatayid prince, who presumably brought his force from that realm; the Right was made up of the units of Buqa Tīmūr, who had come "with an army of Oirat tribesmen," and Köke Ilgei, his original two *hazaras* now apparently fleshed out into a *tümen* (Buqa Tīmūr's force may also have needed bulking up).[89] In addition to these units that were more or less directly under Hülegü's management, three more *tümens* were on their way from the Golden

[86] Needham (1987), 477.

[87] Needham (1995), 176–77, Table 3 for a European siege crossbow and a large Chinese winch-armed crossbow; 484, note for Chinese rockets. I have used the two-foot *pu* to correct Needham's Chinese ranges.

[88] John of Plano Carpini (1955), 36–38.

[89] Rashīd al-Dīn (1998), vol. 2, 483; Juwaynī (1958), vol. 2, 607–8, 618. Supplemental troops could have been impressed as Tainal Noyan had done during Chinggis's Khwarazmian campaign; he conscripted ten thousand Turkmen to enlarge his army as he passed through these same regions (they deserted at the first opportunity, only to be caught by Tainal and slaughtered): Juwaynī (1958), vol. 1, 90.

Horde. Assuming that each named commander led a *tümen*, Hülegü now commanded eight *tümens*.

Hülegü marched via Firuzkuh, Damavand, and Rayy toward the Assassins' castle of Maymun Diz, where their Master was resident, arriving on 7 November 1256.[90] The Left traveled toward the same objective via Khwar and Simnan. The Right proceeded to "Mazandaran,"[91] a region including the extensive pastoral zone where the Gurgan and Atrek Rivers approach the Caspian—a favorite and ample Mongol *qishlaq*[92]—and also the narrow zone between the Elburz Mountains and the Caspian Sea. Hülegü's Right moved west by this shore route, to cross the mountains and attack Maymun Diz if possible, and at least to block the road, lest the Assassin Master obtain support or shelter from the Assassins' castle at Girdkuh. The Golden Horde units also appeared, a *tümen* under Quli b. Orda arrived via Khwarazm and Dihistan, and two more, led by the Batuid princes Balaghai and Tutar approached the Assassin strongholds from the east after entering the Middle East through the "Qipchaq Strait" past Darband. The enemy was encircled.[93]

After the Mongol troops "formed seven coils around" the castle, a circuit "nearly six leagues around," Hülegü surveyed its defenses.[94] Some commanders suggested postponing the siege because of the daunting prospect (on which the Assassins were banking[95]) of again becoming snowbound. It was already late fall, fodder could not be found, and grazing was apparently inadequate, as the animals were losing weight; preparations were being made to requisition flour for the troops and fodder for the animals, and to seize all animals for transportation and as rations from all over northern Iran.[96] But Maymun Diz, although well-fortified and difficult of access, appeared vulnerable.[97] The Mongols' catapults could be placed within range of

---

[90] Juwaynī (1958), vol. 2, 717.
[91] Rashīd al-Dīn (1998), vol. 2, 483.
[92] Smith, J. M. (1999), 52–54.
[93] Rashīd al-Dīn (1998), vol. 2, 361; Juwaynī (1958), vol. 1, 626–27; vol. 2, 716–17.
[94] Rashīd al-Dīn (1998), vol. 2, 484; Juwaynī (1958), vol. 2, 628.
[95] Juwaynī (1958), vol. 2, 619.
[96] Juwaynī (1958), vol. 2, 621–22; Rashīd al-Dīn (1998), vol. 2, 484.
[97] The description, in Willey (1963), of other Assassin castles, Alamut (214–24) and the fortress on Mt. Nevisar Shah (238), in the vicinity of Maymun Diz, shows they were much stronger—essentially inaccessible. The Mongols were fortunate that the Master had not holed up in one of these.

the defenses, probably within about two hundred yards; if the shots could reach the defenses, they could break them. Hülegü, supported by several of his generals, decided to persist, and the following day fighting began. On the second day of combat, 13 November, the 'ox's bows' went into action, picking off the defending Assassins as they exposed themselves.[98] The catapults needed more time, as they were built (at least in part) from local trees, but with one thousand Chinese artillery specialists on the job, work went quickly; the weapons went into action only six days after the start of construction (12–17 November).[99] Once the parts were ready, teams of haulers stationed at about 300-yard intervals moved them "to the top of the hill."[100] From there, the catapults began to smash the Assassins' artillery and walls. Two days later, on 19 November 1256, the Assassin Master surrendered.[101]

Hülegü led a still larger army to Baghdad. Fifteen commanders are named, including Hülegü himself. Two generals, Chormaqan and Baiju, led *tümens* (presumably) from Anatolia, where they had long been stationed. Hülegü's Right Wing included Sönitei, Balaghai, Tutar, Quli, Buqa Tīmūr, and Su'unchaq. The Left had Ketbugha, Qudusun, and Ilgei. The Center comprised Hülegü himself, Köke Ilgei, Uruqtu, and Arghun Aqa; some administrators are also named: Qaraqai, Sayf al-Dīn, Naṣīr al-Dīn Ṭūsī, and 'Alā' al-Dīn 'Aṭā Malik (Juwaynī, our historian), although it is doubtful whether they led troops. Hülegü's entourage also included "all the sultans, maliks, and atabegs of Iran," who probably were commanders—of 'arrow fodder.'[102] These forces encircled the city. The two *tümens* coming from Anatolia via Irbil crossed the Tigris, and approached west Baghdad; they fought, inconclusively at first, with the caliph's field army, but finally swamped it by opening dams of a lake. Six *tümens*, Hülegü's Right Wing, came to the left bank of the Tigris above Baghdad, where four of them proceeded down that bank toward

[98] Juwaynī (1958), vol. 2, 631.

[99] Juwaynī (1958), vol. 2, 629–32.

[100] Juwaynī (1958), vol. 2, 630. The map in Willey (1963), 171, shows trails ascending the southeast side of Maymun Diz to what must have been meant by "the top of the hill." Peter Willey agrees with my view that the Mongol catapults bombarded the northeast corner of the fortress (personal communication).

[101] Juwaynī (1958), vol. 2, 634.

[102] Rashīd al-Dīn (1998), vol. 2, 493. The nominal strength of the putative fifteen *tümens* was 150,000 men, plus the 'arrow fodder.'

the city, and two crossed to join the Anatolian corps. Three *tümens*, forming Hülegü's Left Wing, moved up the Tigris from Khuzistan. And Hülegü, leading four *tümens* and the "sultans, maliks," et al., proceeded from Hamadan to Dinawar (where he left his *a'urughs*), Kirmanshah, Khanaqin, and Ctesiphon. They reached Baghdad on 22 January 1258.[103] The attack began on the 29th, the artillery broke down the walls and towers of the city, and the caliph surrendered on 7 February 1258.[104] A massacre followed.

The Mongols relied in their siege warfare on their catapults, on overwhelming manpower, and, if necessary, on large expenditures of it.[105] Because heavy losses could be expected in taking a city or fortress, the Mongols would take no chances of needing a second siege, when adequate manpower might no longer be available; the enemy soldiery and militias that had resisted their attack were therefore killed at the end.[106] The caliph too was killed.

This effectively ended the Caliphate. Members of the house of ʿAbbās served the Mamluks as puppet-caliphs, and the Ottomans later claimed the title, but the perpetuation was only notional.

Heartbreak

These time-and-motion studies show that Hülegü's army did not take with them their sheep and goats—and families. Nomad wives, helped by their children, manage their families' subsistence animals. Each family needs about one hundred sheep or equivalents to supply its food, so a *tümen* (10,000 men) with their 10,000 families would have, in addition to its 50,000 ponies, at least a million sheep (the equivalent of 200,000 more ponies). Hülegü did not want to take them. One *tümen* with ponies, sheep, and goats would require as much pasture, or fodder, as five *tümens* with ponies only. Moreover, sheep and goats cannot travel more than about 2–3 mpd and still obtain adequate nourishment; short sprints may be manageable, but

[103] Rashīd al-Dīn (1998), vol. 2, 493–95.

[104] Rashīd al-Dīn (1998), vol. 2, 495–97.

[105] For instance, eight *tümens* out of ten were lost by Qubilai during his siege of Yauju during Möngke's war against Sung China in 1256–57. See Rashīd al-Dīn (1998), vol. 2, 415.

[106] Smith, J. M. (1994).

not long distances for a long time. With the sheep and goats, Hülegü might have taken twice as long to get to Baghdad. And if the sheep and goats were left behind, the women and children would have to stay to take care of them—and obtain their own support.

The sources say nothing directly about the familial circumstances of the ordinary soldiers, but Hülegü himself had to leave some of his wives behind in Mongolia. He had four principal wives living when the expedition departed; two came with him: Öljei Khātūn and Doquz Khātūn (his widowed stepmother, described as "influential, and extremely domineering"—Möngke ordered Hülegü to heed her advice). The two others, Yesunjin and Qutui, stayed in Mongolia with Möngke.[107]

Families and flocks left behind as Mongol armies marched to war were called *a'urughs*. The practice was traditional in Inner Asia, and the Mongolian term frequently appears in our story. Hülegü, setting out from Mongolia in 1254, left his *a'urughs* behind with Möngke. Ketbugha, who had already gone, had doubtless done likewise. More *a'urughs*, presumably those of soldiers newly recruited in Central Asia, stayed at Almalyk. Others stopped at Hamadan and Khanaqin on the approach to Baghdad, probably those of the troops from Iran that Hülegü had impressed into the Mongol Center, as well as the establishments of his own wives, Doquz and Öljei, who had traveled with the army.[108]

Whatever plans Yesunjin and Qutui (and the families of the ordinary soldiery) may have made to rejoin Hülegü in Iran were spoiled by the succession-struggle following the death of Möngke in 1259, which stranded them in Mongolia. Not until 1263 was Hülegü able to summon his wives. They started, traveling with Hülegü's son Jumqur, who had also been left behind, and reached Samarqand, only to be further delayed when Jumqur died. They eventually reached Iran in 1268, where "Qutui Khātūn was told of Hülegü Khan's death [four years before], and she cried her eyes out."[109]

If reunion was problematic for Mongol rulers, it was still harder for many ordinary soldiers. The troops raised in Iran would have

[107] Rashīd al-Dīn (1998), vol. 2, 471–72, 479–80.

[108] Rashīd al-Dīn (1998), vol. 2, 473, 479–80, 493, 495, 500. The forces sent by the Golden Horde must have left their *a'urughs* at home, too; this might help explain their reluctance to remain subordinate to Hülegü.

[109] Rashīd al-Dīn (1998), vol. 3, 519–20.

had no difficulty rejoining their families. Of the families left in Mongolia by the (nominally) 22,000 men who departed with Ketbugha and Hülegü—say 22,000 wives and 66,000 children at the time of separation—some wives and younger children might have been able to leave for Iran when Yesunjin and Qutui did. They could have left their subsistence animals with their older children, some of whom would have formed families of their own by that time; this would have speeded the journey and reduced its logistical difficulty. However, other troops in Hülegü's army had no such possibility.

Missing Persons

When the Ögödeid prince, Qaidu, began his effort to reconstitute the *ulus* Ögödei in the late 1260s, he could scarcely scrape up two or three thousand men from its former territories. Its nomads had originally constituted the army of the *ulus*, but the army had been disbanded after the attempted Ögödeid coup against Möngke in 1251, seventy-seven of its top officers had been executed—probably the top officers of seven *tümens* (seven *tümen* commanders and seventy *hazara* commanders of a nominal 70,000 men)—and their soldiers 'distributed' in such a way as left almost none for Qaidu.[110] Hülegü, who shortly came through the region, moving from western Mongolia to the Lake Zaysan area to Almalyk, charged to assemble an army for occupation of the Middle East, very likely assisted in the 'distribution' by taking with him perhaps 60,000, re-forming and rearming them at Hamadan under six new commanders, adding them to his forces, and leading them against Baghdad.[111]

[110] 'Distributed' is the word used by J. A. Boyle in his (partial) translation of Rashīd al-Dīn, Rashīd al-Dīn (1971), 23. 'Dispersed' is Thackston's translation: Rashīd al-Dīn (1998), vol. 2, 306. For the seventy-seven executed officers, see Rashīd al-Dīn (1998), vol. 2, 407.

[111] Rearming: Rashīd al-Dīn (1998), vol. 2, 487: "Hülegü…camped in the plains of Hamadan…[and] began outfitting the army." New Commanders: Rashīd al-Dīn (1998), vol. 2, 493: Sönitei, Su'unchaq, Qudusun, Ilgei, Uruqtu, Arghun Aqa; except for Arghun Aqa, these generals had not been mentioned previously in Rashīd al-Dīn's account of Hülegü's expedition.

Heartbreak II?

Although Hülegü's wives, and perhaps those of his Mongolian soldiers, eventually reached Iran, those of the ex-Ögödeid soldiers probably did not. They had been left in the *a'urugh*s around Almalyk, and probably remained there. Their husbands were now part of Hülegü's army and part of his program as ordered by Möngke to occupy Iran, establish themselves in suitable pastures, and stay.[112] They could not go home, and it was Mongol policy, probably for the logistical reasons discussed above, not to send their wives to soldiers permanently based abroad. For example, Möngke assigned Sali Noyan (Tatar) to Hülegü and gave him command of two *tümen*s previously stationed in the Qunduz–Baghlan–Badakhshan region to hold the Indian frontier. Sali asked how long he would be there, and Möngke replied, "You will be there forever."[113] And his men stayed there without their (original) wives: Sali's troops, and others stationed in eastern Khurasan and even western Iran came to be known as *qarauna*s, and, according to Marco Polo, "They are called Karaunas, that is mongrels, because they are the offspring of Indian mothers and Tartar fathers."[114] The soldiers had had to find new wives.

---

[112] Rashīd al-Dīn (1998), vol. 2, 479: "From the River Oxus to the farthest reaches of the land of Egypt [said Möngke to Hülegü]...Conquer the realm of the rebellious through the might of the great god so that your summer and winter pastures may be many ... [Möngke] imagined that Hülegü would always remain in the realm of Iran..."

[113] Rashīd al-Dīn (1998), vol. 1, 49.

[114] Polo (1980 reprint; original publication 1958), 64 [N.B. pagination may vary among the many reprint editions].

THE *KESHIG* IN IRAN: THE SURVIVAL OF THE ROYAL MONGOL HOUSEHOLD

CHARLES MELVILLE

> Although the rulers of the other sub-divisions of the empire had bodyguards, the Chingizid *keshik* continued only within the Yüan.[1]

> Möngke ordered that two out of every ten of the troops shared out by Genghis Khan among his sons, brothers and nephews, should be picked out and taken off the muster, and transferred to Hülegü's personal estate (*injü*), to accompany him [to Iran] and to be his attendants (*mulāzimān*) here. He also nominated others of his own sons, dependants (*khwīshān*) and intimates (*nököd*) for the same purpose, to set off with the army in the service of Hülegü. For this reason, there are and have always been in this kingdom [Iran] *amīrs* from the family (*urugh*) and kinsmen of each of the *amīrs* of Genghis Khan. Each of them is appointed to his hereditary role and post (*rāh va kār-i mawrūth*).[2]

> [Nadir Shah] all the time selected 1,000 Rustam-like, Isfandiyar-killing warriors and called them the *hamīsha-keshīk*, who were always and constantly present at the Sahib-qiran's court and royal guardhouse (*keshīk-khāna-yi humāyūn*). They were not absent from the exalted court for a moment.[3]

The royal household is both literally the household establishment of the ruler and, in a medieval patrimonial state such as that of the Ilkhans, also the nucleus or core of the imperial government. Nevertheless, the existence of the Ilkhans' household, other than in the generic sense of the *ordo* (*ordū*) or court, has been consistently overlooked: perhaps not surprisingly, in view of the orientation of our sources (both primary and secondary). In this paper I wish to place an accent on the presence of the Mongol household in the Ilkhanate. Among the issues of interest here are to what extent the household provided—or perhaps more accurately, continued to provide—the main officers of state in Mongol Iran, and how this determined the nature of Mongol rule, especially once native traditions

---

[1] Kwanten (1979), 92–93.
[2] Rashīd al-Dīn (1994), 975.
[3] Marvī (1985), 229.

of bureaucratic government reasserted themselves. I will seek to argue that the persistence of household rule in Iran, particularly as ordered around the royal guard (*keshig*), is one of the more enduring legacies of Genghis Khan.[4] In doing so, I will also hope to inject some fresh material into the debate, pursued almost single-handedly by David Morgan, on the question of who ran the Mongol empire.[5]

The Formation of the Keshig *Under Genghis Khan*

The patterns for Mongol government were established by Genghis Khan, who in around 1189 first formed a household of devoted followers from his *nököd* (sing: *nökör*, companions and personal dependents), the patrimony left by Genghis's father and his own personal estate.[6] In preparation for his campaign against the Naimans in 1204, Genghis instituted the decimal arrangement of his troops and created his personal *keshig*, or bodyguard, drawn from these early companions, the sons of relatives and chieftains, and those with a pleasing appearance and special skills.[7] They included a day watch

[4] This paper started life as part of a series of seminars on the royal household, organized at Sabancı University, Istanbul, in December 2002, by Metin Kunt. I am grateful to him for encouraging me to focus on this neglected area. An earlier version of the paper was also presented at a history seminar at SOAS, London, in February 2003, and again benefited from the comments of the participants. I am most grateful to Tom Allsen, whose work (cit. n. 3) raised my interest in the subject in the first place, and who kindly read two drafts of the paper and offered many helpful comments.

[5] Morgan, D. (1982b) and (1996). I too have been circling round this question for some time; see Melville (1990a), 62–64 and (1994), 94–95.

[6] de Rachewiltz, ed. (2004), para. 124 (50–51, 462–66); Barthold (1977), 382–83. See mainly Hsiao (1978), 34–38, and Allsen (1986), esp. 513–21, for what follows, and more recently, Grupper (1992–94).

[7] For the term *keshig*, see for example, Cleaves (1949), 437; Doerfer (1963), 467–70, and Hsaio (1978), 148, n. 10, with further references. I am keenly aware of the difficulty of providing consistent spelling for these and other terms encountered in these texts, which may have a variety of linguistic origins, Mongol, Uighur, Turkish, for all of which different transcriptions are available. *Keshig*, for instance, is equally frequently found as *keshik* (pl. *keshikten, keshigten*), and in Persian as *kezik* (plural *keziktanān*, i.e., with a Persian plural suffix as well). On the whole, my preferred usage is based on the spelling in Persian sources in most cases, while indicating other equivalents on first encounter. For this, I follow de Rachewiltz's commentary on *The Secret History of the Mongols* (de Rachewiltz, ed. [2004]) when possible. I am also grateful to Chris Atwood for his suggestions, but accept all inconsistencies as the product of my own ignorance.

(*turqa'ut*) and night watch (*kebte'üd*) of respectively seventy and eighty men, and a force of one thousand braves (*ba'atut*, Per. *bahādur*). Personal attendants, such as the chamberlain (*cherbi*), steward or cook (*ba'urchi*), quiver bearers (*qorchi*), sword bearers (*üldüchi*, Mo. *ildüchi*) doorkeepers (*e'üdechi*), gelding herders (grooms, or equerries: *akhtachi*, Mo. *aqtachi*) and horse herders (*adu'uchi*), already attached to him in 1189, were Genghis's protectors, domestic helpers, and the guardians of his possessions.[8]

From these rudimentary beginnings, the *keshig* was increased after Genghis Khan's coronation in 1206 to ten thousand men, who accompanied the ruler wherever he went, in order to meet the demands of the expanding empire. The night guard was expanded to one thousand men, the day guard to eight thousand, including the original core force of one thousand *bahadurs*, and a new force was created of one thousand quiver bearers (*qorchi*), who would also perform guard duties in the daytime. Out of eighty-eight commanders appointed at that time, twenty-eight were from the original *nököd* of 1189, and others were their brothers.[9] The day and night guards, *qorchis*, and other domestic officers were divided into four guard shifts, and from these units four *keshigs* were formed, each doing a specified three-day shift in rotation.[10] This fourfold division of the *keshig* had important administrative consequences and is a characteristic feature that permits us to recognize its presence under the Ilkhans, as we shall see.

Members of this household retained their titles, which reveal their basic occupations, such as *qonichi* (shepherd), to which they returned after fulfilling other missions. Apart from these specifically military and personal functions, the *keshig* of 1206 became the central administrative organ of the early empire, with its personnel carrying out

---

[8] de Rachewiltz, ed. (2004), paras. 191–92 (113–14, 689–93); Hsiao (1978), 36; Allsen (1986), 509. Both suggest (35 and 514, n. 75, respectively), that the immediate model for Genghis Khan's guard was the *keshig* of the Kereit Ong Khan, cf. Ratchnevksy (1991), 4, 84; Grupper (1992–94), 40.

[9] de Rachewiltz, ed. (2004), paras. 225–26 (154–55, 821–25); Hsiao (1978), 36.

[10] de Rachewiltz, ed. (2004), paras. 192, 227 (155–57, 825–27), and 229 (157–58, 828–31); it is partly this "positively tedious" way in which the successive shifts of Genghis Khan's night guards are specified that led David Morgan (1996), 67–68, to ask, quite rightly, "whether this looks like a people who had no interest in government and administration?"

assignments in which their 'state' and 'household' roles are indistinct. The main official in charge of civilian affairs was the secretary (or scribe, *bichechi*, in Persian texts, *bitikchi*), with an important supervisory role as well as the function of writing and issuing proclamations and decrees, drawn from the khan's entourage from the outset.[11] Only the *yarghuchi*, or judge (Mo. *jarquchi*), was not definitely associated with the *keshig* of 1206, although the night guards were empowered to reach decisions with him. The *yarghuchi* was responsible for the punishment of thieves and the investigation and trial of rebels, as well as registering the population. It seems, however, that even if not initially, the post of *yarghuchi* quickly became held by a member of the *keshig*.[12]

One further aspect of the formation of the *keshig* should be stressed, namely that many of its members were taken as hostages to guarantee the loyalty of individual commanders and the docility of the conquered peoples. Many such individuals were incorporated into Genghis Khan's day guard.[13] However, for them as for others, membership of the *keshig* was also an honor and an opportunity: they were in an advantageous position to obtain posts, they served apprenticeships, enjoyed special privileges, and were groomed to be the future ruling class. As is frequently stressed, offices were usually held hereditarily (see also below). In short, Genghis Khan's *keshig* was not only his personal guard, hostage camp, and the core unit of the Mongol army, but it also had many domestic and specialized duties. It lay at the heart of government under his first successors and reveals the early administration's intimate relations with, and origins in, steppe society.[14]

---

[11] Hsiao (1978), 38; Farquhar (1990), 2–3.

[12] Hsiao (1978), 38, concerning the first *yarghuchi*, Shigi Qutuqu, perhaps because he was like an adopted son rather than one of the *nököd*. Allsen (1986), 503–4, 508, 510, discussing the career of the chief *yarghuchi*, Menggeser, and later his replacement, Bulghai, indicates that both were in Tolui's *keshig*, having previously served in the household of Genghis Khan. Menggeser, for example, was leader of the *qorchi*s; see Rashīd al-Dīn (1994), 830 and Rashīd al-Dīn (1971), 207. Arghun Aqa, a former *bitikchi* of Genghis Khan, advanced for his knowledge of Uighur, was promoted under Möngke and also carried out the duties of judge (*yarghuchi*) among his other government posts in Khurasan; Lambton (1988), 86; Grupper, (1992–94), 50–51, note; and Lane, G. (1999), 478–79.

[13] Hsiao (1978), 36–37; Ratchnevsky (1991), 94, 106; Grupper (1992–94), 41, 46.

[14] Hsaio (1978), 34; Allsen (1986), 514; Grupper (1994), 48–52.

The Keshig *in the Early Mongol Empire*

On his accession in 1229, Ögödei inherited many members of the *keshig* of Genghis Khan, and it continued its functions of provisioning the imperial encampments (*ordūs*), organizing hunts, supervising the *yam* (postal service, Mo. *jam*), and maintaining the khan's possessions.[15] Ögödei confirmed the elaborate regulations concerning the shifts of the day and night guards, with further detailed instructions and new appointments.[16] As the empire expanded, so more officials were recruited from the native populations to administer the newly conquered realms. Nevertheless, it is clear that Ögödei's household continued to provide some of the most important men of the state, such as Chinqai, a chamberlain in Genghis Khan's household, who authenticated the Chief of the Secretariat's decrees. The *darugha*s, who were appointed to oversee the fiscal administration of the provinces, were also drawn from Ögödei's *nököd*.[17]

Möngke Khan (r. 1251–59) also recruited central government personnel from his household establishment, the elite core of which, Genghis Khan's own 'personal thousand,' had previously been inherited from his father Tolui. Many of the *bitikchi*s and other senior officials had started in either Tolui's or Möngke's household, making it difficult if not impossible to separate the guard, the household, and the central government, which functioned as a single body. The style of his government remained similar at the center, though in the provinces there was heavier reliance on native officials, monitored by officers of the *keshig*; more civilians were given posts, freeing military men for warfare. The *darughachi*s, who were sent to administer the conquered populations and carry out censuses, were selected from the companions of the ruler (*nököd*).[18] Mongol officials were generalists,

---

[15] Allsen (1986), 515. For Ögödei's movements, see Boyle (1977) and for the *yam*, Morgan, D. (2000).

[16] Cf. de Rachewiltz, ed. (2004), paras. 278–80 (209–17, 1019–32), for the detailed arrangements made by Ögödei.

[17] Allsen (1994), 373, 376; Allsen (1986), 515; see also next note. On Chinqai, a Nestorian Christian, see, for example, de Rachewiltz (1983), esp. 284.

[18] Allsen (1994), 396–98, and Allsen (1986), 502–3, 518, citing Buell (1979), 131–34, concerning the appointment of *darughachi*s from the imperial household from the time of Genghis Khan. There is a considerable literature on the office of *darugha*, including the vexed question of its relationship with the office of *basqaq*, recently reviewed by Ostrowski (1998), esp. 271–76; see also below.

and could carry out different tasks and hold more than one office at once (and as a result, could hold more than one title). One later example is the *amīr* Bolad, who at one point held at least five titles simultaneously in the Yüan regime.[19]

As remarked by Tom Allsen, it is a problem of considerable interest to what extent "this pattern [of governance based on patrimonial principles] persisted into the Yüan"—that is, when the Mongol central government moved out of the steppes and into the sedentary lands after Möngke's death in 1259.[20] This move was accompanied, of course, by the political fragmentation of the empire into separate and essentially hostile khanates. It will be helpful first to look briefly at the case of China, which has already been studied to a much greater extent than Iran (thanks not least to far superior surviving documentation), to gain some idea of the questions that arise. To understand the adaptations undergone by the primordial Mongolian administration under the Yüan, and its rather rapid transformation from a clan system to an imperial political organization, is to see the patrimonial character at the core of the original conquest regime.[21]

As for Iran, one reason for the apparent disappearance of this senior and influential group of Mongol officers from our accounts of Ilkhanid government can perhaps be put down to terminology, for such men would typically be described in Muslim sources as *mulāzim*, *muqarrab*, or *khāṣṣa*: the standard terms for the intimates and attendants of the ruler. Another reason, I believe, is that no one has chosen to pay much attention to them, though their presence is unmistakable.[22] I will return to this point later. In contrast to the Ilkhanate, the role of the *keshig* in the Chaghadai realms in Central Asia has received a very clear and thorough treatment by S. M. Grupper, and more recent work by Chris Atwood has focused on

[19] Allsen (1986), 512–13; Allsen (2001), 68–69, for Bolad.

[20] Allsen (1986), 520.

[21] Hsiao (1978), 34. It is a little surprising that Allsen, who was well aware of Hsaio's study, seemed not to recognize that Hsaio had already largely answered his question.

[22] Although for Mostaert and Cleaves (1962), 49, for example, "C'est un fait connu que la garde des ilkhan de Perse était organisée sur le modèle de celle du grand khan"; Luc Kwanten, on the contrary, believes it did not exist outside China (as quoted above). Similarly, there is no reference to the *keshig* or the household, for instance, in Lambton's seminal work (1988) on government institutions, nor George Lane's recent study of the early Ilkhanate (2003).

the Golden Horde.[23] This paper will seek to confirm that despite the lack of focus in our sources, the *keshig* survived in Iran also, not only in the persistence of individual posts (such as the *qorchi*),[24] but as an institution preserving its core function of guarding and serving the ruler and at the focal point of his innermost councils. As elsewhere in the Mongol world, it was the main institution whereby traditional Mongol government was maintained.

The Keshig *under the Yüan*

After the succession of Qubilai, with his greater sensitivity to Chinese practice and the creation of more specialized organs of government, the *keshig* underwent substantial changes and lost jurisdiction in some areas.[25] Nevertheless, its general organization and spirit were deliberately maintained by the rulers, and it remained the cradle of officialdom. The *keshig* was retained as a symbol of Mongol imperial authority and provided an important link between ruler and the Mongol elite. A precise statement of their existence and role is provided by Marco Polo, who numbered them at four guard units of three thousand men.[26]

The *Yüan-Shih* contains important evidence of the *keshig* under the Yüan, which includes not only details of its original form, but changes instituted under Qubilai in 1263. As well as listing the domestic offices of the household, which were held hereditarily, and explaining the rota system of the guard duties, it indicates that command of the

---

[23] Grupper (1992–94). See also Atwood (in press), which is essentially a development of the article by Schamiloğlu (1984). I am very grateful to the author for allowing me to cite his paper, which is to be published in a forthcoming conference proceedings volume, and also for kindly agreeing to read the final draft of my paper and make many valuable comments.

[24] Cf. Haneda (1984), esp. 43.

[25] Hsiao (1978), 39–44, for what follows; also Farquhar (1990), esp. 245–47; Endicott-West (1994), 604–8; Grupper, (1992–94), 61–72. These rather rich summaries of the situation perhaps belie the fact that in Chinese sources too, the *keshig* is a 'submerged' institution, which needs to be sought out among the far better documented references to the regular bureaucracy; Allsen (personal communication).

[26] Polo (1903), book 2, chap. 12: "How the Great Kaan maintains a guard of twelve thousand horse...," vol. 1, 379 (page citation is to the 1929 reprint edition). See also Grupper (1992–94), 90.

four units of the *keshig* were now held hereditarily by the descendants of the 'four heroes,' Boroqul, Bo'orchu, Muqali, and Chila'un. The emperor himself took over command of the first *keshig* after the early death of Boroqul, and after the extinction of Chila'un's line, command of his *keshig* was taken over by the right Grand Councilor (generally a Mongol, cf. the case in Iran, below).[27]

However, the *keshig* lost its primarily military character and function, which was taken over by soldiers of the regular (Chinese) army, and was left guarding the palace only. With the establishment of the main administrative offices (Central Secretariat; Privy Council; Censorship), the *keshig* also lost jurisdiction over administrative matters except for those of the imperial family. Even some domestic functions were shared with Chinese-style organs, founded by Qubilai, for practical reasons or prestige. Thus the Imperial Wine Department was identical with the functions of the *darachi*, and the Imperial Cuisine Department with the *ba'urchi* of the *keshig*. The Court of Imperial Attendants was effectively identical with the role of the *sukurchi* (Mo. *sükürchi*, *shükürchi*); the Court of the Imperial Stud and Carriage with the *akhtachi*, *ula'achi*, and *morinchi*.[28] The Han-lin Academy equated with the traditional tasks of the *bitikchi* and *yarlighchi* (Mo. *jarliqchi*).[29] The relationship of these dual functions was an interesting one, and it seems that they operated together under auspices of both Chinese and Mongol offices: for example, twenty-four *sukurchi*s from the *keshig* worked together with four hundred from the Court of Imperial Attendants. There were eleven *bitikchi*s in the Han-lin Academy in 1275, and four more in 1281, writing sacred decrees, probably detached from the *keshig*. City gatekeepers (*balaqachi*s) shared with officers from *wei* the duty of guarding the gates of Ta-tu (Peking).

Despite the diminution of their role, the *keshig* undoubtedly remained influential, thanks to their proximity to the ruler and being under imperial jurisdiction. Its members were not ranked according to the Chinese bureaucratic system. The original number of around

[27] *Yüan-Shih*, chaps. 98 and 99; Hsiao (1978), 76–77 (for the question of hostages), 92–93. See especially Atwood (in press) on the *keshig* of Qubilai, with references. These four *keshig* heads are not the same as those originally nominated by Genghis Khan; see de Rachewiltz, ed. (2004), para. 227, though the clans of the 'four heroes' were prominent in the command of the day guards, para. 226.

[28] For the Stud and its household officers, see Farquhar (1990), 88–90.

[29] Hsiao (1978), 39. See also Farquhar (1990), 128.

ten thousand was still adhered to, and although it remained an aristocratic organization, lesser ranks were filled by the children of official and military families (often as hostages at court), e.g., from the provinces and especially after the fall of the Southern Sung in 1279. The important connection between the regular army and the *keshig* was thus maintained by the obligation of commanders of one thousand and ten thousand to entrust their sons or younger brothers to the *keshig*. This, combined with the hereditary nature of these attachments, ensured the perpetuation of a system of mutual bonds between the Chinggisids and their military forces, and the survival of the *keshig* as the powerhouse of government down the generations.[30]

In addition to serving as guards and in palace duties, the *keshig* had representation on the Privy Council, and *yarghuchi*s in the Clan Court (administering lawsuits between Mongols and Central Asians) were drawn from their ranks. Even at the end of the dynasty in China, *darughachi*s were drawn from the *keshig*, providing reliable officers in the otherwise crumbling provincial administrations. They continued to bridge household and government functions, often held both household and government titles, and were highly privileged politically and financially. Rations were provided at least from 1281 and a monthly stipend was fixed in 1292; the *keshig* ultimately became a considerable drain on state resources.[31]

Finally, we may note that the *keshig* was evidently not reserved for Mongols alone; naturally, early surrendering officials had sent hostages, but later too, service in the *keshig* was so appealing that nonofficial families tried to penetrate it. The great influx of Chinese commoners threatened the identity of the Mongols and Central Asians; after 1300, repeated decrees were issued in an attempt to prevent Chinese commoners from service in the *keshig*.[32] Despite these attempts to maintain its purity and character, the household organization deteriorated along with the bureaucracy and aristocracy from which its members were drawn.

---

[30] See especially Grupper (1992–94), esp. 63–65.

[31] Hsiao (1978), 94, and 43.

[32] Endicott-West (1989), 85–86. There are certain parallels with the degradation of the Mamluk system in Egypt by the influx of civilians, partly after outbreaks of plague and particularly in the course of the fifteenth century, under the Circassians.

The Mongols in Iran

So much for the situation in China, which provides an exemplary model for the adaptation of Mongol rule to a sedentary setting with its own strongly developed traditions of government. The outstanding points to emerge from this brief review of the fate of the *keshig* in China are (i) that it continued to preserve its separate identity and basic function right through the Yüan period; and (ii) that a duality of functions was introduced (broadly 'military' and 'civilian'), so that effectively there was a Mongol and a Chinese officer or institution charged with the same tasks. We can already state with confidence that a similar development occurred in Mongol Iran.[33] We must be cautious, however, against assuming that identical transformations occurred in both these khanates in the sedentary lands, especially in the face of far less detailed primary sources of information for the study of the administrative history of Iran. If the Mongols entered China and Iran in much the same way, bringing the same essential organizations with them, they encountered different indigenous traditions when they got there and the ground prepared by different regimes before them. In Iran, for instance, the Turkification and militarization of government had been in progress for two centuries under the successive Ghaznavid, Seljuk, and Khwarazmshah regimes, entailing redefinitions and long-term adjustments in the relationships between the men of the pen and of the sword.

The patterns of Mongol occupation of Iran and the territories where they chose to concentrate (in Khurasan and westwards into Azerbaijan and Anatolia) allowed them continue, rather more than was the case in China, the way of life to which they were accustomed. Their form of government largely retained its nomadic character throughout the period.[34] The *ordū* alternated between winter and summer pastures, as did the encampments of the military chiefs. When not at war, the main activity of the Mongols was hunting, although as David Morgan has reminded us, this informality does not mean that they took no interest, or even active involvement in, the government of their conquests: rather the reverse. We shall return to these questions later. The large

[33] The duality of government has been observed by many scholars; see most recently Ostrowski (1998), 270–77.

[34] Melville (1990a), and more recently (2002).

gathering at Ujan, fifty kilometers southeast of Tabriz, in late Dhū al-qaʿda 701/July 1302, with the erection of a great tent in a walled garden enclosure and the personal distribution of ceremonial robes and purses of gold and silver by Ghazan Khan to his loyal officers,[35] shows not only the more formal and hierarchical aspects of court life, but also the political importance of the continuing close relationship between the ruler and his followers.[36] Such events were probably the inspiration for various scenes of court audiences in the illustrated manuscripts of Rashīd al-Dīn's chronicle and other miniature paintings of the period (see pl. 7); it is no accident that the ruler and his entourage are almost invariably depicted outdoors.

Such a mobile and tent-centered life was also reflected in its peripatetic administration, which shows how the basic character of the Ilkhanid court naturally affected the institutions and officialdom associated with it. It is to these that we now turn.

The Keshig *in the Ilkhanate*

The term *keshig* itself is not mentioned very frequently in the Persian sources; most of our direct evidence comes from Rashīd al-Dīn's justly famous chronicle, the *Jāmiʿ al-tawārīkh*, reflecting not only his own wide experience of the Mongol court, but more specifically the provenance of much of his information, received rather directly from Mongol sources.[37] However, the continuing involvement of the khans' officials in affairs of state can also be seen in the names and titles of those performing various tasks throughout the Mongol period, whose affiliations to the household are evident.[38] In what follows I

---

[35] Rashīd al-Dīn (1994), 1303–6; Jackson (1993b), 365; Allsen (1997), 80. For the tent, which took three years to make and one month to erect, see also Āqsarāʾī (1944), 295–96.

[36] Beckwith, C. I. (1984), 35, for the relationship between Germanic sacral kingship and the *comitatus*, citing *Beowulf*. See also Allsen (1997), esp. 52–57, 81. Such lavish largesse also pervades the relations between the shah and his champions throughout Firdawsī's *Shāhnāma*.

[37] For references to the *keshig*, see Doerfer (1963), 467–70; on Rashīd al-Dīn, Morgan, D. (1997) and most recently, Allsen (2001), 84–85.

[38] Allsen (1986), 520, notes the 'suggestive' presence of a *qushchi*, a *buka'ul*, and a *sukurchi* among Qubilai's senior ministers. Cf. Grupper (1992–94), 58, concerning the corporate nomenclature of the imperial guard, and 61–62 for the assumption of its spread to the far reaches of the empire.

shall try to marshal some of the evidence scattered in the sources, and especially in the *Jāmiʿ al-tawārīkh*, not only for the existence of the *keshig* but also for its functioning along the lines already identified above in the early imperial period and in Yüan China. So far as is practical, I will order the discussion into two halves, divided by the reign of Ghazan; as well as surveying the continuities across the period, it is important to seek evidence of change, particularly to what extent Ghazan's conversion to Islam and the ideologically altered regime of his successors might have affected the role of the household.

The Early Ilkhanate: Hülegü to Geikhatu

As we have seen, household officers from among the *nököd* of the khan were already operating in Iran in the period of the early viceroys. Ögödei's general, Chormaghun, was a *qorchi*, and Ketbugha, famous for his defeat at ʿAyn Jalut in 1260, was appointed *ba'urchi* (steward or cook) before being sent west in the vanguard of Hülegü's army in 1256.[39] As is clear from the passage quoted at the outset of this article, Hülegü came at the head of a household partly formed from the legacy of Genghis Khan to the Toluids, that is, long-serving followers whose descendants continued to form the nucleus of his entourage.[40] Hülegü was quick to recruit new adherents to the *keshig*. Grigor of Akner refers to the incorporation of "handsome and youthful sons" of the Armenian and Georgian princes into the *keshig* because of their extreme bravery in battle.[41] Equally to the point, however, is that these were also hostages for the good behavior of the Georgians, who actually continued to serve loyally in the Ilkhanid forces throughout the period.

As for administrators, Aḥmad *bitikchi* (probably a Central Asian Muslim) was sent with Hülegü's forces to help organize the king-

[39] Jackson (1993a) (Chormaghun); for Ketbugha, Rashīd al-Dīn (1994), 976. Allsen (1986), 518. *Ba'urchi* was a post also held later by Bolad Aqa, a cook like his father before him, Allsen (2001), 63, 127.

[40] Shimo (1977), 178–79, makes the point that these troops were nevertheless not all originally Hülegü's own, which might explain the divisions in some units later, in the civil war between Aḥmad and Arghun. See also below, n. 106.

[41] Grigor of Akner (1949), 343–45; Hsiao (1978), 150, n. 40; also Brosset (1849), 540.

dom once conquered. Similarly, the first real administrator of the Ilkhanate was a former official of the Khwarazmshahs, Sayf al-Dīn *bitikchi*, who ultimately fell from power early in Hülegü's reign and was replaced by Shams al-Dīn Juwaynī.[42] The *bitikchi*s, omnipresent in the sources, civilian administrators generally (from their names) but not exclusively recruited from non-Mongols, seem to have been particularly vulnerable to purges and the intrigues at court. In the reign of Arghun, for example, they were accused of hindering the tax-raising efforts of the unpopular Jewish vizier, Saʿd al-Dawla, in Baghdad. He complained of their interference and many of them were executed. In Fars, too, shortly afterwards, many *bitikchi*s were executed for failing to raise sufficient revenues.[43] This may be a sign of increasing assertion of the Persian bureaucracy at the expense of the household officers, at least those in subordinate positions, though it may simply reflect Saʿd al-Dawla's self-aggrandizement. It is interesting that he seems to have created his own mini-bodyguard as a rival power center to that of the great *amīr*s.

Fulfilling their main task as traditionally defined, Aḥmad's general Alinaq used the fact that he was in charge of the *keshig* guarding Arghun to explain why he couldn't go drinking that night,[44] and Rashīd al-Dīn cites examples of the disciplinary role of its members on various occasions. Tukachak, an officer of the *keshig*, was sent to execute Jalāl al-Dīn Simnānī under Arghun,[45] and the *amīr* Mulai, a member of the *keshig*, used his whip on Ṣadr al-Dīn Zanjānī at the start of Ghazan's reign.[46] The *keshig* was also invoked to discipline the cameleers in the reign of Ghazan.[47]

Members of the household are often mentioned performing specific services, most frequently as envoys (*elchi*s) on various missions, too numerous to detail here, both before and after the accession of Ghazan Khan in 1295. It is of interest that on many of these occasions, civilian and military officers are sent together: for example, Ẓahīr al-Dīn Sipahsālār *bitikchi* and Begtemür *qushchi* sent as envoys

---

[42] Rashīd al-Dīn (1994), 980, 1009, 1045, 1049; cf. Aubin (1995), 19–21.

[43] Rashīd al-Dīn (1994), 1173, 1175–76. All the *bitikchi*s listed have Muslim names.

[44] Ibid., 1143.

[45] Ibid., 1174.

[46] Ibid., 1259.

[47] As part of his reforms, ibid., 1539; see also below.

by Hülegü, or Isen Bugha *bitikchi* and Bughdai *akhtachi* sent as envoys by Ghazan.[48] They were regularly sent to the provinces to investigate affairs there; Amīr Nawruz sent *elchis* to Kirman to collect money for the Khurasan army under Baidu and again under Ghazan.[49] Shadi *bitikchi* was sent to Fars in 1266, together with another Mongol officer, to take what was in the treasury and collect the annual taxes. In 1302, Muḥammad *qushchi* was sent to Fars to investigate the alleged usurpation of *injü* (crown) lands and two years later a certain Istaghchaq *sukurchi* was sent to the province with orders to raise funds for the troops defending the frontiers, no doubt part of the same measures to strengthen the army that are mentioned below.[50] Mongol members of the household also accompanied Persian administrators on their tours of duty. When Fakhr al-Dīn Qazwīnī was sent to Anatolia in the reign of Arghun to head the administration (with the ambiguous title *imārat-i rūm*) together with Mujīr al-Dīn, the Mongols' chief revenue inspector for the province, they were accompanied by Iji (*Alchi?) the *totqa'ul* (road guard) and Tuladai (Duladai) the Great *Yarghuchi* of the *ordū*, respectively. In Anatolia as well as Fars, for which rather detailed information is available, the proliferation of posts and the dual structure of government are well-documented in the sources.[51]

On the death of Abaqa (in 1282), the *amīr* Buqa, whose father was a *qorchi*, summoned all the *akhtachis*, *sukurchis*, *qorchis*, and other *muqarrabs* who were the *khāṣṣ* of Abaqa to attend his son Arghun and perform the rites of mourning.[52] In the civil war that followed between Aḥmad Tegüder and Arghun, the loyalties of the household were divided, but we are told that Duladai the *idachi*, Alchi the *totqa'ul*, and others of the *keshig* ('*keziktanān*') and other *mulāzim* of Abaqa took the part of Arghun.[53] Qutui Khātūn, Aḥmad's mother,

---

[48] Ibid., 985, 1246.

[49] Nāṣir al-Dīn Munshī (1983), 78–79, 89, for the dispatch of various *sukurchis* to Kirman under Ghazan.

[50] Lambton (1986–87), 101, 104, 116, 117, cf. Waṣṣāf (1853), 196 (Shadi), 404 (Muḥammad *quschi*), 438 (Istaghchaq).

[51] Āqsarā'ī (1944), e.g., 154, 180–81; see also my forthcoming chapter in the *Cambridge History of Turkey*. For Fars, see Aigle (2005).

[52] Rashīd al-Dīn (1994), 1124.

[53] Ibid., 1131; for Buqa, see 1110. Duladai is here called an *idachi*, but there is little doubt that he is the same as the *yarghuchi* mentioned above. This suggests, as does other evidence, that members of the household were given temporary appoint-

also favored Arghun, and attracted the support of Buqa by clothing him in the personal garments of the Ilkhan Abaqa.[54] Later, as Aḥmad advanced into Khurasan, a group of *qushchi*s came to pay *il* (i.e., submit) to him.[55] The considerable prominence of household officers in the accounts of his brief and contested reign shows that they were greatly affected by it; many lost their lives in the process, for example, Uztemür the *qushchi* and others, executed by Aḥmad for favoring Arghun, and one of the *muqarrab*s of Aḥmad, a grandson of Chormagun, at the start of Arghun's reign.[56]

The later succession crises also inevitably saw the close involvement of the household officers, and their loyalties had a great influence on the outcome. Thus when the domestic slaves (*ev-oghlan*) abandoned the court of Baidu to go over to his rival, Geikhatu, this seems to have been a decisive moment in that power struggle.[57]

Undoubtedly one reason for the maintenance of the close ties between the Ilkhan and his household, other than their institutional or formal mutual dependence, was the fact that the ruling family regularly entered into marriage relations with members of their entourage. Three of Abaqa's daughters were married to household officers: one to a *qushchi*, one to an *idachi* (the same Duladai mentioned above), and one to the son of a *yarghuchi*; similarly, one of Aḥmad Tegüder's daughters was married to a *ba'urchi*. Ghazan Khan himself was the grandson of a *bitikchi*, and married a descendant of a *yarghuchi*.[58] Another reason was the hereditary nature of posts in the household, alluded to by Rashīd al-Dīn in the passage quoted

---

ments as *yarghuchi*s for specific tasks. More work needs to be done on this. Duladai's checkered career would also repay closer study, as a senior figure in Abaqa's *keshig*. Imprisoned by Aḥmad, he served Arghun but was hostile to Buqa. He was a supporter of Baidu and imprisoned by Geikhatu, and later opposed to Ghazan. No more is heard of him after the fall of Nawruz. The term *idachi* or *idechi*, which Rawshan and Mūsawī gloss as *idägächi* (Rashīd al-Dīn [1994], 2307), seems to be equivalent to the Mo. *cherbi*, but with responsibility chiefly for provisions, rather than domestic supervisor; cf. de Rachewiltz, ed. (2004), 445.

[54] Rashīd al-Dīn (1994), 1129.

[55] Ibid., 1139.

[56] Ibid., 1141, 1155. Shimo (1977), 154, notes also the execution of Nikpai *qushchi*, an *amīr* of the Qara'unas, a unit itself divided and, as his study shows, heavily involved in these events. Cf. Allsen (1986), 519–20.

[57] Rashīd al-Dīn (1994), 1184; they were among the last to leave him.

[58] Ibid., 1056–57, 1206, 1215. On such marriages, cf. Grupper (1992–94), 71.

at the start of this paper. Among many examples are Qonjokbal, given the office of *qol-i lashkar* (Command of the Center) in the reign of Aḥmad, inheriting the office of his ancestor, Abatay. Buralghi, son of Amīr Junqur, who was the great *amīr totqa'ul* (Guardian of the Roads) in the reign of Arghun Khan, was given command of all the road guards under Ghazan.[59]

Such information leads us already to anticipate a rather high degree of continuity between the early years of the Ilkhanate and the reign of Ghazan Khan, who is generally thought, in other respects, to have ushered in a new era.

The Later Ilkanid Period: Ghazan to Abū Sa'īd

That Ghazan inherited an operative household cannot be in doubt, and he was brought up surrounded by members of the inner circle of his father, Arghun.[60] That he had his own *keshig* is revealed by several specific statements by Rashīd al-Dīn, referring to both the beginning and end of his reign. Thus in September 1294, before he had become Khan, Ghazan executed a couple of officers of the *keshig* for their undisciplined behavior during his attack on Nishapur.[61] In the winter of 1303, we find the *keshigten* guarding Ghazan during his forty-day retreat (*chilla*); together with the Khwāja-sarai, they were the only people allowed to disturb him.[62]

The activities of the household, however, came under scrutiny during Ghazan's reign, as part of his program of reforms. The *akhtachi*s (grooms) are listed along with other officials, such as *shiḥna*s (governors, cf. *darugha*s), *barschi*s (keepers of hunting leopards), *qushchi*s (falconers), and *qorchi*s (quiver bearers), who habitually abused the *yam* (postal) service by sending out hordes of unnecessary envoys (*elchi*s).[63] The *qorchi*s, together with the *akhtachi*s, were also accused of giving

[59] Rashīd al-Dīn (1994), 1166–67, 1455–56. For Qonjokbal, commander of the Qara'unas unit, see Shimo (1977), 172.

[60] Rashīd al-Dīn (1994), 1209, 1213.

[61] Ibid., 1240.

[62] Ibid., 1318. Their state of permanent attendance on the ruler is also noted elsewhere (1450), together with the fact that they had to supply their own horses and the fodder for them.

[63] Rashīd al-Dīn (1994), 1445–46.

receipts for the inflated purchase of armor and horses in exchange for bribes from the reign of Abaqa onwards, a spiraling fraud in which the *bitikchis* (scribes) were only too ready to participate.[64] The same officials, and especially the *idachis* (provisioners) and their *bitikchis*, were accused of corruption and incompetence in their procurement of food for the *ordū*.[65] Ghazan was obliged to tighten the arrangements for provisioning the *ordūs* of the *khātūns*, and to ensure that regular supplies came in to the wine and stable departments (*sharāb-khāna* and *akhtachi-khāna*).[66] Similarly, the corruption of the *buka'uls* (distributors of spoils of conquest, and later of food and rations), who took bribes and neglected their duties, was one reason for Ghazan's attempt to distribute *iqṭā'* assignments to the army in 1303–4 to ensure the proper upkeep of the military.[67]

Despite these apparent problems with the discipline and service of the household officers, Ghazan seems to have made no attempt to reduce their numbers as time went by. On the contrary, he recruited additional forces to swell the regular army, especially for the adequate defense of the border regions, and also for his own private household. Among his reforms it is mentioned that he encouraged the members of the *keshig* (*keshigten*) to nominate one or two from among their sons and brothers who were not on the regular strength (*shumāra*), so that from every thousand men an additional hundred or two hundred were levied to stay in attendance (at court) for a year, and then return. These men were greatly favored by Ghazan, and ultimately became a force of two to three thousand men who, with the agreement of the *keshig*, attended the ruler (*mulāzim shudand*). Among the same measures, Rashīd al-Dīn also mentions that young boys who had become captured and sold to merchants in the course of the internecine fighting among the Mongol khanates, or others

[64] Ibid., 1490.

[65] Ibid., 1504–6.

[66] Ibid., 1508. This section has been translated by Martinez (1986 [1988]); see 117–18.

[67] Rashīd al-Dīn (1994), 1476–77; trans. Martinez (1986 [1988]), esp. 86–88. The *idachis* and their *bitikchis* are once more singled out for criticism concerning army supplies. The drain on the provinces caused by the demand for supplies (*taghār*) is exemplified by the account of Āqsarā'ī (1944), 145–46. The needs of the *keshig* seem also to have been a component of the *taghār* in Anatolia; ibid., 68. Cf. my 'Anatolia Under the Mongols' (in press). For the significance of the allocation of *iqṭā's*, see recently Amitai-Preiss (2001), with whose conclusions I concur.

sold because of poverty, should be purchased and taken into royal service as *kebte'ülān* (guards of the night watch, i.e., with a redundant additional Persian plural suffix). The *amīr* Bolad was made their commander and the subordinate officers were taken from the household (*muqarrabān-i ḥaḍrat*). In time, the whole force grew almost to a *tümen*, all serving as night guards and entering the ruler's private household estate (*injü-yi khāṣṣ*).[68]

This extension of the traditional *keshig*, or possibly formation of a parallel force equally closely associated with the household, shows that it remained central to the functioning of the Ilkhan's control of events. Ghazan's reforming edicts, which make many other allusions to the unsatisfactory performance of the household officers, show that we are dealing here with an institution that continued to be crucially important at the center of power.[69] Possibly its post holders were becoming out of control and abusing their position. More likely, given Rashīd al-Dīn's inspiration behind the reform program, they were caught in the clash between the competing ideologies of government represented by the decentralizing tendencies of the Mongol establishment, on one hand, and the opposite tendencies of the Persian bureaucracy, hoping with Ghazan's conversion to Islam to recover some lost ground, on the other. Both groups, however, seem to have been almost equally tainted by, and implicated in, the corruption and factionalism of the *ordū*.

That the Mongol household emerged undiminished by the bureaucratic efforts to neuter it is clear from later developments, which we will consider shortly. It is also strikingly confirmed by Ghazan's political testament, preserved by two later Ilkhanid historians, Abū al-Qāsim Qāshānī and Waṣṣāf Shīrāzī, evidently on the basis of a document (*nuskha-yi vaṣāyā*) dictated by Ghazan as death approached.[70] This has not been generally recognized for what it is, probably chiefly

---

[68] Rashīd al-Dīn (1994), 1487–88; Martinez (1986 [1988]), 110–13; an initiative that clearly reflects the earlier precedents of Genghis Khan and Qubilai. One advantage of the ruler purchasing these strays, many of whom came from the families of those who had served with distinction in the time of Genghis Khan, was to deprive the Mamluk slave dealers of acquiring them; cf. al-ʿUmarī (1968), 70, 72; al-Maqrīzī (1943), 525; Ayalon (1994), 3, 6. See also Ratchnevsky (1991), 203.

[69] I am grateful to Tom Allsen for this observation.

[70] al-Qāshānī, Abū al-Qāsim (1969–70), fols. 140v–141r (11–14), presents it as a document; the substantially similar text in Waṣṣāf (1853), 456–58 (cf. Waṣṣāf [1967], 269–70) is given in the form of a speech made by Ghazan to those assembled.

because it is not found in Rashīd al-Dīn, although he does refer to it.[71] Its purpose is to assert Ghazan's attempts to rule justly, to confirm his brother Öljeitü as his successor, and to enjoin on him and on the ruling elite to continue to govern according to the principles that he has established. It is addressed to the *khātūns* and members of the harem; the pillars of the kingdom (*arkān-i mulk*) such as Qutlughshah (who was senior *noyan*); the great *amīrs* (who are listed); [72] the commanders of *tümens* and *hazaras* (thousands) of the Mongol and Persian forces (*cherik*); sultans, *basqaqs*, *maliks*, *atabegs*, governors (*ḥukkām*), and *bitikchis*; and the religious classes, such as *qāḍīs*, *sayyids*, *imāms*, and others, even down to the mass of the townspeople, villagers, and desert dwellers. Waṣṣāf also mentions the advisors (*mushāvarān*) and viziers (Khwāja Rashīd al-Dīn and Khwāja Saʿd al-Dīn).

Not content with this all-embracing audience, Ghazan's testament then specifically singles out the pillars of state (*arkān-i dawlat*; Qāshānī) or intimates and notables (*muqarrabān va nām-āvarān*; Waṣṣāf), listing by name the holders of the following offices: nine *sukurchis* (parasol bearers);[73] nine *akhtachis* (equerries); one *qorchi* (quiver bearer); one *yurtchi* (camp master); ten *ildüchis* (sword bearers); four *bitikchis* (scribes); two *susunchis* (food servers; Mo. *süsünchi*, or *shüsünchi*); nine *idachis* (army provisioners); five *qushchis* (falconers); four *ev-oghlan* (domestic slaves); and other members of the *keshig* (*keziktan*),[74] together with the *īnāqān* and *muqarribān-i ḥaḍrat* (Qāshānī) or *khwājas* and other dependents (*vābastagān*; Waṣṣāf).

This, then, provides a snapshot of the household establishment at the end of the reign of Ghazan Khan (r. 1295–1304), with the names of about sixty of the top officers, all but two or three of whom were

---

[71] Rashīd al-Dīn (1994), 1324, calling it Ghazan's *vaṣiyat-nāma*. Its significance had not escaped A. H. Morton, however, as I recall from several conversations over the years.

[72] Waṣṣāf (1853), 456; Qāshānī (1969–70) has a fuller list of the great *amīrs* earlier in his work, 8–10; see also *Muʿizz al-ansāb* (Paris, Bibliothèque Nationale, ms. anciens fonds, persan 67; hereafter cited as *Muʿizz al-ansāb*), fols. 75v–76v.

[73] al-Qāshānī, Abū al-Qāsim (1969–70), 12, reads "*ankuzkhan*"(?) instead of *sukurchiyan*, to decipher which, from the ms. (fol. 141r, line 8), is admittedly an act of faith.

[74] Instead of the "*keziktanan*" in Qāshānī, Waṣṣāf lists three *khazanchis* (treasurers). One of these, Mihtar (Khwāja) Najīb al-Dīn (Farrāsh), had entered Ghazan's service before he became *khān* and was rewarded by being accepted as one of the *muqarrabān-i ḥaḍrat*, and given a village from the prince's estate (*injü*), see Rashīd al-Dīn (1994), 1221.

evidently Mongols.[75] A more detailed study of this list must await a separate occasion;[76] it has been used in some of my own previous studies to help identify the leading personnel in the late Ilkhanate and the connections between them. More such prosopographical investigations are needed, not only to clarify later relationships, but also looking backwards to discern links and affiliations in the earlier period.[77] The *amīr* Mazuq, mentioned in Ghazan's testament as a *yurtchi*, was a *qushchi* (falconer) under Aḥmad, and was sent on a mission against the Kurds at the start of Arghun's reign.[78] Ramaḍān, of the Baya'ut tribe, named as a *noyan* by Waṣṣāf, is listed as one of Arghun's *amīrs* of the *bitikchis*, was later sent to bring Ghazan news of the death of Geikhatu, and is named as one of the *amīrs* of Ghazan and then Öljeitü.[79] He is distinguished by another important function, countersigning decrees, as we shall see below.

Persistent references in the sources to such officers and their descendants, and more particularly to the continuing succession of household posts within the families of the leading *amīrs* up to the death of Abū Sa'īd in 1335, indicate beyond doubt that in its essential features, the Mongol household continued to function throughout the Ilkhanate. It is interesting to note, for example, that Öljeitü introduced Amīr 'Alī Qushchi and others into his own intimate circle soon after this accession (*īshān-rā anīs-i salvat va jalīs-i khalvat-i khwud gardānīd*).[80]

[75] Only Malik Nāṣir al-Dīn, listed as one of the *bitikchis*, and a certain Amīr 'Alī, an *idachi*, have non-Mongol names. For Nāṣir al-Dīn, see Melville (1997a), 98.

[76] There are many conflicts and difficult readings in the lists of names still to be resolved; even their exact number is not certain. I am currently working on an annotated translation of this important text.

[77] Such an investigation for the early period would be greatly facilitated by Rashīd al-Dīn's *Shu'ab-i panjgāna*, unfortunately still not edited; for the later Ilkhans, see also *Mu'izz al-ansāb*, esp. fols. 73v et seq. This formed the basis of the study of the Tīmūrid establishment by Shiro Ando (1992). For an evaluation of both genealogies for the Chaghatayid Khanate, see Quinn (1989). Thanks to Tom Allsen for insisting on this point.

[78] Rashīd al-Dīn (1994), 1144, 1162. Probably the same as the man listed as a great *amīr*, head of all the *qushchis*, under Abaqa, see *Mu'izz al-ansāb*, fol. 67v.

[79] Waṣṣāf (1853), 456, but later, 468, only as an *amīr* not a great *amīr*; cf. al-Qāshānī, Abū al-Qāsim (1969–70), 11. For his earlier career, *Mu'izz al-ansāb*, fols. 69v (one of *ba'urchis* under Geikhatu), 72r, 74v, 76v (*amīr* of the *bitikchis*) and Rashīd al-Dīn (1994), 1202 (envoy to Ghazan), and also Melville (1999b), 96, n. 87 and Mostaert and Cleaves (1952), 480–81.

[80] al-Qāshānī, Abū al-Qāsim (1969–70), 28–29; he calls 'Alī Qushschi the son of Bayitmish, but in fact they were brothers. Shaikh-'Alī, son of 'Alī Qushchi, and

Before discussing the significance and consequences of this, I shall turn briefly to the persistence of the *keshig* in the post-Mongol period to confirm the proposition that it does not disappear from view but, on the contrary, despite possible modifications in terminology and function that cannot be pursued here, remained a key institution at the center of power.

The Keshig *in Later Persian History*

The continuing nomadic nature of the court and the reflection of this in the duties of some of its officers are confirmed in the *Dastūr al-kātib* of Hindūshāh Nakhjuvānī, writing in the Jalayirid period (c. 1350). It was the job of the *buka'ul*, for example, to distribute the spoils of conquests and keep the chiefs happy with his decisions. The *yasa'ul* (Mo. *jasa'ul*) organized everyone in their proper place on marches and at the time of *quriltai*s and feasts, and in their right position in battle and in the *ordū*.[81] The *yurtchi* selected the *yaylaq*s and *qishlaq*s and ensured that while hunting, everyone knew his proper place—*amīr*s to the right and civilians to the left. This office continues to be attested in the Safavid period.[82] The *bularghuchi* was responsible for staying behind after the *ordū* had left to retrieve lost property, slaves, and animals and for returning them to their correct owners.[83] Officers with such names and titles reappear throughout the Timurid period[84] and the *keshig* clearly remained the key institution under Tīmūr (see pl. 8), maintaining the traditional connection between the guard and Chinggisid dynastic rule.[85] The term *keshig* itself is

---

his father Baybugha were all *qushchi*s. Another example: Buqa, his son Alghu and grandson Dawlatshah were *yarghuchi*s; see Melville (1997a), 104 and (1999a), 22, 32. Note, however, that Alghu is listed as an '*amīr*' in Ghazan's testament and the office of *yarghuchi* is not mentioned. Aubin (1991), 180–84, makes clear too the hereditary position of the senior commanders at the death of Abū Sa'īd.

[81] Nakhjuvānī (1976), vol. 2, 53–57, 57–62; Morgan, D. (1990); cf. Jackson (1993b), 365. The role of *yasa'ul* is essentially described by al-'Umarī (1968), 99.

[82] Nakhjuvānī (1976), 62–67; Yazdī (1987), 369.

[83] Nakhjuvānī (1976), 67–72. This is reminiscent of the work of the so-called Agency of Men and Things Gone Astray, a bureau established under the Yüan, for which no Chinese precedent existed; see Endicott-West (1994), 605.

[84] Gronke (1993), esp. 367; Manz (1989), 169–74, esp. 172; Ando (1992).

[85] Grupper (1992–94), esp. 84–97, citing among other things the *Tuzūkāt-i Tīmūrī* (Davy, ed. [1783], 297–301; page citations are to the 1964 reprint edition).

rather seldom encountered in the Persian sources, usually in its basic sense as guard or attendance on the ruler.[86] If this might suggest a force on the wane over the fourteenth and fifteenth centuries, its higher visibility in the Safavid period belies this impression.

A most important testament comes from Jean Chardin, writing in the third quarter of the seventeenth century. He mentions that the magnates of the Safavid realm discussed all the affairs of state in the *keshik-khāna*, or guardhouse (a special building at entrance to the royal palace, the ʿAlī Qapū in Isfahan). The shah sent petitions that he received to this council and sought its advice.[87] The existence and composition of this council is confirmed by the *Tadhkirat al-mulūk*, written right at the end of the reign of the last Safavid shah, Sultan Ḥusayn (c. 1722), which states that the *keshik-khāna* was a special location for the *dīwān* council and the work of the grand vizier. All the *amīr*s sat there in their proper rank, and only great *amīr*s, dignitaries, great *mustawfī*s, khans of high rank, viziers, and *ṣāḥib-raqam*s could attend.[88] The *keshik-khāna* as council chamber is attested even in the provinces.[89]

Meanwhile, the administrative manuals confirm the continuing role of the *keshig* as the shah's guard; the permanent bodyguard became called the *hamīsha keshik*. Evidence for the existence of both terms is scattered throughout the Safavid chronicles and beyond, into the early Qajar period, witnessing the intimate connection of the *keshig* with the person of the shah.[90] The number of the *qorchi*s (imperial guard) increased in the later Safavid period as the crown (*khāṣṣa*) came to control more resources and revenues at the expense of provincial

[86] Naṭanzī (1957), 199 (*mulāzimat va kishīktanī*); Tihrānī (1964), 550 (*nawbat-i kishīk va pās*). For the household under the Aq Qoyunlu, see Minorsky (1978), 159–60, 165; Woods (1999), 13–14.

[87] Chardin (1811), vol. 5, 237, probably informed by Raphaël du Mans; cf. Doerfer (1963), 468; Floor (2001), 32.

[88] Minorsky (1943), esp. 46, also 43, 50, 56. Also, Mīrzā Rafīʿā (2001), esp. 5 (493), 10 (498), 18 (506). There was evidently more than one guardhouse.

[89] Mashīzī (1990), 540, 560, 588, 639, concerning Kirman.

[90] E.g., Junābādī (1999), 675–76; Maʿsūm (1989), 42, 61; Waḥīd Qazwīnī (1951), 220, 332; Wālih Iṣfahānī (2001), 201; Mīrzā Rafīʿā (2001), 93–94 (581–82); Floor (2001), 125. For Nādir Shāh, see the passage quoted at the outset of this paper (many others are to be found in Marvī's chronicle); it was the captain of the guard, Muḥammad Qulī Khān, who was on duty that night, who organized the murder of Nādir; see Gulistāna (1965), 11–15. For the Qajars, Sārūʾī (1992), 210. The same post, *kishīkchī-bāshī*, was held by Amīr Bahādur Jang under Muẓaffar al-Dīn Shāh at the end of the century.

troops paid from the state (*mamālik*) revenues; this may represent also an expansion of the *keshig* as a whole, though the terms are not entirely interchangeable.[91] The central role of the *keshig* was thus maintained, not only in its primary function as the shah's bodyguard but also at the focus of decision making.

Discussion

It may be felt, then, that there are strong grounds for asserting that the Mongol royal household remained an active establishment in and beyond the Ilkhanid period. Nevertheless, the important role of its officers has rather been implied than entirely demonstrated. Can we detect any specific role in government, or see how the activities of the household affected Mongol rule in Iran?

Fortunately, the answer is at least partly yes. As demonstrated by Francis Woodman Cleaves fifty years ago, the senior officers of the *keshig*, among their other duties, countersigned the orders (*yarligh*, Mo. *jarliq*; Per. *farmān*) issued by the ruler. At least one of these chancery documents, Ghazan's letter to Pope Boniface VIII, dated April 1302, is countersigned with the inscription "on the first day of the *keshig* of Üred. Qutlughshah, Rashīd al-Dawla (Rashīd al-Dīn) and Ramaḍān."[92] This demonstrates first, that the *keshig* did indeed perform its guard shifts according to the rota system established by Genghis Khan. Secondly, the commanders of the four watches (all senior *amīrs*, who came to be called the four *amīr-i ūlūs*), played an important role in authenticating documents. This, indeed, is specifically stated by Rashīd al-Dīn,[93] and later by the Mamluk historian al-ʿUmarī, writing at the time of Abū Saʿīd. He also states that when the senior *amīrs* were not at court (as must have happened frequently), the documents were countersigned by the vizier alone.[94]

---

[91] Haneda (1984), esp. 50–55 (noting also the hereditary nature of the post of *qorchi*); Floor (2001), esp. 137–38, 156–62, 206–7.

[92] Cleaves (1951), 516–22, with evidence of other documents (from the 1330s onwards) dated with reference to the guard shift on duty, and more fully, in Mostaert and Cleaves (1952), 478–82, where the names of the signatories are correctly identified. Atwood (in press) suggests Üred=Oirat. I cannot identify any such prominent *amīr* under Ghazan.

[93] Rashīd al-Dīn (1994), 1467; cf. Mostaert and Cleaves (1952), 479–80.

[94] al-ʿUmarī (1968), 93.

The other striking insight to be gained from this practice is that the vizier has not only become on a par with the Mongol *noyans* (*amīrs*), but has actually been absorbed into the *keshig* system itself. Rashīd al-Dīn first entered the service of Geikhatu as a cook or steward.[95] Furthermore, Rashīd al-Dīn specifically states that he and Qutlugh-shah enjoyed close relations because they were in the same *keshig* (i.e., in the same guard unit).[96] We will recall that in Yüan China, one of the *keshigs* was headed by the right Grand Councilor (generally a Mongol). The situation here is slightly different in that Rashīd al-Dīn and, generally, other viziers after him were not Mongols and did not command a separate guard so much as belong to one of them. The chief minister was thus both inside and yet, to some extent, still outside the system, for he was not a military commander and could act independently in their absence.

In practice the situation may have evolved over time, for on the decree of 1302 and others dated 1292 and 1305, there are only the seals of three *amīrs* and the vizier (Ṣadr al-Dīn Zanjānī in 1292, Saʿd al-Dīn Sāwajī in 1305), suggesting that perhaps the vizier was at least the equivalent of a *keshig* chief. Indeed, we know that Zanjānī, who enjoyed the unlimited confidence of Geikhatu, was created a great *amīr* by him, receiving the trappings of a *noyan* and command of a *tümen*. He also had control of the golden seal (*āl-i zarrīn*, or *altun tamgha*).[97] By the reign of Abū Saʿīd, however, the practice is as described by al-ʿUmarī and Rashīd al-Dīn, with all four commanders obliged to authenticate documents, after which came the vizier's signature.[98] Al-ʿUmarī emphasizes the omnicompetence of the vizier and calls him the "sultan in all but name," and this indeed is the prevailing perception of the situation. Under a vizier such as Rashīd al-Dīn's son, Ghiyāth al-Dīn, who is rather persistently referred to as a man

---

[95] Bar Hebraeus (1932), 496; (1986 reprint edition), 369 (*amr al-nafaqa*). See also Amitai-Preiss (1996b), 25, Allsen (2001), 127.

[96] Rashīd al-Dīn (1994), 1284.

[97] Waṣṣāf (1853), 265; cf. Aubin (1995), 47. For the seal, see Doerfer (1985b), and Herrmann (1997), for the identification of Saʿd al-Dīn on the *yarligh* of 1305, and his remarks on the seals used by the signatories.

[98] See Atwood (in press) for a more detailed discussion. The decrees of 1292 and 1305 are presented by Soudavar (1992), 34–35, and Mostaert and Cleaves (1962), 55–85, respectively.

of the sword as well as the pen, it does seem that the Ilkhan Abū Saʿīd had in effect lost all grip on power.[99]

I believe that viewpoint is at least partly due to the orientation of our sources, issuing exclusively from the bureaucratic milieu and no doubt eager to accentuate their own importance, if only to educate the rulers to this ideal state of affairs. There is an instinctive bias in Western scholarship in the same direction. It is axiomatic of most general treatments of Persian history that successive waves of foreign invaders (particularly in the Mongol period and afterwards), whatever their initial nature, ultimately took over and adapted to the traditional norms of Persian government, overwhelmed by the more advanced sedentary civilization they encountered.[100] Such a formulation, however, discounts or conveniently overlooks the presence of numerous functionaries in the Mongol and post-Mongol period who, as we have seen, played an important role not only in military affairs but also in the supervision of tax collection and provincial government. Their influence and offices derived essentially from their intimate relations with the ruler and their proximity to his presence; they were commissioned, dispatched, and controlled by the ruler and were only at the bidding of the bureaucracy to the extent that the ruler himself might have been. Furthermore, these household connections were forged in, and defined by, the steppe society from which the Mongol empire emerged, and owed little to earlier Perso-Islamic models.

As has been shown by Stephen Blake, however, in practice the two sets of institutions could often be grafted onto one another and coexist in a modified form in a 'patrimonial-bureaucratic empire.'[101] The association of the vizier with the *keshig* might be taken to embody this process of convergence, in which we see the Iranian bureaucracy existing alongside the Ilkhanid household rather than dominating it, and perhaps even struggling to maintain any independence at all

---

[99] See Melville (1990a), esp. 63 for a discussion of al-ʿUmarī's reports in particular, and (1999a), esp. 29, 60–68, for the role of the Ghiyāth al-Dīn.

[100] E.g., Bosworth (1995), 435, and generally implied in Lambton (1988), e.g., 348, though her discussion of the vizierate is rather more cautious, 61–68, esp. 62–63 on the vizier's ambiguous relationship with the *bitikchis* and 67 on his lack of control over the expenditure of the funds he raised. It is not clear how much this changed by the end of the period.

[101] Blake (1979), esp. 82–84 for the household.

from the all-pervading presence of the *bitikchis* and others.

Provisioning the army was regarded as the chief function of the bureaucracy; as emphasized in the *Dastūr al-kātib*, the necessities of the royal court *(khāṣṣa-yi ḥaḍrat)* were the vizier's priority, on which depended the upkeep of the army and other matters.[102] It is clear from the ceremonies at Ujan, mentioned earlier, that Ghazan was anxious to win the support of his subjects by asserting his commitment to Islam and thus to Islamic principles of government and the regulation of society. One aspect of this was the revival of the *sharīʿa* and also of the traditional administration, but it is not really clear how much had changed. On the one hand, we may recall the often-repeated story of Chupan and Irenjin complaining about how they had been eclipsed and the civilians could go along "in the middle of the night" to the ruler without any recourse to the permission or opinions of the *amīrs*.[103] On the other hand, the viziers and chief bureaucrats often arose from the households (*darkhāna-yi umarāʾ*) of the *amīrs* themselves; in the time of Arghun, Ordoqiya promoted Saʿd al-Dawla; under Geikhatu, Taghachar promoted Ṣadr al-Dīn Khālidī; Saʿd al-Dīn Sāwajī was advanced by Nurin Aqa under Ghazan, and Tāj al-Dīn ʿAlīshāh by Amīr Ḥusayn Küregen under Öljeitü. Amīr Chupan also promoted one of his own household, Rukn al-Dīn Ṣāʾin, to the vizierate,[104] which turned out to be a mistake. Later, Abū Saʿīd's promotion of his own favorite (*īnāq*), Musāfir, also proved a poor decision, but it is particularly interesting that Musāfir is said to have been appointed one of the *amīrs* who signed *yarlighs*, apparently thanks to an association with the vizier Ghiyāth al-Dīn. This shows how intertwined the interests of the various groups at court could become. It is evident that the term *īnāq* can be understood as another term for membership of the *keshig*.[105] At best, we might

---

[102] Lambton (1988), 62, 67.

[103] al-Qāshānī, Abū al-Qāsim (1969–70), 195–96, referring to the end of Öljeitü's reign; cf. Lambton (1988), 53–54.

[104] Ḥāfiẓ-i Abrū, *Dhayl-i jāmiʿ al-tawārīkh* (Istanbul, Nurosmaniye Library, ms. 3271), fol. 56v, cited also in Melville (1996), 85. To this list of pairings, we could also add, from an earlier period, the relationship between the Juwaynīs and Sughunchaq Aqa and then with Buqa (himself the son of a *qorchi*, who had risen up through various ranks in Abaqa's household), see Aubin (1995), 30. These contacts and the interdependency of the *dīwān*ians and *noyans* are the stuff of Aubin's pioneering study.

[105] al-ʿUmarī (1968), 99, lines 16–17 on the *īnāqiyya*. For Musāfir, see Melville (1999a), esp. 37, citing Ahrī (1954), 157, tr. 58.

conclude that such distinctions between the Mongol household and the indigenous bureaucratic traditions as they may have existed at the time of Hülegü's arrival in Iran had become much less clear-cut by the time of Abū Saʿīd, but certainly neither had yielded very obviously to the other.

Finally, this identity of interest in obtaining power between the Mongol *amīrs* and the functionaries they patronized also raises the question of the multiplicity of households. Many *amīrs* and other senior officials, as well as the royal *khātūns*, had agents (*nā'ib*, pl. *nuwwāb*) performing personal services. There was evidently also more than one royal *keshig* in the Ilkhanate. We have already seen that Ghazan had his own *keshig* in Khurasan before coming to the throne. Earlier, Taghachar's political role was based on his command of the Qara'unas who came west from Khurasan from the *keshig* of Abaqa. It seems that old *keshigs* continued to function politically after the death of the *khān* they had served.[106] In this, parallels may be pursued with the Mamluk military system that was operating in Egypt and Syria at this same period.

Conclusions

I have tried to show that the Mongol household guard, the *keshig*, entered Iran as the core of Hülegü's entourage and remained active throughout the Ilkhanid period and beyond. As in the early Mongol empire and in Yüan China, and indeed the other regional khanates, the *keshig* was not only the ruler's bodyguard, taking it in turn to protect him day and night, but in a larger sense the whole household, comprising all the officers divided into four rotating guard units. The leadership of these units is more clearly visible in the latter part of the Ilkhanate than at the beginning, vested in four senior *amīrs* (*noyans*) who enjoyed considerable political influence along with their military command.

---

[106] See Shimo (1977), esp. 136–39, 176–77 for Taghachar. I am grateful to Chris Atwood for this reference and for drawing my attention to this point. Further work is needed in this direction. It is not clear whether the Qara'unas are a special case, or whether other such units can be identified. For the links between the Qara'unas and commanders drawn from the *keshig*, see Grupper (1992–94), esp. 53–60.

Not every Mongol soldier or officer, of course, was a member of the ruler's household, and if ambiguity remains it lies in distinguishing the regular army units and their officers from those of the ruler's core guard of approximately one *tümen*, or ten thousand—a figure that, as we have seen, increased under Ghazan. In any event, the practice by the army commanders in sending their sons and brothers not only as hostages but also as privileged members of the household strengthened the connections between the regular army and the elite guard corps. What does seem clear, at least, is that the bulk of the officials about whom we are informed were associated with the ruler's *keshig*. This is suggested not only by the preservation of their traditional domestic posts, such as *ba'urchi*, *sukurchi*, *qushchi*, and *qorchi*, linked to the service of the ruler, but also by their fulfilling tasks on behalf of the court, essentially carrying out the ruler's will. Not surprisingly, the court chronicles focus on what was happening at the *ordū* rather than elsewhere. There are enough specific references to the association of individual personnel with the *keshig* to see it as the real center of power. Undoubtedly, much more work needs to be done on the careers and family or clan backgrounds of those named in the sources to chart the connections between them and with the ruling house. This is particularly so, as it is frequently emphasized that posts were hereditary, as is indeed borne out by many examples.[107]

Thus, we can assert that the Mongols established a patrimonial state in Iran arising out of the household. The influence of the household does not seem to have diminished and little discernible difference is made by the court's conversion to Islam, though the change to a more familiar terminology for the rulers' attendants obscures our view of them at times. The necessary recruitment of non-Mongols into senior posts from an early date, or the conversion of Mongols to Islam, suggests that religion itself was a far less divisive issue for the Mongols than it was for the Persian bureaucrats and historians.[108] In

---

[107] We can only lament the continuing impoverishment of our field, when we compare the resources available for the study of Yüan China, in such a monumental reference tool as the volume edited by de Rachewiltz et al. (1993). Grupper's article (1992–94) on the Barulas tribe is an example of the rich possibilities for further progress.

[108] Was Muḥammad the *sukurchi*, who was *shiḥna* in Baghdad under Geikhatu, a Persian or converted Mongol? Earlier, a certain Amīr ʿAlī is variously referred to in the reign of Arghun as *tamghachi* (collector of *tamgha* commercial tax) in Tabriz, also as *shiḥna* (governor, or *darughachi*), *vālī* and *ḥākim* (governor) there; Rashīd

the Mongol spheres of action, the tax administration (exercised by the *bitikchis*) and application of Mongol law (by *yarghuchis*) remained vigorous and rubbed shoulders rather uncomfortably with the efforts of the Persian bureaucrats to revive their centralizing control. The executive offices seem to have remained personal, and continued to originate in the rulers' household. Power thus continued to be the prerogative of the ruler: lawmaking and arbitrariness were juxtaposed. [109]

It has not been my purpose here to argue that the Mongols were in any way unusual in exercising a form of household government, for such an establishment was, on the contrary, the norm in medieval government across Asia and Europe. Nor were they the first to do so: although we know little about the operation of Seljuk government (as opposed to its caliphal-style bureaucratic structure),[110] it is rather probable that it had many features that are also later found under the Mongols. The guard corps, argued to have been of Central Asian origin,[111] and the ruler's *khāṣṣa* were quickly institutionalized in early Islamic history, and we have only to see the carvings at Persepolis to appreciate the ancient role of the parasol holder.

Neither has my intention been to assert that the Ilkhans ran a household government, in the face of others who perhaps have believed that Mongol government took some other form. I am not aware of any such views, although the question of the origins and model for Mongol administrative organization is not closed.[112] But it is not a question here of whether the Mongols took over their forms of government from the Uighurs, or the Liao (Khitans) or Qara-Khitai, nor even from the Chinese or the Iranians. No doubt many different flavors can be distinguished in the new Mongol brew. On the whole, we are not yet sufficiently well-informed to discern, outside China at least, exactly *how* the Mongols governed; rather, it is a question here of *who* governed. I believe the answer is leaping out of the pages of Rashīd al-Dīn's chronicle: a torrent of names,

al-Dīn (1994), 1157, 1167, 1168, 1171 (executed on the fall of his patron, Buqa).

[109] Rudi Matthee's remarks (1999), 61–62, on the Safavid patrimonial state, echoed here, apply equally well to the Ilkhanate.

[110] Lambton (1968), (1988).

[111] Beckwith, C. I. (1984).

[112] Buell (1979), 124–25, 133–34; Morgan, D. (1986b), 49–50; and especially Ostrowski (1998), 271–72.

largely ignored, of people who made life very difficult for those, like him, who tried to impose a familiar order on an unfamiliar situation. The Mongols proved uncommonly reluctant to change their ways.

It is perhaps an entrenched attitude within Persian studies to see the Ilkhanate as an essentially Iranian monarchy with a few more or less exotic Mongol aspects to it, rather than the pervasively Mongol regime that it was.[113] I hope in this preliminary survey to have brought the Mongol royal household out of the shadows and to have provided evidence of its functioning as one would expect. Many topics and personalities remain to be studied in more detail, particularly the office and officers of the *yarghu*, but I hope to have laid a foundation for further research on the highly durable household establishment, which can appropriately be considered part of the long-term legacy of Genghis Khan.

[113] I am grateful to Chris Atwood for verbalizing this opinion rather more forcefully than I had done myself.

THE ARTS OF THE BOOK IN ILKHANID IRAN

CALLIGRAPHERS, ILLUMINATORS, AND PAINTERS IN THE ILKHANID SCRIPTORIUM[1]

SHEILA S. BLAIR

One of the most important artistic changes that separate the Ilkhanid period from its predecessors in Iran is the increased significance of illustrated books. In architecture, by contrast, most of the forms and building types that had been used in Seljuk times continued to be popular under the Ilkhanids. One need only compare the tomb built at Merv in the 1140s for the Seljuk Sultan Sanjar (exterior diameter twenty-seven meters) with the similar but larger (exterior diameter thirty-nine meters) tomb built a century and a half later for the Ilkhanid Sultan Öljeitü at Sultaniyya: both are massive brick octagons with galleries surrounding pointed domes decorated on the interior with carved and painted plaster.[2] Such architectural continuity was deliberate, for fourteenth-century authors mention that the Ilkhanid rulers' tombs were designed to surpass Sultan Sanjar's tomb at Merv.[3]

In book production, however, there was a major shift from Seljuk to Ilkhanid times, when illustrated books became more common,

[1] This paper was originally presented at a symposium on the Mongols and Mamluks held at Edinburgh University in the summer of 1998 and intended to be included in the conference proceedings. I thank the organizer, Professor Robert Hillenbrand, for allowing me to publish it here with other papers from the symposium on Mongol art held at the Los Angeles County Museum of Art in 2003. Many of the manuscripts discussed in this article were included in the splendid catalogue of the exhibition that was accompanied by this symposium (Komaroff and Carboni, eds., [2002]), and I have included references to their publication there.

[2] Sanjar's tomb at Merv deserves a separate monograph. Meanwhile, the ongoing joint Russian, Uzbek, and British excavations at Merv will enhance our knowledge of medieval Merv; see the interim reports published by Hermann et al. in the journal *Iran* and their picture study, Hermann et al. (2002). For Öljeitü's tomb at Sultaniyya (and Ilkhanid architecture in general), see Wilber (1955), no. 81 (citation is to the 1969 reprint edition). A full bibliography of the building has recently been compiled by Farnaz Tavakoli; Tavakoli (2002).

[3] Rashīd al-Dīn (1998), 685 mentioned, for example, that Ghazan's tomb at Tabriz, no longer extant, was meant to exceed that of Sanjar at Merv, known to the Mongols as the biggest building in the world.

they covered a wider range of subjects, and their illustrations became larger, more complex, and finer in quality.[4] One need only compare a copy of the animal fables *Kalīla wa Dimna* ascribed to thirteenth-century Iran or Anatolia (Istanbul, Topkapı Palace Museum Library H363) with the monumental copy of the *Shāhnāma* made for the Ilkhanid court in the 1330s: the diminutive manuscript of the animal fables (17 x 11 cm) contains small rectangular paintings with simple compositions set on a red ground, whereas the large (written surface 41 x 29 cm, more than six times the written area of the earlier manuscript) copy of the national epic had some two hundred paintings of varied format and style, some with stepped compositions and others containing dozens of figures.[5]

This paper addresses the questions of where, how, and by whom these deluxe books were produced in Ilkhanid Iran. Much is known about book production in later Islamic times and the scriptoria that flourished under the Timurids, Safavids, and Mughals in the fifteenth, sixteenth, and seventeenth centuries.[6] The question of the origin and development of the scriptorium in Islamic lands deserves more attention, and here I amass the evidence about how such books were made during the period of Ilkhanid rule in Iran and adjacent areas during the late thirteenth and early fourteenth centuries.

Ilkhanid manuscripts were produced in various settings. Some calligraphers probably worked independently. Muḥammad ibn Badr al-Dīn Jājarmī, for example, noted in the colophon to his copy of the *Mu'nis al-aḥrār* that he transcribed it in his native town, Isfahan, in Ramaḍān 741/February–March 1341.[7] Since the manuscript was apparently the compiler's original copy, he may well have worked at home. Safavid painters worked in the same way when preparing individual drawings and paintings. Muʿīn Muṣawwir, for example, was kept home by the heavy snows in the winter of 1082/1672 where

[4] This point is developed in Blair (1993a).

[5] For the *Kalīla wa Dimna* manuscript, see Çağman and Tanındı (1986), nos. 25–31; for the Great Mongol *Shāhnāma*, see Grabar, O. and Blair (1980); Komaroff and Carboni, eds. (2002), nos. 36–61.

[6] In general, see Porter (1994); specifically for the Timurids, see Lentz and Lowry (1989), esp. chap. 3; for the Safavids, see Simpson (1993), 105–21; and for the Mughals, see Seyller (1999).

[7] Swietochowski and Carboni (1994); Komaroff and Carboni, eds. (2002), nos. 9–10.

he drew a picture of a tiger attacking a youth, and other Safavid painters also used their residences as their studios.[8]

Jājarmī's manuscript was a modest undertaking: small in format, with six pages of simple strip-like illustrations limited to the twenty-ninth of thirty chapters and a double frontispiece that may have been added later.[9] Larger and more complex projects required a more formal setting, with a bigger bankroll to support specialists in the individual arts of calligraphy, illumination, and illustration,[10] and the largest, finest, and often multivolume manuscripts of the period were made by artists, sometimes working in teams, in more organized scriptoria. Some of these scriptoria were attached to scientific establishments, for the copying of scientific texts was essential to carry out research. Sophisticated scientific instruments were made at the Ilkhanid observatory at Maragha, the first Ilkhanid capital in northwestern Iran,[11] and scientific manuscripts were probably copied for the large library there. The celebrated astronomer Naṣīr al-Dīn al-Ṭūsī certainly used such manuscripts, although he had transcribed his autograph translation of al-Ṣūfī's book of fixed stars (Topkapı Palace Museum Library, Ayasofya 2595) a decade before the observatory was established. His personal copy, dated 647/1249–50, was evidently a prized manuscript, for it passed to the libraries of the Jalayirid Sultan Aḥmad and the Timurid Sultan Ulugh Beg.[12] Maragha remained a center of manuscript production under the Ilkhanids. A celebrated copy of Ibn Bakhtīshū''s *Manāfi'*

---

[8] Farhad (1992), 116–23.

[9] Because of the difference in style between the paintings within the manuscript and the frontispiece, which has taller figures and unusual iconographical features (such as a hat with seven plumes on the ruler's hat, *ṭirāz* bands that run vertically down his sleeve, and a lumpy gold bottle in the foreground), I have always felt that the frontispiece was added later. Stefano Carboni was kind enough to let me examine the painting when it was at the Metropolitan Museum and share with me comments from the conservator there. They suggest that the paper and pigments are the same as those used in the other paintings in the manuscript, but I still find the iconographic details troubling and wonder whether the painting was added (or reworked?) once the manuscript had found a buyer.

[10] Here, I differentiate between illumination, meaning nonfigural decoration, and illustration, meaning paintings with people.

[11] Kennedy (1968), 672. The British Museum owns a celestial globe signed by Muḥammad ibn Hilāl, the astronomer from Mosul, in the year 674/1275–76, which is traditionally assigned to Maragha. There is also one in Dresden.

[12] Çağman and Tanındı (1986), 29. On Naṣīr al-Dīn al-Ṭūsī's career under the Ilkhanids, see George Saliba's contribution to the present volume.

al-ḥayawān (New York, Pierpont Library, M500) datable to the late 690s/1290s was transcribed there.[13] So was a dispersed thirty-part Qur'ān manuscript copied in 738–39/1338–39.[14]

Sufi hospices were another site of manuscript transcription under the Ilkhanids, for Sufis, like scientists, needed manuscripts for instruction and teaching, and these flourishing establishments commissioned deluxe codices, especially of works written by members of the order. One of the richest was the Mawlawī order at Konya, which sponsored deluxe copies of the long *Mathnawī-yi ma'nawī* composed by its founder, Jalāl al-Dīn Rūmī (d. 1273). The earliest copy to survive (Konya, Mevlana Museum no. 51) is a fine manuscript finished in Rajab 677/November–December 1278.[15] Transcribed from an archetype that had been corrected and emended by the author and his assistant Ḥusām al-Dīn Chalabī, it seems to be the first clean copy of the text to survive and is elaborately decorated with twenty full or 'carpet' pages. Other Sufi orders may well have commissioned manuscripts by members of the order, but not all have survived. The Suhrawardī *khānqāh* (hospice) at Natanz, for example, was the residence of the noted Sufi 'Abd al-Razzāq al-Kāshānī, who compiled a Sufi manual and glossary of technical terms at this time.[16]

Members of Sufi *khānqāhs* also commissioned other types of deluxe manuscripts, ranging from copies of the Qur'ān to literary classics. A large thirty-part Qur'ān copied by Ḥusayn ibn Ḥasan nicknamed (*al-mulaqqab bi*) Ḥusām al-Mawlawī, whose final section (New York Public Library, Spencer Arabic ms. 3) is dated Rabī' I 734/November 1333,

---

[13] Komaroff and Carboni, eds. (2002), no. 2. According to its colophon, the Ilkhanid Sultan Ghazan ordered the work translated from Arabic to Persian and entrusted the task to the scribe 'Abd al-Hādī ibn Muḥammad ibn Maḥmūd ibn Ibrāhīm of Maragha.

[14] It was copied by 'Abdallāh ibn Aḥmad ibn Faḍlallāh ibn 'Abd al-Ḥamīd al-Qāḍī al-Qazwīnī. Komaroff and Carboni, eds. (2002), no. 66.

[15] On the manuscript, see Tanındı (1990), 17–22; Blair (2006), chap. 9. The date of the manuscript is sometimes confused. James (1992), 194 and n. 1 reported that the date 677 was a mistake for 667/1268–69, a date repeated in Ettinghausen, Grabar, and Jenkins-Madina (2001), 258. As Zeren Tanındı has kindly informed me, the colophon page is published in Abdülbâki Gölpinarli's edition of the *Mathnawī* (Gölpinarli, ed. [1981]), and the reproduction shows that the date clearly reads 677. This date is accepted by all Rūmī scholars; see Lewis, F. (2000), 307–9.

[16] For the *khānqāh*, see Blair (1986a); for a recent English translation of 'Abd al-Razzāq's glossary, see al-Qāshānī, 'Abd al-Razzāq (1991). The translation gives no information about the earliest surviving manuscripts, as the translator and editor were working from two published editions.

was probably calligraphed by a Mawlawī Sufi at Konya.[17] A copy of the *Shāhnāma* (Cairo, Dar al-Kutub 6006) transcribed by Muḥammad ibn Muḥammad ibn Muḥammad al-Kīshī in 740/1340–41 was made for Urghun Shamsī Kārimī Kāzarūnī. The patron was presumably a *shaykh* in the Kāzarūniyya, the Sufi order that had developed in southern Iran around the tomb of Shaykh Abū Isḥāq (d. 1034). Like the observatory at Maragha, these *khānqāh*s were sufficiently independent to mint their own coins.[18] They also issued decrees stamped with their seals.[19] The Kāzarūnī shrine in Shiraz continued to be a major patron of books into Safavid times, and illustrated manuscripts made there in the early sixteenth century often contain paintings with tall tiled buildings presumably meant to represent the shrine.[20]

The most famous and most productive Ilkhanid scriptoria, especially for illustrated manuscripts, were those established by the historian and vizier Rashīd al-Dīn.[21] These scriptoria were located not only in his tomb complex at Tabriz known as the Rabʿ-i Rashīdī, but also in the pious foundations he established at Sultaniyya, Hamadan, and Yazd as well as those established by Sultan Ghazan at Baghdad and Tabriz and overseen by Rashīd al-Dīn. The vizier ordered manuscripts at least from 705/1305, for the Mamluk chronicler Ibn al-Fuwaṭī (d. 1323) reported that in that year he had met the designer Muḥammad ibn al-ʿAfīf al-Kāshī while he was working on the book of his master and vizier Rashīd al-Dīn.[22] To judge from dated manuscripts

---

[17] See Schmitz (1992), no. V.8; Blair and Bloom (1994), fig. 187. The scribe's name and epithet suggest that he belonged to the Mawlawī order, which was concentrated in Anatolia and had only a few outposts elsewhere. In addition to stylistic evidence, the attribution to Anatolia is strengthened by a later owner's marks in Turkish saying that the volume belonged to a member of a Turkish brotherhood.

[18] Blair (1982), 225–27.

[19] See the example dated 851/1448 stamped with an earlier seal dated 757/1356; Soudavar (1992), no. 28. For an example of such a seal, see Komaroff and Carboni, eds. (2002), no. 167.

[20] Çağman and Tanındı (2002), 43–48.

[21] For a brief biography of his political career and an assessment of his role as a historian, see Morgan, D. (1994). It would be interesting to see whether Rashīd al-Dīn served as model for other patrons like Qiwām al-Dīn Shīrāzī, vizier to the Īnjū governors of Shiraz and patron of at least one copy of the *Shāhnāma* in 741/1341; see Simpson (2000), 217–48.

[22] Ibn al-Fuwaṭī (1962–65), pt. 1, 528, no. 728 cited in Blair (1984), 82 and

produced in these scriptoria and the evidence offered by contemporary chronicles, these scriptoria became increasingly active over the next several decades. The text of the endowment (*waqfiyya*) to the Rabʿ-i Rashīdī, dated Rabīʿ I 709/August 1309, stipulated that every year calligraphers were to produce two multipart manuscripts (a thirty-volume copy of the Qurʾān and a four-volume work on Traditions [*Ḥadīth*]) for the manuscript repository there.[23] Production soon increased, for an addendum to the endowment dated Dhū al-ḥijja 713/March 1314 stipulated that copies of Rashīd al-Dīn's own works also be copied yearly.[24] Following the vizier's execution on 18 Jumādā I 718/17 July 1318, his estates were reportedly plundered, but the scriptorium was revived after his son Ghiyāth al-Dīn assumed the vizierate in 728/1328, and several important manuscripts have been attributed to his patronage there in the 1330s.[25]

At least nine surviving manuscripts can be associated with Rashīd al-Dīn and his scriptoria. The manuscripts divide into the two categories mentioned in the endowment deed to the Rabʿ-i Rashīdī and its addendum: five copies of the vizier's own works and four Qurʾān manuscripts. Parts from three manuscripts of the vizier's universal history or *Jāmiʿ al-tawārīkh* (Compendium of Chronicles) prepared under his supervision survive: an Arabic copy dated 714/1314–15 divided between Edinburgh University Library and the Nour Collection, London; and two Persian copies in the Topkapı Palace Museum Library, Istanbul (H1653 and H1654), dated late Jumādā II 714/October 1314 and 3 Jumādā I 717/14 July 1317, respectively.[26] Two

n. 79 and in a different version in Ivanov (2000), 147–50. Also see DeWeese's contribution to this volume.

[23] Rashīd al-Dīn (1978), 133–34.

[24] Blair (1984), 81–82; Rashīd al-Dīn (1978), 237–38. The section from the addendum is translated by Wheeler M. Thackston in Blair (1995), Appendix I, 114–15.

[25] The most famous is the Great Mongol *Shāhnāma* (Grabar, O. and Blair [1980], chap. 4); Cowen (1989) also attributed a superb copy of the *Kalīla wa Dimna* animal fables dismembered and remounted in the Yildiz album in Istanbul (University Library F1422) to Ghiyāth al-Dīn's patronage, but her attribution is not generally accepted.

[26] The reconstructed Arabic manuscript and the two Persian copies are discussed in Blair (1995), *Compendium*, chap. 1. The first Persian one (H1653), with a colophon on folio 375 at the end of the section on the Fatimids and Nizaris saying that the section was completed at the end of Jumādā II, 714/October 1314, is bound together with replacement pages transcribed by the Timurid historian Ḥāfiẓ-i Abrū in Muḥarram 829/November 1425. The second Persian copy (H1654)

copies of the vizier's theological works entitled *Majmūʿa al-rashīdiyya* also survive: one in Paris (Bibliothèque Nationale, arabe 2324) finished in the months of 710/1310–11 and another in Qatar copied by the same calligrapher at Tabriz between Shaʿbān and Ramaḍān 711/December 1311–February 1312 (pl. 9).[27]

Four thirty-volume manuscripts of the Qurʾān can also be connected with Rashīd al-Dīn. David James brought the first one to scholarly attention: a *juzʾ* from a manuscript copied for the vizier's treasury (*khizāna*) in Ṣafar 715/April 1315 (Istanbul, Topkapı Palace Museum Library EH 248).[28] According to the certificate of commissioning, it was copied by ʿAbdallāh ibn Abī al-Qāsim ibn ʿAbdallāh al-Tuwī al-Rūdrawarī, a calligrapher who apparently hailed from the small town of Tuwi in the Rudrawar district south of Hamadan, Rashīd al-Dīn's hometown.

The second Qurʾān manuscript made in Rashīd al-Dīn's scriptoria is a large (56 x 41 cm) thirty-volume manuscript now in the National Library in Cairo (ms. 72). According to the colophon, it was copied and illuminated by ʿAbdallāh ibn Muḥammad ibn Maḥmūd al-Ḥamadānī in Jumādā I 713/September 1313 at Hamadan, and hence James called it the Hamadan Qurʾān.[29] The colophon specifies that the calligrapher worked there in the *dār al-khayrāt al-rashīdiyya*,

is more complete. Assuming that two copies, one in Arabic and one in Persian, were produced yearly in the scriptorium at Tabriz in the four years between the date of the addendum (1314) and the vizier's death (1318), then a total of eight manuscripts would have been commissioned. Three survive, not a bad rate. There are also individual paintings that were probably detached from volume one of the universal history and now mounted in albums in Istanbul and Berlin (see Rührdanz [1997], 295–306 and Komaroff and Carboni, eds. [2002], nos. 17–32).

[27] My thanks to Francis Richard, who provided detailed notes about the Paris manuscript. It is also published in Richard, F. (1997), no. 12, and Komaroff and Carboni, eds. (2002), no. 5. The Paris manuscript was clearly prepared for Rashīd al-Dīn himself, for the final page (376b) is twice stamped with the seal of his library. Richard, F. (1982), 343–46, also found the same seal on another manuscript in the Bibliothèque Nationale, a copy of Qāḍī Sirāj al-Dīn Maḥmūd ibn Abī Bakr Ādharbāyjānī's *Laṭāʾif al-ḥikma*, completed by Abū Muḥammad Muḥammad ibn Maḥmūd ibn al-Ḥājjī, known as Ḥāmid al-Mukhlaṣī al-Bukhārī, at Konya on 4 Dhū al-ḥijja 684/31 January 1286. The Qatar copy of Rashīd al-Dīn's theological works was purchased at auction from Christie's on 13 October 1998; see Christie's, London (1998), lot 55.

[28] James (1988), no. 46.

[29] Ibid., no. 45. One of the frontispieces is published in Komaroff and Carboni, eds. (2002), fig. 251.

referring not to 'the abode of orthodoxy' as James first translated the phrase, but to the pious foundation established by Rashīd al-Dīn.[30] The calligrapher's place of work explains similarities between this manuscript of the Qur'ān and the one made for Rashīd al-Dīn two years later: regular pages in both manuscripts have five lines of *muḥaqqaq* script surrounded by a border and blue panels.

A third copy of the Qur'ān that can be connected to Rashīd al-Dīn is a dispersed manuscript that James dubbed the anonymous Baghdad Qur'ān.[31] It was transcribed at Baghdad by the renowned calligrapher Aḥmad ibn al-Suhrawardī between 701 and 707 (1302–8). No patron is mentioned, but on formal and stylistic grounds this manuscript is comparable to the two other Qur'ān manuscripts associated with Rashīd al-Dīn. Not only does it have the same general size and format as the other Qur'ān manuscripts (five lines of script on a page 50 x 35 cm), but more specifically, the frontispiece to the second *juz'* has pentagons decorated with scrolls sprouting five tendrils,[32] a feature found only in the Hamadan Qur'ān. James attributed the anonymous manuscript to Öljeitü's patronage, because he thought that the sultan was responsible for three other multipart manuscripts of the Qur'ān. Given the reattribution of the Hamadan Qur'ān, made for Öljeitü but at Rashīd al-Dīn's pious foundation, his assumption is no longer valid and a connection to Rashīd al-Dīn more likely. He is known to have supervised Ghazan's pious foundations in Baghdad and had fine manuscripts read aloud there. It is more probable, therefore, that the anonymous Baghdad copy of the Qur'ān, perhaps begun for Ghazan, was continued under Rashīd al-Dīn.

Rashīd al-Dīn was also involved in the production of a fourth thirty-volume manuscript of the Qur'ān, called by James the Mosul Qur'ān after the place it was transcribed (fig. 23).[33] It was copied between 706 and 710 (1306–11) by the Shi'ite calligrapher 'Alī ibn Muḥammad ibn Zayd ibn Muḥammad ibn Zayd, who proudly enumerates his genealogy all the way back to the Prophet's son-in-law

[30] Corrected in James (1999).

[31] James (1988), no. 39. Two folios from the manuscript are published in Komaroff and Carboni, eds. (2002), nos. 63–64.

[32] Istanbul, Topkapı Palace Museum Library, EH 250, illuminated in Ramaḍān 702/April 1303; see James (1988), 91 and fig. 58.

[33] Ibid., no. 42. Two folios are published in Komaroff and Carboni, eds. (2002), nos. 65.

ʿAlī ibn Abī Ṭālib. Certificates appended to the front of each *juz*ʾ mention that the manuscript was transcribed for Sultan Öljeitü under the auspices of the co-viziers Rashīd al-Dīn and Saʿd al-Dīn Sawajī. James noted how unusual it was to mention viziers in the certificate of commissioning. They may have been in charge of payment and also supervised the uniformity and quality of the large project.

All the manuscripts prepared for Rashīd al-Dīn, both his own works and the multipart copies of the Qurʾān, share several features. All are codices, and they therefore differ from the scrolls used for official correspondence. A few such scrolls have survived, including an edict (*farmān*) issued by the Ilkhanid ruler Geikhatu in 692/1292.[34] Many are depicted in contemporary manuscript paintings, including detached folios probably from a contemporary copy of the first volume of Rashīd al-Dīn's history.[35] Scrolls are also shown in scenes illustrating the reigns of mythical Persian kings and Seljuk sultans in the Arabic copy of Rashīd al-Dīn's Universal History[36] as well as in a painting of Nūshirwān dictating a letter to his scribe for the *khāqān* of China detached from the Great Mongol *Shāhnāma* (pl. 10).[37] Such scrolls represent a long chancellery tradition in Iran.

By contrast, books are depicted in Ilkhanid paintings as codices. Some with flaps represent manuscripts of the Qurʾān or other sacred texts. The scene of Muḥammad's ascension in the Arabic copy of Rashīd al-Dīn's history shows Muḥammad astride the miraculous steed Burāq who offers an attending angel a thick manuscript with a flap, obviously intended as a Qurʾān manuscript.[38] The painting in the same manuscript illustrating the story of Joshua ordering the property taken at Jericho to be destroyed shows the Prophet in front of a red lacquered table supporting a codex with a flap, again intended to represent a holy book.[39]

Codices without flaps in Ilkhanid paintings often represent secular

---

[34] Art and History Trust collection on loan to the Sackler Gallery, Smithsonian Institution, Washington, D.C.; see Soudavar (1992), no. 9; Komaroff and Carboni, eds. (2002), no. 68.

[35] Çağman and Tanındı (1986), pl. 43.

[36] See, for example, Rice, D. T. (1976), nos. 4, 16, 65, and 66.

[37] Dublin, Chester Beatty Library ms. 111; Grabar, O. and Blair (1980), no. 57; Komaroff and Carboni, eds. (2002), no. 60.

[38] Rice, D. T. (1976), no. 36.

[39] Ibid., no. 14.

books. The compilers of the *Rasā'il Ikhwān al-Ṣafā'* hold flapless codices in the frontispiece to a copy transcribed at Baghdad in 686/1287 (pls. 11–12).[40] Similarly, in the Arabic copy of the universal history, a sage proffers a flapless book to king Hūshang to illustrate the text about the king of the world composing a book of maxims.[41] In another detached illustration presumably from vol. 1 of the Universal History, the Mongol figure to the right of the enthroned sultan and his consort holds a flapless book in his lap.[42]

Nevertheless, the distinction between flapped and flapless codices does not hold absolutely for depictions of religious and secular manuscripts. In another detached painting from the Universal History, presumably representing a mobile tent mosque, seated figures study flapless codices open on wooden stands, presumably representing Qur'ān manuscripts set on *raḥla*s.[43] Similarly, a female attendant holds a large flapped book on an inlaid candlestick with the name and titles of Abū Isḥāq, Injuid ruler of Shiraz (r. 1343–53).[44]

In addition to the codex format, the manuscripts made for Rashīd al-Dīn also share similar physical characteristics. They are all large, measuring approximately 50 x 36 cm, with bifolios measuring 72 x 50 cm. These sheets of paper conform to the half-*baghdādī* size described by the Mamluk chronicler al-Qalqashandī.[45] The same large-size sheets were also used in the first surviving copy of Rūmī's *Mathnawī*, suggesting that such innovations as new sizes of paper and even the medium itself may have moved from the secular to the religious domain. All the Qur'ān manuscripts associated with Rashīd

[40] Istanbul, Süleymaniye Library, Esad Efendi 2916. Ettinghausen (1976), 98–99; Komaroff and Carboni, eds. (2002), fig. 253. Also see Hillenbrand's contribution to this volume.

[41] Rice, D. T. (1976), no. 3.

[42] Çağman and Tanındı (1986), pl. 44. The distinction in scroll and codex in the two detached paintings presumably from the same manuscript (Çağman and Tanındı [1986], pls. 43–44) may help us distinguish which parts of the text they illustrate in the way that Rührdanz (1997) has used other significant features of the detached illustrations to connect them to incidents in the text.

[43] Diez A fol. 70, S. 8; Komaroff and Carboni, eds. (2002), no. 31. Also see pl. 15 and fig. 32 in the present volume for examples in other manuscripts.

[44] Museum of Islamic Art, Doha; Komaroff and Carboni, eds. (2002), no. 162. The roundel with the figure holding the flapped book is not visible in the illustration there, but can be seen in the one in Komaroff (1994), 10c. I thank Linda Komaroff, who presciently brought this example to my attention.

[45] On paper, see Bloom (2001) and the same author's article in this volume.

al-Dīn also have fine illumination, with double frontispieces to the separate volumes of the Qur'ān manuscripts. The manuscripts thus fit the specifications laid out by Rashīd al-Dīn in his endowment deed for neat script on good *baghdādī* paper, careful collation with the original that was kept in the library at the Rab'-i Rashīdī, and goatskin binding.

Despite their similarities, there is a clear distinction between the manuscripts of the Qur'ān and the other texts prepared for Rashīd al-Dīn. The manuscripts of the Qur'ān are meticulously and spaciously written with five lines of *muḥaqqaq* script spread out on the large pages. The care with which they are penned is matched by the lavish use of gold, often for opening pages in gold script outlined in black. By contrast, the manuscripts of Rashīd al-Dīn's own works have thirty or more lines per page and are written in a readable and clear but not beautiful *naskh*. They too are copiously illuminated, but with cheaper pigments and less gold.

The distinct physical format confirms the attribution of similar manuscripts to Rashīd al-Dīn's patronage. An anthology of poetry in the India Office Library (Ethé 903, 911, 913 and 1028), for example, may have been prepared for the vizier.[46] Copied by 'Abd al-Mu'mīn al-'Alawī al-Kāshī between Dhū al-qa'da 713 and Dhū al-qa'da 714 (February 1314–February 1315), it has thirty-nine lines of *naskh* written in six columns within a written area measuring 36.5 x 25.5 cm, the same written area used in the other secular manuscripts prepared for Rashīd al-Dīn between 1310 and 1315—the theological treatises and the Arabic and the first Persian copies of the *Jāmi' al-tawārīkh.*

What about the calligraphers and painters who worked in Rashīd al-Dīn's scriptoria? The best-known information about Ilkhanid calligraphers and artists is that recorded by the sixteenth-century chronicler Dūst Muḥammad in the preface to the album he prepared for the Safavid prince Bahrām Mīrzā in 951/1544 (Istanbul, Topkapı Palace Museum Library H2154).[47] The chronicler listed the six famous calligraphers who were followers of Yāqūt al-Musta'ṣimī (d. c. 1298),[48] but gave the name of only one artist active in the Ilkhanid period: Aḥmad Mūsā, who worked during the reign of the Sultan

---

[46] Robinson (1976), nos. 1–53; Komaroff and Carboni, eds. (2002), no. 8.
[47] The preface is published and translated in Thackston (2001), 4–17.
[48] On the problem of identifying Yāqūt's followers, see Blair (2003), 39–47.

Abū Saʿīd (1316–35). The chronicler noted that the painter studied with his father, suggesting that painters, at least by late Ilkhanid times, resembled other craftsmen by working in families.[49] Dūst Muḥammad's evidence about Ilkhanid painters cannot be expanded from signatures, for the first signed painting to survive dates only from the very end of the fourteenth century.[50]

The endowment deed to the Rabʿ-i Rashīdī supplies more information about calligraphers and artists who worked at the beginning of the fourteenth century. The overseer of the endowment was to appoint calligraphers with good legible hands and assign them suitable space to work in the pious foundation. These crafts were not particularly high-status jobs, for calligraphy (*khaṭṭāṭ*), painting (*naqqāshī*), and gilding (*zargarī*), along with farming and conduit-digging, were among the trades assigned to the 220 slaves in the complex.[51] Of the twenty Turkish slaves whose names were given, one named Qutlugh Būqaʿ was called 'the painter' (*naqqāsh*) to distinguish him from two other slaves with the identical name, but such epithets of size, nationality, or profession were added merely to differentiate slaves of the same name.

Signatures in surviving manuscripts also provide information about the people who worked in Rashīd al-Dīn's scriptoria and how they worked. Calligraphers often worked in teams with illuminators and illustrators, and many manuscripts are signed by two people. The clean copy of Rūmī's *Mathnawī*, for example, was copied by Muḥammad ibn ʿAbdallāh al-Qunyawī al-Walīdī and illuminated by Mukhliṣ ibn ʿAbdallāh al-Hindī. Similarly, the anonymous Baghdad Qurʾān was copied by Aḥmad ibn al-Suhrawardī and illuminated by Muḥammad ibn Aybak ibn ʿAbdallāh. The same type of team executed the theological treatise in Paris. The calligrapher Muḥammad ibn Maḥmūd ibn Muḥammad al-Amīn known as *zūd-niwīs al-baghdādī* ('the speedy writer from Baghdad') signed the colophon and

[49] The same was true, for example, for stucco workers; see the present author's article on the Dāmghānī family; Blair (1993c).

[50] Junayd's depiction of 'Humāy and Humāyūn on the Day after their Wedding' in the copy of Khwājū Kirmānī's collected poems transcribed by Mīr ʿAlī ibn Ilyās al-Tabrīzī for the Jalayirid Sultan Aḥmad at Baghdad in Jumādā I, 798/March 1396 (London, British Library, Add. ms. 18113, fol. 45b; color illustration in Blair and Bloom [1994], pl. 38).

[51] Rashīd al-Dīn (1978), 151; Blair (1984), 80.

the right page of the double frontispiece, while the humble servant Muḥammad ibn al-ʿAfīf al-Kāshī signed the left page. Muḥammad ibn al-ʿAfīf was clearly the better artist, for the work on the left page is finer and more regular. He was also the better known artist, for he is mentioned by the Mamluk chronicler Ibn al-Fuwaṭī in his biographical dictionary, [*Talkhīṣ*] *Majmaʿ al-ādāb fī muʿjam al-alqāb*. Muḥammad ibn al-ʿAfīf was not only an illuminator but also an illustrator, for Ibn al-Fuwaṭī described him as a master skilled and adroit in the arts of design and illustration (*ustādh ḥādhiq mahīr fī ṣanʿat al-naqsh wa al-taṣwīr*).[52]

Looking at manuscripts also helps us distinguish the work of different hands. Comparing the two sides of double frontispieces, for example, often shows slight variations and changes in scale that suggest one side was copied from the other. The Mosul Qurʾān (fig. 23), for example, is signed by a single copyist, ʿAlī ibn Muḥammad ibn Zayd, but Martin Lings and Yasin Safadi's examination of the double frontispiece to *juzʾ* 25 in the British Library (Or. 4945) showed that the right page is more brilliant than the left.[53] The decoration on the right side is also slightly larger in scale. A similar distinction appears in the Hamadan Qurʾān, despite the fact that the colophon states that it was both copied and illuminated by ʿAbdallāh ibn Muḥammad ibn Maḥmūd al-Hamadānī. Scrutiny by Michael Rogers showed that the right half of the opening double frontispiece to *juzʾ* 23 is finer than the left half, which may have been the work of an assistant.[54]

Extant manuscripts also give us an idea of how long it took the calligraphers and artists to complete these deluxe books. The longest interval was the six years needed for Aḥmad ibn al-Suhrawardī to pen and Muḥammad ibn Aybak to illuminate the anonymous Baghdad Qurʾān. The dates in the colophons to each individual *juzʾ* (from Ramaḍān 702/April 1303 to 707/1307–8) suggest that the two worked in tandem, and the long time required to complete this fine manuscript may have been necessitated by the fine quality of the calligraphy and the rich illumination. Copying the Mosul

[52] See n. 22, above.
[53] Lings and Safadi (1976), 68. The frontispiece is illustrated in Lings (1976), pl. 25, but the plate is reversed.
[54] Notes made in 1976 for the organizers of the Qurʾān exhibition at the British Library, cited in James (1988), 116, n. 12.

Qur'ān took almost as long (five years), but that manuscript is distinguished by an unusual gap in copying: each surviving *juz'* from the first half of the manuscript is dated to the year 706/1306–7), whereas those from the second half are all dated to different months of 710/1310–11. ʿAlī ibn Muḥammad was apparently a fast worker and could copy some fifteen large *juz'*s within a year. James suggested that he then stopped copying and turned to illumination (with his helper) in the intervening three years.[55] The theological treatise in Paris was also transcribed over a four-year period with a gap in the middle, judging from the colophons at the end of different epistles. The one on folio 56b, for example, says that the *dībācha* was finished by the calligrapher in the middle of Jumādā II 707/December 1306, while others on folios 99b, 144b, 160b, and 376b date his work to 710/1310–11. These teams of artists, therefore, probably worked on several projects simultaneously and often broke off work on one to turn to another.

The text and addendum to Rashīd al-Dīn's endowment stipulate that manuscripts be copied yearly, but the surviving manuscripts of the *Jāmiʿ al-tawārīkh* suggest that this stipulation was overly optimistic.[56] The Arabic copy, with a date of 714/1314–15, was apparently fully illustrated before the scriptorium was disrupted in 718/1318, but the illustrators were apparently under some pressure as the paintings towards the end of the manuscript become more simplified. Production of the first Persian copy (H1653) lagged. Although one section of the text was completed at the end of Jumādā II 714/October 1314, the illustrations were never finished and those at the end of the history of the Turks (from folio 384 onwards) were added only when the manuscript was refurbished under the Timurid Sultan Shāhrūkh.[57] Presumably there was not enough time to compete the manuscript before the vizier's death. The backlog worsened by the time of the second Persian copy (H1654). According to the colophon, copying was finished on 3 Jumādā I 717/14 July 1317, but only the first three illustrations were painted before Rashīd al-Dīn's execution a year later.[58]

---

[55] Ibid., 101.
[56] For further details, see Blair (1995), chap. 3.
[57] Inal (1965), 45–50.
[58] Inal (1963).

Contemporary texts provide only general information about where these scriptoria were located. According to the text of Rashīd al-Dīn's endowment, his library (*dār al-maṣāḥif*) was located in one of the rooms near his tomb and the mosques in the main section (*rawḍa*) of the tomb complex. According to the addendum, the superintendent was to assign the copyists chambers in the Rabʿ-i Rashīdī from among those rooms stipulated for people and tasks. Before the establishment of the Rabʿ-i Rashīdī, however, some calligraphers and artists moved with the royal camp, for Ibn al-Fuwaṭī's encounter with the painter Muḥammad ibn al-ʿAfīf took place in Arran, Sultan Öljeitü's winter camp.

We can suggest further details about the furnishings in Rashīd al-Dīn's scriptoria by comparison to a medieval European scriptorium for a comparable community, the Monastery of St. Gall. The complex comprised a great church for the rule of St. Benedict, surrounded by buildings for the monastic community. It was designed to serve some 270 souls, including 110 monks, and the rest lay followers. The monastic community was thus about the same size as the Rabʿ-i Rashīdī (which had more than 300 employees), but had a larger professional staff. The plan of the monastery has been reconstructed from a unique copy traced on five pieces of calfskin sewn together to form a parchment drawing surface 113 x 78 cm and prepared c. 820–23 from a lost original.[59]

The scriptorium at St. Gall was located on the ground floor below the library and was entered from the north transept. The library in the Rabʿ-i Rashīdī was likewise situated in a convenient location near the mosque and tomb, places in which the manuscripts were used for prayer and recitation. The St. Gall scriptorium contained seven tables for calligraphers along the north and east walls, a large table with shelving racks in the center, and benches along the west and south walls. Walter Horn and Ernest Born pointed out the unusual posture of calligraphers using these desks. Scribes in the early Christian period presumably wrote while holding books in their laps,[60] whereas representations from the ninth and tenth centuries show seated calligraphers with their books supported on lecterns. Scribes

[59] Horn and Born (1979).

[60] They cite the example of the Prophet Ezra, who was depicted this way in the Codex Amiatinus, an early eighth-century Hiberno-Saxon manuscript based on an Italo-Christian prototype of the sixth century.

at the St. Gall scriptorium, however, used solid supports necessitated by the growing popularity of deluxe codices.[61]

Such a situation did not hold in the Islamic lands. The addendum to Rashīd al-Dīn's endowment stipulated spaces for seated calligraphers, and representations of scribes made in Ilkhanid times show artists seated and writing in their laps.[62] Calligraphers and painters are depicted in the same position in later examples such as Muʿīn's famous portrait of his teacher Riḍā done in 1084/1673.[63] Despite the large size of the manuscripts prepared for Rashīd al-Dīn, then, calligraphers and artists in his scriptoria probably did not switch to desks like the ones used at St. Gall. It was probably not only the paucity of wood that made such an innovation unlikely, but also the nature of the support. The papers made in the Ilkhanid domains were some of the finest ever produced, made of smoothly beaten pulp and polished to a high sheen. The reed pen therefore glided over the surface more easily than the quill used on the calfskins at St. Gall, and hence scribes could write easily without propping the writing surface on solid supports.

Many of the practices established at this scriptorium served as models in the royal scriptoria established later in the Iranian lands, especially in Jalayirid and Timurid times when there was a deliberate hearkening back to Ilkhanid traditions and a revival of such canonical figures as the Baghdadi calligrapher Yāqūt al-Mustaʿṣimī.[64] Many other questions, however, remain to be investigated to show how the deluxe books prepared in these scriptoria became an important means of artistic endeavor in the Ilkhanid period. What models did the calligraphers and artists have at hand? How were illustrations transferred from one manuscript to another copy of the same text—by pounces, from pattern books, or simply by imitation? How were the motifs and images disseminated to other media? The answers to these questions may then help us understand other developments in later scriptoria, particularly in the Persian-speaking lands.

---

[61] Horn and Born (1986).

[62] See, for example, the double-page frontispiece depicting the compilers of the *Rasāʾil ikhwān al-ṣafāʾ*; see above, n. 40.

[63] Princeton University Library, Garrett Collection; color illustration in Blair and Bloom (1994), fig. 225. For other portraits of seated artists from Turkish and Mughal albums, see Atıl (1990), figs. 29–30 and no. 79.

[64] On this revivalism in book practices, see Blair (2003).

ERUDITION EXALTED: THE DOUBLE FRONTISPIECE TO THE EPISTLES OF THE SINCERE BRETHREN

ROBERT HILLENBRAND

The two paintings to be discussed in this paper (pls. 11–12) mark the end of an era. Painted in Madinat al-Salam (Baghdad) in Shawwāl 686/November 1287, they introduce[1] a copy of an early Abbasid text from Basra commonly known by its short title: *Rasā'il Ikhwān al-Ṣafā'*. The manuscript is preserved in the Library of the Süleymaniye Mosque in Istanbul (Esad Efendi 3638).[2] The text is a kind of Shi'ite encyclopedia;[3] in early medieval times, some parts of southern Iraq had strong Shi'ite loyalties, or a tendency to oppose the ruling authority.[4] The work was a composite enterprise, and the five authors are duly identified on the first leaf of the frontispiece, fol. 3 verso, above the image (pl. 12). The phrasing of this text is sufficiently curious to be worth noting: "It has been handed down from the *Tatimma Ṣiwān al-Ḥikma* to Ẓāhir al-Dīn Abū al-Qāsim al-Bayhaqī that five of the wise men assembled and they compiled *The Epistles of the Brethren of Purity*. And they were Abū Sulaymān Muḥammad b. Mis'ar al-Bustī known as al-Maqdisī,[5] and Abū al-Ḥasan 'Alī b. Zahrūn[6] al-Zanjānī and Abū Aḥmad al-Nahrajūrī and al-'Awfī and

---

[1] After a preface which extends from fol. 1 recto to fol. 3 recto; Farès (1957), 78.

[2] The most convenient publication of these leaves is that by R. Ettinghausen (1962), 98–103 with three color plates. The fullest publication is that by Farès (see n. 1, above), 78–86.

[3] Marquet (1971), 1073–75.

[4] E.g., H. Djait describes Shi'ism as "the quasi-unique ideology" of Kufa at the end of the ninth century; Djait (1986), 359.

[5] The name appears somewhat differently as "Abū Sulaymān Muḥammad b. Ma'shar al-Ḳudsī al-Bustī, who, according to Abū Sulaymān al-Manṭiḳī, was the author of the *rasā'il* of the Ikhwān al-Ṣafā'"; Goitein (1986), 330a. Yet the text in the Istanbul manuscript clearly has *sīn,* not *shīn,* in the father's name, and reverses the order of the two *nisbas*, while clarifying the distinction between Muḥammad's place of origin and his commonly used name.

[6] Marquet (1971), 1071, gives this name as Hārūn, while Ettinghausen has Zahrān with a long *alif;* but the name is clearly written as Zahrūn with a long *wāw*. Ettinghausen's transcription ([1962], 100) has several minor errors.

Zayd b. Rifāʿa. And the editor of the book was al-Maqdisī." So the scholar who was mentioned first in the list of the five authors and is thus specially honored (and is further singled out by being given his full name, with *kunya*, patronymic, *ism* and *laqab*, plus the name by which he was commonly known—al-Maqdisī) clearly stands out from among his colleagues. The corresponding space above the painting on fol. 4 recto bears the full (rhyming) title of the work: *Rasāʾil Ikhwān al-Ṣafāʾ wa khullān al-wafāʾ* (*The Epistles of the Brethren of Purity and the Friends of Loyalty*) (pl. 11). From the outset, then, the reader is made aware by means of both writing and image that this is a work of multiple authorship. Whether these men were Ismāʿīlīs has been a matter of some contention, as has the identity and number of the authors themselves.[7]

The two paintings, both measuring 20.5 x 18 cm, are meant to be read together. They constitute a double frontispiece, a format which was indeed known in the Byzantine world, but which Arab painters in the thirteenth century made very much their own. Indeed, they tossed off a succession of strikingly original variations on this neglected theme. Sometimes these double frontispieces worked by repetition, with two virtually identical images on facing pages,[8] much in the style of so many Qurʾānic frontispieces.[9] In other cases the artists, as will shortly appear, struck out in a more radical way.[10] The two

[7] Marquet (1971), 1071–76; see also Stern (1964), 405–28; idem (1946–47).

[8] Some of these double frontispieces, such as those of the Paris *Kitāb al-diryāq* of 595/1199 (Farès [1953], pls. 3–4), or of the undated but probably early thirteenth-century *Mukhtār al-ḥikam wa maḥāsin al-kalim* (*The Choicest Maxims and Best Sayings*) of al-Mubashshir (Ettinghausen [1962], 75; see my figs. 24–25) are so similar that the immediate visual impression that they give is that they are identical. In the *Kitāb al-diryāq* the principal differences between the two halves of the double frontispiece are confined to details of dress and of the set of the head. The same goes for the *Mukhtār al-ḥikam*; in this manuscript, moreover, there is a double finispiece whose design is closely related to that of the frontispiece (fig. 26). I am grateful to Dr. Elizabeth Lambourn for lending me her slides of these images, and to Dr. Jaclynne J. Kerner for allowing me to reproduce her slides in this volume.

[9] An early example is the double geometric frontispiece of the Qurʾān of Ibn al-Bawwāb, made in Baghdad and dated 391/1000–1, fols. 8v–9r, which themselves follow two successive pairs of decorative openings in which writing figures prominently (fols. 6v–7r and 7v–8r); after the end of the text there is a double geometric finispiece (fols. 284v–285r), followed by another double decorative opening with multiple lines of writing on each leaf. See, for illustrations of these double-page compositions, Rice, D. S. (1955), pls. 1–5.

[10] Here again, Qurʾāns showed the way: see the double frontispiece of the

Rasā'il leaves under discussion conclude the creative evolution of the Arab frontispiece. As such, they are a marker for the astonishingly rapid rise, flowering, and decline of Arab painting itself. And it all happened in well under a century. This is not to say that Arab painting was finished after 1287. But in the matter of frontispiece design,[11] it marched backwards vigorously. Conventional wisdom has long held that Arab painting as a whole went into permanent decline in the fourteenth century,[12] though the occasional dissenting voice has been raised.[13]

And, by a telling coincidence, just as the Arab frontispiece ran out of steam, the Persian frontispiece, which was destined to have a much longer history, made its debut. The leaves that introduce the Paris copy of Juwaynī's *History of the World Conqueror*, dated 1290 (pl. 13), are infinitely less knowing and subtle than the *Rasā'il* leaves; they have only three figures and their landscape is more cerebral than real (fig. 27).[14] But they carry the seed of a rich future. For that, they have China to thank. And China was essentially a closed book to Arab painters. Yet the Paris frontispiece is transitional in more ways than in its hesitant experiments with a visual vocabulary derived from the Far East. For it looks both backwards and forwards in its subject matter. Backwards in that the principal seated figure, the vizier Juwaynī, is an author portrait, which thus taps into an already millennial tradition whose earliest surviving traces are to be found in late classical times in Rome,[15] and which was then taken up enthusiastically in both Western[16] and Eastern[17] Christianity for

luxury Qur'ān in San'a' attributed by Graf von Bothmer to the Umayyad period (von Bothmer [1987], color pls. 1–2).

[11] See, for example, the frontispiece of Ibn Ẓafar's *Sulwān al-muṭā' fī 'udwān al-atbā'*, datable to the first half of the fourteenth century, in the color facsimile edition (Ibn Ẓafar [1995]), fols. 1v–2r.

[12] Ettinghausen (1962), 179; Ward (1996), 16, 311.

[13] See the arguments presented, on the basis of the Ibn Ẓafar manuscript, by A. S. Melikian-Chirvani (1985), xi–xiii and 166–68.

[14] Richard, F. (1997), 41.

[15] Weitzmann (1977), 11 and figs. II (the *Vergilius Romanus*) and VIII (a Carolingian copy of a fifth-century Terence manuscript).

[16] Friend (1929); Nees (1987), 83 ff.

[17] Friend (1927). Some of these formulaic images made their way into other media, for example ivories; see a probably Egyptian example of the sixth century in which the figure, dressed in tunic and *pallium*, and holding a book in the crook of his arm, strides illusionistically out of a picture space defined by a knotted curtain (Weitzmann, ed. [1979], 542–43, no. 487).

evangelist portraits. But this frontispiece also looks forwards in that Juwaynī, as Ṣāḥib-i Dīwān (the title inscribed, probably later, beside his image), was—after the Mongol Ilkhan himself—the most powerful man in the land. So this is also a ruler portrait, and in that sense the Paris frontispiece foreshadows, not least in its landscape setting, the long line of ruler images that was to dominate the tradition of frontispiece design in Persian painting.[18] None of this is to deny that the standing figure is of greater importance than the vizier;[19] the contrast in body language is enough to ensure that, to say nothing of the striking disparity in costume. This figure could be Hülegü or Abaqa Khan;[20] there is at all events a high likelihood that this is one of the Mongol rulers or a high Mongol dignitary.[21]

The *Rasā'il* leaves, as befits their role as the summative experiment in Arab frontispiece design, are exceptionally rich in content. Accordingly, they lend themselves to quite diverse approaches and interpretations. The present paper will confine itself to five distinct headings only, though plainly these leaves would sustain a much more detailed analysis than this. First, their core subject matter: how they work as author portraits. Secondly, their use of pictorial space, which breaks much new ground. This leads naturally to the third theme, the architectural setting, which will be treated at length since no other Arab frontispiece makes so much of this feature. The fourth theme again focuses on a pioneering aspect of the *Rasā'il* paintings, namely the interplay of figures to construct a narrative more complex than is to be found in any other Arab picture of comparable function in this period. Finally, the paper will attempt to characterize the distinctive style of these paintings and to assess their importance in the history of the Arab frontispiece in the thirteenth century.

[18] A tradition that perhaps culminated in the depiction of the court of Sultan Ḥusayn Bāyqarā in the 1488 copy of Sa'dī's *Būstān* (Lentz and Lowry [1989], 260–61). For a full analysis of this frontispiece, see Prentice (1977), 45–54.

[19] Though the fact that his face has been rubbed out (as has that of his groom), while Juwaynī's face remains as painted—which suggests the anti-Mongol feeling of some later user of the manuscript—reduces his visual impact.

[20] These are the two suggestions made by Richard, F. (1997), 41.

[21] Ettinghausen (1959), 48, transmits the opinion of J. A. Boyle that the figure is likely to be either Hülegü or the Amīr Arghun. Ettinghausen notes that this formulaic representation has as its prototype the classical author inspired by the muse standing beside him (ibid., 49).

The Multiple-Author Portrait

The obvious place to begin is with the principal problem that the painter had set himself—how to depict not one but five authors.[22] The inherent difficulty of that problem is well illustrated by the relative failure of earlier attempts to solve it. These attempts are on the whole characterized by wooden, lifeless, and implausible arrangements of the relevant figures.[23] From the way that the painter of the *Rasāʾil* leaves met this challenge springs most of what is remarkable in this frontispiece. How was he to put over in convincing fashion the concept of multiple authorship, let alone the hierarchies within the team, the milieu within which the book was written, or the readership for which it was intended? Moreover, in the more ambitious Arab frontispieces of the thirteenth century, the emphasis was not confined to the author himself, as was the case in the classical, medieval Western and Byzantine traditions, but extended also to the acquisition and transmission of knowledge. That is a far more complex theme, and it took the author portrait a long way from its origins. This change of direction injected narrative, and with it far more human interest, into a genre that had hitherto tended to the static and formulaic. This broadening of the scope of the author portrait populated the picture space with an entire *dramatis personae*, from students to servants. There was room too for some quirkiness in their interaction.

All this, then, brought a moribund genre back to life. No wonder that no two Arab frontispieces of the thirteenth century that depict authors are the same.[24] No wonder that one experiment crowded on the heels of another. No wonder that the author himself seems to change his nature as readily as a chameleon. In one image, he gives

---

[22] Five authors are mentioned in the text on fol. 3v but six figures dominate the frontal plane. Hoffman (1993), 7 and 17, n. 7, explains the discrepancy as due to reliance on a late antique group portrait. But the desire to create a satisfying visual symmetry may also be at work here, and the addition of the figure identified by Ettinghausen ([1962], 102) as a scribe (fig. 28) was an elegant way of achieving this. No doubt other possibilities could be canvassed.

[23] See Hoffman (1982), 283–84 and, more generally, 255–59 and figs. 86a–91.

[24] Whereas in Byzantine evangelist portraits, for example, the sheer quantity of repetition is astonishing. See Friend (1927), pls. 1–16, 103–6, 125–28, 132–35, 142–43, and 173–75.

a one-on-one practical demonstration to an absorbed student.[25] In another he is the practical businessman, ready—at a price—to grant formal permission to a pair of deferential students to go out into the wide world and teach the material he has dictated to them.[26] The commercial aspect is again to the fore as he sits in his ostentatiously well-stocked shop preparing a drug for an affluent customer (fig. 29).[27] Or he is enthroned in majesty, set on high above his fellow scholars[28] or his pupils or attendants (fig. 30).[29] Sometimes he is shown lecturing to an audience craning to hear his every word, while he himself

[25] Dioscorides, *Hayūlā ʿilāj al-ṭibb*, an Arabic translation of *De Materia Medica*, 626/1229 (probably made in Northern Mesopotamia), now in the Topkapı Palace Museum Library (Ahmet III, 2127), fol. 2v. For a color plate, see Ettinghausen (1962), 71.

[26] See ibid., 67 and 70; color plates on 68–69. For a summary of recent discussion of this double frontispiece, see L. Komaroff in Evans and Wixom, eds. (1997), 429, 432–33. The practical process whose culmination is depicted in these two paintings is described by J. Pedersen (1984), 24–32. For evidence that the artist was a Muslim by the name of ʿAbd al-Jabbār (?) b. ʿAlī, see O. Grabar's review of Farès (1957): Grabar, O. (1959).

[27] This is from another partially dispersed and incomplete Dioscorides manuscript, dated Rajab 621/June–July 1224, now in the Süleymaniye Mosque Library, Istanbul (Ayasofya 3703); see Grube (1959), 173 and Abb. 1 on 171. Professor Grube interprets the central figure as a druggist serving two customers, and this is indeed a plausible suggestion. Nevertheless, such a workaday scene would mark a major departure from the long-established tradition of depicting the author in the opening pages of certain manuscripts (notably of this very type) and it should be remembered that in this case the image (nearly the only one left in this ruthlessly plundered manuscript) occupies fol. 2 recto and thus precedes the beginning of the extant text on fol. 2 verso, which begins with Book 4, so that it is in pole position in the manuscript rather than taking its place in the sequence of later illustrations. Comprising today 155 fols. that encompass Books 4–7, it is not possible to say whether Books 1–3 were removed or were bound as a separate volume, or if it was planned as a truncated version of the text. (I am grateful to Dr. Linda Komaroff for this information.) Moreover, all the other Arabic Dioscorides manuscripts of the thirteenth century that survive and that have figural frontispieces depict Dioscorides himself in them. It may seem preferable, therefore, to interpret the elderly white-haired man rendered in profile to the right, his hand imperiously outstretched, as Dioscorides himself. The composition can be seen in absolute clarity in the colored drawing made by A. Süheyl Ünver in 1939 and published in Brandenburg (1982), 115.

[28] As in the Dioscorides in Bologna (Biblioteca Universitaria, Cod. arab. 2954, dated 642/1244–45, fol. 141 recto), identified by a later user as Dioscorides flanked by Luqmān and Aristotle (Grube [1959], 182). For a color plate, see Brandenburg (1982), 209.

[29] For a color plate of this image (undated; Istanbul, Süleymaniye Mosque Library, Ayasofya 3704, fol. 1 verso), see ibid., 95.

keeps a weather eye on his lord and master, the *amīr* enthroned on the opposite page.[30] No question here about where the power lies—it is with the eagle, not the pigeon; with the frontal image, not the three-quarter or profile one. So while there is the odd image of the standing author holding his book in a Byzantine style which is only lightly Islamized, as in the Oxford Dioscorides,[31] that is exceptional. So, too, is a frontispiece whose theme is exclusively royal, as in the Paris *Kalīla wa Dimna*, probably of the 1220s (fig. 31).[32] Indeed, the intellect rather than political power is exalted in the frontispieces of the thirteenth century. For the most part they proclaim that the pen is mightier than the sword. But the balance was to shift decisively—and for good—in the opposite direction in the fourteenth century and thereafter. This contrast between Arab veneration of learning and Persian veneration of power is, to say the least, instructive. But that is certainly the message of the frontispieces.

Where exactly, then, do the *Rasā'il* leaves belong in this sequence? In simple terms, they are the most developed realization of the concept of multiple authorship in frontispiece design. This theme was itself rare enough. Perhaps its earliest expression is in the little-known double frontispiece to an undated manuscript entitled *Risālat al-Ṣūfī fī al-kawākib*, which ends with a *Poem of the Constellations* sometimes attributed to Ibn al-Ṣūfī but is more likely to date from the twelfth century.[33] Mehdi Mahboubian's theory that it depicts the Buyid ruler 'Adūd al-Dawla on the right and al-Ṣūfī himself on the left[34] is unconvincing, partly because the style puts the paintings around 1200 (and who would wish to honor a potentate who had died some

[30] Farès (1953), 16–17, figs. 3–4. The layout here is as misleading as the caption ("anges baghdadiens"), for it reverses the actual layout in the manuscript itself.

[31] For a good color plate of this image (Bodleian Library, Cod. or. d. 138 [Baghdad, 637/1239–40], fol. 2 verso), see Evans and Wixom, eds. (1997), 402.

[32] Bibliothèque Nationale, arabe 3465. For a brief description, see O'Kane (2003), 49; and Hamid (1966), vol. 1, 224–25 and vol. 2, fig. 55. Hamid notes an inscription on the writing board of a pupil in the stylistically related *Maqāmāt* of al-Ḥarīrī (B.N., ms. arabe 6094, fol. 167) which can be deciphered as stating that the book was made in Damascus, and on this basis concludes that arabe 3465 was also made in Damascus (ibid., vol. 1, 224 and 236 and vol. 2, fig. 64).

[33] Now in the Riza 'Abbasi Museum, Tehran, ms. 570. I am grateful to Dr. Moya Carey, who is currently working on this manuscript, for directing me to a color illustration of this double frontispiece: Vesel (2001), 268–69.

[34] Mahboubian (1970), no. 913 and unnumbered 16.

two centuries previously?), and partly because the right-hand figure holds an astrolabe, scarcely an attribute of authority. He is also smaller than the other man holding the book. And neither figure wears a crown. This painting, then, depicts two scholars—but they do not communicate directly apart from more or less facing each other, as one is in profile and the other in three-quarter view. Each is treated as an independent personage, with the figure to the left treated as the more important one. Vesel's suggestion that the figure holding the astrolabe is Ptolemy is plausible, for al-Ṣūfī's work was based on that of Ptolemy, which al-Ṣūfī revised.[35] There may indeed be an attempt here to distinguish between Islamic and Greek culture, with the taller, more imposing figure of al-Ṣūfī wearing a turban and thus contrasting with his opposite number, who wears a fillet (traditionally associated with classical culture) around his brow. The segmental arch that crowns each picture recurs in other Arab frontispieces,[36] and, like the form of the throne back, the blue-tiled wall and the huge blue scrolls that unfold languidly against a gold backdrop, creates a distinctly Islamic ambience for these images.

The theme of multiple authorship is developed a good deal further in the double frontis- and finispieces to a copy of *The Choicest Maxims and Best Sayings* by al-Mubashshir, a manuscript attributed to Syria and datable to the first half of the thirteenth century (figs. 24–26).[37] This repeats or rings minor changes on the theme of setting six or seven authors each within a separate compartment of an overall ornamental framework, but all so depicted that they connect with each other or with the outside world. The message is plain: erudition involves discussion with your peers, and brings with it the responsibility to inform the rest of the world about your findings. All this is schematically achieved by the poses and gestures of the scholars (presumably themselves the authors of the maxims and sayings of the title). But the simple gold background, lightly embellished with vegetal scrolls, distances these images from reality, although it does serve to simplify the message. This could be summarized, moving

[35] Vesel (2001), 262, 269.

[36] E.g., in the Dioscorides manuscripts of 626/1228–29 and 637/1239–40 (see nn. 25–26 and 31, above). It is only fair to add, though, that it is also found in Syriac manuscripts of this period, as in the evangelist portrait in a Lectionary from Mar Mattai of 1220 (Vatican, Biblioteca Apostolica, ms. Siriaco 559).

[37] Ettinghausen (1962), 74, 76–79; color pl. on 75.

from bottom to top, in the words 'discuss,' 'transmit,' and 'broadcast.' Although the influence of Old Testament prophets or New Testament apostles has been proposed as an explanation of these figures,[38] any such religious origin has been hijacked, so to speak, for secular purposes and for the dissemination of a secular text.

It is this very theme—the acquisition and communication of knowledge—that is taken up and so smoothly and confidently developed in the two *Rasāʾil* leaves. They exude a strong sense of lively debate, of a seminar. There is both humor and urgency here. The debate is largely confined to the left-hand page, fol. 4 recto, while the right-hand page, fol. 3 verso, seems rather to emphasize silence, meditation, and deep thought. Perhaps it is this subdivision between speech and silence that at least partly explains why the two halves of the frontispiece, while generically similar, are not identical. In fol. 4 recto, a servant brings a book as further ammunition in the argument, while another book lies open on the knee of the reclining sage and a third book is held open in the hand of the man with corkscrew eyebrows who is eagerly challenging the central sage. A fan disperses the hot air that is no doubt being generated.

Pictorial Space

It is now time to turn to the second theme, the treatment of pictorial space. This frontispiece is full of spatial adventurousness. Faces are typically in three-quarter view, the angle that best meets the demands of narrative while also involving the viewer. As in Byzantine religious art, the figures are usually not in profile,[39] even though that is the pose that their interchanges would lead us to expect. An all-but-frontal view is also used. People either interact directly through the direction of their glances, which cancel each other out, so to speak, or they turn to the facing page, again keeping the direction of their gaze within the frontispiece as a whole.

Poses are even more varied. People turn their backs, step out towards us, lean back, stoop forward or recline, stand or sit, and

[38] Ibid., 78.

[39] For a concise account of the theological reasons behind this preference, see Demus (1947), 7–9 (page citations are to the 1976 reprint edition).

overlap. In other words, the key central strip is in constant motion. The figures themselves, then, are the major instrument of spatial innovation, and their hand gestures, which are often reciprocal and are broadly at the same level, create a further ripple of movement.

Textiles play their part too. Curtains swirl, loop, and undulate, with internal patterning employed to highlight the sense of movement. But even more noticeable than this is the treatment of clothing, including turbans. The body beneath the drapery is simplified into large ovals, but these are filled with furious activity expressed in churning, eddying folds. The *Rasā'il* leaves illustrate only one variation of an interest in intensely expressive ways of depicting drapery folds with which thirteenth-century Arab painters experimented. Related modes can be seen in the Tehran Ibn al-Ṣūfī, the *Mukhtār al-ḥikam*, the Wasit Qazwīnī, [40] and the London *Na't al-ḥayawān.*[41] In the *Rasā'il* frontispiece, the outlines of sleeves and turban tailpieces resolve themselves into a flurry of cascading pleats and ruffles. It is all rather excitable, even flamboyant. This emphasis on crumpled cloth counterpoints, admittedly in a minor register, the broader movement of the figures themselves. The drapery, then, is part of the overall scheme of spatial mobility; it radiates energy, and a powerful sense of controlled movement expressed through a series of strictly contained vortices.

This drapery technique, like that of the slightly later *Marzubānnāma*,[42] is very closely related to metalwork, perhaps inlaid metalwork[43] as is suggested by the large oval patches denoting the lining of the sleeves or the books held by various figures, but also, perhaps, Byzantine cloisonné enamels.[44] The chrysography—the 'writing in gold' that was such a hallmark of the Byzantine manner—is more marked here than in any other known example of Mesopotamian or Syrian painting. The limited range of colors (black, white, orange, brown, blue, gold)

[40] Ibid., 138.

[41] Contadini (1992).

[42] Simpson (1982), 100, 102, and 104 (figs. 49–51 respectively).

[43] On this general question, see Komaroff (1994), especially figs. 10b–c, 11, and 18a–d, the latter (a brass bowl in Lyons) with the same distinctive use of multiple parallel lines to assert a form.

[44] For a representative selection of relevant images, see Wessel (1969). For superb color close-ups of such work, see Evans and Wixom, eds. (1997), front and back cover (ibid., 88, cat. no. 41).

also recalls metalwork, although in this respect too the immediate parallel is probably the Byzantine cloisonné enamel tradition.

The distinction between the sages, squatting gigantically at the center of each composition (and not just at the center of each lower story) in the frontal plane, and their pygmy servants, placed well back behind the lateral balustrades, is also a triumph of spatial subtlety. The many different overlaps underline this three-dimensional complexity. And part of the spatial interest of these figures lies in their sheer number. No other thirteenth-century frontispiece has so many active figures. They never coalesce into an anonymous mass, like the audiences in the frontispiece to the Paris *Maqāmāt* of 634/1237. Everyone has something to do. There are no walk-on parts. And that theatrical allusion is perhaps not entirely misplaced, for the influence of the contemporary shadow theater may be sensed here,[45] especially in the well-lit but neutral central space occupied by the authors themselves, a space carefully singled out from its surroundings by its size and coloring. The *Rasā'il* leaves are the most stagy of all thirteenth-century frontispieces, cunningly choreographed and with plenty of subplot provided by the servants and the studious occupants of the upper story. The entire space is conceived as a shop front[46] for how learning is acquired. This represents a quantum improvement on the mechanical sexpartite division of architectural space which was a cliché of earlier Arab painting.[47] That said, size is still a function of status, which results in some figures inhabiting rather awkwardly the space allotted to them. Here the contrast between the large fan-waver and the pygmy proportions of the servant opposite, holding a book, is particularly marked, though the former intrudes into the space reserved for the scholars, which may help to explain his greater size. One may note too the elaborate—and perhaps rather labored—spatial device whereby his left arm pushes forward into the frontal plane as he grasps the column to steady himself, while most of his body is behind it.

The side curtains break through the notional frame established

---

[45] The principal source here is P. Kahle; see especially Kahle (1910–11); idem (1940); idem (1954). See also Jacob (1925); Moreh (1987) and idem (1992), Part 3, 87–151, passim.

[46] Cf. the pharmacy discussed in n. 26, above.

[47] Cf. another pharmacy, in the Dioscorides manuscript of 621/1224 (Ettinghausen [1962], 87), or the parturition scene in the Paris *Maqāmāt* (ibid., 121).

by the architecture itself, and this is typical of the spatial energy and expressiveness which permeates both paintings. The effect of these folds of cloth wreathed and wrapped around the columns is to emphasize the third dimension, rather like the column-hugging figures in the St. Petersburg[48] and Paris[49] *Maqāmāt* manuscripts. And yet any literal interpretation of space is excluded, because the curtains, in being wrapped around the outer columns, project well beyond the frame.[50] The same spatial verve makes itself felt in the treatment of the balconies: three of the four people seated there lean their bare elbows casually over the balcony in a device strangely prophetic of the portraiture conventions of the early and High Renaissance with the protruding elbow claiming the frontal plane. Drapery billows out behind their elbows, thus drawing extra attention to the device. By this means, the figures in the balcony serve to link the ground floor with the story above it, and thereby assert their interest and involvement in what is going on below. Similar bridging motifs are known in thirteenth-century *Maqāmāt* manuscripts.[51] In fol. 3 verso, the forward-projecting leg and haunch of each of the two men flanking the senior sage perform much the same spatial function, leading the eye back into the picture (pl. 12). Even the body language is dynamic and expressive, as in fol. 3 verso, where one figure is scribbling furiously with furrowed, knotted brow as though he were a stenographer under pressure. Note too the clenched fists in fol. 4 recto (pl. 11).[52]

Clearly, then, the spatial inventiveness of these paintings extends beyond the figures being depicted, for it includes the architecture and its accessories. Moreover, the artist has succeeded very effectively in so depicting the structure as to suggest three-dimensional space,

---

[48] Ibid., 106 and 107.

[49] Ibid., 114.

[50] A similar device is known in contemporary Armenian manuscript painting, as in the Queen Keran Gospels of 1272 (Evans and Wixom, eds. [1997], 355).

[51] E.g. the scene of Abū Zayd in the tavern in the Paris *Maqāmāt*; Stewart (1967), 95 (page citation is to 1975 reprint edition).

[52] While there is a long tradition of such intensely dramatic depictions of the act of writing, going back indeed to Carolingian times—e.g. the celebrated image of St. Matthew in the Ebbo Gospels (Epernay, Bibliothèque municipale, datable before 823, ms. 1, fol. 18 verso; see Robb [1973], 111, fig. 60)—no continuous chain of transmission between such an image and the *Rasā'il* manuscript can be traced, and it is likely enough that the Arab version of this theme was an original invention.

and especially the recession of the building at its sides. This leads naturally to the third theme of this paper, the architecture itself and the purpose behind its meticulous depiction.

The Architecture

There is a long prehistory for the role of architecture in author portraits, and some review of this rich past is necessary in order to contextualize the *Rasāʾil* paintings. It was of course standard practice in both the Western medieval and the Eastern Christian tradition to place the author figure in some kind of architectural context. Typically, however, this setting has a strong flavor of fantasy. One cannot readily imagine the author actually living in that specific building. This is partly because of the gross discrepancy of scale—after all, the author figure dominates the frontal plane, and his spatial relationship to the building behind him is uncertainly defined—and partly because of the minute and fussy detail of the architecture. It has the air of a model, a doll's house, rather than of an actual building. Yet the Christian tradition demanded a grand building as a backdrop for the more elaborate type of author (usually evangelist) portrait, and the power of that tradition can be sensed even in the most unlikely places. In the only known nonabstract Qurʾānic frontispiece, namely that of the Umayyad luxury Qurʾān in Sanʿaʾ,[53] the human element has of course disappeared. But the architecture remains, and in spades. Even in the most minimalist author portraits, in the Western and Eastern Christian tradition alike, the backdrop, whether it be a simple arch or a sparsely furnished room, suggests an architectural space, though that space has little chance to assert itself given the overpowering scale of the author portrait itself. Thus, whether the setting is elaborate or simple, it is dwarfed and downgraded by the human element. It is plainly of secondary interest and is very seldom conceived as a natural setting for the author's daily work. The cupboard of books seen in the background of the Codex Amiatinus, fol. 5 recto, as Ezra scribbles busily is one of the rare exceptions.[54] Thus the conventions inherited by the Arab

[53] See n. 10, above.
[54] Weitzmann (1977), pl. 48.

painters charged with devising author portraits made it mandatory for them to construct some kind of architectural framework for the figure which was the principal focus of interest.

There was, however, a major difference of meaning between these Arab frontispieces and the Christian ones from which they initially drew inspiration. The Arab author portraits illustrated secular manuscripts, whereas the Christian evangelist portraits introduced a Gospel text, and even when the text was not a Gospel it was much more likely to be religious than secular—a lectionary, perhaps, a set of homilies, or a *menologion*. That religious purpose so central to the image seems to have affected the way that the architectural surround was perceived. It seems to have been regarded as inappropriate to depict an evangelist writing his Gospel in a workaday setting. His task was a sacred one; he himself was a saint; the text that he was composing was the word of God. Hence, of course, his halo, the gold background, and the overall sense of otherworldliness and the supernatural. It was thus only proper that the architecture, too, should partake of that heightened atmosphere: grander, purer, whiter than the buildings of this earth. Whether these Christian painters were deliberately trying to evoke the New Jerusalem is an open question. But when the architecture depicted in these Christian frontispieces rises above minimalism, it tends to acquire a quality at once charged and abstract: charged in the sense that it becomes iconographically meaningful, suggesting as it does a sacred setting, and abstract in the sense that it is an intellectual construct, only incidentally based on real architecture, even if a specific architectural type was the remote inspiration.[55]

It is not easy to determine how far Arab painters were attuned to the deeper resonances of the elaborate architecture in the east Christian frontispieces that they encountered—Byzantine, Syriac,[56] Coptic,[57] Armenian.[58] It seems implausible that the resolutely (and thoroughly archaic) classical vocabulary of these imaginary buildings struck the same kind of chord with them as it did with Byzantine

---

[55] For a detailed discussion of this issue and related ones, see Smith, E. B. (1956); and see ibid., figs. 68–69.

[56] Evans and Wixom, eds. (1997), pl. 253.

[57] Ibid., pl. on 370, 380–81, and pl. 251.

[58] Der Nersessian (1963), figs. 17, 19, 21, 23, 46–47, 49, 51, 182, 196, 198, 200, and 202.

artists. For while Islamic architecture too had its Greco-Roman heritage, a heritage which as it happens was actively being revived in twelfth-century Syria,[59] this could not compare with the unbroken classical tradition so jealously guarded in so many different fields in the Byzantine world, a taproot which nourished the Byzantine imagination and sense of identity for a millennium and more.[60]

Whatever the reason, whether it was mere lack of empathy or an active pious distaste for Christian symbolism, Arab painters gradually discarded the more elaborate architectural confections of East Christian frontispieces. A thirteenth-century Arab Dioscorides employs a much scaled-down architectural setting, though the echo of a consular diptych is palpable, notably in the predella.[61] Several experiments in a minimalist idiom were made. By degrees, too, features derived from Arab domestic interiors and the built environment began to infiltrate these frontispieces, while a geometrical setting with no hint of architecture might be employed. There is no telling what other experiments of this kind were conducted in this exceptionally creative period, when Arab painters were busily rewriting a rule book for frontispiece design that had held sway for at least a thousand years. When one studies the Arab frontispieces dated or datable between 1199 and 1244 as a group, the immediate impression is of an absolute ferment of change. Barely two of them are alike. Most unfortunately, there is no dated Arab frontispiece between 1244 (the date of the Bologna Dioscorides) and 1287 (the date of *The Epistles of the Sincere Brethren*). Who can doubt that in the last decades of the Abbasid caliphate, when (under the enlightened patronage of al-Nāṣir[62] and al-Mustanṣir[63]) Baghdad was fast reclaiming its intellectual primacy in the Muslim world, far more illustrated manuscripts were produced than have survived? For such manuscripts seem to have been at the very peak of fashion at just that time. And while the sack of Baghdad in 1258 was a calamity comparable to that of the sack of Rome in 451, this metropolis (like Rome) obviously recovered quite quickly.

---

[59] The principal study of the topic is Allen (1986); see also Rogers (1971); and, more generally, Grabar, O. (1971) and Hillenbrand, R. (1986).

[60] See Mullett and Scott, eds. (1981).

[61] E.g. Delbrueck (1929), pls. 9–12, 16–21, 23–25, and 32.

[62] Hartmann (1975), 162–68 and 198–205.

[63] Hillenbrand, C. (1993).

So it would be strange if there were no predecessors for the many innovations of design in the 1287 frontispiece.

So what is new about the architectural setting here? To begin with, this is a credible environment for scholarly work: an octagonal pavilion, it seems, a scriptorium which evokes the atmosphere of the *bayt al-ḥikma*, the intellectual powerhouse of the golden age of Abbasid power. The sense of corporate endeavor is very strong. But this building also functions as an instrument of design. As in so many Arab paintings of the thirteenth century, architecture serves as a device to subdivide space.[64] It obligingly expands and contracts to accommodate not just the people that fill it but also the poses that they adopt, and—most importantly—their size. When this is badly done, and the idea is crudely applied, the architectural setting resolves itself into an equal six-part grid in two stories dumped into the frontal plane with no suggestion of depth. But in the *Rasā'il* frontispiece spatial divisions are managed with much more subtlety. The sense of a grid has disappeared altogether, with three unequal divisions on the lower floor and four on the upper story, which is barely half as high as the floor below and thus clearly of lesser importance. And on each of these two floors the spaces themselves are uneven, with the outer flanking compartments taking up markedly less room.

The subdivisions here are therefore distinctly asymmetrical. Yet the painter has taken care to provide a visual justification for this, in that he has boldly attempted to give this building, which is all but identical in both parts of the frontispiece, a solid three-dimensional presence. He has done so by suggesting a polygonal (probably octagonal) structure, perhaps an open kiosk or pavilion, of a kind which has not survived in thirteenth-century Iraqi architecture but is known in the Iranian world four centuries later, for example the Namakdān ('salt cellar') at Herat.[65] The painter achieves the likeness of a polygonal building by giving a marked slant to the lateral walls and emphatically foreshortening their volume. This beveling is accentuated by the triangular cornerpieces on the baseline. These are painted an eye-catching light blue and thus visually lift the side walls away from the main wall which takes up the frontal plane. That same diagonal line continues in the outer wings of the upper

[64] For a general survey of this subject, see Barrucand (1986); eadem (1994).
[65] L. Golombek in Sourdel-Thomine and Spuler (1973), 355 and pl. 348.

story, which are visually distinguished from the inner ones by being left blank and—a painter's trick, this—filled with a gold background. Such close interest in the third dimension implies mathematical calculation, which the casually overlapping figures do not. An equally self-conscious spatial device is the way that the servant waving the fan ducks behind the column and grips it to steady himself as he leans forward to fan the authors. This burgeoning interest in the third dimension foreshadows developments in the next century, but in Persian, not in Arab painting, which regressed in this respect. Indeed, such sophisticated awareness of pictorial space was historically half a century or so ahead of its time. The same can be said for the emphasis on architecture as a complex and coherent setting for group scenes. Here the obvious successor to the *Rasā'il* frontispiece is not the *World History* of Rashīd al-Dīn, where the architectural framework is repeatedly a simplified tripartite one at ground floor level only,[66] but the Great Mongol *Shāhnāma*. Here too the multiple subdivisions of a complex two-story building are crammed with action and human interest,[67] and even a wall depicted at an angle appears once,[68] though this feature, so confidently used in the *Rasā'il* frontispiece, does not come into its own until Jalayirid times.[69]

The precise treatment of the architecture in the *Rasā'il* frontispiece extends to both the overall structure of this scriptorium, with its distinctively recessed sides, and the details of its execution, which testify to the painter's close familiarity with contemporary architectural techniques. This up-to-date knowledge is at the opposite pole to the purely imaginary content of the elaborate architecture in so many evangelist portraits. He is alert to the decorative effect of brickwork with painted rising and horizontal joints, though he favors black rather than the white used in actual buildings. Indeed, these walls may represent a plaster coating incised and painted to resemble actual brick coursing; this was a commonly employed technique in Ilkhanid architecture. The treatment of a coping by bricks in vertical

---

[66] Rice, D. T. (1976), pls. 29, 35, and 69. Sometimes this is expanded, somewhat unconvincingly, to a quadripartite or sexpartite arrangement (ibid., pls. 70 and 34 respectively).

[67] Grabar, O. and Blair (1980), pls. 1, 14, 15, 17, and 52.

[68] Ibid., pl. 46.

[69] Gray (1961), pls. 46 and 54; Sourdel-Thomine and Spuler (1973), color pl. LV.

bond is equally authentic. So is the fanciful segmental arch profile at bottom center, repeated in the outer niches of the upper floor, or the segmental saucer arch of the two central niches on that same floor. These arches caused the painter some difficulty; every one of them is lopsided to some degree. Indeed, not one of the arches in the *Rasā'il* leaves has a normal arched profile. But this is a rare lapse. The three different types of arch are all part of a fashion for decorative arch profiles that enjoyed a brief flurry of popularity in the century following the Mongol invasion of 1220: for example, in the mosque of ʿAlī Shāh at Tabriz,[70] at Veramin,[71] Takht-i Sulayman,[72] and repeatedly at Kashan[73] and Bastam.[74] At the meeting places of the upper bays there is a curious pendant ornament. This building—whether it is a palace, a pavilion, an octagon, or a kiosk (perhaps riparian, to judge by the blue triangles in the lower corners, presumably a reference to water)[75]—is a pretty elaborate and luxurious piece of architecture. The source for this inspiration could be local buildings, as indeed the brickwork suggests, with some quite specific details like the well-marked horizontal and rising joints, the use of specially diminutive bricks for the lintel above the lowest arch, the vertical lay of the coping above it, the use of lighter-colored brick for the base of the balcony, and the fact that this brickwork in general is further highlighted by the use of glaze or dark paint for the joints.[76]

[70] Wilber (1955), 69 and 71.

[71] See Pope and Ackerman, eds. (1938–39), pl. 400. It is of course likely enough that this, like similar luster *miḥrābs* at Mashhad and Qum (Watson [1985], pls. 104a–b and 109; and 103), was actually made in Kashan (see n. 74, below). The same is likely to be true of another luster *miḥrāb* fragment from Qum now in Berlin (Kühnel (1931), fig. 13) and a luster *miḥrāb* in the Jāmiʿ Zīr Dālān at Najaf, which like the Berlin fragment has a decorative arch formed out of calligraphy (Aga-Oğlu [1935], fig. 1), and equally of the tiled (not luster) *miḥrābs* in the Masjid-i ʿAlī and the Masjid-i Kalah, Quhrud (Watson [1975], pls. VIIIa and b respectively).

[72] Melikian-Chirvani (1984), figs. 3–14, 16–17.

[73] Watson (1985), color pl. N and pls. 111, 113, and 125–26.

[74] See Pope and Ackerman, eds. (1938–39), pl. 395 (in the very early fourteenth-century mosque adjoining the tomb tower known as the Kāshānā). For similar arch forms in the interior of that tomb tower, see Hillenbrand, R. (1982), 252–53, figs. 95–96, and—in the porch of that tower—255, fig. 98.

[75] Among the riverine buildings in thirteenth-century Baghdad, where the *Rasā'il* manuscript was produced, the Madrasa al-Mustanṣiriyya, the most famous *madrasa* in the Islamic world at that time, and dedicated—like the building in this frontispiece—to learning, took pride of place (Schmid [1980], Abb. 1–2).

[76] For the quality of Iraqi brickwork of late Abbasid times, as seen in the Mus-

Nor is this all. The painter has noticed that in buildings of high quality a brick incorporating two planes set at an obtuse angle is used in alternating courses when two walls meet at an angle, though his imagination runs ahead of him when he creates unevenly kinked bricks. He has also reproduced accurately the appearance of a wall in typical Ilkhanid common bond, down to the use of headers instead of stretchers in alternating courses at the edge of a wall, or of a row of headers as a lintel above an arch. The arabesque ornament in blue and white tilework, or a combination of tilework and terracotta, is also a feature familiar in Ilkhanid architecture, for example at Sultaniyya[77] and Bastam.[78]

Given the demonstrable accuracy of these details, it seems reasonable to suppose that other features of architecture and its decoration for which no parallels survive may also be founded upon observation rather than fantasy. The balustrades, for example, ebony in color and possibly also in material, are inset with arabesque scrolls, perhaps in ivory although there is a bluish tinge to this inlay work. Arrow- or hourglass-shaped brass (or gilded brass) fittings of a kind familiar from Ilkhanid woodwork, for example the cenotaph of Shaykh Ṣāfī al-Dīn at Ardabil, are set at the short edges of these panels. The columns of the lower story, apparently made of wood, are also very complex.[79] They appear to have *ṭirāz* bands. They have the same silver vase-shaped designs for bases as for capitals and bear patterns that look like Chinese seal script or, more likely, a kufic version of that style. The central part of these columns is painted silver, and may indeed have been silver-plated. Their upper and lower extensions bear successive bands of rectilinear geometric ornament in gold and black, which also occur at the junction of the column and the upper and lower walls. No wooden columns from courtly buildings survive from Ilkhanid times, so this contrast between plain silvered surfaces

tanṣiriyya *madrasa* and the so-called Abbasid palace (probably the Bashīriyya *madrasa*), see ibid., Abb. 1–15, 25–31, and 35–48.

[77] Seherr-Thoss and Seher-Thoss (1968), pls. 40–43 and 45.

[78] Noted in an unpublished paper delivered by J. M. Rogers at the Seventh International Congress of Iranian Art and Archaeology held in Munich in 1976.

[79] Columns with similarly extravagant decoration can be seen in early fourteenth-century Iranian book painting, e.g. the *World History* of Rashīd al-Dīn (Rice, D. T. [1976], pls. 15, 21, 34, and 69; there are also seven porphyry columns depicted in the Edinburgh manuscript), or the Great Mongol *Shāhnāma* (e.g. Pope and Ackerman, eds. [1938–39], pls. 836–37).

and golden decoration furnishes precious evidence for contemporary taste. The few columns illustrated in Ilkhanid painting of the early fourteenth century, however, indicate clearly enough—more than does thirteenth-century Arab painting[80]—that it was the taste of the time to decorate them richly.[81]

But another possible source of inspiration for this architecture takes us right out of the Muslim sphere. Can one perhaps detect here a faint memory (transmitted through East Christian book painting, and therefore perhaps imperfectly understood) of the classical theater? Stage backdrops which distantly recall the *scenae frons* do, after all, often feature in Byzantine religious iconography.[82] A lavish use of curtains, as here, was part of that tradition; so was the use of flanking figures, of perspectival recession and slanted, beveled projection, and of course elaborate architecture. Indeed, it was not rare for Byzantine portraits of evangelists or saints to make great play with a complex architectural setting,[83] while in other Byzantine religious paintings such architecture is inhabited by a group of people.[84]

Yet the overall impression created by this fictive architecture is unmistakably Islamic. Clearly the decoration in the spandrels is well-developed tilework, and that at a time (and in a place) well before such work survives. Similarly, the columns rank as perhaps the most luxuriously decorated examples in thirteenth-century Arab painting. This is in harmony with the ebony and ivory of the gilded brass-plated balustrades, the curtains, the tilework, the fancy arch profiles, and the refined brickwork technique. Altogether an unmistakable message is being sent: the life of scholarship pays.

Finally, what of the curtains? Their elaborate patterning, with pearling at the rims and lavish use of the three-dot motif, their rich

---

[80] Despite the occasional appearance of lightly decorated columns in *Maqāmāt* manuscripts of this period (Ettinghausen [1962], 79 [gold bands] and 93 [gold roundels]); Farès (1957), pl. Vb (bands at top and bottom of the shaft).

[81] See n. 79, above.

[82] E.g. in the early fourteenth-century Kariye Cami in Istanbul (Grabar, A. [1953], 133), or in the Bible of Leo Sakallarios, Constantinople, c. 940 (Evans and Wixom, eds. [1997], 89).

[83] For evangelists, see Friend (1927), figs. 95–98 (Mount Athos, Stauronikita, ms. 43, early tenth century); for a saint, see Evans and Wixom, eds. (1997), 4 (portrait of St. Gregory from *The Liturgical Homilies of St Gregory of Nazianzos*, c. 1150).

[84] Ibid., 108 (*Homilies on the Life of the Virgin* by the monk James, c. 1125–50); 111 (a liturgical roll of c. 1125–50); and 282 (*Izbornik Sviatoslava*, 1073).

coloring, dominated by gold and blue, and their crinkled folds all show that they served as a major constituent element in the architecture, their sumptuousness set off by the plainness of the brickwork. They served equally well to open up a space or to close it off, or to form an honorific canopy over the key figures. They curl luxuriantly around each of the outermost columns and with a fine rhetorical flourish they take the whole scene into the outer margins. This margin-breaking technique creates a certain spatial ambiguity and was later to develop into a means of bringing the action of the painting into the viewer's own space and thus involving that viewer much more closely in what was being depicted. Here it precociously foreshadows the ingenious experiments with this device made by Persian painters in the fourteenth and fifteenth centuries.[85] Their agitated folds and ruffles betray their expressive intent. The central gold and black curtain descends in curvilinear tiers to settle over the central figure in each painting, thereby singling him out from his colleagues. Perhaps this use of the curtain preserves memories of the *chatr*, the parasol used by those of high rank not only to furnish shade but also to single them out and to suggest that they enjoy a divinely bestowed legitimacy.[86] At all events, these curtains—like the architecture of which they are an integral if ephemeral part —are used, as is their color (gold at the center and blue for the outlying sections) to assert a hierarchy. And while there is no serious attempt to depict the interior of this pavilion, so that the figures effectively float against a ground of pale yellow or gold, the architecture is not merely a backcloth for those figures but is properly integrated with them.

Narrative

So much, then, for the architecture. It is now time to consider the figures that inhabit it, and the story that they tell. Very few thirteenth-century frontispieces are as heavily populated as this one, with fourteen people in all, each of whom has his part to play. That in itself is a major achievement, and it indicates how far Arab painting had traveled from the days when a single figure, that of the author,

---

85 Brend (2000), 39–55; Hillenbrand, R. (1992).
86 Sims (1973), 263; L'Orange (1953), 134–38.

dominated the composition, as was the approved fashion in East Christian art. True, the Paris *Maqāmāt* double frontispiece has more people, but only two of them are singled out and the rest (angels excepted) constitute an amorphous audience with their backs to us. Here, by contrast, everyone is in the active mode; and in each leaf every person is treated differently from the rest. Thus the sense of individuality is strong. It may be that the presence of precisely seven people in each leaf is an oblique reference to the fact that the Ikhwān al-Ṣafā᾿ were Ismāʿīlīs; the tradition of using symbolic language was well established among Seveners generally. Alternatively, it may reflect classical precedent,[87] as suggested by Pliny's account of the *Hebdomades* of Marcus Varro (late first century BC), whose text, comprising biographies of seven hundred famous people, was illustrated by one hundred pictures of seven notables apiece.

The obvious place to begin is with the principal figures, who effectively identify themselves by virtue of their larger size and by the fact that they occupy the central opening on each leaf. They are, incidentally, sumptuously dressed, their robes flashily lined with ochre-colored material. These are prosperous scholars, not starving schoolmen pauperized by their thirst for knowledge. Even their servants are well-dressed. This is an aristocracy of the intellect whose members are men of presence and dignity. It is noticeable that not one of them adopts the standard author pose so familiar from the Western and the East Christian traditions, namely standing or seated in a chair. Their poses are quintessentially Islamic: all are on the ground. One reclines, his back against a column; the rest are kneeling or seated with one knee raised.

There is an implicit respect here for the man of learning, and the very process of acquiring, setting down, checking, and transmitting learning is faithfully reproduced. There is no way of telling for sure whether this double frontispiece was intended to be read from the left or from the right, and indeed both practices were followed, rather randomly it seems, in Islamic painting. In the left leaf, fol. 4 recto, several stages of scholarly activity are represented simultaneously. One sage, with a bushy white beard, reclines comfortably on a cylindrical yellow bolster, his back supported against a column.

---

[87] Weitzmann (1959), 116–20. On the connection between literary and pictorial cycles see idem (1970), 41.

Presumably he has been meditating, though his snug, tightly curled pose might suggest that he has nodded off. If so, he is wide awake now and has obviously dreamt up some contribution to the debate, for he is prodding his neighbor in the side to attract his attention, and his other hand is outstretched in a gesture of speech. Nevertheless, his recumbent posture makes it reasonable to regard him as 'The Thinker.' An open book is balanced somewhat precariously on his wrist, as it were in limbo.

The two other figures that share center stage with him—for there is a strong sense of intellect on display here—are engaged in some sort of textual debate, to judge by the open book held by the younger man. His elder, who sports a long but trim pointed beard, puts across a cool objectivity. His rich, long brown-and-gold robe distinguishes him from his two flanking colleagues clad in blue. He does not turn to his interlocutor but instead looks diagonally out of the painting with a tranquil, faintly quizzical expression. His controlled, economical hand gesture suggests a take-it-or-leave-it authority. What a contrast to the black-bearded man, who in his eagerness seems to thrust the book towards his senior. This younger man is distressingly anxious to make his point: hence the pleading angle of his gaze, not to mention his popping eyes, tightly pursed protruding mouth, mobile eyebrows, and furrowed forehead. Scholarly controversy clearly awakens strong emotions in him. He is a direct descendant of the chaffering merchants and disputatious litigants of al-Ḥarīrī's *Maqāmāt* half a century earlier. Discussion, debate, controversy, teaching—there is something of all of these in the tense confrontation pictured here.

A somewhat different sequence of scholarly activity meets the eye in the right frontispiece, the first picture in the book. Here attention focuses on the old man in the center. He is the key figure in this entire double frontispiece, marked out as he is by his rich brown robe worn above a yellow undershirt and decorated with a pattern of triple dots and striated with long vertical lines in gold. The two men flanking him wear blue and thus set him off visually. He alone of all fourteen figures does not wear a turban; instead, his robe covers his head to form a cowl (*ṭarḥa*),[88] as is common practice for prophets in Islamic painting.[89] This, like the curtain terminating directly above

[88] Cf. Simpson (1982), 99.

[89] Cf. Moses and Joshua in the Edinburgh Rashīd al-Dīn manuscript (Rice,

his head, or the way that the flanking figures incline their heads towards him, confers unchallengeable authority upon him, and is a reminder—here, at the very beginning of the book—of its religious content. His words alone are being taken down by a man we must call 'The Scribe,' who balances his codex on his raised knee and writes with a calamus (fig. 28). His frown of anxious concentration, staring eyes, puckered eyebrows, and knotted forehead proclaim the importance of what the old man is dictating. This is 'The Lecturer.' The speaking gesture of his right hand underlines this. He turns away from the scribe as if to maintain his concentration better. His face, as is the case with the other two old men, expresses the serenity conferred by wisdom.

His colleague, distinguished by his spade beard, luxuriant moustache and long black hair escaping from his turban, clutches his raised knee while deeply absorbed in a half-open book; he is obviously 'The Reader.' This man, like the youth on the balcony above, has almond eyes of East Asian origin; the youth has in addition the rounded cheeks and tiny mouth which had long been shorthand for the moon-faced or Buddha-like beauty associated in the eastern Islamic world with East Asia.[90]

What is the point of depicting extra figures in the balcony? All four of them are engaged in intellectual pursuits: they read, whether from scrolls or books, or they listen intently to what is being recited below. In both leaves of the frontispiece one of the figures in the balcony casually rests his arm on the balustrade so that his sleeve billows down towards the main scene, thereby establishing a link with that scene that is both physical and intellectual. They could be interpreted as representing the general audience, young and of mature age alike, for whom these authors wrote. They bring a sense of the wider world to the rarefied intellectual activities taking place below them. Physically they are to some extent excluded from those activities, but their body language proclaims that they too partake of them. This idea was further developed in early fourteenth-century Persian painting. In the Great Mongol *Shāhnāma*, for instance, the windows in the upper stories of the palatial buildings are crammed

D. T. [1976], pls. 10–11 and 14 respectively) and Muḥammad in the Edinburgh al-Bīrūnī manuscript (Hillenbrand, R. [2000], color pl. 13).

[90] Melikian-Chirvani (1974), 34–37.

with women who evince the keenest interest in what is going on below; one can almost hear their excited muttered commentary.[91] Yet the diminutive scale of the men in the balconies, and even more of the servants on the ground floor vis-à-vis the authors themselves, reveals a crucial element of the Islamic world of books: the reverence for intellectual achievement. Many regarded the pen as mightier than the sword. In more senses than one, then, the authors of the *Rasāʾil* are depicted as giants.

Moreover, they are being waited on hand and foot. The servants function as a foil to the main actors, and their humble deportment and diminutive scale underline the importance of their masters. Like the men busily studying in the upper story, they are an innovation in frontispiece design. At one level they are space-fillers, and the fact that their space is so much narrower and more confined than that of the centerpiece in part accounts for this. But those same narrow spaces also have to accommodate the tempestuous undulations of the blue and gold curtains which, being looped, take over the upper portion of those spaces. That said, in the left-hand frontispiece the alert, watchful servant holding a brown book is tiny in comparison with his fan-wielding colleague at the far right, who rises to almost the full height of the opening in which he stands, and yet is crouched over the reclining scholar to whom he tends. And even this latter servant would in turn be dwarfed by the two seated scholars if they stood up. The discrepancies in size are thus not entirely consistent.

In the right-hand frontispiece the two servants are again of pygmy stature. One, with a slightly furtive look on his face and his back turned to the viewer, seems about to sneak off for an unscheduled break.[92] He has had enough of high-octane intellectual discourse. The other—paint loss has largely obliterated his face—approaches his masters with his hand raised, ready to help. Thus all four servants are differently engaged, another sign of that unobtrusive attention to detail which is the hallmark of this double frontispiece. Nevertheless, they are dressed in the same splendiferous robes and turbans as

[91] Grabar, O. and Blair (1980), pls. 6 and 17.

[92] For a comparably subversive vignette from Western medieval painting, depicting a student snoozing during a lecture, see L. de Voltolina, *Liber ethicorum* of Henricus de Allemania, showing the author in Arab dress haranguing his students, Bolognese school, later fourteenth century (Sievernich and Budde [1989], pl. 150). I am grateful to Dr. Stefano Carboni for this reference.

everyone else; nothing in their apparel betrays their modest status. Clearly the desire for a uniform visual tone overrode the demands of naturalism.

Style

Now that the major themes of this paper have been discussed, it remains to consider briefly the hallmarks of this painter's style. He has a distinct preference for the play of line rather than for the bold blocking out of colors, though he does show an acute sensitivity to colors that complement each other, such as blue and gold. His figures naturally arrange themselves in sweeping, flamboyant curves and ovals—turbans, faces, thighs, shoulders, knees, ballooning sleeves. This painter clearly liked to abstract and simplify the human form, and he was fully alive to the expressive potential of these curvilinear volumes. Here too the heritage of the Paris *Maqāmāt* is instantly recognizable.[93] He rejoices in the rhetoric of a fluttering turban-end, the squiggles of its tailpiece, or the cascading folds and shooting sprays of a robe and its secondary internal patterning. These drapery folds employ the distinctive chrysography so familiar in Byzantine mosaics and enamels. Earlier Arab painting had used it confidently, though only on rare occasions, as in the frontispieces of the *Kitāb al-aghānī*.[94] There the impact of Byzantine modes is plain to see, extending even to the choice of a deep ultramarine as a foil to the gold. Here, on the other hand, two complementary colors are employed—sky blue and gray-brown. The lines of the chrysography are thicker than in Byzantine art, and sometimes they acquire a different and more assertive texture altogether because the gold line is bracketed between two dark lines, for example in the delineation of turban folds.[95]

But it is less the technique whereby drapery folds are executed than their complexity which defines the mannerisms of this painter and furnishes a clue to his antecedents. For this obsessive fascination

[93] E.g. the cupping scene, fol. 156 recto.

[94] Rice, D. S. (1953); for color images, see Ettinghausen (1962), 65 and von Folsach (2001), pl. 23.

[95] There was a parallel contemporary fashion for this two-tone effect in luxury Qur'āns (James [1988], 86, fig. 53).

with the intricacies of the folds into which clothing, and in this case headgear as well, fits neatly into a fashion that was already over a century old by this time and was destined to linger on into the fourteenth century. It was, moreover, a cross-cultural fashion, as likely to be encountered in Norman Sicily[96] as in the Mamluk[97] or Ilkhanid[98] realms. The artists who experimented with it did so apparently for sheer love of ornament rather than using these convoluted folds as a vehicle for rendering emotion. They whip up a storm, no question about that, but it is a storm in a teacup. It should be no cause for surprise that artists working in a city that, until a generation before, had been the prime metropolis of the Islamic community should have been *au courant* with contemporary fashions in the world beyond.

What is the role of color here? By the standards of Arab painting earlier in the century, the palette here is indeed reduced. The predominant tonalities are yellow in various shades, grayish brown, and blue, with touches of black and white to accentuate and even highlight key areas or to provide contrast. In chromatic terms, the two halves of the frontispiece mirror rather than complement each other, and this helps to pull together the entire two-page composition. So too does the device of using blue to create a horizontal accent along the top, middle, and bottom of each picture and thus right across the whole double-page spread. Overall, the effect of this particular choice of colors, especially the profusion of a dull gold, is to lend a touch of somber understated magnificence to the entire frontispiece.

The awareness of other cultures and their artistic traditions is not limited to the drapery technique. The hairstyle of the beardless fan-waving youth, with his carefully barbered lock of hair strategically placed in front of his ear and tapering down to his chin, and the elegant thin arch of his eyebrow, are both in full accord with medieval Persian canons of beauty.[99] Yet the two intensely animated figures to the left of each central personage are entirely within the local Iraqi tradition, complete with corrugated brow and pop-eyed stare. And the dusky faces of the servants in the right-hand frontispiece

[96] Demus (1949), pls. 64, 67–70, 73, 75, 79, 83–87, 101–5, and 109a.

[97] Haldane (1978), 17, 20, and 32 and associated plates.

[98] As in al-Bīrūnī's *Āthār al-bāqiya* (*Chronology of Ancient Nations*); see Hillenbrand, R. (2000), color pls. 5–6 and 12–14.

[99] Nurbakhsh (1980).

suggest that they are Indians.[100] Other details tell a similar story. Three different types of halo can be seen in these two paintings. The commonest one, which recurs six times, is a large golden roundel with a double black rim. Next in popularity, with five examples, is a much smaller gold roundel embellished with discreet decorative curlicues on both rims along the central horizontal axis. On one occasion these curls sprout a long leafy tendril which snakes its way to the top of the halo. Such haloes, with their distinctive clustering of ornament in a few carefully chosen places, are already to be found in the *Kitāb al-aghānī* frontispieces,[101] and probably derive from Buddhist sources.[102] The third type of halo, which occurs only once, significantly around the head of the cowled figure who is probably meant to represent al-Maqdisī, has a single thick black rim for the large gold roundel.

Conclusion

It is now time to summarize what claims to importance these leaves of the *Rasā'il* can make. They are legion. The discussion so far has shown that, even after the disastrous sack of Baghdad in 1258 and the fall of the Caliphate, Arab painting was still full of sap[103] and that its artists had the mental capacity to reconfigure the millennial tradition of the frontispiece in new and unexpected ways. In the *Rasā'il* leaves the painter does so by allotting the architecture, which is now wholly contemporary, a far more active role than before, promoting it from a mere backdrop to a believable setting for intellectual activity and an ordering device for very literally putting people in their place and thereby asserting hierarchical distinctions. He also succeeds by developing, more creatively than ever before, the concept of multiple authorship, of intellectual teamwork,[104] with

[100] For parallel types, see Ettinghausen (1962), 108 and 121.

[101] Ibid., 65.

[102] For a general treatment of this theme, see Oh (2003).

[103] Cf. Simpson (1982), 93–94.

[104] This sense of teamwork is precisely what is missing in the group portraits of the early Byzantine period, as in the Vienna Dioscorides of 512 (Weitzmann [1977], pl. 16), in which each physician meditates in isolation, with no interaction with his peers. And while such interaction is indeed depicted in the little-known frontispiece (fig. 32) to the *Kitāb qawā'id al-aḥkām fī ma'rifat al-ḥalāl wa al-ḥarām taṣnīf*

due attention to the processes involved: thinking, reading, writing, discussing, dictating, and teaching. And all this is achieved within a credible built and human environment, rather than in an abstract vacuum. The effect is to humanize learning while maintaining intact its prestige, indeed its charisma. All this involves some quite radical experiments within the very conservative and artificially restricted domain of author portrait iconography, building too upon earlier (though distinctively different) Arab experiments with the double frontispiece.

In style, too, these leaves are nothing less than a radical departure from earlier Arab painting. The principal innovations are in line and color. Figures and textiles in particular are for the most part (faces excepted) doubly outlined in black and gold. The infill of the draperies is a sumptuous swirl of gold sprays, striations, and ovals which infuse the entire painting with dynamism. As in the slightly later *Marzubānnāma*, the combination of black, gold, and silvery white suggests that the painter was influenced by the tonality and the visual impact of inlaid metalwork.[105] Another connection with early Persian painting is the absorbed attention which the artist devotes to the fussy intricacies of drapery, a theme which he takes to new heights of expressiveness, tapping into a clearly defined cross-cultural style that spans well over a century.

The chromatic range is uncharacteristically muted for Arab painting, but the most striking colors in this limited palette are also the most expensive: lapis blue and gold, both of them carefully distributed over most of the painted surface. The emphasis on chrysography points to a continuing respect for the Byzantine tradition. The style of these leaves, then, confirms that Arab painting continued to develop after 1258, and did so within the lines laid down in the previous half-century or so, in everything from figural types to the clothing they wear or the buildings that they inhabit. It remained resolutely deaf to the siren call of Far Eastern art,[106] whereas at this

(*The book of the bases of the ordinances on the subject of the knowledge of what is licit and what is forbidden, compiled by* [al-Ḥillī]), probably of the early fourteenth century (Farès [1957], 87–93 and pls. VI–VII; cf. the review by Grabar, O. [1959], 225), it does not progress far beyond stark juxtaposition.

[105] Cf. for example Ward (1993), 82, pl. 60.

[106] For a minor exception (the Oxford *Maqāmāt* of 738/1337) see Ettinghausen (1962), 152.

very time, as the Paris *History of the World Conqueror* of Juwaynī shows, Iran had fallen once and for all under its spell.

In form the *Rasā'il* leaves continue the double frontispiece design with which the Arabs had experimented so creatively for almost a century. At first glance it seems to return to the simple repetition of the Paris *Kitāb al-diryāq* of 1199. But the central horizontal band of the design, where most of its meaning is concentrated, develops numerous variations within a consistent uniformity of tone, and these variations challenge the viewer to look more closely.

Next, for the first time Arabic script plays a major role in the layout. The name of the book and its author (here, authors) has been moved inwards from the title page. Moreover, the order of those two elements has been reversed, and not by accident either. The names of the authors are embedded in three lines of closely written small scribal *naskh* scarcely vocalized at all, at the top of fol. 3 verso, the first painted page. There is no attempt to highlight their names in any way. Yet the opposite page, fol. 4 recto, has the full title of the book calligraphed in large *riqā'* script as a single banner headline, with every vocalization in place. There could be no clearer way of stating that the book was a team effort, and that teamwork matters more than individual achievement. The way that the script is used therefore teaches a moral lesson.

There is more. This double frontispiece, the swan song of the golden age of Arab painting, celebrates intellectual achievement rather than political power. It is the last double frontispiece to do so: an elegy, then, for the cultural achievement of a people destined to outlast their political eclipse. Its successors, which are mostly Iranian,[107] sing the praises of the ruler and his pastimes. That is a sea change in the subject matter of Islamic painting, and it should not be suffered to go unrecorded.

---

[107] Neither Turkey nor India came close to matching the Iranian achievement in this field, a matter which would bear close examination.

IN THE BEGINNING: FRONTISPIECES AND FRONT MATTER IN ILKHANID AND INJUID MANUSCRIPTS[1]

MARIANNA SHREVE SIMPSON

Anyone who works regularly with Persian illustrated manuscripts is accustomed to opening such a volume and encountering a full-page, and more often than not a double-page, picture. This kind of an image—generally referred to in Islamic manuscript studies as a frontispiece—typically appears among a volume's initial folios, or front matter, which precede its primary text. Given the ubiquity of these compositions, it is remarkable how little scholarly attention has been devoted to this genre of Persian painting, and its history and meaning remain imperfectly understood.[2] Likewise, until recently hardly any consideration had been given to the pictorial frontispiece's position within a manuscript's front matter or to the overall function of these introductory folios within the book as a whole.[3] This paper is an attempt to explore the topic by looking at pictorial frontispieces and front matter within illustrated manuscripts of the Ilkhanid and Injuid periods, that is, the time when Persian book painting began to be practiced in a significant way and to develop into one of Iran's most celebrated and lasting contributions to the arts of the Islamic world. Thus the title, 'In the Beginning,' refers both to the opening leaves within early Persian illustrated manuscripts and to the start of a pictorial tradition. It also applies

---

[1] I am indebted to the following colleagues for numerous courtesies in the preparation of this essay and the symposium presentations from which it derives: Persis Berlekamp, Sheila S. Blair, Stefano Carboni, the late Jerry Clinton, Teresa Fitzherbert, Oleg Grabar, Christy Gruber, Sandy Morton, Oya Pancaroğlu, Francis Richard, Shahla Sohail, Muhammad Isa Waley, Elaine Wright, and Sergei Zhuk.

[2] Simpson (1982), n. 37. For insights into one particular type of frontispiece imagery of the late fifteenth through sixteenth centuries and some interesting assumptions about the genre of Persian frontispieces as a whole, see Bağci (1995), 101–11. See also n. 9.

[3] Wright (1997), chap. 1. This groundbreaking study uses the term 'frontispiece' also to describe certain forms of illuminated folios, both single- and double-page, at the beginning of a manuscript.

to this study, still very much in its initial stages and with more issues to raise than conclusions to draw.

A preliminary point about historiography, terminology, and methodology is in order. As is well known, the origins of the Islamic frontispiece predate the Mongol period and go back to the early thirteenth century when Arabic manuscripts began to feature such introductory compositions. These derive, in their turn, directly from classical and Christian imagery, a long-recognized relationship that has been the focus of renewed and penetrating investigation in recent years.[4] The celebrated frontispiece in the Dioscorides manuscript of 626/1229, for instance, owes its overall form to representations of late antique authors and virtually all of its details to illustrations of the Evangelists in tenth- and eleventh-century Byzantine Gospel books—an artistic heritage that made the Arabic manuscript a natural choice to demonstrate the relations between medieval Christian and Islamic art in the *The Glory of Byzantium* exhibition held at The Metropolitan Museum of Art in 1997.[5] Indeed, it is the venerable tradition of such representations and the subsequent manifestation of analogous compositions in Islamic art that prompted me to survey the literature in Western manuscript studies, with particular attention to recent scholarship, to see how the frontispiece as a pictorial genre in late antique, early Christian, Byzantine, and European medieval art has been defined and discussed.[6] It came as something of a surprise to discover that not much more of substance, meaning synthetic or generic studies, has been written about the non-Islamic frontispiece than about the Islamic frontispiece.[7] This survey did clarify, however, a critical point of terminology—namely, that the

[4] Hoffman (1982) and Hoffman (1993), 6–20. See also Pancaroğlu (2001). Both Hoffman's and Pancaroğlu's work has considerable relevance for the study of early Persian frontispieces.

[5] Hoffman (1993), 6–9; Evans and Wixom, eds. (1997), cat. no. 288 (with extensive bibliography).

[6] For pioneering work on the early history and development of the genre, see Weitzmann (1971), chaps. 1 and 5. Reference to other important studies by scholars of the same generation, including Hugo Buchthal, Kurt Holter and Richard Ettinghausen, may be found in Hoffman (1993).

[7] There are, of course, numerous publications devoted to specific frontispiece images and/or frontispieces in specific types of texts, some of which provide general insights into the significance of the pictorial genre. See, for instance, Salter and Pearsall (1980), especially 108–23; Dauzier (1989); Holladay (1996), 15–18.

kind of picture generally known in Islamic art history as a frontispiece is usually called an author portrait by specialists in early Western manuscripts (fifth–sixth through tenth–eleventh centuries) and a dedication or presentation miniature by specialists in later Western manuscripts (twelfth through fifteenth centuries).[8] Interestingly, the term 'frontispiece' is widely used in studies of European printed books, with particular reference to title pages and title page imagery, and in explicit recognition of the traditional use of the term to mean a building façade.[9] The key distinction in this varied vocabulary seems to be that author portraits and dedication or presentation miniatures emphasize iconography, while frontispieces, borrowed from an architectural context, emphasize placement. In seeking to better understand the early Persian frontispiece the present effort takes up both codicology and iconography, with the discussion first focused on front matter and then on frontispiece imagery.

Manuscript Overview

Eleven early Persian manuscripts, or roughly a third of the known illustrated Ilkhanid and Injuid manuscripts, contain pictorial frontispieces.[10] As a group, they represent a cross-section of the principal

---

[8] Denny (1996), 835–37; Brown (1994), 102. Although the art-historical terms 'author portrait' and 'dedication' or 'presentation miniature' imply a neat distinction, the former can (and often does) include an author presenting his text to a patron.

[9] Corbett and Lightbown (1979), 1–47; Stoichita (1997), 53–55; Smith, M. M. (2000), 12–23 (n. 5 points out a specific instance of art-historical inconsistency in frontispiece terminology) and 147–49 (Glossary, s.v. 'Architectural Frontispiece,' 'Architectural Title-Page,' and 'Frontispiece'); Martin, H.-J. and Chatelain (2000), 354–63; Avcioğlu (2001).

[10] To this corpus of documented manuscripts with pictorial frontispieces, we now may add another work, thanks to Persis Berlekamp's exciting discovery in Istanbul of an *'Ajā'ib al-makhlūqāt* dated 1322; Berlekamp (2004). The Qazwīnī codex opens with a double-page frontispiece that belongs to the princely or royal topos, to be elaborated below. It is included in my Appendix I, but not discussed further here pending more complete publication by Dr. Berlekamp. Also deliberately excluded from this discussion is the frontispiece to a collection of Arabic and Persian alchemical texts entitled *al-Mā' al-waraqī wa al-arḍ al-najmiyya*. Although dated 11 Muḥarram 749/19 July 1339, and thus within the Mongol epoch, this fascinating double-page painting has generally been associated with the Jalayirid dynasty in Baghdad. See Carboni (2002), 222–23; Berlekamp (2003a). Missing as

types of texts that were illustrated during the Ilkhanid and Injuid periods, including histories, fables, and poems. The corpus includes eight dated and three undated manuscripts; most have either documented origins or generally accepted attributions. Three of the dated and one of the undated manuscripts are no longer intact, but enough has survived of these volumes to be able to reconstruct their codicological structure, including the order of their front matter and the place of their frontispieces. All but two works boast a double-page frontispiece, which is here presumed to be the standard format for such compositions, and in their original state the two other volumes may have contained a facing mate to the now-single image. Most of the manuscripts in this corpus are familiar, although only a few have been subjected to monographic study. For the purposes of orientation and introduction, a brief chronology follows here, with further documentation (full text titles, *hijra* dating, scribe, present location, etc.) and selected bibliography for each volume provided in Appendix I.

The two earliest known Ilkhanid-period manuscripts with frontispieces were both created in Baghdad and contain dated colophons: the *Rasā'il Ikhwān al-Ṣafā'*, dated Shawwāl 686/November 1287, usually described as an encyclopedia but more accurately a compendium of knowledge in furtherance of Ismā'īlī doctrine (pls. 11–12), and the *Ta'rīkh-i jahān-gushāy*, a historical chronicle of the Mongol conquests by 'Alā' al-Dīn 'Aṭā Malik Juwaynī, dated 4 Dhū al-ḥijja 689/8 December 1290 (pl. 13). This pair of dated manuscripts brings us to the turn of the century, that is, c. 1300, and to our three undated volumes. First there is the Persian translation and substantial revision by Bal'amī of Ṭabarī's history of the prophets and kings in the Freer Gallery of Art, Washington, D.C. This manuscript, formally entitled

well are single and double-page enthronement scenes which may have originated as frontispieces, but which have long since been detached from their original codex and text and today survive as album paintings. Komaroff and Carboni, eds. (2002), cat. nos. 18–19 (with citations to other examples). See also Esin (1977); Ipşiroğlu (1964), 12–14 and pl. 4, fig. 8; Ipşiroğlu (1973), pls. 22–24 (color reproduction of paintings discussed by Esin). Finally, in this essay Ilkhanid and Injuid manuscripts will be discussed together, glossing over the important distinctions in their dynastic patronage and artistic programs on which so much light had been shed by the recent dissertations of Elaine Wright (see n. 3, above) and Teresa Fitzherbert (Fitzherbert [2001]). See also Wright's and Fitzherbert's contributions to this volume, as well as that of Eleanor Sims.

the *Tarjama-yi ta'rīkh-i Ṭabarī* and nicknamed the Freer Balʿamī, has been recently and rigorously studied by Teresa Fitzherbert who now attributes the work to Iraq, and more specifically to Mosul or perhaps the Jazira, under Ilkhanid rule. Its frontispiece today occupies only a single leaf, but the presence of pigment offset in the lower right-hand corner suggests that originally there was a facing painting, making this once part of a double-page composition (pl. 14). Then there is a small volume of the popular animal fables of *Kalīla wa Dimna* in the Topkapı Palace Museum Library, Istanbul. The origins of this work have fluctuated in the scholarly literature, but, as we shall see, details of its frontispiece also suggest an Ilkhanid attribution, although probably closer to the Tigris than to Tabriz (pl. 15). Finally, the undated manuscripts include a dispersed, but reconstructed, copy of Firdawsī's *Shāhnāma* known as the Freer small *Shāhnāma* after the Smithsonian museum where most of its folios, including the single-page frontispiece, reside (fig. 33). Along with the other so-called small *Shāhnāma*s, this work has been attributed, but not universally accepted, as coming from Baghdad around 1300. A fresh analysis of its frontispiece, also to be considered below, may suggest an attribution closer to the Injuid court, 1330–40.

Returning to the dated sequence, we have another little *Kalīla wa Dimna* dated 707/1307–8 and possibly originating in the city of Shiraz, although this specificity has been recently questioned (pl. 16). There then follow three well-known manuscripts of the *Shāhnāma*, long associated with the Īnjū dynasty and its capital of Shiraz. The first of these is dated Ṣafar 731/November 1330 (pl. 17); the second dated the last day of Jumādā I 733/16 February 1333 (fig. 34); and the third, dispersed but reconstructed, contains a dedication dated Ramaḍān 741/mid-March 1341 (pl. 18). Also dating from February–March 1341 and recently attributed to Isfahan is the poetic anthology compiled by Muḥammad ibn Badr al-Dīn Jājarmī and usually called the *Mu'nis al-aḥrār fī daqā'iq al-ashʿār* (fig. 35). The last manuscript is another *Shāhnāma*, long known as the Stephens *Shāhnāma* after the name of a former owner, with an inscribed ex libris in the middle giving a *terminus ante quem* of 753/1352–53 and also associated with Shiraz (fig. 36).

Front Matter

The straightforward chronology of these early Persian manuscripts belies their varied codicology. Perhaps because of the longstanding association of the word frontispiece with an architectural façade, that is, the front side or face of a building, we tend to assume that pictorial frontispieces would also take visual priority or precedence within the front matter of their manuscripts. Yet as Appendix II reveals, precious few of our eleven Ilkhanid and Injuid manuscripts actually begin with a frontispiece. Indeed, only the two little *Kalīla wa Dimna* volumes, the one attributed to c. 1300 and the other dated 1307–8, definitely had pictures on the initial pair of facing folios (pls. 15–16).[11] A few other manuscripts today open with a frontispiece, including the Freer Balʿamī, the Freer small *Shāhnāma* and the 1341 *Shāhnāma* (pls. 14, 18, and fig. 33), but these volumes are no longer complete and have suffered such codicological abuse over the centuries that the original appearance of their initial folios remains conjectural.

Several other manuscripts in our corpus are embellished on their opening folio 1a (or recto) with an illuminated rosette or *shamsa* that precedes the frontispiece.[12] The oldest such rosette appears in the 1290 *Taʾrīkh-i jahān-gushāy* and consists of a simple circle, surrounded by a band of lotus-like petals with finials, all by itself on the page.[13] The folios 1a in both the 1330 *Shāhnāma* and the 1341 *Muʾnis al-aḥrār* also contain *shamsa*s that are considerably larger and more elaborate in design and illuminated decoration than the 1290 rosette. In addition to more complex central medallions in gold, with subsidiary motifs to the side, these are bracketed at the top and bottom of the page with cartouches that contain the title (and, in the case of the 1330 *Shāhnāma*, the name of the author) of the text to come.[14] So

---

[11] The 1307–8 manuscript actually opens with blank pages on folios 1a, 1b, and 2a. Its frontispiece appears on folios 2b–3a.

[12] Gacek (2001), 80.

[13] Unpublished. The *shamsa*'s uncolored circle is outlined with a thin red line and thicker blue band, and then by an outer band comprised of eight sets of lotus-like petals in pink, blue, and gold, each topped in the center with a finial.

[14] The 1330 *shamsa* consists of a gold central circle, encircled with a thin band of black crosses on a white ground and two other similar, scalloped bands that overlap to form an inner row of pointed, triangular panels, each filled with a lotus blossom, and a outer row of smaller, geometric units filled with leaf-like motifs. Finally, there

in the case of these two manuscripts, the *shamsa* forms part of the illuminated decor of the title page. Furthermore, all three rosettes could have contained dedications: the *shamsa* to the 1341 *Mu'nis al-aḥrār* bears the faint traces of writing, now totally illegible, while the 1290 and 1330 rosettes contain poorly written inscriptions that clearly postdate their manuscripts' production.[15] Assuming that all three rosettes originally had dedicatory inscriptions, then they would have served as ex libris and the folio 1a in both the 1330 and 1341 volumes would have had the dual function of title and dedication page. Be that as it may, the differences in the treatment of the opening folio in these three volumes—the 1290 codex, created under

---

is an outermost ring of lotus petals with diamond-shaped projections. The *shamsa* has a plain background (that is, the page immediately surrounding the rosette is uncolored), but is encased in a square formed by four now rather faint right-sized triangles, filled with floral designs, which function rather like architectural brackets. The panels at the top and bottom are oblong and outlined with a petal border touched in red, blue (or blue-gray), and gold. Their inscriptions are written in white letters, reserved in gold against a background of gold scrolls on a red ground, and flanked by two medallions, each with a large lotus flower. They read: "The book of *Shāhnāma* [from the] writing of Firdawsī, God's mercy upon him."

The corresponding device in the 1341 *Mu'nis al-aḥrār* is today in fragmentary condition, but enough of its decor remains to reveal a gold, eight-lobed rosette defined by a prominent dark blue line and thinner black lines and surrounded by a border of brightly-colored petals and small gold disks. The ground around the *shamsa* is hatched in red and punctuated at the corners with large blue palmette-like medallions. The sole surviving panel beneath the rosette is rectangular and contains a central cartouche with the second part of the manuscript's title (*fī daqā'iq al-ash'ār*) written in white letters that are then reserved in gold and set against gold scrollwork on a red ground. To the right are the remains of a vertical gold frame, edged in blue, which presumably linked the surviving bottom panel with the now-missing one at the top.

For black and white reproductions of these two *shamsa*s, see Swietochowski and Carboni (1994), figs. 8 and 11.

[15] For general remarks on the *shamsa* as ex libris, see Gray, ed. (1979), 35–36. The 1290 *shamsa* is inscribed with the name of Sātilmish ibn Aybak ibn 'Abdallāh al-Malikī, the city of Tabriz, and the date 724/1323–24, which may replace the name of the manuscript's original owner. Richard, F. (1997), 41. The gold circle in the center of the 1330 *Shāhnāma* is filled with a very sloppily written (and thus presumably later) inscription that begins "*bi-rasm*/by order of..." It has been suggested that the 1330 manuscript was prepared for the Ilkhanid vizier Ghiyāth al-Dīn Muḥammad, although this seems implausible. Togan, Z. V. (1963), 2. Wright (1997), 38, gives the misimpression that Togan makes specific reference to a dedication in this *shamsa*. The rosette in the 1341 *Mu'nis al-aḥrār* today contains only faint traces of writing, which cannot be deciphered. Swietochowki and Carboni (1994), 16. The 1341 *Shāhnāma* is the only manuscript under discussion in this study with an original dedicatory inscription in its *shamsa* (actually a pair of facing *shamsas*).

Ilkhanid patronage, with its 'stand-alone' *shamsa*, and the 1330 and 1341 Injuid volumes, with their rosettes bracketed by text titles in cartouches—subscribe to a development that can be traced within the history of early Persian manuscripts as a whole.[16]

In short, a pictorial frontispiece could be either the first visual element in a manuscript or the second, following a *shamsa* (possibly inscribed with a dedication) and/or panels containing text titles. This one-two sequence was not necessarily the norm, however, and the order of front matter folios and the location of the frontispiece within those folios could actually be quite variable.

It is already a given that a frontispiece always precedes its manuscript's primary text; to put it another way, the manuscript's text follows its frontispiece. Sometimes the sequence is immediate, as in the 1290 *Ta'rīkh-i jahān-gushāy* where folio 1a contains the *shamsa*, folios 1b–2a the pictorial frontispiece (pl. 13), and folio 2b the beginning of the text at the top of the page. Likewise in the Topkapı *Kalīla wa Dimna*, the Freer Balʿamī, and the Freer small *Shāhnāma*, the frontispiece verso contains the beginning of the text, with the addition of a headpiece, or illuminated heading (about which more shortly), just above. All the other manuscripts, however, have supplementary text folios that either precede the frontispiece or separate the frontispiece and the primary text. The 1287 *Rasā'il Ikhwān al-Ṣafā'* manuscript, for instance, opens with a prefatory text on folios 2a and 2b–3a (there may have been another folio at the beginning with more of this preface).[17] The next pair, folios 3b–4a, contains the frontispiece, with an explanation of the text's origins and the names of its authors above the right-hand side and the text title above the left side, making this double opening a kind of intermediary title page with both verbal and visual markers (the latter to be discussed later) of its function (pls. 11–12). The actual *Ikhwān al-Ṣafā'* text begins straightaway (that is, without any decorated heading) on folio 4b.

The 1330 *Shāhnāma*, a blessedly complete codex, provides an even better example of how extensive and complex the order of front

---

[16] Wright ([1997], 12–20, 29–31, 36–40) provides important background for and detailed analysis of the distinctions between title pages with *shamsa*s, along with other front matter folios, in manuscripts made under early and later Īnjū patronage and those made under Ilkhanid patronage, including several works included in this study.

[17] A note on folio 1 says that the "beginning is missing."

matter folios can be. As just discussed, its first folio recto (1a) comprises the title page with a *shamsa* and text title in cartouches. The next three openings—folios 1b–2a with an illuminated frame and headings, followed by folios 2b–3a and 3b–4a—contain the so-called old (or older) preface of the *Shāhnāma* in prose.[18] The next pair of double openings on folios 4b–5a contains the frontispiece (pl. 17). This composition is followed on folios 5b–6a by the beginning of Firdawsī's epic text surrounded by an illuminated frame and headings. Other manuscripts in which the sequence of front matter is similar, with a preliminary text followed by a frontispiece and then by the primary text, include the 1333 *Shāhnāma* and the 1352–53 or Stephens *Shāhnāma*. So in these manuscripts the pictorial frontispiece marks the division between the end of the preface and the start of the actual text.[19]

The reverse pattern, so to speak, also obtains, as is demonstrated by the reconstructed 1341 *Shāhnāma*. Here the pictorial frontispiece on folios 1b–2a (pl. 18) precedes at least three double folios containing the old prose preface to the *Shāhnāma*, with the first pair on folios 2b–3a embellished with an illuminated frame and heading and the third (or possibly fourth) on folios 4b–5a featuring a small painting of the author Firdawsī with the court poets of Ghazni. The prose preface ends in five lines at the top of folio 5b. The rest of the page is dominated by a large *shamsa*, which, along with its mate on the facing folio 6a, is inscribed with an original and long-celebrated dedication giving the name of the manuscript's patron, the Īnjū vizier Qiwām al-Dawla wa al-Dīn Ḥasan. This second dedicatory rosette is surmounted by a headpiece that occupies the same space as the five lines of prose text on folio 5b. Finally, Firdawsī's text begins on 6b–7a, framed by an illuminated border and headings.[20] The front matter of the 1341 *Mu'nis al-aḥrār* exhibits a similar sequence; as previously mentioned, its *shamsa* and titles on folio 1a precede the frontispiece on folios 1b–2a. This is followed in turn on folios 2b–3a by a prefatory text with illuminated headings, on 3b–4a by an index to the text (essentially a table of contents), and on folios 4b–5a with

[18] Minorsky (1956); Monchi-Zadeh (1975), 1–15.

[19] Wright (1997), 15, n. 14 draws the same conclusion with regard to the 1330 *Shāhnāma*.

[20] Simpson (2000), 220–25; see especially nn. 20 and 21 for an explanation of the order of the manuscript's prefatory folios.

a chart in a fanciful layout listing the names of Persian poets and embellished with illuminated headings. The poetic text begins on folio 5b, with a headpiece.[21]

These examples by no means exhaust the variations of folio sequence within the front matter of these Ilkhanid and Injuid manuscripts, where the pictorial frontispiece is positively peripatetic. This suggests that there was not yet a standardized order for the initial folios in Persian secular manuscripts during the first half of the fourteenth century, a possibility that would, of course, have to be tested within a much larger corpus of books than the illustrated codices under consideration here. This variability also raises the question as to the codicological role or function of the frontispiece: is it a prelude or preamble to a codex as a physical entity or to the literary text contained within that codex or to some section of that codex's textual contents, such as the prose preface to the *Shāhnāma*? And if the frontispiece as a visual image is meant to connect to the text, what does it signify, iconographically speaking, about that text? Alternatively, if the frontispiece operates independently of the text, does it serve some other artistic, cultural, or historical purpose?

Any solution to these puzzles obviously requires a systematic review of frontispiece imagery. But before undertaking that, there remains one other feature of the manuscripts in the present corpus that deserves some attention, namely the inscribed and illuminated headings that appear so frequently within their initial folios.

One might expect to find, somewhere within each manuscript's front matter, a mention of its text's title and author's name. Yet this occurs in only half of these volumes. As we have just seen, the lines above the *Rasā'il Ikhwān al-Ṣafā'* frontispiece specify the origins of the text's composition, the names of its five authors, and its title (folios 3b–4a; pls. 11–12). The epic text in the Freer small *Shāhnāma* begins with an illuminated headpiece on folio 1b that serves as a title: "The book of the *Shāhnāma* from the writing of the prince of discourse, the peerless Abū al-Qāsim Firdawsī." Similar wording is used at the start of the left-hand *shamsa* in the 1341 *Shāhnāma* (folio 6a). Finally, and again as previously mentioned, the opening folio 1a in both the 1330 *Shāhnāma* and the 1341 *Mu'nis al-aḥrār* contain illuminated cartouches, above and below the *shamsa*, inscribed with

[21] Swietochowski and Carboni (1994), 9–11; Wright (1997), 40, n. 70.

their respective text titles and, in the epic volume, the author's name as well.

These two examples are single-page illuminations, and their separate inscription panels read, of course, from top to bottom. On the following double folios in these and other manuscripts, however, the illuminated headings read across the top from right or verso to left or recto and then across the bottom again from right or verso to left or recto. This textual continuity reinforces the visual unity of the two facing pages, a unity that is further enhanced by the vertical bands that typically join the inscription panels to totally frame or encase the written surface.[22] The prominent placement and decoration of these headings also suggest that they were meant to be read before the text that they bracket and frame. That the illuminated headings provide both a visual and epigraphic introduction to the enclosed text is confirmed by folios 4b–5a in the 1341 *Mu'nis al-aḥrār*. On these facing folios the names of two hundred Persian poets, written in an arresting checkerboard pattern, are framed top and bottom by illuminated headings: "The names of the poets and great men of whom mention is indicated in this compilation are these."

In the *Kalīla wa Dimna* volume of 1307–8, such an introduction appears on two successive openings that follow the frontispiece. Folios 3b–4a consist of symmetrical, full-page illuminations featuring a pair of central diamonds filled with star-tile pattern and offset at the corners with split palmettes, bracketed above and below by Persian inscription panels.[23] The upper headings give the title of the *Kalīla wa Dimna* text, while the lower ones continue with commentary on the text's merits and the esoteric and exoteric meaning of its series of animal fables. Thus, this illuminated and inscribed double folio functions as a title page, comparable to folios 1a in the 1330 *Shāhnāma* and the 1341 *Mu'nis al-aḥrār*, as well as a kind of literary encomium. The top heading on the next opening, folios 4b–5a, contains the Basmala in Persian and the bottom one continues the self-referential

---

[22] Wright (1997), 26, aptly characterizes the same type of illuminated frames, formed of gold strapwork, in an Īnjū Qur'ān as "functioning as the superstructure of the whole composition."

[23] Waley and Titley (1975), figs. 3 and 4. Although unique within our present corpus, these folios very much resemble the composition and decoration of folio 1a in a manuscript dated 759/1358. Gray, ed. (1979), fig. 18; Wright (1997), 17, n. 18.

and self-congratulatory tone about the *Kalīla wa Dimna* stories as on folio 3b–4a. Interestingly, the Basmala is in kufic script, to emphasize its religious content, while the other headings are in *naskh*.

Along with the Basmala, other divine invocations in both Arabic and Persian as well as verses from the Qurʾān appear regularly within our manuscripts' initial illuminated headings. The illuminated heading at the top of the first surviving folio of the 1352–53 or Stephens *Shāhnāma*, comprising the old prose preface, contains the second verse of Sūra 1, while the lower one seems to be a Shiʿite benediction on the Prophet's family.[24] The first full opening in the 1330 *Shāhnāma*, again with the beginning of the old prose preface, has at the top a heading that begins on folio 1b with the Basmala and continues on folio 2a with an Arabic invocation and, at the bottom, continuing across folios 1b–2a, an equivalent expression of piety in Persian verse.[25] The very same Persian invocation also appears at the beginning of the text in the undated *Kalīla wa Dimna* manuscript (folio 2b–3a, top), and on the folios beginning Firdawsī's text in the 1341 *Shāhnāma* (folios 6b–7a, top).[26] A variant form appears at the illuminated heading at the beginning of the text of the Freer Balʿamī (folio 1b), and yet a shorter variant at the beginning of *Shāhnāma* text in the 1333 manuscript (folio 5b).[27] The fact that this expression recurs so frequently, albeit in different versions, suggests that it was a common or standard religious formula for the period.

The 1341 *Shāhnāma* highlights the extent to which Qurʾanic quotations and pious invocations in a mixture of Arabic and Persian permeate the front matter of these manuscripts, and particularly

---

[24] This folio would have been the left side of a double-page opening and the now-missing facing folio to the right would have a corresponding headpiece that presumably would have contained verse 1 of Sūra 1, that is, the Basmala, at the top, as well as the initial words of the now-fragmentary Arabic inscription at the bottom.

[25] Folio 1b, top: Basmala; folio 2a, top: "And we are devoted to him and entrust ourselves to him." Folio 1b–2a, bottom: "In the name of God by whose command existence came into being. The heavens gained their motion, the earth its stability from Him."

[26] For the inscriptions in the 1341 *Shāhnāma*, see Simpson (2000), 224–25 and pls. 12–13. Those at the bottom of folios 6b–7a continue the same pious theme: "The exalted is God, one without equal, whom lords call Lord."

[27] Freer Balʿamī, folio 1b: "In the name of God, the Merciful, the Compassionate." Fitzherbert (2001), 81. 1333 *Shāhnāma*, folio 5b: "In the name of God the Merciful."

those associated with Injuid patronage. The illuminated panels on its folios 2b–3a include the Basmala and the beginning of Sūra 1 at the top and praises to God and the Prophet Muḥammad in Arabic at the bottom. The inscription at the top of folio 6a, right over the dedicatory rosette, contains a fragmentary and rather enigmatic Arabic verse, ending with the word *kitāb*, that may be self-referential. Finally, the illuminations at the top and bottom of folios 6b–7a are inscribed, as mentioned above, with a Persian invocation in praise of God.[28]

Given the lack of any systematic study of the illuminated inscriptions in Ilkhanid and Injuid manuscripts (or any other Persian manuscripts, for that matter), it is difficult to know exactly how to evaluate the relatively small number discussed here. The purpose of those headings that give a text's title and/or author's name and/or evoke its contents, as in the 1330 *Shāhnāma* (folio 1a), the 1341 *Mu'nis al-aḥrār* (folios 1a and 4b–5a), the Freer small *Shāhnāma* (folio 1b), and the 1307–8 *Kalīla wa Dimna* (3b–4a and 4b–5a, bottom) is clear. As for the Qur'anic quotations, the Basmala and the equivalent invocations in Persian, and other pious expressions, these would seem to subscribe to the venerable tradition (or perhaps it should be called an obligation) within Islam of starting both quotidian and extraordinary activities, including oral and written communication, by calling down the blessings of God. That these invocations figure within the illumination of varied works of Persian secular literature (including a prose history, an epic poem, animal fables, and a poetic anthology), and that they repeat regularly at the very least confirms the extent to which Muslim tradition had become ingrained within Mongol culture in Iran, including the arts, by the first half of the fourteenth century.[29]

Frontispieces

As sketched briefly at the outset, the pictorial frontispiece tradition in late thirteenth- and fourteenth-century Persian illustrated manu-

[28] Simpson (2000), 223–25 and pls. 8–13.

[29] Komaroff and Carboni, eds. (2002), 53–59, 117–33. Given that a number of the manuscripts with these inscriptions can be associated with Īnjū style and patronage, it is possible that they reflect some particular dynastic piety.

scripts continued an artistic practice of earlier thirteenth-century Arab illustrated manuscripts, which in turn derived from Western art, including late antique, Early Christian, and Byzantine. In the initial stages of its development, that is, the fifth–sixth centuries AD, full-page frontispieces in Western manuscripts depicted classical authors, such as poets, philosophers, and physicians. With the migration of these images into illustrated Christian texts in the sixth century, the four Evangelists became the most frequently depicted authors in the history of Western book illumination. Sometimes such authors were shown with their muses. Other frontispiece figures also regularly included donors or patrons to whom manuscripts were dedicated, as well as rulers in whose reigns manuscripts were produced. By the eleventh century, certain of these figure types had been combined, with an author often represented in the act of offering his book to a patron or ruler or other protector. Thus the single figure 'portrait' morphed into the dedication scene, which in turn became a popular image in European manuscripts beginning in the twelfth and thirteenth centuries. This period coincides, of course, with the incorporation of the pictorial frontispiece in Arab illustrated manuscripts. During the course of the thirteenth century the repertoire of such opening images in Arab codices developed to encompass three distinctive iconographic types: the author (sometimes called author portrait) or literary *topos*, the princely or royal *topos* (with the prince sometimes also functioning as patron), and the combined author-prince-patron or presentation *topos*. Not surprisingly, given the art-historical continuum between Arab and Persian frontispieces, precisely the same typology characterizes the pictorial frontispiece in Ilkhanid and Injuid manuscripts. In other words, there are basically three types of early Persian frontispieces, none of which is exactly original. As we shall see, however, they become transformed in response to their particular text and time.

The history of the Persian frontispiece begins with the author or literary type, as epitomized by the *Rasā'il Ikhwān al-Ṣafā'* of 1287 (pls. 11–12). The frontispiece to this volume comes directly out of an Arab milieu and the Arab style of manuscript illustration as practiced in Baghdad during the thirteenth century, and depicts the five 'encyclopedia' authors in a two-story architectural setting. The three authors on the left (folio 4a) have books and converse animatedly among themselves; the two on the right are more contemplative and seem to be dictating to a scribe. Attendants, including one energetically fanning the air (possibly heated by too much debate!), flank the sages, while other secondary figures, who may be scribes or students, look down from the balcony above. Despite the quintessentially Arab character of the scene, these venerable authors were clearly inhabiting a new world order following the fall of Baghdad and the regime change of 1258, as evidenced by the presence of at least one attendant, on the far left of folio 4a, represented as a Mongol. Three years later, when the *Ta'rīkh-i jahān-gushāy* volume was produced, the political and cultural changes in Baghdad had become much more overtly manifest, with two figures, one seated and one standing, on the left side of the double-page composition garbed and coiffed *à la Mongole* and the landscape full of Far Eastern motifs (pl. 13). Yet notwithstanding the radical stylistic differences between this frontispiece of 1290 and its 1287 predecessor, it remains a recognizable author type with a seated secretary or scribe taking dictation from a standing muse-like figure. At the same time, it has been fused with what Richard Ettinghausen aptly characterized as the "royal state portrait" type, here referred to as the princely or royal *topos*, since the standing figure is obviously a person of authority.[30] Long ago the seated secretary was labeled 'Alā' Dīn Ṣāḥib Dīwān, which was the official title for 'Alā' al-Dīn 'Aṭā Malik Juwaynī, author of the *Ta'rīkh-i jahān-gushāy* and governor of Baghdad from 1259 to 1282. Modern scholarship has variously identified the man standing and gesticulating in front of Juwaynī as one of several Mongol leaders. Possible candidates include Hülegü, the Ilkhanid ruler and conqueror of Baghdad (r. 1256–65), or his successor Abaqa Khan (r. 1265–82) or the viceroy Amir Arghun.[31] Whatever the figure's exact identity, his superior status is clearly underscored on the facing page by the richly caparisoned horse and attending groom, a motif familiar from the 'princely cycle' in Islamic art. Furthermore, he certainly may be understood as the author's patron.[32] Thus we have here a melding of

[30] Ettinghausen (1959), 50.

[31] Exception has been taken to such efforts at identification, on the grounds that Juwaynī's text contains no suggestion that it was dictated to any Mongol leader and that the image does not fit with descriptions of Mongol protocol. See Soucek (1998), 125.

[32] Ettinghausen (1959), 48–49. Following Ettinghausen, Komaroff and Carboni ([2002], cat. no. 1) observe that the frontispiece is a consolidation in which "the patron is also sort of a muse for the writer." See also Hoffman (1993), n. 9.

two types: the author-cum-literary *topos* and the princely-cum-patron *topos*, with the latter given greater prominence.

Some ten years later, that is, about the turn of the century, Persian frontispiece imagery experienced two simultaneous developments. One is represented by the *Kalīla wa Dimna* manuscript of c. 1300, in which the literary and princely *topoi*, already conflated in the 1290 *Ta'rīkh-i jahān-gushāy*, expand into a full-blown presentation *topos*. The right side of this frontispiece (folio 1b; pl. 15) depicts five seated figures, including a pair of men sitting cross-legged on cushions below who seem to be exchanging an open book and thus may be identified as scholars or authors, and three beardless youths above, whose bookstands and penboxes mark them almost certainly as scribes or students (so here we have a conflated or compressed version of the *Rasā'il Ikhwān al-Ṣafā'* double composition). The dark-bearded figure on the far right, wearing a green robe and striped turban, reappears on the left side of the composition seated on a stool (folio 2a). Here there can be little ambiguity about his authorial role since he offers an open book to the gesturing figure at left. Likewise there can be no mistaking that person's royal or princely status with his golden crown and high-backed throne. Equally clear from their attire and hairstyles is the Mongol identity of the king's four flanking attendants, including two falconers. Given their sartorial relation to the two principal figures in the 1290 *Ta'rīkh-i jahān-gushāy* and their even stronger resemblance to comparable attendant figures in a *Marzubānnāma* manuscript illustrated in Baghdad in 698/1299, these figures would seem to clinch the attribution of this little *Kalīla wa Dimna* manuscript to the last decade of the thirteenth century and to the western part of the Ilkhanid realm, possibly even Baghdad.[33]

Pancaroğlu ([2001], 169) considers that the author is marginalized with respect to the patron.

[33] Characteristically Mongol sartorial details include the falconers' crossover robes (worn also by the enthroned ruler), bunches of hair at their shoulders, and feather headdresses. See Simpson (1982), 103–5, 109–10. It seems unlikely to me that the manuscript could be much earlier than the 1290 *Ta'rīkh-i jahān-gushāy*, where the two principal figures also are presented as Mongol. These features argue against the early thirteenth-century attribution proposed by Pancaroğlu (2001), 162; her identification of the scene will be taken up below. O'Kane's proposed dating of 1260–85 has somewhat greater validity since at least it falls into the Ilkhanid period, although he does not really explain this specific time frame, and does not seem to have taken the details of clothing and hairstyle into account. O'Kane (2003), 228.

Be that as it may, the key point here is that this double-page *Kalīla wa Dimna* painting exemplifies the combination of the literary and princely types of frontispiece imagery. It also turns out to be a unique instance within early Persian frontispieces of such a fusion into a presentation scene.

If the turn of the century, say from 1290 to 1300, when this *Kalīla wa Dimna* manuscript was likely to have been illustrated, marks a moment of typological conflation for the early Persian frontispiece, it also encompasses a period of transition when the combined *topoi* that constitute the presentation *topos* separate out, leaving the princely image as the main frontispiece type. This shift, away from the author *topos* and towards the princely or royal *topos*, seems to be signaled by the Freer *Balʿamī* frontispiece, whose surviving picture depicts a crowned and centrally enthroned ruler, facing forward and with a hawk perched on his right wrist (pl. 14). This figure is surrounded by attendants and advisors, and overflown by two swooping angels or genii.[34] Notwithstanding these heavenly hosts, the scene seems to be set in an interior. And although the king's hierarchy of advisors includes a Muslim *ʿalīm* or man of learning, who seems to be holding a pen in one hand and a scroll or manuscript folios in the other, the composition is clearly not about the presentation of a book. Indeed, Teresa Fitzherbert has suggested that the ruler is presiding over an execution, and the composition, as underscored by the Qurʾanic verse above, is a scene of judgment. We shall return to this interpretation later. For the moment what is important to recognize is that, in terms of the history of Persian frontispiece imagery, we now are passing from the realm of the author and scholarly pursuits into the land of the monarch and princely authority and pastimes.

This new territory—and here of course we are not talking about 'new' in terms of the general history of Islamic frontispiece imagery since earlier Arab frontispieces feature royalty in various guises,[35] but only that it appears to be novel for Persian manuscripts—is clearly staked in the 1307–8 *Kalīla wa Dimna* manuscript (pl. 16). Here the crowned ruler is enthroned in the center, holding a beaker-like cup and looking down slightly to his right. He is surrounded by four

---

[34] In addition to its general resemblance to certain Arab frontispieces (Ettinghausen [1962], 65 and 85), the iconography of this image includes elements absorbed from ancient Near Eastern, Central Asian and Indian art. Simpson (1982), 106–7.

[35] Farès (1961), pls. 8 and 10; Hoffman (1993), figs. 6a and 6b.

close ranks of turbaned courtiers and attendants, all oriented towards the center, including two seated on either side of a table with wine bottles in the foreground and two others who hold up spears over the king's head and beneath a kind of vestigial baldachin or umbrella or curtain above. All this appears on the left, or interior, side of the composition (folio 4a). The facing (right and exterior) side depicts also tightly packed rows of turbaned figures and animals, including the ruler's horse (and possibly also a dog) tended by a small groom in the grassy foreground as well as two cheetahs and a falconer in the upper ranks (folio 3b). And while most of these figures turn towards the ruler on opposite sides, the groom and two other figures aligned above him at the left edge of the scene face in the other direction, as if they were in charge of each row of rank-and-file figures.

Much the same overall concept and treatment of the princely *topos* can be seen in the frontispieces in the three dated *Shāhnāma*s of 1330, 1333, and 1341, particularly in terms of their dual interior/exterior setting and their serried order of figures, who have a very obvious focus on the left side and no apparent centering point on the right (pls. 17–18 and fig. 34). None of these scenes is exactly identical, however, and all three exhibit individual iconographic features. The symmetrical representation of the rulers and their ranked courts on the left side of these double compositions conforms most closely, even down to the direction in which the monarchs face, although their hand gestures vary, as does the placement and design of their thrones. Likewise the number, appearance, and attire of the kings' courtiers and attendants differ. The uppermost right-hand row in the 1333 manuscript, for instance, includes two falconers, plus a third who wears a 'finger perch' but has no bird. In addition, both the king here and the one in the 1330 enthronement seem to be protected by a pair of bodyguards, the equivalent, perhaps, of the spear-bearers in the 1307–8 *Kalīla wa Dimna* frontispiece, who stand directly behind the throne and seem to be scanning the rest of the assembly. All three *Shāhnāma* compositions feature groups of musicians playing in the foreground; in the 1333 manuscript they entertain solo, whereas in the 1330 work they are accompanied by dancers who perform right in front of the throne, a position occupied in the 1341 volume by a table and pair of wine bottles. Both the 1333 and 1341 compositions include winged angels or genii flying before parted curtains or draperies and above the enthroned kings; each of the 1333 pair lifts up a crown, while the 1341 duo together holds a golden platter. These celestial creatures are missing from the 1330 volume, possibly having been painted out or over (with a red curtain) in a modern refurbishment.

Much greater divergence occurs on the right sides of these *Shāhnāma* frontispieces. The 1330 composition repeats the general scheme of the 1307–8 *Kalīla wa Dimna* manuscript with rows of figures (all now depicted as Mongols) and animals, including a pair of cheetahs, who form the king's company. Here, however, the royal entourage is even more numerous and diverse with multiple horses and grooms at the lower right and a seated majordomo-type figure, whom three others entertain with music and drink, at the lower left. The top row of five figures includes one at the far right with a repainted (and therefore no longer particularly Mongol) head carrying a gazelle around his neck, another holding a golden bowl, two carrying geese, and another apparently feeding what looks like a falcon with outstretched wings. Again, as in the earlier *Kalīla wa Dimna* composition, all these retainers are oriented towards the opposite page, except for those at the left edge, including the majordomo and the falconer, who face in the other direction, again as if to lead or direct those coming along behind.

The iconography of the right sides of the 1333 and 1341 *Shāhnāma* frontispieces is totally different. Instead of largely static rows of standing figures, these compositions feature dynamic hunting scenes. That of the 1333 *Shāhnāma* depicts four rows of horsemen, each galloping along in more or less alternate directions with their bows bent and swords drawn. (Actually, only one hunter wields a sword and another, in the upper left, seems to carry no weapon at all.) Their quarry consists primarily of horses or onagers, with a whole herd of equine-like creatures in the center (possibly along with a large feline at the left, being slashed by the lone swordsman) and a trio of hares at the top. The scene is packed so tightly that there is hardly room for anything extraneous, although one spiky plant in the center foreground and a leafy branch at the upper left side have been included to signify the outdoor setting. The hunt in the 1341 *Shāhnāma*, by contrast, takes place in an expansive mountainous landscape, where multicolored peaks edged in gold serve as both the backdrop and the refuge for hunters and prey alike. In the foreground a pair of bearded and mounted men face each other, with their horses very formally posed (each with foreleg raised), on either side of an odd chicken-like creature. They are accompanied by two smaller and beardless riders positioned behind. A large quadruped, resembling an onager, gazes upwards from the center of the mountains, while two archers on foot take aim at four other animals above and at the left side.

Royalty and royal equestrian pastimes are also featured in the single-page frontispiece in the Freer small *Shāhnāma* (fig. 33). Instead of a single, unified field of action, however, this picture plane consists of two superimposed registers, separated and framed by a gold interlace band. The upper register depicts a polo game, with the foreground center dominated by a large crowned king riding a small black horse while facing the viewer and holding up a polo stick. Two other horsemen play vigorously alongside the monarch and four others above, all holding polo sticks at different angles. The lower register contains a hunt, with a crowned king once again in the center, galloping towards the right and raising a sword to slash backwards at a yellow tiger (or possibly a lioness). Behind the king a mounted hunter takes aim with a bow, possibly at the male gazelle already struck by an arrow at right, while three other hunters above go after prey, including two onagers, with weapons of various kinds.

As previously noted, the Freer small *Shāhnāma* has been attributed to Baghdad c. 1300 on the basis of its strong affinity, especially in its figural style, to manuscripts documented or accepted as late thirteenth-century Baghdad production, such as the 1290 *Ta'rīkh-i jahān-gushāy* and the 1299 *Marzubānnāma*.[36] The iconography of its frontispiece, however, is closer (albeit hardly identical) to the right sides of the *Shāhnāma*s created in Shiraz during the Īnjū period, and it now may offer grounds for reconsidering the attribution of the undated *Shāhnāma* to the same milieu.

In addition to its attribution, a question remains about this frontispiece's original configuration and iconography. All the Ilkhanid and Injuid frontispieces belonging to the princely *topos* depict an interior

---

[36] The Freer small *Shāhnāma* is generally discussed together with two other dispersed and small format manuscripts, the so-called First small *Shāhnāma* and the Second small *Shāhnāma*. For the attribution of these works to Baghdad, c. 1300, see Simpson (1979), 272–307. Various reservations have been voiced about this attribution, however, and a recent consideration places these works in a broader temporal and geographic context. See Komaroff and Carboni, eds. (2002), cat. nos. 33–35, where three folios from the First small *Shāhnāma* are attributed to Northwestern Iran or Baghdad, c. 1300–30.

scene, consistently an enthronement, on the left side of the double composition and an exterior scene, featuring either a royal audience (1307–8 *Kalīla wa Dimna* and 1330 *Shāhnāma*) or more frequently a hunt (1333, 1341, 1352–53 *Shāhnāma*s and 1341 *Mu'nis al-aḥrār*, the latter two to be discussed below), on the right. The Freer small *Shāhnāma* composition is the only one with two exterior scenes of royal pleasure in the place reserved in all the other manuscripts for an interior enthronement. It is tempting to speculate but impossible to prove that the small *Shāhnāma* image once had a facing half to its right with an interior enthronement, thus reversing what otherwise would seem to be a common iconographic pattern in early Persian painting.[37] And if the small *Shāhnāma* frontispiece only ever existed as a single folio, perhaps its unusual two-tiered format with crowned kings (or the same king depicted twice?) centered on both top and bottom was intended to provide the comparable focus on a single, dominant royal personage as the enthronement scenes in our other manuscripts.

While unusual, the double-register layout in the Freer small *Shāh-nāma* is not entirely unique. The fragmentary right side of the frontispiece in the 1341 *Mu'nis al-aḥrār* also features multiple registers, in this case three, divided by thin and irregular gold lines (fig. 35). Each zone encloses a separate hunting scene in a distinctive setting. The lower one features a mountainous setting, similar to that in the 1341 *Shāhnāma* but with many more landscape details—including lots of plants, a body of water, and perhaps even snow-capped mountain peaks—and a crowned horseman who gallops on the shore and slices at a tiger (or perhaps a lioness) with a long sword. In the middle zone a mounted archer shoots at a pair of hares dashing away in front of a blue pond. Sadly, this hunter has lost his head due to the damage in the upper part of the painting, so we can only surmise that he too would have been crowned. Most of the upper register is also missing, but the hooves of a brown horse (presumably carrying a rider), some plants, and the bottoms of mountains or hillocks remain visible. Perhaps the most noteworthy aspect of this right half of the frontispiece is that each of the three registers depicts only a single

[37] There is nothing on the Freer painting, such as pigment offset, that might provide a physical clue as to the original existence of a facing scene.

figure, making this more of a solo rather than a collective hunt as in the other manuscripts.

The frontispiece's facing left side consists of an enthronement and is also more condensed than its equivalent scenes in our corpus. Another novelty here is that the enthroned king, who wears a very elaborate Mongol feathered headdress, has been joined by his consort.[38] The royal pair stares attentively at each other, he raising a slender glass as if in a toast and she tightly clutching a napkin or handkerchief. The doubling of royal figures seems to have resulted in a radical reduction in their court and the elimination of some of the characters, like the musicians, dancers, and angels, seen in regular attendance in the other early Persian frontispieces. On the other hand, the queen has gained a handmaiden, who holds a large fan, and the overall setting subscribes to the interiors in the other manuscripts.

The double enthronement recurs in the 1352–53 or Stephens *Shāhnāma,* where the king and queen—he still holding a glass—are once again surrounded by a full court in tightly packed ranks, including musicians and a few figures (fig. 36) like the pair of falconers who seem to have migrated from the facing composition in the 1330 *Shāhnāma.*[39] But now both the angels and the traditional drapery have vanished. Meanwhile, across the way from the enthroned couple, there is a hunting scene that repeats various elements of earlier manuscripts: the conical mountains from the 1341 *Shāhnāma* and *Mu'nis al-aḥrār*, the rows of galloping hunters, and the prominent prey of the 1333 *Shāhnāma*, and the simple shepherd-type figure from the 1330 *Shāhnāma.* New to this otherwise familiar repertoire is the bare-shouldered, knife-wielding man being attacked by a large cheetah (or snow leopard) in the top row.

In short, the development of the early Persian frontispiece typology and iconography begins in Baghdad during the last two decades of the thirteenth century with the literary or author portrait *topos*, and quickly takes on both Mongol cultural and artistic characteristics and

---

[38] The painting has been retouched but its composition is original. Komaroff and Carboni, eds. (2002), cat. no. 9.

[39] Wright ([1997], 44) has proposed that the enthroned couple in the *Mu'nis al-aḥrār* frontispiece may have served as the model for the Stephens *Shāhnāma* rendition of the same theme.

aspects of the royal or patron *topos*.[40] Then comes an equally quick transition around 1300 when the two *topoi* at once conflate into the presentation *topos* and separate out, leaving the royal image—with two complimentary aspects, that is, interior and exterior—as the dominant iconographic type from at least 1307 (and more likely 1300) to 1352–53 in Shiraz and Isfahan and perhaps elsewhere. But while now predominant, this type is hardly static and evolves in various ways, from the single to double enthronement on one side (the left), and from courtiers to hunters and polo players in one, two, and even three fields on the other (typically the right). Meanwhile individual motifs come and go and some come back again: angels or genii are a fleeting phenomenon, whereas wine regularly vies with music for the ruler's attention and sometimes both drink and dancing strike his fancy. But basically we have what seems to be a pretty clear frontispiece history and trajectory over a sixty-five-year period.

Undoubtedly further consideration could yield a much more nuanced reading of this development. For the moment, however, there remains the question of the frontispiece's function and meaning with regard to its location, its typology, and its historical circumstances. Not surprisingly, the early Persian frontispiece seems to play various roles. As part of the front matter of a codex, it serves sometimes as a pictorial entryway through which the reader makes his way into the book, and more frequently as a kind of intermediary stop or point of transition where the reader can pause to reflect on the prefatory pages he has just perused before turning to the text that constitutes the book's main contents. In either case, and to pursue the architectural analogy, the frontispiece forms a kind of visual threshold to a literary construction.

Such a codicologically based function may very well be applicable to all frontispiece paintings, and again we would have to test this notion on more than eleven Ilkhanid and Injuid examples. There is also the possibility that these early Persian frontispieces directly relate, through the particulars of their imagery, to the texts that they adorn and that they introduce some significant aspect(s) of their books' history or contents. Certainly this appears true of the 1287

[40] Pancaroğlu ([2001], 169) sees the royal presence already in the 1287 *Rasā'il Ikhwān al-Ṣafā'* where the scholarly authors, "though prominently depicted, are contextualized in a court-like setting complete with attendants wielding fly-whisks."

Rasā'il Ikhwān al-Ṣafā' composition, which, within our corpus, is the author portrait *par excellence*. Not only does this double folio depict the *Ikhwān al-Ṣafā'* sages engrossed in intellectual activity (including, one may presume, the composing, dictating, and discussing of the very text that follows), but it also identifies the authors by name on the right and states the title of their book on the left. The connection between image and text could not be more immediate, and this frontispiece stands as an extremely individualized example of the author or literary *topos*. It also demonstrates that frontispieces can be both generic or typological and specific or customized.

In fact, the *Rasā'il Ikhwān al-Ṣafā'* may be the most convincing exemplar of an ongoing tendency to personalize the three basic types of early Persian frontispieces largely because it is the most authentic. The 1290 *Ta'rīkh-i jahān-gushāy* frontispiece, for instance, was annotated long ago with the honorific title for the text's author, 'Alā' al-Dīn 'Aṭā Malik Juwaynī, leading modern scholars to identify the seated scribe, doubtless correctly, as Juwaynī. This identification in turn prompted assumptions that the other figure in the scene also must be an actual person who, judging from his stance and attire, had to be a Mongol leader and therefore Juwaynī's patron. And so, as we already have seen, this figure too has been identified (albeit not with the same certainty as Juwaynī) and, in the process, the frontispiece as a whole assumed a specificity and contemporaneity relevant for this manuscript (or at least this text) alone. A similar approach has recently resulted in a possible identification for the frontispiece of the undated *Kalīla wa Dimna* in the Topkapı Palace Museum Library. Oya Pancaroğlu has suggested that this presentation scene, unique within our corpus, depicts on the right side Naṣrallāh Munshī, the author of the Persian translation of *Kalīla wa Dimna*, receiving a copy of the animal fables from an older scholar (possibly 'Abdallāh ibn al-Muqaffa', author of the Arabic version), and, on the left, Naṣrallāh again presenting his book to his enthroned patron, the Ghaznavid ruler Bahrām Shāh.[41]

[41] Pancaroğlu (2001), 162. The author since has expanded on her interpretation of this frontispiece within the context of textual transmission under courtly patronage in a stimulating presentation at a conference on Arab painting held at University of London in September 2004. I am indebted to Dr. Pancaroğlu for sharing her paper in advance of publication and for allowing me to include it within the manuscript's citations in Appendix I.

So, like the *Rasā'il Ikhwān al-Ṣafā'*, the frontispieces in the *Ta'rīkh-i jahān-gushāy* and the Topkapı *Kalīla wa Dimna* have come to be regarded by modern scholars as representations (generally called portraits) of their book's respective authors and patrons. Likewise, a number of other frontispieces, all belonging to the royal *topos* and several illustrating copies of the *Shāhnāma*, have been personalized with specific identities and historical contexts relating to their manuscripts' documented or supposed patrons.[42] By far the strongest argument for such a correlation can be made for the 1341 *Shāhnāma* frontispiece since the subsequent dedicatory rosettes contain a dedication to the manuscript's patron, "the great lord, honorable minister, chief vizier of glorious Fars…the venerable Ḥājjī Qiwām al-Dawla wa al-Dīn Ḥasan."[43] Why shouldn't the vizier be represented at (or at least near) the start of the deluxe copy of the Persian national epic that was made by order of his *kitābkhāna*? Other such identifications are somewhat more speculative, and rest primarily on manuscript dates and/or dynastic history. For instance, the frontal ruler bearing a hawk, a symbol of Mongol authority, in the Freer Bal'amī frontispiece may be Fakhr al-Dīn 'Īsā ibn Ibrāhīm, an Arab Christian who governed the city of Mosul for Ghazan Khan (r. 1295–1304) and who welcomed men of letters, poets and other literati at his residence.[44] Similarly, it has been proposed that the enthroned figure in the center of the left side of the frontispiece in the 1333 *Shāhnāma* represents Sharaf al-Dīn Maḥmūd Shāh who, at the time this manuscript was produced, served as the Īnjū dynasty administrator of the estates in Fars province belonging to the Ilkhan Abū Sa'īd.[45] In this capacity, Maḥmūd Shāh certainly would have had the wherewithal to commission an illustrated *Shāhnāma* and to have directed that his portrait be placed at the beginning of the volume. Likewise, Maḥmūd Shāh's son and

---

[42] There is precedent for such personalization, of course, in Arab painting, and specifically in the frontispieces to several volumes of the *Kitāb al-aghānī*, in which the ruler, sometimes enthroned and sometimes on horseback, wears a robe with *ṭirāz* bands inscribed with the name Badr al-Dīn Lu'lu', vizier of the Zangid dynasty and later *atabeg* of Mosul (1218–59). See Farès (1961), pls. 1, 8, 10, 11, and 12. See also Ettinghausen (1962), 64–65, where it is suggested that the vizier's name may have been added soon after the paintings were completed.

[43] Simpson (2000), 218.

[44] Fitzherbert (2001), 357–71.

[45] Adamova and Giuzal'ian (1985), 29; Komaroff and Carboni, eds. (2002), 216–17.

successor, Abū Isḥāq (r. 1343–57), has been identified tentatively as the prince-cum-patron who sits with his wife in the frontispiece to the *Mu'nis al-aḥrār*.[46]

If these compositions—transferred virtually wholesale from the tradition of Arab frontispiece painting and incorporated into early Persian manuscripts because of the relevance or appropriateness of the royal *topos*, with its symmetrical arrangement of the central enthroned ruler, flanking rows of courtiers and attendants, entertainers below, and angels or genii above—could depict specific personages,[47] then certainly they could also be transformed, through the addition of specific details, from formulaic scenes of homage into representations of special occasions or events. Virtually all the enthroned figures in our manuscripts turn to their right, as if addressing figures on that side. This posture, sometimes reinforced by hands raised in gestures of speech, suggests at the very least that the monarchs are presiding over royal receptions or audiences and that the places closest to the throne and which the kings face are reserved for visiting dignitaries. Such an interpretation has been given, for instance, to the left side of the 1333 *Shāhnāma* frontispiece, where the manuscript's presumed patron, the Īnjū administrator Maḥmūd Shāh, greets an Ilkhanid delegation, identifiable by their Mongol-style hats, moustaches, and beards.[48] And when an enthronement is combined, as in the 1307–8 *Kalīla wa Dimna* and the 1330 *Shāhnāma*, with the facing scene of respectful courtiers arranged in rows, holding animals and objects and seemingly led or guided by an escort, then the audience seems to take on the trappings of gift-giving.[49] Indeed, many of the animals,

---

[46] Wright (1997), 45–46. Here Wright also cites a personal conversation with Stefano Carboni (September 1994) concerning the possibility that the *Mu'nis al-aḥrār*'s enthroned couple might represent Sadi Beg, the sister of the Ilkhanid ruler Abū Sa'īd, with either her husband or her son. While agreeing with Wright that the woman may be the more important figure in this scene and perhaps even the manuscript's patron (because of her position to the right of the man), Carboni's own most recent view is only that the painting doubtless represents a Mongol royal couple, without venturing any specific identifications. Komaroff and Carboni, eds. (2002), 216. Also see Wright's contribution to this volume, n. 51 [ed.].

[47] In addition to identifying the enthroned figure(s), it may eventually be possible to specify the figures who surround the ruler, if not by name, at least by the function they served or the offices they held within the royal household. See Charles Melville's contribution to this volume.

[48] Adamova and Giuzal'ian (1985), 30.

[49] Wright (1997), 39.

particularly the cheetahs and falcons, correspond to descriptions of the kinds of gifts exchanged between the Mongol and Mamluk dynasties during the fourteenth century.[50] In fact, Mongol and/or medieval ceremonial practices may lie behind much of the iconography and significance of our frontispieces, in ways that remain to be investigated.

The Freer Balʿamī offers a far more specific and tantalizing instance of a royal *topos* frontispiece imbued with specific meaning. This enthronement image contains various features not found in the other paintings, such as the Muslim *ʿalīm*, a turbaned figure possibly holding a Mongol patent of authority, and two decapitated bodies (actually, two disembodied heads). In addition, it is surmounted by a verse from the Qurʾān (38:26) invoking Dawūd or David, in which "God empowers David as his deputy on earth and admonishes him to judge men rightly."[51] The combination of these pictorial and epigraphic details embedded in an otherwise standard enthronement has lead Fitzherbert, in her detailed and thought-provoking analysis of the frontispiece, to posit that the setting is a court of law and that the scene is one of execution and judgment. She further interprets the frontispiece as "a sober statement of Mongol and Muslim claims to be God's elect, chosen to rule the earth" during the reign of Ghazan Khan and as a projection of the legitimacy of Ilkhanid rule in both Muslim and Mongol terms.[52] It seems particularly apt that such an image should appear at the very start of a historical text about prophets and kings.

It is perhaps not just a coincidence that the clearest instance of a frontispiece's potential for multiple meanings—one relating to typology (and thus also to its artistic origins), another to its historical context, and yet another to its literary content—comes in a manuscript datable to c. 1300. After all, and as we have seen, the turn of the century (when this manuscript was created) marked a typological shift in frontispiece imagery from the venerable author *topos* to

[50] See the contribution by Donald Little to this volume. For gift-giving in Iran in general, see Wiesehöfer, Matthee, and Floor (2001), 604–17. Unfortunately this article jumps over the medieval era, but fortunately the section on gifting in the Safavid period by Rudi Matthee (609–14) is of great relevance. See also Lambton (1994), 145–58.

[51] Fitzherbert (2001), 12.

[52] Fitzherbert (2001), 52, 370.

the presentation *topos*, in which literary and princely types combine. At the same time the royal *topos* emerges to become the dominant, indeed the sole, form of frontispiece imagery during the first half of the fourteenth century. A clue to this paradigmatic development may be found in our lone presentation frontispiece, also c. 1300, and in turn can lead to a broader sense of the significance of and motivation for early Persian frontispieces as a whole.

As already mentioned, the frontispiece in the little undated *Kalīla wa Dimna* manuscript in Istanbul has been identified as depicting, on the right side, the author of the Persian version of these popular animal fables, Naṣrallāh Munshī, and an older scholar and, on the left, Naṣrallāh and his patron. Certainly the general interpretation of this scene as an author portrait combined with a royal portrait to form a presentation scene is valid. The painting assumes another iconographic identity, however, when considered together with its two illuminated headings at the top and bottom, which happen to be the first two verses of Firdawsī's *Shāhnāma*.[53] Admittedly, these two verses are formulaic and pietistic and correspond in tone and sentiment to those Arabic and Persian invocations to God that appear as illuminated headings of the front matter folios of so many of the manuscripts in our corpus. What is unusual here is that the inscriptions bracketing the *Kalīla wa Dimna* frontispiece come from a recognizable literary (that is, secular) text rather than a standardized repertoire of divine praises, and from a text that, furthermore, is not the one the manuscript contains. This unexpected situation suggests that the frontispiece image is also something other than what one might expect, and that it could represent, on the right, the *Shāhnāma*'s author Firdawsī and the court poets of Ghazni to whom he had to prove his poetic prowess, and on the left, Firdawsī presenting his epic masterwork to his Ghaznavid patron Maḥmūd.

But why would a volume of animal fables open with verses from (and a painting possibly relating to) the Persian national epic? The

---

[53] Firdawsī (1960–71), vol. 1, 12.

In the name of Him whom thought can not transcend
The Lord of wisdom and the soul. Of fame
And rank the Lord as well. The Lord who feeds
Us every day and guides us on our path.

O'Kane ([2003], 48) also has recognized that the *Kalīla wa Dimna* headings contain these *Shāhnāma* verses.

answer may lie in the pictorial history of the *Shāhnāma*, which emerged as the most popular Persian text for illustration in codex form around 1300, just about the time that the Topkapı *Kalīla wa Dimna* was created, and which dominated the illustrative and narrative landscape in Iran for the next half century. Indeed, of the close to three dozen illustrated manuscripts of this period (ranging in literary genre from encyclopedias, bestiaries, and fables to cosmographies, histories, and poetic anthologies), about one-third are volumes of the *Shāhnāma*. More significantly, the *Shāhnāma* "became the vehicle par excellence for the reassertion of Iranian identity at the Mongol court" and the illustrated *Shāhnāma* a dramatic and original expression of Iran's artistic creativity.[54]

The obvious literary distinctions among Ilkhanid and Injuid manuscripts notwithstanding, a loose, thematic connection can be drawn. No matter what their actual prose or poetic contents and whether or not they belong directly, as do the fables of *Kalīla wa Dimna*, to the mirror for princes genre, many of the illustrated works of the Mongol period deal with government and statecraft; with the morality, conduct, and ethics of rulers; and with the rights and responsibilities of kings, including their relation to God.[55] Similar concerns predominate in the *Shāhnāma*, along with the legitimate succession of Iranian monarchs. Given the Ilkhanid and Injuid preoccupation with their legitimacy and their need to proclaim their right to rule Iran in whole or, like the Īnjūs, in part, and given also their evident attraction to and patronage of the Book of Kings and the concomitant rise of the illustrated *Shāhnāma* around 1300 (with its pictorial program dominated by enthronements, hunts, and other princely activities), it is perhaps not too far-fetched to imagine that Firdawsī's epic poem was also the impetus for the typological shift from 'author portrait' to royal representation that took place in frontispiece imagery about the same time.[56] Although the princely frontispieces derive their typological form from the past and can be invested with iconographical (and perhaps even iconological)

---

[54] Melville (2002), 55.

[55] This even pertains to the *Mu'nis al-aḥrār* poetic anthology, which contains one chapter with selections from the *Shāhnāma* and another beginning with a eulogy for a prince of the Seljuq dynasty. Morton (1994), 49–55.

[56] The *Shāhnāma* also may have been the motor for the acceleration of manuscript illustration and visual narration as a whole in this period.

meaning from the present, they may owe their very existence to the critical role played by the *Shāhnāma*, and its compelling vision of kings and kingship, in expressing the ideology of Mongol rule and shaping the practice of Persian painting during the first half of the fourteenth century.

A few final thoughts about Ilkhanid and Injuid frontispieces as a whole, again with an emphasis on their development after 1300, are in order. The nine compositions that can be dated or are datable to the fourteenth century belong to volumes with extensive illustrative programs, mostly of narrative scenes.[57] A pictorial frontispiece thus may have been *de rigueur* for all illustrated manuscripts of the period, a telltale sign at the beginning of a book that other paintings were to follow. Such a composition may also have been regarded as a visual counterpart to the verbal expressions of piety that appear so frequently as illuminated headings on these manuscripts' opening folios. And like these pious invocations, which vary in their use of Arabic and Persian while calling on God, the frontispieces represent variations on the theme of ruler while adhering to the royal or princely *topos*. Through its frontispiece and front matter, each manuscript projects its own unique version of the twin notions of divine authority and princely power. Surely other illustrated volumes of the period, now fragmentary or dispersed, such as the *Jāmiʿ al-tawārīkh* dated 714/1314–15 and the so-called Great Mongol *Shāhnāma*, included within their opening folios propitiatory headings and double-page royal frontispieces intended to convey the same message.

[57] The *Mu'nis al-aḥrār* is the exception here, since its thirty-three small illustrations (on six folios) do not narrate a pictorial 'story.' Instead they depict the poetic terms, symbols and emblems, including zodiacal signs, employed in three sections of chap. 29. For the correlation between the poetic terms and pictorial images, see Swietochowski and Carboni (1994), 17–21, and, in the same volume, Morton (1994), 53–57.

APPENDIX I: ILKHANID AND INJUID MANUSCRIPTS WITH FRONTISPIECES

Chronological listing and selected bibliography

Dated manuscripts

<table>
<tr><td rowspan="2">1287 Rasā'il Ikhwān al-Ṣafā' wa khillān al-wafā'</td><td>folios 3b–4a</td><td>Istanbul, Süleymaniye Mosque Library, Esad Efendi 3638</td><td>Copied by Buzurgmihr ibn Muḥammad al-Ṭūsī in Baghdad, Shawwāl 686/ November 1287</td></tr>
<tr><td colspan="3">Farès (1957); Ettinghausen (1962), 98–102 with color reproductions; Hoffman (1993), 13, 15 and fig. 5a–b; and Robert Hillenbrand's article in the present volume.</td></tr>
<tr><td rowspan="2">1290 'Alā' al-Dīn 'Aṭā Malik Juwaynī, Ta'rīkh-i jahān-gushāy</td><td>folios 1b–2a</td><td>Paris, Bibliothèque Nationale de France, suppl. pers. 205</td><td>Copied by Rashīd al-Khwāfī, 4 Dhū al-ḥijja 689/8 December 1290; attributed to Baghdad (or possibly Maragha)</td></tr>
<tr><td colspan="3">Ettinghausen (1959), 44–52; Fitzherbert (1996), 69–75; Richard, F. (1997), cat. no. 7 with color reproduction; Soucek (1998), 121–25; Sims (2002), 281 and cat. 198 (with color reproduction of folio 1b); Komaroff and Carboni, eds. (2002), 173, fig. 201 (color) and cat no. 1.</td></tr>
<tr><td rowspan="2">1307–8 Abū al-Ma'ālī Naṣrallāh, Kalīla wa Dimna</td><td>folios 2b–3a</td><td>London, British Library, Or. 13.506</td><td>Copied by [Abū] al-Makārim Ḥasan, 707/1307–8; attributed to Iran (possibly Shiraz)</td></tr>
<tr><td colspan="3">Waley and Titley (1975), 42–61; Swietochowski and Carboni (1994), fig. 7; Komaroff and Carboni, eds. (2002), cat. no. 3; O'Kane (2003), 49, 228–29 (Appendix 12).</td></tr>
<tr><td rowspan="2">1322 Qazwīnī, 'Ajā'ib al-makhlūqāt wa-gharā'ib al-mawjādāt</td><td>folios 1b–2a</td><td>Istanbul, Süleymaniye Mosque Library, Yeni Cami 813</td><td>Copied by Muḥammad ibn Mas'ūd ibn Muḥammad ibn Maḥmūd al-Hamad[ānī], 722/1322; attributed to Shiraz</td></tr>
<tr><td colspan="3">Berlekamp (2003b), 97–100, 244–75 (Appendix B), fig. 4b.</td></tr>
</table>

1330 Firdawsī, *Shāhnāma*	folios 4b–5a	Istanbul, Topkapı Palace Museum Library, H. 1479	Copied by Ḥasan ibn ʿAlī ibn al-Ḥusaynī al-Bahmānī, Ṣafar 731/November 1330; attributed to Shiraz
	Çağman and Tanındı (1979), cat. no. 14; Çağman and Tanındı (1986), 51.		
1333 Firdawsī, *Shāhnāma*	folios 1b–2a [reconstructed as folios 4b–5a]	St. Petersburg, National Library of Russia, Dorn 329	Copied by ʿAbd al-Raḥmān al-H...ʿAbdallāh ibn al-Ẓāhir, last day of Jumādā I 733/16 February 1333; attributed to Shiraz
	Adamova and Giuzal'ian (1985), for frontispiece see 28–30 and 41–44 with color reproductions; Swietochowski and Carboni (1994), fig. 6; Digard, ed. (2002), cat. no. 183 (with color reproduction of folio 1b); Adamova (2004), 51–64.		
1341 Firdawsī, *Shāhnāma*	folios 1b–2a [as reconstructed]	Manuscript dispersed. Frontispiece: Washington, D.C., Smithsonian Institution, Arthur M. Sackler Gallery, S1986.113, side 2 and S1986.112, recto	Dedicated to the vizier of Fars, Qiwām al-Dawla wa al-Dīn Ḥasan, end of Ramaḍān 741/mid-March 1341. Copied by Ḥasan ibn Muḥammad ibn ʿAlī ibn Ḥusaynī, known as al-Mawṣilī, dated 20 Dhū al-Qaʿda [741]/7 May [1341]; attributed to Shiraz
	Lowry and Beach (1988), cat. nos. 74–77; Simpson (2000), pls. 6–7 (color).		
1341 Muḥammad ibn Badr al-Dīn Jājarmī, *Mu'nis al-aḥrār fī daqā'iq al-ashʿār*	folios 1b–2a	Manuscript dispersed. Frontispiece: Kuwait, Dar al-Athar al-Islamiyya, LNS 9 MS	Dated Ramaḍān 741/February–March 1341; attributed to Isfahan
	Swietochowski and Carboni (1994), cat. no. 1 with color reproduction; Komaroff and Carboni, eds. (2002), 215–16, fig. 261 (color) and cat. no. 9; Sims (2002), 122 (color).		

<table>
<tr><td rowspan="2">1352–53 Firdawsī, *Shāhnāma*</td><td>folios 4b–5a [as reconstructed]</td><td>Washington, D.C., Smithsonian Institution, Arthur M. Sackler Gallery, LTS 1998.1.1.2 and 1.1.3 [Lent by Mr. and Mrs. Farhad Ebrahimi] (some folios in other collections)</td><td>*Shamsa* on folio 211a inscribed 753/1352–53; attributed to Shiraz</td></tr>
<tr><td colspan="3">Sotheby's, London (1998), lot 41 with color reproduction.</td></tr>
</table>

Undated Manuscripts

<table>
<tr><td rowspan="2">Undated, Abū al-Maʿālī Naṣrallāh, *Kalīla wa Dimna*</td><td>folios 1b–2a</td><td>Istanbul, Topkapı Palace Museum Library, H. 363</td><td>Attributed to c. 1300, Iran</td></tr>
<tr><td colspan="3">Çağman and Tanındı (1979), cat. no. 7 (attributed to end of thir-teenth century); Çağman and Tanındı (1986), 50–51 (attributed to Mesopotamia or possibly Anatolia, later thirteenth century) with color reproduction of frontispiece (no. 25); Pancaroğlu (2001), 162 and fig. 9a–b (atttributed to early thirteenth century); O'Kane (2003), 49, 228 (Appendix 11; attributed to Baghdad, c. 1260–85); Pancaroğlu (2004a); Roxburgh, ed. (2005), cat. no. 37 (attributed to Mosul or Baghdad, late thirteenth century).</td></tr>
<tr><td rowspan="2">Undated, Balʿamī, *Tarjama-yi ta'rīkh-i Ṭabarī*</td><td>folio 1a</td><td>Washington, D.C., Smithsonian Institution, Freer Gallery of Art, 56.16</td><td>Attributed to c. 1300, Iraq (Mosul) or the Jazira</td></tr>
<tr><td colspan="3">Fitzherbert (2001), vol. 1, 12–52 and pls. 1a–m.</td></tr>
<tr><td rowspan="2">Undated, Firdawsī, *Shāhnāma*</td><td>folio 1a [as reconstructed]</td><td>Washington, D.C., Smithsonian Institution, Freer Gallery of Art, 29.25r</td><td>Attributed to c. 1300, Baghdad or 1330s, Shiraz</td></tr>
<tr><td colspan="3">Simpson (1979), 55–84 and Appendix 2.</td></tr>
</table>

APPENDIX II: ORDER OF FRONT MATTER

	1a	1b–2a	2b–3a	3b–4a	4b–5a	5b–6a	6b–7a
1287 *Rasā'il Ikhwān al-Ṣafā'*	–	–/preface	preface	frontispiece with title page	text begins	text	text
1290 *Ta'rīkh-i jahān-gushāy*	*shamsa*	frontis-piece	text begins	text	text	text	text
1307–8 *Kalīla wa Dimna*	–	–/–	frontis-piece	illuminated title page	text begins with illuminated headings	text	text
1330 *Shāhnāma*	*shamsa* with title page	prose preface with illu-minated headings	prose preface	prose preface	frontispiece	text begins with illuminated headings	text
1333 *Shāhnāma*	?	[prose preface]	[prose preface]	prose preface	frontispiece	text begins with illu-minated heading on 5b	text
1341 *Shāhnāma**	?	frontis-piece	prose preface	prose preface	+ prose preface with painting	*shamsa*s with dedi-cation and illuminated heading on 6a	text begins with illuminated headings
1341 *Mu'nis al-aḥrār*	*shamsa* with title page	frontis-piece	preface with illu-minated headings (top only)	index	chart with illuminated headings	text begins	text
1352–53 *Shāhnāma**	?	? prose preface with illu-minated headings on 2a	prose preface	[prose preface on 3b]	frontispiece	text begins with illuminated heading	text

	1a	1b–2a	2b–3a	3b–4a	4b–5a	5b–6a	6b–7a
Topkapı *Kalīla wa Dimna*	–	frontispiece with inscription	text begins with illuminated headings	text	text	text	text
Freer *Balʿamī* *	frontispiece with inscription	text begins with illuminated heading on 1b	text	text	text	text	text
Freer *Shāhnāma* *	frontispiece	text begins with illuminated heading on 1b	text	text	text	text	text

Key

*   Opening folios uncertain; possibly additional folio(s) originally preceded extant folio 1.
–   Blank folio (may include later inscriptions and seals)
?   Original content of this folio uncertain
[ ]   Reconstructed folio content
+   An additional double folio with prose preface may fall here. If so, the actual folio designation would be reconstructed as 3b–3bisa and 3bisa–4a. See above, text n. 20.

PATRONAGE OF THE ARTS OF THE BOOK UNDER THE INJUIDS OF SHIRAZ[1]

ELAINE WRIGHT

One of the earliest existing copies of the *Shāhnāma*—the epic account of the pre-Islamic kings and heroes of Iran—is dated 741/1341 and bears an illuminated frontispiece inscribed with a dedication to Ḥājjī Qiwām al-Dawla wa al-Dīn Ḥasan, who served as vizier to the Injuid rulers of Shiraz. The manuscript includes 108 miniatures, painted in a rather simple but highly distinctive style.[2] In 1936, on the basis of the dedication to Qiwām al-Dīn, Ivan Stchoukine attributed to Shiraz all manuscripts employing a similar miniature style.[3]

One manuscript of this group is a slightly earlier *Shāhnāma*, dated 731/1330.[4] In 1983 Norah Titley published the illuminated *shamsa*-frontispiece of this manuscript, which brought about widespread recognition of an Injuid illumination style and which in turn led to the attribution to Shiraz of all unillustrated manuscripts illuminated in the same style.[5] However, although these two Injuid *Shāhnāmas*,

---

[1] I would like to express my gratitude to the following institutions and individuals for kindly granting permission to reproduce the images included here: the British Library (figs. 37–40); Alexandria Press Ltd. (fig. 41); The Nasser D. Khalili Collection of Islamic Art and Nahla Nassar (fig. 42 and pl. 19); the Collection of Farhad Ebrahimi (fig. 36); and the Dar al-Athar al-Islamiyya, Kuwait (fig. 35).

[2] The manuscript is now widely dispersed with the largest single group of folios (eighty-five) in the Chester Beatty Library, Dublin (Per 110). The folios bearing the dedication to Qiwām al-Dīn are part of the collection of the Arthur M. Sackler Gallery of Art of the Smithsonian Institution in Washington, D.C. (S1986.010 and S1986.0111). The 108 miniatures comprise 106 text illustrations, one double-page frontispiece (counted as one) and a finispiece. See Simpson (2000), 225–26 and, more generally, 217–47 for reproductions of numerous folios (including the dedication folios); see also Swietochowski and Carboni (1994), fig. 9; and Komaroff and Carboni, eds. (2002), figs. 181 and 264–65.

[3] Stchoukine (1936), 1936, 93–94.

[4] Topkapı Palace Museum Library, Hazine 1479.

[5] Titley (1983), 229–33 and fig. 77. This single-page *shamsa*-frontispiece was in fact first published by Waley and Titley in 1975. In 1979 Akimushkin and Ivanov published another *shamsa*-frontispiece (and double-page text-frontispiece) of an undated manuscript in the Russian National Library, St. Petersburg (Dorn 255), which they attributed to the 1330s on the basis of its similarity to the 731/1330

dated 731/1330 and 741/1341, are illustrated in the same basic style, their illumination styles are not totally congruous, for manuscripts produced in Shiraz during the period of Injuid rule can in fact, on the basis of illumination style, be divided into two groups: those that predate 740/1340 and those produced between 740/1340 and the end of Injuid rule in Shiraz in 754/1353. Illuminations of the early period are stylistically both coherent and conservative, and it is the style of this period that has come to be recognized generally as 'the' Injuid style. By comparison, illuminations of the later period are stylistically diverse and therefore do not form an immediately recognizable group.

Early Injuid Illumination

Early Injuid manuscripts employ distinct types and styles of illumination. Especially recognizable is the program of illuminations, or combination of illumination types, used to introduce a manuscript: typically a single-page frontispiece is followed by a double-page frontispiece surrounding the opening lines of text (figs. 37–40). The single-page frontispiece consists of a roundel or *shamsa*, placed between upper and lower panels, which are sometimes linked by a thin frame. The *shamsa* is usually formed through the geometrical interlacing of thin white bands, with the spaces between the interlacing bands filled with lotuses or small palmette-arabesque medallions. A lotus, a palmette-arabesque medallion, or a windmill-type motif might also be placed conspicuously at either end of the two panels that frame the *shamsa*, though a single lotus blossom set on a short stem is the most characteristic motif of this early period. Surrounding either the *shamsa* or panels, or both, is a leaf- or petal-like border. In the double-page text-frontispiece only, a palmette-arabesque is

---

Shāhnāma frontispiece; however, they make no specific mention of a Shiraz attribution, although it was through Waley's and Titley's 1975 publication that they knew of the 731/1330 frontispiece. Even earlier, in 1940, Basil Gray published the *shamsa*-frontispiece of a dispersed 733/1333 *Kalīla wa Dimna* manuscript, noting that in the Bibliothèque Nationale exhibit of 1938 (no. 22), the manuscript was attributed to Shiraz, presumably on the basis of its illustration style. See, respectively, Waley and Titley (1975), fig. 1; Akimushkin and Ivanov (1979), 35, 53, n. 5, and figs. 17 and 19; and Gray (1940), 135 and fig. 1.

sometimes used, in the form of a triangular *ansa* emerging from the outer edge of each half of the frontispiece (fig. 40).

The predominantly gold palette of these frontispieces clearly arises from a conservative adherence to an older, all-gold tradition, one that prevailed from about the ninth century through the late thirteenth century. As in this older tradition, in these Injuid illuminations, forms are delineated by fine black outlines, by the contrasting of two tones of gold, and by the use of the natural color of the unpainted page. Touches of color are used mainly in the leaf or petal borders, with tones of a rusty orange, bluish-grey, and olive green being most common, though a deep red is also sometimes used. Dark blue and green are often used in the double-page text-frontispiece or in the colophon.

Ilkhanid Illumination

In western Iran, the region controlled by the Ilkhanid sultans, artists employed more varied types and programs of illumination. For example, in some multipart Qur'āns, each section is introduced by two double-page frontispieces;[6] in others each section begins with a single, free-standing *shamsa* followed by a double-page text-frontispiece.[7] Secular manuscripts usually employed simpler programs: a single heading, a single- or a double-page frontispiece, or a combination of these might be used, but if a manuscript begins with a *shamsa*, it is almost certainly followed on the next page by a single heading only.[8]

---

[6] As, for example, in the Anonymous Baghdad Qur'ān, dated 701–7/1302–8; for reproductions of the two frontispieces of *juz'* 13 of this manuscript, see James (1988), figs. 51–52.

[7] As, for example, in the Qur'ān copied in Maragha in 738/1338; see James (1988), fig. 128b, and Komaroff and Carboni, eds. (2002), fig. 268.

[8] Examples of Ilkhanid manuscripts in which a *shamsa* is followed by a single heading include the well-known copy of *Manāfi' al-ḥayawān* in the Pierpont Morgan Library, New York (M500), 697/1297 or 699/1300; reproduced in Schmitz, (1997), back slipcover and fig. 2; and a copy of *Marzubānnāma* in the Istanbul Archaeology Museum (ms. 216), 698/1299; reproduced in Simpson (1982), figs. 46–47. In these and most Ilkhanid manuscripts, the *shamsa* is freestanding, with no bordering panels; however, most of the thirty-nine *shamsa*s in each of two extravagantly decorated copies of *al-Majmū'a* of Rashīd al-Dīn are set within an elaborate rectangle. The earlier of these two copies, dated 710/1310, is in Paris (Bibliothèque Nationale,

The style of Ilkhanid illuminations also differs from that used in Injuid manuscripts: the Ilkhanid palette is both brighter and more varied, and the palmette-arabesque, used only occasionally in early Injuid illuminations, is the dominant motif of Ilkhanid illuminations; indeed, numerous examples exist of frontispieces that comprise little else than this single motif and a structure to contain its spiraling energy. Likewise, bands of gold strapwork are a major element in many Ilkhanid illuminations, but are accorded a limited role only in early Injuid illuminations.[9]

Later Injuid Illumination

In about 1340, these Ilkhanid features began to appear in the illuminations of Injuid manuscripts. Unlike illuminations of the early period, those of the later Injuid period, from 1340 onwards, are stylistically diverse. In fact, the single unifying feature of illuminations of the later period is their obvious incorporation, in varying degrees, of traits borrowed from Ilkhanid illuminations.

Of the surviving later Injuid manuscripts that are illuminated, just three are dated. One of these is a Qur'ān and the only Injuid manuscript that actually states that it was copied in Shiraz. Now in the Pars Museum in Shiraz (no. 456), it is dated 745–46/1344–46 and signed by the scribe Yaḥyā al-Jamālī al-Ṣūfī (fig. 41). It was bequeathed to the mosque of Shāh-i Chirāgh in Shiraz (and presumably also commissioned) by Tāshī Khātūn, the mother of Abū Isḥāq, ruler of Shiraz from 744/late 1343 to 754/1353.[10] It is illuminated in a style distinct from that of the early period, for a brightly colored, palmette-arabesque border, and an extensive use of wide bands of gold strapwork are its main decorative features, each of which is characteristic of Ilkhanid illuminations.[11] Yaḥyā's signature in

Arabe 2324); the second, dated 711/1311–12, was sold at auction in 1998 and is now in a private collection. For Arabe 2324, see Richard, F. (1997), 44, cat. no. 12; and Komaroff and Carboni, eds. (2002), 245, cat. no. 5. For the later manuscript, see Christie's, London (1998), lot 55.

[9] For examples of Ilkhanid illuminations see Komaroff and Carboni, eds. (2002), figs. 54, 245, 251, and 268.

[10] James (1988), 163.

[11] The manuscript has not been viewed personally and its illuminations are known

this manuscript suggests that Tabriz, capital to the Ilkhanid sultans throughout much of the dynasty's rule, was indeed the source of these new traits, for it is known that Yaḥyā worked first in Tabriz for the Ilkhanid warlord, Amīr Chūpān Süldüz (d. 728/1328), then in Shiraz for the Īnjūs, and finally for their successors, the Muzaffarids. The exact circumstances under which he made his way to Shiraz are not known, although it has been suggested that after the downfall of the Ilkhanids, Yaḥyā may have ended up in the employ of the grandson of Chūpān Süldüz, Pīr-i Ḥusayn, who was in Shiraz for various periods of time from 740/1339; after the final expulsion of the Chupanids from the city, he would have been taken into the employ of Abū Isḥāq.[12] The visual evidence of the Yaḥyā Qur'ān therefore suggests that by the early 1340s artists as well as scribes had moved from Tabriz and were working in Shiraz. Yaḥyā surely was just one individual in a much larger migration, the ultimate cause of which was the dissolution of Ilkhanid rule in western Iran and the ensuing political and social chaos.

The dispersed Qiwām al-Dīn *Shāhnāma* of 741/1341 also exhibits Ilkhanid traits. One of its three double-page frontispieces consists of two lobed roundels surrounded by gold blossoms and leaves, set against a darker gold ground and delineated by a fine black contour that thickens noticeably at the tip of each petal or leaf.[13] The decoration of many early Injuid manuscripts includes gold florals on a gold ground delineated by a black contour, but only in the 1341 *Shāhnāma* does this specific technique of 'black-tipping' appear. However, it does appear in a painting entitled *Sindukht Becomes Aware of Rudaba's Actions*, one of the dispersed folios from the Great Mongol *Shāhnāma*,

---

only from two published folios; see James (1988), 247 and fig. 115. A Qur'ān in the Chester Beatty Library (Is 1475) is also signed by Yaḥyā and dated 740/1339–40 but has Ottoman illumination; see James (1980), 66.

[12] James (1988), 163–64. A third Qur'ān signed by Yaḥyā and dated 739/1338–39 (Turkish and Islamic Arts Museum, Istanbul, No. Y430) is illuminated in the Ilkhanid style and was probably made in Tabriz. James has noted that the illuminations of this Qur'ān are of a much higher quality than those in the later Yaḥyā Qur'ān in the Pars Museum (No. 456), and therefore has suggested that the illuminations of the Istanbul Qur'ān must be later additions. However, the difference in quality may instead reflect different levels of patronage; see James (1988), 164 and 245, cat. no. 63.

[13] Arthur M. Sackler Gallery of Art, S1986.010 and S1986.0111; for reproductions of each folio, see Simpson (2000), 218, pls. 1–2.

attributed to Tabriz in about 1335.[14] This suggests that knowledge of this painting technique, ultimately of Chinese origin, may have reached Shiraz via a Tabriz artist.[15] Moreover, a miniature in the 741/1341 *Shāhnāma* is painted in the contemporary style of Tabriz[16] and recalls miniatures such as the scene of *Iskandar Enthroned* in the Great Mongol *Shāhnāma*.[17] With the exception of one repainted miniature in the Arthur M. Sackler Gallery,[18] all miniatures in the 741/1341 manuscript are of course in the typical Injuid style. The Ilkhanid-style miniature usually is denounced as a fake or at the very least as a later addition to the manuscript.[19] However, no evidence exists to support this allegation, other than the incongruity of employing two such diverse styles in one manuscript. It is therefore likely that the miniature is indeed contemporary with the 741/1341 manuscript, painted by an artist who had fled Tabriz.[20]

The third of the three dated, later Injuid manuscripts is a copy of *Tarjuma-yi iḥyā'-yi 'ulūm al-dīn*, a Persian translation of al-Ghazālī's great work on theology, dated 744/1344[21] and introduced by what is in fact a typical early Injuid type of single-page frontispiece: the *shamsa* consists of two squares, interlaced to form an eight-pointed star, surrounded by a leaf border and set between two linked panels, the upper of which also has a leaf border. However, it is in fact strikingly different from what one would find in an early Injuid manuscript, for the usual gold palette is offset by an unexpected abundance of blue and green, clearly indicative of the influence of the bright and varied palette of Ilkhanid illuminations.

The Ilkhanid traits present in these three manuscripts dated to the 1340s makes it possible to attribute three undated manuscripts with extensive Ilkhanid traits to this same decade, or perhaps to the

---

[14] Arthur M. Sackler Gallery of Art, S1986.0102; reproduced in Grabar, O. and Blair (1980), 77; Lowry and Nemazee (1988), 81; and Komaroff and Carboni, eds. (2002), fig. 90.

[15] The same technique of black-tipped leaves is used in a number of fifteenth-century Persian drawings of various Chinese motifs preserved in albums in Berlin and Istanbul; see folios reproduced in Lentz and Lowry (1989), 182 ff.

[16] Chester Beatty Library, Dublin, Per 110.4.

[17] Musée du Louvre, No. 7096; reproduced in Grabar and Blair (1980), 113, and Komaroff and Carboni, eds. (2002), fig. 51.

[18] S1986.0099a.

[19] Arberry and Minovi (1959–62), vol. 1, 25.

[20] This was first suggested by James (1992), 124, n. 12.

[21] Topkapı Palace Museum Library, Hazine 231.

early 1350s. These three manuscripts are: certain of the remaining parts of a thirty-part Qur'ān now divided between the Nasser D. Khalili Collection of Islamic Art in London and the Pars Museum in Shiraz;[22] a smaller, single-volume Qur'ān, also part of the Khalili Collection;[23] and the so-called Stephens *Shāhnāma*, now on long-term loan to the Arthur M. Sackler Gallery of Art.[24] In fact, greater Ilkhanid influence is evident in each of these three manuscripts than in any of the three dated manuscripts. As each exhibits similar influence, it will suffice to discuss in detail only the two sections of the thirty-part Qur'ān in the Khalili Collection.

The complete manuscript was copied for Fārs Malik Khātūn, sister of the Injuid ruler of Shiraz, Abū Isḥāq. The endowment notice at the beginning of each part is in the form of a single-page frontispiece, a development of the early Injuid type, in which the once free-standing *shamsa* has been fully integrated into the overall structure of the frontispiece (fig. 42). The inscription states that the manuscript was to be kept in Fārs Malik Khātūn's house until her death, then placed at the head of her tomb—although, as James points out, as the manuscript was still unfinished at the time of her death, it is unlikely that her wish was ever carried out.[25] As in early

[22] QUR182 and no. 417, respectively.

[23] QUR242.

[24] The manuscript is part of the collection of Farhad F. Ebrahimi and is stored in the Arthur M. Sackler Gallery under inventory number LTS 1998.1.

[25] The association of the manuscript with Fārs Malik Khātūn was discovered by David James. In 1988, when discussing the sections of the manuscript now in the Pars Museum, he noted that there appeared to be an earlier inscription beneath the endowment inscription naming the Muzaffarid vizier Tūrān Shāh. Two years later he was able to have the Tūrān Shāh inscriptions removed, not from the Pars sections, but rather from those in the Khalili Collection (QUR182, ff. 2a and 26a). These earlier inscriptions are in the name of Fārs Malik Khātūn. The manuscript is not dated but in its endowment notice the patron's father is referred to as "the late." As he was executed in 1336, this reference provides a definite *terminus post quem* for the dating of the manuscript. Moreover, James has pointed out that Fārs Malik Khātūn was still alive in 1343–44, because the author of the *Shīrāznāma*, writing at that time, comments on building projects then being undertaken by her, namely, a mausoleum over the grave of ʿAlī ibn Bāzghāsh (d. 1279–80), a local saint, as well as the construction of several other buildings at the same site. Another reference, this time to a dispute taking place between the mother and an unnamed sister of Abū Isḥāq, perhaps Fārs Malik Khātūn, was made by Ibn Baṭṭūṭa, who visited Shiraz in 1347–48. Although the whole manuscript was copied for Fārs Malik Khātūn, of the eight surviving parts, only four were also illuminated during her lifetime: Parts 1, 10, 12, and 14 (of which Parts 1 and 12 are in the

Injuid manuscripts, each single-page *shamsa*-frontispiece is followed by a double-page frontispiece surrounding the first lines of text (pl. 19). In these examples, as in the Pars Museum Qur'ān copied by Yaḥyā, gold strapwork no longer merely links the panels of the frontispiece; now it totally enwraps them, functioning as the superstructure of the whole composition.[26] Likewise, use of the palmette-arabesque has increased: as well as forming the side *ansa* of the double-page text-frontispiece (overwhelmingly so in the smaller, single-volume Khalili Qur'ān),[27] it has replaced the petal border of the upper panel in the single-page '*shamsa*'-frontispiece. When the petal border is retained, as it is for the border of the small marginal roundels of the double-page text-frontispieces, it is rendered in a bright palette, as one would expect of Ilkhanid but not (early) Injuid illuminations. The palette as a whole is one of bright contrasts, most noticeable in the large gold blossoms set off against a dark ground, either deep blue or burgundy. Parallels for the placement of large gold blossoms against a deep blue ground are found in contemporary Ilkhanid miniature painting as well as in the illumination of earlier Persian and non-Persian manuscripts.[28] And the placement of the florals in

Pars Museum, no. 417; Parts 10 and 14 are in the Khalili Collection, QUR182). The other four surviving parts were not illuminated until the 1370s, during the reign of the Muzaffarids (754–95/1353–93) and presumably by command of the vizier Tūrān Shāh: Parts 13, 24–25, and 30 (of which Parts 13 and 30 are in the Pars Museum, also as no. 417; Parts 24–25 are in the Khalili Collection, bound together as QUR181). For references and reproductions of folios from both periods of illumination, see Lings (1976), fig. 60; James (1988), 196–97; and James (1992), 122–24 and cat. nos. 29–30.

[26] For the text-frontispiece on fols. 2b/3a, see James (1992), 128–29; and Komaroff and Carboni, eds. (2002), fig. 269.

[27] A double-page text-frontispiece similar to the early Injuid type introduces this manuscript; the palmette-arabesque side *ansa*s extend almost the full length of the frontispiece and wide palmette-arabesque borders frame the upper and lower panels of the frontispiece. Based on similarities in style, James has suggested that this Qur'ān may be from the same workshop as Khalili QUR182, though no documentation exists for the former; for this suggestion and a reproduction of QUR242, see James (1992), cat. no. 31.

[28] For example, they decorate the back of a throne in a miniature of about 1330, now preserved in one of the Istanbul albums (Topkapı Palace Museum Library, Hazine 2153, f. 148b); reproduced in Çağman and Tanındı (1986), fig. 44. Textiles decorated with gold blossoms set against a dark ground are depicted in miniatures in the Great Mongol *Shāhnāma* of about 1335; reproduced in Grabar and Blair (1980), 135, 137, and 165. And the illuminated double-page frontispiece of a *Ṣaḥīḥ* of al-Bukhārī, dated 693/1294 and attributed to Mamluk patronage in either Egypt or

the ends of the panels of both types of frontispiece is reminiscent of frontispieces of the early Injuid era, though the types of florals used are very different.[29]

Although the Fārs Malik Khātūn Qur'ān was copied for an Injuid princess, it does not actually state that it was copied in Shiraz. It is in fact of a much higher quality, in terms of draftsmanship, paper, and pigments, than any of the early Injuid manuscripts;[30] this, along with its obvious Ilkhanid-influenced illumination style, might well tempt one to think that the manuscript had been made-to-order for the princess in another center, probably Tabriz. But the Yaḥyā Qur'ān leaves no doubt that Ilkhanid traits were being employed extensively in Shiraz manuscripts in the later Injuid period. Moreover, the Stephens *Shāhnāma*, which exhibits the same Ilkhanid traits as the Fārs Malik and Yaḥyā Qur'āns, can be placed firmly in Shiraz on the basis of its illustration style. Therefore, the evidence—specifically of the Yaḥyā Qur'ān and the Stephens *Shāhnāma*—allows the Fārs Malik Khātūn Qur'ān to be attributed to Shiraz with considerable certainty.

Changes in Patronage

Manuscripts produced in the later Injuid period are distinguished from those of the early period not only by their obvious incorporation of Ilkhanid traits; a change in patronage is equally indicative of the move from the early to later era. Of the traits that can be

---

Syria (Chester Beatty Library, Ar 4176), consists mainly of large and fleshy palmettes and blossoms painted in gold against a blue ground; see the following note for an example from Persian illuminations.

[29] At least one other copy of the Qur'ān is known with illuminated headings very similar to the frontispiece panels of the Fārs Malik Khātūn Qur'ān. The three headings in the fragment of this Qur'ān, in the Khalili Collection (QUR495), each consist of a central, round-ended cartouche filled with gold palmettes on a burgundy ground; in the ends of the headings, gold blossoms are set on a deep blue ground. The florals are large and robust and several are similar types to those used in Khalili QUR182. The manuscript is not dated, but James suggests a date between 1250 and 1350 and attributes it to "Iran" in general; reproduced in James (1992), 10.

[30] James first speculated that the difference in quality between the Fārs Malik Khātūn manuscript and the (early) Injuid *Shāhnāma* manuscripts could be explained if the former were the work of artists who fled the turmoil of Tabriz; James (1992), 124.

cited as evidence of this change, none is either evenly or consistently employed in all manuscripts. Nevertheless, taken as whole they make explicit the contrast between the two groups of manuscripts.

The first of these traits can be summed up as the higher overall quality of many later Injuid manuscripts in comparison with those of the early Injuid period and refers to the quality of the materials used, the skill of the artists, and the amount of decoration. The higher quality of the Fārs Malik Khātūn Qur'ān has already been commented upon. Of almost equally high quality are the illuminations and paper in the later Injuid Stephens *Shāhnāma*. Rather surprisingly though, the *Shāhnāma* employs the often denigrated early Injuid illustration style. The quality of the illuminations of the dispersed *Shāhnāma* of 741/1341 is close to that of the early Injuid manuscripts, but the manuscript employs a slightly more elaborate illumination program in that it begins with a double- rather than single-page *shamsa*-frontispiece. The manuscript—made for one of the ruler's viziers—also has a greater number of illustrations than either of the two early Injuid *Shāhnāma*s, as does the Stephens *Shāhnāma*.[31] The move to a new level of patronage that these changes might suggest can be explained as a probable—though not exclusive—division between public and private markets, a division for which further evidence is suggested by the treatment of the *shamsa*s of these manuscripts.

In both the 741/1341 *Shāhnāma* and the Fārs Malik Khātūn Qur'ān, the importance of the *shamsa* inscription is proclaimed by the amount of space it occupies (in each case nearly half of the whole frontispiece) and by the use of an elaborate, outlined script set against a decorated ground (fig. 42). The double-page *shamsa*-frontispiece of the 741/1341 manuscript states the title, the name of the patron, and the date, while the '*shamsa*s' of the Fārs Malik Khātūn Qur'ān each function as a *waqfiyya*, detailing the princess's donation of the manuscript. In sharp contrast to these two examples is the small gold

[31] See n. 2, above, for the number of illustrations in the 741/1341 manuscript; the Stephens *Shāhnāma* has 105 text illustrations plus one double-page frontispiece. The 731/1330 *Shāhnāma* includes 92 text illustrations plus a double-page frontispiece; the other early Injuid *Shāhnāma*, dated 733/1333 and now in the Russian National Library, St. Petersburg (Dorn 329), has just 49 text illustrations, plus one double-page frontispiece and one finispiece, though it has been estimated that about 10 percent of the manuscript (possibly including some miniatures) is missing; see Adamova and Giuzal'ian (1985), 159.

space that forms the center of several other Injuid *shamsas* (figs. 37 and 39). The title and name of the author usually appears in the two panels that border the *shamsa*, so the central space presumably was intended for a dedication to the owner. The small size of the space, however, signals the presumed insignificance of the intended dedication and thereby of any owner it might name. But in fact the dedications were probably never added, for most of the *shamsa* centers are now blank or else have later, hastily written inscriptions.[32] It would seem, therefore, that these manuscripts were not made to order but perhaps instead were commercial products, made to be bought and later inscribed by individuals wealthy enough to purchase a decorated manuscript in the market, yet not so wealthy as to be able to commission one of their own design. With the exception of the 744/1344 al-Ghazālī manuscript, these all are part of the early Injuid group.

This does not mean that all early Injuid manuscripts were necessarily the result of commercial production. In fact, in 1963 Zeki Togan stated that the *shamsa* of the 1330 *Shāhnāma* once bore a dedication to Ghiyāth al-Dīn Muḥammad (d. 736/1336), the Ilkhanid vizier and son of Rashīd al-Dīn,[33] presumably indicating that it was made in Shiraz as a gift for him. However, there is today no way of verifying what the inscription once said. Royal or at least courtly patronage might also appear to be indicated by the iconography of the double-page miniature frontispiece, with illuminated borders, in each of the four Injuid *Shāhnāmas* (of which two are early Injuid and two are later Injuid). In three of these manuscripts, the folio on the left portrays a ruler enthroned and surrounded by various combinations of princes, musicians, servants, and other courtiers, while the folio on the right depicts a royal hunt (figs. 34 and 36).[34] In the 731/1330 *Shāhnāma*, the iconography of the double-page miniature is more unusual and may portray the presentation of gifts to a ruler

[32] A few also appear rubbed, as if an earlier inscription might once have existed; for example the *shamsa* of British Library Or. 2676, *Jawāmiʿ al-ḥikāyāt* of Muḥammad ʿAwfī, 732/1332.

[33] Togan, Z. V. (1963), 2. For a different interpretation see Simpson's contribution to this volume, n. 14 [ed.].

[34] For the 733/1333 *Shāhnāma* frontispiece, see Adamova and Giuzal'ian (1985), pls. 1–2; and Swietochowski and Carboni (1994), fig. 6. For the 741/1341 frontispiece, see Simpson (2000), pls. 6–7. Also see Simpson's contribution to this volume.

or other high official on the occasion of Nawrūz.[35] However, while royal imagery as used in these double-page miniatures is well-suited to the *Shāhnāma*, it is not restricted to copies of the *Shāhnāma*, nor does it necessarily indicate royal patronage. Richard Ettinghausen has noted that royal imagery is used in the miniature-frontispiece of several thirteenth- and fourteenth-century manuscripts that cannot be attributed to royal patronage. These, he has suggested, might instead merely be copies of royal manuscripts.[36] In other words, even by this early date, the portrayal of rulers enthroned or engaged in royal pastimes such as the hunt, and perhaps even the depiction of more specific events such as the Nawrūz ceremony, had passed into the 'public' domain to serve as standard frontispiece iconography in both court and non-court manuscripts. Therefore, the royal iconography of a miniature-frontispiece cannot on its own be taken as evidence of royal patronage.[37]

---

[35] I wish to express my gratitude to Teresa Fitzherbert for her comments on this miniature and her suggestion that the figures holding a falcon, geese, a dead gazelle and a gold bowl might be part of a Nawrūz ceremony. Togan assumes that it is the Ilkhanid ruler Abū Saʿīd who is depicted enthroned on the left half of the miniature; see Togan, Z. V. (1963), 2.

[36] Ettinghausen (1962), 64. The manuscripts to which he refers are: 1) the surviving volumes of a copy of *Kitāb al-aghānī*, c. 1218, probably Mosul, with a single-page frontispiece of a ruler enthroned or engaged in a princely activity in each volume (vols. 2, 4 and 11: National Library, Cairo, Adab 579; vol. 20: Royal Library, Copenhagen, No. 168; vols. 17 and 19: Millet Kütüphanesi, Istanbul, ms. Feyzullah Efendi 1566); 2) Nationalbibliothek, Vienna A.F. 10, *Kitāb al-diryāq*, mid-thirteenth century, probably Mosul, with a single-page frontispiece in three registers with an informally seated ruler, a hunt scene and a procession of royal women; and 3) Nationalbibliothek, Vienna, A.F. 9, *Maqāmāt* of al-Ḥarīrī, 734/1334, probably Egypt, with a single-page frontispiece of a ruler enthroned. Reproduced in Ettinghausen (1962), 65, 91 and 148, respectively.

[37] Other early fourteenth-century manuscript frontispieces are: 1) Freer Gallery of Art, No. 29.25a, Freer small *Shāhnāma*, possibly Baghdad, c. 1300, with a single-page frontispiece (perhaps one half of what was originally a double-page miniature) in two registers depicting a royal polo game and a royal hunt; 2) Staatsbibliothek, Preußischer Kulturbesitz, Berlin, Diez A folio 71 s. 46 no. 8, n.d., with a single-page frontispiece of a ruler enthroned; reproduced in Ipşiroğlu (1964), pl. IV, fig. 8; 3) Freer Gallery of Art, No. 57.16, *Ta'rīkh-i Balʿamī* (the so-called *Tarjuma-yi ta'rīkh-i Ṭabarī*), c. 1300, with a single-page frontispiece of a ruler enthroned; 4) Topkapı Palace Museum Library, Istanbul, Hazine 2152, f. 60b, c. 1300, with a double-page miniature of an enthroned ruler on the left half and a two-tiered procession on the right half; reproduced in Ipşiroğlu (1967), 52 and 99; and 5) British Library, Or. 13506, *Kalīla wa Dimna*, 707/1307–8, with a double-page frontispiece of a ruler enthroned on the left half and, on the right half, courtiers with hunting

The evidence for the early Injuid period therefore weighs more heavily in favor of commercial production, with no secure evidence of court production. However, in the later Injuid period, court—and specifically royal—patronage is not in doubt. Manuscripts were commissioned by the Injuid vizier Qiwām al-Dīn, and by both the sister and the mother of the ruler Abū Isḥāq, who himself is known to have commissioned at least three surviving pieces of metalwork[38] and who can perhaps be associated with two manuscripts, though neither actually bears his name. These two manuscripts are a copy of *Mu'nis al-aḥrār*, dated 741/1341,[39] and the undated Stephens *Shāhnāma*. In the double-page miniature-frontispiece included in each, a ruler is shown enthroned with his consort (figs. 35–36).

An enthroned ruler and his consort are also portrayed on one of the three extant pieces of metalwork made for Abū Isḥāq, a candlestick, and also on an undated tray now in the Museum of Fine Arts in Tbilisi. Linda Komaroff has attributed the production of the tray to Shiraz, because the inscription on it refers to the "Inheritor of the Kingdom of Solomon," a title used by the rulers of Fars, who incorrectly regarded Pasargadae and Persepolis as Solomonic sites, and to which they made pilgrimages.[40] The portrayal of an enthroned couple is rare in Islamic art as a whole, yet over twenty such depictions are known from fourteenth-century manuscripts, most of which are thought to have been produced in the Ilkhanid capital, Tabriz, in the 1330s. These images were produced as illustrations to various copies of the *Ta'rīkh-i ghāzānī*, the history of the Mongols that serves

---

leopards and a falcon; reproduced in Waley and Titley (1975) and Swietochowski and Carboni (1994), fig. 7.

[38] 1) A candlestick, now in the Museum of Islamic Art, Doha, Qatar, MW-122-99-Hu; reproduced in Allan (1987), 27, cat. no. 168; Komaroff (1994), 14, fig. 10c, and Komaroff and Carboni, eds. (2002), fig. 224; 2) a bowl in the Musées Royaux d'Art, Brussels, Inv. E.O. 1492; reproduced in Montgomery-Wyaux (1978), fig. 18; and 3) another bowl, in the Hermitage Museum, St. Petersburg, described by Giuzal'ian (1960), 7–9. The latter bowl has not been published, but Komaroff ([1994], 33, n. 53) notes that it relates to both the candlestick and the Brussels bowl in terms of decorative and epigraphic style. However, she also points out that neither bowl is equal in decorative detail and quality to the candlestick.

[39] Dar al-Athar al-Islamiyya, Kuwait, LNS 9 MS.

[40] Komaroff (1994), 9 and fig. 10; and for the Injuids' use of title 'Inheritor of the Kingdom of Solomon,' see Melikian-Chirvani (1971), and Allan (1982), 106–9. Also, in the endowment notice of a Qur'ān (presumably Pars Museum, no. 456), Tāshī Khātūn, mother of Abū Isḥāq, is said to be referred to as "the supreme Khātūn, queen of the Sulaimanī kingdom"; see Ibn Baṭṭūṭa (1958–2000), vol. 2, 307, note 121.

as the first volume of Rashīd al-Dīn's *Jāmiʿ al-tawārīkh*. Unfortunately only a few of these images remain in the manuscripts for which they were made; the other images are preserved in albums in Berlin and Istanbul. These images are of three types, and Karin Rührdanz has shown that each type served a specific function in the text.[41]

The text of the *Ta'rīkh-i ghāzānī* includes a three-part account of each ruler from Genghis Khan to Ghazan, and each account begins with genealogical tables that were illustrated by small images, the largest of which is 65 millimeters square; most are fully colored and each portrays only the enthroned couple, seated on a throne or only on cushions.[42] The second part of each account begins with a double-page enthronement, in which the royal household is arranged before the throne in a standard format.[43] These images might also be used within the body of the text if the passage was very long. Particular announcements, feasts, or receptions given by the ruler and reported throughout the body of the text were illustrated by large, single-page enthronements of the ruler and his consort.[44] Images of enthroned couples therefore served a very specific function within a specific text. Considered within, and extracted from, this context, the depictions of enthroned couples as on the Tbilisi tray, on Abū Isḥāq's candlestick, in the Stephens *Shāhnāma*, and in the *Mu'nis al-aḥrār* manuscript take on a special significance.

Based on parallels between the Tbilisi tray and the enthronement scenes from the albums, Linda Komaroff has suggested that the tray's imagery, in which an enthroned couple is surrounded by members of their court, derives from Ilkhanid painting in Tabriz in about 1330. It therefore is not surprising that the seating arrangement of the couple on the tray follows the typical arrangement used for the *Ta'rīkh-i ghāzānī* miniatures, with the woman placed on the

---

[41] The miniatures have long been recognized as illustrations to the *Jāmiʿ al-tawārīkh*. Karin Rührdanz identified them as relating specifically to *Ta'rīkh-i ghāzānī*; see Rührdanz (1997), 295–306.

[42] For example, Komaroff and Carboni, eds. (2002), fig. 133, which illustrates six miniatures of this type, one fully colored and five that are tinted only (in all but one the consort is seated on the right).

[43] For reproductions, see Çağman and Tanındı (1986), 69, nos. 43–44; Rührdanz (1997), fig. 3; Komaroff (1994), fig. 8; Blair (1995), figs. 59 and 60–61; and Komaroff and Carboni, eds. (2002), figs. 185 and 222.

[44] See Ipşiroğlu (1964), 22 and pl. VII, fig. 11; Rührdanz (1997), fig. 2; Blair (1995), fig. 58; and Komaroff and Carboni, eds. (2002), fig. 84.

right. However, on the candlestick, in the Stephens *Shāhnāma* and in the *Mu'nis al-aḥrār* manuscript, the seating arrangement is reversed, with the woman placed on the left.[45] The candlestick was made for Abū Isḥāq, and although there is no documentary evidence linking the Stephens *Shāhnāma* to Abū Isḥāq, the *Shāhnāma* can at least be attributed to Shiraz during his period of rule. However, the *Mu'nis al-aḥrār* manuscript was copied in Isfahan and is dated 1341. The poet and compiler of this collection of poetry, Muḥammad ibn Badr al-Dīn, was also the calligrapher of the manuscript. As A. H. Morton has noted, in the text, Muḥammad ibn Badr al-Dīn relates that after the death of the Ilkhanid sultan Abū Sa'īd in 1335, Isfahan fell into a state of turmoil, and his once-contented life was transformed into one of relative sorrow.[46] Presumably because of a resulting lack of patronage, Ibn Badr al-Dīn appears to have produced his manuscript on his own initiative, probably intending it for sale or perhaps to present it as a gift to a ruler, a high court official, or some other potential patron. The decoration of the manuscript includes a single-page frontispiece of the early Injuid type.[47] But it has a leaf border in a vibrant and unusual palette used in conjunction with upper and lower panels in which lush gold blossoms are set against a blue ground. The only other close (actually very close) parallel for the decoration of this manuscript seems to be a manuscript now in Paris that can be attributed to Shiraz of the early 1360s.[48] The miniature depicting the enthroned couple is likewise curious. First, considering the specific function of images of enthroned couples and

[45] Carboni states that placement of the woman on the left in the *Mu'nis al-aḥrār* manuscript indicates that she is of higher status than her companion; however, as far as I am aware, there is no literary evidence for this, the assumption being based solely on the fact that it is indeed the ruler himself who usually occupies this position; see Komaroff and Carboni, eds. (2002), 246, cat. no. 9.

[46] Morton in Swietochowski and Carboni (1994), 49–51.

[47] Reproduced in Swietochowski and Carboni (1994), fig. 11.

[48] A copy of Juwaynī's *Ta'rīkh-i jahān-gushāy*, Bibliothèque Nationale, Supplement persane 1375. The frontispiece of the manuscript states that it was made for the library of Kamāl al-Dīn Jamālī al-Islām, whom Richard has identified as Kamāl al-Dīn Ḥusayn Rashīdī, who was appointed vizier to the Muzaffarid ruler Shāh Shujā' after the latter ordered the death of the vizier Qiwām al-Dīn Ḥasan in 764/1362–63; see Richard, F. (1997), 65, cat. no. 24. By 1362, a distinct Muzaffarid style of illumination had developed, in comparison with which the illumination of this manuscript must have seemed rather old-fashioned. The precise combination of colors in the petal border of the *Mu'nis al-aḥrār* manuscript is brighter and more varied than in this manuscript.

the rarity of such images being used outside the context of *Ta'rīkh-i ghāzānī* manuscripts, it seems unlikely that Ibn Badr al-Dīn himself would have included such an image in his manuscript. Second, the image has been repainted at some stage, and although one can only guess when and to what extent, it clearly appears to be a reduced version of the image in the Stephens *Shāhnāma*. It therefore seems that 1341 is surely the date of the copying of the text only; Ibn Badr may have copied the text, and then left the manuscript to be decorated once a suitable recipient or patron was found. Perhaps this was Abū Isḥāq.

The manuscript was copied not long before Abū Isḥāq was appointed governor of Isfahan in late 1341 or early 1342. How much time Abū Isḥāq actually spent in the city itself is not clear, for he soon traveled to Tabriz to join the Chupanid, Malik Ashraf, on his campaign into Fars. The campaign came to an abrupt end in December 1343, and shortly afterwards Abū Isḥāq gained control of Shiraz.[49] Several scenarios concerning the completion of the manuscript are possible. Abū Isḥāq may have obtained the manuscript during his time in Isfahan, or a disheartened Ibn Badr al-Dīn may have himself moved to Shiraz with the unfinished manuscript, eager to benefit from the patronage of the new Injuid ruler and his family. There the manuscript may eventually have been completed, presumably at Abū Isḥāq's command, with the Stephens *Shāhnāma* image serving as the model for the enthronement scene in the *Mu'nis al-aḥrār* manuscript.[50] It is of course also possible that the manuscript

[49] For historical details of this period, see Album (1974), 159–62; Arberry (1960), 139; Boyle (1971), 1208; Ibn Baṭṭūṭa (1958–2000), vol. 2, 306, n. 118; Kutubī (1913), 157–61; and Roemer (1986), 12–13.

[50] That the ruler wears a different headdress in each miniature in no way contradicts this assumption, for on Abū Isḥāq's candlestick he is portrayed twice wearing the simple Mongol cap, which he wears in the *Shāhnāma*, and once wearing the owl-feather head-dress of Mongol rulers and princes, which he wears in the *Mu'nis al-aḥrār* manuscript. (And on the candlestick, his consort is portrayed once wearing the Mongol *bughtaq*.) The depiction of rulers in the dress of their present or former overlords is certainly not without precedent in Islamic art. It should also be noted that Komaroff and Carboni believe that the enthronement scenes on the candlestick should not be regarded "as some form of visual accompaniment to the inscriptions" (which name Abū Isḥāq); however, I disagree, and believe it unlikely that such unusual iconography (for a metal object) would have been chosen to decorate an object which so loudly proclaims the ruler's name unless the iconography was indeed of major significance, namely that it was in fact intended to portray the ruler himself; see Komaroff and Carboni, eds. (2002), 278, cat. no. 162.

remained in Isfahan, being completed for Abū Isḥāq in the period 1353–57, which would explain the similarity of the illuminations to the Paris manuscript of the early 1360s. Whatever the case, it seems unlikely that it could be mere coincidence that of all the fourteenth-century images of an enthroned ruler and his consort, the only four that have no connection with the *Ta'rīkh-i ghāzānī* can each be either directly or indirectly associated with Shiraz, and with the possible exclusion of the undated tray, each can be dated to the later Injuid period. It is also remarkable that, again with the exception of the tray, on each, the standard Ilkhanid imagery is reversed. That one of these images, that on the candlestick, was produced for Abū Isḥāq suggests that perhaps all three, if not all four, were likewise produced for him.[51] Moreover, it is known that copies of Rashīd al-Dīn's

Carboni has stated that the white kerchief held by the woman in the *Mu'nis al-aḥrār* miniature indicates her royal status: see Swietochowski and Carboni (1994), 12; Soudavar holds a similar view, for which see Soudavar (1996), 200, n. 98. Elsewhere Soudavar has discussed the function of the kerchief as a symbol of kinghsip, and its prevalent appearance in enthronement scenes, beginning with the copy of al-Bīrūnī's *al-Āthār al-bāqiyya* dated 1307 and now in Edinburgh (Arab 161); see Soudavar (2003), 9–12. However, that it always (even when held by women) functions as an indicator of royal and hence superior status seems questionable in light of the evidence of at least two other scenes of enthroned couples and their court: 1) Topkapı Palace Museum Library, Hazine 2152, f. 23a, in which the enthroned female holds a brown kerchief and three of the women in the upper register and one in the third register from the top, all seated to the right of the throne, also hold kerchiefs; reproduced in Çağman and Tanındı (1986), 69, no. 43, and Blair (1995), fig. 59; and 2) Staatsbibliothek, Preußischer Kulturbesitz, Berlin, Diez A, f. 70, s. 21, in which the enthroned ruler appears to hold a kerchief and also one woman in each of the top three registers holds a kerchief; reproduced in Rührdanz (1997), fig. 3. In each case there is no other detail of dress or seating arrangement that would indicate that these women are in any way superior to the others depicted around them. (On Abū Isḥāq's candlestick, the enthroned woman holds what looks like a wineskin but is probably intended to represent a kerchief).

51 The twenty-ninth chapter of the *Mu'nis al-aḥrār* manuscript is illustrated, with the first of the three poems in the chapter having been written by the poet Rāwandī in praise of the early thirteenth-century Seljuk ruler of Rum, Sulaymān. Soudavar has speculated that Ibn Badr included this poem in his manuscript, and, in particular, highlighted it by illustrating it, because he intended it as a direct reference to the current Ilkhanid 'puppet' sultan, Sulaymān, husband of Sadi Beg (sister of the Ilkhanid sultan Abū Sa'īd), and therefore, he concludes, it is Sadi Beg and Sulaymān who are depicted in the frontispiece. However, this suggestion overlooks the fact that, as Morton notes, Ibn Badr's illustrating of the poem was in fact nothing new, so to speak, because earlier illustrated versions of the poem surely existed. This is suggested by the version of the poem included in Rāwandī's history of the Seljuks of Iran, *Rāḥat al-ṣudūr*, which is prefaced by a couplet (absent from the 1341 manuscript) that indicates clearly that the poem was to be illustrated. For Soudavar's

Jāmiʿ al-tawārīkh, the first volume of which is of course the *Taʾrīkh-i ghāzānī*, were produced in Tabriz in both Arabic and Persian with the express purpose of being sent to the provinces, and one such copy undoubtedly went to Shiraz. Sent out from the capital, and detailing through both text and image the heritage of the ruling dynasty, the *Taʾrīkh-i ghāzānī* manuscripts served as a statement of the dynasty's perceived right to rule.

The Injuid incorporation of the established imagery of the *Taʾrīkh-i ghāzānī* in new contexts—on a tray and a candlestick, and in two different texts—was unlikely to have been accidental. Rather it was surely an intentional appropriation on the part of the patron of these objects of the original statement of dynastic right to rule imbued in this imagery. As will be discussed below, Abū Isḥāq was the first of the Injuids to see himself as a ruler in his own right, fully independent of the Ilkhanids. As will be seen, the usurping of imagery used by the Ilkhanids to proclaim their dynastic heritage correlates perfectly with Abū Isḥāq's other endeavors to establish his autonomy.

The period of Abū Isḥāq's rule is also notable for the production of copies of the Qurʾān. Four later Injuid Qurʾāns exist, while there are none from the early period. This commissioning of copies of the Qurʾān in the later Injuid period can be seen in the broader light of the patronage of religious works in general at that time by the ruler and members of his family. The Qurʾān copied by Yaḥyā al-Ṣūfī was commissioned by Abū Isḥāq's mother, Tāshī Khātūn, who bequeathed it to the tomb complex of Shāh-i Chirāgh. She also commissioned major renovations to be carried out at the saint's tomb, including the addition of both a *madrasa* and a *zāwiya* (to provide for Qurʾān readers to read continuously at the tomb and for sustenance for the pilgrims who visited).[52] Abū Isḥāq's sister, Fārs Malik Khātūn, commissioned the large thirty-part Qurʾān now divided between the Pars Museum and the Khalili Collection, and two other related Qurʾāns may also have been produced for her.[53] She too was a patron

hypothesis, see Soudavar (1996), 210, n. 98; for Morton's discussion of the poem, see Swietochowski and Carboni (1994), 51–55.

52 James (1988), 163, quoting Ibn Baṭṭūṭa (1958–2000), vol. 2, 307 and n. 121 and 313–14 and n. 135. Neither the *madrasa* nor *zāwiya* survives. It is not clear precisely what buildings already existed at the site; however, a domed structure was built over the tomb between about 628/1230 and 658/1259. No thirteenth-century remains are today visible; see Wilber (1955), 105.

53 The smaller Khalili Qurʾān, QUR242, and another Qurʾān in the Pars Museum,

of architecture: she commissioned the building of a mausoleum over the tomb of a local saint, ʿAlī ibn Bāzghāsh, and was responsible for the construction of several other buildings at the same site.[54] And Abū Isḥāq himself was responsible for repairs to the Khudākhāna, a late thirteenth- or early fourteenth-century structure within the courtyard of the Jāmiʿ ʿAtīq in Shiraz, in which copies of the Qurʾān were preserved and possibly also produced.[55] The early and later Injuid periods therefore are distinguished not only by a change in illumination style but also by a change in patronage, for while commercial production seems to have been predominant in the early period, in the later period court (and specifically royal) patronage flourished. And a most important aspect of this new, royal patronage was the commissioning of copies of the Qurʾān, which appears to have been paralleled by the patronage of religious buildings.

Abū Isḥāq, under whose reign the changes largely took place, was praised as a generous and eager patron of the arts, and renowned poets such as Khwājū Kirmānī and Ḥāfiẓ benefited from his patronage.[56] The fourteenth-century traveler, Ibn Baṭṭūṭa, recorded that Abū Isḥāq wished to be compared to the 'King of India,' who was acclaimed for his generous gift-giving to all those who came to his court.[57] Indeed, the royal patronage characteristic of the later Injuid era perhaps was fostered by a desire on the part of Abū Isḥāq and other members of his family to emulate other rulers.

The Injuids had begun as vassals of the Ilkhanids, who would undoubtedly have served in some capacity as models of kingship for them. They would surely have been well aware of the patronage of the arts in the early years of the fourteenth century on the part of the Ilkhanid sultans and members of their court, specifically the patronage of large, sumptuous copies of the Qurʾān, illustrated copies of the *Jāmiʿ al-tawārīkh*, and the large-format, Great Mongol

Shiraz, no. 427; James ([1992], 124 and n. 11) has suggested that all three might well have been illuminated by the same artist.

[54] See n. 25, above.

[55] The construction of this building has long been attributed to Abū Isḥāq because one of its corner towers bears the date 752/1351. But Galdieri has suggested that the date of construction is in fact about 1281 to 1314 and that the date on the tower refers to renovations, including the addition of the four corner towers, carried out under orders of the Injuid ruler; see Galdieri (1982), 301.

[56] Roemer (1986), 13.

[57] Ibn Baṭṭūṭa (1958–2000), vol. 2, 311 and 313.

Shāhnāma, with its extensive illustration program. Artistic patronage as a requisite to rule was thus a concept with which Abū Isḥāq not only would have been very familiar, but which he may have consciously decided to embody. His actual presence in Tabriz in 1341–42, less than two years before he assumed control of Shiraz, may have been a significant factor in shaping the patterns of patronage of the later Injuid era.

Although the Injuids were in almost every respect independent rulers of Fars by 1325, they continued to rule in the name of the Ilkhanid sultan or, after the death of Abū Saʿīd in 1335, in the name of one of the many Ilkhanids put forth as puppet *khāns*. Abū Isḥāq was the first of the Injuids to act like a fully autonomous ruler. Upon taking control of Shiraz in 744/early 1344, he soon appropriated the twin rights of the *khuṭba* and *sikka* in his own name. Evidence of the speed with which he achieved the latter is provided by the earliest extant coin bearing his name, dated AH 745.[58] Abū Isḥāq was the first Injuid ruler to claim these dual rights of sovereignty, and Kutubī records that by doing so, Abū Isḥāq "rose from the rank of *amīr* to (that of) *sulṭān*,"[59] and thereby established his position as the true sultan of Fars. His expressed desire to equal the generosity of the Sultan of Delhi and his presumed attempt to emulate the artistic patronage of the Ilkhanid sultans thus can be seen as a facet of this more forthright proclamation of kingship.

Although none of the manuscripts of the later Injuid era bear the name of Abū Isḥāq, many can be at least indirectly associated with him, and all are nevertheless a reflection of the political climate of his period of rule. The highly conservative illumination style of the early Injuid era was totally transformed in the 1340s as a result of the dispersal of artists following the downfall of Ilkhanid rule. Undoubtedly encouraged by the political chaos of his time, Abū Isḥāq made the final, symbolic break from the Ilkhanids, a break his predecessors had not seen fit to make and one which may well have stimulated a flourishing of court and specifically royal patronage, a feature of which was the patronage of religious manuscripts and

[58] This is the date of the earliest coin located by Stephen Album; personal communication 11 July 1995. Coins bearing the name Abū Isḥāq are known from as early as AH 719 and 724, but are probably mementos of Shaykh Abū Isḥāq; see Howorth (1888), 692 (page citation is to the 1970 reprint edition).

[59] Album (1974), 159; and Kutubī (1913), 160.

buildings. More idiosyncratic of his reign, however, was his apparent appropriation of Ilkhanid dynastic imagery, through the production of images of enthroned couples, used outside the traditional context of the *Ta'rīkh-i ghāzānī* text.

THOUGHTS ON A *SHĀHNĀMA* LEGACY OF THE FOURTEENTH CENTURY: FOUR ĪNJŪ MANUSCRIPTS AND THE GREAT MONGOL *SHĀHNĀMA*

ELEANOR SIMS

The focus of this article is one group of Īnjū manuscripts, the four illustrated and dated (or datable) copies of Firdawsī's *Shāhnāma* that lie towards one pole of the pictorial history of Shiraz in the second quarter of the fourteenth century.[1] The most salient reason for looking at these four manuscripts together is that they comprise an illustrated series of datable versions of the same text that were presumably produced in the same place over a very short period, perhaps only twenty years. A second reason is that their illustrative programs, together with the *dis*similarity of many aspects of their texts, demonstrate a variety of approaches to the genre of the illustrated *Shāhnāma* at a date still relatively early. Finally, there is the fact that, with one exception, they are single-volume manuscripts that survive almost intact. Dated, respectively, in the years equivalent to 1330, 1333, 1341, and 1352 (or perhaps a bit earlier), I had thought that these four *Shāhnāma* volumes might function as a kind of laboratory in which to examine whatever modes and models of epic images might have been reused or adapted by fourteenth-century Iranian painters who moved away from Tabriz after the effective end of Ilkhanid rule in 736/1335–36: for some had settled in an important, and possibly the oldest, of the Iranian provincial capitals, Shiraz. Indeed, the dispersing of craftsmen from Tabriz and the surrounding area

[1] The most recent comment on them in print—Carboni in Komaroff and Carboni, eds. (2002), 217—is virtually unchanged from anything written since Stchoukine (1936), 83–84 and *passim*; for Stchoukine's advance on the understanding of Īnjū painting as expressed, for instance, in Binyon, Wilkinson, and Gray (1933), 31–33, is very great indeed. The most thorough—even revolutionary—investigation which, when revised and properly published, will surely make us reconsider much of our thinking about 'provincial' Iranian painting in the first half of the fourteenth century is Wright (1997); I am profoundly grateful to Elaine Wright for the revised copy I have been using to prepare this paper, both as it was presented in Los Angeles and as it was reworked for publication.

has been traced for Ilkhanid architecture in various locales, or at least adumbrated,[2] and also for metal wares, mostly inlaid.[3] So I had thought that we were now ready to consider the transmission of pictorial images as they appear in the Great Mongol *Shāhnāma* and reappear—in one guise or another—in the four Īnjū copies of Firdawsī's epic poem. But in preparing this paper for presentation in June 2003, I found that both the material itself and the state of our knowledge of it are still far too incomplete; absent a dedicated campaign of study, the publication record is not yet adequate to the task.[4] Instead I offer what seems to me a useful, if still preliminary, way of considering the four Īnjū *Shāhnāma* volumes: as a coherent group but also one with fascinating variations on a very broad theme. I shall try, as well, to interweave some comments on the way they may relate to the manuscript usually now called the Great Mongol *Shāhnāma*.

The earliest Īnjū *Shāhnāma* is in the Topkapı Palace Museum Library in Istanbul and is dated 731/1330.[5] It is said to contain 286 large folios measuring 375 x 290 millimeters; it thus falls into Wright's category of fourteenth-century manuscripts having the largest folio-area, Group 6 of her Tables 1 and 2.[6] The text is written in six columns of thirty-four lines to a standard page. It also has ninety-two text illustrations, none of which is full-page, and a double frontispiece (pl. 17) that occupies two full, facing pages, along with unrecorded

[2] Blair and Bloom (1995), 14 and *passim*; Sims (2002), 48; the Ilkhanids themselves inherited a similar legacy from Seljuk Anatolia, whence came some of the craftsmen who worked on the first phase of the internal decoration of Öljeitü's great mausoleum at Sultaniyya; see Sims (1988), 149.

[3] The latter material reviewed in Carboni (2002), 221–22, the brief notes signaling the numerous contributions by A.S. Melikian-Chirvani that establish this feature of post-Ilkhanid art history, with more complete references in the bibliography, 301. See also Melikian-Chirvani (1982), 147–51, for an earlier summary. Wright (1997), 13, n. 35, and 17–19, offers precise instances.

[4] Indeed, after Wright (1997), 1–8, 10–17, 98–100, and 176–80, Carboni (2002), chap. 8, especially 216–19 and *passim*, is for the moment the most up-to-date, if also traditionally dismissive, comment about Īnjū illustrated manuscripts.

[5] H. 1479: Karatay (1961), cat. 332, 126–27. The manuscript was first exhibited in public in 1931: see Binyon, Wilkinson, and Gray (1933), cat. no. 23, 43–44, pls. XVB, XVI, XVII; Stchoukine (1936), cat. XIX, 93–94; since 1931 an occasional painting, or a brief comment, has been published but it still awaits publication as a complete monograph. The most recent notice is Çağman and Tanındı, (1986), 50–51, pls. 32–42 in color.

[6] Wright (1997), 80–81.

quantities of *ʿunwān*s and rubrics, all of which occupy a certain amount of space within the frame of the written surface (details, for all four manuscripts, reiterated in the Appendix). Performing a few basic arithmetical operations then permits an approximate calculation of the number of *bayt*s of Firdawsī's text contained in this earliest of recorded, and surviving, Īnjū *Shāhnāma* manuscripts: somewhat less than 58,140, which is close to the canonical number of 60,000.[7]

Next in date is the copy in what is now the Russian National Library in St. Petersburg; it is dated 733/1333.[8] It contains 369 folios not much smaller than the paper of the Topkapı manuscript: 355 x 275 millimeters, but with a smaller 'footprint,' the text copied in only four columns and only thirty-three lines to a standard page. It has fifty illustrations—again, none full-page: a double frontispiece (fig. 34) and a finispiece, and the usual *ʿunwān*s and rubrics. The same arithmetical operations yield a hypothetical number of *bayt*s of Firdawsī's text: somewhat fewer than 48,576, a bit less than 10,000 fewer than the Topkapı manuscript. Giuzal'ian and Adamova had already suggested that this manuscript might have originally had at least four hundred folios (which would add only approximately an additional four thousand verses, still totaling fewer than 52,536);[9] perhaps, too, it would mean that this manuscript might also have had more illustrations than its rather small present complement of 50 text illustrations, although no likely 'candidates' have as yet been identified. They also comment that the folios have been cut

[7] This figure—an approximation of the number of *bayt*s in each manuscript—was calculated by starting from a hypothetical single page: multiplying the number of columns of text by the number of lines in each column; doubling the number—for a folio—but immediately again halving it, since the unit of Persian poetry is a *bayt*, or distich—two lines—to arrive at a standard number of *bayt*s for each folio as if it had neither ornament nor illustration on it; and then multiplying that figure by a multiplicand representing the number of folios *minus* any full pages of illustration or illumination (of which there are few, in the Īnjū manuscripts in question). No deductions were made for ordinary illustrations, which are usually no more than a quarter to a half of a page in height, nor of smaller passages of illumination and *ʿunwān*s; the latter were omitted because, without a careful note of their number and the number of *bayt*s each displaces, it is impossible to know what figure to deduct. I have instead used the necessarily vague phrases, "somewhat less than" or "approximate number."

[8] Dorn 329: briefly mentioned in Stchoukine (1936), 93, n. 1, it has now been published completely, with all the illustrations (or details of them) in color as well as in black and white, in Adamova and Giuzal'ian (1985).

[9] Adamova and Giuzal'ian (1985), 159.

down several times.[10] Its measurements thus seem to be out of fourteenth-century proportion and whether this manuscript then falls into Wright's Group 5 or 6 is, for the moment, uncertain.[11] It also presents a notable peculiarity: even in its cut-down state, its folio size is quite close to that of the Topkapı manuscript, but its layout is one of only four columns, leaving a margin that is already quite wide and might indeed have been wider still. What aesthetic controlled its making?

The third—historically, the key Īnjū *Shāhnāma* manuscript, made for an Īnjū vizier to Abū Isḥāq, al-Ḥasan Qiwām al-Dawla wa al-Dīn—is now quite widely dispersed but recently it has been reconstituted, if only in print.[12] It has the presumable date of 741/1341.[13] The text is copied in six columns of thirty lines on a standard page, and Simpson suggests that it probably had about 325 large folios measuring 370 x 300 millimeters (well in Wright's Group 6).[14] Simpson has also identified 105 folios having illustrations of various kinds; again, none is full-page, with the exception of the double frontispiece (pl. 18); but there are also two finispieces, much illumination and, as usual, *'unwāns* and rubrics that also take up space on the written surface of the manuscript. So the same kind of calculations suggests that this dispersed manuscript originally might have had somewhat less than 58,140 *bayts* of Firdawsī's text: again, close to the canonical number of 60,000.

The last of the four Īnjū *Shāhnāma* manuscripts is the Stephens manuscript; its *shamsa* bears the date of 753/1352–53 but it may be somewhat earlier.[15] It has been sold at auction (at Sotheby's, Lon-

---

[10] Adamova and Giuzal'ian (1985), 159.

[11] Wright (1997), 80–81.

[12] Simpson (2000), 217–47.

[13] Simpson (2000), 218–19, cautions that we may have to widen the date bracket slightly, to 740–42/1339–43, because the rubbed last digit, traditionally read as '1,' might also have been either a '0' or a '2.'

[14] Wright (1997), 80–81.

[15] In the continuing delay in publication of the papers arising from a meeting in Edinburgh in the late summer of 1995, I repeat my comment concerning the date of the manuscript, although it was written before Wright's thesis had been completed: "The crux of the problem is that the manuscript is defective and lacks its final colophon, and the date...753 (February 18, 1352 to February 5, 1353), occurs in a partially rubbed *shikasta* inscription in a *shamsa* that was possibly painted later but—if so—may well repeat the original date. Along with the date 753 is written the name 'Maḥmūd' but, tantalizingly, the words are rubbed away before

don) at least three times in the last quarter of a century;[16] its present owners have placed it on loan to the Arthur M. Sackler Gallery at the Smithsonian Institution in Washington, D.C. The most recent sale catalogue suggests that it has 322 folios[17] measuring 291 x 210 millimeters; it thus falls into Wright's Group 4,[18] being much smaller than the other three, at least as it has come down to us. That sale catalogue also lists only one hundred paintings; however, seven more folios, bearing eight pictures, have now been identified.[19] Thus I use the number of 329 folios, with four columns of text in thirty-three lines, as the basis from which to calculate the number of *bayt*s it might have contained: well fewer than 43,229, taking into account its double frontispiece and its at least 108 text-illustrations, *'unwān*s, and also one large folio of illumination. This is by far the smallest number of *bayt*s presently contained in any of the four Īnjū *Shāhnāma* manuscripts, although its illustrative complement is the highest of all four (using Simpson's hypothetical figure of 105 folios for the 1341 volume, having illustrations of some kind). Even calculating by the number of folios recorded in the 1931 London exhibition—334—raises the number to only 43,890 *bayt*s. This is approximately 5,000 fewer *bayt*s now contained by the St. Petersburg manuscript of 733/1333, a fact more than faintly surprising when it is recalled that the *layout* of these two manuscripts is the same—four columns of thirty-three lines

---

and behind the name. To compound the uncertainty, the folio on which this *shamsa* occurs was, at one point in the past, misbound."

[16] Sotheby's, London (1976), Lot 190, 80–83, interleaved illustrations, and color frontispiece; Sotheby's, London (October 8–9, 1979), Lot 260, 126–33; Sotheby's, London (1998), Lot 41, 54–57, with many color illustrations and a color detail on the cover; the *shamsa* with the date of 752—said to have been recopied—is illustrated in color on 55.

[17] Sotheby's, London (1998), 54.

[18] Wright (1997), 80–81.

[19] They are incompletely, and incorrectly, noted in the most recent sale catalogue. To date, they include: two, on one folio, in the Harvard University Art Museums (1934.25); see only Schroeder, (1942), cat. II, 28–34, pl. II; one in the Metropolitan Museum of Art (57.51.32), see only Grube, (1963), 288, fig. 3; two in the Freer Gallery of Art (44.56 and 46.16), the latter unpublished, and one each, both still unpublished, in the Cleveland Museum of Art (45.387), and the Royal Ontario Museum (967.315); the eighth, *The Travail of Rudaba at the Birth of Rustam*, is perhaps the best known, for it was exhibited in London in 1931, Exhibition 532[a]; Binyon, Wilkinson, and Gray (1933), cat. 22, 43, pl. XIIIA, and is now in the Nasser D. Khalili Collection, ms. 920; its publication by the present author, with all relevant literature, is forthcoming.

each—although the folio size of the two manuscripts is remarkably different (at least, at present). Thus, despite their similar layouts, the 'look of each book' is also remarkably different. Whether we can yet say what this may tell us is unclear.

If size is any criterion, the so-called Great Mongol *Shāhnāma* remains the grandest of fourteenth-century *Shāhnāma* manuscripts.[20] Its folios now measure over half a meter in height and just less than 375 millimeters in width; its text, on a written surface measuring 410 x nearly 300 millimeters, is also copied in six columns but in only thirty-one lines. Its pictures are correspondingly large, although none that survive is full-page in size. It might originally have been a work of perhaps as many as three hundred folios bound in two volumes;[21] it is now a fragment of just over sixty folios with—at least early in the twentieth century—fifty-eight paintings.[22] Its lack of fixed documentation includes the fact that no frontispiece or colophons are today recorded; nor has any additional scribal note (or any evidence for a date or place of copying) ever been detected on any of the surviving folios with (or on the few without) illustrations. Thus, when it was produced is uncertain, apart from the collective conviction that it is surely Ilkhanid and was made in Tabriz. Since 1980, a date of around 1335 has been broadly accepted for its completion, although one study of the past decade pushes the date back to between 1330 and 1335;[23] another, written with compelling passion, proposes a far longer span of time that stretches over two decades, from 1314 to 1336, and also argues that the manuscript in question should be interpreted as Dūst Muḥammad's *Abū-Saʿīdnāma*.[24] That its sponsor was Ghiyāth al-Dīn Muḥammad, son of Rashīd al-Dīn, succeeding his father as vizier to the last Ilkhanid ruler—Abū Saʿīd—who ruled

[20] Komaroff and Carboni, eds. (2002), 155–67, and the technical comments, 227–32, represent the most recent additions to a very large bibliography; the most thorough study is still that of Grabar and Blair (1980), with all paintings illustrated in black and white, although the then-current bibliography must be culled from the cumulative notes on 191–202; the most thought-provoking (as well as more recent) is Soudavar (1994), 95–218; the standard reference, by which all surviving paintings must have been identified since its publication just before World War II, remains Brian (1939), 97–112.

[21] Blair (1989), 125–31.

[22] One—Brian 16—was destroyed, possibly inadvertently, in 1937; illustrated in Grabar and Blair (1980), 89.

[23] Swietochowski and Carboni (1994), 12.

[24] Soudavar (1994).

from 1328, has not been seriously questioned since 1980.

Another way to compare the pictorial aspect of this magnificent fragment of Firdawsī's text with any, and all, of the four Īnjū *Shāhnāma* manuscripts is by means of the shape of the pictures. Wright has rightly made us aware that shape is not a gratuitous feature in illustrated manuscripts in the second quarter of the fourteenth century. Broadly speaking, pictures in manuscripts of this period are completely bounded by rulings and, in shape, are usually rectangular, square, or stepped; the latter may be either symmetrical or asymmetrical, including those specifically shaped to accommodate the narrative, as in the Stephens manuscript picture, *Kay Khusraw Attacks Gang Dizh* (fig. 43). Rectangular pictures may extend the full width of the written surface but they need not (even though this does not always yield a square picture); by far the majority are horizontally aligned but already some are vertical.

Thus, the Great Mongol *Shāhnāma* has a great number of rectangular paintings—twenty-nine aligned horizontally and eight vertically; twelve are square, and surprisingly, only nine are stepped, five symmetrically so—all but one used for enthronement scenes, and four being specifically shaped to the narrative needs of the text.[25] As to the four Īnjū manuscripts, the earliest, of 731/1330, has a distinct pictorial profile: about half of its more than ninety text illustrations are stepped, eighteen for symmetrical enthronement scenes, and twenty-eight for dramatic points in the narrative; forty-four of those remaining are horizontal rectangles, all but two extending the full width of the six-column written surface. The manuscript of 733/1333 has a very different look: twenty horizontally rectangular pictures in it occupy the full four-column width of the written surface, while another seven extend over three columns; nine are square pictures and fourteen are stepped, usually asymmetrically so for dramatic text-points, as opposed to symmetrical throne-scenes.[26] The shapes of the pictures in the 741/1341 manuscript have been summarized by Simpson: approximately half of the 105 text illustrations are rectangular and extend the full width of the written surface; "a small

[25] This analysis is based on the illustrations in Grabar and Blair (1980); it need hardly be added that, for this wreck of a once-splendid manuscript, such a breakdown is utterly defective as a tool and only reminds us how little of it has survived.

[26] This analysis is based on the illustrations in Adamova and Giuzal'ian (1985).

handful occupy the middle four columns of text," and more than forty are stepped.[27] The rectangular group includes many scenes which, in the two earlier manuscripts, would have been presented in a stepped format but have, here, been flattened into wide rectangles, such as *Yazdigird Shahriyār Enthroned*.[28] In the last (the Stephens) manuscript, the rectangular pictures (which are virtually all horizontal) are surprisingly numerous—ninety-three, and none are square; there are fifteen stepped pictures, again four symmetrical, mostly for enthronement scenes, while eleven are asymmetrically stepped. This tendency within so 'controllable' a series of manuscripts, the move—probably within two decades—from at least half the pictures being stepped to the great majority being horizontally rectangular in shape, does seem to suggest some kind of chronological development. Whether it is to be called a 'progression' should perhaps remain moot, for the moment.

As I was cogitating on the formal relationships between the Īnjū manuscripts and the Great Mongol *Shāhnāma*, as well as the data—or lack of it—regarding dates and patrons, Elaine Wright reminded me of the surprising, if virtually unnoticed, assertion of Zeki Velidi Togan, made in 1963: that this earliest of the Īnjū *Shāhnāma* volumes had been made for the son of Rashīd al-Dīn. The English translation says that the manuscript "was prepared for the treasury of Ghiyāth al-Dīn ibn Rashīd al-Dīn," a phrase that does sound much like a translation of the usual *shamsa* text.[29] Whatever may eventually prove to be the correct reading of the text in question, this manuscript was indisputably completed in 731/1330, a fact stated in the colophon, which has never been tampered with. It is, then, of interest to recall that the celebrated graduate seminar at Harvard in 1975, which took published shape as 'Grabar and Blair,' had come to the collective conclusion that the Great Mongol *Shāhnāma* was only begun between November 1335 and May 1336, about five years later than the Īnjū-style *Shāhnāma* manuscript: ordered, planned, and sponsored by the same Ghiyāth al-Dīn for his Ilkhanid overlord.[30] This seems a

---

[27] Simpson (2000), 226.

[28] Lowry, Beach, et al. (1988), 85.

[29] Togan, Z. V. (1963), 2 and 23; Wright (1997), 20–21; shortly before the symposium in 2003, Wright added that she had always thought this inscription to be a later addition.

[30] Grabar and Blair (1980), 48.

chronological disjuncture of some significance, whatever the *shamsa* inscription in the earliest of the Īnjū *Shāhnāma* manuscripts might originally have said.

Hence, the primary question arising from such considerations seems to be this: how is it that the Great Mongol *Shāhnāma*, a Tabrīzī manuscript completed in about 1335–36, might have had any influence on a presumably Shiraz manuscript finished five years prior, in 1330? Other questions are: how might a pictorial relationship between these two volumes, so apparently different in so many ways, be explained? And could there have been any personal connection between the putative sponsor of both manuscripts, one so 'provincial' a *Shāhnāma* as the Topkapı volume of 1330, destined to enhance the position of a mere petty dynastic governor in Shiraz, albeit a person of ancient Iranian stock, the other a supremely ambitious, almost awe-inspiring copy of the same text, conceived in Tabriz for the glorification of a now-Iranicized (and also now Muslim) ruling family of East Asian origin? Even if the original inscription purporting to make the connection no longer exists—or may only have existed for Togan—it seems to me that the overarching question should be framed more or less in this manner: just what might an earlier, unquestionable, written date of completion, in a manuscript bearing a certain physical resemblance to the Great Mongol *Shāhnāma*, signify in terms of, first, the date of completion of the latter, and second, the places of execution, the intended functions, and the material relationship between these two manuscripts? Quite apart from whatever relationship the earliest Īnjū *Shāhnāma* may bear to the later three Īnjū copies of the same text? Or to any of the other illustrated fourteenth-century copies that have come down to us, at least ten contemporary manuscripts, some of whose dates and places of production still remain uncertain?

Save for one immediately obvious reply—that the Great Mongol *Shāhnāma* was surely in the making for several decades, as Soudavar has proposed,[31] its influence thereby potentially in the general purview of others concerned with the making or the sponsoring of illustrated manuscripts—I do not propose to attempt to deal with these questions. Instead, I offer some observations on aspects that both link and differentiate the four *Shāhnāma* manuscripts of the Īnjū series, and

[31] Soudavar (1994), 171–79.

then comment on several reflections of the Great Mongol *Shāhnāma* that I suggest are visible in one or another of the Īnjū four.

Breadth of conception and sheer physical size, historical focus, astonishing imagination combined with extraordinary material veracity, and a high quality of style and execution: these are among the fundamental differences between what survives of the Great Mongol *Shāhnāma* and any of the other illustrated fourteenth-century copies of Firdawsī's epic. Even in its fragmentary state, it tends to blind with its magnificence, obscuring some of what I think can be seen as conceptual similarities between the same illustrated text points, or in compositional renditions of different episodes. Consider two images in which a hero battles a horrendous, if imaginary, beast, *Bahrām Gūr Slays the Dragon*, from the great Tabriz manuscript and from the St. Petersburg Īnjū volume;[32] besides the subject, the two have very little in common. As for the overall character of such pictures in which heroes battle such imaginary but awful creatures, *Isfandiyār Slays the Dragon*, from the earliest Īnjū volume, well justifies a description of the fairly large paintings of the 1330 manuscript as 'action-packed': a pictorial conception in which many figures in a small painting virtually fill the vertical picture-space in their enaction of heroic or evil deeds. In this manuscript, as indeed in all the Īnjū *Shāhnāma* volumes, the figures are usually set against simple red or yellow grounds which may be varied by the addition of mountainous terrain—often shown as distinctively cone-shaped mountains—and the rudimentary settings of thrones, tents, and pennons. In them, we are still aware of myriad pictorial conventions of the Seljuq, Zangid, and Mamluk past,[33] as well as those of more ancient Iranian wall paintings, which is the way the red and ocher-yellow Īnjū ground color has traditionally been interpreted and as I have come to think is surely correct.[34] The drawing is not always as slapdash as Īnjū painting is usually said to be, and in this manuscript, the surfaces are more continuously covered by pigment than are the paintings in the 1341 manuscript, for example.

---

[32] Sims (2002), 309.

[33] Sims (2002), figs. 39, 42–49, 54, and 55 provide useful comparisons in just one place; others (better reproduced, moreover) could be cited from many publications.

[34] Marshak, 11–12 in Sims (2002), and 48; building on the work of Arnold (1923), 95–97, and *idem*, (1924); repeated by—among others—Gray (1960), 58; Adamova and Giuzal'ian (1985), 161; and most recently by Carboni (2002), 219.

In another fourteenth-century compositional type, a figure, or a pair of them, sits on a throne at the raised center of a symmetrically stepped composition in an interior: for instance, *Isfandiyār Approaches Gushtāsp*[35] in I Tatti, Florence, and the earliest Īnjū example *Rustam Entertained by Kay Khusraw'* (fig. 44). That this standard composition for a formal image or event—court scenes of enthronement or audiences, for weddings, or important parleys—should occur in both manuscripts is hardly worth remarking; the formula is ancient, found all over the Near East, and recurs continually in Iranian manuscript illustration.[36] What is rare, however, in pictures in any of the Īnjū manuscripts, unlike the great Tabriz manuscript, is a single figure set in a landscape, especially a realistically presented one such as that in which Bahrām Gūr hunts onager.[37] A related image (fig. 45) can be seen on the underside of a contemporary piece of inlaid brass, its flat shape and everted spout of Chinese derivation but its inlaid decoration thoroughly Islamic: the mounted figure is similar to that in the Tabriz volume, even to the nimbus setting off the profile of the crowned head. It underscores the consistently creative use of transferred images that characterizes the arts of the book in this period.

Sometimes an exceptional subject calls forth an exceptional fourteenth-century picture. The fatal encounter of Rustam and Isfandiyār is a good example. Different moments of the episode are illustrated in good paintings in both the Īnjū 1330 and 1341 manuscripts (figs. 46–47), and also in the Stephens manuscript, even if the latter is not as good a picture. But the scene in the Tabriz manuscript is extraordinary, before which all the Īnjū pictures pale in comparison: it is the celebrated image of Rustam slaying Isfandiyār with the forked arrow,[38] the tree in the foreground echoing the shape of the fatally wounded younger hero, and so eloquently recapitulating in pictorial terms the import of Rustam's rash act.

Whatever the temporal relationship between the Great Mongol *Shāhnāma* and the earliest of the Īnjū manuscripts may prove to be, there is no doubt that paintings in the two later Īnjū volumes, of

---

[35] Sims (2002), 213.

[36] A pictorial/thematic composition explored, and illustrated, by Sims (2002), 114–26, 213–17, and 318–20.

[37] Brian 51: Komaroff and Carboni, eds. (2002), 156.

[38] Brian 21: Komaroff and Carboni, eds. (2002), 161.

1341 and before 1353, could have made use of pictorial ideas in the Tabriz manuscript, and did, even if at first the parallels are virtually unrecognizable. One such example is *Bahrām in the House of the Peasants*. In the Tabriz manuscript (fig. 48),[39] the picture is a satisfying vertical rectangle, its architectural setting modulated to suggest a stepped composition whose potential voids are instead filled with a tree and a deep blue sky, its figures remarkably large and expressive. In the 1341 manuscript (fig. 49), the same image has been flattened out, compressed into a long rectangle with only a rudimentary landscape and a smaller rectangular mat for Bahrām, while the palette is both lightened and limited. Yet the formal elements of the composition are the same: both rulers sit at the left of the picture, framed by the curve of a tree at the margin, and in a similar pose, with outer leg drawn up; both are crowned, and dressed in garments decorated with large golden floral patterns; and in both the cow is humped and spotted, placed in the center of the picture facing left, being milked by the peasant woman sitting beneath her. The story is not frequently illustrated—only six instances are listed in the 1969 Index,[40] and of these six, half are fourteenth-century: the two just discussed, and a third, from the Second small *Shāhnāma*, although it is entirely different in its composition and its details.[41] Different as the Īnjū and the Tabriz pictures at first appear, the parallel seems clearly established by the formal elements of the composition.

A more complex set of parallels is afforded by one of the oldest of Iranian stories and images to be enshrined in Firdawsī's *Shāhnāma*, that of Bahrām Gūr and his harpist Āzāda. In the pictures in both the Tabriz manuscript[42] and the earliest of the Īnjū volumes, Bahrām Gūr and Āzāda hunt gazelle in a hilly landscape and present us with some of the potential post-Sasanian variations on an ancient Iranian pictorial theme: Bahrām, crowned and riding on a single-humped but shaggy-necked camel, has just released an arrow at the pairs of gazelles fleeing to the right, but Āzāda already lies under the feet of the beast.

[39] Brian 50: Sims (2002), 251.

[40] Norgren and Davis (1969).

[41] Brooklyn Museum of Art, 36.239: reproduced in Simpson (1979), fig. 43 (but identified, variously, as both 36.238 and 36.239). The derivation from 'a common pictorial tradition' had already been noted in Grube (1962), 34.

[42] Brian 47: Komaroff and Carboni, eds. (2002), fig. 110.

The episode occurs in all four of the Īnjū manuscripts but not in either of the small *Shāhnāmas*, nor in the Freer or Gutman copies;[43] this is surely a kind of 'diagnostic' feature to be kept in mind. In the four Īnjū copies, however, the images clearly come from the same pictorial stemma: the camels are all large-headed and shaggy, Bahrām usually faces left and either draws his bow or has just released an arrow at a fleeing single pair of gazelles, while Āzāda always lies on her face beneath the camel's feet (in three instances her head to the left),[44] and she is always dressed in same dark robe patterned with large white flowers (or dots), her headdress lost in the fall. The variations are minor: in the 1333 version Bahrām on his camel has been flipped and faces right—as also in the Tabriz picture, which is perhaps contemporary?—and Āzāda's harp has somehow wound up around her neck.

The age of the image by which this old story is told may be inferred from versions painted on Seljuk *mina'i* wares, for instance, a dish in Berlin and a bowl in New York. The dish offers a particularly useful parallel, since the figures stand out clearly against a white background; less clear is the image on the bowl, the space around the primary unit of Bahrām-Āzāda-the camel 'obscured' not only by the trampled Āzāda under the camel's hooves but also by the gazelles of the challenge and landscape filler elements, while the camel's distinctive hairiness is merely rendered as short parallel lines traced against its neck.[45] In both ceramic versions, and surely on many more examples, the clothing is still Seljuk, but the shaggy, large-headed Bactrian camel, which appears to be a long-standard part of the image, is already in its 'classical' place, facing left and bearing Bahrām, whose bow is drawn and at the ready, with his ill-fated harpist behind him. Both ceramic versions, moreover, are strikingly similar to another Seljuk-style image of Bahrām and Āzāda on the back of an emphatically shaggy camel, a pen drawing in one register of a hitherto unpublished page of Muzaffarid drawings in the Topkapı Palace Museum Library.[46] If the Tabriz version of the

---

[43] Simpson (1979), Appendices 2, 3, and 4, the relevant sections on 362–63, 374, and 380; and Masuya (1994), 140–41.

[44] Sims (2002), 307, from the Stephens manuscript.

[45] The dish: Museum für islamische Kunst, Berlin (I.5667), Farmer (1966), 30–31, Abb. 13 in color; the bowl: Metropolitan Museum of Art (57.36.13), illustrated in Sims (2002), 306 in color.

[46] H. 2158, fol. 98r: Komaroff and Carboni, eds. (2002), fig. 221.

episode is, again, one of the less impressive paintings in this usually magnificent manuscript, it might also be seen as the pictorial source—one, at least—of the entire Īnjū series which is, for all its evident 'primitive' qualities, manifestly cast in the newer, illustrative mode rather than the medieval one of multiple images. And it is a remarkably consistent series, once initiated; its first appearance makes use of the Seljuk model (unlike the Tabriz picture which flips the human and animal groups but does no more, perhaps because it is so very old a story), adjusting tiny details of clothing and setting the scene in mountainous landscapes; while the next three in the series make only minimal changes in the formula, such as the direction in which Bahrām faces, and whether his bow is drawn or already released.

Two more pictorial features, I would suggest, link the Great Mongol *Shāhnāma* and the four Īnjū volumes and, equally, set them apart from the small, Freer, and Gutman manuscripts. One is the appearance of Mongol feathered headdresses, so prevalent in some of the contemporary (and often astonishingly large) wash-colored drawings on bare ground.[47] But they seem quite rare in the Tabriz manuscript and I have only been able to find two instances, in *Īraj Slain by His Brothers, Salm and Tūr*, and in *Afrāsiyāb Slays Nawdar.*[48] They are equally rare in the Īnjū series, and in what survives of the Gutman manuscript, in which I have found only one,[49] while they are not so rare in the small *Shāhnāma*s and the Freer copy. Surely this is another 'diagnostic' feature of some significance, whatever it will ultimately prove to be.

*Dīw*s are most infrequent in the Tabriz manuscript, although here we really must affirm that 'absence of evidence is not evidence of absence,' for who knows what images might have been originally illustrated in it? A related picture—and it is hard not to see it as once having been part of the great Mongol *Shāhnāma*—does show a pair of them,[50] being crucial to the story of Kay Khusraw's victory over

[47] The exhibition brought together sixteen of them, cat. nos. 17–32, and Mongol feathered headgear representing many ranks can clearly be seen in nine of them: Komaroff and Carboni, eds. (2002), 18–23, 25, and 30–31, figs. 35, 39, 68, 84, 86, 133–34, 220, and 222.

[48] Brian 6 and 13, respectively: Grabar and Blair (1980), 69 and 83.

[49] Swietochowski and Carboni (1994), 84: *Ẓāl Delivers Sām's Letter to Manūchihr.*

[50] Topkapı Palace Museum Library, H. 2153, fol. 55r: Sims (2002), 188.

them. They are shown as classically *dīw*-like: sturdy humanoids with horned feline heads, golden eyes, long canine side-teeth, and exaggeratedly long claw-like digits, naked save for short skirts; whereas one of the few *dīw*s in the Īnjū series—Akwān, from the Stephens manuscript (pl. 20)—seems to have dropped by from a Halloween masquerade, dressed in cropped red pants and a leopard-skin quiver, with a fox-like head and thick red lips. He is, moreover, an unusually well-defined Īnjū *dīw*; few if any of the others, in the entire Īnjū *Shāhnāma* series, are so specifically conceived, and most look like stuffed scarecrows. This, too, must surely serve as some kind of 'diagnostic' feature, probably meaning that we shall eventually be permitted to exclude the still unplaced fourteenth-century manuscripts from whatever textual and pictorial traditions lie behind both the Great Mongol *Shahnama* and the entire Īnjū series.[51]

As for these four Īnjū manuscripts, we ought, now, to summarize at least their material similarities and differences (tabulated in the Appendix). The earliest, of 1330, is closest to the third of the series, being only faintly larger in (its present) folio size and the approximate number of *bayt*s of Firdawsī's text it contains, and its layout is also in the six-column format. This is, we should recall, also the format used for the Great Mongol *Shāhnāma.* As for its paintings, those in this first Īnjū *Shāhnāma* are the most varied of the four in their shape as well as the best in terms of the solidity of their application of pigment. And they breathe that indefinable something that gives the impression of a provincial attempt, however vain, at reaching for the kind of pictorial magnificence of the Great Mongol *Shāhnāma*, if only in its taste for pictures of complex shape and its predilection for garments decorated with large golden floral ornament. Had its painters perhaps seen—or heard—something about the great *Shāhnāma* taking shape in the *khān*'s atelier and tried, around 730/1330, to emulate what they had heard of, perhaps even presenting it to the *khān*'s vizier, Ghiyāth al-Dīn?

The second in the series, dated very shortly thereafter, in 1333, has a folio size that is, even in its cut-down state, still not much smaller than the first, though its format is one of only four columns:

[51] The two small *Shāhnāma*s, and the Freer and Gutman manuscripts, as well as another dispersed manuscript written on a large folio with thirty-four lines of text to an undecorated page.

this is a progressive trait for the time, suggests Wright.[52] Its picture-complement is by far the smallest of the group and, while this may only signify that many have been lost, the pictorial quality is in any case not high, even if it is quite lively. Was this manuscript the first of the series to have been made in Shiraz, in a truly provincial emulation of the first, finished only two years prior? In any event, both are dated before the effective end of the Ilkhanid dynasty, in 736/1335–36. The last two were made in the second period of Īnjū bookmaking, after 1340, and, while their colophons do not say they were made in Shiraz, there seems little doubt that they were. The third of the series was made for Qiwām al-Dīn, vizier to Abū Isḥāq Īnjū. It has a folio size virtually equal to the earliest manuscript, as has been noted, and is also copied in six columns, with a still-undetermined number of illustrations that may eventually establish it as having had the largest pictorial program of all four manuscripts. Many of its pictures appear to have flattened their models down into unimaginative horizontal rectangles; others are quite interestingly composed and drawn, with a certain calligraphic freedom and originality. In overall quality it seems the least fine of the four; its paper is soft and not well-polished, and consequently the surfaces are all quite rubbed and badly abraded, while its application of paint is truly the most slapdash of the four. On the other hand, both Wright and Simpson have commented on the extensiveness and quality of its illumination, which argues for both thought and money lying behind its commission, if not in its execution.[53]

The last of the series is, in its folio size and also in terms of the amount of poetry it contains, the smallest; yet at the moment its pictorial program is the largest of the four, the great majority being rectangular. Simplicity of format, however, does not always mean simplicity of conception, and Wright has commented on the effectiveness of the stepped compositions in this manuscript and its setting of specific text points to dramatize the reading of the texts.[54] The quantity of its variant readings may not be unconnected with the limited number of the *Shāhnāma* text verses it contains; indeed, the variant texts may well confer upon it a value quite unrelated to

---

52 Wright (1997), 69–72, *passim*.

53 Wright (1997), 11 and 19–20; Simpson (2000), 223–25.

54 Wright (1997), 123–24.

that of its many illustrations, which may have been even greater in number than 108, for its program seems truncated and is especially sparse for the reign of Bahrām Gūr, whose feats are so particularly well-illustrated in the Great Mongol *Shāhnāma*.[55] If there are missing pictures, there would also be missing text on the folios around them, which would then increase the hypothetical number of *bayt*s of text originally contained in this manuscript. Finally, it appears to have suffered most at the hand of those who would 'improve' it, for many of the paintings have been noticeably retouched (if not completely repainted), although their vivid liveliness still stands out within the unmistakable Īnjū pictorial canon.

The direction these disparate pictorial observations will eventually lead us remains, for the moment, unknown. Among other problems, which can surely be resolved by the application of both thought and time, is that of the pictorial programs of each of the Īnjū manuscripts. These have not yet been firmly established, although I suspect that we are coming close. I suspect, too, that in many cases our visual expectations need some focal readjustment to be able to shift from the magnificence of 'the kind of painting which is current at the present time,' of which the Great Mongol *Shāhnāma* is the example *par excellence*, to the still quite old-fashioned conception of book illustration demonstrated by volumes made in Shiraz in the second quarter of the fourteenth century. I do not doubt, however, that, as a group, the illustrations in the Īnjū series of *Shāhnāma* manuscripts are far more interesting—and perhaps also more important to the history of this art—than they have previously been considered, and I dare to suggest that I am not alone in so thinking.

---

[55] Only two are so far known: one picture still in the manuscript—on folio 32r, *The Infant Bahrām Gūr Presented to His Father*—and *Bahrām Gūr Hunts with Āzāda*, now in the Metropolitan Museum of Art; see n. 18, above.

APPENDIX

Details of Four Īnjū Shāhnāma *Manuscripts*

Manuscript	H. 1479	Dorn 329*	Dispersed	Stephens
Date	731/1330	733/1333	741/1341	752/1352–53
Number of folios	286 (?)	369	325 (?) postulated	322 (>334?)
Page size (in millimeters)	375 x 290	355 x 275	370 x 300	291 x 210
Written-surface size	289 x 224	288 x 215	285 x 240	222 x 150
Number of text columns	6	4	6	4
Number of lines per column	34	33	30	33
Number of pictures	92	50 (now)	105 +?	108
Double-frontispiece	1	1	1	1
Finispiece(s)	none recorded	1	2	none recorded
Approximate number of *bayts*	<58,140	<48,576	<58,140	<43,229

* The measurements for this manuscript were kindly provided to me by Olga Yastrebova, of the Russian National Library, Department of Oriental Manuscripts.

THE ARTS AND ARTISTIC INTERCHANGE

PAPER: THE TRANSFORMATIVE MEDIUM IN ILKHANID ART

JONATHAN M. BLOOM

Paper, which had been introduced to the Islamic lands in the eighth and ninth centuries, began to play a major role in Iranian artistic production from the thirteenth century, approximately at the moment when the Mongol Ilkhans came to rule the region. Since the ninth century, writers in the Islamic lands had used paper for copying books on a great variety of subjects, and in the tenth century, Iranian calligraphers began using paper for making copies of the Qur'ān. Artists, however, seem to have taken little notice of this new medium, tending to work directly in their chosen media, be they textiles, metalwork, pottery, or wood. In the thirteenth century, however, illustrated books begin to appear in greater numbers in larger formats, and artists begin to use paper not only as a medium for sophisticated painting and drawing but also as an intermediary medium for the creation of works of art in other media.[1] It is tempting, indeed, to hypothesize that this new exploration of the potential of paper was a direct result of the Mongol conquests and of the increased contact with China, which remained at the forefront of papermaking technology throughout the period, but the available evidence does not yet support such a conclusion. Artists' increasing use of paper in their work seems to have been part of a greater phenomenon in Islamic society from the thirteenth century, as paper and particularly larger sheets of paper became cheaper and more widely available for use by all members of the culture, not only those in the literate (and scribbling) classes. Rather than speculate on *why* this happened, in the following pages I propose to discuss *how* this happened.

About one half of the West Asian objects displayed in the exhibition *The Legacy of Genghis Khan* in New York and Los Angeles were works on paper (cat. nos. 1–68), and as some of these—Rashīd al-Dīn's

[1] Bloom (2001).

Compendium of Chronicles, for example—are multileaved manuscripts, the number of works on paper seemed preponderant to any visitor to the exhibition or reader of the catalogue.[2] As for the other objects, it is possible to imagine that a drawing on paper was somehow involved in their creation, whatever the media in which the works were ultimately executed.

Signatures on several works on paper, for example, lead us directly to other works of art. The magnificent colophon page from a volume of the so-called Anonymous Baghdad Qur'ān contains the signature of the calligrapher Aḥmad [ibn] al-Suhrawardī, who came from a well-known family of mystics and was probably the grandson of the Sufi master Shihāb al-Dīn Abū Ḥafṣ 'Umar al-Suhrawardī (1145–1234).[3] Aḥmad was one of the six disciples of the noted Baghdadi calligrapher Yāqūt al-Musta'ṣimī, who is said to have transcribed the Qur'ān thirty-three times. Aḥmad's most famous work is this dispersed large-format (each leaf is 50 cm high) manuscript in thirty volumes, which was copied at Baghdad between 1302 and 1308, with illumination (*tadhhīb*) by Muḥammad ibn Aybak ibn 'Abdallāh, who signed each of the extant volumes as well. Although the surviving parts mention no patron, the size and luxury of the manuscript along with the dates of the colophons suggest that it was begun under the auspices of Ghazan (d. 1304) and completed for his successor Öljeitü.

Aḥmad may also have calligraphed an even larger manuscript of the Qur'ān in thirty volumes (which was not in the exhibition), which was also illuminated by his partner Muḥammad ibn Aybak. Made for Öljeitü between 1306 and 1313, it was bequeathed to his mausoleum at Sultaniyya.[4] According to the Safavid chronicler Qāḍī Aḥmad, Aḥmad ibn al-Suhrawardī also designed many architectural inscriptions in Baghdad. For example, he is said to have written the complete text of Qur'ān Chapter 18, *Sūra al-kahf* ('The cave') for the congregational mosque there, but the building has not survived. Lest we imagine Aḥmad standing on the scaffolding with a big brush, Qāḍī Aḥmad says explicitly that masons reproduced Aḥmad al-

---

[2] Komaroff and Carboni, eds. (2002). This seemed particularly true of the exhibition as presented in New York, where many, if not most, of the works on paper were displayed together in separate rooms. In Los Angeles, by contrast, works on paper were integrated with objects in other media throughout the galleries.

[3] Komaroff and Carboni, eds. (2002), cat. nos. 63, 64.

[4] James (1988), cat. no. 40.

Suhrawardī's designs in baked brick worked in relief.[5]

Aḥmad al-Suhrawardī's contemporary, the calligrapher Ḥaydar (d. 1325–26), was another disciple of Yāqūt al-Mustaʿṣimī. He was a renowned teacher whose pupils included his own son, such famous calligraphers as ʿAbdallāh Ṣayrafī, and the Ilkhanid viziers Tāj al-Dīn ʿAlī Shāh and Ghiyāth al-Dīn (the son of Rashīd al-Dīn). Ḥaydar earned the nickname 'writer in large characters' (Pers. *gunda-nawīs*), presumably because of his masterful work designing architectural inscriptions in carved stucco. Although none of his manuscripts is known to have survived (and hence they were not displayed in the exhibition), two examples of his work in this medium survive in Iran: a lovely band (1307–8) across the intrados of the north *īwān* of the mosque in the shrine complex at Natanz (fig. 50), and the superb *miḥrāb* (1310) in the winter prayer hall of the Friday Mosque at Isfahan (fig. 51).[6] Each area of the brilliant composition is worked in a distinct pattern; each pattern is worked simultaneously on several levels. The outer rectangular frame, for example, has a ground of double arabesque scrolls sprouting carved and stippled palmettes, which supports an elegant inscription in *thuluth* script. A comparison with the inscription at Natanz, which is flatter and less crisp, shows that Ḥaydar only designed these inscriptions by making drawings that other craftsmen of varying talents could execute. Another indication of Ḥaydar's role (or lack of one) at Natanz is that the inscription is placed so that it can only be read when one's back is facing the *qibla*.[7]

Paper also played an important role in the career of the designer-calligrapher Aḥmad Shāh al-Naqqāsh, who was born in Tabriz in the early fourteenth century and became a leading calligrapher under the Jalayirids by the middle of the fourteenth century.[8] Blair, who also

---

[5] Qāḍī Aḥmad (1959), 60.

[6] Turner, ed., (1996), s.v. 'Haydar.'

[7] Blair (1986b), 395, fig. 10.

[8] Another designer-calligrapher, Muḥammad Shāh *al-naqqāsh*, copied a collection of *dīwāns* now in the Chester Beatty Library; his name also appears on the stucco inscription on the dado around the shrine of Pīr-i Bakrān (1303–12) at Linjan. The *minbar* from Na'in (1311) was ordered by a merchant and was signed by yet another designer, Maḥmūd Shāh ibn Muḥammad of Kirman. Of typical form and size (5.2 x 1 x 3.2 m), it is made of jujube wood. The triangular sides are composed of rectangular panels within a mortised frame. The panels and frame are carved with shallow 'beveled style' arabesques, the balustrade is a lattice of interlaced octagons, and larger raised panels with stellate designs are used for emphasis on the canopy and the lintel.

delineated his career, originally suggested that Aḥmad Shāh worked in a "variety of media," but I believe—and I think she now does too—that the evidence suggests that he produced designs that were realized by others in a variety of media. According to the Safavid chronicler Qāḍī Aḥmad, Aḥmad Shāh was hired by the Jalayirid sultan 'Uways to "write in the buildings at Najaf," tombsite not only of the Prophet's son-in-law 'Alī but also of Shaykh 'Uways's father, Ḥasan Jalāyir, who had died in 1356. It seems to me most unlikely that the calligrapher would have been willing or able to ascend a scaffold and do the actual interior design. Instead, he must have designed the inscriptions on paper which were then executed by others. For this work, the calligrapher received the sobriquet *zarīn-qalam*, or 'golden pen.'[9]

Aḥmad Shāh also designed the epigraphic decoration of the Mirjaniyya, the funerary complex founded by Mirjan ibn 'Abdallāh ibn 'Abd al-Raḥmān in Baghdad and completed in 758/1357 during the reign of 'Uways. Aḥmad Shāh is mentioned in an inscription dated 758/1357–58 on the lintel over the well, another over the door from the mosque to the bazaar, and the endowment inscription over the portal to the Khān 'Urtma. Blair believes that he also designed the long endowment inscription dated 758/1357 around the *muṣallā, miḥrāb,* and *īwān* of the mosque, and had a hand in the other epigraphic decoration of the complex. In Baghdad, Aḥmad Shāh is called 'the designer (*naqqāsh*) from Tabriz known as the Golden Pen.'[10] A decade later Aḥmad Shāh *al-naqqāsh* actually signed a Qur'ān manuscript dated 766/1364–65, now in the Reza 'Abbasi Museum in Tehran, where his nickname is given as the 'golden pen of Shiraz' (*zarīn qalam al-shirāzī*) thereby connecting him to a group of four related candlesticks in Lyon, Paris, and Cleveland.[11] One of them was made for and probably designed by Aḥmad Shāh al-Naqqāsh, thereby providing the basis for the attribution of the entire group to the city of Shiraz.

---

[9] According to Blair (1985), 54–55, in his account of the pupils of the great calligrapher Yāqūt al-Musta'ṣimī, the seventeenth-century chronicler Qāḍī Aḥmad conflated our Aḥmad Shāh with Mubārak-Shāh, one of Yāqūt's actual pupils, who was active in the early fourteenth century, penning, among others, a Qur'ān manuscript dated 1313 presently in Baltimore.

[10] Ibid., 53–55.

[11] Musée des Beaux-Arts, Lyon E538-54; Cleveland Museum of Art 51.539; Musée du Louvre, Paris 7530 and 6034.

Although artists such as Ḥaydar and Aḥmad Shāh must have used preparatory drawings on paper, few such drawings are known to have survived from the Ilkhanid period, most of them in albums in Istanbul and Berlin. None was shown in the exhibition, but since some were illustrated in the accompanying catalogue, their absence may be due to the practical considerations the organizers faced in securing some loans.[12] These drawings are, of course, fragile things. When they were used, they must have been quite literally used to shreds, as the designs were repeatedly studied, copied, traced, transferred, pricked, and corrected. Indeed, some of the drawings in the Istanbul and Berlin albums attributed to the fifteenth century are believed to be copies of fourteenth-century originals.[13]

Of the drawings included in the exhibition, none can be considered a preparatory drawing. For example, a large colored drawing (8 x 11 3/8 in.) of a landscape exhibited only in New York is said to be from a manuscript of Rashīd al-Dīn's *Compendium of Chronicles*.[14] That explanation, however, raises as many questions as it answers: what exactly would it have illustrated, with its leafless spiny forest crossed by a roiling river? Then again, its level of finish seems to suggest that it was not a preparatory drawing for something else. Muḥammad ibn Maḥmūdshāh al-Khayyām's drawing in ink and gold of a Mongol archer on horseback is attributed to the early fifteenth century.[15] The use of gold and the prominent signature indicate that this wasn't a preparatory drawing, but a finished drawing meant to be enjoyed as it is.

Quite apart from surviving drawings, there is still ample evidence that such drawings were used. For example, the *ʿarḍadāsht*, or progress report, prepared in the early fifteenth century on the activities of the Timurid design studio, said that in the studio "there was a design by Mīr Dawlatyār for a saddle. Khwāja Mīr Ḥasan copied it, and Khwāja Mīr Ḥasan's son Mīr Shamsuddīn and Ustādh Dawlat-Khwāja are busy executing it in mother-of-pearl."[16] According to the sixteenth-century Safavid chronicler Dūst Muḥammad, the artist Mīr Dawlatyār, who had made the design, had been active

---

[12] Komaroff (2002), figs. 221, 223, 225, 226.
[13] Komaroff (2002), fig. 223.
[14] Komaroff and Carboni, eds. (2002), cat. no. 29, and fig. 168.
[15] Ibid., cat. no. 20 and fig. 220.
[16] Thackston (2001), 43–44.

at the court of the Ilkhan Abū Sa'īd (r. 1316–35)—that is, several generations *before* the *'arḍadāsht* was composed—where he was known for his pen-and-ink drawings.[17] Mīr Dawlatyār's drawing, therefore, must have been nearly a century old when it was used in the Timurid design studio. The matter-of-fact quality in which the author of the *'arḍadāsht* mentions this drawing suggests that it was by no means unique, so such drawings must have been produced regularly in the thirteenth and fourteenth centuries to be saved and consulted in the fifteenth.

Many of the tiles from the palace at Takht-i Sulayman, decorated in the 1270s, are decorated with—among other subjects—images of phoenixes and dragons, Chinoiserie motifs that Linda Komaroff has shown are derived from representations of these mythical creatures on Chinese and Central Asian textiles woven in colored silk and gold.[18] While it is possible to imagine that potters might have seen luxurious textiles in public and semipublic places—whether as clothing, canopies, or banners—it is still much easier to imagine that someone else, with cleaner hands, made intermediary drawings of dragons and phoenixes, and that potters used these drawings as inspiration for their work.[19]

In an article published nearly a decade ago, Komaroff showed how the presence of certain motifs on fourteenth-century metal wares can best be explained by the use of paper designs, even though none of the actual designs used is known to survive.[20] For example, a candlestick in the exhibition (no. 162) made by Sa'd ibn 'Abdallāh in the mid-fourteenth century is decorated on the base with four large medallions containing figural compositions depicting enthronements. These are very similar to the enthronements depicted on a drawing in Berlin, believed to be a fifteenth-century copy of a fourteenth-century original. Komaroff correctly imagined that drawings of this type would have been used in the design of metalwares that she aptly characterized as "paintings in silver and gold." Although such metalwares are technically products of a craft tradition, their

---

[17] Komaroff (2002), 186.

[18] Komaroff and Carboni, eds. (2002), 175–77.

[19] Komaroff (2002), 186, although on 183–84 she notes that "This is not to suggest that all manner of Persian artists had direct access to these expensive imported goods."

[20] Komaroff (1994), 2–34.

decoration is closely related to contemporary imagery on paper.

The intermediary of paper designs has also been used to explain the similarities between certain types of architectural decoration and Qur'ān illumination in Ilkhanid Iran. For example, at Öljeitü's tomb at Sultaniyya, erected between 1307 and 1313, a ring of galleries on the exterior overlooks the surrounding plain. The two dozen gallery vaults display an enormous variety of geometric and epigraphic motifs carved in the plaster and painted in red, yellow, green, and white (fig. 52). Many of the strapwork panels closely resemble the designs found on contemporary manuscript illumination by the likes of such illuminators as Muḥammad ibn Aybak ibn ʿAbdallāh, suggesting not that Ilkhanid stucco carvers spent their free time studying Qur'ān frontispieces but that Ilkhanid designers, presumably illuminators such as Muḥammad ibn Aybak, also produced drawings on paper which other artisans could realize on different scales in different media.[21]

In his essay for the catalogue, Stefano Carboni takes this idea one step further, suggesting that "the styles of illumination on frontispieces [by such Baghdad illuminators as Muḥammad ibn Aybak] probably influenced designs used for other ornamental purposes," not only the exterior gallery vaults at Sultaniyya, but also on the lampas textile from the Cooper-Hewitt Museum that was displayed in the exhibition (and illustrated in the catalogue next to the Sultaniyya vaults).[22] Although the similarities are indeed persuasive on the page where the textile is displayed on the diagonal, they are somewhat less so when the entire textile is reconstructed (pl. 21). Instead, the textile design now resembles the star-and-cross tiles found commonly on Ilkhanid walls, whether the set from the Victoria and Albert Museum in the exhibition or those from the Ilkhanid summer palace at Takht-i Sulayman.[23]

Excavators at the site of Takht-i Sulayman discovered hundreds of fragments of cast-plaster elements, which they determined were the remains of a *muqarnas* vault that once stood in the palace.[24] Making the *muqarnas* units from plaster and assembling the vault, which must have resembled the one that survives at Natanz (fig. 53), was probably a pretty messy business that involved wet materials and dirty

[21] Blair and Bloom (1994), 8.
[22] Carboni (2002), 206 and figs. 248 and 249.
[23] Komaroff and Carboni, eds. (2002), fig. 120.
[24] Naumann, R. (1977).

hands. The master builder may have planned the vault on paper, but when it came time for the workmen to put it together onsite, the actual working drawing—the *aide-mémoire* that helped the artisans assemble the prefabricated elements in the correct order—was transferred to the less-expensive and more durable medium of plaster. Such a plaster plaque was indeed found at the site and is the earliest surviving architectural drawing from the Islamic lands.[25] Surely paper and not plaster plans were used by the second quarter of the fourteenth century when the plan for Rukn al-Dīn's funerary complex in Yazd—which included a *madrasa*, hostel for *sayyid*s, hospice for Sufis, bazaar, and bath—was drawn up in Tabriz and sent to Yazd.[26] It is difficult, however, to know what exactly these 'plans' must have been—were they measured drawings showing the layout of buildings or only designs for decoration? If they were plans in the sense we understand the word today, they would reveal a new level of conceptual sophistication as the builders in Yazd would have known how—and been willing—to decode the instructions previously encoded in Tabriz.

Builders and decorators in the Ilkhanid period, however, can be shown to have used paper in other ways. For example, a fragment of a tile frieze from Öljeitü's tomb at Sultaniyya was displayed in the exhibition.[27] Made of pieces of earthenware, which were glazed, cut, and assembled as a mosaic, the design is a perfect example of the technique of 'complete mosaic faience' or 'complete tile mosaic,' in which an architectural surface is entirely covered by a pattern arrangement of small pieces of tile which have surface glazes of different colors.[28] Several areas from the interior of the sultan's mausoleum, including the capitals, shafts, and bases of the engaged colonnettes between the wall panels of the first stage of decoration, were also decorated in this technique. The elements are cut from dark blue, light blue, and white tile and fitted together in intricate curvilinear patterns as closely as the elements would permit.[29] Elsewhere in

---

[25] Ibid.

[26] Iraj Afshar has produced clear evidence for the use of plans drawn on paper for the Rabʿ-i Rashīdī at Tabriz. See Rogers (1989), 135; Jaʿfarī (1960), 88–89; and Blair (1986a), 33.

[27] Komaroff and Carboni, eds. (2002), fig. 143 and cat. no. 121.

[28] Wilber (1939), 16.

[29] Ibid., 45.

the interior, a related technique was used for the background to some of the inscriptions written in terracotta, where prefabricated hexagons, each formed of three tile squares alternating with three rhombuses around a central triangle, were laid in staggered rows.[30] Perhaps the finest surviving example is at the sides of the doorway leading to the mosque room on the south; they are decorated with a magnificent design of ten-pointed stars in complete mosaic (fig. 54).[31] On the exterior of the building, the great *muqarnas* cornice is covered with areas of complete mosaic faience worked in somewhat coarser geometric patterns. Most of the tile decoration at Sultaniyya, however, is in a different style, in which strips or other pieces of glazed earthenware and terracotta are inserted into a plaster surface to form geometric patterns (pl. 22).

In the 1930s, Donald Wilber, who had studied the evolution of Persian tilework, saw what he called 'complete mosaic faience' to be the logical culmination of a development begun centuries before, as Iranian builders increasingly inserted bits of terracotta and glazed earthenware into wall surfaces to decorate them with patterns. According to Wilber, over the course of the thirteenth century the amount of tile surface gradually expanded at the expense of the interstitial plaster, although this linear development was somewhat obscured by the temporary hiatus in building caused by the Mongol invasions. The late Michael Meinecke demonstrated that in the thirteenth century some Iranian craftsmen emigrated to central Anatolia, where they also used the complete mosaic technique in such buildings as the Gök Medrese in Tokat.[32]

Wilber suggested that complete tile mosaic was first used in Iran to decorate the tomb of Ghazan Khan (d. 1304) as well as the buildings of the Rabʿ-i Rashīdī (before 1318), for he found fragments of tile mosaic in the ruins of these buildings outside Tabriz.[33] The first Iranian examples of complete tile mosaic *in situ*, however, are on the tomb of Öljeitü at Sultaniyya, from which the fragment in the exhibition came. In the following decades artisans took the technique to other parts of the country where it flourished, as for example in

[30] Sims (1988), 146 and figs. 21, 22.
[31] Ibid., 146 and fig. 29.
[32] Meinecke (1976), vol. 1, 165–66.
[33] Wilber (1939), 42–44. Chahriyar Adle has also studied the ruins of Ghazan's tomb; Adle (1985).

the magnificent tilework on the portal of the Congregational Mosque at Yazd.[34]

The focus on *who* first developed complete tile mosaic and *where* has obscured investigation into *how* it was done, namely that 'incomplete' and 'complete' tile mosaic, despite their visual similarities, are quite different techniques. As Meinecke already noted, the first is a direct technique in which the artisan places and fits tiles directly onto or into the plaster wall surface, perhaps guided by an underdrawing on the wall. Complete tile mosaic, by contrast, is an indirect technique in which the design is first worked out on paper and then transferred to a large surface, usually the workshop floor. Only then does the tilecutter cut tiles into pieces using a paper or pasteboard template, bevel the tile edges so they fit closely together, and then match them *face down* on the pattern. Once fitted together, the tile pieces are covered with a thin layer of plaster and then the resulting plaque is affixed to the wall.[35] Thus, while strapwork patterns or even the hexagonal backgrounds to the Sultaniyya inscriptions could have been done directly by eye, complete tile mosaic, particularly with intricate curvilinear and geometric designs, demanded the use of large sheets of paper to design the patterns, make cartoons, and cut the tiles. The availability of large sheets of paper in Ilkhanid Iran has long been established. Large sheets were also available in central Anatolia, where tile mosaic was also produced in the thirteenth century. The earliest surviving manuscript of Jalāl al-Dīn Rūmī's *Mathnawī*, for example, was copied on 312 large (50 x 32 cm; half-*baghdādī* size) pages of thick paper in 1278, probably at Konya.[36]

Ilkhanid craftsmen in Iran also used paper to design stucco and luster tiles. The calligrapher Ḥaydar, we have already seen, must have designed but not executed the inscription in the *īwān* of the mosque at Natanz (fig. 50), although it bears his 'signature.' A set of two large luster tiles in the exhibition, probably the cover for the tomb of Shaykh ʿAbd al-Ṣamad adjacent to that very mosque at Natanz, is prominently 'signed' as the "work of the builder Ḥ asan ibn ʿAlī' (*ʿamal-i Ḥasan bin ʿAlī bin Bābawayh al-Bannā'*) on the spandrels on either side of the central arch.[37] What exactly do these 'signatures' mean?

---

[34] Wilber (1939), 46–47.
[35] Meinecke (1976), vol. 1, 165–66.
[36] Raby and Tanındı (1993), 3–4.
[37] Komaroff and Carboni, eds. (2002), cat. no. 116 and fig. 237.

The medieval Persian builder Ḥasan ibn ʿAlī was descended from the Bābawayhs, an old family of learned men in the city of Qum whose most famous member was the Twelver theologian Shaykh-i Ṣadūq (d. 911). One might interpret this information to mean that Ḥasan ibn ʿAlī was a very talented individual who not only built buildings (hence his epithet *al-bannāʾ*) but also decorated them with tiles. However the set of tiles is also inscribed much less prominently, upside down on the right side of the bottom margin, by "the hand of the poor servant, ʿAlī ibn Muḥammad ibn Faḍlallāh," who "wrote it" in the month of Shawwāl of the year 9 and [?], which must be 709, equivalent to March 1310.

In 1986 Sheila Blair published an article on the career of Ḥasan ibn ʿAlī, in which she determined that he had signed several other works, including the capitals on the colonettes supporting the inscription band encircling the walls beneath the spectacular *muqarnas* dome at Natanz, under which these very tiles once lay.[38] Each of the (eight) attached colonettes has a single word in interlaced kufic script just below the capitals. Looking at the capitals, Blair was able to recognize the words *ʿamal-i Ḥasan-i ʿAlī-yi [A]ḥmad-i [Ba]baw[ayh]*, "the work of Ḥasan b. ʿAlī b. Aḥmad b. Bābawayh," and then another *ʿAlī*, which she construed as another part of this same man's name.[39]

Blair also noted that Ḥasan b. ʿAlī's name also appears on a stucco *miḥrāb* dated 736/1335–36 in the shrine of Abū al-Faḍl and Yaḥyā at Mahallat-i Bala, a village some twenty-five kilometers from the town of Delijan on the main road between Qum and Isfahan (fig. 55). Blair noted that the stucco work was poorly done, with stiff and shallow carving. Even the simplest words were misspelled, so she suggested, somewhat reluctantly, that the poor quality of the execution might be due to Ḥasan b. ʿAlī's advanced age. But there is another way of interpreting the same information: in all these cases Ḥasan b. ʿAlī may have been simply the designer of the work of art, which was actually executed by someone else. The drawing for the Natanz tiles would have been prepared by Ḥasan b. ʿAlī and realized by ʿAlī ibn Muḥammad ibn Faḍlallāh; the Natanz inscription would have been designed by Ḥasan b. ʿAlī and realized by an extremely talented stucco carver whose name (or part of it) was ʿAlī.

38 Blair (1986b).
39 Blair (1986a), 62.

In contrast, the Mahallat-i Bala *miḥrāb* would have been designed on paper by Ḥasan b. ʿAlī and realized by an incompetent hack in a remote location.

Oliver Watson, in writing about Persian luster potters of the Ilkhanid period, came to somewhat different conclusions. He noted that the most common form of signature was *katabahu* ('decorated,' or literally 'wrote'), which is used fullest in the phrase *katabahu baʿda mā ʿamilahu wa ṣanaʿatuhu*, "decorated after he had made it and fashioned it."[40] Although noting that such technical terms are "notoriously difficult to identify precisely, if indeed they were ever used in a precise fashion," Watson suggested "with due reserve" that *ṣanʿa* referred to design, leaving *ʿamila* to indicate the purely ceramic processes, and *kataba* to refer to the actual painting.[41]

For example, the medium-sized *miḥrāb* (or tomb cover) from the Imāmzāda Yaḥyā, Veramin (now in the Hermitage, fig. 56), bears an inscription squeezed in at the bottom of the central arch stating that it was made (*ṣanaʿat*) by ʿAlī ibn Aḥmad ibn ʿAlī al-Ḥusaynī *kātib*, 'the scribe,' an expression that Watson interpreted to mean 'designed.'[42] This ʿAlī was also the father of our Ḥasan ibn ʿAlī of the Bābawayh family whose design work (*ʿamal*) appears at Natanz. A somewhat less prominent inscription in the lower left margin states that this same set of tiles was made by (*ʿamila*) Yūsuf ibn ʿAlī Muḥammad, a fourth-generation descendant of the Abū Ṭāhir family of Kashan who also signed many other pieces. Watson understood him to be the artisan who actually did the ceramic tile. The decoration was completed or 'written' (*kataba*) (by an anonymous decorator?) on 10 Muḥarram 705/3 August 1305.

Although the name of Ḥasan's father, ʿAlī ibn Aḥmad *the scribe*, appears most prominently, it is poorly written and squeezed into the space, whereas Yūsuf's name fits the space well. If the terms are used consistently, the word *ʿamal* means 'design' and *ṣanʿa* means 'fabrication,' so that Yūsuf ibn ʿAlī was the designer and Ḥasan the fabricator.[43] In any event, many of these 'signatures' should be

[40] Combe, Sauvaget, and Wiet (1931), no. 5195; Watson (1985), 176, 179.

[41] Combe, Sauvaget, and Wiet (1931), no. 5195; Watson (1985), 176, 179.

[42] Watson (1985), 136, 176, and 179, no. 2.a(a).

[43] Oddly enough, the term *sanʿa* is used in the opposite sense to mean 'design' on the wooden *miḥrāb* dated 643/1245–46 in the Madrasa al-Halawiyya in Aleppo. See Herzfeld (1954–55), nos. 101 and 102.

understood as brand names rather than traces of the master's hand, much in the way that Ralph Lauren didn't actually make any of the clothes bearing his name that people wear.

Whatever the actual roles these individuals played, their activities involved the use of paper patterns and templates. The results of this type of collaboration can be seen in the luster tomb cover dated 1310 now in the Calouste Gulbenkian Foundation, Lisbon (fig. 57), where an anonymous artisan appears to have used a standard design that was then 'customized' for the patron, Shams al-Dīn Ḥusayn Nājī b. Tīmūr-Bugha, who, according to the inscription in white, ordered "these *miḥrāb*s and inscriptions" in 710/1310.[44] No artisan's name appears to be mentioned, but it seems clear from the script that some less-talented individual did the white inscription, which is poorly fitted to the space allotted: the date is spelled out entirely and the year is qualified by three otiose adjectives, *hijriyya, nabawiyya,* and *muṣṭafawiyya*, simply to fill out the space.

This hierarchical relationship of craftsmen in the Ilkhanid period should be contrasted with the cooperation of apparently unrelated potters a century earlier, when the evidence of signatures shows that they worked as equals on different aspects of a project. According to Watson, the most important of these partnerships was that between Abū Zayd and Muḥammad ibn Abī Ṭāhir, who worked together at both Qum and Mashhad in the early twelfth century.[45] The difference is that the increased availability of paper during the thirteenth century not only allowed for an increasing specialization of labor in Ilkhanid art, in which design was becoming divorced from execution, but also allowed for a greater homogeneity in the arts, as artisans traveled from one city to another not only with their memories of work they had done but also with the very designs they had used to make them.

It is very tempting to believe that this new use of paper was directly related to the Mongol conquest of Iran. For example, in her essay accompanying the exhibition, Linda Komaroff suggested that the increased importance of drawloom weaving under Ilkhanid patronage may have encouraged artists in other media to use

[44] Mota and Guerreiro, eds. (1972), no. 4.
[45] Watson (1985), 124.

paper as an intermediary stage between inspiration and creation.[46] I myself prefer to see the increased use of paper as part of a larger phenomenon in the central and eastern Islamic lands in which the artists of the Ilkhanid period were willing and able participants. For example, already by the early thirteenth century in northern Mesopotamia, the builder Yaḥyā ibn Ibrāhīm built tower XXXIX at Diyar Bakr according to plans (*tarsīm*) drawn up by his Artuqid overlord Maḥmūd.[47]

Certainly this trend cannot be separated from the increased size of paper and of books in Ilkhanid Iran, but there is ample evidence that it had begun earlier and also happened elsewhere. Whatever the reason, however, as artists began to use paper to work out design problems and transfer motifs from one medium to another, the qualities of freshness and spontaneity, which had characterized much early Islamic art, become increasingly characteristic of works on paper, while the finished products in other media become more cerebral and meticulous in execution. One could say that this happened to the arts of the book as well, as paintings of the Timurid and Safavid periods retain little of the spontaneity seen in the Ilkhanid works (as demonstrated in the exhibition). This momentous change of working habits, in which artistic design is a separate process from execution, was due largely to the increased use of paper. This new working method would come to characterize much of Islamic art in the period after the Mongol invasions, and it is for this reason that the Ilkhanid period is truly one of the transformative moments in the history of Islamic and Persian art.

---

[46] Komaroff (2002).
[47] Blair (2000), 523.

CHINESE MOTIFS IN THIRTEENTH-CENTURY ARMENIAN ART: THE MONGOL CONNECTION

DICKRAN KOUYMJIAN

In 1977 I presented a paper entitled 'Far Eastern Influences in Armenian Miniature Painting in the Mongol Period.'[1] It focused on two headpieces (pls. 23–24) in the Lectionary of Prince (later King) Het'um II, copied and illustrated in Cilicia in 1286.[2] They depict Chinese dragons, phoenixes, lions, and flying birds. The principal conclusions were two. First, Chinese motifs were integrated in Armenian art by the 1280s in an aesthetically satisfying way. Second, Armenian artists incorporated both motifs and stylistic aspects of Chinese and Chinese-inspired Mongol art perhaps prior to the neighboring Muslim tradition but certainly independent of it. As an addendum, I suggested that Far Eastern works of art may have been partly responsible for a pronounced stylistic change in Cilician painting of the late thirteenth century.[3]

An expanded study, published in 1986 in the Haïg Berbérian Festschrift,[4] incorporated new material: late thirteenth-century Islamic miniatures[5] and a depiction of a Chinese dragon on a gold

---

[1] Kouymjian (1977); the paper formed part of a panel entitled Patronage and Symbolism in Medieval Armenian Art, sponsored by the Society for Armenian Studies during the Eleventh Annual Meeting of the Middle East Studies Association in New York. It was distributed in mimeographed form.

[2] Erevan, Matenadaran, Repository of Ancient Manuscripts (henceforth M), M979, fols. 293 and 334, as is visible on the folios, though they are listed as fols. 295 and 335 in Der Nersessian and Agemian (1993), figs. 516–17 (in color).

[3] In the mimeographed version of 1977, 7–9; in the published version (see the following note), 461–68.

[4] Kouymjian (1986), 415–68.

[5] The 1977 version referred to the *Manāfi' al-ḥayawān* executed in Maragha in the 1290s (Pierpont Morgan Library, ms. no. 500, fol. 55) as showing the first trace of Chinese influence in Islamic painting; miniatures from the manuscript have been widely reproduced; see, for example, Gray (1961), 22 and 24; Pope (1945), esp. pl. 114; Komaroff and Carboni, eds. (2002), fig. 169. However, Marianna Shreve Simpson pointed out earlier traces in a manuscript of the *History of the World Conqueror* of 'Aṭā Malik Juwaynī now in the Bibliothèque nationale de France, Supplément persan, no. 205, fols. 1–2. This two-page frontispiece is seemingly the earliest example of Islamic painting with Chinese influences (cloud bands, garments, horse trappings).

embroidered piece of silk (figs. 58–59). This textile is visible in a donor portrait of a Gospel book of 1289 commissioned by Archbishop John, brother of Cilician King Het'um I; it serves as the tunic under his luxurious cope or is a piece of silk sewn onto that undergarment.[6] Among the themes treated in the article were the use of Chinese elements in Islamic art of the Ilkhanid and Timurid periods, the Armenian-Mongol alliance, visits of Armenian aristocracy to the Mongol and Ilkhanid courts and the exchange of gifts, Cilician ports as the major trading centers for East-West commerce, Chinese objects that might have served as the models for the motifs (fig. 60 and pl. 25), the date of Takht-i Sulayman and the dragon and phoenix tiles,[7] the stylistic influences of Chinese art on Armenian painting, especially landscapes,[8] and the effect of all of this on post-1300 manuscript illustration.

In light of more recent studies, including the *Legacy of Genghis Khan* catalogue,[9] I will here reexamine my earlier premises. Relying on the excavation reports of Elisabeth and Rudolf Naumann and the studies of A. S. Melikian-Chirvani and Yolande Crowe,[10] I initially accepted a date near the end of Abaqa's reign, circa 1282, for the Takht-i Sulayman tiles (figs. 61–62), which are now assigned by inscriptions to the 1270s.[11] Though I referred to Chinese ceramics,

The manuscript was executed in Ilkhanid court circles in 689/1290; Juwaynī was an important court official. His *Ta'rīkh-i jahān-gushāy/History of the World Conqueror* (Juwaynī, 1912–58), Part I, already reproduces the frontispiece between pages xx–xxi; cf. Ettinghausen (1959), figs. 1–2; Komaroff and Carboni, eds. (2002), fig. 201.

[6] Erevan, M179, fol. 141v. Sirarpie Der Nersessian, who had read the mimeographed version of the 1977 paper, brought the dragon textile to my attention.

[7] Takht-i Sulayman was not discussed at all in the 1977 paper, but covered in detail in the 1986 article, Kouymjian (1986), 444–56.

[8] This latter section was expanded in Kouymjian (1986), 461–68, and several illustrations were added.

[9] Komaroff and Carboni, eds. (2002).

[10] Naumann, E. and Naumann, R. (1969). See also Naumann, R. and Naumann, E. (1976), and Naumann, R. (1977); neither of the latter works was available for the 1986 study. Crowe (1976); A. S. Melikian-Chirvani, who had been studying the inscriptions on the Takht-i Sulayman tiles, dated them at the time to the period 1280–90; see Melikian-Chirvani (1984).

[11] Komaroff and Carboni, eds. (2002), figs. 59, 79, 95, 97, 100, 101, and 205. Luster tiles excavated from the site bear the dates 670, 671, and 674 AH (AD 1271–73, and 1275–76); see the essay in the exhibition catalogue by Tomoko Masuya (Masuya [2002]), 84 with no further reference, but discussed in her doctoral dissertation, Masuya (1997), 350, 354, and 368–70.

bronzes, and lacquers as possible sources for the repertory of exotic animals in the headpieces, I emphasized the importance of textiles, especially because of the dragon in silk visible in the manuscript of 1289 (figs. 58–59).[12]

Rather than reiterate the discussion of twenty-five years ago, this paper will present the essential background for an intelligent understanding of how the works in question came into being, and then, based on the new data, especially Chinese and Central Asian textiles, expand the discussion into the role of royal patronage in the selection of the motifs and their seamless integration into the painting of the Armenian kingdom of Cilicia during a moment of exceptional leadership and prosperity.

For more than fifty years, coinciding with the second half of the thirteenth century, the Armenian kingdom of Cilicia had friendly relations with the Mongols, even concluding an alliance several times renewed.[13] From the successive journeys by Smbat, Constable of Armenia, in 1247–50[14] and then his brother King Het'um in 1253–55[15] to the death of Ghazan Khan in 1304, Armenian princes and kings traveled to the Great Mongol court in Central Asia or to the various residences of the Ilkhanids of Iran,[16] especially under

---

[12] It should be noted that during research for the 1986 article, Jean-Paul Desroches, then Conservator of the Musée Guimet in Paris, also suggested bronze mirrors as a source of the motifs because they were common items of export. Yet the heraldic, princely, perhaps imperial, aspect of the phoenixes and dragons in the Armenian examples at such an early date might preclude items with such motifs as suitable for commercial transactions (but see author's Addendum [ed.]). Crowe (1976), 298, has remarked that "diplomatic gifts, although of best quality, were not readily available on the open market." However, in contradiction to this notion, Heyd thought that only expensive goods were brought from the East, especially those not affected in price by the length of the journey, like precious silk; quoted by Manandian (1965), 197.

[13] On Armenian-Mongol relations see, Galstian (1964) (in Armenian); Der Nersessian (1962), reprinted in Der Nersessian (1973b); Boase (1978), 25–29; Mutafian (1988), vol. 1, 423–29; Mutafian (1993), 54–61.

[14] On Smbat's journey, see Richard, J. (1986).

[15] On the famous journey of Smbat's brother King Het'um, see Kirakos Ganjakets'i (1961), 364–72, and the translation of this section with commentary, Boyle (1964).

[16] The most convenient treatment of the Ilkhanids is still found in Boyle (1968). Of course the works of Masuya cited in n. 11 above, especially her contribution to the exhibition catalogue, is indispensable for residences of the Ilkhans. On the residences of the Ilkhans and Armenian contacts, see also Soucek (1998).

Hülegü (1256–65), his son Abaqa (1265–82), and grandson Arghun (1284–91).

The dragon textile in the miniature of 1289 (figs. 58–59) was perhaps a gift to Bishop John from one of his brothers.[17] This would seem the most logical way for the entry of precious objects with Chinese motifs into court circles. According to Armenian sources, such gifts could have come directly from the Mongol court at Qaraqorum or from the Mongol rulers based in Iran. Smbat the Constable, we are told by his cousin, the historian Het'um of Korikos, had taken with him rich presents for the Mongol *khāns* on his journey of 1247–50.[18] Though there is no mention of his bringing back any gifts in the sources, it must be assumed that the customary exchange took place. It is a well-known fact that the emperors of China—and presumably by extension their Mongol usurpers—always gave more lavish presents than they received as a way of overwhelming foreigners with the might and wealth of their empire. Concerning his brother the king's voyage three years later, not only are we told by Smbat himself in the *Chronicle* attributed to him that King Het'um took presents that were so marvelous they excited the envy of those who saw them,[19] but Het'um the historian also tells us that Möngke Khan sent the Armenian monarch home with great gifts (*granz dons*) and honors.[20] At the beginning of his *History*, written in 1307, he also comments about the exceptional artistic and artisan skills of the Chinese.[21] Another contemporary historian, Grigor of Akner, also states that

[17] If it were given just after their voyages, it would be an item gifted in the 1250s, a rather early date. A date in the 1270s or 1280s would be more reasonable, but by then the silk could have been acquired commercially or as a present during a later voyage to the Ilkhanid court, for which see below.

[18] Hayton (1906), 164; Backer (1877), 177; Smbat (1980), 98–99. For further details on Smbat see the article by Richard, J. (1986).

[19] Smbat (1980), 98: "Le roi prit tous ces présents qui excitaient la convoitise de ceux qui les regardaient, se rendit auprès du khan Mangu, auquel il les offrit." Vardan (1862), 148; English trans., Thomson (1989), 216, says that Het'um first went to visit Batu, "the great king of the North," and then on to the court of Möngke in Qaraqorum.

[20] Hayton (1906), 164; for a modern French translation, Backer (1877), 178: "e lui [Möngke] fist mercis de grans dons e de granz graces." See also Der Nersessian (1962), 263; Der Nersessian (1973b), 347.

[21] "E verraiement l'om voit venir de celui pays tantes choses estranges, et merveilloses, e de sotil labour, que bien semblent estre la plus soutils gens du monde d'art e de labour de mains," Hayton (1906), 121; Backer (1877), 126; cf. Der Nersessian (1973b), 348: "Hetoum returned...laden with gifts."

Het'um went with much treasure and was honored by the *khān*,[22] while Vahram of Edessa says the king returned to Armenia with great honors.[23] The journeys of Smbat and Het'um could have provided the direct channel from Qaraqorum for the entry of gifts into the royal court of Armenia under whose patronage, some thirty years later, the manuscripts bearing Chinese motifs were executed.

But an intermediate route from the Mongol court in northwestern Iran could have served just as well for the exchange of such diplomatic gifts. King Het'um I and his son Levon II paid many visits to the Ilkhans Hülegü, Abaqa, and Arghun from the 1250s to the 1280s, and several of these sojourns are well recorded by Armenian historians. In July 1264 Het'um visited Hülegü, probably in Tabriz, bearing many gifts. The *khān* in turn dispatched him to Armenia with honor and great wealth.[24] Before July 1269, Levon II, perhaps with his father, journeyed to the Ilkhanid court to receive approval from Abaqa Khan for succession to the Armenian throne; Smbat the Constable reports that Levon was received with consideration and sent back to Cilicia with numerous presents.[25] Levon visited Abaqa again in 1272 and obtained military assistance from him.[26] A decade later, he visited Arghun Khan to pay his respects.[27] The later trip would have had to be after Arghun's succession in 1284 but before Levon's own death in 1289. Any, probably all, of these visits would have involved the exchange of diplomatic gifts between the Armenian aristocracy and the Mongol rulers. Though such gifts have neither survived (though the miniature of the dragon textile we

---

[22] Grigor of Akner (1949), 325.

[23] Vahram (1869), 519: "Ils [the Mongols] lui donnèrent parole d'amitié et un traité de paix. Il s'en revint comblé d'honneurs."

[24] Vardan (1862), 156; Vardan describes a gathering which he calls a *quriltai* (Arm. *Khurult'ay*), "[P]resent were all their subjects with many notable gifts—kings and sultans, such as, in our [Vardan's] sight, the king of Armenia, Het'um, and the king of Georgia, Dawit', and the prince of Antioch, and many sultans from the regions of Persia"; Thomson (1989), 220. Grigor of Akner says, "with such honor and great wealth he dispatched the king of the Armenians to his country"; Grigor of Akner (1949), 341.

[25] This had to be before Het'um's death on July 15, 1269. Smbat in his *Chronicle* relates the event as follows: "Lewon, baron des Arméniens, se rendit en Orient, auprès du khan Abaga qui le reçut avec considération et le renvoya en Cilicie avec de nombreux présents," Smbat (1980), 123; cf. Der Nersessian (1973b), 375.

[26] Abaqa sent ten thousand men and came to Armenia in person several months later, according to Smbat (1980), 124.

[27] Der Nersessian (1973b), 349.

assume is a faithful rendering) nor been textually described, some, perhaps all, were undoubtedly of Chinese manufacture or inspiration since the Mongols ruled China and were already fascinated by its arts and fashions.

The history of East-West trade before the Ilkhanids, as well as the relationship and exchanges between Hülegü and his successors in Iran and his brothers Qubilai in China and Möngke in the homeland, have been covered in this conference and its catalogue, as has the adoption of Chinese ways by the Mongols and their special affection for silks woven with golden thread.[28] Armenians also had access to Chinese art through the Mongol connection. By the 1280s, a decade before some of the first significant borrowings of Chinese modes in Islamic art[29] (excepting Takht-i Sulayman and Viar, to be discussed below), evidence of Chinese influence is found in the illuminations of the two Armenian religious manuscripts already mentioned (pls. 23–24 and figs. 58–59).

The latter of these, a Gospel manuscript executed for Archbishop John (Yovhannes) in 1289, has as its last miniature a donor portrait depicting the aged cleric performing an ordination (fig. 58).[30] On the archbishop's tunic or alb, a liturgical garment worn under the chasuble, there is an isolated motif of a Chinese dragon woven in gold with red outlines (fig. 59). The head of the dragon is raised vertically in profile, while the neck, body, and tail wind upward. The three visible feet have three or four claws.[31] In front of its open mouth is a leaf-like object, perhaps intended to be a flaming pearl. In any case

---

[28] This has been reiterated by nearly every contributor to the catalogue in the respective chapters, often referring specifically to an earlier exhibition at the Metropolitan Museum and the Cleveland Museum of Art in 1997–98, Watt, J. C. Y. and Wardwell (1997). In addition, note should be made of Thomas Allsen's seminal work, Allsen (1997) [ed.].

[29] The earliest examples of Chinese motifs in Islamic art are subtle ones found, for example, in the decoration of a Kashan luster-painted ceramic dish of 1268–69 in the David Collection, Copenhagen; see Komaroff and Carboni, eds. (2002), cat. no. 128, fig. 3.

[30] Erevan, M197, fol. 141v, not executed at the monastery of Akner as believed by some authorities; see Der Nersessian and Agemian (1993), 96–97; Kouymjian (1986), 418–19, figs. 1a–1b (detail of dragon); color reproductions in Mutafian (1993), 55; Der Nersessian and Agemian (1993), fig. 645.

[31] When I originally studied this miniature, I thought I saw four claws, but the fourth claw, especially on the right front leg, may be a leaf. The hind legs or feet show three claws. As brother of King Het'um, the number three would place him in the proper subordinate rank of a prince, on which question see below.

the silk would have to have been woven before the execution of the Gospel in 1289, the same year as Bishop John's death.[32] No doubt Der Nersessian's supposition that it is a piece of Chinese silk used as an undergarment is correct,[33] but it is hard to say if the entire tunic was made of a Chinese silk or if the dragon was just a piece sewn on its front. The dragon's resemblance to authentic Chinese silks is striking, as is evident from two textiles in the exhibition: a splendid red silk of the Jin Dynasty (1115–1234) in the Metropolitan Museum of Art with rows of coiled golden dragons with five claws facing in different directions,[34] and a smaller fragment in the Cleveland Museum of Art (fig. 60) dated to the contemporary Mongol Yüan Dynasty (1279–1368) depicting rows of golden dragons with three claws in nearly the identical coiled position within roundels.[35]

John, as the brother of King Het'um I and Smbat the Constable, both of whom had been received by the Mongol *khāns* at Qaraqorum,

---

[32] John wears a chasuble decorated with four-pointed stars in gold (intended as stylized crosses with arms of equal length?) on a red ground. The shape is similar to 'cross' tiles, as they are called, from Takht-i Sulayman; Komaroff and Carboni, eds. (2002), 175, fig. 204, 237, fig. 278; Kouymjian (1986), 448, fig. 14, after a reconstruction of eight-pointed dragon and phoenix tiles with cross tiles proposed by Naumann, E. and Naumann, R. (1969), fig. 11; Komaroff and Carboni, eds. (2002), 176, fig. 205. Might this suggest that the chasuble was woven in Ilkhanid Iran?

[33] Der Nersessian (1977); English edition Der Nersessian (1978), 160, "An example of…imported silk clothes exists in the portrait of Archbishop John…adorned with a Chinese dragon…sewn onto the bottom of his cope"; color illustrations in Mutafian (1993), 55; Der Nersessian and Agemian (1993), fig. 645. Der Nersessian has spoken of this fabric more than once; Der Nersessian (1970), reprinted in eadem (1973b), 595: "[Jean, i.e. Bishop John] semble avoir eu une prédilection pour les beaux tissus car dans son portrait de l'an 1287 [sic] il porte, sous la chasuble, une tunique de soie chinoise ornée du motif caractéristique du dragon"; Der Nersessian and Agemian (1993), 158: "The material of Archbishop John's alb…came from an entirely different region. A gold dragon, standing upright with gaping jaws, is woven on white ground; the gold has flaked from the greater part of the foliate ornament around the dragon…. I believe that we do not have an imitation of Chinese ornament, but an actual textile like the Italian material of the chasuble [in the miniature of 1274]…Chinese silk might have been brought by one of John's brothers…both of whom had visited the Mongol court, or it may have been an imported silk that Bishop John could have used as his alb."

[34] New York, MMA, 1989.205, 74.5 x 33.2 cm; first published in Watt, J. C. Y. and Wardwell (1997), no. 30, 116–17; Komaroff and Carboni, eds. (2002), cat. 181, 174, fig. 202.

[35] Cleveland Museum of Art (Edward I. Whittemore Fund, 1995.73), 20 cm square, with alternating rows of roundels with phoenixes (only partially visible on the fragment) and dragons; Watt, J. C. Y. and Wardwell (1997), no. 42, 153; Komaroff and Carboni, eds. (2002), cat. 183, fig. 206.

may have acquired this Chinese silk as a gift from one of them. Yet in three earlier portraits in manuscripts also commissioned by him, he is wearing robes without any clear trace of Far Eastern design. In the first of these, a Gospel of 1263, he is shown ordaining a deacon;[36] he wears a plain red-violet cope over a plain white alb or tunic with an embroidered gold band at the hemline. His liturgical cuffs (maniples) and his white miter with two small red squares are also embroidered in gold and studded with jewels and pearls. In a miscellany of Old and New Testament books in Erevan dated 1263–66,[37] he is seen kneeling, as the donor of the manuscript before his namesake St. John the Evangelist, wearing virtually the same white miter with gold embroidery as in the manuscript of 1263, with embroidered cuffs of gold, but longer and different and with a blue-black cope over a white alb that appears to be embroidered in gold with a plain hem. The third portrait is on a single folio in Brussels detached from a Gospel manuscript of 1274 in the Morgan Library, where Bishop John is bareheaded wearing a chasuble of *fleurs-de-lis* of Italian (Sicilian) manufacture.[38] His tunic seems to be plain white and without a decorated hem.

A decade and a half later, in the portrait of 1289 (fig. 58), he wears essentially the same gold-embroidered white miter, without red squares (already missing in the portrait of 1266) and bejeweled gold embroidered cuffs. The outer cope or chasuble is once

[36] Washington, D.C., Freer 56.11, fol. 293, Gospels copied for Bishop John by the priest T'oros at the hermitage of Grner in Cilicia; Der Nersessian (1963), 55–72, fig. 195; color reproduction in Der Nersessian and Agemian (1993), fig. 644.

[37] Erevan, M4243, fol. 15, copied by the scribe Step'annos Vahkats'i in a monastery in Bardzrberd in Cilicia; Der Nersessian and Agemian (1993), 82–84, fig. 307; Guevorkian (1982) (in Armenian, Russian, and French), pls. 21–22, in color; Mutafian (1993), color reproduction, 64. The gold design is very blurred on the tunic, which is not dead white like the miter.

[38] New York, Pierpont Morgan Library, ms. no. 740, executed in Sis in 1274, Gospel of Marshall Oshin. The single folio was formerly in the Feron-Stoclet Collection in Brussels, Der Nersessian convincingly demonstrated that it belonged to the Morgan Library manuscript; Der Nersessian and Agemian (1993), 158–59 and fig. 646; see also Thomas Mathews's more recent discussion; Mathews (1998), 168 and fig. 78. The miniature has since been acquired by the Morgan Library (ms. M.1111), for which see Merian (1998–2000). Der Nersessian identified the material of the chasuble as of Sicilian manufacture rather than French; Der Nersessian (1970), reprinted in Der Nersessian (1973b), 595 with reference to Beaulieu (1967), 267–69.

again different,[39] as is the alb, the object of our interest. It appears to be different from any of the previous three. Though the gold paint depicting the border has in part flaked off, showing the yellow underpainting, below it there is an irregular white area partially overlapping the colored triangles that make up the frame of the miniature. It is the bottom of the tunic and from it, protruding into the same frame, are Archbishop John's golden slippers. Taken together, the four surviving portraits of the clergyman in his liturgical robes underline, as Der Nersessian had already remarked,[40] his penchant for the finest fabrics whether from East or West and his eagerness (with the artists' complicity) to show them off whenever he could. The tunic of 1289 with the dragon was either sewn onto a plain white alb, similar to the one he wears in the Marshall Oshin Gospel of 1274, or less likely an integral part of an entire garment fashioned from a Chinese silk acquired later in life, a vestment he was clearly proud of. It is probably safe to conjecture that the silk textile with the Chinese dragon was only used as or on the tunic after 1274 and perhaps only acquired after that date.

The other manuscript, executed earlier in 1286, is a luxuriously illuminated Lectionary containing a more organically integrated group of Chinese elements.[41] Though neither the name of the scribe nor artist is preserved, we know Prince Het'um, son of the reigning king, Levon II, commissioned the manuscript. The first chapter heading with Chinese elements[42] (pl. 23) shows a wide, richly decorated band

---

[39] See n. 32, above.

[40] See n. 33, above.

[41] Erevan, M979; like the Gospel of 1289, it has never been fully published nor described. Der Nersessian provided a list of some 130 marginal miniatures in Appendix II of her *Miniature Painting in the Armenian Kingdom of Cilicia*, 165–67 and reproduced many of the full-page illuminations in the same book. Earlier studies of the manuscript include: Azaryan (1964); Dournovo (1952), album in Russian and Armenian with color plates; Dournovo (1961), a reduced album with color plates in English and French versions; Dournovo and Drampian (1967–69), text in Armenian, French, and Russian, an expanded version of the other albums; Narkiss and Stone, eds. (1979), *passim*; Velmans (1980).

[42] Erevan, M979, fol. 293, lection for 6 April, the Annunciation to the Virgin; Kouymjian (1986), 421–25, figs. 2a–e (details); color reproduction in Der Nersessian and Agemian (1993), fig. 516. Earlier literature and reproductions: Sakisian (1939), reprinted in Sakisian (1940), fig. 38, references in this article to the latter; Dournovo (1961), 126–27; Dournovo and Drampian (1967–69), pl. 43; Azaryan (1964), fig. 134; Der Nersessian (1969), 2–9, 110, fig. 22, reprinted in Der Nerses-

tapering toward a central round frame decorated with a symmetrical scroll of *fleur-de-lis*, in which is a beardless bust against a plain gold background of the youthful Christ Emmanuel, a common feature of twelfth- and thirteenth-century Cilician Armenian manuscripts.[43]

On each side of Christ are gray-brown Chinese-inspired lions in an upright position prancing toward the central circle but with head turned forward with eyes slightly askance toward Christ, whose own eyes look toward the left. Each animal's mouth and nose is highly stylized, forming a trilobed leaf motif; from the top of the head, sharp, flame-shaped crops of hair point upward. Their tails are knotted in the Chinese manner.[44] Lions were introduced into Chinese art along with Buddhism. Buddha was considered a lion among men. These felines are seen as symbols of power and protectors of temples or the image or icon around which they are placed. Just below the frame is another pair of like animals of a bright blue color, crouching on all fours. They display the same tightly curled hair, bushy tails, and ears, but somewhat different faces. Their tails also seem shorter. Their appearance on textiles is rarer than in other media. Among numerous examples one might cite a pair of lunging lions at the top of an imposing sixth-century Qi Dynasty stele[45] and a winged pair of them seated upright as guardians on a late Tang Dynasty (618–907) Buddhist altar cloth.[46] Closer in style to the Armenian example are wingless lions prancing forward with flame-like manes on a Central Asian *kesi* (tapestry) of the early Mongol period.[47] How-

---

sian (1973b), 509–15, fig. 261; Beckwith, J. (1970), 139, pl. 259; Der Nersessian (1978), 155, fig. 116.

[43] The first Armenian manuscript with Christ Emmanuel in the headpiece of the incipit of St. Matthew is from a Cilician Gospel book of 1166 copied by the scribe Kozma at Hromkla, Erevan, M7347, fol. 13; Der Nersessian and Agemian (1993), 3–4, fig. 9; others are discussed by her, for which see the index, 197.

[44] Discussion of the knotted tail in Masuya (2002), 97 and Crowe (1991), 157.

[45] Zurich, Rietberg Museum, Eduard von der Heydt Collection, inventory no. RCh 116; Sirén (1959), 74, 79, illustration on 75. I would like to thank Jorrit Britschgi of Zurich for this reference.

[46] Paris, Musée Guimet, a painted textile showing a pair of phoenixes above an incense burner flanked by the lions; from the mission of Paul Pelliot, Musée Guimet (1976), 60, no. 302; Kouymjian (1986), 437, fig. 6.

[47] Cleveland Museum of Art, purchased from the J. H. Wade Fund (1991.3). Watt, J. C. Y. and Wardwell (1997), no. 19, 80–82. On page 80 a fragment of another *kesi* (perhaps the same unidentified except from Central Asia, thirteenth century) with these lions. And another fragment with various animals, but including a prancing gray lion, with curly mane like our lions, is shown in figs. 20, 68 (provenance not

ever, a late Tang or Liao Dynasty (907–1125) upright gilt bronze lion has a face and pug nose similar to our animals,[48] and a Sung Dynasty (960–1279) ceramic with a seated lion scratching its left ear has similar curls and a trilobed nose.[49] In the headpiece, just below the lower lions' hindquarters, are violet-colored monsters with wide open mouths and long serpentine tongues, giving them a menacing appearance. Each has a truncated serpentine or fish body, marked by accordion elements ending in a strange light violet-colored base; others are found in the vertical band to the right. They, too, are dragons, but a legless, non-Chinese reptile variety.[50] The Chinese lions protect Christ from these menacing dragons.[51]

Above the bust of Christ are three pairs of birds, one pair gracefully hovering at the top. Flying birds are common in Chinese art, whether ducks, cranes, or the fabulous phoenix. Though birds with spread wings about to fly are depicted in late twelfth- and thirteenth-century Armenian canon tables,[52] they lack the naturalistic quality of those of the Lectionary.[53] Generally, in Near Eastern art up to the Mongol period, birds are not shown in flight.[54] Finally, in the

given, Eastern Central Asia, eleventh–twelfth century). One might also mention the addorsed and winged golden lions because of their curly manes on a silk lampas shown in the exhibition, Cleveland Museum of Art, Wade Fund (1989.50); ibid., no. 35, 142–43; Komaroff and Carboni, eds. (2002), nos. 39, 64, fig. 58.

[48] Victoria and Albert Museum (1970), 40, no. 42; Kouymjian (1986), 434–35, fig. 4.

[49] Prodan (1960), pl. 15; Kouymjian (1986), 436, fig. 5.

[50] Kouymjian (1986), figs. 2c, 2e, 3d, and 336–41 for a detailed discussion of these creatures.

[51] Lydia Dournovo had already suggested this function as the reason for their presence in the miniature; Dournovo (1961), 126; cf. Kouymjian (1986), 433–34 and nn. 18 and 21.

[52] Baltimore, Walters Gallery of Art, ms. no. 538, Gospel executed in 1193 at Poghoskan, Cilicia, fols. 5, 7, 11, Der Nersessian (1973a), figs. 28, 30, 32; Venice, Mekhitarist Congregation, ms. no. 1635, Gospel of 1193, Cilicia, fols. 4, 7v, Der Nersessian (1936), vol. 2, figs. 42–43; Baltimore, Walters Gallery of Art, ms. no. 539, Gospel of 1262 executed by T'oros Roslin at Hromkla, fols. 4, 9v, 383v, Der Nersessian (1973a), figs. 46, 51, 132.

[53] In her final posthumous monograph of 1993, Der Nersessian commented on these birds, "[C]haracteristic features of Chinese art…can (also) be seen in the drawing of birds with sweeping lines, their tails and wings swinging upward like those of the Chinese flying cranes." Der Nersessian and Agemian (1993), 124.

[54] "Before the spread of Mongol taste about 1300 birds in Near Eastern art never convincingly fly, at most they stand in profile with wings raised, or in the heraldic frontal stance with wings displayed." Lane, A. (1957), 12. This is certainly

top center of the composition is an eight-spoked rosette, reminiscent of the Buddhist Wheel of the Law.[55]

The second chapter heading (pl. 24) is less well-known.[56] Its formal arrangement is similar to the other, with a complex vertical decoration to the right. The center of the headpiece is an empty trilobed arch, whose flanking spandrels are filled with a dragon and phoenix facing each other. From the viewer's position the dragons are given preference: their blue heads with white highlights are shown with open mouth, nose turned up, both eyes visible and directed frontally. They have paws of four claws spread out like pinwheels. Confronting the dragons are phoenixes with brown bodies and heads and blue wings, the tips of which end in soft pink flared feathers. The birds are rendered vertically by the requirements of the composition with their heads in profile, beaks open, pointed directly into the dragons' mouths. Their bodies, however, are spread out in aerial view. The characteristic tails with long flowing streamers are reduced to short, deep pink tufts (seen at the bottom of the spandrels) probably due to the exigencies of space, though there is a form of Chinese phoenix with a short tail but no long streamers.[57] In any case, the dragon

---

the case with most of the Armenian examples. See also Ettinghausen (1959). There are, however, some notable exceptions, e.g., in late twelfth–early thirteenth-century manuscript illustrations; see, for instance, the *Kitāb al-diryāq* manuscript in the Bibliothèque Nationale de Paris (ms. arabe 2964), illustrated in Ettinghausen (1962), 84–85. A good instance in the Mongol art of Iran is the large jar in the Metropolitan Museum of Art (acc. no. 56.185.3) dated 1282–83; see Komaroff and Carboni, eds. (2002), cat. no. 129. I would like to thank Linda Komaroff for pointing out these examples.

[55] Usually depicted as a wheel with eight spokes representing the eight-fold path; the wheel represents the endless cycle of birth, death, and reincarnation. The Wheel of the Law (*dharmachakra*) stands for the teachings of Buddha, which provide a path to enlightenment.

[56] Erevan, M979, fol. 334, readings for the Feast of the Transfiguration (Vardavar in Armenian); Kouymjian (1986), 426–33, figs. 3a–d (with details); color illustrations in Dournovo (1952), pl. 35; Korkhmazian, Drampian, and Hakopian (1984), fig. 119; Der Nersessian and Agemian (1993), fig. 517; see also Azaryan (1964), fig. 134.

[57] Best illustrated in the large (143 x 135 cm) Yüan canopy with two phoenixes in the Metropolitan Museum of Art (1988.82), Watt, J. C. Y. and Wardwell (1997), no. 60, 196–99; Komaroff and Carboni, eds. (2002), no. 184, 179, fig. 210, the phoenix on top, see also fig. 82, 196, in Watt, J. C. Y. and Wardwell (1997), showing a Yüan relief carving with two phoenixes; the one lacking streamers is above. See Rawson (1984), 100, where it is suggested that the difference in tail feathers has to do with the gender of the bird.

phoenix combat does not occur in Chinese art as far as I am aware until the Ming Dynasty (1368–1644), making this Armenian miniature a curious predecessor of a later Chinese convention.[58]

In the center above the arch is a single, almost heraldically placed, Chinese phoenix (pl. 24). Its coloring is the same as the others. It is positioned almost identically to phoenixes described as 'soaring' on a thirteenth-century Jin Dynasty (1115–1234) silk in the Los Angeles County Museum of Art (pl. 25).[59] The head of the Armenian example is turned like those on the silks and the streaming tails are prominent, though one is hidden under its body; they are arranged symmetrically and are very long, winding down and then looping upward above the phoenix's spread wings. The whole bird is visible, revealing fine, soft, furry tufts of feathers and on both sides at the back of the wings, additional pointed feathers are reminiscent of the pointed flames on the lion manes. The entire form is rendered extremely gracefully with well-understood proportions.

Floating above and to each side of this phoenix is a pair of eight-pointed rosettes representing the Buddhist Wheel of Law as in the earlier headpiece. The rest of the decoration is similar to the other headpiece. It should be pointed out that most of the profusion of animals and other motifs of the Lectionary are *not* inspired by Chinese art and are not of concern to this study. One should note, however, the deer in the upper corners of the headpiece, which may have a Chinese inspiration.

One group of figures seems to be copied with almost no modification from Chinese models. It includes the dragon-phoenix motif, the heraldic phoenix, and the single dragon on Archbishop John's garment. In the latter case (fig. 58), we are confronted by a faithfully copied piece of Chinese cloth of silk and gold.[60] The single phoenix

---

[58] Rawson (1984), 100.

[59] There is a better known fragment with the same design and color scheme in the Cleveland Museum of Art, John L. Severance Fund (1994.292), Watt, J. C. Y. and Wardwell (1997), no. 31, 118–19; Komaroff and Carboni, eds. (2002), no. 180, 197, fig. 207. Also see Watt, J. C. Y. and Wardwell (1997), no. 32, 120–21, for another related textile.

[60] It is less likely a fabric produced in Armenia with a Chinese motif, though Armenia was known for its fine textile industry and contemporary miniatures display the rich apparel worn by Armenian aristocracy, no doubt some imported from East and West. A manuscript of 1268–69, attributed to T'oros Roslin, in the Freer Gallery of Art, Washington, D.C., 32.18, 535, shows Christ wearing such a garment

in the headpiece is rendered in such a way that it too must have been copied from Jin or Yüan silks. The dragon-phoenix motif is well known from Chinese textiles,[61] including honorary robes, ceramics, bronze mirrors, and later Ming lacquers.

Despite the difference in medium, the painted Armenian dragons and phoenixes resemble those on the tiles from Takht-i Sulayman (figs. 61–62).[62] Their source was surely the same: China, either directly or through the Mongol courts in Central Asia or Iran. The possibility that East Asian craftsmen actually were in part responsible for the design of certain of the Ilkhanid ceramics has no echo in the Armenian experience.[63] Whether we speak of the 1270s or 1280s or even the 1290s, in my opinion, the only authentic Chinese-looking animals in the art of the Near East before 1300 are the Armenian ones and the Takht-i Sulayman tiles, along with the monumental dragon carved at the neighboring site of Viar (fig. 63), dated like

---

when he appears to the Disciples after the Resurrection; Der Nersessian (1963), fig. 165, color reproduction in Der Nersessian (1978), 135, fig. 98. There are many other such examples, as in the costumes of Prince Leo and Princess Keran, in a manuscript executed in 1262 at Hromkla by T'oros Roslin, Jerusalem, Armenian Patriarchate, J2660, fol. 228; for color illustration, see Sotheby's, London (1967), lot no. 1; Der Nersessian and Agemian (1993), fig. 640; or in another portrait of the same Leo and Keran, now king and queen, and their children being blessed by Christ flanked by the Virgin and John the Baptist in a Gospel of 1272 copied by the scribe Avetis probably in the Cilician capital Sis, Jerusalem, Armenian Patriarchate, J2563, fol. 380; ibid., fig. 641.

[61] A silk lampas fragment from the Yüan Dynasty (1279–1368) acquired in 1995 by the Cleveland Museum of Art (Edward I. Whittemore Fund, 1995.73), 20 cm square, shows the dragons and phoenixes individually woven in roundels in gold on a dark green-black ground, Watt, J. C. Y. and Wardwell (1997), no. 42, 153; Komaroff and Carboni, eds. (2002), no. 183, 176–77, fig. 206.

[62] The closest in feeling are on the large luster titles with both dragons and phoenixes, but never together on the same tile, and for the phoenix the eight-pointed star tiles in *lajvardina*; Komaroff and Carboni, eds. (2002), no. 99, fig. 97; dragon from the Metropolitan Museum of Art, no. 100, fig. 100, phoenix from the Victoria and Albert Museum, no. 84, fig. 101, star tiles from Arthur M. Sackler Gallery, Washington, or the phoenix on a hexagonal tile from Berlin, Komaroff and Carboni, eds. (2002), no. 103, fig. 95. For the exhibition at the Los Angeles County Museum of Art, there was an entire wall of these tiles or their reproductions mixing dragon and phoenix tiles based on the reconstruction on paper by the Naumanns; see Komaroff and Carboni, eds. (2002), fig. 205, and the original archaeology photo, fig. 92. For these same or similar phoenix and dragon tiles from Takht-i Sulayman, see Kouymjian (1986), figs. 10–14.

[63] On the possible use of Chinese craftsmen by the Ilkhans see Rossabi (2002), 35.

the tiles to the reign of Abaqa (1265–82).[64] Though individual dragons and phoenixes from Takht-i Sulayman resemble those in the Armenian miniatures, the phoenix and the dragon are never shown together on a single tile as they are in the Lectionary, but rather are juxtaposed in various geometric arrangements,[65] much like the Chinese silks. However, there is little evidence to suggest that dragons and phoenixes in China were depicted in opposition to one another in this period. Silks probably provided models for each motif, but in the Lectionary the artist apparently more freely interpreted the design in a way that was going to become common in Chinese art in the Ming Dynasty.

Though the earlier date (1270s) of the Takht-i Sulayman ceramics would allow the possibility that Armenian envoys could have seen the palace of Abaqa during one of the well-documented official visits to the Ilkhanids (see above), it is possible to imagine that a talented artist or patron could have visually united the separate dragons and phoenixes and portrayed these animals (fearsome to Western eyes) without recourse to a model or knowledge of the symbolic meaning of these creatures in Chinese art. Thus, we must conclude that the use of similar artistic features in Cilician Armenia and the Ilkhanid court at virtually the same moment was done quite independently.

In discussing the integration of Far Eastern elements in Armenian painting in my earlier study, I posed the question of how far the Chinese influence went, especially if it affected the general style of contemporary Cilician art. I concluded that it might have been partly responsible for the increased mannerism and a change in the background landscapes in a number of highly charged, mannered narrative miniatures from manuscripts of the 1270s and 1280s, including both the Lectionary and the Gospels of 1289.[66] Gnarled trees, jagged mountains, and different ground planes are the attributes that most closely resemble what was to happen in Islamic painting in

---

[64] Marco Brambilla was kind enough to inform me in the early 1980s of this monumental Chinese dragon carved in stone in a single unit with a *miḥrāb* near the village of Viar, thirty kilometers south of Sultaniyya. He also sent me a fine photograph of the monument. See Curatola (1982); Komaroff and Carboni, eds. (2002), 110, fig. 127. Viar was perhaps the site of a Buddhist Monastery (*vihara* in Sanskrit); see Blair (2002), 110.

[65] Kouymjian (1986), 461–68.

[66] Ibid.

the 1290s and the following decades in such works as the illustrated *Compendium of Chronicles* of Rashīd al-Dīn and the Mongol *Shāhnāmas*. Even a minor marginal scene in the Lectionary of 1286 seems inspired by Chinese landscapes (fig. 64). The false prophet Baalam is shown riding an uphill path with a crouching lion, not unlike the Chinese examples in the headpiece, blocking his path.[67]

Deer are also quite prevalent in these late thirteenth-century manuscripts. Could those in the upper corners of the dragon-phoenix headpiece actually be *djeiran* (pl. 24), the Chinese deer, with their mushroom antlers, as in several objects (a silk, a bronze, tiles, plaques) in the exhibition?[68] Nearly identical headpieces from two contemporary, but undated Cilician manuscripts, also suggest the presence of *djeiran* and perhaps *qilin*, the massive deer-lion-bull-like Chinese creatures. The headpiece of the incipit of St. Matthew (fig. 65) in a Gospel of the 1270s or 1280s[69] shows in the center a grazing animal, probably a donkey, directly above which is a recumbent deer. To the left and the right, flanking these tranquil animals, are two massive creatures on their hind legs, with wide open and menacing jaws of their moose-like heads; these are copied from Chinese *qilin*.[70] The

[67] Erevan, M979, fol. 10; Korkhmazian, Drampian, and Hakopian (1984), fig. 113; Der Nersessian and Agemian (1993), fig. 433 and Der Nersessian's discussion, 124: "Contrary to the Armenian custom, the artist...has tried to represent a small landscape and indicate the distance by a diagonal line and the place of the lion in the background."

[68] A lovely Jin Dynasty brocade, gold thread on red, of a recumbent *djeiran*, Cleveland Museum of Art, H. J. Wade Fund (1991.4), Watt, J. C. Y. and Wardwell (1997), no. 29, 114–15; Komaroff and Carboni, eds. (2002), cat. no. 138, 68, fig. 63. A bronze mirror stand from the Song, Jin, or Yüan Dynasty in the form of a recumbent *djeiran* from the Victoria and Albert Museum (M. 730-1910), Komaroff and Carboni, eds. (2002), cat. no. 195, 68, fig. 67, also reproduced in Watt, J. C. Y. and Wardwell (1997), 114, fig. 46. A hexagonal tile from Takht-i Sulayman now in Berlin, Deutsches Archäologisches Institut (DAI 2), Komaroff and Carboni, eds. (2002), no. 87, 185, fig. 218; two gilt bronze plaques from fourteenth century Iran, London, Nasser D. Khalili Collection (JLY 503), ibid., no. 152, 195, fig. 235, the upper plaque with a grazing deer-*djeiran* similar to the Armenian examples.

[69] Erevan, M7651, fol. 10, a Cilician Gospel; Buschhausen and Buschhausen (1981), fig. 19; Der Nersessian and Agemian (1993), fig. 431.

[70] Though they look menacing, the role of the *qilin* was (like the lion) a protector whose appearance coincides with the birth of a sage or an illustrious ruler. The manifestation of *qilin* could also indicate imperial authority and wisdom as well as the benevolence of an emperor's rule. For comparable examples from Ilkhanid, Timurid, and early Safavid Iran, see a fourteenth-century drawing from an album, Berlin, Staatsbibliothek (Diez A fol. 73, S. 46, #6), Komaroff and Carboni, eds.

other miniature is also a headpiece from a late thirteenth-century Missal showing the same four animals in the same poses, though the frames of the two miniatures are rendered differently.[71] In the floral band in the right hand margin of the latter illumination is a lion seated upright resembling those in the Christ Emmanuel headpiece (M979, fol. 293; pl. 23) and even more closely those in the British Library *Kalīla wa Dimna* of 1306.[72]

After 1300 all such elements of Chinese art disappear from Armenian painting; royal patronage declines as does the wealth and security of the Armenian kingdom menaced by the Mamluks of Egypt and abandoned by the Mongols after the conversion to Islam of Ghazan Khan and the Ilkhanid court. By the early fourteenth century, Mongol traits, especially facial features, are borrowed directly from the Islamic art of Iran, which by then had integrated Chinese and Central Asian elements as its own. Armenian scribes and artists were active in western Iran producing from time to time figures and decoration inspired by Ilkhanid painting, as, for instance, the Annunciation from a Gospel copied and painted by Mkhit'ar of Ani in Sultaniyya in 1356–57.[73]

Returning to our dragons and phoenixes, they were particularly appropriate for members of the Armenian court, the king and queen, princes and princesses, or Bishop John, a king's brother and another king's uncle, since these animals were associated with the imperial rulers of China and, after its conquest by the Mongols, with the rulers of Central Asia and the western regions including the Ilkhanids.[74] The Chinese emperor himself sat on a dragon throne and wore robes with dragons, while emblems with dragons were common for

(2002), 190, fig. 225; an early fifteenth-century drawing from the same album in the Staatsbibliothek, Berlin (Diez A fol. 73, S. 54, #1), ibid., 190, fig. 226; and a marginal painting from a Tabriz manuscript of the second quarter of the sixteenth century in the Keir Collection, London, Musée du Louvre (2001), cat. no. 71, 106.

[71] Vienna, Mekhitarist Congregation, ms. no. 1303, a Missal copied by the scribe T'oros; Buschhausen and Buschhausen (1981), 92–96, fig. 18.

[72] London, British Library (Or. 13506), copied by [Abū] al-Makārim Ḥasan in Iran in 1307–8; Komaroff and Carboni, eds. (2002), cat. no. 3, 218, fig. 266.

[73] Erevan, M7740, fol. 1v; Korkhmazian, Drampian and Hakopian (1984), fig. 163.

[74] Tomoko Masuya points out that "The Great Khans in China followed this Chinese tradition, and indeed, it was during the Yüan period that the imperial monopoly over these two motifs (the dragon and phoenix) was firmly established." Masuya (2002), 96.

his courtiers.[75] An imposing Yüan mandala (c. 1330–32) with imperial donor portraits of Emperors Wenzong and Mingzong offers a near contemporary example (fig. 66).[76] A dragon with five claws is clearly represented on the latter's blue outer garment and on the red sleeves of his undergarment; his younger brother, to the left, has the same dragon shirt and overgarment, but its light beige color makes it difficult to see the dragon.[77] The five-clawed imperial dragon was iconographically reserved for the emperor himself (and the Mongol Great Khans); the four-clawed dragon was used by princes (thus Hülegü, in taking the title Ilkhan, deferring to his brother Qubilai, the Great Khan and Emperor of China).[78] In consequence, the dragon tiles at Abaqa's palace at Takht-i Sulayman have four claws (fig. 61), as do those in the phoenix-dragon headpiece in the Lectionary (pl. 24). The kings of Armenia regarded their relationship with the central Mongol authority the same way the Ilkhanids felt about it.[79] Archbishop John, as a prince, would of course use a dragon with three claws in respect to his brother the king.

[75] See the general discussion of the meaning of these symbols for the Chinese in the exhibition catalogue: "The dragon and phoenix are considered good omens and are two of the oldest and most popular mythical animals in Chinese culture. Most importantly, both were symbols of sovereignty in China. Often forming a pair, they were used as decorative motifs on imperial belongings… [I]t was during the Yüan period that the imperial monopoly over these two motifs was firmly established. The code…issued in 1314 prohibits the appearance on robes of officers, vessels, plates, tents, or carts of any design using the dragon with five claws and two horns, or the phoenix." Ibid., 96; Kouymjian (1986), 431.

[76] Metropolitan Museum of Art, purchase, Lila Acheson Wallace Gift, (1992.54), silk *kesi*, 245.5 x 209 cm; Komaroff and Carboni, eds. (2002), cat. no. 185, 108–9, figs. 125–26; Watt, J. C. Y. and Wardwell (1997), no. 25, 95–99.

[77] Though both catalogues cited in the previous note have closeups of these two emperors seated in Buddhist style, that on 95 of Watt, J. C. Y. and Wardwell (1997) is larger and in color.

[78] Masuya (2002), 97: "[T]he presence of only four claws on the dragons at Takht-i Sulayman may have expressed the Ilkhans' respect for the suzerainty of the Great Khans, who claimed for themselves the exclusive use of the five-clawed dragon"; similarly, see Komaroff (2002), 177, n. 27: "One notable difference is in the number of dragon's claws, five in the textiles, four in the [Takht-i Sulayman] tiles…. [T]he omission of one claw in the Ilkhanid version of this royal motif may be a sign of deference to the Great Khan."

[79] It is more difficult to say how the Mongols felt toward the Armenian kings and their state—no doubt with the respect that an ally who provided troops to the conquering army deserved. In Rashīd al-Dīn's *Compendium of Chronicles*, there is a section, short to be sure, on Armenia, unfortunately not translated in the section of the *Compendium* on Christian states, Rashīd al-Dīn (1951), or in the more recent extensive translation, Rashīd al-Dīn (1998).

As a complement, the phoenix represented the empress; her crown bore the fabled bird, the Feng Huang—not really a phoenix, but assimilated with the animal of Greek mythology from early times.[80] In China the Feng Huang-phoenix (like the dragon) was one of the four animals representing the cardinal directions. It ruled over the southern parts of heaven and, therefore, represented warmth, summer, and the sun, and was said to appear to glorify a successful ruler and a peaceful reign. Its dominant position in the royal Lectionary of Het'um II is clearly parallel to that of Christ, the king of peace and justice, on the other headpiece.

The Lectionary of 1286, commissioned by the Prince Het'um soon to become king, is the most magnificent surviving example of the ruling family's consistent artistic patronage. His mother Princess (later Queen) Keran and father King Levon were patrons of two of the finest gospels of the Cilician kingdom. In that of 1262, painted by T'oros Roslin, the princely couple appears in silken robes under the outstretched hands of Christ; in the Queen Keran Gospels of 1272 (fig. 67), they are seen together with their children, including (next to the king) the eldest Prince Het'um, successor to the throne and patron of the Lectionary with the Chinese motifs. Though there are no donor portraits in the Lectionary, I think that the king and queen, parents of the young prince, inspired our headpieces (pls. 23–24). If my conjecture has merit, Levon and Keran are represented by the dragon-phoenix motif, the anonymous artist fully aware of their use for the emperor and empress in the Sino-Mongol court, but also probably by the Ilkhanids if the tiles of the royal foundation at Takht-i Sulayman are any indication,[81] suggesting that in the summer palace the consorts (*khātūns*) lived together with the

---

[80] The dragon and phoenix motifs were already used in the Han Dynasty (206 BC–220 AD) and seem to have attained a high level of popularity in Chinese art under the Sung (960–1279). But the animals were not shown in confrontation until the Ming Dynasty (1368–1644); see Rawson (1984), 100. A silk fragment found in a Chinese excavation of 1949 dated to the Chu Kingdom, about 300 BC, shows a standing woman painted on a white silk banner. Above her head is a dragon and phoenix, which may represent a struggle between good and evil. The image of the silk reproduced on an Internet site (http://home.seechina.com.cn/html/arts/2bh-e.html) is difficult to make out. Even if this were to be a *bona fide* combat between these animals, it is too far removed to relate to the discussion presented here.

[81] "The inclusion in the design scheme [at Takht-i Sulayman] of dragons and phoenixes, Chinese symbols of rulership, was…a deliberate importation of foreign imagery that had special significance for the Ilkhans." Masuya (2002), 102.

khāns.[82] Furthermore, the dominant, heraldic phoenix at the top of the headpiece is a direct tribute to Queen Keran, the great lady of the arts. The other headpiece with Christ Emmanuel probably stood for King Levon and his realm, one of peace and justice as symbolized by the Wheel of the Law, a kingdom blessed by Christ, guarded by lions, and governed by the rule of law. [83] Whether the idea of a headpiece for each member of the royal couple is ultimately justified or not, clearly the phoenix that dominates one headpiece symbolizes a kingdom of harmony and tranquility, probably alluding to or even celebrating the short-lived peace treaty of 1285 concluded with the Mamluks, who under Baybars and Qalāʿūn had thrown Cilician Armenia into total disarray.

The integration of these potent Chinese symbols is so organic in this lavish manuscript full of well-assimilated European, Near Eastern, and Iranian influences that their presence seems quite natural. Unfortunately, this brilliant syncretic moment of Armenian art was to vanish in the fourteenth century along with the Cilician kingdom and its royal patrons.

Addendum on the Dragon-Phoenix Motif

In Chinese art the motif of the dragon and phoenix pictured together, associated with emperor and empress, first became popular in the Ming Dynasty (1368–1641) as a decoration on all sorts of luxury items. Specialists in Chinese or Mongol art prior to the late fourteenth century have questioned me when I suggested, apparently by conjecture, that the artist of the Lectionary of 1286 borrowed this theme from an earlier Chinese or Chinese-inspired Mongol work of art. They knew of no example and asked if I could point to any. My own search turned up none. Together these scholars corrected an assumption I had made, *a priori*, that because the dragon and the phoenix were popular animals individually in Chinese art

---

[82] The tiles with the dragons representing the Ilkhans and the phoenixes their consorts should reinforce the idea that at Takht-i Sulayman they lived together under the same roof.

[83] The guardian lions under the Christ Emmanuel represent symbolically the king [Levon, Leo, Leon, Lion]. The lion was already the royal emblem used on the coins of the dynasty for generations; numerous examples in Bedoukian (1962), *passim*.

as far back as the Han Dynasty and because I knew of so many examples of them together in Ming art, this duet must have existed as a common motif in Yüan art from which it was passed on to an Armenian artist. None of these scholars proposed a solution to my dilemma, but I thank each of them for their critical spirit. I was forced to conclude that the confronted dragons and phoenixes painted in the Armenian Lectionary a full century earlier than the Ming Dynasty are enigmatic.

During the correction of the final proofs of this communication, Lukas Nickel, Chair of Art History of East Asia, Zurich University, sent me an email from London (2 February 2005) announcing the discovery of what I now call 'the missing link.' A bronze mirror found in a late Liao Dynasty (907–1125) tomb clearly shows the motif. Nickel reports, "Tomb M10, belonging to Zhang Kuang-zheng, died 1058 and buried in 1093 (strange difference, but noted as such). The tomb is among a group of tombs of the same time, in Xuanhua, Hebei province." The reference is *Excavation Report of the Liao Dynasty Frescoed Tombs at Xuanhua: Report of Archaeological Excavation from 1974–1993* (Beijing: Cultural Relics Publishing House, 2001, vol. 1, 49), in Chinese, but with an English title. The accompanying illustration (a line drawing) that Nickel sent shows a dragon with three claws and a phoenix with five long trailers facing each other at some distance hovering around a round object, no doubt meant to be a pearl. In the field are cloud bands. The mirror's phoenix resembles much more the one above the trilobed arch of the Armenian headpiece than those confronting the dragons, where they are much reduced in form to accommodate the very limited space in the spandrels. Nickel cautions, however, that "the Liao were by no means Chinese, so if they started this tradition, I would not expect it to be Chinese, but influenced by [a] Central Asian, steppe, or more Western tradition."

Perhaps more important for the tenor of this study and those preceding it is an assumption I made that the phoenix and dragon inspired by Chinese artistic representations were shown in conflict in the Armenian miniature. Yolande Crowe (email of 2 August 2004) was the first to caution me that though the dragon may look fierce to Western eyes, in China he was regarded as an auspicious symbol. "The problem arises when we think that we are looking at two beasts in combat. That is our non-Chinese reaction. In fact dragon and phoenix are not in combat in a Chinese context." Linda Komaroff (email of 18 February 2005) affirmed the notion and suggested that the dragon and phoenix "should be viewed as complimentary opposites like yin and yang." Lukas Nichol commented (email of 9 March 2005), "[J]udging from my experience I would be most surprised if the meaning were conflict. The Chinese quest for harmony in everything connected to tombs would suggest that the balance between both powers should matter, not conflict."

There is still the question of how the bringing together of these Chinese creatures in a headpiece of the Armenian Lectionary of 1286 came about. Was it simply the fertile imagination of an artist who saw them represented separately in imported textiles or even together in separate bands like a number of well-known Yüan silks? Personally I think not. The artist, I believe, knew that the phoenix represented the empress and the dragon the emperor, in his context the queen and king of Armenia. If my suggestion has merit, namely that the lion-Christ Emmanuel headpiece represented King Levon, Het'um's father, and the phoenix-dragon one dominated by an heraldic phoenix stood for his consort Queen Keran, Het'um's mother, then the combining of the two creatures is not accidental but a conscious depiction of harmony in the Cilician royal household.

POTTERY UNDER THE MONGOLS

OLIVER WATSON

In the book *The Legacy of Genghis Khan*, which accompanied the exhibition in New York and Los Angeles, there are (for the ceramic historian) a pleasingly high number of ceramics: fifty-six items out of a total of 206—more than a quarter of the whole.[1]

Was the importance of ceramics fully recognized in the mix of materials that make up the material culture of an age? Alas, no. Of these fifty-six items, forty-eight were tiles, mostly from the royal palace at Takht-i Sulayman. There were only eight vessels shown, a mere one twenty-sixth of the total number of exhibits. But on reflection, this representation is, in its context, realistic and fair. For the subtitle of the book and exhibition is *Courtly Art and Culture in Western Asia*, and a sober assessment of the evidence suggests that at every period ceramic vessels (as opposed to tilework) are not a 'courtly' art, but a commercial trade directed not at the highest levels of society but at the levels below—the 'middle classes.'

While a 'royal' interest in ceramics is usually absent, nevertheless the ceramic industry provides rich case studies of the progress of visual culture generally, and it is possible to see reflected in ceramic products not only stylistic and technical fashions, but if we are lucky also economic conditions and trade relations. Indeed in thirteenth-century Iran, it is in ceramics that we see the clearest impact of the Mongol invasions and have ample material illustrating the artistic changes that the Mongols brought in their wake.

Ilkhanid ceramics have been overshadowed in study and appreciation by their immediate predecessors—the wares of the pre-Mongol period.[2] For many decades prior to the Mongol invasions, Iran enjoyed an extraordinary period of ceramic development in a phenomenon that still awaits satisfactory explanation given the

---

[1] Komaroff and Carboni, eds. (2002).

[2] I use the term 'pre-Mongol' to cover the period from the middle of the twelfth century to the incursions of the Mongols into Iran in the 1220s, a period it is very misleading to continue to call 'Seljuk,' but which defies an easy dynastic label.

apparent political and economic turmoil of the time. In a period of little over half a century, the ceramic industry was transformed, and widespread new markets for new luxury products developed. This transformation required two distinct elements: the development of new ceramic technology, and the existence of customers who were able and prepared to buy the resulting products. The technology arrived from Egypt at some point in the mid-twelfth century: the fine frit ceramic body and the luster decoration technique were probably introduced by migrating potters.[3] Both techniques were quickly established and developed to a degree of technical perfection and artistic sophistication never before seen. New types of decoration were additionally invented or refined. Incised and carved decoration followed traditional methods in both clay and fritware.[4] Molding, a technology borrowed from the manufacture of simple unglazed wares, was taken to new heights and fully exploited the potential of new colored glazes.[5] Most luxurious of all was *mina'i*—ware with overglaze-enameled decoration. Complicated to make, requiring (like luster ware) two firings with all the attendant costs and risks, *mina'i* represented, along with luster, the apogee of ceramic production. Additionally, it was a completely new invention unlike luster, which already had a long history.[6]

For fully fifty years, from the 1170s to the 1220s, all these technologies were in constant development and production. Around 1200, yet another new decorative technique was invented: underglaze painting. Though less glamorous than luster or *mina'i* (and with a single firing, certainly less expensive), it was the most important technological breakthrough and provided potters throughout the Islamic world with their basic decorative technology (and on the frit body, their basic fabric material) from this moment onward.[7]

---

[3] Watson (1999a) and Watson (2004), chap. 5.

[4] Both are found in clay and frit-bodied wares in Egypt and also in earlier clay-bodied wares in Iran; see Watson (2004), sections I and Ib.

[5] Molded clay-bodied wares, both unglazed and glazed, had been made across the Islamic world from early times; it was in unglazed wares that the molding process had been most fully exploited. See Watson (2004), section A.

[6] Watson (2004), section P.

[7] The moment of invention of underglaze painting is difficult to discern; precursors are seen in Egypt, and both Egypt and Syria introduced the full-blown technique at about the same time as Iran. In Iran, however, we can see a clear trajectory from earlier carved and slip-painted earthenware techniques into underglaze-painted fritware; see Watson (1979) and (2004), nos. K5–K9 and section N.

So the customer at the luxury ceramic bazaar in Iran around the year 1210 would have been able to choose from a selection of wares of unparalleled variety and splendor: *mina'i*, luster, underglaze painting, molded wares, pierced and carved decoration, and all with an astonishing quality of material, fineness, and variety of shape and skill in decoration.

The best of these wares were made at Kashan, which probably had a monopoly over the luster and *mina'i* techniques, and could produce the finest, thinnest-walled vessels in the other techniques. Kashan wares were traded all over Iran and further afield to Syria and Egypt in the west, to Azerbaijan and further north, and to Afghanistan and further east. In all these places Kashan shards and vessels are found alongside locally made variants that are occasionally of high quality but occur only in the simpler techniques—molding, carving, and underglaze painting.

What makes this trade especially remarkable are the peculiar characteristics of luxury ceramics in which they differed from most other 'luxuries' similarly traded: they had no intrinsic value and they were fragile—break them, and their value disappears. The materials of which they were made were essentially worthless, costing little more than the labor to dig and prepare them. Once fired, they were not recyclable.[8] The pots had value only as a result of the work put into them and resources like the kiln-heat, neither of which could be reclaimed. Once broken they lost virtually all their value, even the few pennies that glass, for example, still possessed as material for recycling. Yet they are relatively heavy and fragile—expensive to transport, and continually at risk of breakage. They cannot be compared with luxury textiles, which formed a medium of exchange and capital saving as well as the major material of display and prestige, nor with metal, where the value of the (recyclable) materials must have formed a considerable percentage of cost of the finished article and the overwhelming fraction of the value of precious metal objects. The market for luxury ceramics required customers who were prepared and could afford to put surplus cash into such ephemeral and risky pleasures.

[8] It is for this reason that they form the largest part of archaeological finds. All other common materials were repairable (textiles, metalwork, wood) or recyclable (all the above, and glass).

Furthermore, the patrons for these wares were not 'royal.' In spite of the widespread use of inscriptions and despite the use of an apparently 'royal' iconography,[9] there are but a handful of objects with dedications to named patrons (all in the pre-Mongol period)—a pitiful fraction of thousands of vessels and shards that survive. The named patrons are all unidentified, and were evidently minor figures of the upper echelons, not true wielders of power. This does not give the appearance of an industry serving primarily a courtly milieu: 'royal' iconography does not necessarily imply 'royal' patronage; rather, it may indicate a general middle-class aspiration or identification.[10]

We can follow the industry at Kashan in a detail unavailable for earlier ceramics, thanks to the numerous dated and signed pieces that survive; the existence of such numbers of documentary pieces is also a comment on both the prestige and monopoly enjoyed by the major workshops in Kashan. The signed and dated pieces appear to reflect the hierarchy in cost, which at this period must link directly to the prestige of the vessels. Luster and *mina'i* are the most frequently dated or signed, while cheaper techniques record far less instances.[11] Luster, which survives in large quantities and records more actual instances of signatures and dates than *mina'i*, is more frequently signed and dated than the cheaper techniques such as underglaze-painted or molded wares. Plain monochrome wares, the most numerous product, have no recorded dates or signatures.

Over ninety documentary luster vessels are recorded with dates ranging from 574/1178 to 624/1226, and the names of perhaps six different potters. Ten pieces of *mina'i* are dated between 573/1178 and 616/1219, with three different potters' names. The cheaper underglaze-painted vessels are even less frequently dated—eight pieces from 601/1204 to 613/1216, and no signatures are yet recorded.[12]

---

[9] See, e.g., Hillenbrand, R. (1995).

[10] Watson (1985), 108. Compare, for example, the number of patrons' names found on Ayyubid and Mamluk metalwork, or even on Mamluk incised slipwares.

[11] For luster wares, see Watson (1985), and for *mina'i* see Watson (1994); both lists are now in need of updating as new examples are published. The figures given here reflect what has additionally come to my attention, both published and unpublished.

[12] One underglaze-painted tombstone of Ilkhanid date bears the name of a member of a Kāshānī potting family, see Watson (1975), but no underglaze-painted vessels are signed.

Molded glazed wares record one name which occurs on several pieces apparently from the same master mold.[13]

The manufacture of vessels appears to dominate the Kashan industry, though major luster tile projects in Qum (602/1205) and Mashhad (612/1215) survive, and the scatter of other luster tiles of very fine quality dating from 600 up to the Mongol invasions indicate that tile production must have been much more extensive than the surviving remains indicate.[14]

The exact significance of these statistics can be debated, given how much material inevitably does not survive. But a consistent pattern does appear to emerge from all the evidence available: Kashan as the sole center producing the most sophisticated wares, and producing in large quantities for export, and the dominance of a few individuals—Abū Zayd and the Abū Ṭāhir family in particular. The extraordinary innovation and maintenance of very high artistic and technical standards over a period of decades is both clearly evident and remarkable.

What is also clear is the impact of the Mongol invasions and the subsequent establishment of the Ilkhanid state. Dated luster vessels are recorded in many years from 574/1179 and in an uninterrupted sequence from 600/1203 up to 614/1217. In 614/1217 fourteen pieces are recorded, in 615/1218 five pieces, in 616/1219 also five pieces, and in 617/1220 a single piece. There are then single pieces dated 619/1222, 621/1224 and 624/1226.[15] Then nothing is recorded until 660/1261, a gap of thirty-five years. Given the scale of production between 600/1203 and 616/1219, this gap is most

[13] Ḥasan al-Kāshānī—in the Freer Gallery, see Atil (1973), pl. 22, and also a piece in the Metropolitan Museum of Art, New York (68.223.9) and one in the Brooklyn Museum (86.227.89). The David Collection, Copenhagen, possesses half of a two-piece mold (which includes the signature) used to make such bowls (32/1977). The small molded bottle in the Nasser D. Khalili Collection of Islamic Art, London dated 534/1139 and signed by ʿAlī Bahūnī needs further examination before it can be confidently included in the corpus; see Grube (1994), no. 148.

[14] Watson (1985), 123–31. Tiles in the 'monumental style' (which do not bear inscriptions) indicate that there was a not inconsiderable tile production before the year 600/1202. Star tiles must have been made for schemes of wall revetment that required at least dozens of tiles, possibly (like the Mashhad installation) hundreds of tiles, so single individual dated stars indicate a much larger original production.

[15] Watson (1985), 199, nos. 60–62. None of these three pieces is published in a way that enables the inscription to be seen and verified and the dates may therefore need to be revised.

plausibly interpreted as the collapse of the market. The Mongols' impact on Kashan itself may have been small ("relatively spared" according to *The Encyclopaedia of Islam*[16]) but the impact on their wider market is quite marked and precisely reflects the years of the Mongol invasions through Iran, starting in the east in 1219. While it is in luster that the impact may be most clearly seen (as they are most frequently inscribed), we have no reason to believe that the production of *mina'i*, underglaze-painted, or other simpler techniques were not similarly affected. In other words, the decline that can be seen in the luster market indicates a decline in the market for luxury ceramic vessels altogether.

The production of luster tiles does not grind to a halt in quite the same way. Seventeen individual pieces and two big surviving installations indicate a substantial level of production up to 617/1220. Then a large *miḥrāb*—perhaps the most technically demanding of all luster tile production—is dated Ṣafar 623/February 1226: the technical quality is excellent, and no skill appears to have been lost.[17] Five individual star tiles, remnants of larger tiling schemes, date between 624/1226 and 631/1233.[18] Then in 640/1242 another *miḥrāb* is installed in the shrine of Mashhad, and by a member of the Abū Ṭāhir family. Smaller than the earlier 'large *miḥrāb*s' and, to judge from available photographs, uncertain in technical quality with running glaze and varied colors.[19] Then a gap of almost fifteen years occurs until resumption of production in earnest.

The Ilkhanid Revival

Three luster tiles are dated in the 650s/1250s, but from 660/1261 an enormous production suddenly starts again, with numerous tiling schemes involving stars, friezes, and *miḥrāb*s in constant demand up until 740/1339.[20] The resumption of vessel manufacture is also

[16] Calmard (1978), 695.

[17] Watson (1985), 131, 185.

[18] Watson (1985), 190 and nos. 19–22. The readings on these tiles also need to be verified.

[19] Watson (1985), 131, fig. 109.

[20] Watson (1985), 131–49.

indicated by pieces dated from the 660s/1260s.[21] The Kashan industry is set back on course, and at a time that precisely reflects the establishment of the Ilkhanid dynasty. The new Ilkhanid production shows a clear shift in priorities, fashions and techniques.

Tiles

Tiles dominate luster production. The pre-Mongol tile industry had supplied the two major Shiʿite shrines in Qum and Mashhad; other tiles may have been for either secular or religious use. As far as we can see, the Mongol demand for tiles is generated again from Shiʿite centers, but more widespread and varied. Of the twenty-odd buildings recorded, the vast majority are Shiʿite tombs, or tombs whose occupants demonstrate in one way or another an attachment to the Shiʿite sect, and luster tiles do not occur in areas of strong Sunni leaning in spite of the numerous building works in such areas in the Ilkhanid period.[22] The Ilkhanid renovations at the palace of Takht-i Sulayman provide the only unambiguous evidence for the use of luster decoration in a secular building. This mixture of use presents some problems of interpretation, whatever perspective we take. The funerary association of the luster tiles is quite marked, for luster tiles are always associated with tomb chambers, not with the prayer halls or mosques proper, even when these occur as part of the same complex.[23] The Shiʿite association is strongly indicated by the use of luster at the major shrines (Qum, Mashhad, Najaf), and even if the preponderance of Imāmzādas with luster tiles is now exaggerated by the preferential survival of these buildings, the lack of luster in major Sunni centers or shrines is still puzzling.

[21] Watson (1985), 200, nos. 63 ff.

[22] Watson (1985), appendix II, 183–88.

[23] The two exceptions are the *miḥrāb* from the Maidan mosque in Kashan, and the tiles in the Mosque of ʿAlī, in Quhrud. The *miḥrāb*, dated 623/1226, predates the fifteenth-century building which housed it by several centuries, and must have been transferred from an earlier unknown building. The ʿAlī mosque was founded by a patron who had a vision of Imām ʿAlī, and thus the building also functions as a shrine, not simply as a local mosque. See Watson (1985), 153–54, 185, 187. The *miḥrāb* is now in the Museum für Islamische Kunst, Berlin, the distinctive six-pointed luster tiles from the ʿAlī Mosque are hopefully still *in situ*, though a luster plaque from the building was sold at Christie's, London, 15 October 1996, as lot 323.

As for the secular use of luster, can we really imagine if the tiles had strong associations with the funerary buildings of a particular sect, that they would readily be chosen simply as luxury decoration within palaces? One possible way to resolve this conundrum is to forge a link through Sufism and through popular beliefs that merged Sufism, Shiʿism, and indeed Iranian nationalism through the invocation of the *Shāhnāma*. The *Shāhnāma* is very frequently quoted on tiles (when non-Qurʾānic), and of course it forms a major part of the decoration on the Takht-i Sulayman tiles. *Shāhnāma* texts and secular quatrains also appear quite unequivocally on tiles intended for religious buildings.[24] Could it be that the use of luster at Takht-i Sulayman, with the important frieze of *Shāhnāma* texts, is to be linked with a wider world of religious belief, rather than being just a claim for secular royal legitimacy?

Patronage

The Takht-i Sulayman tiles are so far the only real evidence for a 'royal' interest in local ceramics. A royal, or at least courtly, interest in ceramic vessels may or may not be discernable in the extensive archaeological finds from the site, but these lamentably remain unpublished, like the finds of so many major Islamic archaeological sites. We are left to surmise from the internal evidence of the pots themselves; this suggests, as usual, that we are back in the area of commercial manufacture. A paucity of dated vessels (around twenty pieces dated between 660 and 700, and less than ten throughout the following century), no signed pieces, no pieces bearing the name of a patron: this gives even less a picture of a royal or 'commission-driven' industry than that of the pre-Mongol period.

Only *lajvardina* ware—the continuation of pre-Mongol *minaʾi* enameled ware, often on a dark blue ground—has been claimed to be of 'royal' status, following a reference in the letters of Rashīd al-Dīn. Arthur Lane explains it thus:

> There is a curious and unexplained passage in a letter received in 1308 by the vizier Rashīd al-Dīn at Tabriz; it describes various gifts being sent to him via Basra by ʿAlāʾ al-Dīn Muḥammad Shāh I, Sultan

[24] Watson (1985), 155–56.

> of Delhi (1295–1315). These included objects of 'china' (the word normally used of Chinese wares)—'*lajvard* dishes and drinking-bowls; royal bowls (i.e., large ones) with floral designs; big sherbet-bowls with "seven-color" decoration; wine-ewers in *lajvard* ornamented with gold designs; and *lajvard* saucers and flat dishes.'[25]

Lane rightly observes that no early fourteenth-century Chinese ware matches this description, and concludes that *lajvardina* ware was being sent as a diplomatic gift back to Iran from India whence it must have been originally traded. This idea gives us some pause for thought: are *lajvardina* wares, grand though they appear to be, really the stuff of international diplomatic gifts? Would they be grand and novel enough to impress Iran's most powerful servant, made as they were in a province of Iran and readily available at the time, one would have thought, in Tabriz's teeming bazaars?[26] And a technique that was already old and well-known—*lajvardina* tiles had been installed in Takht-i Sulayman some thirty years before.

There is another explanation that both rests on and supports the argument that the Rashīd al-Dīn letters are a later compilation.[27] For while there are no early fourteenth-century Chinese ceramics that match these descriptions, there are wares in the fifteenth and sixteenth centuries that certainly do. Skimming the catalogue of Ming porcelains of the British Museum, for example, one finds a series of wares that could have been chosen to illustrate Rashīd al-Dīn's putative letter: wares with decoration on a blue ground, large bowls with polychrome enameled decoration, and wares with gilt decoration.[28] These mostly happen to be dated first half of the sixteenth century, but the arrival in Iran of similar wares in the previous century is demonstrated by similar pieces of the Chenghua and Hongzhi periods (1465–87 and 1488–1505) still preserved in Iran.[29] The collection

[25] Lane, A. (1957), 7–8.

[26] The only documentary *lajvardina* vessel is the sole dated piece—dated after the Ilkhanid period—of Rajab 776/December 1334 now in the Museum für Islamische Kunst, Berlin; see Klinge, Zick-Nissen, and Klein (1973), no. 222.

[27] Morton (1999).

[28] Harrison-Hall (2001), nos. 9:53–9:108.

[29] Thompson and Canby, eds. (2003), nos. 11.2 and 11.9. The first is a blue-and-white dish with the reverse painted in dark blue under a lighter blue glaze; the second, a bowl decorated with polychrome enamels. Blue-and-white porcelain had been imported into the Middle East in quantities since it was first made in the early fourteenth century, but production had not developed by the time of Rashīd al-Dīn's death in 1318.

of Chinese porcelain in Istanbul includes a small number of enameled wares of the late fifteenth and early sixteenth centuries, which indicates their availability in the Middle East, even if they were not common.[30] The record of a fifteenth- or sixteenth-century diplomatic gift of rare Chinese porcelains interpolated into the so-called Rashīd al-Dīn letters is, on the whole, a more plausible explanation than that Kashan Ilkhanid *lajvardina* ware was involved.

Style

There is something distinctive about potting and painting styles in the Ilkhanid period that distinguish them from the wares of the pre-Mongol period.[31] The vessels are often thicker, with less subtle profiles and little experiment with translucency. Bowl shapes may exaggerate pre-Mongol forms (e.g., the bowl with the T-rim) or derive from those of newly-imported Chinese celadon (flat dishes with broad rims and upturned edges, or smoothly flaring bowls).[32] An apparently new shape is the bowl with the articulated wall forming a broad, in-sloping rim.[33] The coloring in many wares is somber to the extent that Lane labels it the "age of blue and black."[34] An extraordinary gray slip ground characterizes one particular class of Sultanabad ware.[35] The painting style also becomes somewhat less refined, with simpler animal, figural, or floral ornament. Even more than in the case of the pre-Mongol painted wares, certain standard motifs and compositions occur regularly (animals against foliage, standing figures, panels of conventional ornament).[36] We see for the first time the Chinese lotus and phoenix (though dragons are found

[30] Krahl and Erbahar (1986), vol. 2, 536, nos. 751–56, 1631–32, and 1661–64.

[31] Watson (2004), section Q.

[32] 'T-rim': Watson (2004), nos. Q.5 and Q.11; Lane, A. (1957), pl. 4; compare with Watson (1985), fig. 87. Dish: Watson (2004), no. Q.13; Lane, A. (1947), pl. 74b; Lane, A. (1957), pl. 86b. For the Chinese model, see Krahl and Erbahar (1986), vol. 1, 210 and nos. 64 ff. Flaring bowl: Watson (2004), nos. Q.4, Q.9, Q.18, etc.; Lane, A. (1947), pls. 64a, 75a, 93, and 96b; Lane, A. (1957), pl. 6a. For the Chinese model, see Krahl and Erbahar (1986), vol. 1, no. 1.

[33] Watson (2004), Q.6, Q.7; Lane, A. (1947), pl. 89; Lane, A. (1957), pl. 86a.

[34] Lane, A. (1957), 10.

[35] Morgan, P. (1995) and Watson (2004), nos. Q.11–14.

[36] See, e.g., Atil (1973), nos. 69–75.

only on tiles from Takht-i Sulayman).[37] However, the painters show signs of familiarity with contemporary book illustration, from which they on occasion adopt a 'frame' that may cut the scene abruptly, such as half an animal entering from the side.[38]

Although the above is a fair characterization of the generality of Ilkhanid ceramics it is, like all generalizations, subject to exceptions, and almost all the criteria listed above are contradicted to some extent by one ware or another. Indeed the variety of Ilkhanid wares and the variety of approaches they embody have been overshadowed by the conventional concentration on the 'classic' wares—Sultanabad, luster, and *lajvardina*.[39] In fact, there is as great a diversity in this period as in the previous.

Variety of Ilkhanid Ceramic Production

We can identify many distinct types, some of which have distinct subtypes. As in pre-Mongol times, we are left to distinguish wares by their formal qualities, given the dearth of archaeological information. As in the pre-Mongol period, it is probably the case that the finest wares were made in a single center, with simpler techniques being more widespread. The evidence of Abū al-Qāsim, backed up in the case of tiles by evidence from inscriptions, confirms the continuing manufacture at Kashan of a wide range of ceramics, including luster and overglaze enameled wares, both vessels and tiles.[40]

[37] The lack of dragons has been explained by their being restricted to Imperial use, as sometimes in China; see Morgan, P. (1995). This explanation is, however, undermined by the occurrence of dragons on metalwork with anonymous dedications; see, e.g., Melikian-Chirvani (1982), no. 93.

[38] Watson (2004), no. Q.7.

[39] These, for example, with the addition of the dated molded jar of 681/1282 and one celadon copy, are the only types that figured in *The Legacy of Genghis Khan* exhibition; Komaroff and Carboni, eds. (2002).

[40] See Allan (1973) and Watson (1985). Abū al-Qāsim's treatise on precious stones of 700/1300 contains an appendix with a detailed description of the production of pottery. Abū al-Qāsim himself comes from one of the major families of luster potters from Kashan, with a grandfather, father, and brother all documented as potters.

Luster (fig. 68)

Ilkhanid luster is much more uniform than pre-Mongol wares in the vessel shapes, designs, and quality of decoration. The painting style is simpler than that often found in the pre-Mongol period, and is identical to that of the contemporary luster tilework.[41] There is every reason to think that these were made by the same potters who made the luster tiles in Kashan, and that they still had a monopoly over the technique they enjoyed in the pre-Mongol period. Though inscriptions play a much less prominent role than before, more than a dozen vessels are dated between 660/1261 and 683/1284; no signatures of potters have been recorded. It would be surprising if the 680s/1280s saw the end of luster vessel production, as luster tile production is well documented as continuing unabated into the 730s/1330s, though the lack of later dated vessels is puzzling. While vessels appear to be much less prolific than in the pre-Mongol period and many are simpler in manufacture and design, items such as impressively large jars show that there was still considerable talent and ambition among the potters, as might be expected of the those who continued to make such impressive tiling schemes.[42]

Lajvardina (pl. 26 and fig. 69)

Lajvardina is the continuation of *mina'i* ware into the Ilkhanid period.[43] It shows the most dramatic instance of the 'new style': the color is

[41] See, e.g., Watson (1985), pl. H, figs. 88–96.

[42] See, e.g., Pope and Ackerman, eds. (1938–39), pls. 700–1; for the tiles see Watson (1985), chap. 10.

[43] Gold leaf decoration is known in pre-Mongol *mina'i* wares, but is rare and is used in a subordinate role to enhance other enamel colors. The decoration on *lajvardina* ware, like *mina'i*, is highly prone to be 'enhanced' by overpainting and regilding. Such work, carried out recently for the purposes of sale, may or may not follow the original decoration. The use of acetone to detect paint (fired enamel should not be affected) has been found in more than a few instances to remove all decoration completely! See Watson (2004), 87, no. LNS 206 C. This difficulty may account for the surprising lack of any study of *lajvardina* ware, or indeed of any substantial body of illustrations. The sherd illustrated in text fig. 69, from an archaeological context, has not been repainted as have most 'complete' pieces. It gives us confidence that the technique was produced to the highest standards—the interlocking geometric design is constructed from tiny individual strips of gold leaf

usually (though not always) dominated by a dark blue glaze with the main designs depicted in cut gold leaf with red, white, and black enamel outlines and details.[44] And the motifs, far from the figural scenes of *mina'i* ware, are largely abstract and geometric, the exception being on the tiles where much more elaborate decoration is known. It is reasonable to suppose that these are also a monopoly of the potters of Kashan. There are tiles of *lajvardina* technique in the palace of Takht-i Sulayman that presumably date from the 670s/1270s,[45] but the only documentary piece is a bowl of rather simple quality with a post-Ilkhanid date of Rajab 776/December 1334.[46]

Celadon (fig. 70)

Copies of Chinese celadon form a major new ware in the Ilkhanid period. They are mostly close copies of the Chinese, imitating the porcelain and transparent blue-green glaze with a frit body under an opaque turquoise glaze. Two vessel shapes predominate: the flat dish with broad rim, often with molded fish as a decoration, and the bowl with smoothly curved sides, often with carved lotus leaves on the exterior.[47] This ware, simple in technique, may have been made in many centers, and may have been made for a considerable while: the Chinese models continue into the fifteenth century. There are no documentary pieces.

---

in a circular cartouche measuring not more than 5 cm in diameter. Most publications rely on the illustration of the same, or very similar pieces. The famous and extensively reproduced dish in the Louvre is unique in being the application of enamel and gilding to what otherwise is a plain celadon copy of a dish with raised fish; see Lane, A. (1947), pl. 74b; Komaroff and Carboni, eds. (2002), fig. 239.

[44] Klinge, Zick-Nissen, and Klein (1973), nos. 223–24; Lane, A. (1947), pl. 75a; Hayward Gallery (1976), nos. 369–70. For *lajvardina* ware on a non-blue ground, see Atil (1973), no. 75; Watson (2004), no. Q.4.

[45] Komaroff and Carboni, eds. (2002), figs. 98, 101–2, 106, 275, 278.

[46] Klinge, Zick-Nissen, and Klein (1973), no. 222.

[47] Komaroff and Carboni, eds. (2002), fig. 238; Lane, A. (1957), pl. 86b; Folsach (2001), no. 243; Metropolitan Museum of Art (1987), no. 54.

Sultanabad (fig. 71)

Sultanabad is a name given to a group of related wares first described in detail by Arthur Lane.[48] I have taken the liberty of restricting the name 'Sultanabad' to only the first two of the three groups identified by Lane. These two share a common style of painting, and are sufficiently related to suggest that they are the products of a common center. The find in the early twentieth century of a hoard of pieces in excellent condition appears to be entirely composed of just these two groups, which gives further support to the belief that they are products of the same center.[49] Where that center is located is not certain. The reported find-spot of this hoard (or hoards) is in the vicinity of the modern city of Sultanabad in northwest Iran, which gives its name to the ware. It may be that they were made in this area, though it can also be argued that they are the products of Kashan, given their quality and stylistic relation to contemporary luster ware. A large number of pieces from this hoard appears to have been acquired by Kelekian, and was published by him in 1910: eight of these are now in the al-Sabah Collection in Kuwait.

The two types of 'Sultanabad' wares share a common set of vessel shapes, and are distinguished primarily by the nature of the background of the painting. In the first group, it is the white body (or a white slip overlaying it) against which the motifs are depicted in reserve. In the second, a gray-green slip provides the background and a white slip is then used for the main motifs.[50] In both groups, the whole ground is decorated with a tapestry of foliage against which the main motifs are often in danger of disappearing. In the first group, there is ample use of blue and turquoise which, with the thick black outlining, achieves the required somber tonality. In the slip-painted ware, this is achieved by the dark ground alone, against which the main motifs stand more clearly delineated.

A provincial version of the slip-painted group, crudely made and decorated with angular drawings of flying birds, started to appear in the art trade in numbers in the 1970s, when it was attributed to

[48] Lane, A. (1957), 10–13.

[49] Watson (2004), 373, and nos. Q.5–12. Kelekian (1910) also attributes luster wares to Sultanabad, and the three pieces now in the al-Sabah Collection may also have formed part of the same hoard.

[50] For this second group, see Morgan, P. (1995).

Bujnurd and other sites in northeast Iran. Its discovery in archaeological contexts would reassure the more skeptical observers among us about its dating and origins.[51] It is sometimes attributed to the lands of the Golden Horde, though the basis for this is unclear.

Underglaze-painted Wares

Fully developed underglaze painting was invented in Iran only around the year 1200,[52] but in the two decades before the disruption of the Mongol invasions, it appears to have been taken up with alacrity and spread far beyond its apparent source of Kashan. It is not surprising, therefore, that we find a proliferation of wares decorated in this technique in the Ilkhanid period. In addition to the 'Sultanabad' ware mentioned above, there is one particular high-quality type that is tempting to attribute to Kashan. The others could well have been made elsewhere, possibly in multiple locations.

Panel style (fig. 72)

A style in which the surface of the vessel is divided into small concentric panels which are filled with a limited variety of conventional patterns, notably sketchy arabesques, interlaces, and groups of dots (usually in threes). Less common are running foxes and lotus sprays.[53] The design is outlined in black, with much cobalt blue and lesser touches of turquoise. Center panels in more elaborate and finely painted vessels can contain figures depicted in the same manner as on Sultanabad wares.[54] This, along with the occurrence of the same style of decoration in luster painting, points to Kashan as the main center of production.[55] The quality of the ware, however, varies considerably, from the fairly simple to the finest-made and most meticulously painted pottery of the Ilkhanid period as a whole.[56]

---

[51] Watson (2004), nos. Q.15–17.

[52] Watson (1979).

[53] Watson (2004), no. Q.18; Lane, A. (1957), pl. 6.

[54] Lane, A. (1957), pl. 6b.

[55] Compare Lane, A. (1957), pl. 6b and Lane, A. (1947), pl. 64a.

[56] Lane, A. (1957), pl. 6b illustrates an extraordinary object: the bowl is very

Polychrome Painted (figs. 73–74)

There is a wider variety of underglaze-painted wares in the Ilkhanid period than is normally recognized. Of particular note is a ware in which manganese purple is often added to the usual black, blue, and turquoise palette. Two styles are to be noted. In the first, animal figures are shown against rather wiry foliage (fig. 73), the type specimen being the footed bowl in the Victoria and Albert Museum dated Ramaḍān 672/March 1274.[57] Other designs in the same technique include a cruciform interlace (fig. 74) and a quadripartite arabesque.[58] Pierced rims, in this and the panel style above, connect the wares to the so-called white ware described below.

Black Under Turquoise (figs. 75–76)

A distinct variety of black painting under a turquoise glaze is worthy of note (fig. 75). The vessel shapes follow the norm for Ilkhanid pottery, but the painting follows a distinctive style of foliate design, in which broadly depicted leaves and simple palmettes are filled with peacock-eye motifs.[59] A bowl with a deeply serrated rim in the al-Sabah Collection, Kuwait, shows a fox, and a bowl with a 'T-rim' in the Victoria and Albert Museum is dated Rabīʿ I 676/August 1277 (fig. 76).[60] Intriguing is a 'waster' in a simple version of this style said to have been found at Sultaniyya in northwest Iran.[61] This ware forms a link with the past and the future of Ilkhanid pottery. Black-under-turquoise decoration is one of the first to be found in the manufacture of the new fritwares in Iran in the twelfth century, and the Ilkhanid ware is evidently a continuation of this earlier

---

finely molded, and the painting is of an exquisite fineness and detail. The technical quality of the piece is of the highest order, but the painting style relates it to many others whose quality is that more normally found in Ilkhanid pottery.

[57] Pope and Ackerman, eds. (1938–39), no. 153, pl. 781a; Lane, A. (1947), pl. 94; see also Lane, A. (1947), pls. 95b, 96a; Atil (1973), no. 72; Bagherzadeh (1988), nos. 94 and 168.

[58] Lane, A. (1947), pls. 95a and 96b; Soustiel (1985), nos. 256 and 263, more likely to be dated 706/1306 than a century later.

[59] Lane, A. (1947), pl. 93.

[60] Watson (2004), no. Q.22; the dated piece in the Victoria and Albert Museum is unpublished.

[61] Rice, D. T. (1932).

tradition. One bowl decorated in the distinctive Ilkhanid manner has walls with molded fluting, copying a Chinese celadon type.[62] Exactly the same type of bowl with identical fluting in the al-Sabah Collection is decorated with the 'beaver-tailed bird' and has been attributed to fifteenth-century Samarqand[63]—evidence, perhaps, for the continuation of the Ilkhanid tradition into the fifteenth century, and for the transfer to Samarqand by Tīmūr of the Iranian potters responsible.

White Wares (fig. 77)

The prevalence of a somber tonality in the Ilkhanid period is remarkable, and led Arthur Lane to characterize it as the "age of blue and black."[64] But this should not blind us to the simultaneous production of wares with a very different aesthetic. There are wares that rely simply on the whiteness of the material for their main effect, with a minimal amount of underglaze painting. Others include extensive piercing of the rims with a pattern of holes, which are then filled with glaze to provide little translucent windows.[65] The designs remain simple and do not nearly reach the complexity and sophistication sometimes seen in pre-Mongol wares.[66] However, they still predate the Chinese use of the same technique by several centuries.

Monochrome-glazed Wares (fig. 78)

Little is known of the monochrome wares of the Ilkhanid period other than the famed copies of Chinese celadon that have perhaps caught the fancy of collectors more than other wares. A group of large jars with molded decoration, two of which are dated in the late thirteenth century,[67] perhaps illustrate the artistic pinnacle of a

---

[62] Bonham's, London, 11 October, 2000, lot 451.
[63] Watson (2004), no. U.6.
[64] Lane, A. (1957), 10.
[65] Lane, A. (1947), pl. 89b; Palazzo delle Esposizioni (1990), no. 66.
[66] Lane, A. (1947), pl. 89a.
[67] Jars dated 681/1282 and 683/1284 in the Metropolitan Museum of Art, New York, and the Freer Gallery, Washington, D.C., respectively; see Komaroff and Carboni, eds. (2002), fig. 212 and Atil (1973), no. 77.

continuing manufacture of functional ware that had been made in the Middle East for centuries and was certainly prolific and highly varied in the pre-Mongol period (fig. 78). We await the publication of excavation reports to confirm the reality.

Spread of Styles

The Iranian pottery industry was very active from the 1260s at least into the middle of the fourteenth century. Luster production appears to have all but ceased around the year 1340 for reasons unknown,[68] but *lajvardina* ware carried on to the end of the century, and underglaze painting became the standard technique for fine ceramics from this moment onwards.

From the point of view of Ilkhanid ceramics, it is surprisingly not its legacy in Iran that is of particular note, but its spread, both in style and technology, to lands far beyond the confines of Iran. This involves two distinct wares: underglaze-painted wares in the 'panel style,' and wares painted in the Sultanabad style, both with and without raised white slip.

The spread of techniques of manufacture and styles of decoration across the Islamic world has become a recognized feature of the ceramic industry. It was first recognized in the history of luster decoration, where its course can be traced across many countries and centuries: from glass decoration in eighth-century Syria and Egypt, to ceramic decoration in ninth- and tenth-century Iraq, back to Egypt in the eleventh and twelfth centuries, and again to Syria and Iran (and possibly Spain) in the later twelfth and following centuries.[69] This story has captured the attention of many scholars, but no less impressive is the spread of the use of glazing in any form across the Islamic world in the ninth century, and the spread of decorated opaque white-glazed wares from Iraq as far as Spain in the West and Central Asia in the East during the ninth and tenth centuries.[70] In the mid-twelfth century, we can follow the spread of the fritware technology from Egypt, where it appears to have been invented, to

[68] For the end of luster production, see Watson (1985), 142, 157.
[69] Watson (2004), 38–40.
[70] Watson (2004), 35–38.

Syria and Iran, simultaneously accompanied by the luster technique and other modes of decoration.[71] This eastward trajectory in the twelfth century is followed in the later thirteenth and fourteenth centuries by a contrary westward movement, this time of Ilkhanid 'panel' and Sultanabad styles to the lands of the Golden Horde, to Syria, and to Egypt.

The Golden Horde wares are known to us only through a few well-published pieces, and these seem to suggest a distinct manner of decoration. The iconic piece in the Hermitage from excavations in Sarai Berke, published by Lane half a century ago, is in the raised-slip Sultanabad style but includes a stippled rim and a band of blue hatching (fig. 79).[72] The rather simple painting style is matched by other pieces found in or attributed to the lands of the Golden Horde.[73] The stippled rim and hatching are also found in a series of bowls painted in a rather angular and distinctive variation of the panel style, and might indicate that this entire group is also to be attributed to the same region.[74] A jug of the same style was excavated at Sarai Berke.[75]

The wares from Syria and Egypt in both Sultanabad and panel styles are better known, with plentiful archaeological finds from Hama in Syria and ample shard material from Fustat.[76] In Egypt, the panel style develops into a considerable industry,[77] and continues in variant form into the fifteenth century.

This transference of the Ilkhanid styles is of some interest. In earlier movements of this kind, as outlined above, styles of painting have simply accompanied techniques, and it is clear that the techniques are the more important element, adding substantially to the repertoire of the local pottery industry. In this transfer of Ilkhanid methods,

---

[71] Watson (1999a).

[72] Lane, A. (1957), pl. 5; also Dar al-Athar al-Islamiyya (1990), no. 69.

[73] Dar al-Athar al-Islamiyya (1990), 65; Watson (2004), 77, LNS767C; Folsach (2001), no. 223.

[74] See, e.g., Jenkins (1983), no. 83; Soustiel (1985), fig. 279; Galeries nationales du Grand Palais (1977), no. 141.

[75] Dar al-Athar al-Islamiyya (1990), no. 70.

[76] It is not yet possible to distinguish the Syrian from the Egyptian production: for 'Syrian' material see Riis and Poulsen (1957), nos. 744–61, 764–65 and also Lane, A. (1957), pls. 10–11; Watson (2004), no. R.3; for 'Egyptian,' see, e.g., Lane, A. (1957), 15–20, esp. 19.

[77] Watson (2004), R.4, R.7, and esp. R.8.

it is mostly just a style of decoration that is transferred, as happens again in the fifteenth century when blue-and-white Chinese styles of painting appear to have spread from Samarqand westward.[78] The only new technique involved, that of decorating with a raised slip, is something of an oddity—a curiosity of a technique, not terribly important, and one that had little future life. Unlike the previous transfers of opaque white glaze, luster decoration, or the fritware body, it was not something that radically transformed anything. This comment may not hold true for the potteries of the Golden Horde, for the arrival of Ilkhanid methods may have been the area's first establishment of fine pottery production. If this is the case, then we might see a contingent of potters from Iran bringing with them their entire set of methods and expertise—fritware body, vessel shapes, and underglaze painting technique including the Sultanabad raised-slip style.[79] However, Syria and Egypt had well-established pottery industries, already capable of producing fine-quality underglaze-painted fritwares in the twelfth century. What is apparently transferred is the style of painting alone (and the curious use of raised slip).

It may be that this indicates we are dealing with the movement of craftsmen, not just ideas. The potters bring with them their habits of manufacture. If this is the case, we must then imagine that the immigrants from Iran were able to settle in the midst of an already well-established industry and to make a considerable impact. The styles they introduce become prevalent in fourteenth-century manufacture in both Syria and Egypt. And in Egypt, at least, they are copied by local craftsmen. The most prolific and competent potter in the 'panel' style signs himself as *al-ustādh al-miṣrī* (the Egyptian master),[80] as if in defiance of so many of his contemporaries and rivals whose names suggest a foreign origin. Yet the style of his painting is one that leads directly back to Ilkhanid Iran.

---

[78] Golombek, Mason, and Bailey (1996).

[79] It is not certain whether pre-Mongol fine pottery discovered in this area is locally made, or imported from Iran.

[80] Lane, A. (1957), pl. 16b.

Conclusions

To summarize, the Ilkhanid pottery industry was evidently flourishing through the thirteenth and fourteenth century. Though less studied than 'Seljuk' pottery, very many pieces survive in a wide variety of styles and qualities. It is a popular ware in the sense of serving a wide market, and there is no evidence for vessel manufacture being directed at a court elite. This holds true even if styles of painting on occasion follow 'elite' taste. A great variety of styles were made, more than usually recognized in the commonly quoted 'classic sequence.'[81] We are able to say little of where it was produced in Iran, whether through a centralized or distributed organization of production. However, there are strong indications that Kashan continued to be a major, if not the predominant, center. The production of very similar wares in the lands of the Golden Horde and in Mamluk Syria and Egypt pose questions as yet unanswered. How were the styles and techniques actually transferred? Why and when? How did they succeed?

[81] For the 'classic sequence,' see Watson (1999a).

PERSIAN POETRY ON ILKHANID ART AND ARCHITECTURE

BERNARD O'KANE

The flowering of Persian as a literary language was first apparent at the court of the Samanids in the ninth to tenth centuries.[1] But this was not immediately accompanied by its use on works of art and architecture. This seems to have been first accomplished by, rather surprisingly, Turkish dynasties on the periphery of the Islamic world, the Ghaznavids and Qara-Khanids, whose familiarity with Arabic was certainly much less than with Persian, the language of the majority of their subjects. By far the majority of Persian inscriptions of this period appear on monuments rather than on artifacts. With regard to the Seljuks in central Iran, like the Buyids before them, their proximity to the center of Arabic civilization in Baghdad and their relationship to the Abbasid caliphate were such that they did not appear to question the primacy of Arabic on their monuments.

It is only in the second half of the twelfth century that we begin to find examples of the decorative arts with Persian inscriptions, occasionally poetic, produced under the smaller dynasties that succeeded the breakup of the Seljuk state. This trickle of examples becomes a steady stream after the advent of the Mongols. This paper is intended to highlight some of the examples that illustrate this change in attitude, and also to suggest why it might have occurred at this time.

The change therefore begins just before the Ilkhanid period, in pottery and tiles of the late twelfth and thirteenth centuries (mostly luster-painted examples). Persian verses occur on these more often than on any other medium, sometimes sharing the epigraphic program with Arabic, but often appearing alone. Very few of these have an inscription that identifies their patron, indicating that they were most likely made for any wealthy patron who could afford them,

[1] For the background to this see Lazard (1975). This paper is condensed from a larger study, *The Appearance of Persian on Islamic Works of Art*, which was given as the Yarshater Lecture Series at SOAS, London, in December 2002. A fuller treatment will be found in its forthcoming publication.

such as the urban mercantile or landed class. Even so, the inscriptions sometimes flattered the patron, as in the quatrain on a luster bowl from the Victoria and Albert Museum:

May your wealth and fame be evermore
May your fortune surpass all limits
So that whatever you drink out of this bowl
May, O Prince, leader of the world, add pleasure to your life.[2]

A rather different type of quatrain is found on a luster bowl dated to 604/1207:

I wished to take the veil off from your moonlike face
I wished to have a bite of those lips sweet as sugar
She said, 'Why talk of pincers, you who burn like a candle in my love
Are you not afraid that your head might be cut off in the attempt?'[3]

I will return shortly to the interpretation of such love poetry, for this is one of the most frequent types of inscription found not only on bowls, which these two examples dated 1210 and 1217 have, but also on a series of luster dado tiles in both secular and religious monuments from the middle of the thirteenth century onwards. Unfortunately not many of these tiles are left *in situ*, such is their portability and the insatiable appetite of collectors for them, but the original location of some of them is certain. All the tiles from the *khānqāh* of Pīr-i Ḥusayn near Baku (1284–86), are now in the Hermitage Museum, for example (fig. 80).[4] Similar panels were removed from the Imāmzāda Jaʿfar in Damghan and many comparable tiles dated to 1266 are known from the latter monument (fig. 81).[5] But the largest known source of inscribed tiles from this period is the palace at Takht-i Sulayman, built from 1272 onwards by the Mongol ruler Abaqa Khan. This was a Sasanian site which incorporated a famous fire temple and a spring that bubbles forth from the unfathomably deep lake at the center of the site. It was known through Iranian sources to have played a major role in the ritual of Sasanian coronation.[6] The magnificent tile revetment of

[2] Bahrami (1949), 121, pl. XLIX.
[3] Ibid., 121, pl. LXIV (formerly in the Tillinger Collection, Tehran).
[4] Best illustrated in Piotrovsky and Vrieze, eds. (1999), 217, no. 190.
[5] Watson (1985), 132–33.
[6] Melikian-Chirvani (1991), 35–36.

the building contained many luster examples with inscribed verses, and thanks to the work of scholars such as A. S. Melikian-Chirvani, ʿAbdallāh Qūchānī, and more recently Tomoko Masuya, we have extremely detailed information about the verses and the poets who wrote them.[7] The magnitude of the production is shown by one type of Takht-i Sulayman tile, of which around nineteen hundred fragments are known. They have yielded 114 different complete verses and ninety-three other verse fragments. The authors of some of these verses have remained unidentified, but the works of forty-three different poets have been found in the identified portions, with the eleventh-century mystic Abū Saʿīd and the thirteenth-century panegyric and Sufi poet Kamāl Ismāʿīl, topping the popularity tables.[8] A series of frieze tiles from the site with *Shāhnāma* verses have also been identified.

Shāhnāma episodes that are quoted on the tiles include several that relate to the exploits of the Sasanian king Kay Khusraw, to whom the founder of the palace, Abaqa Khan, was compared as a second Kay Khusraw.[9] Another conqueror with whom the Mongols identified was Alexander, a foreign ruler who becomes revered by his Iranian subjects.[10] Later, illustrations of his exploits form an unusually large part of the cycle of painting of the Great Mongol *Shāhnāma*. Verses from his sojourn in India are also found on the tiles[11] and his ultimate quest for the Water of Life, mirroring the Sufi's quest for fulfillment in God, may have been associated with the spring that forms the deep lake at the center of the site.

One surprising feature of the *Shāhnāma* verses on the tiles is that they are frequently not from the climax of episodes in the story, but from their beginnings. However, in this way they may have

[7] Melikian-Chirvani (1988); Melikian-Chirvani (1991); Melikian-Chirvani (1996); Qūchānī (1992); Masuya (1997).

[8] Masuya (1997), 377–400 and 677–88.

[9] Melikian-Chirvani (1991), 85. In an interesting variation of the Ghazni palace, two of the original verses of the *Shāhnāma* changed the line from the third to the second person singular, metaphorically comparing the ruler to the kings of Iran; Melikian-Chirvani (1984), 304. However, the possibility that Melikian-Chirvani has confused verses that were deliberately altered with mere variant readings is discussed in Masuya (1997), 492–504.

[10] The likelihood of the Mongols' identification with Alexander is increased by the prominence of episodes from his life illustrated in the Great Mongol *Shāhnāma*; see Grabar, O. and Blair (1980), 112–35.

[11] Melikian-Chirvani (1984), 284; Melikian-Chirvani (1997), 159.

functioned as an *aide-mémoire* to viewers, many of whom might have learned portions of the *Shāhnāma* by heart, or they could have aided *Shāhnāma* reciters, professionals who could narrate the entire epic or at least its important parts.

Many of the star tiles have erotic quatrains inscribed on them; that quoted earlier from the bowl also appears on the Takht-i Sulayman tiles. These should not be taken at face value, or at least not just at face value. Sufi poetry, first directed exclusively towards God, was frequently blended with the admiration of a beautiful face in which God's beauty reveals itself to the loving mystic; this had become a standard feature of Persian poetry by the twelfth century. This could also be represented in figural images on pottery, as in the nude figure in the water on a plate in the Freer Gallery, which has been interpreted as a revelation of God's beauty, beckoning towards the mystic.[12]

The most cogent argument for the interpretation of these quatrains as being symbolic of divine rather than earthly love is that they also frequently occur on luster tiles that decorated the walls of religious buildings.[13] The same verses occur on the tiles of the Imāmzāda Ja'far and the Pīr-i Ḥusayn *khānqāh* mentioned earlier, and there are some that are still found in a small village mosque near Kashan, the Masjid-i 'Alī (pl. 27). These, datable between 1303 and 1307, have erotic quatrains, *Shāhnāma* quotations, as well as many Qur'ānic inscriptions.[14] Several also have figural images, as have many of those from the earlier religious buildings mentioned. These were obviously no barrier to their being used as decoration of a religious monument, but another point to be made about the figural decoration, be it animals or human figures, is that it bears no correspondence with the poetry around the tiles. Surprising as it seems, the calligraphers of the poetry seem to have paid no attention to the images decorating the tiles.

What source did the tile makers use for this great variety of verses? Such is the variety that they probably had access to a compendium of quatrains. One such, the *Majālis al-nafā'is*, was written between 1285 and 1294 and contains 4125 quatrains conveniently divided

---

[12] Guest and Ettinghausen (1961).
[13] Watson (1985), 155.
[14] Watson (1975).

into subject matter, of which thirty-three are found on the Takht-i Sulayman tiles. Very likely something similar was used by the potters; this is also suggested by the way in which quatrains by two different authors are frequently found on the same tile.[15]

Even in an area normally thought remote from Persian speakers, the Golden Horde capital at New Saray, now in southern Russia, we find a tile decorated with extensive Persian verses, although so far not completely deciphered. The shape and coloring do not have exact parallels in Ilkhanid Iran, although the source of its inspiration can hardly be doubted.[16]

Despite the prominence of Persian on tiles and pottery in this period, not many examples on metalwork are known. To take a sample from a representative collection, of the forty-two objects catalogued in the Victoria and Albert Museum collection, only three have inscriptions in Persian.[17] All are wine bowls; other wine bowls with Persian verses are in collections in Paris, London, Tbilisi, and Tehran (fig. 82).[18] The following verses are found on several of them:

> O sweet beverage of our pleasures
> O transparent Fount of Mirth
> If Alexander had not seen you
> O world-revealing bowl of Mani
> How could his mind have conceived
> The notion of the fount of life?[19]

The mention of Mani, always cited as the exemplar of painting, relates to the beautiful images that the cup reflects and which incline the owner, like Alexander, towards the search for the fountain of youth, another metaphor for the Sufi's quest for God.[20]

It is interesting to note that here the verses are enclosed within cartouches. This, unlike contemporary examples in Arab architecture as in Mamluk Egypt, later comes to be a visual clue leading us to expect poetry within such a frame.

Although a few candlesticks of this period also have Persian

[15] Masuya (1997), 398–400.
[16] Komaroff and Carboni, eds. (2002), fig. 28.
[17] Melikian-Chirvani (1982), nos. 84–85.
[18] Ibid., 147; Melikian-Chirvani (1973), 60–61.
[19] Melikian-Chirvani (1982), 188.
[20] Cf. ibid., 332, 343.

inscriptions,[21] the majority is found on objects relating to serving and drinking wine. This may at first seem surprising but, as even the casual reader of Ḥāfiẓ will know, there is a strong linkage of poetry, Sufism, and wine drinking.

On architecture in the early fourteenth century, other than the examples with luster tiles there are still extremely few that use Persian inscriptions, although some of the surviving examples are of great interest.[22] They are mostly from northwestern and western Iran. One is on a stone tympanum from Kubachi, probably from a secular building as it shows two wrestlers below the field of the verses.[23] Another secular building is a *caravansaray* north of Marand, between Tabriz and Julfa; the partially deciphered verses in kufic that Khanikoff saw in the nineteenth century are still visible on its portal (fig. 83).[24] The inscription on the mosque at Asnaq (dated 733/1333), in the same area, is interesting for the pride that the craftsman took in his work. The main portal and the lower inscriptions are in Arabic, but there are two quatrains above the windows, the first giving the date, the second as follows:

īn masjidīst a'ẓam az sang-i kanda kār
Ustad-i īn amal Malikshāh-i nāmdār
Az dam-i tīsha īn hama naqqāshīyish bikard
Dastish durust bād khudāyish nigahdār (fig. 84)

This is a most great mosque of carved stone
The master of this work is the famous Malikshāh
He made all its decoration with the point of an adze
May his hand be steady and may God protect him.

The other inscription that gives the date is in the first person: "I wrote the facts on the door of the mosque so that anyone may read them after a hundred years; I wrote its date on carved stone, it was seven hundred and thirty-three *hijra*." This echoes some from the

---

[21] One such example is a candlestick datable to the second half of the thirteenth century now in the Louvre (inv. no. 7530); see Melikian-Chirvani (1973), 56–58.

[22] At the mosque at Ani a government decree (of Abū Saʿīd) was written in Persian: Khanykov (1852–56), 61–67.

[23] Ivanov (1984), 57–60.

[24] Wilber (1955), cat. no. 85 (it is located some 25 kilometers north of Marand, rather than the 13 kilometers noted by Wilber); Khanykov (1862), 116. Wilber's unconfirmed report, that it had been destroyed between 1942 and 1945, is fortunately untrue; Wilber (1955), 177.

previous centuries in metalwork and textiles and that of the tile worker of the Sirçali Madrasa in Konya.[25]

In Hamadan in western Iran we have a unique building, the so-called Buqʿa-yi Khiḍr, a mausoleum datable to the early fourteenth century with extensive carved stucco kufic inscriptions on the interior (fig. 85).[26] The inscription around the *miḥrāb* is Qur'ānic, but the extensive verses around the interior walls are from the *Shāhnāma*, the only example known in this context outside of the luster tiles that we examined earlier. Appropriately, in this case they are the opening verses in praise of the Creator of the world.

At this point it is worth casting a look backwards to see how the use of Persian and Persian poetry on works of art changed up to the Mongol period, and to examine the factors behind these changes. First of all, if Persian and Arabic are found together on works of art they are so far undifferentiated in terms of script. There are only occasional uses of Persian on monumental epigraphy, particularly in examples from northwest Iran. On metalwork, the start made by a number of Ghurid examples in the late twelfth century mostly fizzled out, only returning in a few vessels related to wine drinking of the early fourteenth century. The only media to this date that used Persian regularly were luster pottery and tiles. The import that the use of Persian carried was therefore clearly not the same for different media. Luster pottery was perhaps less of a luxury ware than metalwork or the finest textiles, and may have been distributed to a wider non-princely clientele to whom Arabic may have been incomprehensible.

A number of features may have contributed to this increased use. We have seen that many luster pottery pieces, and especially tiles, contain verses on unrequited love, which are to be given a Sufi interpretation.[27] This mirrors the newfound importance of Sufism within society, one in which Sufis—far from being the recluses of previous centuries—collaborated with the state authorities, examples being Jalāl al-Dīn Rūmī (d. 1273), who served the Anatolian Seljuk vassals of the Mongols and ʿAlā' al-Dawla Simnānī (d. 1336), who

[25] O'Kane (1979), 345. For earlier craftsmen's signatures, see Ettinghausen (1970), 123–24. See also the first-person Persian inscription on the door of the mosque of ʿAlī at Quhrud: Watson (1975), 69–70.

[26] Mostafavi (1953), 202–03.

[27] Watson (1985), 150–53.

served Arghun Khan. One poet, Ibn Yamīn Faryūmadī (d. 1368), the eulogist of several small Khurasani rulers, even criticizes the excessive spending to embellish *khānqāhs* in one of his works,[28] a state of affairs that is mirrored, for example, by building activity in Yazd, where fourteen *khānqāhs* are known to have been built in the fourteenth century.

The Sufi masters most often expressed themselves through poetry, and not only their own poetry appears on objects but also that of earlier masters such as Firdawsī. It is worth remembering that the founder of the illuminationist school of Sufism, Suhrawardī and his followers, offered mystical glosses on the *Shāhnāma*.[29] This might be one of the reasons for its appearance on luster tiles that were used to adorn the interiors of religious buildings. In a secular context, such as the dadoes of Takht-i Sulayman, such mystical interpretations may not have been out of place, but of course they were also combined with, in the case of their Mongol patrons, a desire to situate themselves within the Persian cultural orbit and to make favorable comparisons with themselves and Iranian heroes of old.

These messages would of course have reached a larger audience by being in the vernacular. This desire to reach a wider public is also paralleled in Ilkhanid historiography, which increasingly used Persian rather than Arabic.[30] A similar shift is visible in the patronage of the arts of the book, which although continuing to make magnificent illuminated Qurʾāns, now started to produce illustrated rivals in the form of either historical texts, such as Rashīd al-Dīn's *Compendium of Histories* or poetical works such as the Great Mongol *Shāhnāma*.

One more social group may have helped tilt the balance towards Persian—the craftsmen. The greater number of craftsmen's signatures known on architecture from this period is also a reflection of their newfound confidence of their importance within society, and what better way to advance this than by advertising their work in the language of most of their customers.[31] The pride in their work shown by the makers of metalwork, textiles, and architecture was in each case expressed in Persian poetry.

---

[28] Potter (1994), 79.
[29] Melikian-Chirvani (1984), 312–31.
[30] Morgan (1982a), 109–24; Meskoob (1992), 87.
[31] Ettinghausen (1970), 119–20.

A number of different factors therefore contributed to the popularity of Persian poetry at this time. Paramount is its significance to Sufism and the patronage of Sufism by the court. The coming into being of a market for non-royal patrons was also of importance, as was the role of the craftsmen in displaying their knowledge of their native language and their pride in their accomplishments. The result was that the display of Persian on works of art moved from being a marginal activity in peripheral areas to, for the first time, the center stage of works of art at the core of the Persian heartlands.

STATE AND RELIGION IN ILKHANID IRAN

HOROSCOPES AND PLANETARY THEORY: ILKHANID PATRONAGE OF ASTRONOMERS

GEORGE SALIBA

One year after the fall of Baghdad to Hülegü Khan and several hundred miles to the north, ground was broken for the construction of an astronomical observatory in the city of Maragha, in modern-day northwest Iran. The fact that the project was authorized by the same Hülegü Khan, and creatively funded by him, has been taken to mean that Hülegü was a believer in astrology. Otherwise, why build an observatory? What I intend to consider here is just how serious was his interest in astrology, and how relevant was the work done in that observatory to the fulfillment of that interest.

Astrology Proper?

Astrology is a term that is rather ambiguous. In ancient and medieval times, it covered a variety of topics, and it is difficult to determine which of those topics would have been of concern to Hülegü (pl. 28). The theoretical foundation of astrology, on the other hand, is rather simple and may be easily summarized as follows. From ancient times, it was observed that the revolutions of celestial bodies such as the sun and the moon had a detectable influence on the changing of the seasons, the movement of tides, the human menstrual cycles and all such phenomena, which very few people would deny. From there it was easy to extrapolate that if the most observable planets like the sun and the moon had such detectable influences, then would not the other planets have similar influences, even if slightly less obvious and more subtle?

The next step in the conception of astrological theory was the perception that the planets were in continuous motion, and that it was the motion itself that seemed to cause the varying observable effects that we see all around us. Most notably, the seasons were obviously a by-product of the various positions of the sun. So whatever planetary influences one needed to investigate, that influence itself had to be related to the temporal positions of the planets in the sky. And to calculate those positions one needed a very sophisticated knowledge of astronomy proper. So, one could argue that the building of an observatory was the first step to determining the necessary planetary positions, which would ultimately lead to astrological investigations.

But the building of an observatory by itself need not always lead to astrological investigations, for one may have other legitimate astronomical and calendrical questions that could be answered by such an enterprise. So which of those concerns was the overriding factor in the establishment of the Maragha observatory? Some background material is in order.

Ilkhanid Interest in Astrology

To start with, the extant historical sources attest to the fact that the Ilkhanid rulers themselves seem to have had a complex and ambivalent interest in astrology. Ambivalent because we do not know of any of the rulers having had a specific technical horoscope cast for him at his time of birth, and yet we know that they sought and nurtured astronomers who could, in principle, cast such horoscopes.

Even their interest in the most important astronomer of the time, the Shiʿite scholar Naṣīr al-Dīn al-Ṭūsī (d. 1274), who later became the director of the Maragha observatory, is itself ambiguous, as it is hard to determine for certain if this interest was driven by Ṭūsī's knowledge of astrology or by his political acumen, as we shall soon see. What we do know is that Ṭūsī was captured at the time of the Mongol invasion of the Ismāʿīlī stronghold of Alamut, and he seems to have immediately become a close companion and advisor to Hülegü Khan.

But we are also told that Hülegü's brother Möngke had a genuine interest in the mathematical sciences, as evidenced by his having solved some of the difficult problems of Euclidean geometry on his own, and thus wanted to have Ṭūsī sent to him once he was captured.[1] The prevailing opinion is that Möngke was interested in having Ṭūsī erect for him an observatory of his own at his capital in Qaraqorum. Furthermore, we are also told that Möngke had already

[1] For the details of this relationship with Ṭūsī, see Sayılı (1960), 189 ff.

attempted to construct such an observatory in Dadu (Beijing), but the project did not come to fruition until the reign of his successor Qubilai (r. 1257–94).

It was this Möngke, then, who was the first to express an interest in Ṭūsī and to have written to Hülegü, and requested Ṭūsī from him after the fall of the Ismāʿīlī stronghold. He may very well have had genuine astronomical interests of his own, as was the case two centuries later with the great Timurid prince and scientist Ulūgh Beg (d. 1449), the grandson of Tīmūr. But the fall of Alamut in 1256 coincided with Möngke's preoccupation with other conquests further east, and his death almost immediately thereafter, in 1257, left the matter of Ṭūsī's fate completely undecided.

What seems to have happened then was that Hülegü found himself with an astronomer at hand who was no longer needed by his brother Möngke. At that point the sources become ambiguous again as to who suggested to whom that Ṭūsī should be commissioned to build another observatory, but this time in the city of Maragha, under Hülegü's jurisdiction. The standard accounts speak of Hülegü taking a liking to Ṭūsī and granting him enough revenues to build his observatory, while others speak of Ṭūsī approaching Hülegü with the subject first.[2] Determining who asked whom first does have some bearing as to who the interested party was in the project, and may shed light on the actual purposes for which the project was proposed in the first place. If Hülegü had a genuine interest in astrology, it would then stand to reason that he himself would encourage the most eminent astronomer of the day to build such an observatory. If not, then it must have been Ṭūsī who convinced Hülegü of the plan in order to secure his own position.

Since the sources do not speak of Hülegü as having had any scientific interests similar to those of his brother, one may assume that the idea of an observatory was forced upon him by the circumstances and not by any genuine scientific or astrological concern of his own. But it may be assured, too, that he would not be adverse to having in his retinue a prominent astronomer who was well-equipped to cast a horoscope every now and then should the need arise.

There is yet a third dimension to the relationship between Ṭūsī and Hülegü that should concern us at this point. While detailing the fall

[2] Sayılı (1960), 190–91.

of Baghdad to the Mongols, Ayyubid and Mamluk sources spoke of the intrigues that went on before the fateful date of 1258. Someone like Ibn Aybak al-Ṣafadī (1296–1363),[3] the notable historian and man of letters who occupied various official posts in the first part of the fourteenth century in almost every city between Cairo and Aleppo that did not fall to the Mongols, had an interesting account of the conquest of Baghdad. In particular, and in his biography of the last Abbasid vizier Ibn al-ʿAlqamī (d. 1259), he says that that vizier was himself an undeclared fanatic Shiʿite (*rāfiḍī*, to use his language) who was at odds with the equally fanatic Sunni Dawādār at the court of the last Abbasid caliph al-Mustaʿṣim (d. 1258). The caliph's son took the side of the Dawādār, which left Ibn al-ʿAlqamī in a precariously vulnerable position. That led Ibn al-ʿAlqamī to correspond with the Mongols and to encourage them to attack Baghdad.

Therefore the Shiʿite connection between Ṭūsī and Ibn al-ʿAlqamī may have been a deciding factor in Hülegü's favoring Ṭūsī, and for his retaining him as a personal advisor (or even a vizier, but with no authority over endowment money at first, as we are told by Ṣafadī). This relationship may have also played a decisive role in Hülegü's acceptance of the advice of Ṭūsī when the latter spoke definitively against the judgment of the astrologers who had warned Hülegü against the sacking of Baghdad. It was Ṭūsī who assured Hülegü that the attack would bring him no personal harm. Of course the invaluable help of the insider Ibn al-ʿAlqamī ensured that nothing would go wrong.[4]

Now, the ultimate success of the attack on Baghdad obviously called for a reward for Ṭūsī and the utter derision and humiliation for Ibn al-ʿAlqamī, as all collaborators throughout history are prone to receive. What better reward to bestow upon Ṭūsī than to allow him to save from destruction of the Abbasid capital all the books that he needed for his pet project, namely, the observatory that every astronomer dreamed of having?[5]

This version of the story suggests at once the motivation for the construction of the Maragha observatory, the mundane pragmatic

[3] Ṣafadī (1981), vol. 1, 179–189.

[4] Ibid., 184 ff.

[5] Ibid., 179 says that the number of books was four hundred thousand and that they were mostly stolen from Baghdad, *Shām* (Syria), and the Jazira (upper Mesopotamia).

interests of the Mongol patron in conquest and acquisition of further wealth and authority, and at the same time relegates astrological concerns to an afterthought. Had Ṭūsī not been involved directly in the conquest of Baghdad by having countered the original pessimistic prognostications of the astrologers,[6] it is unlikely that Ṭūsī would have been granted his observatory.

But with Ṭūsī in a favored position and having all the expenses for the project, whether in books or in salaries and instruments taken from the religious endowments that were just conquered, much to the chagrin of the religious legal scholars as reported by Ṣafadī, Hülegü was in a win/win situation.[7] In other words, Hülegü incurred no expenses whatsoever from his own treasures for this project, and by giving Ṭūsī his pet project assured him of his loyal service.

To further confirm this interpretation, that is, Hülegü's purely pragmatic interest in Ṭūsī himself rather than his astrology, we are told of an early encounter between the two in which Hülegü asked Ṭūsī, point-blank, about the utility of astrology since its pronouncements were inevitable in any event. To which Ṭūsī could only give the standard response that had already been given by Ptolemy a millennium earlier, saying that it was better to be warned about forthcoming events even if one could not avert them.[8]

What emerges from these accounts is that Hülegü seems to have been a reluctant patron, willing to support Ṭūsī but at no real cost to himself. And like the shrewd scientist he was, Ṭūsī seems to have taken advantage of the situation. With his fantastic salesmanship he must have convinced Hülegü that he needed enough funds to operate the observatory for a period of thirty years, the approximate time it takes the slowest planet, Saturn, to go once around the sun. He must have argued that he needed to observe all the planets at various points in their revolution, even the slowest of them, in order to update their positions and produce new tables that would be required for any serious casting of any horoscope. No such horoscope was ever recorded for Hülegü, and the vague statement preserved in Ṣafadī that Hülegü would not do anything without consulting with

[6] Ibid., 192.

[7] Ibid., 179 ff.

[8] This account is also preserved in Ṣafadī (1981), 179.

Ṭūsī may have more to do with Ṭūsī's political and administrative advice rather than his astrological predictions.[9]

In fact, the same Ṣafadī tells us that when Ṭūsī explained to Hülegü why he needed thirty years to finish the observations, Hülegü promptly replied by saying: "try to finish in twelve." Ṭūsī is supposed to have only said that he would indeed try to do so.[10] These exchanges do not strike me as the conversations one would have with someone who really believed that his life depended on the results obtainable from astrology.

The only time Hülegü was subjected to Ṭūsī's astrological chicanery was the instance when Hülegü had ordered the death of his erstwhile confidant and chief of staff (chief of the *dīwān*) ʿAlāʾ al-Dīn al-Juwaynī (1226–83). Juwaynī's brother appealed to Ṭūsī for help. It was then that Ṭūsī sought audience with Hülegü in the middle of the night, accompanied by someone carrying incense, himself carrying a staff, an astrolabe, and the whole astrological paraphernalia.[11] He went through all the standard motions of lifting the astrolabe towards the sky, lowering it, murmuring this or that, and demanded to see Hülegü. When he was brought to him, he told the startled Hülegü that he had calculated a horoscope for him and found out that he was undergoing a critical moment (*qaṭʿ*) that could only be avoided if he were to set free all the prisoners in his domain. Hülegü went along with the request and allowed Juwaynī to go free. The trick apparently worked as all the sources seem to gloat while reporting it.[12] In reality, Hülegü may have indeed welcomed any intervention to rescue a friend, a confidant, and a loyal servant whom he had probably condemned to death in a moment of anger.

The position of astrology in Hülegü's mind was probably very simple. He would go along with the astrologers when their judgment suited his political purposes, and would not hesitate to dismiss their advice, as he did with the sacking of Baghdad, when he could find a counteropinion. The impression one gets is that astrological predictions were to be consulted but not necessarily followed, and would certainly be obeyed if they could rescue a friend.

[9] Ibid., 182.
[10] Ibid., vol. 1, 183.
[11] Sayılı (1960), 202–3.
[12] See the sources cited in ibid., 202–3.

When asked to supply funds for the building of an observatory, Hülegü seemed to have gone along as well. In his mind he had probably computed that it would not cost him anything. Besides, it was a good ornament for his court, and seemed to fit with images of other courts of the day. But throughout, he was never seen to have adamantly demanded astrological predictions. At one point he even entertained dispensing with Ṭūsī altogether when he was tired of humoring him.

In a rare human instance, he is reported by Khondmir[13] to have threatened Ṭūsī by telling him that he would have had him killed had he not needed the time to complete his observations. And in that apparently joking environment Ṭūsī's most notable colleague and student, Quṭb al-Dīn al-Shīrāzī (d. 1311), who was also present, chimed in by saying that he would complete the observations should his master Ṭūsī be dispensed with. In the lightness of the atmosphere the remark was not taken seriously; Ṭūsī was never really threatened, but Shīrāzī was chastised by Ṭūsī for butting in with his poor joke at that time. To add insult to injury the brash Shīrāzī interjected that he was not joking, and that he was in earnest about his ability to continue the work. In any event, the whole episode seems to reflect a lighthearted and joking atmosphere among friends rather than an ominous need to have the royal astrologer around at all times.

Incidentally, Shīrāzī's joke had serious repercussions. Of all the astronomers that were mentioned in the introduction of the *Zīj-i Ilkhānī*, the nominal *chef d'oeuvre* of the Maragha observatory, the name of Shīrāzī is noticeably missing. And when one of Ṭūsī's sons asked Shīrāzī to complete the *zīj* after Ṭūsī's death, Shīrāzī supposedly refused to do so, on account of that omission.[14]

In the end, even when Ṭūsī had his observatory, and despite his desire to have a new set of astronomical tables based on fresh observations lasting for thirty years, fate caught up with him and he died in 1274 without completing the project. Like all projects undertaken by a group rather than an individual, the end results tend to suffer once the principal investigator was no longer present. Thus the observational legacy of the Maragha observatory, as enshrined in the *Zīj-i Ilkhānī*, seems to have missed the mark.

---

[13] Quoted in ibid., 206–7; name so spelled, ibid., 435.
[14] Ibid., 214–15.

As a result, the only astronomical tables that were indeed based on fresh observations that were conducted in the Maragha observatory and could have been used for fresh astrological computations were those that were apparently produced single-handedly by Yaḥyā b. Abī al-Shukr al-Maghribī (d. 1283).[15] This Maghribī was one of the astronomers who had worked as an astrologer in Damascus and was saved when he fell prisoner to the Mongols at a battle in that city and screamed: "astrologer, astrologer." He was then spared from death and was sent to join Ṭūsī's team in Maragha. This is as much as one can document by way of Hülegü's actual reliance on, and interest in, astrology.

As for Hülegü's son Abaqa, we are told that he was reluctant at first to assume his father's mantle after the latter's death in 1265.[16] Who wouldn't be? Abaqa changed his mind only when Ṭūsī cast a horoscope and determined the most propitious moment for him to ascend the throne.[17] But who is to say whether or not Abaqa only pretended to believe in astrological predictions since the prognostication suited his purposes? Was it not better to have it said that he was destined by the stars to become the next potentate rather than to have him fight his brothers for the throne? No doubt any modern-day politician would gladly 'believe' in astrology if the end result meant getting elected.

The net result is that after all the attention and expenditure that were devoted to Ṭūsī's pet project at Maragha, the final output, as we have just noted, does not seem to support an urgent belief in the need for new observational material in order to produce astrological predictions. So what was the extent of the Ilkhanid belief in astrology that would have motivated their patronage of the Maragha observatory? Not much belief, if any, but nice to have.

Bait and Switch and the Building of the Maragha Observatory

So why was this observatory built if it only meant having Ṭūsī raise all the resources he needed for a royal observatory—complete with

[15] Saliba (1994a), 163–86.
[16] Sayılı (1960), 203.
[17] Ibid., 203.

a first rate engineer and astronomer like Mu'ayyad al-Dīn al-ʿUrḍī (d. 1266),[18] a group of the best astronomers as assistants, a library of four hundred thousand books that had been confiscated by Ṭūsī before the sacking of Baghdad (in stark contrast to the more recent sacking of Baghdad where the books were put to the torch), and endowment funds for about twenty years devoted to the project—only to achieve the paltry production of astronomical tables? As was just said, the only set of astronomical tables produced at that institution, based on observations conducted there between the years 1262 and 1274, was that of Maghribī. That in itself is no mean activity, and any astronomer would have been proud to produce such a result as efficiently as was fashioned by Maghribī. But Maghribī is scarcely known, and his tables lingered in total obscurity until two decades ago when I managed to reassess this astronomer's work and discovered, by sheer accident, that he was indeed the accomplished Maragha astronomer whose name appeared a few times in the medieval sources.[19] But was that the Ilkhanid's expected result?

Quṭb al-Dīn al- Shīrāzī, on the other hand, did not even produce any tables that we know of, and as we have already seen, even refused to complete the tables of his master Ṭūsī. Ṭūsī himself produced his groundbreaking work, *al-Tadhkira fī ʿilm al-hay'a*, while the observatory was still under construction, and this text was based on research that he had completed before he even came to Maragha.[20] Besides, *al-Tadhkira* had nothing to do with astronomical tables or astrological predictions.

Similarly, the famous engineer and astronomer Mu'ayyad al-Dīn al-ʿUrḍī, who was specially recruited by Ṭūsī to build the observatory, produced no tables of his own, either. And in an earlier work, which he too wrote before he came to Maragha, he bemoaned the fact that he had no fresh observations to challenge the Greek astronomical tradition that he was criticizing, although he did nothing of the sort when he was at Maragha.[21] ʿUrḍī may be excused, for he died in

[18] This ʿUrḍī has left us a treatise about the instruments that he had built especially for the Maragha observatory; see Jourdain (1809), vol. 4.

[19] See sources cited in Sayılı (1960), 214.

[20] This work of Ṭūsī is now edited with a translation and commentary by J. Ragep; Ṭūsī (1993).

[21] Saliba (2001), 219, where ʿUrḍī expressly states that he did not have observations for his new astronomy.

1266, some five years after the observatory went into production, and apparently barely had enough time to produce a treatise describing the instruments he built there.[22] So what were these astronomers doing if they were not busy producing tools for astrological predictions? Why were the Ilkhanids 'supporting' these activities?

As far as the Ilkhanids were concerned, and here we are talking about Hülegü and his son Abaqa who were directly involved with the Maragha observatory, such support did not come from the royal treasury *per se*. Instead it came from a quasi-official source, namely, the revenues from the religious endowments that the royal house was clever enough not to use for its own purposes. In fact all the blame that the later sources heap upon Ṭūsī are only half motivated by his participation in the destruction of the Abbasid Caliphate; the other half was for his appropriation of the revenues of the religious endowments, or at least one tenth of them, for the purposes of the observatory.[23] Up to that time the Ilkhanids were still promoting Buddhism, flirting with Christianity, and supporting Shiʿites like Ṭūsī against their predominantly Sunni subjects, and did not care much about the fate of religious endowments.

On the part of the astronomers, the real bait-and-switch game seems to have been played by Ṭūsī himself and his willing accomplices were his friends and students. As we have just stated, both Ṭūsī and ʿUrḍī had either completed their theoretical astronomical work, as in the case of ʿUrḍī, or had done all the preliminary research for it as was done by Ṭūsī, before they had ever set foot in Maragha. Furthermore, the kind of work they had accomplished was pure theoretical astronomy, having nothing to do with astrological predictions, and was obviously directed at highly esoteric issues having to do with cosmology and philosophy. Had Ṭūsī told Hülegü that he required funds to establish an astronomical research institute, for that is what he actually ended up doing, in order to investigate cosmological problems relating to the very foundations of astronomical planetary theories, Hülegü would have indeed ordered his head cut off. What Ṭūsī seems to have done instead was to sell Hülegü the benign dream of better astrological horoscopes—a project that was entertaining, acceptable at a political court such as that of Hülegü,

[22] See Jourdain (1809).
[23] Ṣafadī (1981), vol. 1, 182.

and somehow useful as in the case of Abaqa when it added some luster to his claim to the throne.

In reality, what astronomers like Ṭūsī, ʿUrḍī, and Shīrāzī wanted to do was to pursue their critique of Greek astronomy. And that critique had already begun to yield fruit just prior to the building of the observatory, as is already obvious in the earlier works of ʿUrḍī and Ṭūsī. Once the observatory was built, they could continue with their theoretical work, and on the side carry out some observations as was done by Maghribī.

Shīrāzī, on the other hand, seems to have combined the results already achieved by Ṭūsī and ʿUrḍī and to venture into new areas of his own. He wrote two commentaries on Ṭūsī's work that was just mentioned, one around the year 1272 when Ṭūsī was still alive, and another after his death in 1283. In both instances the commentaries were indeed voluminous and amounted to more than 250 folios of densely written mathematical astronomy. Unlike other commentaries, Shīrāzī's presented not only a synthesis of the results already achieved by Ṭūsī and ʿUrḍī, and evaluative statements as to which of the two options proposed by those earlier astronomers came closer to what Shīrāzī saw as the truth, but also included some of his own novel ideas.[24] His attempt to solve the problem of the motions of the planet Mercury, for example, not only surpassed the solution that was proposed by ʿUrḍī before him, but also completed this entirely missing section in Ṭūsī's *al-Tadhkira*. Indeed, Mercury was the one planet that Ṭūsī could not solve and he admitted as much in his critique of the Greek version of its theory. Mercury was such a challenge that Shīrāzī felt he had to respond. And respond he did. In his later commentary, he even managed to propose some nine solutions for the motion of this planet: eight of them were admittedly imperfect, while only one proved valid. He claimed that he had demonstrated the faults of seven of them and left it to the brightest students to tell which of the last two was valid.[25]

It was this kind of highly significant research that animated those who were engaged with the Maragha observatory. The results they obtained had a lasting effect on the astronomical output of future generations, up until the European Renaissance when those earlier

[24] See Kennedy (1966), esp. 373 ff. for the original work of Shīrāzī.
[25] Saliba (1997), esp. 115 and 120.

works were appropriated by such distinguished founders of modern science as Copernicus (d. 1543) and Kepler (d. 1630).

More important, this type of research also became the new benchmark to which later astronomers strove to add their own initiatives. People like Ibn al-Shāṭir of Damascus (d. 1375), who is usually included among the Maragha astronomers although he lived a century later and never set foot in Maragha, were to carry this research even further, producing their own impact on later astronomers.[26] Ibn al-Shāṭir's lunar model turned out to be identical to that of Copernicus. And so was his technique for the solution of the motions of the planet Mercury when compared to that of Copernicus.

In the Islamic sphere, later astronomers who pursued this research in planetary theories like Qushjī (d. 1474) and Khafrī (d. 1550) are just beginning to be appreciated, and their work is beginning to be coherently related to the achievements that were set in full motion by this group of brilliant astronomers who managed to assemble in Maragha.[27]

Conclusion

Returning to Maragha and to the Ilkhanid patronage of that observatory, one might say that the Ilkhanids seem to have unwittingly patronized what could be justly called the first astronomical research institute in medieval Islam. But they certainly never knew how far their patronage had taken the astronomers, and that their institution would one day go far beyond the prescribed purposes for which it was first established.

---

[26] See the edition of the theoretical work of this astronomer, *Nihāyāt al-Sūl*, by the present author (Ibn al-Shāṭir [forthcoming]). For other descriptions of his work, see Kennedy and Ghanem (1976) and Saliba (1987), reprinted in Saliba (1994a), 233–41.

[27] See Saliba (1993); Saliba (1994b); Saliba (1997); Saliba (2000).

REFLECTIONS ON A 'DOUBLE RAPPROCHEMENT': CONVERSION TO ISLAM AMONG THE MONGOL ELITE DURING THE EARLY ILKHANATE

JUDITH PFEIFFER

Introductory Remarks

The study of conversion to Islam among the Mongols has recently received a strong impetus through Devin DeWeese's seminal work on Baba Tükles and the Islamization of the Golden Horde.[1] For the Ilkhanate, Charles Melville,[2] Reuven Amitai,[3] and Cüneyt Kanat[4] have devoted articles to the Ilkhans Ghazan Khan's and Aḥmad Tegüder's conversions to Islam, and earlier scholarship, undertaken by Muṣṭafā Ṭāhā Badr in the 1950s[5] and Fu'ād 'Abd al-Mu'ṭī al-Ṣayyād[6] and Muḥammad Aḥmad Muḥammad[7] in the 1970s and 1980s focused on these Ilkhans' conversions as well. Nonetheless, research on conversion to Islam among the Mongols of the Ilkhanate is still in its infancy. It is in this sense that the following thoughts are presented here, namely as a starting point, rather than a conclusive answer to a complex issue.

When talking about conversion to Islam in the Ilkhanate we normally think of Ghazan Khan, his vizier Rashīd al-Dīn, and the reforms implemented under their patronage. That there were earlier converts on the lower echelons of Mongol society is well known, and DeWeese's contribution to this volume provides further insightful examples. In this paper, I will focus on conversion to Islam among the Mongol elite in the *early* Ilkhanate, a period which for the purposes of this paper shall be defined as the four decades between the

[1] DeWeese (1994).
[2] Melville (1990b), 159–77.
[3] Amitai-Preiss (1996a), 1–10; idem (1999), 27–46; Amitai (2001), 15–43. On the Ilkhan Öljeitü's conversion to Shī'ī Islam, see Pfeiffer (1999), 35–67.
[4] Kanat (2002), 233–47. See also Pfeiffer (2003).
[5] Badr (1950).
[6] al-Ṣayyād (1979); see also idem (1987).
[7] Muḥammad (1989).

Mongol conquest of Baghdad in 656/1258 and Ghazan Khan's conversion to Islam in 694/1295.

Among the historical works of the period, Rashīd al-Dīn's (d. 718/1318) *Jāmiʿ al-tawārīkh* has become the dominant source of knowledge on the Ilkhanate in twentieth-century European and North American scholarship. Rashīd al-Dīn's bias in favor of his patrons Ghazan Khan and Öljeitü, and the line of Hülegü-Abaqa-Arghun-Ghazan Khan, is well known.[8] For converts prior to Ghazan Khan this means that their conversions are not particularly stressed or fleshed out by Rashīd al-Dīn—thus, information on the Islamic reforms of the earlier convert Ilkhan Aḥmad Tegüder is not provided by Rashīd al-Dīn, but has to be culled from Waṣṣāf (fl. 728/1328),[9] such lesser and as yet unpublished sources as Juwaynī's (d. 681/1283) *(Dhayl) Tasliyat al-ikhwān*,[10] and contemporary Mamluk and Christian sources.[11] With these reflections in mind, let us turn to those conversions that occurred prior to Ghazan Khan's.

There are several dimensions to the phenomenon in question. These include, but are not restricted to, conversion to Islam among the Mongol *amīrs* prior to the Ilkhans' conversions; conversion to Islam among the Chinggisid elite; marriage politics and conversion in the Ilkhanate; and the role of Sufis in Ilkhanid conversions. In the following discussion, I shall give a quick overview of the first aspect, and go into some detail with regard to the fourth, namely the role of Sufis in Ilkhanid conversions.[12]

Conversion to Islam among the Mongol elite in the Ilkhanate seems to have been a long process, extending over several generations. While the Muslim *shahāda* is found on all of the first Ilkhan Hülegü's (and before him on some of Genghis [Chinggis] Khan's

---

[8] See, e.g., Aubin (1995), 23. There exist several editions and also translations into various European languages of Rashīd al-Dīn's *Jāmiʿ al-tawārīkh*. In the following, I shall quote after the recent edition by Rawshan and Mūsawī, Rashīd al-Dīn (1994), and the translation by Thackston, Rashīd al-Dīn (1998).

[9] Waṣṣāf (1853) 110; 113–15 (page citations are to the 1959–60 reprint edition); idem (1856), 219, 231–35, trans. 205; 215–18. On Waṣṣāf, see Pfeiffer (in press).

[10] *(Dhayl) Tasliyat al-ikhwān*, Paris, Bibliothèque Nationale, ms. Supplément Persan 206, fols. 1b–41b, here fol. 33a.

[11] al-Yūnīnī (1954), vol. 4, 141.

[12] For a more detailed discussion of the second and third issues listed above, see Pfeiffer (2003), chap. 2.

and Möngke Khan's) coins,[13] there is no doubt that Hülegü never converted to Islam, and his son Abaqa, his grandson Arghun, and even his great-grandson and later convert to Islam Ghazan Khan were all Buddhists for part, if not all of their lives.[14] The inscriptions on Ilkhanid coins are a good example of the way in which the Mongol elite of the Ilkhanate appropriated the existing, predominantly Muslim, discourse, and integrated it into their own worldview. Whereas Abbasid gold *dīnārs* had borne the message "With God is the Command in the Past and in the Future,"[15] the new message on the *dīnārs* minted under Hülegü immediately after the conquest of Baghdad reads:

> Say: "Oh God! Lord of Sovereignty! You give sovereignty to whom You please, and You withdraw sovereignty from whom You please: You exalt whom You wish, and You abase whom You wish."[16]

This inscription is likewise Qur'ānic. While using the Arabic script and language, and even the religious discourse prevalent in the area, the Qur'ānic quotation expresses the message of divinely sanctioned Mongol world domination, which is well known from other documents of the time.[17] As Thomas Allsen puts it,

> We are accustomed to thinking about Chinese, Tibetan, or Muslim influence among the nomads. Such formulas have validity of course but leave a misleading impression; placed in such a framework the nomads appear as passive recipients, overcome by wily, culturally more sophisticated neighbors and rivals. To my mind, it is more helpful to think in terms of the nomads' active and selective appropriation of sedentary culture, material and spiritual.[18]

This is what 'conversion to Islam' most probably meant in most

---

[13] For numismatic evidence, see al-Bakrī (1966), 95–106, especially 98–99; and, in general, Aykut and Pamuk (1992).

[14] On Buddhist practices among the early Ilkhans, see Rashīd al-Dīn, *Jāmiʿ al-taṣānīf-i Rashīdī*, Paris, Bibliothèque Nationale, ms. arabe 2324, fols. 200a–206b, here 203a. For former Buddhist structures (mainly caves) from the Ilkhanid period that were converted into Islamic complexes probably under Ghazan Khan, see Ball (1976), 103–63; and idem (1979), 329–40.

[15] *li'llāhi al-amru min qablu wa min baʿd*: Qur'ān 30:4 (al-Rūm).

[16] *quli 'llāhumma mālika al-mulki tu'tī al-mulka man tashā'u wa tanziʿu al-mulka mimman tashā'u wa tuʿizzu man tashā'u wa tudhillu man tashā'*: Qur'ān 3:26 (Āl-i 'Imrān). See al-Bakrī (1966), 95–106, especially 98–99.

[17] On this concept, see Voegelin (1940–41), 378–413.

[18] Allsen (2002b), 28.

cases: the selective appropriation of elements that were felt to be enriching, with the possible exclusion of others (such as, potentially, the performing of ablutions under running water) that were not approved of from a Mongol point of view or sanctioned by Mongol customs.[19] More than that, as some of the reforms implemented by the Muslim converts among the Ilkhans, the Ilkhans Aḥmad Tegüder (r. 1282–84), Ghazan Khan (r. 1295–1304), and Öljeitü (r. 1304–16) demonstrate, the Mongols used religious—including local religious—discourse to solve social and political issues *internal* to Mongol society.

Conversion to Islam among the Mongol Amīrs

Muslim historiographical literature generally has paid less attention to those classes that do not rule or write; while sultans, theologians, and poets (to name a few) are relatively well represented by composers of chronicles and biographical dictionaries, members of the military elites—like the peasantry and individual, non-writing, wandering dervishes of this period—have seldom found audiences that would commemorate their existence.

Information on conversion to Islam among the lower echelons of the Mongol society is rather terse, though some information is available on Mongol *amīrs*. Thus, the Qonqirat *amīr* Mūsā Küregen, a maternal grandson of Genghis Khan, obviously underwent a conversion experience, if only by accepting a new name; Rashīd al-Dīn states that one of Hülegü Khan's daughters, Ṭaraqay,

> was given [i.e., married] to Mūsā Küregen from the Qonqirat tribe, Genghis Khan's grandson through his daughter [Tümelün].[20] His name had been Toghā Tīmūr. A learned man (*dānishmandī*) who was his tutor (*adīb-i ū*) gave him the name Mūsā. He was Martay Khātūn's brother.[21]

[19] For the Mongols' concern to keep the water clean, and how Genghis Khan's son Chaghadai saved a Muslim, who was performing his ablutions in a lake, from his brother Ögödei's wrath, see Jūzjānī (1881), vol. 2, 1108–9.

[20] There is a blank in all of the manuscripts used by Rawshan/Mūsawī, Rashīd al-Dīn (1994), vol. 3, 1858; Thackston, Rashīd al-Dīn (1998), vol. 2, 476 suggests that this woman was Genghis Khan's daughter Tümelün.

[21] Rashīd al-Dīn (1994), vol. 2, 971; Rashīd al-Dīn (1998), vol. 2, 476.

The unidentified "learned man" should be Mūsā Küregen's 'converter,' but as this example shows, the information is extremely concise. Other examples of early converts among the Turco-Mongol elite of the Ilkhanate known by name are the formerly Buddhist governor of Eastern Iran during Ögödei Qa'ān's reign (r. 1229–41), the Uighur Körgüz, who died c. 640/1242–43, and converted to Islam toward the end of his life;[22] and the Mongol general Bayju, governor of Anatolia who, according to the Mamluk chronicler al-Nuwayrī, asked to be washed and buried according to the Muslim customs in the late 1250s.[23] Another example of an early convert is a certain Shaykh 'Alī. The ninth/fifteenth-century Mamluk historian al-Maqrīzī reported that in the year 681/1282, Shaykh 'Alī, a Muslim convert from the (Mongol) Oirat tribe, had arrived in Egypt, where he produced a number of miracles.[24]

Richard Bulliet and John E. Woods have used onomastic shifts in establishing conversion patterns of larger populations, where a Muslim name is the sole indicator that a conversion may have taken place.[25] Applied to the Ilkhanate, and based on Rashīd al-Dīn's

[22] Juwaynī's notice contains a 'conversion narrative' in a gist, but is extremely concise and in this typical for the laconic description of conversions among the echelons of the Mongol elite below the *khān*: "Towards the end of his life, [Körgüz] had become a Muslim and had abandoned the religion of idolatry." This is rather little in the biography of one of the foremost governors in the western Mongolian Empire, to whom Juwaynī devoted an entire chapter of his *Ta'rīkh-i jahān-gushāy* (1997), 505. See also D'Ohsson (1834), vol. 3, 121; Arnold (1913), 230.

[23] Bayju "was said to have converted to Islam before his death, and when death approached him, he decreed that he should be washed and buried according to the custom of the Muslims" ("*wa qīla innahu kāna qad aslama qabla mawtihi, wa lammā ḥaḍarathu al-wafāt awṣā bi-an yughsala wa yudfana 'alā 'ādat al-Muslimīn*"); al-Nuwayrī (1964), vol. 27, 384. According to Peter Jackson, Western sources (related to the exchange of envoys between St. Louis and Eljigidei) report that Bayju "was a pagan and was surrounded by Muslim advisors." Jackson (1989), 1a–2b, here 1b; Jackson's source is d'Achery (1723), vol. 3, 627.

[24] al-Maqrīzī (1845), vol. 2/1, 53.

[25] See Bulliet (1979), and Woods (1990), esp. 10–12. Note that Woods, 10, distinguishes between various subgroups of Muslim names in the Timurid context, such as "Turko-Mongol (e.g., Möngke), Turko-Iranian (e.g., Ṭaghāy Shāh), Iranian (e.g., Rustam), Turko-Arabic (e.g., Allāhbirdī), Irano-Arabic (e.g., Muḥammad Darwīsh) and Arabic (e.g., 'Abd Allāh)." Since in the context of this investigation the absolute numbers of converts among the Mongol elite are too low to allow for further conclusions (Woods worked with hundreds of names, here we are dealing with a few dozen), such a diversified distinction among Muslim names has not been attempted.

genealogical work *Shuʿab-i panjgāna*, this method has yielded the following results: starting with Hülegü's reign, the percentage of *amīrs* with Perso-Muslim names[26] increases under the Ilkhans as time proceeds, though Baidu is missing due to the author's specific bias, and Ghazan Khan's reign is badly represented, as the manuscript breaks off abruptly in the middle of the list of *amīrs*:[27]

Table 1. Mongol *amīrs* in the Ilkhanate with Perso-Muslim names according to the *Shuʿab-i panjgāna*

Ilkhan	absolute number of *amīrs*	absolute number of *amīrs* with Perso-Muslim names	percentage of *amīrs* with Perso-Muslim names	generation
Hülegü (d. 1265)	74	5	6.8 %	I.
Abaqa (r. 1265-81)	67	7	10.4 %	II.
Aḥmad Tegüder (r. 1282–84)	26	3	11.5 %	II.
Arghun (r. 1284–91)	69	9	13.0 %	III.
Geikhatu (r. 1291–94)	46	14	30.4 %	III.
Ghazan Khan (r. 1295–1303)	19	4	21.0 %	IV.

Worthy of note is the particularly steep rise to over 30 percent of Muslim names among the (non-Muslim) Ilkhan Geikhatu's *amīrs*, an issue that will be followed up below.

The implied adoption of Islam among the Mongol elite during the third generation after Hülegü is confirmed by outside sources. The Indian historians Iṣāmī (fl. 1350)[28] and Baranī (fl. 1284–1356)[29] report the arrival of Muslim converts from among the Mongol elite of the Ilkhanate in northern India "since the reign of Sultan Ghiyāth al-Dīn

[26] These are 'Zangī,' 'Khalīfa,' 'Sayf al-Dīn Bitikchī,' 'Mūsā Gūrgān [Küregen],' and 'Nawrūz.' These are five out of seventy-four listed *amīrs*. *Shuʿab-i panjgāna*, Istanbul, Topkapı Sarayı Müzesi Kütüphanesi, ms. Ahmet III, 2937, under Hülegü Khan.

[27] The following numbers are based on the *Shuʿab-i panjgāna*, Istanbul, Topkapı Sarayı Müzesi Kütüphanesi, ms. Ahmet III, 2937.

[28] Iṣāmī (1948), 187–88, 254, 298 (cited in Siddiqui [1993], 51–63, here 57, n. 7).

[29] Baranī (1862–64), 133, where the Mongols in Sultan Muʿizz al-Dīn Qayqubād's (r. 684–89/1286–90) retinue, who had reached the Delhi Sultanate during the reign of his predecessor Balbān, are described as '*naw-musalmān*,' 'recent [convert] Muslims.' See also Siddiqui (1993), 51–63, here 57, n. 7.

Balbān (1266–87)."[30] Thus, potentially as early as the 660/1260s, significant numbers of Muslim converts among the (possibly non-Hülegüid) Mongol troops were found in the territories of the Ilkhanate. All in all, we learn about single converts among the *amīrs* long before the conversion of the first Hülegüid convert, Aḥmad Tegüder (1282–84), and potentially even before the arrival of the founder of the Ilkhanid dispensation in the area, Hülegü, in 1256.

Evidence from contemporary documents points in the same direction. Some of the signatures on one of the few original documents extant from this time provide good examples for the close interactions between the local and Mongol elites. Nūr al-Dīn [b.] Jājā's endowment deed (*waqfiyya*) of Kırşehir from 1272 attests to this,[31] as the document was recorded in a bilingual Mongol/Arabic form, and signed (among others) by Mongol dignitaries.[32] In the Mongolian version of this document, several dozens of Mongol *noyans* pledge not to intervene with the *waqf* under the threat of being "hit by the punishment of the Eternal God."[33] While it is not clear whether and how many of the Mongols who signed the document were Muslims at that time, the fact that they testified that they would abide by the rules of this document shows at least that a very close interaction and mutual respect existed between the Muslim *waqf* founder and the Mongol *amīrs* in the region.[34]

Anatolia seems to have been a place where the Islamization of the Mongols attached to the Ilkhanate may have taken place earlier than elsewhere. A great number (four *tümen*, i.e., forty thousand men) of Mongols were stationed there one to two generations before the arrival of Hülegü and his troops,[35] and fifteenth-century hagiographic narratives relating Hülegü's (!) conversion to Islam as the 'condition'

---

[30] See Siddiqui (1993), 51–63, here 57.

[31] On the probably Turkmen Nūr al-Dīn [b.] Jājā (Caca Oğlu), see, e.g., Āqsarā'ī (1944), 75; Jalālī, ed. (1999), 101; Bar Hebraeus (1932), vol. 1, 509 (page citation is to the 1976 reprint edition).

[32] Temir, ed. (1959), 80, 162–65; also 178.

[33] The modern Turkish translation reads "*ebedî tanrısının cezasına çarpılsınlar.*" See Temir (1959), 162.

[34] According to Bar Hebraeus (1932), vol. 1, 443, at least one of the individuals listed among the Mongol *noyans* who signed the deed, Samdaghu Noyan, was Christian (page citation is to the 1976 reprint edition). He described him as "Samdâghû, a Christian Mongol, a splendid young man."

[35] See Sümer (1969), 1–147.

(*sharṭ*) under which the Sufi saint Hacı Bektaş permitted the Mongols to enter Anatolia ("*al-Rūm*") may be distant repercussions of this.[36]

The Role of Sufis in Ilkhanid Conversions

We have seen above the remarkably steep increase of Muslim names among Mongol *amīr*s under Geikhatu Khan. While he himself is not known to have been a Muslim,[37] two of his wives (ʿĀʾisha and Pādishāh Khātūn) certainly were.[38] One of the few, and among the earliest of the original documents from the Ilkhanid period that have come down to us stems from Geikhatu Khan's reign (r. 690–94/1291–

[36] Firdevsî-i Rûmî (1986), 145–51. We know from the versified version of Hacı Bektaş's *Vilāyetnāme* that 'Tatars' were settled in the region of Kırşehir, the founder of the Bektaşi order's place of refuge during the uprising of Baba Isḥāq against the Seljuq overlords, shortly before the Mongol's decisive victory over Seljuq forces at Kösedağ in 1243. According to legend, Hacı Bektaş established himself in Kırşehir. Kırşehir, which from the fifteenth century onward became an important center of Bektaşi activities, competing to a certain extent with what became later seen as 'mainstream' religious movements of Anatolia, such as the Mevleviyye in Konya, became the place where a major Mongol camp settled during the second half of the thirteenth century. The possible remains of an observatory from the same period likewise suggest Mongol activities there; Sayılı and Ruben (1947). The 'Tatars' settled there were resettled in the east during Tīmūr's time, but their presence in Kırşehir during the preceding century is well attested. Hacı Bektaş's *Vilāyetnāme* explicitly claims that the saint had converted a number of Mongols to Islam.

[37] According to the medieval Christian chronicler Het'um, Geikhatu adhered neither to (the Christian) belief, nor to any (Christian?) law, nor did he adhere to any other religion: "Cilz Quegato ne avoit ne tenoit foy ne loy ne creance nulle." Het'um (1998), 300. Had Geikhatu openly professed his Islam, Het'um would certainly have stressed this, as he did so with other Ilkhans. A certain affinity to Sufi *shaykh*s, as reflected in the *farmān* discussed below, can be observed. Note that Geikhatu had spent many years in Anatolia, an area where there was a vibrant intellectual and social life, enriched through the participation of various Sufi orders and movements (see, e.g., Köprülü [1993]; Ocak [1989]; idem [1992]). Muslim sources do not indicate Geikhatu's (potential) Islam in any explicit way.

[38] ʿĀʾisha Khātūn, a Jalāyir, was the mother of Geikhatu's first three daughters. Ṣafwat al-Dīn Pādishāh Khātūn from the Qara-Khitaids of Kirman, daughter of Burāq Ḥājib's and later his successor Quṭb al-Dīn's wife Qutlugh Terken Khātūn, was first married to the Ilkhan Abaqa and then to Geikhatu. Pādishāh Khātūn was highly educated and was also a poetess, and later female poets, such as Jihān bt. Masʿūd Shāh, took her as an example (for Jihān's *Dīwān,* mentioning Pādishāh Khātūn as her model in the preface, see, Blochet [1900], 221–22). Pādishāh Khātūn built *madrasas* and was famous for her piety: according to her own poetry, she wore a Muslim headcover (*maqnaʿa*). Shabānkāraʾī (1984), 202.

95).[39] The text was translated and published by Abolala Soudavar, and was part of the exhibition that provided the framework of the conference during which this paper was presented. The contents of this *farmān*, dated early Jumādā II/May 1293, harmonize with the above findings: in Irinjin Turji's [Geikhatu's Buddhist name][40] name, and supported by the Mongol *amīrs* Shiktür, Aq-Buqa, and Toghachar,[41] it decrees tax exemptions for the benefit of a dervish lodge in the village Mandashīn near Ardabil.[42]

The name of the founder of this endowment, the 'Great Amīr Beitmish Aqa,' is mentioned in the *Jāmiʿ al-tawārīkh* as one of the *amīrs* both during Arghun and Geikhatu Khan's reigns as 'Beitmish Qushchi,' i.e., Beitmish the Falconer, and he is listed in the *Shuʿab-i panjgāna* under Geikhatu Khan's predecessor Arghun Khan as the leader of ten thousand (*amīr tümen*).[43]

That Beitmish endowed a village to a dervish hospice and that he beseeched the Ilkhan for a protective document both suggest the extent of contact between the Mongol elite and individual Sufis as

[39] The original is part of the collection of the Art and History Trust, Arthur M. Sackler Gallery, Smithsonian Institution, Washington, D.C. (LTS 1995.2.9). For color facsimiles (in reduced size) and an English translation, see Soudavar (1992), 34–35, and Komaroff and Carboni, eds. (2002), 50 (commentary, 210).

[40] Rashīd al-Dīn (1994), vol. 2, 1189, relates that Geikhatu had been given his Buddhist name 'Irenjin Tūrjī' by the Uighur *bakhshīs*, which is also the name that appeared on the official records ("*bar yarlīgh-hā Īrjī Tūrjī nibishtand*"; Shabānkāraʾī [1984], 266), and on Geikhatu's coins in Arabic script. See, e.g., Aykut and Pamuk (1992), 69. Geikhatu Khan's coins are rather rare, and gold coins became known only in 1985. Ibid., 69.

[41] The above three *amīrs* are listed in exactly this order on top of the list of *amīrs* as given by Rashīd al-Dīn in the *Shuʿab-i panjgāna* (under Geikhatu). Rashīd al-Dīn writes that the Jalāyir Shiktür, who had already been held in high esteem under Abaqa and Arghun Khan, had reached such an authority under Geikhatu that the latter appointed him as his representative. The Jalāyir Aq Buqa was the son of the great Ilka Noyan, and the grandfather of the famous Shaykh Ḥasan, founder of the Jalayirid dynasty (Sümer (1969), 1–147, here 12). The Suqai'ut *amīr* Toghachar defected to Baidu towards the end of Geikhatu's reign; he was executed by Ghazan Khan. Toghachar was a famous leader of the Qara'unas; see Shimo (1977), 131–81, here 135–39, 170, 177.

[42] Soudavar (1992), 34. In a note accompanying the translation, Soudavar clarified that the village of Mandashīn (Mendejin) is situated at 48°15' N, 37°25' E; ibid., 53, n. 23. See also Herrmann (2004), 52.

[43] *Shuʿab-i panjgāna*, under the entries '*Ṣūrat-i Kaykhātū Khān wa shuʿba-yi farzandān-i ū*,' and '*Ṣūrat-i Arghūn Khān wa shuʿba-yi farzandān-i ū*' (Istanbul, Topkapı Sarayı Müzesi Kütüphanesi, ms. Ahmet III, 2937, unfoliated). Beitmish does not appear among the *amīrs* listed under Hülegü, Abaqa, and Aḥmad Khan.

well as Sufi groups. (Whether Beitmish was a Muslim, and what this meant, remain open questions.) Nevertheless, his case indicates that Islam may have spread among the Mongol elite even in cases where their names might not reveal this.[44] To say the least, Beitmish's endowment shows that he believed in the benefit of such patronage, and had great respect for those who run and attended the Sufi lodge.

The fact that the tax-exempt hospice stood under the surveillance of the tax collectors who were responsible for the district of Ardabil harmonizes with the information found in narrative sources: Geikhatu's daughter Qutlugh-Malik[45] is known to have venerated Shaykh Zāhid Ibrāhīm, *pīr* (spiritual master) of the eponymous founder of the Ṣafawī order and later Safavid dynasty, Ṣafī al-Dīn Ardabīlī.[46] Abolala Soudavar pointed out that the above *farmān* from the time of Geikhatu may have been related to property that was later incorporated into the Safavid shrine in Ardabil.[47] On the other hand, information contained in the later, fourteenth-century Ṣafawī source[48] *Ṣafwat al-ṣafā* indicates that the relationship between the piously-minded *shaykh* and the Mongol elite does not seem to have been untroubled, and if anything, this particular group was probably not among the active converters—at least this is how it is portrayed in this source. In stark contrast to later Bektashi claims to have

---

[44] In fact, names alone may not always be good indicators for a given individual's religious affiliation: while Aḥmad Tegüder was a Muslim, none of his children bore Muslim names, though a Turkification is clearly discernible. His three sons were called Qaplanchi, Arslanchi, and Noqa(y)chi, and his oldest daughters were called Küchük, Könchek, and Chichek. In fact, Aḥmad Tegüder appears to have been conversant in Turkish, as Rashīd al-Dīn (1994), vol. 2, 1129–30; (1998), vol. 3, 550–51, reports that he addressed Shaykh ʿAbd al-Raḥmān as his 'father,' using the Turkic (as well as Persian) word '*bābā*,' and that he called the Sufi *shaykh* Īshān Menglī his 'brother' (T. *qarındāsh*). In Aḥmad Tegüder's second letter addressed to Qalāʾūn, Aḥmad Tegüder also addresses ʿAbd al-Raḥmān as his 'father,' thus transferring the terminology into Arabic (*abūnā*); Baybars al-Manṣūrī (1998), 243. For an English translation of this letter, see Pfeiffer (2006), 167–202.

[45] She was married to the Mangqūt *amīr* Qutlughshah. This information, not contained in the *Jāmiʿ al-tawārīkh*, can be gleaned from the *Shuʿab-i panjgāna* (Istanbul, Topkapı Sarayı Müzesi Kütüphanesi, ms. Ahmet III, 2937, under the entry '*Ṣūrat-i Kaykhātū Khān wa shuʿba-yi farzandān-i ū*').

[46] E.g., Ibn-i Bazzāz (1994), 1102–3.

[47] Soudavar (1992), 35; see also Fragner (1980), 19.

[48] On this particular source and its historical background and ideological baggage, see Sohrweide (1965), 95–223, here 97–117; also see Mazzaoui (2006), 303–310.

converted the Mongols to Islam, the Ṣafawī hagiographic source *Ṣafwat al-ṣafā* is careful to establish the Ṣafawī *ṭarīqa*'s independence from Mongol patronage.

According to the *Ṣafwat al-ṣafā*, Geikhatu Khan's daughter Qutlugh-Malik sent Shaykh Zāhid Ibrāhīm gifts, including food and a cloak (*khirqa*), from her income from a naphtha well (*maʿdan-i nafṭī*). Despite the fact that this income was legally permissible (*ḥalāl*), as one of the *shaykh's* disciples pointed out, the *shaykh* did not consume or distribute among his disciples the gifts that Qutlugh-Malik made to the *khānqāh*, nor did he wear the *khirqa* she had sent to him. Nonetheless, Shaykh Zāhid granted the fulfillment of Qutlugh-Malik's written requests, which came true at the very moment he read her letters.[49] Shaykh Zāhid's argument to refuse her gifts was that the presents reeked of "Turkishness, royal origin, and connections to the military elite."[50] This argument may reflect the ethos of the period during which this source was composed, though it could also indicate that there were considerable tensions between the piously minded Sufi circles, specifically those around Shaykh Ṣafī of Ardabil and Shaykh Zāhid Ibrāhīm of Gilan, and the ruling Ilkhanid elite.

There are a number of similar stories in the same (hagiographic) source, which stress the theme of the independence of the Ṣafawī Sufi *shaykhs* from the Ilkhanid rulers, including the famous Mongol convert Ghazan Khan: one day, an unnamed *shaykh*, who was much revered by the Mongol *amīr* Qutlughshah, entered into competition with Shaykh Zāhid Ibrāhīm, who was, according to this account, none less than Ghazan Khan's master. Ghazan Khan invited the two together with their disciples to a banquet, where Shaykh Zāhid stood out by not touching the food he was offered, whereas the other *shaykh* served himself freely.[51] Ghazan, who wanted to learn *waraʿ*

---

[49] Ibn-i Bazzāz (1994), 1102–3.

[50] "*chun nām-i Turkī wa pādishāh-zādagī wa amīrī bar sar dārand, dilam riḍā namīdahad.*" Ibn-i Bazzāz (1994), 899. His contemporary and to a certain extent rival Sufi 'Alā' al-Dawla Simnānī (659 736/1261–1336) commended Shaykh Ṣāfī al-Dīn for exhorting the Muslims to the remembrance (*dhikr*) of God's name, and for eating that which is permissible (*ḥalāl*), which, "during these times in which the world is full of (bad) innovations and people who eat what is forbidden (*ḥarām*)" was sufficient for Simnānī to wish him success: "*Khudāyash tawfīq-i khayr dihād.*" Amīr Iqbālshāh, *Fawāyid-i Shaykh 'Alā' al-Dawla* (fl. 724/1323), in Simnānī (1988), 176.

[51] For a similar narrative, albeit in a Lamaist context, see, Stuart, ed. (1995), 40 ('Debating Philosophic Theory').

and *taqwā*, temperance and fear of God, from his master's *ṭarīqa*, was pleased with the result: how could he learn these qualities from anyone who was not different from himself, but who ate the very bread he offered to him?[52] The second test consisted in the calling of reciters (*qawwāls*): they were asked to start their *samāʿ* (mystical dance), but whoever would get up and join them in the *samāʿ*, his head would be cut off with the sultan's sword. The *qawwāls* started to sing, and no one dared to move from fear of the sultan's sword. Suddenly, one of the disciples (*murīds*) of Shaykh Zāhid got up without regard for the sultan's *farmān* or his sword, proceeded into the middle of the place, and started his *samāʿ*, upon which the sultan burst into tears, flinging his sword to the side, and exclaiming that this was what he wanted the people to learn, namely that for the one who is transported in true ecstasy of love, the sultan, the *farmān*, and the sword do not exist. The sultan won the argument, and the *amīr* Qutlughshāh had to admit his sovereign's victory and his Sufi master's superiority.[53] Like so many other narratives, this one as well bears on the parallel between spiritual authority and worldly power.

A very similar attitude was taken by Shaykh Ṣafī's contemporary, the former theologian and Sufi 'convert' 'Alā' al-Dawla Simnānī (659–736/1261–1336),[54] who was concerned how to use the wealth donated to him by the Ilkhan Arghun prior to his own, Simnānī's, withdrawal from the people of the world (*ahl al-dunyā*). Thus, Simnānī, who had been close to Abaqa Khan and then Prince Arghun during his adolescence, described how he experienced a sudden religious crisis, expressed in a trance situation, when he entered the battle field on Arghun's side against the army of the Muslim Aḥmad Tegüder. The consequent ethical conflict led him to withdraw from the Ilkhan's

---

[52] Ibn-i Bazzāz (1994), 150.

[53] Ibn-i Bazzāz (1994), 150–51.

[54] On Simnānī and his works, see Elias (1995). As Jürgen Paul (1999), 364–65, has observed in his review of Elias' work, the role of Simnānī in the Ilkhanid political realm is not given as much attention as one might wish for, which is probably largely due to the fact that Elias based his work mainly on works written by Simnānī rather than by his contemporaries, which reflect Simnānī's wish for reclusion from 'the world,' and in particular Mongol potentates. See especially Simnānī (1988), 118 (for Simnānī's 'conversion' to Sufism on the battlefield against Aḥmad Tegüder and his subsequent attempts to leave the service of Ilkhan Arghun); 185–88 and 189–90 (on Simnānī's attempts to evade Amīr Chupān's invitations, including a narrative about his earlier attempts to avoid Arghun Khan); 226 (on his position on converting gifts from Arghun Khan into *ṣadaqa*).

service as well as from worldly service altogether. Many years later, his disciple Amīr Iqbālshāh asked Simnānī, inquiring about using the lands that were restituted with the support of the Ilkhans:

> "If someone were to restore the dead land to life, if [...] in this restoration he orders people to work by force, would the yield of that land be forbidden (*ḥarām*) or lawfully earned (*ḥalāl*)?" [Simnānī] replied that its income would be lawfully earned (*ḥalāl*), but the injustice of having made the people work by force will be his accountability ('will be on his neck').[55]

The *shaykh* told his disciple how he himself had made a decision in a similar case, related to the substantial gifts he had received from Arghun Khan. After withdrawing from the Ilkhan's service, he followed the advice of the "*'ulamā' wa 'uqalā-yi Īrān*" regarding such matters: these monies and items were not to be returned to the Ilkhan, because it was obvious that they had not belonged to him in the first place. It was also not advisable to keep them. Instead, he decided that it would be better to donate money as alms (*ṣadaqa*), and convert the land property and other immobilia into endowments (*waqf*): "*bihtar ān-ast ki nuqūd-rā ṣadaqa kunī wa amlāk-rā waqf sāzī.*" The *shaykh* is said to have fared well with this decision. But he did keep one item: a prayer rug (*muṣallā*) that was once given to him by a Jew. When that as well started to haunt him in a dream, he gave it away as *ṣadaqa,* and slept well ever after.[56]

Thus, 'keeping a distance' from the Mongol rulers was seen as a virtue, whereas accepting their service and gifts did not harmonize with at least the later views of those Sufi circles whose accounts have come down to us.[57] Nevertheless, some of the Ilkhans appear

---

[55] "*agar kasī zamīn-i mayyit-rā iḥyā kunad, agar dar ān iḥyā kardan [...] mardum-rā ba-zūr kār farmāyad, dakhl-i ān zamīn ḥarām bāshad yā ḥalāl?" [Shaykh 'Alā' al-Dawla Simnānī] farmūd ki dakhl-i ān ḥalāl bāshad, ammā maẓlima-yi ān-ki khalq-rā ba-zūr kār farmūda bāshad, dar gardan-i ū buwad.*" *Fawāyid-i Shaykh 'Alā' al-Dawla,* in Simnānī (1988), 226. Compare Qur'ān verse 30:50: "Contemplate (O man!) the memorials of Allāh's Mercy! How He gives life to the earth after its death" (*unẓurū ilā āthāri raḥmati Allāh kayfa yuḥyī al-arḍa ba'da mawtihā*). This verse appears frequently in the literature of the 'post-Mongol revival.' It occurs in the Qur'ān in the context of the distinction between believers and unbelievers, and is ubiquitous in the Juwaynī letters and Waṣṣāf's *Tajziyyat al-amṣār,* e.g., Waṣṣāf (1856), 218, trans. 203.

[56] *Fawāyid-i Shaykh 'Alā' al-Dawla,* in Simnānī (1988), 226–27.

[57] The Sufi ethos of maintaining distance from worldly rulers predates the Mongol invasions; as 'Umar al-Suhrawardī (d. 632/1234) expressed it, "it is the custom of the Sufis to seek seclusion, isolation, and solitude for the sake of God's fear, to avoid

to have been successful in making endowments to Sufi lodges during the period in question, and some Sufi circles, in turn, seem to have accepted these without further qualms. A document composed by Shams al-Dīn Juwaynī regarding an unnamed Ilkhan's (*pādishāh-i jahān*) annual donation (*idrār*) of one thousand *dīnār*s from the income of Anatolia (*muqaddamāt az maḥṣūl-i Rūm*) in perpetuity to the Sufi lodge (*zāwiya*) of a certain Shaykh Humām al-Milla wa al-Dīn is preserved in a fourteenth-century copy of an *inshā'* collection in St. Petersburg.[58]

While this document is undated, the death date of the author of the letter, Shams al-Dīn Juwaynī (5 Shaʿbān 683/17 October 1284),[59] provides the year 1284 as the *terminus ante quem.* The document is thus an indication of the imperial patronage of Muslim institutions during the early Ilkhanate.[60] Expressing the same concern as Ṣafī al-Dīn and Simnānī regarding the legality of the funds to be endowed, it also contains further indications for the uneasy relationship between the local Muslims and the Mongol rulers.

That the Mongols were attracted to wonder-working saints is well known. What is difficult to assess is the exact nature of this relationship. The above examples all involved members of what became more or less 'established' Sufi orders with worldly possessions, including shrines, as well as ample literary evidence for their existence in the form of the very hagiography from which the above examples were cited. Less prominent(ly represented) individuals also played impor-

---

the company of kings and sultans and to abandon all intercourse." Najm al-Dīn Rāzī (1982), 45–46. As his long explanations, the recourse to the encouragement by al-Suhrawardī, and the reference to (not quoted) Qur'ānic evidence justifying his service to the Seljuq Sultan show, the Sufi *shaykh* Najm-i Rāzī (Dāya) was obviously not very much at ease with his conscience for seeking the Seljuq Sultan's company in the 1220s; see Najm al-Dīn Rāzī (1982), 45–48.

[58] "*...banā bar īn muqaddamāt az maḥṣūl-i Rūm bar sabīl-i idrār ʿalā al-dawām wa al-istimrār mablagh-i yak hazār dīnār muqarrar shud ba-abwāb-i awqāf-i ānjā sāl ba-sāl ān-rā bī quṣūr wa iḥtibās ba-way mīrasānand...*" See *al-Mukātabāt wa al-murāsalāt,* St. Petersburg, ms. C816=4305 (Rosen, no. 282), fols. 207a–207b, here 207b.

[59] Shams al-Dīn Juwaynī was executed on 5 Shaʿbān 683/17 October 1284 early in the reign of Arghun Khan, and he was never active in his chancery.

[60] All this, of course, is only valid under the premise that the documents contained in this *inshā'* collection can be taken at face value. I have not been able to identify Shaykh Humām al-Milla wa al-Dīn either in the extant parts of Ibn al-Fuwaṭī's biographical dictionary or in Rashīd al-Dīn's *Jāmiʿ al-tawārīkh.* It appears as though he was a local official who, like so many, does not appear in the larger narrative histories.

tant roles, especially in mediating between the Mongol elite and the local population, a fact that should not be forgotten when listening to the much 'louder' voices of the hagiography of their famous Ṣafawī and (proto-) Kubrawī contemporaries and rivals. Thus a certain Qalandar dervish with the name Īshān[61] (Ḥasan) Menglī,[62] whose tent was pitched in the Ilkhan Aḥmad Tegüder's camp, facilitated Rashīd al-Dīn's access to this Ilkhan: it was through Ḥasan Menglī's mediation that Rashīd al-Dīn received what was apparently his only audience with this Ilkhan. The same Īshān Menglī is known to have celebrated common Sufi ceremonies with Aḥmad Tegüder, who addressed him as his brother (T. *qarındash*).

Such intimacy seems to have aroused jealousy. As Hanna Sohrweide pointed out, the Ṣafawī hagiographic work *Ṣafwat al-ṣafā* (written in the mid-fourteenth century and later remodeled) is rather hostile vis-à-vis Qalandar dervishes.[63] In fact, it describes in an almost gleeful tone how the abovementioned Ḥasan Menglī was executed after his patron had been deposed. According to the author, Ibn-i Bazzāz, Ḥasan Menglī was a godless man surrounded by the scum of society, but close to the sultan with whom he shared his drug addiction, and so envious of Shaykh Zāhid that he planned on the extirpation of his entire order (*ṭarīqa*):

> ...there was someone with the name Ḥasan Menglī, who was the *nā'ib* and *khalīfa* of the Ya'qūbiyān, and he was close to Sultan Aḥmad. Because Ḥasan Menglī followed the path of 'permissiveness' (*ibāḥat*),[64]

[61] On this term, which, especially in Central Asia, denotes holy men, see Sohrweide (1965), 95–223, here 103, n. 54. Sohrweide holds that the word *īshān* means—especially in Central Asia—"ein Heiliger, ein frommer Mann," adding "Im Yasavi-Orden war dieser Titel üblich." Further, with regard to Īshān Menglī, Sümer (1969), 1–147, here 56, n. 28, stated that "...buradaki îşân kelimesi [...] şübhesiz *Tükistan*'da din ve tarikat adamlarına verilen *îşân* sözünün aynıdır." See also Mélikoff (2000), 275–89, here 277. In a narrative used by DeWeese (1994), 463, the word '*īshān*' is attached to the less 'unorthodox' of two Sufi brothers, though in the case of Īshān Menglī, we are clearly dealing with a figure who has entered the path of *ibāḥa;* see below.

[62] Orbélian (1864), 238, who pointed out that Ḥasan Menglī belonged to Aḥmad Tegüder's 'confidants,' called him 'Hasan Manli-Chekh.'

[63] "*ğam'ī az qalandar wa muwallah wa abnā-i īšān az mardum-i bī tamyīz*"; see Sohrweide (1965), 95–223, here 104, n. 62.

[64] The term *ibāḥa* apparently includes the use of drugs and the departure from all kinds of social constraints, which was typical for Qalandar/Jawlaqī dervishes; in fact, it was the path of the 'founder' of the Qalandariyya, Jamāl al-Dīn Sāwī; see Ocak (1992), 27. Note that this 'freeing from all social constraints' is exactly

> and of taking inebriating [drugs], Sultan Aḥmad had found pleasure in him, and together they indulged in immorality (*fusūq*), and a number of Qalandar [dervishes] and forsaken souls (*muwallah*)[65] and dervishes (*īshān*) from among the people without discernment had gathered around Ḥasan Menglī. And when the signs of the right guidance of Shaykh Zāhid, may God sanctify his soul, became world-conquering like the sky, Ḥasan Menglī burned in the fire of envy, and by creating trouble and fighting fiercely, he kindled the fire of rage in Sultan Aḥmad. He invented the lie that "The Zāhidiyān and the son of Shaykh Zāhid—Jamāl al-Dīn ʿAlī—have assassinated forty of the members of this group, and have thrown them into the water. Messengers have to be dispatched, and retribution (*qiṣāṣ*) needs to be taken from Jamāl al-Dīn ʿAlī." This calumny and slander he had invented by himself and he deeply changed the disposition of Sultan Aḥmad.[66]

Further following the narrative of the *Ṣafwat al-ṣafā*, these events coincided with matters that were of greater immediate importance to the Ilkhan, as his nephew Arghun rose against him claiming the throne.[67] 'Sultan Aḥmad' left in the direction of Ardabil, where he was welcomed by the religious nobility of the town (*a'imma wa ʿamāyim-i Ardabīl*).[68] Seeing these people in the vicinity of the Ilkhan made Ḥasan Menglī even more furious, and he started spreading rumors, finding an open ear with the Ilkhan, who, however, refused his renewed proposal to send messengers, asking Menglī to be patient until he had settled things with Arghun.[69] After that, the Ilkhan Aḥmad promised, he would "go in person to take blood revenge and extirpate the house and family and eradicate the vestiges of the Zāhidiyān."[70] However, these plans came to naught, as

---

what may have been appealing to Aḥmad Tegüder, allowing him to transgress, during his *samāʿ* sessions, all protocols imposed by the Mongol society of which he was part.

[65] According to Ocak (1992), 39, similarly, 231, the term *Muwallaha* was synonymous with the terms *Qalandariyya* and *Jawlaqiyya* during the seventh/thirteenth to ninth/fifteenth centuries: "Buraya kadar verilen bilgilerden çıkan sonuç şudur ki, Kalenderîler Sûriye, Irak ve Mısır'da *Kalenderiyye, Cavlakiyye* (veya *Cevâlika*) ve *Müvellihe* adı altında tanınıyorlardı."

[66] Ibn-i Bazzāz (1994), 217–18.

[67] Ibid., 218.

[68] Ibn-i Bazzāz mentions that among this group was a certain Khwāja Kamāl al-Dīn, who was approached in secret by the then minister Shams al-Dīn—the thread is not followed up, Ibn-i Bazzāz does not disclose what went on between the two.

[69] Ibn-i Bazzāz (1994), 218.

[70] "*ṣabr mībāyad kardan tā man az īn lashkar-u-muḥāraba-yi Arghūn bāz gardam ba nafs-i*

the Ilkhan Aḥmad Tegüder was soon deposed and executed by his Mongol kin.

Ḥasan Menglī, "who had kindled [the] fire [of wrath of Sultan Aḥmad against Shaykh Zāhid and his descendants]," was taken, and the people "boiled him in a cauldron until he was thoroughly cooked."[71] This 'punishment in kind,'[72] i.e., the 'boiling' of the one who had 'kindled fire,' which moreover countered his own alleged lies—the Ṣafawī Sufis' *drowning* of a group of Qalandar dervishes—is doubly affirmed by two couplets, one in Arabic and one in Persian:

> If God were to punish humankind for their sins
> He would prepare hell for them every day.[73]
> Because of that rage ('fire') of a raw thought which he had in his mind
> He reached maturity ('became well cooked') through time.[74]

This is the worst, and at the same time, the liveliest account that has survived on this otherwise rather obscure figure. Evoking the fires of jealousy inside of Ḥasan Menglī and the fire of wrath he kindled in Aḥmad Tegüder, this account 'proves' at the same time that Ḥasan Menglī was not a saint after all: had he been a true saint, he could not have perished through boiling.[75] It appears as though it is exactly these silenced Sufis that had a high standing during Aḥmad Tegüder's reign.

Another Sufi *shaykh* who was prominent during this Ilkhan's reign,

---

khwud birawam wa qiṣāṣ kunam wa qaṭ'-i khāna wa khānadān wa qal'-i āthār-i Zāhidiyān bukunam." Ibid., 218. If this had really happened, history might have gone quite a different path, as the family in question is that of the later Safavid dynasty.

71 "*Wa Ḥasan Menglī-rā ki ātash mīfurūkht bigiriftand wa dar qazghān bijūshānīdand wa muharrā gardānīdand.*" Ibid., 219.

72 Note that among the forms of punishment mentioned in medieval Muslim sources those which imply that the punishment is in some way related to the offense particularly stand out.

73 "*fa-law akhadha Allāhu al-'ibāda bi-dhanbihim / a'adda lahum fī kulli yauwmin jahannamā;*" Ibn-i Bazzāz (1994), 219.

74 "*z'ān ātish-i fikr-i khām k'ū dāsht ba-dil / khush pukhtagī kard zi-dawrān ḥāṣil;*" the 'rounds' implied here may be the rounds Ḥasan Menglī made in the kettle, just as much as the word *dawrān, davarān* refers to the life cycle, i.e., time, which makes man experienced, i.e., 'cooked.' Ibid., 220.

75 Fire ordeals were a widespread means of asserting the truthfulness of suspects both in the Middle East and in Europe during this time; see the chapter 'The Oven-Pit: Ordeal, Sacrifice, and Sacred Enclosure in Forging a Community' in DeWeese (1994), 243–90; for the European context, see Bartlett (1986).

a certain Kamāl al-Dīn ʿAbd al-Raḥmān, is a case in point for the limited use of the distinction between 'popular' and 'established' Sufis which has been maintained by a number of scholars: being probably of Turkic background and born in northern Iraq, ʿAbd al-Raḥmān's father served as a chamberlain to the last Abbasid caliph, and ʿAbd al-Raḥmān himself took apparently 'classical' *madrasa* education with the famous Mosul *shaykh* and Qur'ān exegete Muwaffaq al-Dīn al-Kawāshī.[76] He apparently had sufficient experience in financial matters to grow into a position that had previously been held by a man of the stature of Naṣīr al-Dīn Ṭūsī: like Ṭūsī under Hülegü, so ʿAbd al-Raḥmān became overseer of all the pious endowments in the Ilkhanate under Aḥmad Tegüder.

It should also be pointed out that it was ʿAbd al-Raḥmān who headed Aḥmad Tegüder's second embassy to the Mamluk sultan on the latter's special request. In the letter that the *shaykh* carried, Aḥmad Tegüder had called him his "right and left hand." While a certain exaggeration may have been involved, Rashīd al-Dīn, who said very little about these embassies, made it rather clear that it was upon Shaykh ʿAbd al-Raḥmān's and the vizier Shams al-Dīn Juwaynī's advice that the Ilkhan sent the first embassy to Egypt:

> With Shaykh ʿAbd al-Raḥmān's and Ṣāḥib Shams al-Dīn's approval [the Ilkhan Aḥmad Tegüder] sent Mawlānā Quṭb al-Dīn Shīrāzī, the most learned man in the world, on an embassy to Egypt on 19 Jumādā I 681 (25 August, 1282).[77]

This passage is confirmed by the text of the actual letter that has come down to us. In this letter Aḥmad Tegüder had asserted that he had taken the decision to send an embassy to the Mamluk Sultan Qalā'ūn against the decision which the major Mongol princes and *amīrs* had taken during a *quriltai*.[78] Not surprisingly, the *amīrs* felt ignored by the Ilkhan, which is expressed even in the otherwise very concise *Shu'ab-i panjgāna*.[79]

---

[76] On al-Kawāshī, see al-Yūnīnī (1954), vol. 4, 104–5; see also Ibn al-Ṣuqāʿī (1974), 42–43; and Ibn al-ʿImād (1932), vol. 5, 366.

[77] Rashīd al-Dīn (1998), vol. 3, 551 (transliteration adapted); see also Rashīd al-Dīn (1994), vol. 2, 1130.

[78] See, e.g., Ibn ʿAbd al-Ẓāhir (1961), 7. For a translation, see Pfeiffer (2006), 167–202.

[79] See, e.g., Rashīd al-Dīn on the Suldus *amīr* Su'unjaq and the Jalāyir Shiktür Noyan, *Shuʿab-i panjgāna*, Istanbul, Topkapı Sarayı Müzesi Kütüphanesi, ms. Ahmet III, 2937, under Aḥmad Khan.

And yet, Shaykh ʿAbd al-Raḥmān participated in the same *samāʿ* sessions as the likes of Ḥasan Menglī, who is described by the contemporary Armenian historian Stepanos as a Jawlaqī (Qalandar) dervish and by Rashīd al-Dīn as the head of the adherents of Bābī Yaʿqūb. More than that, we hear that during these *samāʿ* sessions, the Ilkhan Aḥmad Tegüder called Ḥasan Menglī his 'brother,' and ʿAbd al-Raḥmān his 'father.' The sources are too terse, and at times contradicting, to allow for a judgment, but these few glimpses on one of the major *shaykhs* from Aḥmad Tegüder's reign should show that a sharp distinction between 'high' and 'popular' (rudimentarily 'shamanist') Sufism is not a meaningful way of categorization. Rather, I would suggest investigating the individual lives of such persons to allow drawing the first lines of a more complex—if seemingly less complete—picture.

From the little information from contemporary sources that has survived it can be derived that both Ḥasan Menglī and the above-mentioned ʿAbd al-Raḥmān were of considerable importance during the reign of Aḥmad Tegüder.[80] Particularly noteworthy are the communally celebrated *samāʿ* sessions described by Rashīd al-Dīn, who attested that Aḥmad Tegüder

> held Shaykh ʿAbd al-Raḥmān in such reverence that he called him *bābā* (father) and he called Īshān Menglī, a disciple of Bābī Yaʿqūb who resided in Arran, his *qarındash* (brother). He used to go often to his tent, which was near the back gate of the *ordū,* and participate in *samāʿ*, paying little attention to matters of finance and state.[81]

Rashīd al-Dīn and other contemporary authors stress the daily routine and intensity with which Aḥmad Tegüder engaged in Sufi ceremonies, attesting to the importance of this ritual in this Ilkhan's life.[82] Rather than explaining Aḥmad Tegüder's relationship with ʿAbd al-Raḥmān and Ḥasan Menglī as personal, private encounters

---

[80] The fact that someone like Rashīd al-Dīn, who became very powerful during the later Ilkhans' reigns, who had already been a court physician during Aḥmad Tegüder's brother and predecessor Abaqa Khan's reign, and who certainly knew well how to find his 'way in,' chose to use Menglī as his way to approach the Ilkhan, shows how close Menglī was to the ruler during Aḥmad Tegüder's reign.

[81] Rashīd al-Dīn (1998), vol. 3, 550–51 (translation and transliteration adapted); idem, (1994), vol. 2, 1129–30.

[82] See also Galstian (1962), 38 ("From the manuscript of Bishop Stepanos"). I am indebted to İlker Evrim Binbaş for translating this passage into English.

between 'converters' and 'convert,' it might be more meaningful to understand these individuals as part of Aḥmad Tegüder's attempt to create an additional space of authority *outside* of the Mongol customs, established human relationships, and inherited hierarchies. It was the *samāʿ* rituals that allowed Aḥmad Tegüder to recreate the hierarchies in the human geography of which he was part.[83] The hierarchical relationships expressed in the names 'brother' and 'father' that Aḥmad Tegüder used when addressing the members of the Sufi community with whom he celebrated should reflect that such a deconstruction and reorganization of relationships may have indeed been intended. Like Chinggis Khan before him, and so many (from the Chinggisid perspective even more 'lateral') rulers after him, Aḥmad Tegüder cultivated relationships with individuals who were able or claimed to be able to establish a connection to the other world, attaching a sacredness to his rule that could counterweigh such 'this-worldly' issues as lateral succession, marriage politics, and *amīrs*' needs for appreciation and reward.

While it is not known to what extent Sufi converters were involved in the Mongol elite's Islamization, Aḥmad Tegüder's active patronage of the Sufis should in turn have allowed him to attract those members of the Mongol elite who had already converted to Islam—which might be numerically reflected in the steep increase of Muslim names among the Mongol *amīrs* during the generation following Aḥmad Tegüder's reign.

Preliminary Conclusions

The preceding discussion has shown that conversion to Islam among the Mongol elite in the Ilkhanate was a long process. Conversion to Islam among the Mongol elite in the Nile-to-Oxus region appears to have occurred from the 650s/1250s onwards, preceding the formation of the Hülegüid appanage and extending over several generations.

---

[83] For the importance of the seating order in Turco-Mongol societies, and the rituals attached to it, see, e.g., Ibn Faḍlān (1939), 159–60 (§ 46a); İnan (1968), 241–54; and McChesney (1983), 33–70. A description of the sitting order (regarding only the royal family) at the court of Özbek Khan can be found in Ibn Baṭṭūṭa (1958-2000) vol. 2, 483–85. Miniature paintings of the time reflect this seating order; see, e.g., Masuya (2002), 80, 82, figs. 84, 85, and 86, cat. nos. 19 and 30.

Up to 30 percent of converts to Islam are found among the highest ranking Mongol *amīrs* in the Ilkhanate from the third generation after Hülegü onwards, i.e., before Ghazan Khan's conversion to Islam.

In Aḥmad Tegüder's case in particular, *samāʿ* sessions appear to have played a central role in his daily efforts to consolidate his power, adding a sacred dimension to his authority. Contemporary evidence in the form of legal documents shows that there existed substantial contacts between the Mongol elite and local Sufi constituencies, though the later Sufi hagiography conveys an uneasiness about having accepted Mongol 'donations,' expressed in legal reasoning regarding the acceptance of such 'gifts.'

'Sufis without memory,' i.e., without a shrine and hagiographical literature, emerge as dynamic, though at times reviled, agents in the narrative sources—attesting to their importance in their own time. In the Mongol armies the Muslim Turkic contingents may have been the pioneers in the veneration of local saints, though even less is known about these than the Sufi saints.

RELIGIOUS DIVERSITY UNDER ILKHANID RULE C. 1300 AS REFLECTED IN THE FREER BALʿAMĪ

TERESA FITZHERBERT

A recent study has concluded that the Freer Gallery of Art's illustrated copy of Balʿamī's fourth/tenth-century *History*, also known as *Tarjama-yi ta'rīkh-i Ṭabarī,*[1] was produced in the Jazira c. 1300, and possibly for a Christian governor of Mosul.[2] Although the quality of the manuscript's illustrations indicates provincial production, the abbreviated redaction of the text and subject matter chosen for illustration strongly suggest it was designed for teaching the young, or recent converts to Islam, destined for high government or military office under the Ilkhans.[3] The manuscript as a whole may be seen as focusing on lessons and parallels of particular relevance to the nascent Islamic state following Ghazan's official conversion to Islam in 694/1295,[4] and particularly after the removal in 696/1297 of the

[1] Freer Gallery of Art, Smithsonian Institution, Washington, D.C., ms. F1957.16, 1947.19 and 1930.21. As Elton Daniel has pointed out, *Tarjama-yi ta'rīkh-i Ṭabarī* (*Translation of the History of Ṭabarī*) is one of the most unfortunate titles ever given to a book, since it gives no credit to Balʿamī for his substantial supplements and annotations to al-Ṭabarī's text; Daniel (1990), 284–87. For further close textual study supporting this argument see Peacock (2003). Peacock refers throughout to Balʿamī's text as his *Ta'rīkhnāma.* I would like to express my thanks to Elton Daniel for copies of his currently unpublished papers, and to Andrew Peacock for providing me with a copy of his thesis.

[2] Fitzherbert (2001), currently in preparation for publication as Freer Gallery of Art Occasional Papers (new series). I would like to express my particular thanks to Massumeh Farhad and Ann Gunter for their ongoing guidance and support, and to Neil Greentree for his skillful photography of the manuscript.

[3] Following a preface (in Persian), the text begins with Adam and the last folio describes the death of the Caliph al-Muqtafī in 295/908. As the final three lines of text have been cropped, it is now not possible to say with certainty whether the text continued or a colophon has been lost. However, since some copies end with the reign of al-Muqtafī, only a single folio may be missing; otherwise the text is complete. Although originally a single volume, the manuscript is now bound in two parts.

[4] Extant folios 368; thirty-seven paintings, excluding the frontispiece, occur at irregular intervals through the text as follows: 1) rulers of ancient Iran, pre-Islamic prophets and kings, ff. 1b–157, 24 illus., ratio c. 1:6; 2) Prophet's public life, ff. 157b–223a, 7 illus., ratio c. 1:9; caliphal period, ff. 223b–368b, 6 illus., ratio c.

religiously intolerant kingmaker, the Mongol general Nawrūz, when Ghazan's policies of state consolidation included restoring relations with the Christian communities.[5]

If a date of c. 1300 is correct, this manuscript is not only among the earliest surviving copies of Balʿamī's text, but also appears to be the only illustrated version surviving from the fourteenth century.[6] Since pictures in historical texts may provide insights into how the past was presented to a contemporary audience, the Freer manuscript offers an important additional source for the historiography of the Mongol period, providing insights into Ilkhanid Iran at a watershed in its religious and political history. Despite its worn condition, the manuscript's frontispiece provides a rare glimpse of the religiously and culturally inclusive ideals of the Ilkhanid state at this time.

The originality of the frontispiece (pl. 14 and figs. 86–87) lies not in its form but in its message. Alone among its predecessors, contemporaries, and, as far as I am aware, its successors, it depicts a judgment scene and includes a quotation from the Qurʾān. In its composition it adheres to the time-honored formula of a centrally enthroned ruler, flanked by supporters, backed by guards, and overflown by angels, as for example in the frontispiece to vol. 17 of the *Kitāb al-aghānī*, produced sometime between 1215 and 1219, depicting an image of the *atabeg* ruler of Mosul, Badr al-Dīn Lu'lu', in the guise of a Turk (fig. 88).[7]

1:24. Themes in the cycle may be identified as follows: aspects of conversion to monotheism–33; military affairs, tactics and ruses–14; state administration, including judgments, assessing evidence and diplomacy–13; transfer of political power–10; and rites of passage from youth to manhood–5. Paintings may illustrate more than one theme.

[5] For example, work on the monastery of St. John the Baptist at Maragha, suspended during the troubles, was continued; Ghazan presented the Nestorian Patriarch, Yahbh-Allaha III, with a replica of the great gold seal, originally presented to him by the Great Khan Möngke (r. 649–58/1251–60) in 1281, which had been pillaged from the Patriarchal residence in 1297. The Patriarch's presence was required at the royal camp through the summer of 697/1298; in 699–700/1300 Ghazan spent three days as his guest at Maragha; on the 13 *Īlūl* (September) 701/1301 the new monastery church was completed and consecrated; in 702–3/1303 Ghazan again visited the Patriarch at Maragha and on each of his visits bestowed honors upon him, Budge, trans. (1928), 83–85 and 240–54; Fiey (1975a), chap. 8, 68–73.

[6] The next securely dated and illustrated Balʿamī manuscript is in the Chester Beatty Library, Dublin, ms. Persian 144, dated 874/1469–70; Arberry and Minovi (1959–62), 79. In 1998, another illustrated, but undated, copy in a late-Timurid style was sold in Paris; Drouot-Richelieu (1998), 73–79.

[7] A *mamlūk* of Mosul's last independent Zangid ruler, Badr al-Dīn Abū al-Faḍāʾil

While painting style is not the focus of this paper, an idiosyncratic feature is shared by the *Kitāb al-aghānī* and Balʿamī frontispieces and will be returned to later in this paper—namely, that the wings of the angels issue not from their backs but from their haloes.

Despite its formulaic composition, the enthronement scene in the Balʿamī is headed by a quotation from the Qurʾān (fig. 87) and footed, not by musicians, dancers, and servants of the commissariat, but by a scene of execution. The vertical sequencing of the iconography reads from the top as:

1) the opening to Sūra 38:26, in which God empowers Dawūd (David) as his deputy on earth and admonishes him to judge rightly between men;

    "[*Yā dāwūdu innā jaʿal*]*nāka khalīfatan fī al-arḍi fa'ḥkum bayna al-nāsi bi al-ḥaqq*..."
    "O David! Lo! We have set thee as a viceroy in the earth; therefore judge aright between mankind..." (fig. 87)

2) an enthroned Mongol ruler surrounded by civilian and military supporters;
3) the ultimate sanction of authority, the sentence of death.[8]

The frontispiece thus declares that the Biblical-Qurʾānic Creator has invested the Ilkhanid ruler as the rightful successor to King David, state-founder *par excellence* for Jews, Christians, and Muslims, with the ultimate sanction over life and death under the Divine mandate.

The centrally enthroned Mongol with a hawk on his right wrist sits at the apex of a hierarchy of advisors. The ruler lacks *ṭirāz* armbands or a turban. Although this area of the image is badly worn, what remains points to him wearing a headdress of owl and eagle

---

Lu'luʾ b. ʿAbdallāh al-Nūrī al-Atabakī, was granted a caliphal diploma in 628–29/1231, and thereafter ruled virtually independently until his death in 657/1259. He was an Armenian from Rum, not a Turk; see Patton (1991), in general and 13 in particular for his ethnic background. His patronymic, b. ʿAbdallāh, suggests that his father converted to Islam.

[8] Unless stated otherwise, right and left refer to the viewer's right and left. The lower section of the composition is extremely abraded, and therefore difficult to read; however, two pairs of feet visible at the foot of the painting and pointing to the left cannot be reasonably matched to the two heads below the throne, which point to the right. A figure at the far right of the damaged area, for whom only the top of a turban and the heel of an axe may now be identified, suggests an executioner.

feathers. To the right of the ruler a Muslim divine is seated with a text in his hands; to the left of the ruler a smaller, turbaned figure holds a circular or oval gold object, probably a cup. Next to him sits a figure with exaggerated Mongol features holding an oblong tapered object with red markings; the shape of this object suggests an enameled glass beaker of Syrian design.

Supporters to the rear of the throne display traditional insignia of office: to the left, a Turkic quiver bearer; in the center, the parasol bearer;[9] and flanking the throne two trident bearers, the one on the right coiffed with Sasanian-type hair ribbons. Together with the inscription, the depiction of Muslim, Turkic, and anachronistic Sasanian figures suggests a configuration intended to show a Mongol ruler in a religious and dynastic sequence, thus presenting a complex religious and political situation in simple and positive terms.

Images of a hawk on the wrist of a 'mounted' royal hunter (fig. 94) or in court scenes on that of a court falconer (*bāzchī*)[10] are common, but a hawk shown on the wrist of an enthroned ruler, as here, is rare.[11] For the Mongols, birds of prey represented the link with the all-powerful sky god Tengri,[12] and through their ability to soar to the heavens they also represented the flight of the spirit at the

---

[9] For officers at the Mongol court, see Charles Melville's paper in this volume.

[10] For examples, see Marianna Shreve Simpson's contribution to this volume.

[11] To date I have identified five examples: 1) candlestick dated 622/1225, possibly Artuqid, Museum of Fine Arts, Boston; see Rice (1949), 339–40, especially 337, fig. c (VII) and Rice (1957), 317–20, fig. 40f; 2) thirteenth-century stem cup from the Tomb of Sayyid Baṭṭāl Ghazi in western Anatolia, Türk ve Islam Eserleri Müzesi, Istanbul, inv. no. 102; see Baer (1977), 299–33, fig. 1; 3) Ilkhanid period tray, British Museum, inv. no. OA 1878.12–30.706, Henderson Bequest; see Ward (1993), 87, no. 66; 4) stucco relief from the larger palace at Kubadabad, Ince Minareli Medresesi, Konya; see Roux (1982), 25 and fig. 11; and 5) a gold medallion, struck at the feast of Nawrūz, 360/970–71, in the name of the Buyid *amīr* 'Izz al-Dawla, Bibliothèque Nationale, Paris; see Ilisch (1985), 11, no. 39.

[12] According to Roux, 'Tengri' is the oldest Turco-Mongol word known, and by the second century BC it had subsumed all other words for deities; Roux (1982), 110. In the *Jāmiʿ al-tawārīkh*, the form of words used by Mongols in swearing oaths is given as: "Oh Lord of the sky and the earth…" [*Ay khudā-yi āsmān wa zamān*], for example, Rashīd al-Dīn (1994), vol. 1, 373. This tended, often conveniently, to blur distinction between the God/Allāh of People of the Book and that of the Mongols, particularly when formal imprecations were required. A notable case in point is Ghazan's letter to Pope Boniface VIII in 1302, some seven years after his official conversion to Islam, which, nonetheless, is written in Uighur script and uses traditional Mongol epithets for the Almighty; Mostaert and Cleaves (1952), 471.

moment of death.[13] Power of flight attributed to the Mongol shaman was often signified by feathers attached to their shoulders.[14] Chinggis (Genghis) Khan claimed descent from Tengri. Juwaynī quotes the shaman, Teb-Tengri, as pronouncing that: "God has spoken with me and has said: 'I have given all the face of the earth to Temüjin and his children and named him Chinggis Khan. Bid him administer justice in such-and-such a fashion.'"[15] In the *Secret History of the Mongols* Chinggis Khan is likened to, and likens himself to, a gyrfalcon.[16] The Armenian monk-chronicler, Grigor of Akanc', records a tradition that the Chinggisid law code, the *yāsa*, was delivered by an eagle with the power of speech and golden feathers.[17] Budge notes that the Ilkhan Geikhatu (r. 690–94/1291–95) conferred a golden *pāyza* of the *sunqur* (gyrfalcon) class on the Nestorian Patriarch Mar Yahbh-Allaha, when he visited him at Maragha.[18]

Hawks and falcons as symbols of authority were already embedded in the iconography of thirteenth-century Jazira and Anatolia prior to

---

[13] The metaphor for death, "He has become a falcon," continued in Mongol use after their conversion to Islam; Roux (1984), 253 and 258.

[14] For a general discussion of magical flight, see Eliade (1964), 477–82; for hawks and flight in Mongol shamanism, see Eliade (1964), 481, and Roux (1984), especially 62–63 and 103. Roux also cites Ohlmarks on the Mongol practice of attaching feathers to the Shaman's shoulders; Ohlmarks (1939), 211–12. An Ilkhanid-period winged figure, standing at an enthroned figure's right but from whom he turns away towards the left, appears in one of the medallions of the so-called Nisan Tası in the Tekke of Jalāl al-Dīn Rūmī, in Konya, which bears an inscription to the last Ilkhan, Abū Sa'īd (r. 716–36/1316–35). This enthroned figure is turbaned with a *taylasān*, and holds a staff on the top of which a pointed ovoid, somewhat like a bird's head, has been placed horizontally as a knob, while the figure to his left, also turbaned, holds some kind of long-handled spade or reversed banner, illustrated in Baer (1973–74), 23 and fig. 28, medallion (e). The exact iconography of this group is at present unclear; however, that the turbaned ruler should also claim jurisdiction over the traditional Mongol beliefs of his subjects seems plausible, and the winged figure to the ruler's right and a turbaned one to his left is not unlike the configuration in the Bal'amī frontispiece.

[15] Juwaynī (1958), vol. 1, 39.

[16] Cleaves, trans. (1982), 15, para. 63; Boyle (1974), 184, quoting Rashīd al-Dīn (1959–60), vol. 1, 286.

[17] Allsen (1997), 61–62; Grigor of Akanc' (1949), 289 and 291.

[18] Budge, trans. (1928), 75. Budge does not provide a primary source for this information, and I have not been able to trace it in Bar Hebraeus's Chronography. The falcon appears on Geikhatu's coinage but only on local copper issues of little significance. The hawk is not known on Ilkhanid gold coinage, and on silver only from the reign of Arghun (r. 683–90/1284–91). I am grateful to Stephen Album for this information.

submission to Mongol rule—for example, the carved stone inscription from the walls of Konya, reading '*al-sulṭān*' and flanked by two single-headed birds of prey, dated by Gierlichs to 618/1221, now in the Ince Minareli Medresesi (fig. 89).[19] An intriguing example, although probably of later date, much restored and currently with no known exact thirteenth-century parallel, is the carved stone lintel above the portal of the so-called Governor's House in Amadiya, north of Mosul (fig. 90). Here, a bird of prey pinions with its talons the gaping jaws of two dragons. The iconography of this portal, whatever its date, indicates the enduring legacy of the hawk as a symbol of authority in the area.[20]

Bearing in mind the potency of bird of prey imagery among the Turks and Mongols, to find one on the wrist of an Ilkhanid enthroned figure of authority, and juxtaposed with Sūra 38:26 from the Qur'ān, becomes less surprising. What we see in the Balʿamī frontispiece, therefore, is an instance of Mongol symbols of religious and temporal authority neatly synchronized with comparable traditions already potent among the conquered peoples—a process not dissimilar to the pragmatic 'meshing' of terminologies for the one supreme God.[21] While the image implies religious and historical continuity, the fact that a court of law is depicted, with the ruler flanked by a Muslim cleric and a group including Mongol secular figures, also suggests that both the Muslim *sharīʿa* and the Mongol *yāsa* may be represented.

Sūra 38:26 is one of two in the Qur'ān that specifically mention the Caliphate and were therefore commonly cited in justification of caliphal rule.[22] As a whole, Sūra 38 may be seen as prefigur-

[19] Inv. no. 880; Gierlichs (1996), cat. 36, 191–92 and pl. 35, 1–2; and Redford (1993) 221 and fig. 13. I am very grateful to Scott Redford for permission to publish his photograph.

[20] I am most grateful to Joachim Gierlichs for guidance on this building. Although it is problematic, I have included this photograph two reasons: first, as an interesting example of the legacy of the bird of prey image; and second, because it predates by some twenty-five years the photographs from the 1970s available to Gierlichs at the time he was writing, and shows the building prior to significant alteration and/or dilapidation that occurred in the intervening period. I am most grateful to Anthony Kersting for his permission to publish it. For a thoughtful discussion of this monument, see Gierlichs (1998), 349–60. For fourteenth-century examples of birds of prey on Anatolian tombstones, see Öney (1969), 292–301.

[21] See n. 12, above.

[22] The other is Sūra 2:30, in which God tells the angels he is appointing Adam as caliph on the earth; Watt, W. M. (1971), 564–74, and Crone and Hinds (1986), 4–6.

ing many of the personalities and much of the subject matter in Balʿamī's text and its cycle of illustrations. It describes how God establishes his kingdom on earth, through the mediation of prophets and kings, with a repeated emphasis on the need for vigilance against apostasy; it includes accounts of the Creation, the Fall, messianic visions of heaven and hell and the Day of Judgment. A quotation from Sūra 38 is, therefore, an excellent introduction to Balʿamī's text and particularly at a period of reestablishment of Muslim rule. More importantly, perhaps, the inclusion of the word of God in the image significantly alters the hierarchy of the iconography, giving the enthroned ruler second billing. In effect, it turns a religious and judicial statement into one of legitimization.

In terms of Islamic religious theory, an authority stemming from God through King David may be understood as encompassing all members of the 'People of the Book'—Jews, Christians, and Muslims, and with pseudo-Sasanians present, perhaps also Zoroastrians. In the Balʿamī frontispiece a Mongol figure of authority, with no Muslim insignia, has been placed at the heart of this salvatic vision. Ghazan used Sūra 38:26 to head an important *yarligh* on land reform, closely associated with another dated 3 Rajab 699/26 March 1300, issued at Kushaf near Mosul soon after his victorious return from the first Syrian campaign.[23] This *yarligh* also identifies crimes to be punished according to the *yāsa*.[24] May contemporary events help explain this unusual recoding of a traditional frontispiece formula?

Between 1299 and the spring of 1303, Ghazan mounted three Syrian campaigns; the first was crowned with some success, the second was abandoned because of bad weather, and the third resulted in a comprehensive Mongol defeat.[25] Since in 1299 mosques at Ra's al-ʿAyn, near Mardin, had been desecrated during a Mamluk incursion into Ilkhanid territory, Ghazan obtained a *fatwā* for *jihād*. By 31 December Ghazan was in possession of Damascus, and by 8 March 1300 he himself had returned to Mosul, leaving behind in Syria a

[23] In the *yarligh*, verse 26 is paired with the *ḥadīth*, "The justice of an hour is worth forty years of prayer."

[24] Rashīd al-Dīn (1941), 221–22. See also Spuler (1955), 387–88 and Lambton (1988), 92–93.

[25] Raff (1973), 1; Raff's article is available only in typescript but is widely circulated and cited. I am most grateful to Reuven Amitai-Preiss for providing me with a copy.

garrison of occupation. If there was a time for Ilkhanid triumphalism subsequent to the fall of Baghdad in 1258, this was surely it! He had shone in the role of *ghāzī* and *pādshāh-i islām* as well as proving himself the best qualified member of the house of Chinggis and Hülegü to rule a horde that was still configured for war.

However, at this time in Damascus the Hanbalite theologian Aḥmad ibn Taymiyya (661–728/1263–1328) was also vastly enhancing his prestige by assuming the role of verbal antagonist to the Mongols.[26] This culminated in 702/1302 in his closely argued *fatwā*,[27] detailing the heterodox nature of Mongol beliefs and exhorting Mamluk troops to treat their campaign as *jihād*.[28]

Ibn Taymiyya's polemic provides a useful foil for Ilkhanid aspirations at this time: it reflects both Ghazan's wish for the Ilkhanid state to be accepted into the Muslim fold, with himself as a warrior for the faith, and his attempt to synchronize Chinggisid ideology with Islam. Ibn Taymiyya turns the ideological weapons of the Mongols against themselves,[29] declaring that Ghazan equated the Prophet with "...an infidel and polytheistic prince who the Mongols believe is the son of God, analogous to what the Christians believe of Christ..."; he also compares Chinggis Khan to the ilk of Namrūd and Pharaoh, and declares him more harmful than Musaylima the Liar.[30] Namrūd, Pharaoh and Musaylima are all pictured in the cycle of illustrations in this manuscript.

That the Syrian campaigns should elicit anti-Mongol polemic is not surprising. However, this view from the Sultanate also appears to parody the message of 'inclusive' Mongol and Muslim kingship expressed in the frontispiece. If so, then perhaps the iconography reflects not only matters of internal concern within the Ilkhanid state but also sensitivity to external Mamluk propaganda.

Is religious diversity also conveyed in the cycle of illustrations? The lines immediately above and below the paintings provide keys to the actions depicted. However, illustrations may also reflect a story that closely precedes or follows it. The subjects for illustration appear to have been chosen with care, since when the stories are read

---

26 Ibid., 4; Laoust (1971), 951.
27 Raff, 6.
28 Ibid., 4–5.
29 Ibid., 44.
30 Ibid., 45–49.

in sequence, certain topics persistently recur throughout the cycle, creating a strong impression of thematic unity within the whole. Even those illustrating the life of the Prophet do not operate as a discrete mini-cycle. A single story may carry more than one lesson; however, the topic most frequently returned to is that of conversion to monotheism—that is, to Judaism and Islam, including an overarching theme that God supports his chosen people. There is also a fascinating number of permutations of problems associated with conversion, in particular, the divisive effects on the family and wider community of failure to convert and apostasy.[31] However, in marked contrast to the Edinburgh al-Bīrūnī manuscript, in the Balʿamī there is a total absence of images depicting the physical destruction of idols;[32] by contrast, the paintings draw attention to the spiritual superiority of God's chosen ones, their ability to subjugate the spirit world with his assistance and miraculously survive sentences of death.

Two images, for instance, are associated with trial by fire. The first (fig. 91) depicts Ibrāhīm cast into the fire by Namrūd, King of Bābil (Babylon), an ardent idolater, for claiming God's superiority over the ruler and his gods.[33] Ibrāhīm is shown standing unharmed in the midst of the flames, which God has turned into flowers and aromatic herbs; he praises God and is ministered to by angels.[34]

The second is from the history of pre-Islamic Arabia (fig. 92).[35] Here, Jewish doctors from Medina, together with a copy of the Torah, have been subjected to trial by fire by the idolatrous Tubbaʿ, Himyarite ruler of the Yemen; they and the scriptures emerge unscathed.

---

[31] See n. 4, above.

[32] For example, 'Ibrāhīm destroys the idols' in *Āthār al-bāqiya ʿan al-qurūn al-khāliya* of al-Bīrūnī, dated 707/1307–8, possibly Maragha or Tabriz, Edinburgh University Library, Arab. 161, fol. 88b; for discussion, see Soucek (1975), 114 and fig. 5.

[33] F1957.16, fol. 24b; see Milstein (1987), 127 and fig. 2; mentioned without illustration in Allen (1985), 125; Brosh and Milstein (1991), 30, n. 45, and in Milstein, Rührdanz, and Schmitz (1999), 119. In the upper section of the painting (not illustrated), Namrūd and a companion, with a helpful shove from a beefy *dīw*, are shown flying heavenwards in a basket drawn by vultures to challenge God; however, in both scenes Namrūd's face has been badly thumbed.

[34] The depiction of angels is contrary to the text, in which Balʿamī is critically outspoken against al-Ṭabarī for giving credence to accounts of their presence on this occasion. As in the frontispiece, the wings of these angels sprout from their haloes.

[35] F1957.16, fol. 126a, not previously published. So far, I have not found this subject depicted in the fourteenth century or later.

The doctors then further demonstrate God's power by exorcising an evil spirit from a temple, indicated by a Buddhist-inspired sculpture in an alcove.[36] However, as recorded in the text, the evil spirit flees in the form of a black dog, which disappears into the ground. This persuades the Tubbaʿ and his people to convert to Judaism. In the text, the Jews are portrayed as custodians of the Mosaic tradition who foretell the coming of Muḥammad.

DeWeese has noted the role played by Ibrāhīm in myth patterns associated with conversion to Islam.[37] In particular, Ibrāhīm personifies the Prophet, who broke with his own family to do God's will; breaking with the traditions of their ancestors was clearly an important issue for Mongol converts.[38] With particular reference to the conversion of the Golden Horde, DeWeese discusses Ibrāhīm and the concept of trial by fire together with parallels in Inner Asian and Islamic societies.[39] The custom of purification by passing between fires is described by Ibn Shaddād (613–84/1217–85), sent to Hülegü with a mission from the last Ayyubid ruler of Aleppo and Damascus in 657/1259:

> A group of Mongols came upon us, and with them were shamans (*qāmāt*). They inspected all of our people, and the beasts with us. Then they set up fires on two sides and passed through them with us, while beating us with sticks.[40]

In certain shaman traditions of Central and North Asia, the entrance to the underworld is guarded by dogs.[41] There is an extensive literature on the role of dogs and wolves in Mongol myth and legend, more often as forces for good rather than evil, and both feature

[36] The same type of sculpture is used in the Edinburgh al-Bīrūnī example cited above; see n. 32. The choice of image probably reflects the proliferation of Buddhist temples and monasteries prior to Ghazan's official conversion, especially in the reign of his father, Arghun (r. 683–90/1284–91).

[37] DeWeese (1994), especially 24 and 244–45.

[38] For example, Amitai-Preiss cites the feat of casuistry required in order to accommodate Ghazan's conversion with his having married his father's widow, according to Mongol custom, and his refusal to divorce her, Amitai-Preiss (1996a), 2–3.

[39] DeWeese (1994), 244–62. An example of incineration to test religious veracity is recorded for the late fifteenth century; idem, 249–50.

[40] Amitai-Preiss (1991), 354–55.

[41] Eliade (1964), 251; however, I have not yet found an exact parallel for this in other sources.

significantly in creation myths.[42] For example, perhaps the best known regards the origin of Chinggis Khan in the *Secret History of the Mongols*, which opens thus: "There was a bluish wolf which was born having [his] destiny from Heaven above. His spouse was a fallow doe."[43] The form of the dog used in the Balʿamī image is close to one of a wolf on a fragmentary cobalt and luster tile, probably from the palace built by Abaqa at Takht-i Sulayman, and therefore dateable to the 1270s (pl. 29a).[44] However, since many of the Mongol dog/wolf beliefs conflicted with Islam, the inclusion of an image showing the exorcism of a dog, especially at a period of Mongol conversion, suggests the choice may have held greater significance than mere pattern book pasting.

A second unusual subject chosen for illustration depicts the purification of Muḥammad's heart, in preparation for his prophethood, by three divine messengers (fig. 93).[45] The text describes how the Prophet was sent to live with his wet nurse, Ḥalīma. When three years old, he used to go into the desert every day with ʿAbdallāh, his milk brother. One day, three men came from the mountain and carried Muḥammad away from his companion. The men then laid Muḥammad on the ground and slit open his chest and belly; one of them removed his heart, cut it into two halves and removed black blood from it before returning it to its place. Another of the men then rubbed the wound, which healed instantly, leaving Muḥammad in no pain but feeling weak and cold.

The method of cleansing Muḥammad's heart finds an echo in shaman practices in Central and North Asia. A cure for illness and 'the rape of the soul' was said to lie in opening up the body and removing the offending part, after which the body would heal instantly.[46] Mostaert has discussed the role of evisceration of animals in traditional Mongol medicine, which included using newly removed organs as

---

[42] For example, Roux (1984), especially 177–95, and Golden (1997), 87–97. I am very grateful to Charles Melville for suggesting sources.

[43] Cleaves, trans. (1982), 1. White (1991) suggests a translation of "wild she-dog" for "fallow doe," 137.

[44] Freer Gallery of Art and Arthur M. Sackler Gallery, Washington, D.C., F1973.14; perhaps fortuitously due to opacity of the glaze, the color of the wolf on this tile is gray-blue rather than deep cobalt.

[45] F57.16, fol. 138a; see Soucek (1988), 198 and fig. 2. To date, I have not found another illustration of this incident.

[46] Eliade (1964), 251.

poultices to draw out infected blood from wounds.[47] It seems possible, therefore, that familiarity with such procedures may have rendered this scene less shocking and more meaningful to recent Mongol converts than to established Muslim communities.

Another religiously complex image is the first of two concerned with the battle at the wells of Badr, in the second year of the *hijra* (pl. 30).[48] The painting depicts a sequence of incidents described in the text, but the lines adjacent the painting are concerned, first and foremost, with the Muslim convert ʿUbayda being fatally struck on the thigh by the unconverted Meccan warrior ʿUtba, and the Prophet's promise to the dying ʿUbayda of paradise for those who die in the cause of *jihād*. The description of God sending an angelic host to secure victory for the Muslims occurs on the following folio. During the battle, the Prophet and Abū Bakr are described as withdrawing to a hut where they prostrate themselves and call upon God for assistance. Nonetheless, in the painting the Prophet is shown on a wall-eyed black horse, galloping behind the battle lines, wielding a sword, and gazing over his left shoulder at the approaching heavenly squadron.

As Raya Shani has previously pointed out,[49] the Prophet's pose with the attendant angel owes a debt to the figure of the royal hunter in the frontispiece to vol. 20 of the *Kitāb al-aghānī*, dated 616/1219 (fig. 94).[50] However, that we are also dealing with a generalized repertoire image from the Jazira and Anatolia is suggested by the relief-carved stucco figure of a royal hunter, probably part of a frieze of repeat designs, from the larger palace at Kubadabad, founded in 1227 on the southwestern shore of Lake Beyşehir, and now in the Ince Minereli Medresesi in Konya (fig. 95).[51] These examples provide prototypes for the image, but they do not explain why, contrary to the text, the Prophet is shown as a cavalryman in killing mode.

---

[47] Cleaves (1954), 428–44, especially 444.

[48] F1957.16, fol. 182a; see Soucek (1988), 195–96 and fig. 5; mentioned without illustration in Milstein, Rührdanz, and Schmitz (1999), 168.

[49] Conference paper delivered at The Art of the Mongols: its Precursors, Contemporary Context and Legacy, held at the University of Edinburgh, 31 July–2 August, 1995. I am most grateful to Raya Shani for providing me with a copy of her paper.

[50] Royal Library, Copenhagen, Cod. Arab. CLXVIII, on permanent loan to the David Collection, no. D1/1990; see Folsach (2001), 45 and no. 24.

[51] Redford, Beach, and Luzzadder-Beach (2000), 78–79 and ill. 20.

A possible answer may lie in the deeply rooted cult and ethos of the Christian warrior saints of the Eastern Christian Churches, most notably Saints George and Theodosius, who were revered by both the Christian and Muslim communities of the Jazira and Anatolia.[52] St. George, *Hazrat* Jurjays, was a patron saint of Mosul.[53] In the Freer text, the calligrapher has improvised a way of differentiating the section heading for this saint (pl. 29b): apart from the first twelve folios which suggest experimentation, all the section headings are written with a pen and in a bright red ink; however, the one for *Hazrat* Jurjays is a deep plum color and was probably written with a brush rather than a pen. The heading is also followed by the abbreviation for a blessing, the only occurrence of this type of abbreviation in a section heading in this manuscript—a small but telling act of reverence.

Datable to between 1282 and 1304, the wallpaintings of the Kırk Dam Altı Kilise at Belisirama in eastern Cappadocia are dedicated to St. George. The saint appears both as the mounted knight (fig. 96) and between donors, who are identified as a certain Georgian lady, Thamar, and her turbaned husband, the Emir and Consul Basil, with the Seljuk Sultan Masʿūd II and the Byzantine Emperor Andronicus II also named in the inscriptions (fig. 97).[54] It seems likely, therefore,

[52] According to tradition, St. George was born in Mitelene (Malatya) and suffered martyrdom in Lydda during the reign of Diocletian (284–305). However, in Balʿamī's text he is described as a Palestinian. On the conflation of St. George with the Judeo-Christian Prophet Elijah and the Muslim prophet al-Khiḍr, see Hastings (1920), 81–82. On the shared shrine of Mar Behnam, some twenty-three miles from Mosul, with its plaque in Uighur script calling down blessings on Ghazan and his house and the association of this shrine with the Biblical Elias, the Qur'ānic Khiḍr Elias and probably the ancient god of spring, Tammus, see Fiey (1959), 50 and Fiey (1975a), 71.

[53] Fiey (1959), 105–6, and also 57–58, where Fiey, citing Rich (1836), vol. 2, 46, recalls a popular legend of how St. George, in the company of the local saint, Mar Matta, the eponym of the monastery near Mosul, and the Prophet Jonah (*Nabī* Yūnus), sent by God to convert the people of Nineveh, on the far bank of the Tigris opposite Mosul, appeared on the ramparts during the siege of the city by Nādir Shāh in 1743. Ibn Baṭṭūṭa provides an enthusiastic description of his visits to the shrines of Nabī Jurjays and Nabī Yūnus, while visiting Mosul in the 1330s. Ibn Baṭṭūṭa, (1958–2000), vol. 2, 348–50 and 349, nn. 272 and 273.

[54] Restle (1967), vol. 1 (Text), no. LX, 176–77, and vol. 3 (Plates), ills. 515–16; Thierry, N. and Thierry, M. (1963), ch. XIII, 201–9, pls. 93–94. I am very grateful to Oya Pancaroğlu for telling me about this church, and for providing me with a copy of her paper 'The Itinerant Dragon Slayer: Forging Paths of Image and Identity in Medieval Anatolia' prior to publication; see Pancaroğlu (2004b).

that an instinctive feeling that it would be unseemly to depict the Prophet other than actively participating in the battle might account for this significant departure from the text and Muslim tradition.

An additional link with the Christian communities of the Jazira is suggested by certain figural and architectural forms found in some of the Balʿamī's paintings, and in the Vatican Library's Syrian Orthodox Lectionary, copied in 1260/1571 (Greek), at the Monastery of Mar Mattai, near Mosul.[55] For example, on fol. 181b of the Balʿamī, the heresiarch Bābak is depicted under siege in his mountain fastness, parleying with the Caliph al-Muʿtaṣim's brilliant Central Asian general from Ushtrushana, the Afshīn Ḥaydar (fig. 98).[56] The figure of Bābak may be compared to that of St. Simeon (fig. 99)[57] and also to the venerable, bearded, and turbaned figure in discussion with a companion as Christ approaches Jerusalem (fig. 100).[58] The Afshīn's furled banner, with its crescent moon finial, has replaced St. Simeon's tree. The triangular brick corner battlements of unequal size, on Bābak's rooftop, resemble the triangular supports rising at the front and back of the saint's prayer stall; triangular battlements flanking a central dome echo the city gate into Jerusalem.[59] In addition, the wings of the angel shown visiting St. Simeon during his prophetic dream issue not from its back but from its halo. This idiosyncratic feature has already been noted for attendant angels in the Balʿamī

[55] Biblioteca Apostolica Vaticana, ms. Syriaco 559, published by Leroy with a colophon date (fol. 250b) of 1220/1531 (Greek); Leroy (1964) 301–2. The colophon was subsequently convincingly reread by Fiey as 1260/1571 (Greek), that is, two years after the fall of Baghdad to Hülegü, whose wife was the Nestorian Christian Kereit princess, Doqūz Khātūn; Fiey (1975b), 59–64.

[56] Marteau and Vever (1913), vol. 1, pl. 47, no. 52; Schulz (1914) vol. 1, pl. H; Blochet (1926), pl. 2.

[57] Syriaco 559, fol. 48a.

[58] Syriaco 559, fol. 105a.

[59] Surviving evidence of preliminary underdrawing suggests that the parapet of Bābak's tower was originally fortified with a triangular brick type of crenelation, now overlaid by the poorly drawn dome, perhaps to emphasize the religious-political confrontation. Using a Christian prototype for the figure of Bābak might also be seen as provocative; I am grateful to Julie Meisami for her view. However, the story adjacent to the image relates how Bābak outwits the Afshīn and temporarily escapes; thematically, therefore, it falls more happily within the category of military affairs, tactics, and ruses, rather than that of problems associated with conversion (see n. 4, above). It is, of course, possible that the designer of the manuscript, who selected the subjects to be depicted, and the artist(s), who carried out the work, were not singing from identical hymn sheets!

frontispiece and those ministering to Ibrāhīm in the fire (fig. 91), as well as in the frontispiece to vol. 17 of the *Kitāb al-aghānī* (fig. 88), representing Badr al-Dīn Lu'lu', who collaborated with the Mongols and remained in power in Mosul until his death, aged eighty, in 1259.

For whom, then, might the Balʿamī have been designed?[60] Ghazan's governor in Mosul was a known bibliophile named Fakhr al-Dīn ʿĪsā ibn Ibrāhīm.[61] Stefano Carboni has suggested him as a possible patron, or at least recipient, for the British Library's Qazwīnī manuscript.[62] For information on Fakhr al-Dīn ʿĪsā we have largely to thank Ibn al-Ṭiqṭaqā, who composed for him a mirror for princes in thanks for hospitality while caught by bad weather in Mosul in 1302. Ibn al-Ṭiqṭaqā is unusual in that he grasps the nettle of justifying Hülegü's destruction of the Caliphate on the grounds that a just infidel ruler is preferable to rule by an unjust believer. He supports this contention with an opening anecdote describing how, following the sack of Baghdad in 1258, Hülegü posed this question to the jurists in the Mustanṣiriyya Madrasa, who, after due deliberation, declared in favor of the just infidel.[63]

Also, Ibn al-Ṭiqṭaqā is specific in saying that he composed his text for Fakhr al-Dīn ʿĪsā with teaching in mind, including children, thereby pointing to what must surely have been a major problem of the period: how to explain the fall of the Caliphate to younger generations. Perhaps it was this that spurred the patron of the Freer Balʿamī to recode the iconography of the frontispiece to express religious and political continuity and add to an otherwise rarely illustrated text a cycle of images that were carefully selected and adapted to appeal to a culturally complex Ilkhanid society.

Rashīd al-Dīn describes the demise of Ghazan's governor in the spring of 1303, roughly a year after Ibn al-Ṭiqṭaqā's visit: "...the people of Mosul raised their cries for help to the seventh heaven

[60] In my opinion the ruler in the frontispiece should be read as a coded generic image, in the manner of such frontispieces as those in the *Kitāb al-aghānī*, rather than as a personal portrait.

[61] Ibn al-Ṭiqṭaqā (1895), 1–34; Ibn al-Ṭiqṭaqā (1910), VII–XXVIII and Ibn al-Ṭiqṭaqā (1947); Kritzeck (1959), 157–84.

[62] *ʿAjā'ib al-makhlūqāt*, undated, Or. 14140, Carboni (1992), especially 533–37.

[63] Ibn al-Ṭiqṭaqā (1895), Arabic text 21. I am grateful to Charles Melville for noting that this anecdote is also put into the mouth of Ghazan.

against the hand of oppression and injustice of Fakhr-i ʿĪsā al-Naṣrānī, Fakhr-i ʿĪsā the Christian..." He goes on to describe how Ghazan tricked him into thinking he was confirming his governorship of Mosul, but had him killed after a few days.[64]

The epithet 'al-Dīn' was used by Christians as well as Muslims;[65] however, even if Fakhr al-Dīn ʿĪsā had converted to Islam, Rashīd al-Dīn clearly doubted his sincerity. According to Karl Jahn, an alternative version in the *Ta'rīkh-i Ghāzānī* says that he was executed according to the *yāsa*; since Muslims were tried according to the *sharīʿa*, it would appear that he was not given the benefit any doubt. If so, the execution scene in the frontispiece takes on a searing irony.

If the Balʿamī manuscript was copied and illustrated at the behest of Fakhr al-Dīn ʿĪsā, Christians or recent converts to Islam are likely to have been employed. A religiously pragmatic attitude on the part of the patron, particularly if more interested in practicalities than dogma, at a period when Ghazan's policies were aimed at state consolidation, may help to explain some of the unusual features of the illustrative cycle: for example, the unexpected freedom with which models from other traditions were included and adapted, the selection of unusual subject matter, and also the preponderance of illustrations relating to conversion. Indeed, if the Freer Balʿamī was produced in Mosul, the city protected by *Hazrat* Jurjays, looking west across the Tigris to the walls of Nineveh and the shrine of *Nabī* Yūnus (fig. 101) and south to the Babylon of Ibrāhīm and Namrūd, and remains of the Sasanian palace at Ctesiphon, then quires of Balʿamī's text will have read as local history.

Balʿamī's text was overtaken, if never entirely eclipsed, by Rashīd

---

64 " ...*ahl-i mawṣil az dast-i ẓulm wa taʿaddī-yi fakhr-i ʿīsā naṣrānī al-ghiyāth ba-falak-i haftum rasānidand, farmān shud kih sulṭān najm al-dīn chūn bi-mawṣil rawad kār-i ū tamām kunad, sulṭān ūrā ba-farīb-i ānkih nā'ibī ba-way dihad baʿd az chand rūz halāk kard...,"* Rashīd al-Dīn (1941), 148.

"...the people of Mosul raised their cries for help to the seventh heaven against the hand of oppression and injustice of Fakhr-i ʿĪsā, the Christian; and the order was given that when Najm al-Dīn should arrive in Mosul he should bring his [Fakhr-i ʿĪsā's] affairs to an end; the Sultan, deceiving him (Fakhr-i ʿĪsā) on the pretext that he would give him the deputyship [of Mosul], killed him after a few days..." I am grateful to Julie Scott Meisami for clarifying this text.

65 For example, Fakhr al-Dīn ʿAbd al-Masīḥ, vizier to the Zangid ruler, Nūr al-Dīn who, in the 1170s, built the mosque named after him in Mosul; Tabbaa (2002), 339.

al-Dīn's *Jāmiʿ al-tawārīkh*. Begun for Ghazan and completed for Öljeitü, it placed the Mongols securely within a magisterial religious as well as historical global sweep and also displayed them in paint. Nonetheless, if I am correct, the Freer Balʿamī had already blazed a significant trail and shown the value of painting as a subtext to history during the crucial process of integrating the Ilkhanid state into the *Dār al-Islām*.

THE MONGOL LEGACY OF PERSIAN *FARMĀNS*

ABOLALA SOUDAVAR

Introduction

Uzun Ḥasan's (r. 1453–78) successive defeats of two renowned rulers, the Qara-Quyunlu ruler of Tabriz, Jahānshāh (r. 1438–67), and the Timurid ruler of Herat, Abū Saʿīd (r. 1451–69), drove him into the realm of the great conquerors of the Iranian plateau who had each generated their own brand of legitimacy. If Uzun Ḥasan wished to gain a lasting recognition, his victories had to be translated into a new formulation of dynastic legitimacy as well. In the post-Mongol era, Turco-Mongol rulers had traditionally elevated a puppet Chinggisid ruler to the throne and/or married a Chinggisid princess in order to gain legitimacy.[1] By the time Uzun Ḥasan rose to power, there were simply no Chinggisids to be found. Inevitably, any new theory of legitimacy had to be based on Islamic tenets, mixed with Turkoman beliefs, and garbed in a Persianate robe.[2] The problem of bringing such a heterogeneous group of beliefs into harmony, however, was not a new one; it had been previously encountered when the Mongols first espoused Islam. The formulae devised then influenced those concocted later on.

Through the analysis of the headings used in a recently discovered edict of Uzun Ḥasan, I shall try to demonstrate the close relationship between Mongol *farmāns* and those of the following ruling dynasties of Iran, especially the Aq-Quyunlus, in this paper.

[1] The marrying of Chinggisid princesses entitled warlords such as Tīmūr to become *gūrkāns* (i.e., son-in-laws to the House of Genghis [Chinggis]).

[2] After the defeat of Jahānshāh, and following earlier Islamic practices, a robe of investiture was requested from the Mamluk court of Sultan Qaytbay of Egypt, where an Abbasid caliph had resided since the fall of Baghdad in 1258. Uzun Ḥasan's second victory necessitated a new legitimizing theory; Woods (1999), 114.

The Edict

This majestic *farmān* of Uzun Ḥasan is an edict related to a charitable institution that because of a missing end part bears no date, nor does it reveal for which shrine or religious institution it was issued. The incomplete text is written in gold and blue *taʿlīq* script, and comes after an elaborate set of headings. It is the latter that is of interest to this study.[3] It comprises six different sections:

– Section 1 displays a verse from the Qurʾān and is prefaced with a statement to that effect: "Quoth God; May he be praised and exalted." The preface is written in a small *rayhān* script in blue ink. The Qurʾānic verse is written in a majestic *thuluth* in gold with black outlining (fig. 102):

اطيعوا الله واطيعوا الرسول واولي الامر منكم

4:59: Obey God and obey the Apostle and those in authority from among you

– Section 2 quotes two other verses from the Qurʾān, prefaced with the statement: "Quoth God; May he be blessed and exalted," in a similar *rayhān* script as above. The verses are written in (a) majestic *thuluth* in gold with black outlining at the bottom, (b) blue *muhaqqaq* in the middle, and (c) decorative kufic at the top in blue (fig. 103):

(a) انّ الذين يعملون الصالحات انّ لهم اجراً

(b) حسناً

(c) ممّا كثير فيه ابداً

18:2–3: Those who do good deeds, they shall have a goodly reward, staying in it for ever.

– Section 3 displays a verse from the Qurʾān and is prefaced with a statement to that effect: "Quoth God; May he be praised and exalted." The preface is written in a small *rayhān* script in blue ink. The verses are written in a majestic *thuluth* in gold with black outlining, one half straight and the other upside down (fig. 104)

[3] This edict is in a private collection from which I could only obtain a color photocopy. For lack of seeing the original, I am unable to give accurate information about dimensions and other characteristics. The analysis of the main text written in Arabic is beyond the scope of this study.

التعظيم لامر الله
والشفقة على خلق الله

Ḥadīth: Respect shall be for God's orders, and compassion shall be for God's creatures.

– Section 4 is positioned as a subheading of the previous section, since it appears in symmetry with its preface as another inconspicuous blue line of script. In reality, it is an independent line and displays a traditional adage used in edicts (fig. 104):

القدرة لله تعالي

Power is for God, The Most Exalted (to exercise)

– Section 5 is written in a majestic gold and blue *muhaqqaq* in an elaborate script with intertwined letters (fig. 105):

بالقوّة الاحدية والعناية الصمدية والمعجزات المحمدية والدولة البايندرية

By the power of The Unique, and the solicitude of The Eternal, and the Muḥammadan Miracles, and the fortunes (*dawla*) of the Bayāndur Clan.

– Section 6 comprises the standard *tughra* of Uzun Ḥasan that combines the sign of the Bayāndur clan—the paramount Aq-Quyunlu clan named after Uzun Ḥasan's supposed ancestor, Bayāndur Khan—with the saying (fig. 106):

Orders are for God (to issue them) الحكم لله

followed by:

Abū al-Naṣr Ḥasan Bahādur has said (*syūzūmīz*) (fig. 107)

ابو النصر حسن بهادر سيوزوميز

Analysis

Section 1

Islamic legitimacy was primarily based on the Qur'ān. Two verses therein provided the possibility for mortals to claim acting as God's deputy (*khalīfa*) on earth:

2:30: And when your Lord said to the angels, I am going to place in the earth a *khalīfa*

38:26: O David! surely We have appointed you as a *khalīfa* on earth

The appropriation of the title *khalīfa* by Turco-Mongol rulers, however, would have been problematic since, as the title of past caliphs, it implied religious leadership, and al-Ghazālī had argued that it behooved only those with a Qurayshi lineage (*nasab-i quraysh*) to be in such position.[4] Turco-Mongols could obviously not claim descent from an Arab tribe. They did not have to. For verse 4:59, which appears at the top of this edict, was more useful and more versatile. Indeed, it placed 'those in authority' on par with God and his Prophet in terms of the obedience that was due to them. In essence, every ruler or kinglet could claim to be 'in authority'; hence, he had to be obeyed.

The Aq-Quyunlu panegyrists however, added a new twist to the interpretation of 4:59. Since the numerical value of its last word (منكم), in the *abjad* computation, added up to that of 'Ḥasan Beg' (i.e., Uzun Ḥasan), they argued that his authority had effectively been foretold by the Qur'ān.[5] The prominent top line of this edict thus reflects the very legitimization efforts of Uzun Ḥasan's panegyrist to promote him as the new emperor of the Islamic lands.

Sections 2 & 3

In a fifteenth-century manual for scribes entitled *Manāẓir al-inshā'*, its author describes how *farmān* headings must be appropriately chosen, and gives the example that if the text is about helping somebody it should start with the invocation هو المعين (He is the helper); or if it is about grants it should be prefaced with هو الكريم (He is the generous).[6] Similarly, *ḥadīth* or Qur'ānic quotations of an edict must reflect, and reinforce, its purpose and subject matter. Thus,

[4] Laoust (1970), 247. Nevertheless, these verses are sometimes boldly inserted into Turkoman *farmāns* (Mudarrisī-i Ṭabāṭabā'ī [1974], 31), and some other times cautiously (Nawā'ī, ed. [1962–63], 320). In his panegyrics however, Jalāl al-Dīn Dawānī goes so far as calling Uzun Ḥasan "The Shadow of God, and the Caliph of God, and the Deputy of the Prophet"; Woods (1999), 105. In an odd way, the multiplicity of divine attributes weakens the eulogy since they can become contradictory: it is demeaning for God to have a deputy who is also a deputy of his own messenger!

[5] Woods (1999), 103. In addition, through similar cabalistic exercises, they were also able to claim that Uzun Ḥasan's victory over Jahānshāh Qara-Quyunlu was foretold in the Qurʿān; ibid., 102.

[6] Gāvān (2002–3), 215.

the headings in sections 2 and 3, which speak about charitable acts, must indicate that the purpose of the edict was to relegate authority or confirm an existing one over a charitable and/or religious institution.

The text of a similar *farmān* by Uzun Ḥasan, reportedly two meters long and 33 centimeters wide, written in gold, and comprising headings similar to our section 1, 3, and 6, has been published by Mudarrisī.[7] It confirms the trusteeship (*tawliya*) of two Raḍawī *sayyids* over the endowments of the Fatima Shrine of Qum and the adjacent *masjid* of Imām Ḥasan al- ʿAskarī. It came in the wake of two other *farmāns*, one issued by Tīmūr (r. 1370–1405) and the other by Jahānshāh Qara-Quyunlu, both confirming the trusteeship of the ancestors of the Raḍawī *sayyids*, who all descended from the eighth Imām of the Shiʿites, ʿAlī al-Riḍā, the brother of said Fatima.[8] Since the *farmān* of Uzun Ḥasan for the Raḍawī *sayyids* is dated 12 Shaʿbān 874/14 February 1470, which coincides with the year of his first visit to Qum, and considering the strong similarity between this *farmān* and the one under study, we may perhaps assume that the latter was issued for the same purpose (and for members of the same family of *sayyids*) on the occasion of one his two subsequent visits to Qum in the winters of 1471–72 and 1473–74. The third visit came in the aftermath of the crushing defeat that the Ottomans inflicted upon him in Bashkent (August 1473). Defeat had to be overshadowed by propaganda and pomp. And most probably, similar to Ismāʿīl I's defeat at Chaldaran (1514) that led to the production of the most lavishly illustrated *Shāhnāma* (the one that was subsequently called the Ṭahmāsp Shāhnāma), the elaborate decoration of this *farmān* and its magnificent *invocatios* were formulated in reaction to the Bashkent defeat.

Section 4

The tradition of the adage in section 4 goes back to the Seljuk era, to which period must be attributed the earliest extant *farmān* specimen of the Iranian lands. It is an edict from the Eldiguzid Muḥammad b. ʿUthmān b. Uzbek, dated 630/1233 and first published by Her-

[7] Mudarrisī-i Ṭabāṭabāʾī (1974), 62–66.
[8] Ibid., 38–43.

rmann in 1994 (fig. 109).[9] Herrmann, though, failed to understand the meaning of a bold graffito incorporated near the top of the *farmān,* which should read as our section 4:

القدرة لله تعالي

The writing of this adage continued in Timurid times, and was even expanded in an edict issued by Tīmūr to include two other similar sayings:[10]

(1) الحكم لله تعالي ، (2) القدرة لله تعالي ، (3) الملك لله تعالي

(1) and (2) of course appear in our present edict, and (3) which means 'kingship belongs to God, The Most Exalted,' is very much in the same vein. Even though they all imply that the ruler is acting through powers invested to him by God, in form, they are shrouded in a veil of humility that presents the ruler as a simple agent of God and not as an authoritarian despot.

Section 5

Contrary to the humble form of the previous heading, section 5 is authoritative and empowers the edict with forces of various origins. The first two invoke powers emanating from God and the third from the Prophet Muḥammad, although the role of 'Muḥammadan Miracles' as a source of power is not very clear; one suspects its inclusion in this heading was to create a connecting bridge to the fourth one. The latter is by far the most interesting one, since it recognizes for the Bayāndur clan powers equivalent to those emanating from God and the Prophet Muḥammad. To better understand this, we shall backtrack its formulation to Mongol times and argue that it was rooted in a Turco-Mongol tribal belief.

The closest parallel to the section 5 formula is encountered in the above-mentioned *farmān* of Jahānshāh concerning the trusteeship of the Qum shrine, which, incidentally, reinforces the assumption of its connectivity with our edict. It reads:

---

[9] Herrmann (1994), 299.

[10] Ḥāfiz-i Abrū (1949), 12. The edict was addressed to Tīmūr's son, 'Umar Bahādur.

[11] Rashīd al-Dīn (1957), vol. 3, 430.

[12] This fragment was first published in Pelliot (1936), and subsequently in Cleaves (1953).

بالقدرة الكاملة الاحدية والقوة الشاملة الاحمدية

"By the most complete godly powers and the all-encompassing Muḥammadan strength"

It has no tribal ingredients and appears to be a more Islamicized version of the *invocatio* that Rashīd al-Dīn had formulated for the *farmāns* of the Ilkhan Ghazan (r. 1295–1304):

بقوت الله تعالي ومیامن الملت المحمدية

"By the power of God, The Most Exalted, and the good fortunes of the Muḥammadan nation" (*millat al-Muḥammadiya*) [11]

Although clad in an Islamic garb, this *invocatio* is recognizing a power attached to the Muḥammadan nation as a group of people, and almost independent from God's will. It is a tribal concept that appears even more forcefully in a Uighur edict of the Ilkhan Abū Saʿīd (r. 1316–35). This edict remains as a fragment in the Tehran Museum and contains only three lines:[12]

[1] mongke tngri-yin küchündür
[2] Muqamad baighambar-un umat-dur[13]
[3] yeke suu jali-yin ibegendür
By the Might of Everlasting Sky (Tengri)
By (the power of) the nation of the Apostle Muḥammad
By the protection (?) of the Great Shining Fortune.[14]

Abū Saʿīd had visibly transformed what was known as the *ummat-i musulmān* (the Muslim community) into a clan/tribe grouping led by a victorious leader, the apostle (*baighambar*, Pers. *payghambar*) Muḥammad, in the same way that the Mongol nation had been forged by the successful campaigns of Chinggis (Genghis) Khan.

---

[13] The underlined word was first read by Pelliot as *imān-dur*, then suggested an Arabic word امّة instead of *imān*; Pelliot (1936). Others read it as *himmat* or *niʿmat* and Cleaves came up with the reading *imadtur* (in the support of); Cleaves (1953), 26 and 40–42. None of these makes sense, and it is clear from the context, and in comparison with Ghazan's edicts, that it should be read as *ummat* as in *ummat-i Muslimān.*

[14] Cleaves translated this third sentence as "In the Protection of the Great Fortune Flame," even though he admits that the etymology of the word *jalī* is unclear. In consideration of the pattern of using foreign terms in these Turkic formulae, it seems that *jalī* represents the Arabic word *jalī* (manifest, shining) and that the whole sentence reflects a power derived from a Fortune akin to the Iranian *farr/khvarna* whose main attribute is brilliance.

Thus, similar to the Iranian tribes who believed in the concept of the Aryan *khvarna* (the Fortune tied to the Aryan nation),[15] Turco-Mongols, who had also descended from the Central Asian steppes onto the Iranian plateau, seem to have believed in a fortune tied to a clan or tribe. No matter how strong was their adherence to Islam, their tribal beliefs persisted. Even though Abū Saʿīd was a second generation convert to Islam and had been brought up according to Irano-Islamic ethics, the opening invocation [1] of his *farmān* verges on blasphemy (if judged by Islamic standards). For, despite some Ottomanists' contention that Tengri referred to a monotheistic god and was therefore equivalent to Allah, the fact is that for the Mongols it represented a specific god, a sky god, and word combinations containing *tengri* were all sky related.[16] Moreover, [1] follows the exact formula used by Güyüg (r. 1246–48) in his letter addressed to Pope Innocent IV (see fig. 108).[17] If an Iranian prince would have started his letters in the post-Islamic period with an invocation addressed to Ahura-Mazda and in the manner of his Sasanian predecessors, he would have certainly been accused of blasphemy. One cannot plausibly argue that Güyüg was a monotheist, nor does it make sense to say that by 'Tengri' Abū Saʿīd meant 'Allah.' Less hampered by Islamic orthodoxy in a Turkic context, Abū Saʿīd saw no need to abide by strict Islamic rules in his Uighur *farmān*.

More surprising, though, is the invocation of the Bayāndur Fortune alongside godly powers in a Persian-Islamic context, and by an Aq-Quyunlu ruler whose dynasty was renowned for religious orthodoxy. It is clearly a testimony to the importance of tribal beliefs, and to the esteem that Turco-Mongol rulers held for Ilkhanid models and formulae.

---

15 *Yashts* 18:2–5 of the *Avestā*; see for instance Dustkhvāh, trans. (2000–1), vol. 1, 481–82.

16 Even and Pop, trans. (1994), 342–43. The name *Tengri-wīrdī* (Tengri-given) for instance, is more akin to *Mihr-dād* (Mithra-given) than *Allāh-dād* or *Allāh-wīrdī* (Allah-given). Tengri may have been used later on in lieu of a generic term for god, even though when Shaybānī Khan uses it, one has the distinct impression that he still refers to the sky-god (see Kiliç [1997], 65, where mistranslations occur, for instance "*Lik tingriga irur bu revshan*..." has wrongly been translated "but my light comes from God," instead of "it is clear for Tengri..."; I am indebted to Wheeler Thackston for this remark).

17 For a complete reproduction see Natalini et al., eds. (1991), 67; for a translation see Lupprian (1981), 188–89.

Section 6

The title-signature of Uzun Ḥasan is yet another example of mixing tribal traditions with Islamic doctrines. In a little noted remark in his seminal work on the Aq-Quyunlus, Woods draws attention to the fact that the word *lillāh* in the first segment of the Uzun Ḥasan *tughra* was conceived to reflect the *tamgha* sign (i.e. the brand that tribes used to mark their herds with) of the Bayāndur clan, as depicted—among others—by the historian Rashīd al-Dīn Faḍlallāh (d. 1319) in his *Jāmiʿ al-tawārīkh.*[18] Indeed, as evidenced in fig. 109, the dotted line pattern was all that was required to produce *lillāh*. The x-marked line was added on top, in order to incorporate the Bayāndur *tamgha* sign into the heading. Shaping the name of God into a cattle brand was certainly not an expression of Islamic piety. Previously, Persian scribes had incorporated the bow and arrow of Seljuk chieftains into their *farmān* headings. It led to the creation of the *tughra*, the bow and arrow-shaped calligraphy of the ruler's name (see appendix). At that early stage however, the *tughra* did not incorporate any religious invocation. The mix of tribal and Islamic tenets into the same title-signature is one step further than Seljuk or Ilkhanid scribes had dared to take.

Another interesting feature in Uzun Ḥasan's *tughra* is the use of the word *syūzūmīz* ('our words,' i.e., has said) that originated in Mongol times. As people of the steppes, the Mongols were not a talkative people. Hence, when their *khān* spoke, it was perceived as an order, and was called a *yarliq* (literally 'words of'). And when the spoken word had to be transmitted in written form, a person of trust, who had so close an access to the *khān* as to be able to hear his utterances, needed to vouch for it. Louis XI of France used to say that the most trusted person of his realm was his barber who held a knife on his throat everyday. Similarly, the most trusted persons of a Mongol *khān* were his *keshig*, the officers who stood guard or were on duty before his tent, and which included the *ba'urchi*, the kitchen superintendent. Because of their easy access to the *khān*, the *keshig* officers could easily kill or poison him.

Thus, on the back of a Uighur letter of Ghazan to Pope Boniface VIII in 1302, we have an attestation by his trusted *keshig* officers:

---

[18] Woods (1999), 26.

> It's *üjig* (correct). First day of the *keshig* (guard) of Üred (?), Qutlughshāh, Rashīd al-Dawla (*Erisidküle*), Ramaḍān (*Iramadan*).[19]

Three things need to be noted in this attestation. Firstly, Rashīd is named according to his initial *kunya* Rashīd al-Dawla, and not Rashīd al-Dīn by which he is better known. Whereas the administration people and historians respectfully called him Rashīd al-Dīn (especially after writing commentaries on the Qurʾān), among the Mongols he was still referred to by his initial *kunya*. Secondly, it should be of no surprise to see his name written in the company of the *amīr* Qutlughshāh's as members of the same *keshig*, for Rashīd al-Dīn himself recounts that when he was wrongly accused of demeaning this *amīr* before Ghazan, upon seeing him Qutlughshāh exclaimed: "We have been together in one *keshig*, and nothing has ever come between us to cause anger. Why have you attacked me before the emperor?"[20] Thirdly, while Rashīd al-Dīn was obviously not a military man to stand guard by the imperial tent, the reason that he was included in the *keshig* was that prior to his ascension to the vizierate he was a *ba'urchi*, and according to one account "Ghazan would not eat except from his hand and the hands of his son."[21]

The same type of countersigning on the back of an imperial document appears, for instance, in the case of a letter of Öljeitü to King Philippe IV of France in 1305 and a *farmān* of Abū Saʿīd dated 1320, both written in Uighur.[22] While conservatism was a characteristic of Turkic bureaucratic procedures, Persian officials eager to have their names included on the face of the document rather than on the back were probably waiting for an opportune moment to modify this countersigning procedure. The reign of the feeble Geikhatu (r. 1291–95) provided such an occasion. To give weight to a *yarliq* issued in the name of this ineffective Ilkhan, the vizier Aḥmad Khālidī Zanjānī, known as Ṣadr al-Dīn (d. 1298), devised a new procedure:

---

[19] Cleaves (1951), 516. Cleaves was unable to decipher the name that he transcribed as *Erisidkül;* but it is clear that after dropping the prothetic vowel, which Turkic people add before foreign names starting with an 'r' (Ramaḍān, for instance, was spelled *Iramadan* in the same line), it is clear that it should be understood as Rashīd al-Dawla, the initial *kunya* of Rashīd.

[20] Rashīd al-Dīn (1957), vol. 3, 326. The false accusations had come from the vizier Ṣadr al-Dīn (see below).

[21] Allsen (2001), 127.

[22] Cleaves (1951), 508 and 523; Cleaves (1953), 33.

on an order issued in 1292, instead of having the *keshig* countersign the *yarliq*, he added below the Ilkhan's name the name of the three most powerful military commanders—Shiktur, Toghachar, and Aq-buqa—as officers who repeated (i.e., vouched for) the 'word' of the Ilkhan (fig. 110). And to differentiate their 'words' from the 'word' of Geikhatu, he used the term *suzindin* ('words of them,' in a plural form) after their names, which was synonymous with the honorific plural *yarliqindin* written after the name of the Ilkhan. In the process, Ṣadr al-Dīn was also able to sneak in his own name (below those of the *amīrs*) followed by the same term *suzi* ('his word') in singular form.[23]

Perhaps Ghazan understood the negative effect of this change of procedure on the Ilkhan's authority and banned it, since we have no such specimen surviving from his time. But beginning with the reign of Öljeitü, we see powerful *amīrs* affixing their names once again on *farmāns*, followed by the words *suzi* or *suzindin* (depending on the number of *amīrs* involved).[24] Half a century later, Tīmūr would do the same and mention the name of his puppet Chinggisid *khān* at the top followed by *yarlqindin*, and then mention his own name followed by *suzumiz*, a more honorific version of *suzi*.[25] When the last of Tīmūr's Chinggisid puppets died and Tīmūr found no replacement for him, he simply scratched the top line. Thus began the tradition of prefacing *farmāns* with the name of a Turco-Mongol ruler followed by *suzumiz*, or *syūzūmīz* (which followed the western pronunciation of the same word).[26]

Appendix

There are two main schools of thought on the origins of the word *tughra*. The first sees it derived from a Turkic secretarial emblem called *tughragh*, and the second as an effort by Persian scribes to shape

---

[23] The *farmān* begins with: "Irinjin–turji (i.e., Geikhatu) *yarliqindin*; Shiktur, Toghachar, Aq-buqa, *suzindni;* Aḥmad-i Ṣāḥib Dīwān (i.e., Ṣadr al-Dīn) *sozi*"; Soudavar (1992), 34–35.

[24] See, for instance, Herrmann (1997), 332.

[25] Fekete (1977), pls. 1 and 3.

[26] Fragner (1999), 287.

the name of the ruler into a bow-like element called *turgha/turghay,* subsequently mispronounced as *tughra.*[27]

The primary argument for the first school is a remark by Maḥmūd al-Kāshgarī in his *Dīwān lughāt al-turk* lexicon, written between 1075 and 1094:

> the *tughragh* is the seal (*ṭābiʿ*) and signature (*tawḳīʿ*) of the king [in] Oghuz dialect (*ghuzziyya*) and not known to the [Western] Turks; I do not know its origin.[28]

There are several problems, though, with Kāshgarī's account:
1. As Kāshgarī himself admits he does not know what the origin of his *tughragh* is, and since then, no philologist has been able to provide a satisfactory etymology for it.
2. The spelling *tughragh* appears only in a unique surviving manuscript of Kāshgarī's lexicon copied two centuries after the original, and chances are that if the author himself did not misspell *tughragh,* a later scribe did.
3. One can envisage the drop of the last 'gh' in everyday parlance, but then one expects it to resurface in other combinations of the word; for instance, one should have had *tughraghi* instead of *tughrayi* (i.e., the person in charge of drawing the *tughra*). In addition, the drop of the last letter does not explain the transformation of the short 'a' into a long one.

More generally, when nomadic tribes rise to power and establish control over an empire, by necessity they have to rely on the bureaucratic practices of their predecessors, as well as their scribes and functionaries. As a result, bureaucratic practices tend to be very traditional. When rudimentary transaction instruments (such as the incised sticks that the Mongols used for the dispatch of horses) can even be traced back to Achaemenid bureaucratic practices,[29] it should be of no surprise to see the Sasanid royal epithet *bagh* (Lord) adopted by Turkic rulers as *bäg* (which eventually led to the popular Turkic epithet *beyg/beg*).[30] In the same vein, since Balādhurī relates from

---

[27] Doerfer (1963), 342–345; Iqbāl-i Ashtiyānī (1970), 533–34; Muʿīn (1974), vol. 2, 2227; Cahen (1943–45), 168.

[28] Bosworth et al. (2003). The term *tughra* is perhaps more commonly rendered as *ṭughrā,* as in Bosworth [ed.].

[29] Soudavar (2006a), vol. 2, 235–36.

[30] *Bäg* is first attested in the eighth-century inscriptions from the banks of the

Ibn al-Muqaffaʿ that "whenever a Sasanid king issued an edict, he had his stylized signature (*tawqīʿ*) added to it,"[31] one would expect that when Turkic rulers had their names written as a signature on top of their edicts, it was in following of an existing—non-Turkic—bureaucratic practice.

The *tughra*, however, was not a simple signature but one with a distinct characteristic: it had a curved line crossing the name,[32] often described by Persian poets as a crescent, eyebrow, or a bow.[33] The fourteenth-century Persian lexicon *Ṣiḥah al-furs*, and the twelfth/thirteenth-century poet Qawāmī-yi Raḍī, in particular, describe it as a bow-like curve. The description of the latter carries weight since the poet Qawāmī was a friend and a panegyrist of Ṭughrāʾī, who was appointed to the Tughra Office of the Seljuk chancellery in 512/1118.[34] Earlier on, in a poem in praise of Tāj al-Mulk Abū al-Ghanāʾim Marzbān b. Khusraw Fīrūz Shīrāzī, the *tughra* officer of the Seljuk Malikshāh (r. 1072–92), Muʿizzī-yi Nishābūrī specifically describes it as a bow and arrow combination at the very time that Kāshgarī was composing his lexicon.[35]

From time immemorial, the bow represented a symbol of power. The Assyrians and the Achaemenids depicted their rulers with a bow, and the rebellious satrap Datames (d. 360 BC) who struck coins in his own name held a bow in his hand.[36] Similarly, the Parthians, who descended on the Iranian plateau from the northeast, had their coins struck with the effigy of a ruler holding a bow in his hand, and the Seljuks, who centuries later followed the same route, had a bow and arrow emblem struck on their coinage. A study by Bulliet shows how, in a tacit division of the empire between Tughril Beg (r. 1038–63) and his brother Chaghri Beg, the Seljuk coinage for the territories west of Nishapur bore the bow and arrow sign of Tughril, and those to the east of Nishapur bore the emblem of Chaghri Beg, even though both types of coinage were issued in the name of Tughril.[37] What

---

Orkhan River; Bazin (2003). For a discussion on the evolution of the Achaemenid word *baʔa* (god) into a royal epithet *bagh* (Lord), see Soudavar (2006b), 162.

[31] Balādhurī (1866), 465.

[32] Tabrīzī (1982), 1355; Doerfer (1963), 344.

[33] Dihkhudā (1994), vol. 9, 13640–41.

[34] Ṣafā (1989), vol. 2, 696–97.

[35] Iqbāl-i Ashtiyānī (1971), 534.

[36] Soudavar (2003), 1–3.

[37] Bulliet (1994), 295.

this discrepancy between the written word and the signage shows is that for the Seljuk power base, i.e., for the Ghuzz tribesmen, tribal emblems were more important than the written name. It therefore seems quite natural that Persian scribes would try to incorporate this cherished emblem of the Seljuk rulers into their signature, in the same way that centuries later they incorporated the Bayāndur *tamgha* into Uzun Ḥasan's title-signature.

Even though we do not have a *tughra* specimen from an imperial Seljuk *farmān*, we can guess from a 1325 edict of Muḥammad b. Tughluq in Delhi how it might have looked, since chancery scribes carried their practices from Iran to India (fig. 111).[38] When compared to coins issued in Tughril's domain bearing his bow and arrow mark (fig. 112), even though the 'nūn' letter of the Tughluqid *farmān* provides a concave line, its relationship to the Turkic tribal emblem jumps to the eye. On the other hand, since the heading of the Eldiguzid *farmān* of our fig. 109 does not have a crossing curved line, we must assume that in Seljuk times, the *tughra* was reserved for the rulers of the house of Seljuk. After their demise, though, it is probable that scribes of the successor dynasties began imitating it. Eventually, all title-signatures were referred to as *tughra*, whether or not they had a bow-like line.

The above scenario ties in well with Kāshgarī's remark that the *tughra* originated with the Ghuzz (Oghuz) people, whom he disdainfully calls the *ghuzziya*. Since the Seljuks were the most prominent clan of the Ghuzz tribes to ascend to power, the advent of the *tughra* must surely be associated with them. Clearly, the Qara-Khanids who were their predecessors, and with whom Kāshgarī was affiliated, did not have a *tughra* sign. Because the Seljuks were initially clients of the Qara-Khanids, it would have been normal for Kāshgarī to treat them with contempt and avoid elaborating on a sign that his kinsmen never had.

Moreover, like the Persian Achaemenids, who had to rely on Elamite and Mesopotamian scribes and who adopted Aramaic as the bureaucratic language of the empire, the Seljuks had to rely on Persian scribes and on the Persian language as the *lingua franca* of their empire. It then seems quite plausible that the Persian scribe

---

[38] For a complete image and description, see Robinson et al. (1976), 283–84, pl. 150.

who first incorporated the Seljuk bow into the stylized signature of his king misunderstood and mispronounced the Turkic word *turghay*, and as a result, in the Persian bureaucratic parlance, *tughra* gained currency. If the *tughra* was indeed first devised for Tughril, then the transition from *turghay* to *tughra* might have been facilitated by its affiliation to a ruler whose name started with the letters '*t-gh-r*.'

Finally, it seems that in designing their *tughras* with arrows piercing a convex bow, the Ottoman scribes followed to some extent the emblem of the descendants of Chaghri Beg, whose line ruled as the Great Seljuks in Iran and Anatolia.[39] To this day, Persian calligraphers call the curved line of an Ottoman-like *tughra*, the *kaman* (bow), and its three elongated *alifs* *nīza* (spear, arrow).[40]

[39] Bulliet (1974), 293.
[40] The late calligrapher and scholar Aḥmad-i Suhaylī-yi Khunsārī who designed my own *tughra* mentioned it to me.

CONCLUDING REMARKS

THE MONGOL EMPIRE IN WORLD HISTORY

DAVID MORGAN

Empires seem to have become rather fashionable in the last few years. We might notice, for example, Niall Ferguson's book about the biggest of them all, the British Empire[1] (which would have been bigger still, but for the unfortunate misunderstandings of the 1770s), with its argument that that empire was on the whole a thoroughly good thing—or, at the very least, that it was much preferable, with all its faults, to any likely alternative at the time. I should note that I have no particular prejudice in favor of the British Empire: being of Welsh descent, I represent, one might argue, the first victims of English colonial expansion. Now, according to some, the United States is in the process of acquiring an empire of sorts. Like many other specialists in the history of the Middle East, I have given all too many talks on Iraq in the twentieth century during and since 2003. But in any case, even had I chosen to stick firmly to the Mongol Empire—in the words of John Masson Smith, "the thirteenth century's only superpower"—this would not have kept me out of Iraq's current difficulties. A Maureen Dowd op-ed piece in the *New York Times*, one that was somewhat critical of Secretary of Defense Rumsfeld, included, improbably, a quotation from my *The Mongols*.[2] And Saddam Hussein, before his fall and disappearance, was wont to invoke the alleged parallel of the Mongol invasion of Iraq in 1258: a somewhat ill-omened precedent, one might have thought, in view of what happened to the last Abbasid caliph at Mongol hands. Saddam might have been wiser to restrict himself his other exemplars, Nebuchadnezzar and his fellow Takriti (albeit a Kurd), Saladin.

Saddam was not the first of America's enemies to talk about a Mongol parallel. Usama bin Laden, in one of his recorded messages,

---

[1] Ferguson (2003).

[2] Maureen Dowd, 'What Would Genghis Do?,' *New York Times*, 5 March 2003, A23, reprinted in Maureen Dowd, *Bushworld: Enter at Your Own Risk* (New York: G. P. Putnam's Sons, 2004), 322–24.

speaking of the first Gulf War, likened General Colin Powell and then-Secretary of Defense Cheney to Hülegü. Ian Frazier, feeling that Americans would probably have little or no idea what Usama was talking about, has published an explanatory article in the *New Yorker*.[3] However, I propose to resist the temptation to explore further potential parallels, such as whether it might be appropriate to term the Mongol Empire a 'coalition of the willing.'

Most of us who spend our time studying the Mongol Empire are, if my experience is anything to go by, asked several times a year how we came to be interested in so apparently esoteric a subject. In my own case, at the age of fourteen, I was lent a copy of Michael Prawdin's *The Mongol Empire: Its Rise and Legacy*—not, perhaps, a very good book, but sufficient to get me going. Not long afterwards, I chose Boyle's excellent translation of Juwaynī, then recently published (1958), as a school prize. I was amazed by the empire's sheer size—smaller than the British Empire at its greatest extent in the 1920s, but unlike it, occupying contiguous territory—and by its astonishing military achievement. What accompanied the Mongols' military conquests—death and destruction on a vast scale—is no doubt still what people most readily associate with the Mongols: and let us not try to pretend that it did not happen. But there is a great deal more to the Mongol impact on world history than havoc and massacre.

Here there has been a major historiographical shift in the last fifteen or twenty years. Art historians have long appreciated that, from their point of view, the Mongol period was strikingly constructive and fertile. The exhibition that was the occasion for the symposium whose proceedings are published here, and the symposium itself, provided an eloquent demonstration of that. Historians were perhaps slower to catch up, and for too long tended to follow, a little uncritically, the contemporary chroniclers' interest in campaigns, battles, massacres, intrigue, and factional struggles. But much has changed, as illustrated vividly in an article published a few years ago by Professor Peter Jackson.[4] This was a discussion of what has happened to the

---

[3] Ian Frazier, 'Invaders: Destroying Baghdad,' *The New Yorker*, 25 April 2005, 48–55.

[4] Jackson (2000). There is much subsequent work that could now be added to what Jackson considered, not least his own pathbreaking *The Mongols and the West*; Jackson (2005).

field since the publication of the last general survey, as it happens my *The Mongols* of 1986. The answer was: a very great deal, of some of which I at least was unaware.

The most significant single contributor to this rethink, in my opinion, has been Professor Thomas Allsen, in numerous articles and in three books, most especially the last two published. These were *Commodity and Exchange in the Mongol Empire*,[5] which was concerned especially with the fate of Muslim textile workers who were sent east by their captors to serve the Mongols' insatiable appetite for gold brocade, and the much more wide-ranging *Culture and Conquest in Mongol Eurasia*[6]—in my opinion the most important single book on the Mongols to have been published since I first read Prawdin around forty-five years ago. The book demonstrated the active Mongol role not just in providing some kind of 'Pax Mongolica,' but in facilitating transasiatic cultural transmission in a wide variety of fields—historiography, geography and cartography, astronomy, agriculture, cuisine, medicine, printing. We might note that Allsen does not discuss art: his evidence is written materials, not visual or artifacts, which shows persuasively that the positive side of the Mongol impact was by no means only about art. One of Allsen's major innovative strengths is the way in which he brings together Chinese and Persian sources, and makes them illuminate each other. All this is far from saying, of course, that Allsen is unique; the contrary is shown by Jackson's article, by the bibliography of the exhibition catalogue,[7] and by the six essays which introduce Professor Paul Buell's admirable *Historical Dictionary of the Mongol World Empire.*[8]

A brief survey of the contributions published in this volume will illustrate, I think, what remarkable progress continues to be made in Mongol Empire studies. Devin DeWeese, in his examination of the surviving sections of Ibn al-Fuwaṭī's biographical dictionary—a book which has previously been somewhat neglected except by art historians—demonstrates how an author who lived through most of the period of Mongol rule in western Asia, and who was a librarian in both Maragha and Baghdad, can provide us with rich material

[5] Allsen (1997).
[6] Allsen (2001).
[7] Komaroff and Carboni, eds. (2002), 289–308.
[8] Buell (2003).

on, among other things, cultural accommodation between Persians and Mongols, polyglotism, and the crucial issue of the conversion of the Mongols to Islam. Judith Pfeiffer also examines the latter issue, concentrating on the period 1258 to 1295, that is, before the definitive conversion associated with Ghazan Khan. She suggests that the Mongols' approach was one of 'selective appropriation' of Islamic elements. She also attempts, cautiously, an interesting variation on Richard Bulliet's well-known methodology of estimating conversion by looking for specifically Muslim nomenclature, in this case Muslim names among Mongol *amīrs* who appear in Rashīd al-Dīn's *Jāmiʿ al-tawārīkh*. Teresa Fitzherbert, in her study of religion in the Freer Balʿamī manuscript of c. 1300—not a text which was often illustrated—contends that it shows the contemporary shift towards and adaptation to Islam among the Mongols of the Ilkhanate. The notable jurist Ibn Taymiyya's anti-Mongol *fatwā* of 1302 (much studied still today in some Islamist circles) puts in an appearance; and Ibn Taymiyya also features in Donald Little's case study of the Ilkhanid diplomatic mission to the Mamluk government in 1301. It would appear that in 1326 the Ilkhan Abū Saʿīd interceded, unsuccessfully, for Ibn Taymiyya, who was at that time imprisoned in Damascus: ironic, in view of his earlier damning opinion on the Mongols and their conversion to Islam. The mission of 1301 provides interesting evidence, from what we know about the gifts provided, of opportunities for cultural exchange.

Bert Fragner continues his fascinating argument, first advanced in a paper published in 1997,[9] that the Ilkhanid Mongol kingdom in some sense marked the beginning of modern Iran. He considers the significance of various indigenous Persian elements as well as the acquisition of characteristically East Asian governmental devices such as the square seal. Charles Melville, in his persuasive discussion of the previously largely ignored survival of the Mongol *keshig* (royal guard, and center of Mongol administration) in the Ilkhanate, which he shows operated alongside the Iranian bureaucracy, emphasizes rather the pervasively Mongol character of the regime. Attention is also drawn to the continued significance of the *keshig* by Abolala Soudavar in his paper on how the Mongol legacy may still be traced in a much later Aq-Quyunlu *farmān* of Uzun Ḥasan. Eastern influence on Iran is the

[9] Fragner (1997).

prevailing impression in Dietrich Huff's account of the excavations at Takht-i Sulayman, where Chinese motifs are conspicuous in both the architecture and the iconography of decoration. It would seem, to judge from Mark Kramarovsky's account of Jochid metalwork, that while the first generation of Mongol invaders brought artistic features with them to the future territories of the Golden Horde, the East Asian influence there was much more ephemeral than it was in the Ilkhanate. Similarly, Dickran Kouymjian demonstrates that Chinese dragons and phoenixes like those found at Takht-i Sulayman are featured in Armenian art in the late thirteenth century—before they make a widespread appearance in Persian art—but that they disappear after around 1300. Bernard O'Kane, on the other hand, shows how Persian poetry became a much more prominent feature in art and architecture during the Mongol period, and in particular how the increased popularity of Sufism led to an increased use of poetry from that tradition.

One of the deficiencies of scholarship on the Ilkhanate used to be its excessive concentration on the center. For example, J. A. Boyle's extremely useful chapter on the dynastic and political history of the Ilkhanate in the fifth volume of the *Cambridge History of Iran* (1968) provides a clear narrative of events, but the reader learns very little about what may have been going on in the provinces. Several papers in this volume help to redress the balance, particularly in connection with artistic developments in the Fars of the Injuid dynasty. Elaine Wright discusses book patronage under the Injuids, suggesting that some earlier manuscripts may have been commercial productions, whereas later manuscripts of higher quality can be seen as showing a more developed level of elite patronage. Eleanor Sims considers four Injuid manuscripts and their relation to the celebrated book which we are now required to call the 'Great Mongol' rather than the 'Demotte' *Shāhnāma.* That astonishing manuscript (a number of leaves from which were displayed in the exhibition) has often been thought, since the appearance of Oleg Grabar and Sheila Blair's *Epic Images and Contemporary History: The Illustrations of the Great Mongol Shahnama* in 1980, to have been the result of patronage on the part of the vizier Ghiyāth al-Dīn, son of the great Rashīd al-Dīn. Indeed, Dr. Sims maintains that the attribution has "not…been seriously questioned." Ghiyāth al-Dīn is indeed a perfectly plausible patron, perhaps the most likely, but there does not in fact seem to be any actual hard evidence that this was the case.[10] The discussion, as is well-known, was taken much further by Abolala Soudavar in a fascinating article, indeed a virtual monograph, 'The Saga of Abu-Sa'id Bahādor Khān: The Abu-Sa'idnāmé.'[11] There it was argued that the manuscript constituted nothing less than "an epic history of the Mongols," which might be right, but again seems (at least to me) to be highly speculative.

Marianna Shreve Simpson also sheds light on the art of the Injuid dynasty. Like Teresa Fitzherbert, she considers the Freer Balʿamī as well as the double frontispiece of a 1287 Baghdad manuscript of the letters of the Ikhwān al-Ṣafā'. She sees continuity of artistic development, and suggests that the new interest in illustrating the *Shāhnāma* provided the impetus for a shift from author portraiture to royal representation. Robert Hillenbrand, who examines the same Ikhwān frontispiece, seems to see less continuity, arguing that it is evidence of the survival of the older style of 'Arab' painting after the cataclysm of 1258. He contends that the frontispiece "celebrates intellectual achievement rather than political power," as is prominent in later Persian painting. It might be observed that the association of intellectual achievement with political power is a phenomenon which is still to this day a feature of Iranian society, something nicely encapsulated in the original subtitle of Roy Mottahedeh's justly famous *The Mantle of the Prophet*, a study of a twentieth-century lightly fictionalized *mullā*. The subtitle was *Learning and Power in Modern Iran*.[12]

Other papers provide persuasive evidence of cultural and commercial prosperity in the Ilkhanate after recovery from the impact of the initial invasions. Sheila Blair collects information on the great expansion of the production of illustrated books: who did it, and how. She pays particular attention to the scriptorium of Rashīd al-Dīn, while Jonathan Bloom, following on from his remarkable book *Paper Before Print: The History and Impact of Paper in the Islamic World*,[13] shows how the increased use of paper was significant not only in the manufacture of big books but also as a design intermediary for art in

---

[10] See my review; Morgan, D. (1982c).

[11] Soudavar (1996).

[12] Mottahedeh (1986). In later paperback reprints, the publishers changed the subtitle to the much less illuminating, but possibly more saleable, *Religion and Politics in Iran*.

[13] Bloom (2001).

other forms and materials. Oliver Watson shows how flourishing the pottery industry was, and that it served a popular, not just an elite, market. Incidentally, he demonstrates how a letter in the collection formerly attributed to Rashīd al-Dīn, which contains a reference to fifteenth/sixteenth century Chinese porcelain, argues persuasively in favor of the case made (in my opinion, but not that of quite everyone, conclusively, by A. H. Morton[14]) that the letters are spurious. Ralph Kauz discusses the trade of Kish and its rivalry, more or less on equal terms, with Hormuz, while pointing out that the rulers of Kish were much more closely involved with the Mongols than were their competitors. George Saliba examines the observatory built by Hülegü for Naṣīr al-Dīn Ṭūsī at Maragha, and shows how important work was done there in astronomy (but not in astrology). He notes that the observatory was paid for by loot from Baghdad, a salutary reminder that not everything in the Mongol realm was characterized by sweetness and light.

One paper takes us all the way back to Mongolia itself: Noriyuki Shiraishi's discussion of the excavations of Avraga, which he believes to have been the site of Chinggis Khan's winter palace. The results are of great interest: as he says, historians have tended to the view that, in a quotation he includes from one of them, "nomadism is no friend to the archaeologist."[15] However, it should be noted that not all scholars are convinced that the identification is correct. Dr. Igor de Rachewiltz, in his magisterial annotated translation of the *Secret History*, indeed asserts that it is "totally unwarranted."[16] Lastly, John Masson Smith, Jr. offers another in his long series of studies in Mongol military history, providing a 'time and motion study' of Hülegü's campaign as he moved west, which seems to show convincingly, contrary to what has sometimes been assumed, that the soldiers were not accompanied on the expedition by their families, flocks, and herds.

The impression conveyed by these papers is certainly a positive one, on the whole: the Mongols, in the recent historiography of politics and culture under their rule, do seem to be coming in out of the cold.[17] It is worth considering, in conclusion, what may be

---

[14] Morton (1999).
[15] Morgan, D. (1986b), 30.
[16] de Rachewiltz, ed. (2004), vol. 1, 502.
[17] For a strongly argued case on these lines, see Lane, G. (2003). For a short

regarded as the legacy, the enduring impact of the Mongol Empire in the lands which it comprised or influenced. Let us proceed from east to west.

The Chinese have at times tended to take a fairly benevolent view of the Mongols despite the destruction they wrought, especially in the north of the country. This is perhaps mainly for two reasons: under the Mongols, China expanded for the first time into Yunnan; and the Mongols brought political unity back to China after centuries of division—a unity which has never since been lost for long, if one discounts Taiwan since 1949 (and even there the theory of 'One China' remains official policy on both sides of the strait). One can argue that the Great Wall of China was a Mongol legacy, in a way. It is true that there was no Great Wall in existence at the time of the Mongol invasions (and hence it is hardly surprising, contrary to what was argued by Frances Wood,[18] that Marco Polo failed to notice it). But the Great Wall that we see today, built much later under the Ming Dynasty, was designed to keep at bay the Mongols of its day. One can also encounter favorable views of the Mongols in Japan, which may have something to do with the fact that the Japanese, aided by the weather in the shape of the *kamikaze*, the Divine Wind, defeated them. In the early 1990s I was acting as series adviser for a four-part television documentary series on the Mongols, *Storm from the East*.[19] The series was produced jointly by the BBC in England and NHK in Japan. I was slightly startled to be told by one of the Japanese team that the Mongol Empire was not only East Asia's gift to the West, but that more specifically it had caused the Italian Renaissance. The evidence adduced for this was a 1306 painting of the Robe of Christ in Padua. The trim around the robe had long been taken to be a geometric design, but in fact, I was told, it is a text in Phagspa, the new script devised on the orders of the Great

---

discussion of current trends in Ilkhanid historiography, see my 'The Mongols in Iran: A Reappraisal'; Morgan, D. (2004). The most recent biography of Chinggis Khan, Jack Weatherford's *Genghis Khan and the Making of the Modern World* (Weatherford [2004])—briefly a *New York Times* bestseller—makes, as its title indicates, very large claims indeed for its hero.

[18] Wood (1995), 96–101. For further references and discussion, see Jackson (2005), appendix 1, 363–66.

[19] See the excellent and beautifully illustrated accompanying book of the same name by the series producer, Robert Marshall (Marshall [1993]), and the review article on it by T. N. Haining (Haining [1994]).

Khan Qubilai for the writing of Mongolian. This is indeed correct, and undeniably remarkable, even if it still seems something of a leap from that to causing the Renaissance.

In Central Asia, while 'national' identities may be a product of the Soviet period and to a great extent artificial, it does seem that the groupings of peoples that are there today are not, for the most part, pre-Mongol. As Professor Peter Golden remarks, "Although...the principal Turkic groupings...were already well-established by the year 1200 in the lands in which we today find them, it is, nevertheless, the Činggisid era and its turbulent events that is largely responsible for giving them their modern appearance."[20] The old tribal groupings were broken up by Mongol conquest and military reorganization,[21] and were redistributed in ways that ultimately gave rise to today's ethnic Turkic units—Kazakhs, Uzbeks, and so forth. Nor did the specific Chinggisid legacy soon disappear: a proposal for the forthcoming second volume of the *Cambridge History of Inner Asia* described the period 1500–1750 as 'The Chinggisid Revival.' But in the post-Soviet world of Central Asia, the search for a founding national hero, notably in Uzbekistan, has led not to Chinggis but to Tamerlane, despite the fact that he was dead a century before a single Uzbek set foot in Transoxania.

Regarding Iran I need say little, as much of this volume is concerned with the Mongol impact there. After the initial destruction, the immediate results were a broadening of horizons and the marked significance of cross-cultural artistic and other influences so persuasively illustrated by these papers, as well as in the exhibition and its catalogue. In the longer term, there is the possibility of an important Ilkhanid role in the creation of modern Iran, as is argued by Bert Fragner and mentioned above. As evidence of an enduring impact, one might cite the Qajar myth of descent from a Mongol in Hülegü's entourage. So far as the remainder of the Middle East is concerned, it may be that the legacy was not quite so positive: the destruction of Baghdad (though there is evidence of speedy revival) and the relegation of Iraq to the status of a somewhat neglected frontier province. Some have argued that the termination of the Abbasid caliphate

[20] Golden (1992), 283.

[21] See Morgan, D. (1986b), 90, and Togan, I. (1998), index under 'detribalization.'

gave a boost to the spread of Sufism. Another boost was arguably to the Mamluks, who avoided incorporation into the Mongol Empire, and hence to Egypt as the surviving bastion of Islamic civilization. Historians of the Ottoman Empire have for the most part proved singularly reluctant to pay serious attention to its possible Mongol antecedents, despite the fact that much of Anatolia was for long an Ilkhanid province. An exception is Professor Rudi Lindner,[22] and a more revolutionary suggestion has come from Professor Colin Heywood,[23] for whom the still-mysterious appearance of the Ottoman emirate around 1300 was in fact part of the fallout from political troubles in the Golden Horde—or rather in the Noghai horde after its ruler's defeat and death in 1299 and the turbulent events, including a large-scale displacement of Turko-Mongol peoples, that followed. If the Mongols were indeed responsible, albeit inadvertently, for the foundation of what was to become the Ottoman Empire, then their legacy was a potent one indeed.

The Russians did not emulate the Chinese in their view of their Mongol conquerors. There appear to have been two, apparently contradictory, reactions. First there was a tendency at the time of the conquest to, in effect, deny that it had happened: Charles Halperin calls this "the ideology of silence."[24] Then the Mongols were blamed for all the ills which were ever after to befall Russia—the brutality of the political system, slowness of state formation, and so on. Foreign scapegoats have their uses, and not only in Russia. Arguably the major lasting Mongol legacies were the rise of the previously not very important city of Moscow (whose rulers made themselves useful to the Golden Horde as tax collectors), and the increasing centrality of the Orthodox Church—all the more so after the Mongols had converted to Islam—as a major symbol of Russian identity.

Most of the rest of Europe was, of course, not conquered by the Mongols. The late Archibald Lewis[25] took the view that this might be the explanation of that interminably discussed phenomenon, 'the rise of the West'—everywhere else was so battered by the Mongols that Europe was left with no effective competitors. One would have

[22] Lindner (1999).
[23] Heywood (2000).
[24] Halperin (1984).
[25] Lewis, A. R. (1988).

to point out that this theory falls foul of the rather long gap in time between the Mongol failure (or disinclination) to conquer Europe, and that continent's rise to global hegemony, quite apart from the doubts one might justly have about whether the world's other civilizations were, after Chinggis Khan, in anything like the terminal decline Lewis seems to imagine. If one is disinclined to ascribe the Renaissance to the Mongols, their most conspicuous impact on Europe was probably in terms of European knowledge of the world. We should recall that Christopher Columbus, when he sailed westwards across the Atlantic, was heading for Cathay, the land of the Great Khan. His copy of the 1485 edition of Marco Polo is still extant in Seville (though Professor John Larner[26] believes it to be improbable that he had read it before setting off on his first voyage). Presumably the most devastating Mongol legacy to Europe, though unintentional, was the Black Death—if one accepts W. H. McNeill's view of its origins[27]—that is, that it traveled across Asia from China, along the Mongol imperial trade routes, before arriving in 1346 at Kaffa in the Crimea, from where it spread westwards, causing far more deaths than all the Mongol military campaigns put together.

Lastly, what of Mongolia itself? Various Mongol groups were locally powerful in the centuries after the expulsion of the Yüan Dynasty from China in 1368, but ultimately all were absorbed into the expanding empires of czarist Russia and Ch'ing China. Eventually, the Mongols, together with the other steppe nomads, lost the military edge they had had before the development of firearms. But it is worth remembering that it was a very long time before any handgun could match the composite bow of the steppe cavalry archer in accuracy, range, rate of fire, or power of penetration. The fine historical novelist Bernard Cornwell, in an appendix to his *Harlequin*,[28] which is set during the Hundred Years' War and features the battle of Crécy, suggests that as late as 1815, had the Duke of Wellington's troops been equipped with (and had a lifetime's training in the use of) longbows rather than smoothbore muskets at Waterloo, they would have performed far more impressively than they (or their French opponents) did.

---

[26] Larner (1999), 153 ff.

[27] McNeill (1989), chap. 4.

[28] Bernard Cornwell, *Harlequin* (London: HarperCollins, 2001), 484. On this whole matter, see Chase (2003).

The same argument would apply to the steppe bow. Essentially, Mongolia, once the center of a world empire, slipped back into its pre-Chinggisid comparative obscurity, in the twentieth century to be divided between two Communist empires (though the Mongolian Peoples' Republic never formally became part of the USSR). In the 1990s, after the collapse of the Soviet Union, Mongolia—unlike Inner Mongolia, which remained an integral part of China—achieved real independence, though at vast economic cost. Chinggis Khan once again became the preeminent national hero.[29] This had not been possible while the country was under Soviet domination. In 1962, stamps were issued to commemorate a possible date for the eighth centenary of Chinggis's birth. They were available only in the West,[30] and the official responsible for commissioning them was punished. How marked the change had been was vividly illustrated to me around 1991 when the Mongolian ambassador to Britain, Mr. Ochirbal, kindly told me that he had enjoyed reading my *The Mongols*, but that he thought I had been "rather hard on Chinggis Khan." That was not an opinion that any Mongolian official would have been wise to express a decade earlier.

In 2003 an article, with precisely as many authors as this volume (led by Dr. Chris Tyler-Smith of Oxford), appeared in an electronic journal, the *American Journal of Human Genetics*.[31] This was entitled 'The Genetic Legacy of the Mongols,' and it argued, on the basis of research into the DNA of the Y chromosome, that something like one half of one percent of the male population of the entire world (that is, sixteen million men) are descended from Chinggis Khan, or at any rate from one of the great man's own ancestors who lived around a century and a half before his birth. I had a long telephone conversation with a science journalist at the *New York Times* about this, and in due course a piece based on the article appeared, with contributions from Morris Rossabi as well as me.[32] I freely confess that the science is quite beyond me. But if there is indeed anything

[29] On the contemporary cult of Chinggis Khan, see Man (2004), Part IV.

[30] The stamps are illustrated in Bawden (1968), pl. 17. Professor Bawden told me that he had bought them from a dealer in London.

[31] Zerjal et al. (2003).

[32] Nicholas Wade, 'A Prolific Genghis Khan, It Seems, Helped People The World,' *New York Times*, 11 February 2003, F3.

in the argument, then the impact of the Mongol Empire is clearly far from exhausted, and it marks something of a change in perception if Chinggis Khan should now be remembered for peopling the world, rather than for depopulating large parts of it.

BIBLIOGRAPHY

Achery, 1723
Achery, Luc d'. *Spicilegium: sive, Collectio veterum aliquot scriptorum.* Edited by Étienne Baluze. New ed. 3 vols. Paris: Montalant, 1723.

Adamec, ed., 1976
Adamec, Ludwig W., ed. *Historical Gazetteer of Iran.* Vol. 1, *Tehran and Northwestern Iran.* Graz: Akademische Druck- u. Verlagsanstalt, 1976.

Adamec, ed., 1989
Adamec, Ludwig W., ed. *Historical Gazetteer of Iran.* Vol. 3, *Abadan and Southwestern Iran.* Graz: Akademische Druck- u. Verlagsanstalt, 1989.

Adamova, 2004
Adamova, Ada T. 'The St. Petersburg Illustrated Shahnama of 733 Hijra (1333 A.D.) and the Injuid School of Painting.' In *Shahnama: The Visual Language of the Persian Book of Kings*, edited by Robert Hillenbrand. Aldershot, England: Ashgate, 2004.

Adamova and Giuzal'ian, 1985
Adamova, Ada T., and Leon T. Giuzal'ian. *Miniatyury rukopisi poemy 'Shakhname' 1333 goda.* Leningrad: 'Iskusstvo,' Leningradskoe otdelenie, 1985.

Adle, 1985
Adle, Chahriyar. 'Tessons du Sanb-Qâzân de Tabriz (696–Circa 704/1297–Circa 1305).' Unpublished typescript, 1985.

Aga-Oglu, 1935
Aga-Oglu, Mehmet. 'Fragments of a Thirteenth-Century Mihrab at Nedjef.' *Ars Islamica* 2 (1935): 128–31.

Ahrī 1954
Ahrī Abū Bakr. *Ta'rīkh-i Shaikh Uvais.* Translated and edited by J. B. van Loon. The Hague: Uitgeverij Excelsior, 1954.

Aigle, ed., 1997
Aigle, Denise, ed. *L'Iran face à la domination mongole.* Tehran: Institut français de recherche en Iran, 1997.

Aigle, 2005
Aigle, Denise. *Le Fârs sous la domination mongole. Politique et fiscalité (XIIIe–XIVe s.).* Studia Iranica, Cahier 31. Paris: Association pour l'avancement des études iraniennes, 2005.

Akimushkin and Ivanov, 1979
Akimushkin, Oleg F., and Anatol A. Ivanov. 'The Art of Illumination.' In *The Arts of the Book in Central Asia, 14th–16th Centuries*, edited by Basil Gray. London: Serindia, 1979.

Album, 1974
Album, Stephen. 'Power and Legitimacy: The Coinage of Mubariz al-Din Muhammad

ibn al-Muzaffar at Yazd and Kirman.' *Le monde iranien et l'Islam* 2 (1974): 157–71.

Allan, 1973
Allan, James. 'Abu'l-Qasim's Treatise on Ceramics.' *Iran* 11 (1973): 111–20.

Allan, 1982
Allan, James. *Islamic Metalwork: The Nuhad Es-Said Collection*. London: Sotheby, 1982.

Allan, 1987
Allan, James. 'Islamic Metalwork.' *Louisiana Revy* 27, no. 3 (1987): 24–25, 100.

Allen, 1985
Allen, Terry. 'Byzantine Sources for the *Jami al-tawarikh* of Rashid al-Din.' *Ars Orientalis* 15 (1985): 121–36.

Allen, 1986
Allen, Terry. *A Classical Revival in Islamic Architecture*. Wiesbaden: L. Reichert, 1986.

Allsen, 1986
Allsen, Thomas T. 'Guard and Government in the Reign of the Grand Qan Möngke, 1251–59.' *Harvard Journal of Asiatic Studies* 46, no. 2 (1986): 495–521.

Allsen, 1987
Allsen, Thomas T. *Mongol Imperialism: The Policies of the Grand Qan Möngke in China, Russia, and the Islamic Lands, 1251–1259*. Berkeley: University of California Press, 1987.

Allsen, 1994
Allsen, Thomas T. 'The Rise of the Mongolian Empire and Mongolian Rule in North China.' In *The Cambridge History of China*. Vol. 6, *Alien Regimes and Border States, 907–1368*, edited by Herbert Franke and Denis Twitchett. Cambridge and New York: Cambridge University Press, 1994.

Allsen, 1996
Allsen, Thomas T. 'Biography of a Cultural Broker: Bolad Ch'eng-Hsiang in China and Iran.' In *The Court of the Il-Khans, 1290–1340*. Oxford Studies in Islamic Art, vol. 12, edited by Julian Raby and Teresa Fitzherbert. Oxford: Oxford University Press, 1996.

Allsen, 1997
Allsen, Thomas T. *Commodity and Exchange in the Mongol Empire: A Cultural History of Islamic Textiles*. Cambridge and New York: Cambridge University Press, 1997.

Allsen, 2001
Allsen, Thomas T. *Culture and Conquest in Mongol Eurasia*. Cambridge and New York: Cambridge University Press, 2001.

Allsen, 2002a
Allsen, Thomas T. 'The Circulation of Military Technology in the Mongolian Empire.' In *Warfare in Inner Asian History (500–1800)*, edited by Nicola Di Cosmo. Leiden and Boston: Brill, 2002.

Allsen, 2002b
Allsen, Thomas T. *Technical Transfers in the Mongolian Empire*. Bloomington: Department of Central Eurasian Studies, Indiana University, 2002.

Amitai, 2001
Amitai, Reuven. 'The Conversion of the Ilkhan Tegüder Ahmad to Islam.' *Jerusalem Studies in Arabic and Islam* 25 (2001): 15–43.

Amitai-Preiss, 1991
Amitai-Preiss, Reuven. 'Evidence for the Early Use of the Title *Ilkhan* among the Mongols.' *Journal of the Royal Asiatic Society* 3rd ser., no. 1 (1991): 353–61.

Amitai-Preiss, 1994
Amitai-Preiss, Reuven. 'An Exchange of Letters in Arabic between Abaqa Ilkhan and Sultan Baybars (A.H. 667/A.D. 1268–69).' *Central Asiatic Journal* 38 (1994): 11–33.

Amitai-Preiss, 1995
Amitai-Preiss, Reuven. *Mongols and Mamluks: The Mamluk-Ilkhanid War, 1260–1281*. Cambridge: Cambridge University Press, 1995.

Amitai-Preiss, 1996a
Amitai-Preiss, Reuven. 'Ghazan, Islam and Mongol Tradition: A View from the Mamluk Sultanate.' *Bulletin of the School of Oriental and African Studies* 59, no. 1 (1996): 1–10.

Amitai-Preiss, 1996b
Amitai-Preiss, Reuven. 'New Material from the Mamluk Sources for the Biography of Rashid al-Din.' In *The Court of the Il-Khans, 1290–1340*. Oxford Studies in Islamic Art, vol. 12, edited by Julian Raby and Teresa Fitzherbert. Oxford: Oxford University Press, 1996.

Amitai-Preiss, 1999
Amitai-Preiss, Reuven. 'Sufis and Shamans: Some Remarks on the Islamization of the Mongols in the Ilkhanate.' *Journal of the Economic and Social History of the Orient* 42 (1999): 27–46.

Amitai-Preiss, 2001
Amitai-Preiss, Reuven. 'Turko-Mongolian Nomads and the *Iqta'* System in the Islamic Middle East (ca. 1000–1400 AD).' In *Nomads in the Sedentary World*, edited by Anatoly M. Khazanov and André Wink. Richmond, Surrey: Curzon Press, 2001.

Amitai-Preiss and Morgan, eds., 1999
Amitai-Preiss, Reuven, and David O. Morgan, eds. *The Mongol Empire and its Legacy*. Leiden and Boston: Brill, 1999.

Ando, 1992
Ando, Shiro. *Timuridische Emire nach dem Mu'izz al-ansab: Untersuchung zur Stammesaristokratie Zentralasiens im 14. und 15. Jahrhundert*. Islamkundliche Untersuchungen, Bd. 153. Berlin: Schwarz, 1992.

Andrews, 1981
Andrews, Peter A. 'Ejen Qoriy-a, the Tent of Chinggis Qan at Ejen Qoriy-a, and their Authenticity.' *Journal of the Asian-Mongolian Society* 7, no. 2 (1981): 1–49.

Andrews, 1999
Andrews, Peter A. *Felt Tents and Pavilions: The Nomadic Tradition and its Interaction with Princely Tentage*. London: Melisende, 1999.

Āqsarā'ī, 1944
Āqsarā'ī, Karīm al-Dīn Maḥmūd. *Musāmarat al-akhbār wa musāyarat al-akhyār*. Edited by Osman Turan. Ankara: Türk Tarih Kurumu Basımevi, 1944. Reprint, 1999.

Arberry, 1960
Arberry, A. J. *Shiraz: Persian City of Saints and Poets*. Norman: University of Oklahoma Press, 1960.

Arberry and Minovi, 1959–62
Arberry, A. J., and Mojtaba Minovi. *The Chester Beatty Library: A Catalogue of the Persian Manuscripts and Miniatures*. 3 vols. Dublin: Hodges, Figgis, 1959–62.

Arnold, 1913
Arnold, Thomas W. *The Preaching of Islam: A History of the Propagation of the Muslim Faith*. 2nd ed. New York: C. Scribner's Sons, 1913.

Arnold, 1923
Arnold, Thomas W. 'The Survival of Sasanian Motifs in Persian Painting.' In *Studien zur Kunst des Ostens. Josef Strzygowski zum sechzigsten Geburtstage von seinen Freunden und Schülern*, edited by Heinrich Glück. Vienna: Avalun-Verlag, 1923.

Arnold, 1924
Arnold, Thomas W. *Survivals of Sasanian and Manichaean Art in Persian Painting*. Oxford: Clarendon Press, 1924.

al-ʿAsqalānī, 1974
al-ʿAsqalānī, Ibn Ḥajar. *al-Durar al-kāmina fī aʿyān al-mi'at al-thāmina*, vol. 3. Hyderabad, India: Osmania University, 1974.

Atil, 1973
Atil, Esin. *Ceramics from the World of Islam*. Washington, D.C.: Smithsonian Institution, 1973.

Atil, 1990
Atil, Esin. *Islamic Art and Patronage: Treasures from Kuwait*. New York: Rizzoli, 1990.

Atwood, in press
Atwood, Christopher P. 'Ulus Emirs, Marriage Partners, and Kesig Shifts: The Evolution of a Classic Mongol Institution.' In *Imperial Statecraft: Political Forms and Techniques of Governance in Inner Asia*, edited by D. Sneath, in press.

Aubin, 1953
Aubin, Jean. 'Les princes d'Ormuz du XIIIe au XVe siècle.' *Journal Asiatique* 241 (1953): 77–138.

Aubin, 1969
Aubin, Jean. 'La survie de Shilau et la route du Khunj-o-Fal.' *Iran, Journal of the British Institute of Persian Studies* 7 (1969): 21–37.

Aubin, 1991
Aubin, Jean. 'Le quriltai de Sultân-Maydân (1336).' *Journal Asiatique* 276 (1991): 175–97.

Aubin, 1995
Aubin, Jean. *Émirs mongols et vizirs persans dans les remous de l'acculturation*. Studia Iranica,

Cahier 15. Paris: Association pour l'avancement des études iraniennes, 1995.

Avcioğlu, 2001
Avcioğlu, Nebahat. 'Ahmed I and the Allegories of Tyranny in the Frontispiece to George Sandys's *Relation of a Journey*.' *Muqarnas* 18 (2001): 203–26.

Ayalon, 1994
Ayalon, David. 'Mamluk: Military Slavery in Egypt and Syria.' In *Islam and the Abode of War*. Aldershot, England: Variorum Reprints, 1994.

Aykut and Pamuk, 1992
Aykut, Tuncay, and Şevket Pamuk. *Ak Akçe. Moğol ve İlhanlı Sikkeleri / Mongol and Ilkhanid Coins*. Istanbul: Yapı Kredi Yayınları, 1992.

al-ʿAynī, 1992
al-ʿAynī, Badr al-Dīn Maḥmūd ibn Aḥmad. *ʿIqd al-jumān fī taʾrīkh ahl al-zamān*. Edited by Muḥammad Muḥammad Amīn. 4 vols. Cairo: al-Hayʾa al-Miṣriyya li-al-Kitāb, 1992.

Azaryan, 1964
Azaryan, Levon. *Kilikyan manrankarch'ut'yune, XII–XIII dd. / Cilician Miniature Painting, XIIth–XIIIth Centuries*. Yerevan: Haykakan SSR GA Hratarakch'ut'yun, 1964.

Backer, 1877
Backer, Louis de. *L'Extrême Orient au Moyen-Age d'après les manuscrits d'un Flamand de Belgique et d'un prince d'Arménie*. Paris: E. Leroux, 1877.

Badr, 1950
Badr, Muṣṭafā Ṭāhā. *Mughūl Īrān bayna al-masīḥiyya wa al-Islām*. Cairo: Dār al-Fikr al-ʿArabī, 1950.

Baer, 1973–74
Baer, Eva. 'The Nisan Tası: A Study in Persian-Mongol Metal Ware.' *Kunst des Orients* 9 (1973–74): 1–46.

Baer, 1977
Baer, Eva. 'A Brass Vessel from the Tomb of Sayyid Battal Ghazi: Notes on the Interpretation of Thirteenth-Century Islamic Imagery.' *Artibus Asiae* 39 (1977): 299–335.

Bağci, 1995
Bağci, Serpil. 'A New Theme of the Shirazi Frontispiece Miniatures: The *Divān* of Solomon.' *Muqarnas* 12 (1995): 101–11.

Bagherzadeh, 1978
Bagherzadeh, Firouz. *Iran Bastan Museum. Oriental Ceramics: The World's Great Collections*, vol. 4. Tokyo: Kodansha, 1978.

Bahrami, 1949
Bahrami, Mehdi. *Gurgan Faïences*. Cairo: Le Scribe égyptien, 1949.

al-Bakrī, 1966
al-Bakrī, Mahāb Darwīsh. 'al-ʿUmla al-islāmiyya fī al-ʿahd al-Īlkhānī.' *Sumer* 22, no. 1/2 (1966): 95–106.

Balādhurī, 1866
Balādhurī, Aḥmad ibn Yaḥyā. *Liber expugnationis regionum/Futūḥ al-buldān.* Edited by M. J. de Goeje. 2nd ed. Leiden: Brill, 1866.

Ball, 1976
Ball, Warwick. 'Two Aspects of Iranian Buddhism.' *Bulletin of the Asia Institute of Pahlavi University* 1, no. 4 (1976): 103–63.

Ball, 1979
Ball, Warwick. 'The Imamzadeh Maʿsum at Vardjovi: A Rock-Cut Il-Khanid Complex near Maragheh.' *Archäologische Mitteilungen aus Iran* 12 (1979): 329–40.

Bar Hebraeus, 1932
Bar Hebraeus (Ibn al-ʿIbrī). *The Chronography of Gregory Abû'l Faraj 1225–1286, the Son of Aaron, the Hebrew Physician, commonly known as Bar Hebraeus.* Translated by E. A. Wallis Budge. 2 vols. London: Oxford University Press/H. Milford, 1932. Reprint, 1976; reprint, *Ta'rīkh al-zamān*, translated by Isḥāq Armalah, Beirut: Dār al-Mashriq, 1986.

Baranī, 1862–64
Baranī, Ziyā' al-Dīn. *Tārīkh-i Fīrūzshāhī/The Tarikh-i Feroz-shahi of Ziaa al-Din Barni, commonly called Ziaa-i Barni.* Edited by Sayyid Aḥmad Kha'n, W. Nassau Lees and Kabīr al-Dīn. Calcutta: Asiatic Society of Bengal, 1862–64.

Barros, 1973
Barros, João de. *Asia. Dos feitos que os Portuguezes fizeram no descubrimento e conquista dos mares et terras do Oriente.* Facsimile version, 1777–78 ed. Lisbon: Livraria Sam Carlos, 1973.

Barrucand, 1986
Barrucand, Marianne. 'Les representations d'architectures dans la miniature islamique en Orient du début du XIIIe au début du XIVe siècle.' *Cahiers Archéologiques* 34 (1986): 119–41.

Barrucand, 1994
Barrucand, Marianne. 'Architecture et espaces architectures dans les illustrations des *Maqamat* d'al-Hariri du XIIIe siècle.' In *The Art of the Saljuqs in Iran and Anatolia*, edited by Robert Hillenbrand. Costa Mesa, Calif.: Mazda, 1994.

Barth, 1964
Barth, Fredrik. *Nomads of South Persia: The Basseri Tribe of the Khamseh Confederacy.* Oslo: Oslo University Press, 1964.

Barthold, 1977
Barthold, V. V. *Turkestan down to the Mongol Invasion.* Edited by C. E. Bosworth. 4th ed. London: Luzac, 1977.

Bartlett, 1986
Bartlett, Robert. *Trial by Fire and Water: The Medieval Judicial Ordeal.* Oxford and New York: Clarendon Press and Oxford University Press, 1986.

Bates, 1973
Bates, Daniel G. *Nomads and Farmers: A Study of the Yörük of Southeastern Turkey.* Ann Arbor: University of Michigan Press, 1973.

Bawden, 1968
Bawden, Charles R. *The Modern History of Mongolia.* London: Weidenfeld & Nicolson, 1968.

Baybars al-Manṣūrī, 1998
Baybars al-Manṣūrī, Rukn al-Dīn. *Zubdat al-fikra fī ta'rīkh al-Hijra.* Edited by Donald S. Richards. Beirut and Berlin: Das Arabische Buch/Orient-Institut der DMG, 1998.

Bazin, 2003
Bazin, L. 'Beg.' In *The Encyclopaedia of Islam,* CD-ROM. Leiden: Brill, 2003.

Beaulieu, 1967
Beaulieu, M. 'Les ornaments liturgiques à Notre Dame de Paris aux XIVe et XVe s.' *Bulletin Monumental* 125 (1967): 267–69.

Beckwith, C. I., 1984
Beckwith, C. I. 'Aspects of the Early History of the Central Asian Guard Corps in Islam.' *Archivum Eurasiae Medii Aevi* 4 (1984): 29–43.

Beckwith, J., 1970
Beckwith, John. *Early Christian and Byzantine Art.* Harmondsworth, England: Penguin, 1970.

Bedoukian, 1962
Bedoukian, Paul Z. *Coinage of Cilician Armenia.* Numismatic Notes and Monographs, no. 147. New York: American Numismatic Society, 1962.

Benjamin of Tudela, 1966
Benjamin of Tudela. *The Itinerary of Benjamin of Tudela: Critical Text, Translation and Commentary.* Translated and edited by Marcus Nathan Adler. Reprint of 1907 London ed. New York: P. Feldheim, 1966.

Berlekamp, 2003a
Berlekamp, Persis. 'Painting as Persuasion: A Visual Defense of Alchemy in an Islamic Manuscript of the Mongol Period.' *Muqarnas* 20 (2003): 35–59.

Berlekamp, 2003b
Berlekamp, Persis. 'Wonders and their Images in Late Medieval Islamic Culture: "The Wonders of Creation" in Fars and Iraq, 1280–1388.' Ph.D. diss., Harvard University, 2003.

Berlekamp, 2004
Berlekamp, Persis. 'Narrative Images in a Neoplatonic Frame: An Inju Arabic Qazwīnī Manuscript Dated 1322, and the Transition from Arab to Persian Painting.' Paper presented at the Arab Painting: Text and Image in Illustrated Arabic Manuscripts Conference, School of Oriental and African Studies, University of London, 17–18 September 2004 (conference proceedings forthcoming, London and New York: I. B. Tauris).

Binyon, Wilkinson, and Gray, 1933
Binyon, Laurence, James V. S. Wilkinson, and Basil Gray. *Persian Miniature Painting, including a Critical and Descriptive Catalogue of the Miniatures Exhibited at Burlington House, January–March, 1931.* London: Oxford University Press, 1933.

Blair, 1982
Blair, Sheila S. 'The Coins of the Later Ilkhanids: Mint Organization, Regionalization and Urbanism.' *American Numismatic Society Museum Notes* 27 (1982): 211–30.

Blair, 1984
Blair, Sheila S. 'Ilkhanid Architecture and Society: An Analysis of the Endowment Deed of the Rab'i Rashidi.' *Iran* 22 (1984): 67–90.

Blair, 1985
Blair, Sheila S. 'Artists and Patronage in Late Fourteenth-Century Iran in Light of Two Catalogues of Islamic Metalwork.' *Bulletin of the School of Oriental and African Studies* 48, no. 1 (1985): 53–59.

Blair, 1986a
Blair, Sheila S. *The Ilkhanid Shrine Complex at Natanz, Iran.* Cambridge: Harvard University Center for Middle Eastern Studies, 1986.

Blair, 1986b
Blair, Sheila S. 'A Medieval Persian Builder.' *Journal of the Society of Architectural Historians* 45 (1986): 389–95.

Blair, 1989
Blair, Sheila S. 'On the Track of the "Demotte" *Shahnama* Manuscript.' In *Les Manuscrits du Moyen-Orient: Essais de codicologie et de paléographie.* Varia Turcica 8, edited by Francois Déroche. Paris: Maisonneuve, 1989.

Blair, 1993a
Blair, Sheila S. 'The Development of the Illustrated Book in Iran.' *Muqarnas* 10 (1993): 266–74.

Blair, 1993b
Blair, Sheila S. 'The Ilkhanid Palace.' *Ars Orientalis* 23 (1993): 239–48.

Blair, 1993c
Blair, Sheila S. 'Dāmgānī.' In *Encyclopaedia Iranica*, edited by Ehsan Yarshater. Costa Mesa, Calif.: Mazda, 1993.

Blair, 1995
Blair, Sheila S. *A Compendium of Chronicles: Rashīd al-Dīn's Illustrated History of the World.* Nasser D. Khalili Collection of Islamic Art, vol. 27. London: Nour Foundation in association with Azimuth Editions and Oxford University Press, 1995.

Blair, 2000
Blair, Sheila S. 'Decoration of City Walls in the Medieval Islamic World: The Epigraphic Message.' In *City Walls in Early Modern History*, edited by James D. Tracy. Cambridge: Cambridge University Press, 2000.

Blair, 2002
Blair, Sheila S. 'The Religious Art of the Ilkhanids.' In *The Legacy of Genghis Khan: Courtly Art and Culture in Western Asia, 1256–1353*, edited by Linda Komaroff and Stefano Carboni. New York, New Haven, and London: Metropolitan Museum of Art and Yale University Press, 2002.

Blair, 2003
Blair, Sheila S. 'Yaqut and His Followers.' *Manuscripta Orientalia* 9, no. 3 (2003): 39–47.

Blair, 2006
Blair, Sheila S. *Islamic Calligraphy*. Edinburgh: Edinburgh University Press, 2006.

Blair and Bloom, 1994
Blair, Sheila S., and Jonathan M. Bloom. *The Art and Architecture of Islam, 1250–1800.* The Pelican History of Art. New Haven and London: Yale University Press, 1994.

Blake, 1979
Blake, Stephen. 'The Patrimonial-Bureaucratic Empire of the Mughals.' *Journal of Asian Studies* 39, no. 1 (1979): 77–94.

Blochet, 1900
Blochet, Edgar. *Catalogue de la collection des manuscrits orientaux, arabes, persans et turcs*. Paris: E. Leroux, 1900.

Blochet, 1926
Blochet, Edgar. *Les enluminures des manuscrits orientaux—turcs, arabes, persans—de la Bibliothèque nationale.* Paris: Éditions de la Gazette des beaux-arts, 1926.

Bloom, 2001
Bloom, Jonathan M. *Paper Before Print: The History and Impact of Paper in the Islamic World.* New Haven: Yale University Press, 2001.

Boase, 1978
Boase, T. S. R. *The Cilician Kingdom of Armenia.* New York: St. Martin's Press, 1978.

Bosworth, 1995
Bosworth, C. E. 'Dīvān, ii. Government Office.' In *Encyclopaedia Iranica*, edited by Ehsan Yarshater. Costa Mesa, Calif.: Mazda, 1995.

Bosworth et al., 2003
Bosworth, C. E., et al. 'Tughra.' In *The Encyclopaedia of Islam*, CD-ROM. Leiden: Brill, 2003.

von Bothmer, 1987
Bothmer, H.-C. Graf von. 'Architekturbilder im Koran. Eine Prachthandschrift der Umayyadenzeit aus dem Yemen.' *Pantheon* 45 (1987): 4–20.

Boulanger, ed., 1956
Boulanger, Robert, ed. *Les Guides Bleus: Moyen-Orient.* Paris: Hachette, 1956.

Boyle, 1961
Boyle, J. A. 'The Death of the Last 'Abbasid Caliph: A Contemporary Muslim Account.' *Journal of Semitic Studies* 6 (1961): 145–61.

Boyle, 1964
Boyle, J. A. 'The Journey of Het'um I, King of Little Armenia, to the Court of the Great Khan Möngke.' *Central Asiatic Journal* 9, no. 3 (1964): 175–89.

Boyle, 1968
Boyle, J. A. 'Dynastic and Political History of the Il-Khans.' In *The Cambridge History of Iran.* Vol. 5, *The Saljuq and Mongol Periods*, edited by J. A. Boyle. Cambridge: Cambridge University Press, 1968.

Boyle, 1971
Boyle, J. A. 'Īndjū.' In *The Encyclopaedia of Islam,* new ed., edited by H. A. R. Gibb, J. H. Kramers, E. Levi-Provencal, and J. Schacht. Leiden and London: Brill/Luzac, 1971.

Boyle, 1974
Boyle, J. A. 'The Attitude of the Thirteenth-Century Mongols Towards Nature.' *Central Asiatic Journal* 22 (1974): 177–85.

Boyle, 1977
Boyle, J. A. 'The Seasonal Residences of the Great Khan Ögedei.' In *The Mongol World Empire, 1206–1370.* London: Variorum Reprints, 1977.

Brandenburg, 1982
Brandenburg, Dietrich. *Islamic Miniature Painting in Medical Manuscripts.* Basel: Editiones Roche, 1982.

Brend, 2000
Brend, Barbara. 'Beyond the Pale: Meaning in the Margin.' In *Persian Painting from the Mongols to the Qajars: Studies in Honour of Basil W. Robinson,* edited by Robert Hillenbrand. London and New York: I. B. Tauris, 2000.

Bretschneider, 1910
Bretschneider, Emil. *Mediaeval Researches from Eastern Asiatic Sources,* vol. 2. London: Kegan Paul, Trench, Trübner & Co., 1910.

Brian, 1939
Brian, Doris. 'A Reconstruction of the Miniature Cycle in the Demotte *Shah Namah.*' *Ars Islamica* 6 (1939): 97–112.

Brosh and Milstein, 1991
Brosh, Na'ama, and Rachel Milstein. *Biblical Stories in Islamic Painting.* Jerusalem: Israel Museum, 1991.

Brosset, 1849
Brosset, M.-F. *Histoire de la Géorgie,* vol. 1. St. Petersburg: Impr. de l'Académie Impériale des Sciences, 1849.

Brown, 1994
Brown, Michelle. *Understanding Illuminated Manuscripts: A Guide to Technical Terms.* Malibu, Calif.: J. Paul Getty Museum in association with the British Library, 1994.

Budge, trans., 1928
Budge, E. A. Wallis, trans. *The Monks of Kûblâi Khân, Emperor of China, or, The history of the life and travels of Rabban Ṣâwmâ, envoy and plenipotentiary of the Mongol khâns to the kings of Europe, and Markôs who as Mâr Yahbh-Allâhâ III became Patriarch of the Nestorian Church in Asia.* London: Religious Tract Society, 1928.

Buell, 1979
Buell, Paul D. 'Sino-Khitan Administration in Mongol Bukhara.' *Journal of Asian History* 13, no. 2 (1979): 121–51.

Buell, 2003
Buell, Paul D. *Historical Dictionary of the Mongol World Empire.* Lanham, Md.: Scarecrow Press, 2003.

Bulliet, 1974
Bulliet, R. W. 'Numismatic Evidence for the Relationship between Toghril Beg and Chaghri Beg.' In *Near Eastern Numismatics, Iconography, Epigraphy and History: Studies in Honor of George C. Miles*, edited by Dickran Kouymjian. Beirut: American University of Beirut, 1974.

Bulliet, 1979
Bulliet, Richard W. *Conversion to Islam in the Medieval Period: An Essay in Quantitative History*. Cambridge: Harvard University Press, 1979.

Buniiatov, 1981
Buniiatov, Z. M. 'Gars an-Ni'ma as-Sabi i Kamal ad-Din ibn Fuvati ob istorii karakhanidov.' *Pis'mennye pamiatniki Vostoka, 1974* (1981): 5–10.

Buschhausen and Buschhausen, 1981
Buschhausen, Heide, and Helmut Buschhausen. *Armenische Handschriften der Mechitharisten-Congregation in Wien*. Vienna: Delphin-Druck, 1981.

Busse, 1961
Busse, Heribert. 'Persische Diplomatik im Überblick: Ergebnisse und Probleme.' *Der Islam* 37 (1961): 202–45.

Çağman and Tanındı, 1979
Çağman, Filiz, and Zeren Tanındı. *Topkapı Saray Museum: Islamic Miniature Painting*. Istanbul: Tercuman Art and Cultural Publications, 1979.

Çağman and Tanındı, 1986
Çağman, Filiz, and Zeren Tanındı. *The Topkapı Saray Museum: The Albums and Illustrated Manuscripts*. Translated and edited by J. M. Rogers. Boston: Little, Brown and Company, 1986.

Çağman and Tanındı, 2002
Çağman, Filiz, and Zeren Tanındı. 'Manuscript Production at the Kazaruni Orders in Safavid Shiraz.' In *Safavid Art and Architecture*, edited by Sheila R. Canby. London: British Museum Press, 2002.

Cahen, 1943–45
Cahen, C. 'La Tughra Seldjukide.' *Journal Asiatique* 234 (1943–45): 167–72.

Calmard, 1978
Calmard, J. 'Kā͟shān.' In *The Encyclopaedia of Islam*, new ed., edited by H. A. R. Gibb, J. H. Kramers, E. Levi-Provencal, and J. Schacht. Leiden: Brill, 1978.

Carboni, 1992
Carboni, Stefano. 'The Wonders of Creation and the Singularities of Ilkhanid Painting: A Study of the London Qazwini, British Library Ms. Or. 14140.' Ph. D. diss., University of London, 1992.

Carboni, 2002
Carboni, Stefano. 'Synthesis: Continuity and Innovation in Ilkhanid Art.' In *The Legacy of Genghis Khan: Courtly Art and Culture in Western Asia, 1256–1353*, edited by Linda Komaroff and Stefano Carboni. New York, New Haven, and London: Metropolitan Museum of Art and Yale University Press, 2002.

Chao, 1975
Chao, Kung. *Men-da bei-lu/Polnoe opisanie Mongolo-Tatar: Faksimile ksilografa*. Translated

by Nikolai Ts. Munkuev. Pamiatniki Pis'mennosti Vostoka, no. 26. Moscow: Nauka, 1975.

Chardin, 1811
Chardin, Chevalier Jean. *Voyages du chevalier Chardin en Perse, et autres lieux de l'Orient.* Edited by L. Langlès. New ed. 10 vols. Paris: Le Normant, Imprimeur-Libraire, 1811.

Chase, 2003
Chase, Kenneth W. *Firearms: A Global History to 1700.* Cambridge and New York: Cambridge University Press, 2003.

Chen Dazhen, 1986
Chen Dazhen. *Dade Nanhai zhi canben* 大德南海志殘. Guangzhou: Guangzhou shi difangzhi yanjiusuo, 1986.

Chen Jiarong, Xie Fang, and Lu Junling, 1986
Chen Jiarong, 陳佳榮, 謝方 Xie Fang, and 陸峻嶺 Lu Junling. *Gudai Nanhai diming huishi* 古代南海地名匯釋. Beijing: Zhonghua shuju, 1986.

Christie's, London, 1998
Christie's, London. *Islamic Art and Manuscripts.* Sale cat., 13 October 1998.

Cleaves, 1949
Cleaves, F. W. 'Mongolian Names and Terms in the *History of the Nation of Archers.*' *Harvard Journal of Asiatic Studies* 12, no. 3–4 (1949): 400–43.

Cleaves, 1951
Cleaves, F. W. 'A Chancellery Practice of the Mongols in the Thirteenth and Fourteenth Centuries.' *Harvard Journal of Asiatic Studies* 14 (1951): 493–526.

Cleaves, 1953
Cleaves, F. W. 'The Mongol Documents in the Musée de Téhéran.' *Harvard Journal of Asiatic Studies* 16 (1953): 27–33.

Cleaves, 1954
Cleaves, F. W. 'A Medical Practice of the Mongols in the Thirteenth Century.' *Harvard Journal of Asiatic Studies* 17 (1954): 428–41.

Cleaves, trans., 1982
Cleaves, F. W., trans. *The Secret History of the Mongols*, vol. 1. Cambridge and London: Published for the Harvard-Yenching Institute by Harvard University Press, 1982.

Collins, 1975
Collins, L. J. D. 'The Military Organization and Tactics of the Crimean Tatars during the Sixteenth and Seventeenth Centuries.' In *War, Technology and Society in the Middle East*, edited by V. J. Parry and M. E. Yapp. London: Oxford University Press, 1975.

Combe, Sauvaget, and Wiet, 1931
Combe, Étienne, Jean Sauvaget, and Gaston Wiet. *Répertoire chronologique d'épigraphie arabe.* Cairo: Institut français d'archéologie orientale, 1931.

Contadini, 1992
Contadini, Anna. 'The *Kitab na't al-hayawan* (Book on the characteristics of animals,

British Library Or. 2784) and the "Ibn Bakhtishu" illustrated bestiaries.' Ph.D. diss., University of London, 1992.

Corbett and Lightbown, 1979
Corbett, Margery, and R. W. Lightbown. *The Comely Frontispiece: The Emblematic Title-Page in England, 1550–1660.* London, Henley, and Boston: Routledge & Kegan Paul, 1979.

Cowen, 1989
Cowen, Jill Sanchia. *Kalila wa Dimna: An Animal Allegory of the Mongol Court.* New York and Oxford: Oxford University Press, 1989.

Crone and Hinds, 1986
Crone, Patricia, and Martin Hinds. *God's Caliph: Religious Authority in the First Centuries of Islam.* University of Cambridge Oriental Publications, no. 37. Cambridge and New York: Cambridge University Press, 1986.

Crowe, 1976
Crowe, Yolande. 'The Islamic Potter and China.' *Apollo* (1976): 296–301.

Crowe, 1991
Crowe, Yolande. 'Late Thirteenth-Century Persian Tileworks and Chinese Textiles.' *Bulletin of the Asia Institute* N.S. 5 (1991): 153–61.

Curatola, 1982
Curatola, Giovanni. 'The Viar Dragon.' *Quaderni del Seminario di Iranistica, Ural-Altaistica e Caucasologia dell'Università degli Studi di Venezia* 9 (1982): 71–88.

Damm, 1968
Damm, Bernhard. *Geologie des Zendan-i Suleiman und seiner Umgebung.* Wiesbaden: F. Steiner, 1968.

Daneshvari, 1986
Daneshvari, ʿAbbas. *Animal Symbolism in Warqa wa Gulshah.* Oxford Studies in Islamic Art, vol. 2. Oxford: Oxford University Press, 1986.

Daniel, 1990
Daniel, Elton L. 'Manuscripts and Editions of Balʿami's *Tarjamah-yi Tarikhi Tabari.*' *Journal of the Royal Asiatic Society* Part 2 (1990): 282–321.

Dar al-Athar al-Islamiyya, 1990
Dar al-Athar al-Islamiyya. *Masterpieces of Islamic Art in the Hermitage Museum.* Kuwait: Dar al-Athar al-Islamiyya, 1990.

Dauzier, 1989
Dauzier, Martine. 'L'image-porche ou la première page enluminée dans les romans médiévaux.' In *From Sign to Text: A Semiotic View of Communication,* edited by Yishin Tobin. Amsterdam and Philadelphia: John Benjamins, 1989.

Davy, ed., 1783
Davy, Major, ed. *Tuzūkāt-i Tīmūrī/Institutes Political and Military...by the Great Timour,* 1783. Reprint, with an introduction by Mojtaba Minovi, Tehran: Asadī, 1964.

Delbrueck, 1929
Delbrueck, Richard. *Die Consulardiptychen und verwandte Denkmäler.* Berlin: W. de Gruyter, 1929.

Demus, 1947
Demus, Otto. *Byzantine Mosaic Decoration: Aspects of Monumental Art in Byzantium*, 1947. Reprint, London: Routledge & Kegan Paul, 1976.

Demus, 1949
Demus, Otto. *The Mosaics of Norman Sicily*. London: Routledge & Paul, 1949.

Denny, 1996
Denny, Don. 'Author Portrait.' In *The Dictionary of Art*, edited by Jane Turner. London: MacMillan, 1996.

Der Nersessian, 1936
Der Nersessian, Sirarpie. *Manuscrits arméniens illustrés des XIIe, XIIIe et XIVe siècles de la Bibliothèque des pères Mekhitharistes de Venise*. 2 vols. Paris: E. de Boccard, 1936.

Der Nersessian, 1962
Der Nersessian, Sirarpie. 'The Kingdom of Cilician Armenia.' In *A History of the Crusades*, edited by K. M. Setton, R. C. Wolff, and H. W. Hazard. Philadelphia: University of Pennsylvania Press, 1962.

Der Nersessian, 1963
Der Nersessian, Sirarpie. *Armenian Manuscripts in the Freer Gallery of Art*. Washington, D.C.: Freer Gallery of Art, 1963.

Der Nersessian, 1969
Der Nersessian, Sirarpie. 'Miniatures ciliciennes.' *L'Oeil* 179 (1969).

Der Nersessian, 1970
Der Nersessian, Sirarpie. 'Deux exemples arméniens de la Vierge de Miséricorde.' *Revue des Études Arméniennes* N.S. 7 (1970): 187–202.

Der Nersessian, 1973a
Der Nersessian, Sirarpie. *Armenian Manuscripts in the Walters Art Gallery*. Baltimore: Trustees of the Walters Art Gallery, 1973.

Der Nersessian, 1973b
Der Nersessian, Sirarpie. *Études byzantines et arméniennes/Byzantine and Armenian Studies*. 2 vols. Leuven: Impr. orientaliste, 1973.

Der Nersessian, 1977
Der Nersessian, Sirarpie. *L'Art arménien*. Paris: Arts et métiers graphiques, 1977.

Der Nersessian, 1978
Der Nersessian, Sirarpie. *Armenian Art*. London: Thames and Hudson, 1978.

Der Nersessian and Agemian, 1993
Der Nersessian, Sirarpie, and Sylvia Agemian. *Miniature Painting in the Armenian Kingdom of Cilicia from the Twelfth to the Fourteenth Century*. 2 vols. Washington, D.C.: Dumbarton Oaks Research Library and Collection, 1993.

Derman, 1998
Derman, M. Uğur. *Letters in Gold: Ottoman Calligraphy from the Sakip Sabanci Collection, Istanbul*. New York: Metropolitan Museum of Art, 1998.

DeWeese, 1994
DeWeese, Devin A. *Islamization and Native Religion in the Golden Horde: Baba Tükles and*

Conversion to Islam in Historical and Epic Tradition. University Park: Pennsylvania State University Press, 1994.

Digard, ed., 2002
Digard, Jean-Pierre, ed. *Chevaux et cavaliers arabes dans les arts d'Orient et d'Occident.* Paris: Institut du monde arabe/Éditions Gallimard, 2002.

Dihkhudā, 1994
Dihkhudā, 'Alī Akbar. *Lughat-nāma.* 15 vols. Tehran: Mu'assasah-i intishārāt wa chāp-i dānishgāh-i Tihrān, 1994.

Djait, 1986
Djait, Hichem. 'al-Kūfa.' In *The Encyclopaedia of Islam,* new ed., edited by H. A. R. Gibb, J. H. Kramers, E. Levi-Provencal, and J. Schacht. Leiden: Brill, 1986.

Doerfer, 1963
Doerfer, Gerhard. *Türkische und mongolische Elemente im Neupersischen, unter besonderer Berücksichtigung älterer neupersischer Geschichtsquellen, vor allem der Mongolen- und Timuridenzeit.* 4 vols. Wiesbaden: F. Steiner, 1963.

Doerfer, 1985a
Doerfer, Gerhard. 'Āl Tamġā.' In *Encyclopaedia Iranica,* edited by Ehsan Yarshater. London, Boston, and Henley: Routledge & Kegan Paul, 1985.

Doerfer, 1985b
Doerfer, Gerhard. 'Altūn Tamġā.' In *Encyclopaedia Iranica,* edited by Ehsan Yarshater. London, Boston, and Henley: Routledge & Kegan Paul, 1985.

Dournovo, 1952
Dournovo, Lydia. *Hin haykakan manrankarch'ut'yun/Ancient Armenian Miniature Paintings.* Yerevan, 1952.

Dournovo, 1961
Dournovo, Lydia. *Armenian Miniatures.* London: Thames and Hudson, 1961.

Dournovo and Drampian, 1967–69
Dournovo, Lydia, and R. G. Drampian. *Haykakan manrankarch'ut'yun/Miniatures Arméniennes.* Yerevan, 1967–69.

Drouot-Richelieu, 1998
Drouot-Richelieu, Paris. *Art Ottoman et Arts d'Orient.* Sale cat., 6–7 April 1998.

Dulaurier, 1858
Dulaurier, É. 'Les Mongols d'après les historiens arméniens.' *Journal Asiatique,* 5th ser., 11 (1858).

Dustkhvāh, trans., 2000–1
Dustkhvāh, Jalīl, trans. *Avestā.* 6th ed. Tehran: Murvārīd, 2000–2001.

Eliade, 1964
Eliade, Mircea. *Shamanism: Archaic Techniques of Ecstasy.* Translated by Willard R. Trask. Rev. and enl. ed., Bollingen Series, no. 76. London: Routledge & Kegan Paul, 1964.

Elias, 1995
Elias, Jamal J. *The Throne Carrier of God: The Life and Thought of 'Alā' ad-Dawlah as-Simnānī.* Albany: State University of New York Press, 1995.

Endicott-West, 1989
Endicott-West, Elizabeth. *Mongolian Rule in China: Local Administration in the Yuan Dynasty*. Cambridge: Council on East Asian Studies, Harvard-Yenching Institute, Harvard University Press, 1989.

Endicott-West, 1994
Endicott-West, Elizabeth. 'The Yüan Government and Society.' In *The Cambridge History of China*. Vol. 6, *Alien Regimes and Border States, 907–1368*, edited by Herbert Franke and Denis Twitchett. Cambridge and New York: Cambridge University Press, 1994.

Engels, 1978
Engels, Donald W. *Alexander the Great and the Logistics of the Macedonian Army*. Berkeley: University of California Press, 1978.

Epstein, 1969
Epstein, Hellmut. *Domestic Animals of China*. Farnham Royal, England: Commonwealth Agricultural Bureaux, 1969.

Esin, 1977
Esin, E. 'Pair of Miniatures from the Miscellany Collections of Topkapi.' *Central Asiatic Journal* 21 (1977): 13–35.

Ettinghausen, 1959
Ettinghausen, Richard. 'On Some Mongol Miniatures.' *Kunst des Orients* 3 (1959): 44–65.

Ettinghausen, 1962
Ettinghausen, Richard. *Arab Painting*. Geneva: Skira, 1962. Reprint, 1977.

Ettinghausen, 1970
Ettinghausen, Richard. 'The Flowering of Seljuq Art.' *Metropolitan Museum Journal* 3 (1970): 113–31.

Ettinghausen, Grabar, and Jenkins-Madina, 2001
Ettinghausen, Richard, Oleg Grabar, and Marilyn Jenkins-Madina. *Islamic Art and Architecture 650–1250*. 2nd ed., The Pelican History of Art. New Haven and London: Yale University Press, 2001.

Evans and Wixom, eds., 1997
Evans, Helen C., and William D. Wixom, eds. *The Glory of Byzantium: Art and Culture of the Middle Byzantine Era, A.D. 843–1261*. New York: Metropolitan Museum of Art, 1997.

Even and Pop, trans., 1994
Even, M. D., and R. Pop, trans. *Histoire secrète des Mongols, Chronique Mongole du XIIe siècle*. Paris: Gallimard, 1994.

Farès, 1953
Farès, Bishr. *Le Livre de la Thériaque: Manuscrit arabe à peintures de la fin du XIIe siècle conservé à la Bibliothèque Nationale de Paris*. Cairo: Institut français d'archéologie orientale, 1953.

Farès, 1957
Farès, Bishr. 'Philosophie et jurisprudence illustrées par les arabes.' In *Mélanges Louis Massignon*. Damascus: Institut français de Damas, 1957.

Farès, 1961
Farès, Bishr. *Vision Chrétienne et Signes Musulmans.* Cairo: Institut français d'archéologie orientale, 1961.

Farhad, 1992
Farhad, Massumeh. 'An Artist's Impression: Mu'in Musavvir's *Tiger Attacking a Youth.*' *Muqarnas* 9 (1992): 116–23.

Farmer, 1966
Farmer, Henry George. *Islam. Musikgeschichte in Bildern.* Bd. 3, Lfg. 2, *Musik des Mittelalters und der Renaissance.* Edited by H. Besseler and M. Schneider. Leipzig: Deutscher Verlag für Musik, 1966.

Farquhar, 1990
Farquhar, David M. *The Government of China under Mongolian Rule.* Stuttgart: F. Steiner, 1990.

Fedorov-Davydov, 2001
Fedorov-Davydov, German A. *The Silk Road and the Cities of the Golden Horde.* Edited by Jeannine Davis-Kimball. Berkeley: Zinat Press, 2001.

Fekete, 1977
Fekete, L. *Einführung in die Persische Paläographie.* Budapest: Akademiai Kiado, 1977.

Ferguson, 2003
Ferguson, Niall. *Empire: The Rise and Demise of the British World Order and the Lessons for Global Power.* New York: Basic Books, 2003.

Fiey, 1959
Fiey, J. M. *Mossoul chrétienne. Essai sur l'histoire, l'archéologie et l'état actuel des monuments chrétiens de la ville de Mossoul.* Beirut: Impr. Catholique, 1959.

Fiey, 1975a
Fiey, J. M. *Chrétiens syriaques sous les Mongols (Il-Khanat de Perse, XIIIe–XIVe s.), Corpus Scriptorum Christianorum Orientalium,* vol. 362, subsidia, Tomus 44. Leuven: Secrétariat du Corpus SCO, 1975.

Fiey, 1975b
Fiey, J. M. 'Hulagu, Doquz Khatun...et Six Ambons?' *Le Muséon* 88 (1975): 59–68.

Firdawsī, 1960–71
Firdawsī. *Shāhnāma/Shākh-nāme: kriticheskii tekst.* Edited by E. E. Bertels et al. 9 vols. Moscow: Idārah-i' Intishārāt-i Adabiyyat-i Khavar, 1960–71.

Firdevsî-i Rûmî, 1986
Firdevsî-i Rûmî. *Manzûm Hacı Bektâş Veli Vilâyetnâmesi.* Translated by Bedri Noyan. Aydın, Turkey: B. Noyan, 1986.

Fitzherbert, 1996
Fitzherbert, Teresa. 'Portrait of a Lost Leader: Jalal al-Din Kharazmshah and Juvaini.' In *The Court of the Il-Khans.* Oxford Studies in Islamic Art, vol. 12, edited by Julian Raby and Teresa Fitzherbert. Oxford: Oxford University Press, 1996.

Fitzherbert, 2001
Fitzherbert, Teresa. '"Bal'ami's Tabari": An Illustrated Manuscript of Bal'ami's

Tarjama-yi Tārīkh-i Ṭabarī in the Freer Gallery of Art, Washington (F57.16, 47.19 and 30.21).' Ph.D. diss., University of Edinburgh, 2001.

Floor, 2001
Floor, Willem M. *Safavid Government Institutions.* Costa Mesa, Calif.: Mazda, 2001.

Folsach, 2001
Folsach, Kjeld von. *Art from the World of Islam in the David Collection.* Rev. and expanded ed. Copenhagen: Davids Samling, 2001.

Fong and Watt, J. C. Y., 1996
Fong, Wen C., and James C. Y. Watt. *Possessing the Past: Treasures from the National Palace Museum, Taipei.* New York: Metropolitan Museum of Art, 1996.

Fragner, 1980
Fragner, Bert G. *Repertorium persischer Herrscherurkunden. Publizierte Originalurkunden (bis 1848).* Freiburg: Klaus Schwarz Verlag, 1980.

Fragner, 1997
Fragner, Bert G. 'Iran under Ilkhanid Rule in a World Historical Perspective.' In *L'Iran face à la domination mongole,* edited by Denise Aigle. Tehran: Institut français de recherche en Iran, 1997.

Fragner, 1999
Fragner, Bert G. 'Farmān.' In *Encyclopaedia Iranica,* edited by Ehsan Yarshater. New York: Bibliotheca Persica, 1999.

Fragner, 2001
Fragner, Bert G. 'The Concept of Regionalism in Historical Research on Central Asia and Iran (A Macro-Historical Interpretation).' In *Studies on Central Asian History in Honor of Yuri Bregel,* edited by Devin DeWeese. Bloomington: Research Institute for Inner Asian Studies, Indiana University, 2001.

Franke, H., 1974
Franke, Herbert. 'Siege and Defense of Towns in Medieval China.' In *Chinese Ways in Warfare,* edited by Frank A. Kierman, Jr. and John K. Fairbank. Cambridge: Harvard University Press, 1974.

Franke, H., 2000
Franke, Herbert. 'Nationalitätenprobleme im chinesischen Mittelalter.' *Münchner Beiträge zur Völkerkunde* 6 (2000): 279–90.

Franke, U., 1979
Franke, U. 'Die Baukeramik vom Taht-i Suleiman, Azerbaigan, Iran.' M.A. thesis, University of Göttingen, 1979.

Friend, 1927
Friend, A. M., Jr. 'The Portraits of the Evangelists in Greek and Latin Manuscripts.' *Art Studies* 5 (1927): 115–47.

Friend, 1929
Friend, A. M., Jr. 'The Portraits of the Evangelists in Greek and Latin Manuscripts, II.' *Art Studies* 7 (1929): 3–29.

Gabriel, 1952
Gabriel, Alfons. *Die Erforschung Persiens; die Entwicklung der abendländischen Kenntnis der Geographie Persiens.* Vienna: A. Holzhausens, 1952.

Gacek, 2001
Gacek, Adam. *The Arabic Manuscript Tradition: A Glossary of Technical Terms and Bibliography.* Leiden and Boston: Brill, 2001.

Galdieri, 1982
Galdieri, Eugenio. 'Un exemple curieux de restauration ancienne: La xoda-xane de Chiraz.' In *Art et Société dans le monde Iranien,* edited by Chahriyar Adle. Paris: Éditions Recherche sur les civilizations, 1982.

Galeries nationales du Grand Palais, 1977
Galeries nationales du Grand Palais. *L'Islam dans les collections nationales.* Paris: Éditions des Musées nationaux, 1977.

Galstian, 1962
Galstian, A. G. *Armianskie istochniki o mongolakh: izvlecheniia iz rukopisei XIII–XIV vv.* Moscow: Izd-vo vostochnoi literatury, 1962.

Galstian, 1964
Galstian, A. G. 'The First Armeno-Mongol Negotiations.' *Patma-Banasirakan Handes* 1 (1964): 91–105.

Gāvān, 2002–3
Gāvān, ʿImād al-Dīn Maḥmūd. *Manāẓir al-inshāʾ.* Edited by Maʿṣūmah Maʿdankan. Tehran: Farhangistān-i Zabān va Adab-i Fārsī, 2002–3.

Gibb et al., 1960–2002
Gibb, H. A. R., J. H. Kramers, E. Levi-Provencal, and J. Schacht, eds. *The Encyclopaedia of Islam,* new ed. Leiden: Brill, 1960–2002.

Gierlichs, 1996
Gierlichs, Joachim. *Mittelalterliche Tierreliefs in Anatolien und Nordmesopotamien: Untersuchungen zur figürlichen Baudekoration der Seldschuken, Artuqiden und ihrer Nachfolger bis ins 15. Jahrhundert,* Istanbuler Forschungen, Bd. 42. Tübingen: Ernst Wasmuth Verlag, 1996.

Gierlichs, 1998
Gierlichs, Joachim. 'Das "Drachenportal" in ʿAmadiya.' *Baghdader Mitteilungen* 29 (1998): 349–60.

Giuzal'ian, 1960
Giuzal'ian, Leon T. 'Three Injuid Bronze Vessels.' In *XXV International Congress of Orientalists: Papers Presented by the USSR Delegation.* Moscow: Oriental Literature Pub. House, 1960.

Goitein, 1954
Goitein, S. D. 'Two Eyewitness Reports of an Expedition of the King of Kish (Qais) against Aden.' *Bulletin of the School of Oriental and African Studies* 16 (1954): 247–57.

Goitein, 1986
Goitein, S. D. 'al-Ḳuds.' In *The Encyclopaedia of Islam,* new ed., edited by H. A. R. Gibb, J. H. Kramers, E. Levi-Provencal, and J. Schacht. Leiden: Brill, 1986.

Golden, 1992
Golden, Peter B. *An Introduction to the History of the Turkic Peoples.* Wiesbaden: O. Harrassowitz, 1992.

Golden, 1997
Golden, Peter B. 'Wolves, Dogs and Qipcaq Religion.' *Acta Orientalia Academiae Scientiarum Hungaricae* 50 (1997): 87–97.

Golombek, 1988
Golombek, Lisa. 'The Draped Universe of Islam.' In *Content and Context of Visual Arts in the Islamic World*, edited by Priscilla P. Soucek. University Park and London: Published for the College Art Association of America by the Pennsylvania State University Press, 1988.

Golombek, Mason, and Bailey, 1996
Golombek, Lisa, Robert B. Mason, and Gauvin A. Bailey. *Tamerlane's Tableware: A New Approach to Chinoiserie Ceramics of Fifteenth-and Sixteenth-Century Iran*. Costa Mesa, Calif.: Mazda Publishers in association with Royal Ontario Museum, 1996.

Gölpinarli, ed., 1981
Gölpinarli, Abdülbâki, ed. *Mesnevî tercemesi ve Serhi*. Istanbul: Inkilap ve Aka Kitabevleri, 1981.

Grabar, A., 1953
Grabar, André. *Byzantine Painting*. Translated by Stuart Gilbert. Geneva: Skira, 1953.

Grabar, O., 1959
Grabar, Oleg. Review of Bishr Farès, *Philosophie et jurisprudence illustrées par les arabes*. *Ars Orientalis* 3 (1959): 225–26.

Grabar, O., 1971
Grabar, Oleg. 'Survivances classiques dans l'art de l'Islam.' *Annales Archéologiques Syriennes* 21: Proceedings of the 9th International Congress of Classical Archaeology (1971): 371–80.

Grabar, O. and Blair, 1980
Grabar, Oleg, and Sheila Blair. *Epic Images and Contemporary History: The Illustrations of the Great Mongol Shahnama*. Chicago: University of Chicago Press, 1980.

Gray, 1940
Gray, Basil. 'Fourteenth-Century Illustrations of the *Kalila wa Dimna*.' *Ars Islamica* 7 (1940): 134–40.

Gray, 1961
Gray, Basil. *Persian Painting*. Geneva: Skira, 1961.

Gray, ed., 1979
Gray, Basil, ed. *The Arts of the Book in Central Asia, 14th–16th Centuries*. Boulder, Colo.: Shambhala, 1979.

Grigor of Akner, 1949
Grigor of Akner. 'History of the Nation of Archers (The Mongols) by Grigor of Akanc', Translated by R. P. Blake and R. N. Frye. *Harvard Journal of Asiatic Studies* 12, no. 3–4 (1949): 269–399.

Gronke, 1993
Gronke, Monica. 'Courts and Courtiers, v. Under the Timurid and Turkman Dynasties.' In *Encyclopaedia Iranica*, edited by Ehsan Yarshater. Costa Mesa, Calif.: Mazda, 1993.

Grube, 1959
Grube, Ernst J. 'Materialien zum Dioskurides Arabicus.' In *Aus der Welt der islamischen Kunst. Festschrift für Ernst Kühnel zum 75. Geburtstag*, edited by Richard Ettinghausen. Berlin: Verlag Gebr. Mann, 1959.

Grube, 1962
Grube, Ernst J. *Muslim Miniature Paintings from the XIII to XIX Century from Collections in the United States and Canada.* Venice: N. Pozza, 1962.

Grube, 1963
Grube, Ernst J. 'The Miniatures of Shiraz.' *Bulletin of the Metropolitan Museum of Art* N.S. 21 (1963): 285–95.

Grube, 1994
Grube, Ernst J. *Cobalt and Lustre: The First Centuries of Islamic Pottery.* Nasser D. Khalili Collection of Islamic Art, vol. 9. London: Nour Foundation in association with Azimuth Editions and Oxford University Press, 1994.

Grupper, 1992–94
Grupper, S. M. 'A Barulas Family Narrative in the *Yuan Shih*: Some Neglected Prosopographical and Institutional Sources on Timurid Origins.' *Archivum Eurasiae Medii Aevi* 8 (1992–94): 11–97.

Guest and Ettinghausen, 1961
Guest, Grace D., and Richard Ettinghausen. 'The Iconography of a Kashan Luster Plate.' *Ars Orientalis* 4 (1961): 25–64.

Guevorkian, 1982
Guevorkian, Astyhik. *Miniatures arméniennes. Portrait.* Yerevan, 1982.

Gulistāna, 1965
Gulistāna, Abū al-Ḥasan. *Mujmal al-tawārīkh.* Edited by Mudarris Razavī. Tehran: Ibn Sīnā, 1965.

Ḥāfiẓ-i Abrū, 1949
Ḥāfiẓ-i Abrū, 'Abdallāh b. Luṭfallāh b. 'Abd al-Rashīd. *Dhayl-i ẓafarnāma-yi Niẓām al-Dīn-i Shāmī.* Edited by Bahman Karīmī. Tehran: Bungāh-i Maṭbū'ātī-yi Afshārī, 1949.

Ḥāfiẓ-i Abrū, 1996–2000
Ḥāfiẓ-i Abrū, 'Abdallāh b. Luṭfallāh b. 'Abd al-Rashīd. *Jughrāfiyā-yi Ḥāfiẓ-i Abrū.* Edited by Ṣādiq Sajjādī. 3 vols. Tehran: Markaz-i nashr-i mīrāth-i maktūb, 1996–97, 1999–2000.

Haining, 1994
Haining, Thomas Nivison. Review of Robert Marshall, *Storm from the East. Journal of the Royal Asiatic Society,* 3rd ser. 4, no. 2 (1994): 251–54.

Haldane, 1978
Haldane, Duncan. *Mamluk Painting.* Warminster: Aris and Phillips, 1978.

Halperin, 1984
Halperin, Charles. 'The Ideology of Silence: Prejudice and Pragmatism on the Medieval Religious Front.' *Comparative Studies in Society and History* 26, no. 3 (1984): 442–66.

Hamid, 1966
Hamid, I. S. 'Mesopotamian School and the Place of Painting in Islam.' Ph.D. diss., University of Edinburgh, 1966.

Hammer-Purgstall, 1842–43
Hammer-Purgstall, Joseph, Freiherr von. *Geschichte der Ilchane, das ist der Mongolen in Persien, 1200–1350*, 1842–43. Reprint, Amsterdam: Philo Press, 1974.

Han and Deydier, 2001
Han, Wei, and Christian Deydier. *L'or de la Chine Ancienne.* Paris: Éditions d'art et d'histoire, 2001.

Haneda, 1984
Haneda, Masashi. 'L'évolution de la garde royale des Safavides.' *Moyen Orient et l'Océan Indien* 1 (1984): 41–64.

Harb, 1978
Harb, Ulrich. *Ilkhanidische Stalaktitengewölbe.* Berlin: Reimer, 1978.

Harrison-Hall, 2001
Harrison-Hall, Jessica. *Catalogue of Late Yuan and Ming Ceramics in the British Museum.* London: British Museum, 2001.

Hartmann, 1975
Hartmann, Angelika. *an-Nāṣir li-Dīn Allāh (1180–1225): Politik, Religion, Kultur in der späten 'Abbāsidenzeit.* Berlin and New York: de Gruyter, 1975.

Hastings, ed., 1920
Hastings, James, ed. *Encyclopaedia of Religion and Ethics,* vol. 11. Edinburgh and New York: C. Scribner's Sons/T. & T. Clark, 1920.

Hayton, 1906
Hayton. 'Fleur des histoires de la terre d'Orient.' In *Recueil des historiens des Croisades: Documents arméniens*, vol. 2, edited by H. Omont. Paris: Imprimerie nationale, 1906.

Hayward Gallery, 1976
Hayward Gallery. *Arts of Islam.* London: Arts Council of Great Britain, 1976.

Hermann et al., 2002
Hermann, Georgina, Stuart Laidlaw, Helena Coffey, and K. Kurbansakhatov. *The Monuments of Merv.* London: British Institute of Persian Studies, 2002.

Herrmann, 1994
Hermann, Gottfried. 'Ein früher persischer Erlaß.' *Zeitschrift der Deutschen Morgenländischen Gesellschaft* 144 (1994): 284–99.

Herrmann, 1997
Herrmann, Gottfried. 'Zum persischen Urkundenwesen in der Mongolenzeit: Erlasse von Emiren und Wesiren.' In *L'Iran face à la domination mongole*, edited by Denise Aigle. Tehran: Institut français de recherche en Iran, 1997.

Herrmann, 2004
Herrmann, Gottfried. *Persische Urkunden der Mongolenzeit.* Wiesbaden: Harrassowitz, 2004.

Herzfeld, 1954–55
Herzfeld, Ernst. *Inscriptions et Monuments d'Alep, Matériaux pour un Corpus Inscriptionum Arabicarum, Deuxième Partie: Syrie du Nord.* Cairo: Institut français d'archéologie orientale, 1954–55.

Het'um, 1998
Het'um. *Die Geschichte der Mongolen des Hethum von Korykos (1307) in der Rückübersetzung durch Jean le Long "Traitiez des estas et des conditions de quatorze royaumes de Aise" (1351).* Edited by Sven Dörper. Frankfurt am Main and New York: Peter Lang, 1998.

Heywood, 2000
Heywood, Colin. 'Filling the Black Hole: The Emergence of the Bithynian Atamanates.' In *The Great Ottoman-Turkish Civilisation,* vol. 1, edited by Kemal Çiçek et al. Ankara: Yeni Türkiye, 2000.

Hillenbrand, C., 1993
Hillenbrand, Carole. 'al-Mustanṣir.' In *The Encyclopaedia of Islam,* new ed., edited by H. A. R. Gibb, J. H. Kramers, E. Levi-Provencal, and J. Schacht. Leiden: Brill, 1992.

Hillenbrand, R., 1982
Hillenbrand, Robert. 'The Flanged Tomb Tower at Bastam.' In *Art et Société dans le monde Iranien,* edited by Chahriyar Adle. Paris: Éditions Recherche sur les civilizations, 1982.

Hillenbrand, R., 1986
Hillenbrand, Robert. 'The Classical Heritage in Islamic Art: The Case of Medieval Architecture.' *The Scottish Journal of Religious Studies* 7 (1986): 123–40.

Hillenbrand, R., 1992
Hillenbrand, Robert. 'The Uses of Space in Timurid Painting.' In *Timurid Art and Culture: Iran and Central Asia in the Fifteenth Century,* edited by Lisa Golombek and Maria Eva Subtelny. Leiden, New York, and Cologne: Brill, 1992.

Hillenbrand, R., 1995
Hillenbrand, Robert. 'Images of Authority on Kashan Lustreware.' In *Islamic Art in the Ashmolean.* Oxford Studies in Islamic Art, vol. 10, part 2, edited by James W. Allan. Oxford: Oxford University Press, 1995.

Hillenbrand, R., 2000
Hillenbrand, Robert. 'Images of Muhammad in al-Biruni's *Chronology of Ancient Nations.*' In *Persian Painting from the Mongols to the Qajars: Studies in Honour of Basil W. Robinson,* edited by Robert Hillenbrand. London and New York: I. B. Tauris, 2000.

Hinz, 1991
Hinz, Walther. *Islamische Währungen des 11. bis 19. Jahrhunderts umgerechnet in Gold.* Wiesbaden: Harrassowitz, 1991.

Hirth and Rockhill, eds., 1966
Hirth, Friedrich, and William Woodville Rockhill, eds. *Chau Ju-Kua: His Work on the Chinese and Arab Trade in the Twelfth and Thirteenth Centuries, entitled Chu-fan-chi.* Amsterdam: Oriental Press, 1966.

Hoffman, 1982
Hoffman, Eva R. 'The Emergence of Illustration in Arabic Manuscripts: Classical Legacy and Islamic Transformation.' Ph.D. diss., Harvard University, 1982.

Hoffman, 1993
Hoffman, Eva R. 'The Author Portrait in Thirteenth-Century Arabic Manuscripts: A New Islamic Context for a Late-Antique Tradition.' *Muqarnas* 10 (1993): 6–20.

Hoffmann, 1997
Hoffmann, Birgitt. 'Iran under mongolischer Herrschaft.' In *Die Mongolen in Asien und Europa*, edited by Stephan Conermann and Jan Kusber. Frankfurt am Main and New York: Europäischer Verlag der Wissenschaften/P. Lang, 1997.

Holladay, 1996
Holladay, Joan A. *Illuminating the Epic: The Kassel Willehalm Codex and the Landgraves of Hesse in the Early Fourteenth Century*. Seattle and London: College Art Association in association with University of Washington Press, 1996.

Horn and Born, 1979
Horn, Walter, and Ernest Born. *The Plan of St. Gall: A Study of the Architecture and Economy of, and Life in, a Paradigmatic Carolingian Monastery*. Berkeley: University of California Press, 1979.

Horn and Born, 1986
Horn, Walter, and Ernest Born. 'The Medieval Monastery as a Setting for the Production of Manuscripts.' *Journal of the Walters Art Gallery* 44 (1986): 16–47.

Horst, 1967
Horst, Heribert. 'Eine Gesandtschaft des Mamluken al-Malik an-Nasir am Ilkhan-Hof in Persien.' In *Der Orient in der Forschung*, edited by Wilhelm Hoenerbach. Wiesbaden: Harrassowitz, 1967.

Houtsma, ed., 1913–38
Houtsma, M. Th., ed. *Enzyklopaedie des Islam: Geographisches, ethnographisches und biographisches Wörterbuch der muhammedanischen Völker*. 5 vols. Leiden: Brill, 1913–38.

Howorth, 1888
Howorth, Henry H. *History of the Mongols, from the 9th to the 19th Century, Part III: The Mongols of Persia*, 1888. Reprint, Taipei: Ch'eng Wen, 1970.

Hsiao, 1978
Hsiao, Ch'i-ch'ing. *The Military Establishment of the Yüan Dynasty*. Harvard East Asian Monographs, vol. 77. Cambridge: Council on East Asian Studies, Harvard University Press, 1978.

Huff, 1977
Huff, Dietrich. 'Takht-i Suleiman. Vorläufiger Bericht über die Ausgrabungen im Jahre 1976.' *Archäologische Mitteilungen aus Iran* N.S. 10 (1977): 211–30.

Huff, 1993
Huff, Dietrich. 'Architecture sassanide.' In *Splendeur des Sassanides: L'empire perse entre Rome et la Chine (224–642)*. Brussels: Musées royaux d'Art et d'Histoire, 1993.

Huff, 1999
Huff, Dietrich. 'Traditionen iranischer Palastarchitektur in vorislamischer und islamischer Zeit.' In *Bamberger Symposium: Rezeption in der islamischen Kunst, vom 26.6.–28.6.1992*, edited by Barbara Finster, Christa Fragner and Herta Hafenrichter. Stuttgart: F. Steiner, 1999.

Huff, 2000
Huff, Dietrich. 'Takht-i Suleiman. Tempel des sasanidischen Reichsfeuers Atur Gushnasp.' In *Archäologische Entdeckungen. Die Forschungen des Deutschen Archäologischen Instituts im 20. Jahrhundert*, edited by Klaus Rheidt, Angelika Schöne-Denkinger and A. Nünnerich-Asmus. Mainz: Philipp von Zabern, 2000.

Huff, 2005
Huff, Dietrich. 'From Median to Achaemenian Palace Architecture.' *Iranica Antiqua* 40 (2005): 371–95.

Huff, forthcoming
Huff, Dietrich. 'The Functional Layout of the Fire Sanctuary at Takht-i Sulayman.' In *Proceedings of the Conference on Current Research on Sasanian Archaeology and History, November 3–4, 2001, Durham*, edited by D. Kennet. Forthcoming.

Ibn-i Bazzāz-i Ardabīlī, 1994
Ibn-i Bazzāz-i Ardabīlī. *Ṣafwat al-ṣafā*. Edited by Ghulāmriḍā Ṭabāṭabā'i Majd. Tabriz: Ghulāmriḍā Ṭabāṭabā'i Majd, 1994.

Ibn 'Abd al-Ẓāhir, 1961
Ibn 'Abd al-Ẓāhir, Muḥyī al-Dīn. *Tashrīf al-ayyām*. Edited by Murād Kāmil and Muḥammad 'Alī al-Najjār. Cairo: Tur§thun§, 1961.

Ibn 'Abd al-Ẓāhir, 1976
Ibn 'Abd al-Ẓāhir, Muḥyī al-Dīn. *al-Rawḍ al-ẓāhir fī sīrat al-Malik al-Ẓāhir*. Edited by 'Abd al-'Azīz Khuwayṭir. Riyadh, 1976.

Ibn al-Balkhī, 1921
Ibn al-Balkhī. *The Fārsnāma of Ibnu'l-Balkhi*. Edited by Guy Le Strange and Reynold Alleyne Nicholson. London: Luzac, 1921.

Ibn al-Dawādārī, 1960
Ibn al-Dawādārī, Abū Bakr ibn 'Abd Allāh. *Kanz al-durar wa-jāmi' al-ghurar*. Edited by Hans Robert Roemer. Cairo: Deutsches Archäologisches Institut, 1960.

Ibn al-Dawādārī, 1971
Ibn al-Dawādārī, Abū Bakr ibn 'Abd Allāh. 'Vorwort.' In *Kanz al-durar wa-jāmi' al-ghurar*, edited by Ulrich Haarmann. Cairo: Deutsches Archäologisches Institut, 1971.

Ibn al-Fuwaṭī, 1962–65
Ibn al-Fuwaṭī. *Talkhīṣ majma' al-ādāb fī mu'jam al-alqāb*. Edited by Muṣṭafā Jawād. 3 vols. Damascus: Wizārat al-thaqāfa wa al-irshād al-qawmī, 1962–65.

Ibn al-Fuwaṭī, 1995
Ibn al-Fuwaṭī. *Majma' al-ādāb fī mu'jam al-alqāb*. Edited by Muḥammad al-Kāzim. 6 vols. Tehran: Vizārat-i Farhang va Irshād-i Islāmī, 1995.

Ibn al-'Imād, 1932
Ibn al-'Imād, 'Abd al-Ḥayy ibn Aḥmad. *Shadharāt al-dhahab fī akhbār man dhahab*. 8 vols. Cairo: Maktabat al-Qudsī, 1932.

Ibn al-Shāṭir, forthcoming
Ibn al-Shāṭir. *Nihāyāt al-sūl.* Edited by George Saliba. Forthcoming.

Ibn al-Ṣuqāʿī, 1974
Ibn al-Ṣuqāʿī, Faḍl Allāh ibn Abī al-Fakhr. *Tālī kitāb wafāyāt al-aʿyān.* Translated and edited by Jacqueline Sublet. Damascus: al-Maʿhad al-Faransī bi-Dimashq li-al-Dirāsāt al-ʿArabiyya, 1974.

Ibn al-Ṭiqṭaqā, 1895
Ibn al-Ṭiqṭaqā, Muḥammad ibn ʿAlī. *al-Fakhrī: Histoire du khalifat et du vizirat, depuis leurs origines jusqu'à la chute du khalifat ʿAbbaside de Bagdadh (II–656 de l'hégire=632–1258 de notre ére), avec des prolégomènes sur les principes du gouvernement, par Ibn At-Tiktaka.* Translated by Hartwig Derenbourg. Paris: E. Bouillon, 1895.

Ibn al-Ṭiqṭaqā, 1910
Ibn al-Ṭiqṭaqā, Muḥammad ibn ʿAlī. *[al-Fakhrī] Histoire des dynasties musulmanes.* Translated by Émile Amar, *Archives Marocaines,* vol. 16. Paris: E. Leroux, 1910.

Ibn al-Ṭiqṭaqā, 1947
Ibn al-Ṭiqṭaqā, Muḥammad ibn ʿAlī. *al-Fakhrī: On the Systems of Government and the Moslem Dynasties, composed by Muhammad son of ʿAli son of Tabataba, known as the rapid talker, may God have mercy on him.* Translated by C. E. J. Whitting. London: Luzac, 1947.

Ibn Baṭṭūṭa, 1958–2000
Ibn Baṭṭūṭa. *The Travels of Ibn* Baṭṭūṭa, *A.D. 1325–1354.* Translated by C. Defrémery and B. R. Sanguinetti. Edited by H. A. R. Gibb. 5 vols. Cambridge: Published for the Hakluyt Society at the University Press, 1958–2000.

Ibn Faḍlān, 1939
Ibn Faḍlān, Aḥmad. *Ibn Faḍlān's Reisebericht (Riḥlat Ibn Faḍlān).* Edited and translated by A. Zeki Validi Togan. Leipzig: F. A. Brockhaus, 1939.

Ibn Ẓafar, 1995
Ibn Ẓafar, Muḥammad ibn ʿAbd Allāh. *Sulwān al-muṭāʿ fī ʿudwān al-atbāʿ.* Edited by Muḥammad Aḥmad Damaj. Facsimile ed. Beirut: Muʾassasat ʿIzz al-Dīn li-al-Ṭibāʿa wa al-Nashr, 1995.

Ilisch, 1985
Ilisch, L. 'Münzgeschenke und Geschenkmünzen in der mittelalterlichen islamischen Welt.' *Münstersche Numismatische Zeitung* 15, no. 1 (1985): 1–12.

Inal, 1963
Inal, Güner. 'Some Miniatures of the *Jamiʿ al-Tavarikh* in Istanbul, Topkapi Museum, Hazine Library no. 1654.' *Ars Orientalis* 5 (1963): 165–75.

Inal, 1965
Inal, Güner. 'The Fourteenth-Century Miniatures of the *Jamiʿ al-Tavarikh* in the Topkapi Museum in Istanbul, Hazine Library no. 1653.' Ph.D. diss., University of Michigan, 1965.

İnan, 1968
İnan, Abdülkadir. "Orun' ve 'ülüş' meselesi. *İ*-Mevki-Orun Hukuku.' In *Makaleler ve İncelemeler,* edited by Abdülkadir İnan. Ankara: Türk Tarih Kurumu Basımevi, 1968.

Ipşiroğlu, 1964
Ipşiroğlu, M. Ş. *Saray-Alben: Diez'sche Klebebände aus den Berliner Sammlungen.* Wiesbaden: F. Steiner, 1964.

Ipşiroğlu, 1967
Ipşiroğlu, M. Ş. *Painting and Culture of the Mongols.* London: Thames and Hudson, 1967.

Ipşiroğlu, 1973
Ipşiroğlu, M. Ş. *Islâmda Resim: Yasaği ve Sonuçlari.* Istanbul: Doğan Kardeş Matbaacilik Sanayii, 1973.

Iqbāl-i Āshtiyānī, 1971
Iqbāl-i Āshtiyānī, ʿAbbās. *Majmūʿa-yi maqālāt-i ʿabbās-iqbāl-i āshtiyānī.* Edited by Muḥammad Dabīrsiyāqī. Tehran: Khayyām, 1971.

Iqbāl, ʿA., 1950–55
Iqbāl, ʿAbbās. ʻḤabash ʿAmīd-i Turkistānī.' In *60. Doğum Yılı Münasebetiyle Zeki Velidi Togan'a Armağan.* Istanbul: Maarif, 1950–55.

Iqbāl, M., 1937
Iqbāl, Moḥammad. 'Ibn al-Fuwatî.' *Islamic Culture* 11 (1937): 516–22.

Iqtidārī, 1966–67
Iqtidārī, Aḥmad. *Khalīj-i Fārs.* Tehran: Ibn Sīnā, 1966–67.

Iṣāmī, 1948
Iṣāmī, ʿAbd al-Malik. *Futūḥ al-Salāṭīn.* Edited by A. S. Usha. Madras: University of Madras Press, 1948.

Ivanov, 1984
Ivanov, Anatol A. 'Novoe chetenie nadpisi na timpane s bortsami iz seleniya Kubachi.' *Epigrafika Vostoka* 22 (1984): 57–60.

Ivanov, 2000
Ivanov, Anatoly. 'The Name of a Painter who Illustrated the *World History* of Rashid al-Din.' In *Persian Painting from the Mongols to the Qajars: Studies in Honour of Basil W. Robinson,* edited by Robert Hillenbrand. London and New York: I. B. Tauris, 2000.

Jackson, 1990
Jackson, Peter. 'Bāyjū.' In *Encyclopaedia Iranica,* edited by Ehsan Yarshater. London and New York: Routledge & Kegan Paul, 1990.

Jackson, 1993a
Jackson, Peter. 'Čormāgūn.' In *Encyclopaedia Iranica,* edited by Ehsan Yarshater. Costa Mesa, Calif.: Mazda, 1993.

Jackson, 1993b
Jackson, Peter. 'Courts and Courtiers, iv. The Mongol Period.' In *Encyclopaedia Iranica,* edited by Ehsan Yarshater. Costa Mesa, Calif.: Mazda, 1993.

Jackson, 2000
Jackson, Peter. 'The State of Research: The Mongol Empire, 1986–1999.' *Journal of Medieval History* 26, no. 2 (2000): 189–210.

Jackson, 2005
Jackson, Peter. *The Mongols and the West, 1221–1410*. Harlow, England and New York: Pearson Longman, 2005.

Jacob, 1925
Jacob, Georg. *Geschichte des Schattentheaters im Morgen- und Abenland.* 2nd enlarged ed. Hanover: Orient. Buchhandlung Heinz Lafaire, 1925.

Jaʿfarī, 1960
Jaʿfarī, Jaʿfar ibn Muḥammad ibn Ḥasan. *Tārīkh-i Yazd*. Tehran: Bungāh-i Tarjuma wa Nashr-i Kitāb, 1960.

Jalālī, ed., 1999
Jalālī, Nādira, ed. *Tārīkh-i Āl-i Saljūq dar Ānāṭūlī*. Tehran: Āyina-yi Mīrāth, 1999.

James, 1980
James, David. *Qur'ans and Bindings from the Chester Beatty Library: A Facsimile Exhibition.* London: World of Islam Festival Trust, 1980.

James, 1988
James, David. *Qur'ans of the Mamluks*. London: Alexandria Press/Thames and Hudson, 1988.

James, 1992
James, David. *The Master Scribes: Qur'ans of the 10th to 14th Centuries AD*. Nasser D. Khalili Collection of Islamic Art, vol. 2. London: Nour Foundation in association with Azimuth Editions and Oxford University Press, 1992.

James, 1999
James, David. *Manuscripts of the Holy Qur'an from the Mamluk Era*. Riyadh: King Faisal Center for Research and Islamic Studies, 1999.

Jenkins, 1983
Jenkins, Marilyn. 'Islamic Pottery: A Brief History.' *Bulletin of the Metropolitan Museum of Art* 40, no. 4 (Spring, 1983).

John of Plano Carpini, 1955
John of Plano Carpini. 'History of the Mongols.' In *The Mongol Mission*, edited by Christopher Dawson. London: Sheed and Ward, 1955.

Jourdain, 1809
Jourdain, M. 'Mémoire sur les instruments employée à l'Observatoire de Méragha.' *Magasin Encylopédique* 4 (1809).

Junābādī, 1999
Junābādī, Mīrzā Beg. *Rawḍat al-Ṣafawiyya*. Edited by Ghulāmriḍā Ṭabāṭabā'i Majd. Tehran: Mawqūfāt-i Maḥmūd Afshār Yazdī, 1999.

Juwaynī, 1912–58
Juwaynī, ʿAlā' al-Dīn ʿAṭā Malik. *Ta'rīkh-i jahān-gushāy/History of the World Conqueror*. Edited by Mīrzā Muḥammad ibn ʿAbd al-Wahhāb-i-Qazwīnī. 3 vols. Leiden: Brill, 1912–58.

Juwaynī, 1958
Juwaynī, ʿAlā'' al-Dīn ʿAṭā Malik. *The History of the World-Conqueror*. Translated by J. A. Boyle. 2 vols. Cambridge: Harvard University Press, 1958.

Juwaynī, 1997
Juwaynī, 'Alā' al-Dīn 'Aṭā Malik. *Genghis Khan: The History of the World Conqueror.* Translated by J. A. Boyle. Edited by David O. Morgan. Manchester and Paris: Manchester University Press and UNESCO Publishing, 1997.

Jūzjānī, 1881
Jūzjānī, 'Uthmān. *Ṭabaḳāt-i-Nāṣirī.* Translated by H. G. Raverty. 2 vols. London: Gilbert & Rivington, 1881.

Kahle, 1910–11
Kahle, P. 'Islamische Schattenspielfiguren aus Ägypten.' *Der Islam* 1 and 2 (1910–11): 264–99 and 143–95.

Kahle, 1940
Kahle, P. 'The Arabic Shadow Play in Egypt.' *Journal of the Royal Asiatic Society* (1940): 21–34.

Kahle, 1954
Kahle, P. 'The Arabic Shadow Play in Medieval Egypt (Old Texts and Old Figures).' *Journal of the Pakistan Historical Society* 2 (1954): 85–97.

Kanat, 2002
Kanat, Cüneyt. 'İlhanlı Hükümdarı Teküdar'ın Müslümanlığı Kabulü ve Bunun Memlûk Devleti'ndeki Yankıları.' *Türklük Araştırmaları Dergisi* 12 (2002): 233–47.

Karashima, 1989
Karashima, Noboru. 'Trade Relations between South India and China during the 13th and 14th Centuries.' *Journal of East-West Maritime Relations* 1 (1989).

Karatay, 1961
Karatay, Fehmi Edhem. *Topkapı Sarayı Müzesi Kütüphanesi Farsça yazmalar kataloğu.* Istanbul: Topkapı Sarayı Müzesi, 1961.

Kauz and Ptak, 2001
Kauz, Ralph, and Roderich Ptak. 'Hormuz in Yuan and Ming Sources.' *Bulletin de l'École française d'Extrême-Orient* 88 (2001): 39–46.

Kelekian, 1910
Kelekian, Dikran G. *The Kelekian Collection of Persian and Analogous Potteries, 1885–1910.* Paris: H. Clarke, 1910.

Kennedy, 1966
Kennedy, E. S. 'Late Medieval Planetary Theories.' *Isis* 57 (1966): 365–78.

Kennedy, 1968
Kennedy, E. S. 'The Exact Sciences in Iran under the Seljuks and Mongols.' In *The Cambridge History of Iran.* Vol. 5, *The Saljuq and Mongol Periods*, edited by J. A. Boyle. Cambridge: Cambridge University Press, 1968.

Kennedy and Ghanem, 1976
Kennedy, E. S., and Imad Ghanem. *The Life and Work of Ibn al-Shāṭir.* Aleppo: University of Aleppo, 1976.

Khanykov, 1852–56
Khanykov, N. 'Note sur le yarligh d'Abou-Saïd-Khan conservé sur les murs de la mosquée d'Ani.' *Mélanges Asiatiques* 2 (1852–56): 61–67.

Khanykov, 1862
Khanykov, N. 'Mémoire sur les inscriptions musulmanes du Caucase.' *Journal Asiatique* 5ᵉ série, 20 (1862).

Khodzevich, 1988
Khodzevich, L. P. 'O Proiskhozhdenii Siueta na Odnoi Unikal'noi Poiasnoi Garniture iz Lazovskogo Gorodishcha.' In *Materialy po Etnokul'turnym Sviaziam Narodov Dal'nego Vostoka v Srednie Veka*, edited by V. D. Lenkov, A. M. Pevnov, and E. V. Shavkunov. Vladivostok, 1988.

Kiliç, 1997
Kiliç, N. 'Change in Political Structure: The Rise of Shebani Khan.' In *L'héritage timouride: Iran, Asie Centrale, Inde, XVᵉ–XVIIIᵉ siècles*, edited by Maria Szuppe. Tashkent and Aix-en-Provence: Edisud, 1997.

Kirakos Ganjakets'i, 1961
Kirakos Ganjakets'i. *Patmut'iwn Hayots'/Universal History*. Edited by K. A. Melik'-Ohanjanyan. Yerevan: Haykakan SSR Gitut'yunneri Akademiayi Hratarkch'ut'yun, 1961.

Kleiss, 1971
Kleiss, Wolfram. *Zendan-i Suleiman: die Bauwerke*. Wiesbaden: F. Steiner, 1971.

Klinge, Zick-Nissen, and Klein, 1973
Klinge, Ekkart, Johanna Zick-Nissen, and Adalbert Klein. *Islamische Keramik*. Düsseldorf: Hetjens-Museum in cooperation with the Museum für Islamische Kunst, Berlin-Dahlem, 1973.

Komaroff, 1994
Komaroff, Linda. 'Paintings in Silver and Gold: The Decoration of Persian Metalwork and its Relationship to Manuscript Illustration.' *Studies in the Decorative Arts* 2, no. 1 (Fall 1994): 2–34.

Komaroff, 2002
Komaroff, Linda. 'The Transmission and Dissemination of a New Visual Language.' In *The Legacy of Genghis Khan: Courtly Art and Culture in Western Asia, 1256–1353*, edited by Linda Komaroff and Stefano Carboni. New York, New Haven, and London: Metropolitan Museum of Art and Yale University Press, 2002.

Komaroff and Carboni, eds., 2002
Komaroff, Linda, and Stefano Carboni, eds. *The Legacy of Genghis Khan: Courtly Art and Culture in Western Asia, 1256–1353*. New York, New Haven, and London: Metropolitan Museum of Art and Yale University Press, 2002.

Köprülü, 1993
Köprülü, Mehmed Fuad. *Islam in Anatolia after the Turkish Invasion (Prolegomena)*. Translated and edited by Gary Leiser. Salt Lake City: University of Utah Press, 1993.

Korkhmazian, Drampian, and Hakopian, 1984
Korkhmazian, Emma, Irina Drampian, and Hravard Hakopian. *Armenian Miniatures of the 13th and 14th Centuries from the Matenadaran Collection*. Leningrad: Aurora, 1984.

Kouymjian, 1977
Kouymjian, Dickran. 'Far Eastern Influences in Armenian Miniature Painting in the Mongol Period.' Paper presented at the panel on Patronage and Symbolism in Medieval Armenian Art, 11th Annual Meeting of the Middle East Studies Association, New York, 1977.

Kouymjian, 1986
Kouymjian, Dickran. 'Chinese Elements in Armenian Miniature Painting in the Mongol Period.' In *Armenian Studies/Études arméniennes: In memoriam Haig Berbérian*, edited by Dickran Kouymjian. Lisbon: Calouste Gulbenkian Foundation, 1986.

Krachkovskaia, 1946
Krachkovskaia, V. A. *Izraztsy mavzoleia Pir-Khuseina*. Tbilisi: Izd-vo Akad. nauk gruz. SSR, 1946.

Krahl and Erbahar, 1986
Krahl, Regina, and Nurdan Erbahar. *Chinese Ceramics in the Topkapi Saray Museum, Istanbul: A Complete Catalogue*. Edited by John Ayers. 3 vols. London and New York: Sotheby's Publications, 1986.

Kramarovsky, 2000
Kramarovsky, Mark. *The Treasures of the Golden Horde (In Tatar, Russian, and English)*. St. Petersburg: Slaviia, 2000.

Kramarovsky, 2001
Kramarovsky, Mark. *Zoloto Chengizidov: kul'turnoe nasledie Zolotoi Ordy (The Gold of the Chinggisids: The Cultural Legacy of the Golden Horde)*. St. Petersburg, 2001.

Kramarovsky, 2004
Kramarovsky, Mark. *Rannie Dzhuchidy: Khronologia i Problema Kul'turogeneza in Ermitazhnye Chteniia Pamiati B. B. Piotrovskogo*. St. Petersburg, 2004.

Krawulsky, 1978
Krawulsky, Dorothea. *Iran, das Reich der Ilḫane*. Wiesbaden: Reichert, 1978.

Krawulsky, 1989
Krawulsky, Dorothea. *Mongolen und Ilkhane: Ideologie und Geschichte*. Tübingen: Verlag für Islamische Studien, 1989.

Kritzeck, 1959
Kritzeck, James. 'Ibn al-Tiqtaqa and the Fall of Baghdad.' In *The World of Islam: Studies in Honour of Philip K. Hitti*, edited by James Kritzeck and R. Bayly Winder. London and New York: Macmillan/St. Martin's Press, 1959.

Kropp and Pfeiffer, eds., in press
Kropp, Manfred, and Judith Pfeiffer, eds. *Theoretical Approaches to the Transmission and Edition of Oriental Manuscripts*. Würzburg: Ergon Verlag, in press.

Kühnel, 1931
Kühnel, Ernst. 'Dated Persian Lustred Pottery.' *Eastern Art* 3 (1931): 221–36.

Kuribayashi and Choijinjiab, 2001
Kuribayashi, H., and Choijinjiab. *Genchohishi mongorugo zentango gobisakuin (Word- and Suffix-Index to The Secret History of the Mongols)*. CNEAS Monograph Series, no. 4. Sendai: The Center for Northeast Asia Studies, Tohoku University, 2001.

Kutubi, 1913
Kutubi, Mahmud. 'Account of the Muzaffari Dynasty.' In *Ta'rikh-i guzida of Hamdu'llah Mustawfi-i Qazwini. Reproduced in facsimile form from manuscript dated A.H. 857 (A.D. 1453)*, edited by Edward G. Browne. London: Luzac, 1913.

Kwanten, 1979
Kwanten, Luc. *Imperial Nomads: A History of Central Asia, 500–1500*. Leicester: Leicester University Press, 1979.

Lambton, 1968
Lambton, Ann K. S. 'The Internal Structure of the Saljuq Empire.' In *The Cambridge History of Iran*. Vol. 5, *The Saljuq and Mongol Periods*, edited by J. A. Boyle. Cambridge: Cambridge University Press, 1968.

Lambton, 1986–87
Lambton, Ann K. S. 'Mongol Fiscal Administration in Persia.' *Studia Islamica* 64 and 65 (1986 and 1987): 79–99 and 97–123.

Lambton, 1988
Lambton, Ann K. S. *Continuity and Change in Medieval Persia: Aspects of Administrative, Economic, and Social History, 11th–14th Century*. Albany: Bibliotheca Persica/ SUNY Press, 1988.

Lambton, 1992
Lambton, Ann K. S. 'Naḳḳāra-k͟hāna.' In *The Encyclopaedia of Islam*, new ed., edited by H. A. R. Gibb, J. H. Kramers, E. Levi-Provencal, and J. Schacht. Leiden: Brill, 1992.

Lambton, 1994
Lambton, Ann K. S. '*Pishkash*: Present or Tribute.' *Bulletin of the School of Oriental and African Studies* 57 (1994): 145–58.

Lane, A., 1947
Lane, Arthur. *Early Islamic Pottery*. London: Faber and Faber, 1947.

Lane, A., 1957
Lane, Arthur. *Later Islamic Pottery*. London: Faber and Faber, 1957.

Lane, G., 1999
Lane, George. 'Arghun Aqa: A Mongol Bureaucrat.' *Iranian Studies* 32, no. 4 (1999): 459–82.

Lane, G., 2003
Lane, George. *Early Mongol Rule in Thirteenth-Century Iran: A Persian Renaissance*. London and New York: RoutledgeCurzon, 2003.

Laoust, 1970
Laoust, Henri. *La politique de Ǧazālī*. Paris: P. Geuthner, 1970.

Laoust, 1971
Laoust, Henri. 'Ibn Taymiyya.' In *The Encyclopaedia of Islam*, new ed., edited by H. A. R. Gibb, J. H. Kramers, E. Levi-Provencal, and J. Schacht. Leiden and London: Brill/Luzac, 1971.

Larner, 1999
Larner, John. *Marco Polo and the Discovery of the World*. New Haven and London: Yale University Press, 1999.

Lazard, 1975
Lazard, G. 'The Rise of the New Persian Language.' In *The Cambridge History of Iran*. Vol. 4, *From the Arab Invasion to the Saljuqs*, edited by R. N. Frye. Cambridge: Cambridge University Press, 1975.

Le Strange, 1905
Le Strange, Guy. *The Lands of the Eastern Caliphate*. Cambridge: Cambridge University Press, 1905. Reprint, 1930; reprint, London: F. Cass, 1966.

Lentz and Lowry, 1989
Lentz, Thomas W., and Glenn D. Lowry. *Timur and the Princely Vision: Persian Art and Culture in the Fifteenth Century*. Los Angeles: Los Angeles County Museum of Art, 1989.

Leroy, 1964
Leroy, Jules. *Les manuscrits syriaques à peintures conservés dans les bibliothèques d'Europe et d'Orient; contribution à l'étude de l'iconographie des églises de langue syriaque*. 2 vols. Paris: P. Geuthner, 1964.

Lewis, A. R., 1988
Lewis, Archibald R. *Nomads and Crusaders, A.D. 1000–1368*. Bloomington: Indiana University Press, 1988.

Lewis, F., 2000
Lewis, Franklin. *Rumi: Past and Present, East and West: The Life, Teaching and Poetry of Jalal al-Din Rumi*. Oxford and Boston: Oneworld, 2000.

Lindner, 1999
Lindner, Rudi. 'How Mongol Were the Early Ottomans?' In *The Mongol Empire and its Legacy*, edited by Reuven Amitai-Preiss and David Morgan. Leiden and Boston: Brill, 1999.

Lings, 1976
Lings, Martin. *The Quranic Art of Calligraphy and Illumination*. London: World of Islam Festival Trust, 1976.

Lings and Safadi, 1976
Lings, Martin, and Yasin Hamid Safadi. *The Qur'an: Catalogue of an Exhibition of Qur'an Manuscripts at the British Library, 3 April–15 August 1976*. London: World of Islam Publishing for the British Library, 1976.

Little, 1998
Little, Donald P. 'Historiography of the Ayyubid and Mamluk Epochs.' In *The Cambridge History of Egypt*. Vol. 1, *641–1517*, edited by Carl F. Petry. Cambridge and New York: Cambridge University Press, 1998.

Liu Yingsheng, 1985
Liu Yingsheng, 劉迎勝. 'Cong 'Bu'ali shendao beiming' kan Nanyindu yu Yuan chao ji Bosiwan de jiaotong 從不阿里神道碑銘看南印度與元朝及波斯灣的交通.' *Lishi dili* 7 (1985): 90–95.

Liu Yingsheng, 1992
Liu Yingsheng, 劉迎勝. 'An Inscription in Memory of Sayyid Bin Abu Ali: A Study on the Relationship between China and Oman from the 11th–15th Centuries.' In *Papers Submitted at the International Seminar on the Silk Roads Held at Sultan Quaboos University, Muscat, Sultanate of Oman, 20–21 November 1990*, edited by

Malallah bin Ali Habib Al-Lawaty. The Ministry of National Heritage and Culture, Sultanate of Oman, 1992.

L'Orange, 1953
L'Orange, Hans Peter. *Studies on the Iconography of Cosmic Kingship in the Ancient World.* Instituttet for Sammenlignende Kulturforskning, series A: Forelesninger, vol. 23. Oslo: H. Aschehoug, 1953.

Lopez and Raymond, 1955
Lopez, Robert S., and Irving W. Raymond. *Medieval Trade in the Mediterranean World.* New York: Columbia University Press, 1955.

Lowry and Beach, 1988
Lowry, Glenn D., and Milo C. Beach. *An Annotated and Illustrated Checklist of the Vever Collection.* Washington, D.C.: Arthur M. Sackler Gallery in association with University of Washington Press, 1988.

Lowry and Nemazee, 1988
Lowry, Glenn D., and Susan Nemazee. *A Jeweler's Eye: Islamic Arts of the Book from the Vever Collection.* Washington, D.C.: Arthur M. Sackler Gallery in association with University of Washington Press, 1988.

Lupprian, 1981
Lupprian, K. E. 'Die Beziehungen der Päpste zu Islamischen und Mongolischen Herrschern im 13. Jahrhundert anhand ihres Briefwechsels.' *Studi e Testi* 291 (1981): 182–89.

Mahboubian, 1970
Mahboubian, Mehdi. *Treasures of Persian Art after Islam: The Mahboubian Collection.* New York: Plantin Press, 1970.

Maidar and Maidar, 1972
Maidar, D., and T. Maidar. 'Kamennaya colonna iz Avragyn balgas (Column Base Stones from Avraga Fortress).' *Arkheologiin Sudlal (Studia Archeologica, Institute Historiae Academiae Scientiarum Mongoli)* 5 (1972): 151–56.

Man, 2004
Man, John. *Genghis Khan: Life, Death, and Resurrection.* London and New York: Bantam Press, 2004.

Manandian, 1965
Manandian, Hakob A. *The Trade and Cities of Armenia in Relation to Ancient World Trade.* Translated by Nina G. Garsoian. Lisbon: Livraria Bertrand, 1965.

Manz, 1989
Manz, Beatrice Forbes. *The Rise and Rule of Tamerlane.* Cambridge and New York: Cambridge University Press, 1989.

al-Maqrīzī, 1845
al-Maqrīzī, Aḥmad ibn ʿAlī. *Histoire des Sultans Mamlouks de l'Égypte/Kitāb al-sulūk li-maʿrifat duwal al-mulūk.* Translated by Étienne Quatremère. 2 vols. Paris: Oriental Translation Fund of Great Britain and Ireland, 1845.

al-Maqrīzī, 1943
al-Maqrīzī, Aḥmad ibn ʿAlī. *Kitāb al-sulūk li-maʿrifat duwal al-mulūk.* Edited by Muḥammad Muṣṭafā Ziyāda. 4 vols. Cairo: Lajnat al-Ta'līf, 1943.

Marquet, 1971
Marquet, Y. 'Ikhwān al-Ṣafā".' In *The Encyclopaedia of Islam*, new ed., edited by H. A. R. Gibb, J. H. Kramers, E. Levi-Provencal, and J. Schacht. Leiden and London: Brill/Luzac, 1971.

Marshak, 2002
Marshak, Boris I. 'Pre-Islamic Painting of the Iranian Peoples and its Sources in Sculpture and the Decorative Arts.' In *Peerless Images: Persian Painting and its Sources*, edited by Eleanor Sims. New Haven and London: Yale University Press, 2002.

Marshall, 1993
Marshall, Robert. *Storm from the East*. London: BBC Books, 1993.

Marteau and Vever, 1913
Marteau, G., and H. Vever. *Miniatures persanes, tirées des collections de MM. Henry d'Allemagne, Claude Anet, Henri Aubry...et exposées au Musée des arts décoratifs, juin–octobre 1912*, vol. 1. Paris: Bibliothèque d'art et d'archéologie, 1913.

Martin, H.-J. and Chatelain, 2000
Martin, Henri-Jean, and Jean-Marc Chatelain. *La Naissance du livre moderne (XIVe–XVIIe siècles)*. Paris: Éditions du Cercle de la librairie, 2000.

Martin, H. D., 1950
Martin, Henry Desmond. *The Rise of Chingis Khan and his Conquest of North China*. Baltimore: Johns Hopkins Press, 1950.

Martinez, 1986 [1988]
Martinez, A. P. 'The Third Portion of the Story of Gāzān Xān in Rašīdu'd-Dīn's *Ta'rīx-e Mobārak-e Gāzānī*.' *Archivum Eurasiae Medii Aevi* 6 (1986 [1988]): 41–127.

Marvī, 1985
Marvī, Muḥammad Kāẓim. *'Alam-ārā-yi Nādirī*. Edited by Muḥammad Amīn Riyāḥī. 3 vols. Tehran: Kitābfurūshī Zuvvār, 1985.

Mashīzī, 1990
Mashīzī, Mīr Muḥammad. *Tadhkira-yi Ṣafawiyya*. Edited by M. I. Bāstānī Pārīzī. Tehran: Nashr-i 'Ilm, 1990.

Ma'ṣūm, 1989
Ma'ṣūm, Mīrzā Muḥammad. *Khulāṣat al-akhyār*. Edited by Irāj Afshār. Tehran: Intishārāt 'Ilmī, 1989.

Masuya, 1994
Masuya, Tomoko. 'The Condition of the Metropolitan Museum's Small *Shahnama* and the Reconstruction of its Text.' In *Illustrated Poetry and Epic Images: Persian Painting of the 1330s and 1340s*, edited by Marie Lukens Swietochowski and Stefano Carboni. New York: Metropolitan Museum of Art, 1994.

Masuya, 1997
Masuya, Tomoko. 'The Ilkhanid Phase of Takht-i Sulaiman.' Ph.D. diss., New York University, 1997.

Masuya, 2002
Masuya, Tomoko. 'Ilkhanid Courtly Life.' In *The Legacy of Genghis Khan: Courtly Art and*

Culture in Western Asia, 1256–1353, edited by Linda Komaroff and Stefano Carboni. New York, New Haven, and London: Metropolitan Museum of Art and Yale University Press, 2002.

Mathews, 1998
Mathews, Thomas F. 'The Genius of the Armenian Painter.' In *Treasures in Heaven: Armenian Art, Religion and Society*, edited by Thomas F. Mathews and Roger S. Wieck. New York: Pierpont Morgan Library, 1998.

Matthee, 1999
Matthee, Rudolph P. *The Politics of Trade in Safavid Iran: Silk for Silver, 1600–1730, Cambridge Studies in Islamic Civilization.* Cambridge and New York: Cambridge University Press, 1999.

Mayer, 1952
Mayer, L. A. *Mamluk Costume.* Geneva: A. Kundig, 1952.

Mayhew, Plunkett, and Richmond, 1996
Mayhew, Bradley, Richard Plunkett, and Simon Richmond. *Lonely Planet: Central Asia.* Hawthorn, Australia: Lonely Planet, 1996.

Mazzaoui, 2006
Mazzaoui, Michel M. 'A "New" Edition of *Ṣafvat al-ṣafā*.' In *History and Historiography of Post-Mongol Central Asia and the Middle East*, edited by Judith Pfeiffer and Sholeh A. Quinn. Wiesbaden: Harrassowitz, 2006.

McChesney, 1983
McChesney, Robert D. 'The Amirs of Muslim Central Asia in the XVVIIth Century.' *Journal of Economic and Social History of the Orient* 26 (1983): 33–70.

McNeill, 1989
McNeill, William H. *Plagues and Peoples.* New ed. New York: Anchor Books, 1989.

Meinecke, 1976
Meinecke, Michael. *Fayencedekorationen seldschukischer Sakralbauten in Kleinasien.* 2 vols. Istanbuler Mitteilungen, Beiheft 13. Tübingen: Verlag Ernst Wasmuth, 1976.

Melikian-Chirvani, 1971
Melikian-Chirvani, A. S. 'Le Royaume de Saloman, les inscriptions persanes de sites achéménides.' *Le monde iranien et l'Islam* 1, no. 4 (1971): 1–41.

Melikian-Chirvani, 1973
Melikian-Chirvani, A. S. *Le bronze iranien.* Paris: Musée des arts décoratifs, 1973.

Melikian-Chirvani, 1974
Melikian-Chirvani, A. S. 'L'évocation littéraire du bouddhisme dans l'Iran musulman.' *Le Monde Iranien et l'Islam* 2 (1974): 34–37.

Melikian-Chirvani, 1982
Melikian-Chirvani, A. S. *Islamic Metalwork from the Iranian World, 8–18th Centuries.* London: Victoria and Albert Museum, 1982.

Melikian-Chirvani, 1984
Melikian-Chirvani, A. S. 'Le *Shah-Name*, la gnose Soufie et le pouvoir mongol.' *Journal Asiatique* 272, no. 3–4 (1984): 249–337.

Melikian-Chirvani, 1985
Melikian-Chirvani, A. S. *Sulwān al-muṭāʿ fī ʿudwān al-atbāʿ: A Rediscovered Masterpiece of Arab Literature and Painting.* Kuwait: Shuwaikh, 1985.

Melikian-Chirvani, 1988
Melikian-Chirvani, A. S. 'Le Livre des Rois, miroir du destin.' *Studia Iranica* 17 (1988): 7–46.

Melikian-Chirvani, 1991
Melikian-Chirvani, A. S. 'Le Livre des Rois, miroir du destin II.—Takht-e Soleyman et la symbolique du *Shah-Name*.' *Studia Iranica* 20 (1991): 33–148.

Melikian-Chirvani, 1996
Melikian-Chirvani, A. S. *Les frises du Shah Name dans l'architecture iranienne sous les Ilkhan.* Studia Iranica, Cahier 18. Paris: Association pour l'avancement des études iraniennes, 1996.

Melikian-Chirvani, 1997
Melikian-Chirvani, A. S. 'Conscience du passé et résistance culturelle dans l'Iran mongol.' In *L'Iran face à la domination mongole*, edited by Denise Aigle. Tehran: Institut français de recherche en Iran, 1997.

Mélikoff, 2000
Mélikoff, Irène. 'La montagne et l'arbre sacré de Hadji Bektach.' *Turcica* 32 (2000): 275–89.

Melville, 1990a
Melville, Charles. 'The Itineraries of Sultan Öljeitü, 1304–16.' *Iran* 28 (1990): 55–70.

Melville, 1990b
Melville, Charles. '*Pādshāh-i Islām*: The Conversion of Sultan Maḥmūd Ghāzān Khān.' *Pembroke Papers* 1 (1990): 159–77.

Melville, 1994
Melville, Charles. 'The Chinese-Uighur Animal Calendar in Persian Historiography of the Mongol Period.' *Iran* 32 (1994): 83–98.

Melville, 1996
Melville, Charles. 'Wolf or Shepherd? Amir Chupan's Attitude to Government.' In *The Court of the Il-Khans, 1290–1340.* Oxford Studies in Islamic Art, vol. 12, edited by Julian Raby and Teresa Fitzherbert. Oxford: Oxford University Press, 1996.

Melville, 1997a
Melville, Charles. 'Abu Saʿid and the Revolt of the Amirs in 1319.' In *L'Iran face à la domination mongole*, edited by Denise Aigle. Tehran: Institut français de recherche en Iran, 1997.

Melville, 1997b
Melville, Charles. 'Ebn al-Fowaṭī.' In *Encyclopaedia Iranica*, edited by Ehsan Yarshater. Costa Mesa, Calif.: Mazda, 1997.

Melville, 1999a
Melville, Charles. *The Fall of Amir Chupan and the Decline of the Ilkhanate, 1327–1337: A Decade of Discord in Mongol Iran.* Papers on Inner Asia, no. 30. Bloomington: Research Institute for Inner Asian Studies, Indiana University, 1999.

Melville, 1999b
Melville, Charles. 'The Ilkhan Öljeitü's Conquest of Gilan (1307): Rumour and Reality.' In *The Mongol Empire and its Legacy*, edited by Reuven Amitai-Preiss and David O. Morgan. Leiden: Brill, 1999.

Melville, 2002
Melville, Charles. 'The Mongols in Iran.' In *The Legacy of Genghis Khan: Courtly Art and Culture in Western Asia, 1256–1353*, edited by Linda Komaroff and Stefano Carboni. New York, New Haven, and London: Metropolitan Museum of Art and Yale University Press, 2002.

Melville, in press
Melville, Charles. 'Anatolia under the Mongols.' In *The Cambridge History of Turkey*, vol. 1, edited by Kate Fleet. Cambridge: Cambridge University Press, in press.

Meng-Ta Pei-Lu and Hei-Ta Shih Lüeh, 1980
Meng-Ta Pei-Lu, and Hei-Ta Shih Lüeh. *Chinesische Gesandtenberichte über die frühen Mongolen 1221 und 1237*. Asiatische Forschungen, Monographienreihe zur Geschichte, Kultur und Sprache der Völke Ost- und Zentralasiens, Bd. 56. Wiesbaden: Harrassowitz, 1980.

Merian, 1998–2000
Merian, Sylvia. 'Un feuillet appartenant à la Collection Feron-Stoclet acquis par la Pierpont Morgan Library de New York.' *Revue des Études Arméniennes* N.S. 27 (1998–2000): 417–20.

Meskoob, 1992
Meskoob, Shahrokh. *Iranian Nationality and the Persian Language*. Translated by Michael C. Hillmann. Edited by John R. Perry. Washington, D.C.: Mage Publishers, 1992.

Metropolitan Museum of Art, 1987
Metropolitan Museum of Art. *The Islamic World*. New York: Metropolitan Museum of Art, 1987.

Milstein, 1987
Milstein, Rachel. 'Nimrod, Joseph and Jonah: Miniatures from Ottoman Baghdad.' *Bulletin of the Asia Institute* 1 (1987): 123–38.

Milstein, Rührdanz, and Schmitz, 1999
Milstein, Rachel, Karin Rührdanz, and Barbara Schmitz. *Stories of the Prophets: Illustrated Manuscripts of the Qiṣaṣ al-Anbiyā'*. Costa Mesa, Calif.: Mazda, 1999.

Minorsky, 1943
Minorsky, Vladimir. *Tadhkirat al-mulåk: A Manual of Safavid Administration (circa 1137/1725): Persian text in facsimile (B.M. Or. 9496)*. E. J. W. Gibb Memorial Series, N.S. 16. London: Luzac, 1943.

Minorsky, 1956
Minorsky, Vladimir. 'The Older Preface to the *Shah-Nama*.' In *Studi Orientalistici in onore di Giorgio Levi Della Vida*. Rome: Instituto per l'Oriente, 1956.

Minorsky, 1978
Minorsky, Vladimir. 'A Civil and Military Review in F§rs in 881/1476.' In *The Turks, Iran and the Caucasus in the Middle Ages*. London: Variorum Reprints, 1978.

Mīrzā Rafī'ā, 2001

Mīrzā Rafī'ā, Muḥammad. 'Dastūr al-mulūk.' In *Daftār-i Tārīkh. Jild-i awwal: Majmū'a-yi asnād wa manābi'-i tārīkh*, edited by Irāj Afshār. Tehran: Mawqūfāt-i Maḥmūd Afshār Yazdī, 2001.

Monchi-Zadeh, 1975

Monchi-Zadeh, Davoud. *Topographisch-historische Studien zum iranischen Nationalepos*. Wiesbaden: F. Steiner, 1975.

Montgomery-Wyaux, 1978

Montgomery-Wyaux, Cornelia. *Métaux islamiques*. Brussels: Musées royaux d'art et d'histoire, 1978.

Moreh, 1987

Moreh, Shmuel. 'The Shadow Play (*Khayāl al-Ẓill*) in the Light of Arabic Literature.' *Journal of Arabic Literature* 18 (1987): 46–61.

Moreh, 1992

Moreh, Shmuel. *Live Theatre and Dramatic Literature in the Medieval Arab World*. Edinburgh: Edinburgh University Press, 1992.

Morgan, D., 1982a

Morgan, David O. 'Persian Historians and the Mongols.' In *Medieval Historical Writing in the Christian and Islamic Worlds*, edited by David O. Morgan. London: School of Oriental and African Studies, University of London, 1982.

Morgan, D., 1982b

Morgan, David O. 'Who Ran the Mongol Empire?' *Journal of the Royal Asiatic Society* N.S. 2 (1982): 124–36.

Morgan, D., 1982c

Morgan, David O. Review of Oleg Grabar and Sheila Blair, *Epic Images and Contemporary History: The Illustrations of the Great Mongol Shahnama*. *Bulletin of the School of Oriental and African Studies* 65, no. 2 (1982): 364–65.

Morgan, D., 1985

Morgan, David O. 'Aḵtājī.' In *Encyclopaedia Iranica*, edited by Ehsan Yarshater. London, Boston, and Henley: Routledge & Kegan Paul, 1985.

Morgan, D., 1986a

Morgan, David O. 'The "Great *Yasa* of Chingiz Khan" and Mongol Law in the Ilkhanate.' *Bulletin of the School of Oriental and African Studies* 49 (1986): 163–76.

Morgan, D., 1986b

Morgan, David O. *The Mongols*. Oxford and New York: Blackwell, 1986.

Morgan, D., 1990

Morgan, David O. 'Bokāvol.' In *Encyclopaedia Iranica*, edited by Ehsan Yarshater. London and New York: Routledge & Kegan Paul, 1990.

Morgan, D., 1994

Morgan, David O. 'Rashīd al-Dīn Ṭabīb.' In *The Encyclopaedia of Islam*, new ed., edited by H. A. R. Gibb, J. H. Kramers, E. Levi-Provencal, and J. Schacht. Leiden: Brill, 1994.

Morgan, D., 1996
Morgan, David O. 'Mongol or Persian: The Government of Ilkhanid Iran.' *Harvard Middle Eastern and Islamic Review* 3 (1996): 62–76.

Morgan, D., 1997
Morgan, David O. 'Rašīd al-Dīn and xazan Khan.' In *L'Iran face à la domination mongole*, edited by Denise Aigle. Tehran: Institut français de recherche en Iran, 1997.

Morgan, D., 2000
Morgan, David O. 'Reflections on Mongol Communications in the Ilkhanate.' In *Studies in Honour of Clifford Edmund Bosworth*. Vol. 2, *The Sultan's Turret*, edited by Carole Hillenbrand. Leiden: Brill, 2000.

Morgan, D., 2004
Morgan, David O. 'The Mongols in Iran: A Reappraisal.' *Iran* 42 (2004): 131–36.

Morgan, P., 1995
Morgan, Peter. 'Some Far Eastern Elements in Coloured-Ground Sultanabad Wares.' In *Islamic Art in the Ashmolean*. Oxford Studies in Islamic Art, vol. 10, part 2, edited by James W. Allan. Oxford: Oxford University Press, 1995.

Morton, 1994
Morton, A. H. 'The *Mu''nis al-ahrar* and its Twenty-Ninth Chapter.' In *Illustrated Poetry and Epic Images: Persian Painting of the 1330s and 1340s*, edited by Marie Lukens Swietochowski and Stefano Carboni. New York: Metropolitan Museum of Art, 1994.

Morton, 1999
Morton, A. H. 'The Letters of Rashid al-Din: Ilkhanid Fact or Timurid Fiction.' In *The Mongol Empire and its Legacy*, edited by Reuven Amitai-Preiss and David O. Morgan. Leiden: Brill, 1999.

Mostaert, 1956
Mostaert, Antoine. 'Matériaux Ethnographiques rélatifs aux Mongols Ordos.' *Central Asiatic Journal* 2 (1956): 241–94.

Mostaert and Cleaves, 1952
Mostaert, Antoine, and F. W. Cleaves. 'Trois documents mongols des Archives Secrétes Vaticanes.' *Harvard Journal of Asiatic Studies* 15 (1952): 419–506.

Mostaert and Cleaves, 1962
Mostaert, Antoine, and F. W. Cleaves. *Les lettres de 1289 et 1305 des ilkhan Argun et Öljeitü à Philippe le Bel.* Cambridge: Harvard, 1962.

Moṣṭafavī, 1953
Moṣṭafavī, M. T. *Hagmatāna: āsār-i tārīkh-i Hamadān va faṣlī dar bāra-yi Abū 'Alī Sīnā.* Tehran, 1953.

Mota and Guerreiro, eds., 1972
Mota, Maria Manuela Marques, and Glória Guerreiro, eds. *Persian Art: Calouste Gulbenkian Collection.* Lisbon: Calouste Gulbenkian Foundation, 1972.

Mottahedeh, 1986
Mottahedeh, Roy P. *The Mantle of the Prophet: Learning and Power in Modern Iran.* London: Chatto and Windus, 1986.

Mudarrisī-i Ṭabāṭabā'ī, 1974
Mudarrisī-i Ṭabāṭabā'ī, Ḥussein. *Farmānhā-yi turkamānān-i qarā-Quyunlu wa aq-Quyunlu.* Qum: Chāpkhāna-yi Ḥikmat, 1974.

Muḥammad, 1989
Muḥammad, Muḥammad Aḥmad. *Islām al-Īlkhāniyyīn.* Cairo: Sharikat al-'afā li-al-Ṭibā'a wa al-tarjuma wa al-nashr, 1989.

Mu'īn, 1974
Mu'īn, M. *Farhang-i fārsī.* 4 vols. Tehran, 1974.

Mullett and Scott, eds., 1981
Mullett, Margaret, and Roger Scott, eds. *Byzantium and the Classical Tradition: University of Birmingham Thirteenth Spring Symposium of Byzantine Studies, 1979.* Birmingham: Centre for Byzantine Studies, University of Birmingham, 1981.

Musée du Louvre, 2001
Musée du Louvre. *L'étrange et le merveilleux en terres d'Islam.* Paris: Réunion des musées nationaux, 2001.

Musée Guimet, 1976
Musée Guimet. *La route de la soie.* Paris: Éditions des musées nationaux, 1976.

Mustawfī, 1915–19
Mustawfī, Ḥamdallāh. *The Geographical Part of the Nuzhat al-qulūb.* Translated by Guy Le Strange. 2 vols. Leiden and London: Brill/Luzac, 1915–19. Reprint, Frankfurt am Main: Institute for the History of Arabic-Islamic Science at the Johann Wolfgang Goethe University, 1993.

Mutafian, 1988
Mutafian, Claude. *La Cilicie au carrefour des empires.* 2 vols. Paris: Belles Lettres, 1988.

Mutafian, 1993
Mutafian, Claude. *Le royaume arménien de Cilicie: XIIe–XIVe siècle.* Paris: CNRS Éditions, 1993.

Najm al-Dīn Rāzī, 1982
Najm al-Dīn Rāzī, 'Abd Allāh ibn Muḥammad. *Mirṣād al-'ibād/The Path of God's Bondsmen from Origin to Return: A Sufi Compendium.* Translated by Hamid Algar. Delmar, N.Y.: Caravan Books, 1982.

Nakhjuvānī, 1976
Nakhjuvānī, Hindūshāh. *Dastår al-kātib*, vol. 2, edited by 'A. 'A. 'Alīzādeh. Moscow, 1976.

Narkiss and Stone, eds., 1979
Narkiss, Bezalel, and Michael E. Stone, eds. *Armenian Art Treasures of Jerusalem.* New Rochelle, N.Y.: Caratzas Bros., 1979.

Nāṣir al-Dīn Munshī, 1983
Nāṣir al-Dīn Munshī. *Simṭ al-'ulā.* Edited by 'Abbās Iqbāl. Tehran: Asāṭīr, 1983.

Nāṣir-i Khusraw and Rastegar, 1993

Nāṣir-i Khusraw and Nosratollah Rastegar. *Safarname: Das Reisetagebuch des persischen Dichters Nāṣir-i zusrau.* Translated by Uto von Melzer. Edited by Manfred Mayrhofer. Graz: Leykam, 1993.

Natalini et al., eds., 1991
Natalini, Terzo, et al., eds. *Archivio segreto Vaticano.* Florence: Nardini, 1991.

Naṭanzī, 1957
Naṭanzī, Muʿīn al-Dīn. *Muntakhab al-tawārīkh-i Muʿīnī.* Edited by Jean Aubin. Tehran: Ḥaydarī, 1957.

Naumann, E. and Naumann, R., 1969
Naumann, Elisabeth, and Rudolf Naumann. 'Ein Kösk im Sommerpalast des Abaqa Chan auf dem Tacht-i Sulayman und seine Dekoration.' In *Forschungen zur Kunst Asiens. In Memoriam Kurt Erdmann,* edited by Oktay Aslanapa and Rudolf Naumann. Istanbul: Istanbul Universitesi Edebiyat Fakültesi, 1969.

Naumann, R., 1963
Naumann, Rudolf. 'Eine keramische Werkstatt des 13. Jahrhunderts auf dem Takht-i-Suleiman.' In *Beiträge zur Kunstgeschichte Asiens. In Memoriam Ernst Diez,* edited by Oktay Aslanapa. Istanbul: Istanbul Universitesi Edebiyat Fakültesi, 1963.

Naumann, R., 1971
Naumann, Rudolf. 'Brennöfen für Glasurkeramik.' *Istanbuler Mitteilungen* 21 (1971): 173–90.

Naumann, R., 1977
Naumann, Rudolf. *Die Ruinen von Tacht-e Suleiman und Zendan-e Suleiman und Umgebung.* Berlin: Reimer, 1977.

Naumann, Huff, et al., 1965
Naumann, Rudolf, Dietrich Huff, et al. 'Takht-i Suleiman und Zendan-i Suleiman. Vorläufiger Bericht über die Ausgrabungen in den Jahren 1963 und 1964.' *Archäologischer Anzeiger* (1965): 619–802.

Naumann, Huff, et al., 1975
Naumann, Rudolf, Dietrich Huff, et al. 'Takht-i Suleiman. Bericht über die Ausgrabungen 1965–1973.' *Archäologischer Anzeiger* (1975): 109–204.

Naumann, Kleiss, et al., 1961
Naumann, Rudolf, Wolfram Kleiss, et al. 'Takht-i Suleiman und Zendan-i Suleiman. Vorläufiger Bericht über die Ausgrabungen im Jahre 1960.' *Archäologischer Anzeiger* (1961): 28–67.

Naumann, Kleiss, et al., 1962
Naumann, Rudolf, Wolfram Kleiss, et al. 'Takht-i Suleiman und Zendan-i Suleiman. Vorläufiger Bericht über die Grabungen im Jahre 1961.' *Archäologischer Anzeiger* (1962): 633–93.

Naumann, Kleiss, et al., 1964
Naumann, Rudolf, Wolfram Kleiss, et al. 'Takht-i Suleiman und Zendan-i Suleiman. Vorläufiger Bericht über die Ausgrabungen im Jahre 1962.' *Archäologischer Anzeiger* (1964): 1–77.

Naumann, R. and Naumann, E., 1976
Naumann, Rudolf, and Elisabeth Naumann. *Takht-i Suleiman. Katalog der Ausstellung.* Munich: Prähistorischen Staatssammlung, 1976.

Nawāʾī, ed., 1962–63
Nawāʾī, ʿAbd al-Ḥusayn, ed. *Asnād wa mukātabāt-i tārīkhi-yi Irān*. Tehran: Bungāh-i Tarjuma wa Nashr-i Kitāb, 1962–63.

Needham, 1987
Needham, Joseph. *Science and Civilisation in China*. Vol. 5, part 7, *Military Technology: The Gunpowder Epic*. Cambridge: Cambridge University Press, 1987.

Needham, 1995
Needham, Joseph. *Science and Civilisation in China*. Vol. 5, part 6, *Military Technology: Missiles and Sieges*. Cambridge: Cambridge University Press, 1995.

Nees, 1987
Nees, Lawrence. *The Gundohinus Gospels*. Cambridge, Mass.: Medieval Academy of America, 1987.

Norgren and Davis, 1969
Norgren, Jill, and Edward Davis. 'Preliminary Index of Shah-Nameh Illustrations.' Ann Arbor: University of Michigan, 1969.

Nurbakhsh, 1980
Nurbakhsh, Javad. *What the Sufis Say*. New York: Khaniqahi-Nimatullahi Publications, 1980.

al-Nuwayrī, 1964
al-Nuwayrī, Aḥmad ibn ʿAbd al-Wahhāb. *Nihāyat al-arab fī funūn al-adab*, vol. 27, edited by Saʿīd ʿAbd al-Fattāḥ ʿĀshūr. Cairo: al-Muʾassasa al-Miṣriyya al-ʿĀmma li-al-Taʾlīf wa-al-Tarjama wa-al-Ṭibāʿa wa-al-Nashr, 1964.

al-Nuwayrī, 1997
al-Nuwayrī, Aḥmad ibn ʿAbd al-Wahhāb. *Nihāyat al-arab fī funūn al-adab*, vol. 33, edited by Muṣṭafā Ḥijāzī. Cairo: Dār al-kutub al-Miṣriyya, 1997.

al-Nuwayrī, 1998
al-Nuwayrī, Aḥmad ibn ʿAbd al-Wahhāb. *Nihāyat al-arab fī funūn al-adab*, vol. 32, edited by Fahīm M. Shaltūt. Cairo: Dār al-kutub al-Miṣriyya, 1998.

O'Kane, 1979
O'Kane, Bernard. 'The Friday Mosques of Asnak and Saravar.' *Archäologische Mitteilungen aus Iran* N.F. 12 (1979): 341–51.

O'Kane, 1993
O'Kane, Bernard. 'From Tents to Pavilions: Royal Nobility and Persian Palace Design.' *Ars Orientalis* 23 (1993): 249–68.

O'Kane, 2003
O'Kane, Bernard. *Early Persian Painting: Kalila and Dimna Manuscripts of the Late Fourteenth Century*. London and New York: I. B. Tauris, 2003.

Ocak, 1989
Ocak, Ahmet Yaşar. *La révolte de Baba Resul ou la formation de l'hétérodoxie musulmane en Anatolie au XIIIe siècle*. Ankara: Impr. de la Société turque d'histoire, 1989.

Ocak, 1992
Ocak, Ahmet *Yaşar. Osmanlı İmparatorluğunda marjinal Sûfîlik: Kalenderîler (XIV–XVII. Yüzyıllar)*. Ankara: Türk Tarih Kurumu Basımevi, 1992.

Oh, 2003
Oh, L. J. 'The East Asian Characteristics of Ilkhanid Royal Manuscripts.' *Persica* 19 (2003): 69–105.

Ohlmarks, 1939
Ohlmarks, Ake. *Studien zum Problem des Schamanismus.* Lund, Sweden: C. W. K. Gleerup, 1939.

Ohsson, 1834
Ohsson, Constantin d'. *Histoire des Mongols, depuis Tchinguiz-Khan jusqu'à Timour Bey, ou Tamerlan.* 4 vols. The Hague and Amsterdam: Les frères Van Cleef, 1834.

Öney, 1969
Öney, G. 'Tombstones in the Seljuk Tradition with Bird, Double-Headed Eagle, Falcon and Lion Figures in Anatolia.' *Vakiflar Dergisi* 8 (1969): 292–301.

Orbélian, 1864
Orbélian, Stephanos. *Histoire de la Siounie.* Translated by M. Brosset. St. Petersburg: L'Académie impériale des sciences, 1864.

Osawa, 2005
Osawa, Masami. 'One of the Forms of Iron Producing in the Mongol Empire Obtained from Forge-Related Objects Found at Avraga Site.' In *Avraga 1.* New Directions in Mongolian Archaeology, vol. 1, edited by Shimpei Kato and Noriyuki Shiraishi. Tokyo: Doseisha, 2005.

Osten, Naumann, et al., 1961
Osten, Hans Henning von der, Rudolf Naumann, et al. *Takht-i Suleiman. Vorläufiger Bericht über die Ausgrabungen 1959*, Teheraner Forschungen, Bd. 1. Berlin: Verlag Gebr. Mann, 1961.

Ostrowski, 1998
Ostrowski, D. 'The *tamma* and the dual-administrative structure of the Mongol Empire.' *Bulletin of the School of Oriental and African Studies* 61, no. 1 (1998): 262–77.

Palazzo delle Esposizioni, 1990
Palazzo delle Esposizioni. *Le Mille e una notte: ceramiche persiane, turche e ispano moresche.* Faenza: Gruppo Editoriale Faenza, 1990.

Pancaroğlu, 2001
Pancaroğlu, Oya. 'Socializing Medicine: Illustrations of the *Kitab al-Diryaq.*' *Muqarnas* 18 (2001): 155–72.

Pancaroğlu, 2004a
Pancaroğlu, Oya. 'Beyond the Frontispiece: The Visual Dimension of Narrative Beginnings in Early Illustrated Manuscripts.' Paper presented at the Arab Painting: Text and Image in Illustrated Arabic Manuscripts Conference, School of Oriental and African Studies, University of London, 17–18 September 2004 (conference proceedings forthcoming, London and New York: I. B. Tauris).

Pancaroğlu, 2004b
Pancaroğlu, Oya. 'The Itinerant Dragon Slayer: Forging Paths of Image and Identity in Medieval Anatolia.' *Gesta* 43, no. 2 (2004): 151–64.

Paterson, 1990
Paterson, W. F. *A Guide to the Crossbow*. N.p.: Society of Archer-Antiquaries, 1990.

Patton, 1991
Patton, Douglas. *Badr al-Din Lu'lu': Atabeg of Mosul, 1211–1259*. Seattle: University of Washington Press, 1991.

Paul, 1999
Paul, Jürgen. Review of Jamal J. Elias, *The Throne Carrier of God: The Life and Thought of 'Alā' ad-Dawlah as-Simnānī*. *Der Islam* 76 (1999): 364–65.

Paulsen, 1956
Paulsen, Peter. *Axt und Kreuz in Nord- und Osteuropa*. Bonn: Rudolf Habelt Verlag, 1956.

Peacock, 2003
Peacock, A. S. 'Abu 'Ali Bal'ami's Translation of al-Tabari's History.' Ph.D. diss., University of Cambridge, 2003.

Pedersen, 1984
Pedersen, Johannes. *The Arabic Book*. Translated by G. French. Edited by Robert Hillenbrand. Princeton: Princeton University Press, 1984.

Pegolotti, 1936
Pegolotti, Francesco Balducci. *La Pratica della Mercatura*. Edited by Allan Evans. Cambridge, Mass.: Mediaeval Academy of America, 1936.

Pelliot, 1936
Pelliot, Paul. 'Les documents mongols du Musée de Téhéran.' *Athar-é Iran* 1 (1936): 37–46.

Pelliot, 1959
Pelliot, Paul. *Notes on Marco Polo*. 3 vols. Paris: Impr. nationale, 1959.

P'eng and Wang, 1983
P'eng Ta-ya, and Wang Kuowei. *Wang Kuowei yishu (The Notes of Wang Kuowei)*, vol. 8. Shanghai: Shanghai shutien ch'upanshe, 1983.

Pfeiffer, 1999
Pfeiffer, Judith. 'Conversion Versions: Sultan Öljeitü's Conversion to Shi'ism (709/1309) in Muslim Narrative Sources.' *Mongolian Studies* 22 (1999): 35–67.

Pfeiffer, 2003
Pfeiffer, Judith. 'Conversion to Islam among the Ilkhans in Muslim Narrative Traditions: The Case of Aḥmad Tegüder.' Ph.D. diss., University of Chicago, 2003.

Pfeiffer, 2006
Pfeiffer, Judith. 'Aḥmad Tegüder's Second Letter to Qalā'ūn (682/1283).' In *History and Historiography of Post-Mongol Central Asia and the Middle East*, edited by Judith Pfeiffer and Sholeh A. Quinn. Wiesbaden: Harrassowitz, 2006.

Pfeiffer, in press
Pfeiffer, Judith. '"A turgid history of the Mongol empire in Persia:" Epistemological reflections concerning an edition of Vaṣṣāf's *Tajziyat al-amṣār wa tazjiyat al-a'ṣār*.' In *Theoretical Approaches to the Transmission and Edition of Oriental*

Manuscripts, edited by Manfred Kropp and Judith Pfeiffer. Würzburg: Ergon Verlag, in press.

Pfeiffer and Quinn, 2006
Pfeiffer, Judith, and Sholeh A. Quinn. *History and Historiography of Post-Mongol Central Asia and the Middle East.* Wiesbaden: Harrassowitz, 2006.

Piacentini, 1975
Piacentini, Valeria Fiorani. *L'emporio ed il regno di Hormoz (VIII–fine XV sec. d. Cr.), vicende storiche, problemi ed aspetti di una civiltà costiera del golfo persico.* Memorie dell'Istituto lombardo-accademia di scienze e lettere, vol. 35, fasc. 1. Milan: Istituto lombardo di scienze e lettere, 1975.

Piacentini, 1992
Piacentini, Valeria Fiorani. *Merchants, merchandise, and military power in the Persian Gulf (Sūriyānj/Shahriyāj-Sīrāf).* Atti della Accademia nazionale dei lincei, Memorie, ser. 9, vol. 3, fasc. 2. Rome: Accademia nazionale dei lincei, 1992.

Piotrovsky and Vrieze, eds., 1999
Piotrovsky, Mikhail B., and John Vrieze, eds. *Earthly Beauty, Heavenly Art: Art of Islam.* Amsterdam and London: De Nieuwe Kerk/Lund Humphries, 1999.

Polo, 1903
Polo, Marco. *The Book of Ser Marco Polo, the Venetian, concerning the Kingdoms and Marvels of the East.* Translated by Henry Yule. Edited by Henri Cordier. 3rd rev. ed. 2 vols. London: John Murray, 1903. Reprint, 1929; reprint, 1st Indian ed., New Delhi: Munshiram Manoharlal Publishers, 1991.

Polo, 1958
Polo, Marco. *The Travels of Marco Polo.* Translated by R. E. Latham. Harmondsworth, England: Penguin, 1958. Reprint, 1980.

Pope et al., 1937
Pope, Arthur U. et al. 'The Institute's Survey of Persian Architecture: Preliminary Report on Takht-i Sulayman.' *Bulletin of the American Institute for Iranian Art and Archaeology* 5 (1937): 71–109.

Pope, 1945
Pope, Arthur Upham. *Masterpieces of Persian Art.* New York: Dryden Press, 1945.

Pope and Ackerman, eds., 1938–39
Pope, Arthur Upham, and Phyllis Ackerman, eds. *A Survey of Persian Art from Prehistoric Times to the Present.* 6 vols. London and New York: Oxford University Press, 1938–39.

Porter, 1994
Porter, Yves. *Painters, Paintings, and Books: An Essay on Indo-Persian Technical Literature, 12–19th Centuries.* Translated by S. Butani. 1st ed. New Delhi: Manohar, Centre for Human Sciences, 1994.

Potter, 1994
Potter, Lawrence G. 'Sufis and Sultans in Post-Mongol Iran.' *Iranian Studies* 27 (1994): 77–102.

Prentice, 1977
Prentice, V. R. 'The Illustration of Sa'di's Poetry in Fifteenth-Century Herat.' Ph.D. diss., Harvard University, 1977.

Prodan, 1960
Prodan, Mario. *La poterie T'ang*. Paris: Arts et métiers graphiques, 1960.

Qāḍī Aḥmad, 1959
Qāḍī Aḥmad. *Calligraphers and Painters: A Treatise by Qāḍī Aḥmad, Son of Mīr-Munshī (circa A.H. 1015/A.D. 1606)*. Translated by V. Minorsky. Edited and intro. by B. N. Zakhoder. Washington, D.C.: Freer Gallery of Art, 1959.

al-Qāshānī, 'Abd al-Razzāq, 1991
al-Qāshānī, 'Abd al-Razzāq. *A Glossary of Sufi Technical Terms*. Translated by Nabil Safwat. Edited and revised by David Pendlebury. London: Octagon Press, 1991.

al-Qāshānī, Abū al-Qāsim, 1969-70
al-Qāshānī, Abū al-Qāsim b. 'Ali b. Muḥammad. *Tārīkh-i Ūljaytū*. Edited by Mahin Hambly. Tehran: Bungāh-i Tarjuma wa Nashr-i Kitāb, 1969–70.

Qūchānī, 1992
Qūchānī, 'Abdallāh. *Ash'ār-i Fārsī-yi kāshīhā-yi Takht-i Sulaymān/Persian Poetry on the Tiles of Takht-i Sulayman, 13th Century*. Tehran: Markaz-i Nashr-i Dānishgāhī, 1992.

Quinn, 1989
Quinn, Sholeh. 'The *Mu'izz al-Ansāb* and *Shu'ab-i Panjgānah* as Sources for the Chaghatayid Period of History: A Comparative Analysis.' *Central Asiatic Journal* 33, no. 3–4 (1989): 229–53.

Raby and Fitzherbert, eds., 1996
Raby, Julian, and Teresa Fitzherbert, eds. *The Court of the Il-Khans, 1290–1340*. Oxford Studies in Islamic Art, vol. 12. Oxford: Oxford University Press, 1996.

Raby and Tanındı, 1993
Raby, Julian, and Zeren Tanındı. *Turkish Bookbinding in the 15th Century: The Foundation of an Ottoman Court Style*. London: Azimuth Editions on behalf of l'Association Internationale de Bibliophilie, 1993.

de Rachewiltz, 1983
Rachewiltz, Igor de. 'Turks in China under the Mongols: A Preliminary Investigation of Turco-Mongol Relations in the 13th and 14th Centuries.' In *China Among Equals: The Middle Kingdom and its Neighbors, 10th–14th Centuries*, edited by Morris Rossabi. Berkeley and Los Angeles: University of California Press, 1983.

de Rachewiltz, ed., 2004
Rachewiltz, Igor de, ed. *The Secret History of the Mongols: A Mongolian Epic Chronicle of the Thirteenth Century*. 2 vols. Leiden and Boston: Brill, 2004.

de Rachewiltz et al., eds., 1993
Rachewiltz, Igor de, Hok-lam Chan, Hsiao Ch'i-ch'ing, and Peter W. Geier, eds. *In the Service of the Khan: Eminent Personalities of the Early Mongol-Yüan Period (1200–1300)*. Asiatische Forschungen, Bd. 121. Wiesbaden: Harrassowitz, 1993.

Raff, 1973
Raff, Thomas. *Remarks on an Anti-Mongol Fatwa by Ibn Taimiya*. Leiden, 1973.

Rashīd al-Dīn, 1836
Rashīd al-Dīn. *Histoire des Mongols de la Perse*. Translated by Étienne Quatremére, 1836. Reprint, Amsterdam: Oriental Press, 1968.

Rashīd al-Dīn, 1941
Rashīd al-Dīn. *Tā'rīḫ-i-Mubārak-i-Ġāzānī des Rašīd al-Dīn Faḍl Allāh Abī-l-zair: Geschichte der Ilḫāne Abāġā bis Gaiḫātū (1265–1295)*. Edited by Karl Jahn. Prague: Verlag der Deutschen Gesellschaft der Wissenschaften und Künste, 1941.

Rashīd al-Dīn, 1951
Rashīd al-Dīn. *Histoire universelle de Rašīd al-Dīn Faḍl Allāh Abūl'Khair*. Vol. 1, *Histoire des Francs*, edited by Karl Jahn. Leiden: Brill, 1951.

Rashīd al-Dīn, 1952
Rashīd al-Dīn. *Sbornik letopisei*, vols. 1–2. Translated by O. I. Smirnova. Moscow and Leningrad: Akademiya nauk SSSR, 1952.

Rashīd al-Dīn, 1957
Rashīd al-Dīn. *Jāmiʿ al-tawārīkh*. Translated by A. K. Arandas. Edited by ʿAbd al-Karīm ʿAlīzāda. 3 vols. Baku: Farhangistān-i ʿUlūm-i Jumhūr-i Shuravī-i Sūsīyālistī-i Āẕarbāyjān, 1957.

Rashīd al-Dīn, 1959–60
Rashīd al-Dīn. *Jāmiʿ al-tawārīkh*. Edited by Bahman Karīmī. 2 vols. Tehran: Iqbāl, 1959–60.

Rashīd al-Dīn, 1971
Rashīd al-Dīn. *The Successors of Genghis Khan*. Translated by J. A. Boyle. New York: Columbia University Press, 1971.

Rashīd al-Dīn, 1978
Rashīd al-Dīn. *Waqfnāmah-i Rabʿ-i Rashīdī*. Edited by Mojtabā Minovī and Īrāj Afshār. Tehran, 1978.

Rashīd al-Dīn, 1980
Rashīd al-Dīn. *Die Indiengeschichte des Rašīd ad-Dīn: Einleitung, vollständige Übersetzung, Kommentar und 80 Texttafeln*. Translated by Karl Jahn. Vienna: Verlag der Österreichischen Akademie der Wissenschaften, 1980.

Rashīd al-Dīn, 1994
Rashīd al-Dīn. *Jāmiʿ al-tawārīkh*. Edited by Muḥammad Rawshan and Muṣṭafā Mūsawī. 4 vols. Tehran: Nashr-i Alburz, 1994.

Rashīd al-Dīn, 1998
Rashīd al-Dīn. *Jamiʿu't-Tawarikh: Compendium of Chronicles; A History of the Mongols*. 3 vols. Sources of Oriental Languages and Literature 45. Translated by W. M. Thackston. Cambridge: Harvard University, Department of Near Eastern Languages and Civilizations, 1998.

Ratchnevsky, 1991
Ratchnevsky, Paul. *Genghis Khan: His Life and Legacy*. Translated and edited by Thomas Nivison Haining. Oxford and Cambridge: Blackwell, 1991.

Rawlinson, 1841
Rawlinson, H. C. 'Notes on a Journey from Tabriz through Persian Kurdistan to the Ruins of Takhti Soleiman….' *Journal of the Royal Geographical Society of London* 10 (1841): 1–64.

Rawson, 1984
Rawson, Jessica. *Chinese Ornament: The Lotus and the Dragon*. New York: Holmes & Meier, 1984.

Redford, 1993
Redford, Scott. 'Thirteenth-Century Rum Seljuq Palaces and Palace Imagery.' *Ars Orientalis* 20 (1993): 219–36.

Redford, Beach, and Luzzadder-Beach, 2000
Redford, Scott, Timothy Paul Beach, and Sheryl Luzzadder-Beach. *Landscape and the State in Medieval Anatolia: Seljuk Gardens and Pavilions of Alanya, Turkey*. Oxford: Archaeopress, 2000.

Reinert, 1997
Reinert, B. "Aṭṭār.' In *Encyclopaedia Iranica*, edited by Ehsan Yarshater. London and New York: Routledge & Kegan Paul, 1997.

Restle, 1967
Restle, Marcell. *Byzantine Wall Painting in Asia Minor*. Translated by Irene R. Gibbons. 3 vols. Recklinghausen: Bongers, 1967.

Rice, D. S., 1949
Rice, D. S. 'The Oldest Dated "Mosul" Candlestick.' *Burlington Magazine* 91 (1949): 334–40.

Rice, D. S., 1953
Rice, D. S. 'The Aghani Miniatures and Religious Painting in Islam.' *Burlington Magazine* 95 (1953): 128–34.

Rice, D. S., 1955
Rice, D. S. *The Unique Ibn al-Bawwab Manuscript in the Chester Beatty Library*. Dublin: E. Walker, 1955.

Rice, D. S., 1957
Rice, D. S. 'Inlaid Brasses from the Workshop of Ahmad al-Dhaki al-Mawsili.' *Ars Orientalis* 2 (1957): 283–326.

Rice, D. T., 1932
Rice, David Talbot. 'Some Wasters from Sultanieh.' *Burlington Magazine* 60 (1932): 252.

Rice, D. T., 1976
Rice, David Talbot. *The Illustrations to the 'World History' of Rashid al-Din*. Edited by Basil Gray. Edinburgh: Edinburgh University Press, 1976.

Rich, 1836
Rich, Claudius James. *Narrative of a residence in Koordistan, and on the site of ancient Nineveh, with journal of a voyage down the Tigris to Bagdad and an account of a visit to Shirauz and Persepolis*. 2 vols. London: J. Duncan, 1836.

Richard, F., 1982
Richard, Francis. 'Muhr-i Kitābkhāna-yi Rashīd al-Dīn Faíl-Allāh Hamadānī.' *Ayanda* 8, no. 6 (Shahryar 1361/August–September 1982): 343–46.

Richard, F., 1997
Richard, Francis. *Splendeurs persanes: manuscrits du XIIe au XVIIe siècle*. Paris: Bibliothèque Nationale de France, 1997.

Richard, J., 1986
Richard, Jean. 'La lettre du Connétable Smbat et les rapports entre Chrétiens et Mongols au milieu du XIIIème siècle.' In *Armenian Studies/Études arméniennes: In memoriam Haig Berbérian*, edited by Dickran Kouymjian. Lisbon: Calouste Gulbenkian Foundation, 1986.

Riefstahl, 1922
Riefstahl, Rudolf Meyer. *The Parish-Watson Collection of Mohammedan Potteries*. New York: E. Weyhe, 1922.

Riis and Poulsen, 1957
Riis, P. J., and V. Poulsen. *Hama: Fouilles et recherches de la Fondation Carlsberg, 1931–1938. Les Verreries et Poteries Médiévales*. Copenhagen: Fondation Carlsberg, 1957.

Robb, 1973
Robb, David Metheny. *The Art of the Illuminated Manuscript*. South Brunswick, N.J.: A. S. Barnes, 1973.

Robinson, 1976
Robinson, B. W. *Persian Paintings in the India Office Library: A Descriptive Catalogue*. London: Sotheby Parke Bernet, 1976.

Robinson et al., 1976
Robinson, B. W., Ernst J. Grube, G. M. Meredith-Owens, and R. W. Skelton. *Islamic Painting and the Arts of the Book*. London: Faber and Faber, 1976.

Rockhill, 1914–15
Rockhill, William Woodville. 'Notes on the Relations and Trade of China with the Archipelago and the Coasts of the Indian Ocean during the Fourteenth Century.' *T'oung Pao* 15, 16 (1914–15).

Roemer, 1986
Roemer, H. R. 'The Jalayirids, Muzaffarids and Sardabars; Timur in Iran; The Successors of Timur.' In *The Cambridge History of Iran*, Vol. 6, *The Timurid and Safavid Periods*, edited by Peter Jackson and Laurence Lockhart. Cambridge: Cambridge University Press, 1986.

Rogers, 1971
Rogers, J. M. 'A Renaissance of Classical Antiquity in North Syria (11th–12th Centuries).' *Annales Archéologiques Syriennes* 21: Proceedings of the 9th International Congress of Classical Archaeology (1971): 347–61.

Rogers, 1972
Rogers, J. M. 'Evidence for Mamluk-Mongol Relations, 1260–1360.' In *Colloque international sur l'histoire du Caire*. Cairo: UAR Ministry of Culture, 1972.

Rogers, 1989
Rogers, J. M. Review of Bernard O'Kane, *Timurid Architecture in Khurasan*. *Bulletin of the Asia Institute* 3 (1989): 129–38.

Rorex et al., 1974
Rorex, Robert A., Wen Fong, and Shang Liu. *Eighteen Songs of a Nomad Flute: The Story of Lady Wen-chi*. New York: Metropolitan Museum of Art, 1974.

Rosenthal, 1968
Rosenthal, Franz. *A History of Muslim Historiography*. 2nd rev. ed. Leiden: Brill, 1968.

Rosenthal, 1971
Rosenthal, Franz. 'Ibn al-Fuwaṭī.' In *The Encyclopaedia of Islam,* new ed., edited by H. A. R. Gibb, J. H. Kramers, E. Levi-Provencal, and J. Schacht. Leiden and London: Brill/Luzac, 1971.

Rossabi, 1997
Rossabi, Morris. 'The Silk Trade in China and Central Asia.' In *When Silk Was Gold: Central Asian and Chinese Textiles,* edited by James C. Y. Watt and Anne E. Wardwell. New York: Metropolitan Museum of Art in cooperation with the Cleveland Museum of Art, 1997.

Rossabi, 2002
Rossabi, Morris. 'The Mongols and their Legacy.' In *The Legacy of Genghis Khan: Courtly Art and Culture in Western Asia, 1256–1353,* edited by Linda Komaroff and Stefano Carboni. New York, New Haven, and London: Metropolitan Museum of Art and Yale University Press, 2002.

Roux, 1982
Roux, Jean-Paul. *Études d'iconographie islamique: quelques objects numineux des Turcs et des Mongols.* Paris and Leuven: Association pour le développement des études turques/Editions Peeters, 1982.

Roux, 1984
Roux, Jean-Paul. *La religion des Turcs et des Mongols.* Paris: Payot, 1984.

Roxburgh, ed., 2005
Roxburgh, David J., ed. *Turks: A Journey of a Thousand Years, 600–1600.* London: Royal Academy of Arts, 2005.

Rührdanz, 1997
Rührdanz, Karin. 'Illustrationen zu Rasid al-dins *TaŞrih-i Mubarak-i Gazani* in den berliner Diez-Alben.' In *L'Iran face à la domination mongole,* edited by Denise Aigle. Tehran: Institut français de recherche en Iran, 1997.

Ṣafā, 1989
Ṣafā, Ẓabīḥ Allāh. *Tārīkh-i adabīyāt-i Īrān.* 3rd ed. 6 vols. Tehran: Firdaws, 1989.

Ṣafadī, 1981
Ṣafadī, Ṣalāḥ al-Dīn Khalīl ibn Aybak. *al-Wāfī bi al-wafayāt,* vol. 1. Wiesbaden: F. Steiner, 1981.

Sakisian, 1939
Sakisian, Arménag. 'Thèmes et motifs d'enluminure et de décoration arméniennes et musulmanes.' *Ars Islamica* 6 (1939): 66–87.

Sakisian, 1940
Sakisian, Arménag. *Pages d'art arménien: enluminure, tapis, tissus royaux, sculpture sur bois, orfèvrerie, faïences, iconographie.* Paris: Fonds Melkonian, 1940.

Saliba, 1987
Saliba, George. 'Theory and Observation in Islamic Astronomy: The Work of Ibn al-Shatir.' *Journal for the History of Astronomy* 18 (1987): 35–43.

Saliba, 1993
Saliba, George. 'Al-Qushji's Reform of the Ptolemaic Model for Mercury.' *Arabic Sciences and Philosophy* 3 (1993): 161–203.

Saliba, 1994a
Saliba, George. *A History of Arabic Astronomy: Planetary Theories During the Golden Age of Islam.* New York: New York University Press, 1994.

Saliba, 1994b
Saliba, George. 'A Sixteenth-Century Arabic Critique of Shams al-Din al-Khafri.' *Journal for the History of Astronomy* 25 (1994): 15–38.

Saliba, 1997
Saliba, George. 'A Redeployment of Mathematics in a Sixteenth-Century Arabic Critique of Ptolemaic Astronomy.' In *Perspectives arabes et médiévales sur la tradition scientifique et philosophique grecque*, edited by Ahmad Hasnawi, Abdelali Elamrani-Jamal, and Maround Aouad. Leuven: Peeters, 1997.

Saliba, 2000
Saliba, George. 'The Ultimate Challenge to Greek Astronomy: Hall ma la Yanhall of Shams al-Din al-Khafri (d. 1550).' In *Sic Itur Ad Astra: Studien zur Geschichte der Mathematik und Naturwissenschaften, Festschrift für den Arabisten Paul Kunitzsch zum 70. Geburtstag*, edited by Menso Folkert and Richard Lorch. Wiesbaden: Harrassowitz, 2000.

Saliba, 2001
Saliba, George. *The Astronomical Work of Mu'ayyad al-Din 'Urdi: A Thirteenth-Century Reform of Ptolemaic Astronomy.* 3rd rev. ed. Beirut: Center for Arab Unity Studies, 2001.

Salter and Pearsall, 1980
Salter, Elizabeth, and Derek Pearsall. 'Pictorial Illustration of Late Medieval Poetic Texts: The Role of the Frontispiece or Prefatory Picture.' In *Medieval Iconography and Narrative: A Symposium*, edited by Flemming Gotthelf Andersen. Odense: Odense University Press, 1980.

Sārūʾī, 1992
Sārūʾī, Muḥammad. *Tārīkh-i Muḥammadī.* Edited by Ghulāmriḍā Ṭabāṭabāʾi Majd. Tehran: Amīr Kabīr, 1992.

Sayılı, 1960
Sayılı, Aydın. *The Observatory in Islam and its Place in the General History of the Observatory.* Ankara: Türk Tarih Kurumu Basımevi, 1960.

Sayılı and Ruben, 1947
Sayılı, Aydın, and Walter Ruben. 'Preliminary Report on the Results of the Excavation, Made under the Auspices of the Turkish Historical Society, in the Caca Bey Madrasa of Kırşehir, Turkey.' *Belleten* 11, no. 44 (1947): 682–91.

al-Ṣayyād, 1979
al-Ṣayyād, Fuʾād ʿAbd al-Muʿṭī. *al-Sulṭān Maḥmūd Ghāzān Khān al-Mughūlī wa iʿtināquhu al-Islām.* Cairo: Maktabat al-Anjlū al-Miṣriyya, 1979.

al-Ṣayyād, 1987
al-Ṣayyād, Fuʾād ʿAbd al-Muʿṭī. *al-Sharq al-Islāmī fī ʿahd al-Īlkhāniyyīn (usrat Hūlākū Khān).* Doha: University of Qatar, Markaz al-wathāʾiq wa al-dirāsāt al-insāniyya, 1987.

Schamiloğlu, 1984
Schamiloğlu, U. 'The *Qaraçı* Beys of the Later Golden Horde: Notes on the Orga-

nisation of the Mongol World Empire.' *Archivum Eurasiae Medii Aevi* 4 (1984): 283–97.

Schippmann, 1971
Schippmann, Klaus. *Die iranischen Feuerheiligtümer*. Berlin and New York: de Gruyter, 1971.

Schmid, 1980
Schmid, Hansjörg. *Die Madrasa des Kalifen al-Mustansir in Baghdad: eine baugeschichtlichte Untersuchung der ersten universalen Rechtshochschule des Islam*. Mainz: Philipp von Zabern, 1980.

Schmitz, 1997
Schmitz, Barbara. *Islamic and Indian Manuscripts and Paintings in the Pierpont Morgan Library*. New York: Pierpont Morgan Library, 1997.

Schmitz, 1992
Schmitz, Barbara, with contributions by Latif Khayyat, Svat Soucek, and Massoud Pourfarrokh. *Islamic Manuscripts in the New York Public Library*. New York and Oxford: Oxford University Press and The New York Public Library, 1992.

Schön, 1990
Schön, Dorit. *Laristan, eine südpersische Küstenprovinz: ein Beitrag zu seiner Geschichte*. Vienna: Verlag der Österreichischen Akademie der Wissenschaften, 1990.

Schroeder, 1942
Schroeder, Eric. *Persian Miniatures in the Fogg Museum of Art*. Cambridge: Harvard University Press, 1942.

Schulz, 1914
Schulz, Philipp Walter. *Die persisch-islamische Miniaturmalerei*, vol. 1. Leipzig: K. W. Hiersemann, 1914.

Schwarz, 1896
Schwarz, Paul. *Iran im Mittelalter nach den arabischen Geographen*. 4 vols., 1896. Reprint, 2 vols., Hildesheim and New York: G. Olms, 1969.

Schwarz, 1914
Schwarz, Paul. 'Hurmuz.' *Zeitschrift der Deutschen Morgenländischen Gesellschaft* 68 (1914): 531–43.

Seherr-Thoss and Seherr-Thoss, 1968
Seherr-Thoss, Sonia P., and Hans Christoph Seherr-Thoss. *Design and Color in Islamic Architecture: Afghanistan, Iran, Turkey*. Washington, D.C.: Smithsonian Institution Press, 1968.

Seyller, 1999
Seyller, John W. *Workshop and Patron in Mughal India: The Freer Rāmāyaṇa and Other Illustrated Manuscripts of 'Abd al-Raḥīm*. Artibus Asiae Supplementum, vol. 42. Zurich: Museum Rietberg, 1999.

Shaanxi Historic Museum, n.d.
Shaanxi Historic Museum. *Exhibition of Cultural Relics from the Tomb of Princess Chenguo of the State of Liao*. N.p., n.d.

Shabānkāra'ī, 1984
Shabānkāra'ī, Muḥammad ibn 'Alī ibn Muḥammad. *Majma' al-ansāb*. Edited by Mīr Hāshim Muḥaddith. Tehran: Amīr Kabīr, 1984.

al-Shabībī, 1950–58
al-Shabībī, Muḥammad Riḍā. *Mu'arrikh al-'Irāq Ibn al-Fuwaṭī*. 2 vols. Baghdad, 1950–58.

Shafī'ī Kadkanī, 1999
Shafī'ī Kadkanī, Muḥammad Riḍā. *Ẓubūr-i pārsī: Nigāhī be zindagī va ghazalhā-yi 'Aṭṭār*. Tehran: Āgāh, 1999.

Shani, forthcoming
Shani, R. 'The Veneration of 'Ali in Mongol Art and Architecture.' *The Art of the Mongols: Its Precursors, Contemporary Context and Legacy. A Symposium held at the University of Edinburgh, 31 July–2 August, 1995*. Forthcoming.

Sharaf al-Dīn 'Alī Yazdī, 1957–58
Sharaf al-Dīn 'Alī Yazdī. *Ẓafarnāma*. Edited by Muḥammad 'Abbasī. 2 vols. Tehran: Amīr Kabīr, 1957–58.

Shavkunov, 1990
Shavkunov, E. V. *Kul'tura Chzhurchzhenei-udige XII–XIII vv. i problema proiskhozhdeniia tungusskikh narodov Dal'nego Vostoka*. Moscow: Nauka, 1990.

Shimo, 1977
Shimo, Hirotoshi. 'The Qarāūnās in the Historical Materials of the Īlkhanate.' *Memoirs of the Research Department of the Toyo Bunko* 35 (1977): 131–81.

Shiraishi, 2001
Shiraishi, Noriyuki. *Chingisu kan no kokogaku (Archaeological Studies on Genghis Khan)*. Tokyo: Doseisha, 2001.

Shiraishi, 2002
Shiraishi, Noriyuki. *Mongoru teikokushi no kokogakuteki kenkyu (Archaeological Research on the History of the Mongol Empire)*. Tokyo: Doseisha, 2002.

Shiraishi, 2004
Shiraishi, Noriyuki. 'Seasonal Migrations of the Mongol Emperors and the Peri-urban Area of Kharakhorum.' *International Journal of Asian Studies* 1, no. 1 (2004): 105–19.

Siddiqui, 1993
Siddiqui, Iqtidar Husain. 'Indian Sources on Central Asian History and Culture 13th to 15th Century A.D.' *Journal of Asian History* 27, no. 1 (1993): 51–63.

Sievernich and Budde, 1989
Sievernich, Gereon, and Hendrik Budde. *Europa und der Orient, 800–1900*. Berlin and Gütersloh: Berliner Festspiele/Bertelsmann Lexikon Verlag, 1989.

Simnānī, 1988
Simnānī, Aḥmad ibn Muḥammad. *'Alâ'üddevle Simnânî: Küçük Eserleri (Opera Minora)*. Edited by Wheeler M. Thackston. Cambridge: Harvard University, Office of the University Publisher, 1988.

Simpson, 1979
Simpson, Marianna Shreve. *The Illustration of an Epic: The Earliest Shahnama Manuscripts.* New York and London: Garland Publishing, 1979.

Simpson, 1982
Simpson, Marianna Shreve. 'The Role of Baghdad in the Formation of Persian Painting.' In *Art et Société dans le monde Iranien*, edited by Chahriyar Adle. Paris: Éditions Recherche sur les civilizations, 1982.

Simpson, 1993
Simpson, Marianna Shreve. 'The Making of Manuscripts and the Workings of the *Kitab-Khana* in Safavid Iran.' In *The Artist's Workshop*, edited by Peter M. Lukehart. Washington, D.C.: National Gallery of Art, 1993.

Simpson, 2000
Simpson, Marianna Shreve. 'A Reconstruction and Preliminary Account of the 1341 *Shahnama*, with Some Further Thoughts on Early *Shahnama* Illustration.' In *Persian Painting from the Mongols to the Qajars: Studies in Honour of Basil W. Robinson*, edited by Robert Hillenbrand. London and New York: I. B. Tauris, 2000.

Sims, 1973
Sims, Eleanor. 'The Garrett Manuscript of the Zafar-Name: A Study in Fifteenth-Century Timurid Patronage.' Ph.D. diss., New York University, 1973.

Sims, 1988
Sims, Eleanor. 'The "Iconography" of the Internal Decoration in the Mausoleum of Uljaytu at Sultaniyya.' In *Content and Context of Visual Arts in the Islamic World*, edited by Priscilla P. Soucek. University Park and London: Published for the College Art Association of America by the Pennsylvania State University Press, 1988.

Sims, 2002
Sims, Eleanor. *Peerless Images: Persian Painting and its Sources.* New Haven and London: Yale University Press, 2002.

Sirén, 1959
Sirén, Osvald. *Chinesische Skulpturen der Sammlung Eduard von der Heydt.* Zurich: Museum Rietberg, 1959.

Sīstānī, 1998–99
Sīstānī, Irāj Afshār. *Jazīrat-yi Kīsh, morvārīd-i Khalīj-i Fārs.* Tehran: Hīrmand, 1998–99.

Smbat, 1980
Smbat. *La Chronique attribuée au connétable Smbat.* Translated by Gérard Dédéyan. Paris: R. Geuthner, 1980.

Smirnov, 1909
Smirnov, I. I. *Vostochnoe Serebro.* St. Petersburg, 1909.

Smith, E. B., 1956
Smith, E. Baldwin. *Architectural Symbolism of Imperial Rome and the Middle Ages.* Princeton: Princeton University Press, 1956.

Smith, J. M., 1984
Smith, John Masson, Jr. "Ayn Jalut: Mamluk Success or Mongol Failure?' *Harvard Journal of Asiatic Studies* 44, no. 2 (1984): 307–45.

Smith, J. M., 1994
Smith, John Masson, Jr. 'Demographic Considerations in Mongol Siege Warfare.' *Archivum Ottomanicum* 13 (1993–94): 329–34.

Smith, J. M., 1997
Smith, John Masson, Jr. 'Mongol Society and Military in the Middle East: Antecedents and Adaptations.' In *War and Society in the Eastern Mediterranean, 7th–15th Centuries*, edited by Y. Lev. Leiden: Brill, 1997.

Smith, J. M., 1999
Smith, John Masson, Jr. 'Mongol Nomadism and Middle Eastern Geography: Qishlaqs and Tümens.' In *The Mongol Empire and its Legacy*, edited by Reuven Amitai-Preiss and David O. Morgan. Leiden: Brill, 1999.

Smith, J. M., 2000
Smith, John Masson, Jr. 'Dietary Decadence and Dynastic Decline in the Mongol Empire.' *Journal of Asian History* 34, no. 1 (2000): 35–52.

Smith, M. M., 2000
Smith, Margaret M. *The Title-Page: Its Early Development, 1460–1510*. London and New Castle, Del.: The British Library/Oak Knoll Press, 2000.

Sohrweide, 1965
Sohrweide, Hanna. 'Der Sieg der Ṣafaviden in Persien und seine Rückwirkungen auf die Schiiten Anatoliens im 16. Jahrhundert.' *Der Islam* 41 (1965): 95–223.

Song Lian, 1976
Song Lian, 宋濂. *Yüan-Shih* 元史. Beijing: Zhonghua shuju, 1976. Reprint, 1995.

Sotheby's, London, 1967
Sotheby's, London. *Catalogue of Twenty-Three Important Armenian Illuminated Manuscripts*. Sale cat., 14 March 1967.

Sotheby's, London, 1976
Sotheby's, London. *Important Oriental Manuscripts and Miniatures: The Property of the Hagop Kevorkian Fund*. Sale cat., 12 April 1976.

Sotheby's, London, 1979
Sotheby's, London. *Important Oriental Miniatures, Manuscripts and Qajar Lacquer*. Sale cat., 8–9 October 1979.

Sotheby's, London, 1998
Sotheby's, London. *Oriental Manuscripts and Miniatures*. Sale cat., 29 April 1998.

Soucek, 1975
Soucek, Priscilla P. 'An Illustrated Manuscript of al-Biruni's *Chronology of Ancient Nations*.' In *The Scholar and the Saint: Studies in Commemoration of Abu'l Rayhan al-Biruni and Jalal al-Din Rumi*, edited by Peter J. Chelkowski. New York: New York University Press, 1975.

Soucek, 1988
Soucek, Priscilla P. 'The Life of the Prophet: Illustrated Versions.' In *Content and Context of Visual Arts in the Islamic World*, edited by Priscilla P. Soucek. University Park and London: Published for the College Art Association of America by the Pennsylvania State University Press, 1988.

Soucek, 1998
Soucek, Priscilla P. 'Armenian and Islamic Manuscript Painting: A Visual Dialogue.' In *Treasures in Heaven: Armenian Art, Religion and Society*, edited by Thomas F. Mathews and Roger S. Wieck. New York: Pierpont Morgan Library, 1998.

Soudavar, 1992
Soudavar, Abolala. *Art of the Persian Courts: Selections from the Art and History Trust Collection.* New York: Rizzoli, 1992.

Soudavar, 1996
Soudavar, Abolala. 'The Saga of Abu-Sa'id Bahādor Khān. The Abu-Sa'idnāmé.' In *The Court of the Il-Khans, 1290–1340.* Oxford Studies in Islamic Art, vol. 12, edited by Julian Raby and Teresa Fitzherbert. Oxford: Oxford University Press, 1996.

Soudavar, 2003
Soudavar, Abolala. *The Aura of Kings: Legitimacy and Divine Sanction in Iranian Kingship.* Costa Mesa, Calif.: Mazda, 2003.

Soudavar, 2006a
Soudavar, Abolala. 'Achaemenid Bureaucratic Practices and the Safavid Falsification of their Early History.' In *Proceedings of the Fifth Conference of the Societas Iranologica Europaea, Ravenna, 6–11 October, 2003*, vol. 2, edited by A. Panaino and R. Zipoli. Milan, 2006.

Soudavar, 2006b
Soudavar, Abolala. 'The Significance of Av. *či?ra*, OP. *čiūa*, MP. *čihr*, and NP. *čehr*, for the Iranian Cosmogony of Light.' *Iranica Antiqua* 41 (2006): 151–85.

Sourdel-Thomine and Spuler, 1973
Sourdel-Thomine, Janine, and Bertold Spuler. *Die Kunst des Islam.* Berlin: Propyläen-Verlag, 1973.

Soustiel, 1985
Soustiel, Jean. *La céramique islamique, Le guide du connaisseur.* Fribourg and Paris: Office du Livre/Vilo, 1985.

Spuler, 1939
Spuler, Bertold. *Die Mongolen in Iran: Politik, Verwaltung und Kultur der Ilchanzeit 1220–1350.* Leipzig: J. C. Hinrichs, 1939.

Spuler, 1952
Spuler, Bertold. *Iran in früh-islamischer Zeit: Politik, Kultur, Verwaltung und öffentliches Leben zwischen der arabischen und der seldschukischen Eroberung, 633 bis 1055.* Wiesbaden: F. Steiner, 1952.

Spuler, 1955
Spuler, Bertold. *Die Mongolen in Iran: Politik, Verwaltung und Kultur der Ilchanzeit 1220–1350.* 2nd ed. Berlin: Akademie-Verlag, 1955.

Spuler, 1968
Spuler, Bertold. *Die Mongolen in Iran: Politik, Verwaltung und Kultur der Ilchanzeit 1220–1350.* 3rd ed. Berlin: Akademie-Verlag, 1968.

Stchoukine, 1936
Stchoukine, Ivan. *La peinture iranienne sous les derniers 'Abbasides et les Il-Khans*. Bruges: Imprimerie Sainte Catherine, 1936.

Steingass et al., 1957
Steingass, Francis Joseph, John Richardson, Charles Wilkins, and Francis Johnson. *A Comprehensive Persian-English Dictionary*. London: Routledge & Kegan Paul, 1957.

Stern, 1946–47
Stern, S. M. 'The Authorship of the Epistles of the Ikhwan-as-Safa.' *Islamic Culture* 20 and 21 (1946–47): 367–72 and 403–04.

Stern, 1964
Stern, S. M. 'New Information about the Authors of the "Epistles of the Sincere Brethren."' *Islamic Studies* 3, no. 4 (1964): 405–28.

Stewart, 1967
Stewart, Desmond. *Early Islam, Great Ages of Man*. New York: Time, Inc., 1967. Reprint, 1975.

Stiffe, 1896
Stiffe, Arthur. 'Ancient Trading Centers of the Persian Gulf: II. Kais, or al-Kais.' *Geographical Journal* (June 1896).

Stoichita, 1997
Stoichita, Victor I. *The Self-Aware Image: An Insight into Early Modern Meta-Painting*. Cambridge and New York: Cambridge University Press, 1997.

Stuart, ed., 1995
Stuart, Kevin, ed. *Mongol Oral Narratives: Gods, Tricksters, Heroes, & Horses*. Bloomington, Ind.: Mongolia Society, 1995.

Sümer, 1969
Sümer, Faruk. 'Anadolu'da Moğollar.' *Selçuklu Araştırmaları Dergisi* 1 (1969): 1–147.

Swietochowski and Carboni, 1994
Swietochowski, Marie Lukens, and Stefano Carboni. *Illustrated Poetry and Epic Images: Persian Painting of the 1330s and 1340s*. New York: Metropolitan Museum of Art, 1994.

Tabbaa, 2002
Tabbaa, Yasser. 'The Mosque of Nur al-Din in Mosul 1170–1172.' *Annales Islamologiques* 36 (2002): 339–60.

Tabrīzī, 1982
Tabrīzī, Muḥammad Ḥusayn b. Khalaf-i. *Burhān-i qāṭiʿ*, vol. 5, edited by Muḥammad Muʿīn. 4th ed. Tehran: Amīr Kabīr, 1982.

Tanındı, 1990
Tanındı, Zeren. '1278 Tarihli en Eski Mesnevi'nin Tezhipleri.' *Kültür ve Sanat* 2, no. 8 (1990): 17–22.

Tavakoli, 2002
Tavakoli, Farnaz. *A Bibliography of Sultaniyeh*. Tehran: Conservation and Revitalization Deputy, Iranian Cultural Heritage Organization, 2002.

Teixeira, 1902
Teixeira, Pedro. *The Travels of Pedro Teixeira, with his 'Kings of Harmuz' and Extracts from his 'Kings of Persia.'* Translated by William F. Sinclair. Edited by Donald W. Ferguson. London: Printed for the Hakluyt Society, 1902.

Temir, ed., 1959
Temir, Ahmet, ed. and trans. *Kırşehir Emiri Caca Oğlu Nur el-Din'in 1272 Tarihli Arapça-Moğolca Vakfiyesi.* Ankara: Türk Tarih Kurumu Basımevi, 1959.

Thackston, 2001
Thackston, Wheeler M. *Album Prefaces and Other Documents on the History of Calligraphers and Painters.* Studies and Sources in Islamic Art and Architecture, Supplements to Muqarnas. Leiden and Boston: Brill, 2001.

Thierry, N. and Thierry, M., 1963
Thierry, Nicole, and Michel Thierry. *Nouvelles églises rupestres de Cappadoce: Région du Hasan Dagi (New Rock-Cut Churches of Cappadocia).* Paris: C. Klincksiek, 1963.

Thompson, 2004
Thompson, Jon. *Silk, 13th to 18th Centuries: Treasures from the Museum of Islamic Art, Qatar.* Doha: National Council for Culture, Arts and Heritage, 2004.

Thompson and Canby, eds., 2003
Thompson, Jon, and Sheila R. Canby, eds. *Hunt for Paradise: Court Arts of Safavid Iran, 1501–1576.* Milan: Skira, 2003.

Thomson, 1989
Thomson, Robert. 'The Historical Compilation of Vardan Arewelc'i.' *Dumbarton Oaks Papers* 43 (1989), 125–226.

Tihrānī, 1964
Tihrānī, Abū Bakr. *Kitāb-i Diyārbakriyya.* Edited by Osman Turan. Ankara: Türk Tarih Kurumu Basımevi, 1964.

Titley, 1983
Titley, Norah M. *Persian Miniature Painting and its Influence on the Arts of Turkey and India.* London: British Library, 1983.

Togan, I., 1998
Togan, Isenbike. *Flexibility and Limitation in Steppe Formations: The Kerait Khanate and Chinggis Khan.* Leiden and New York: Brill, 1998.

Togan, Z. V., 1963
Togan, Zeki Validi. *On the Miniatures in Istanbul Libraries.* Istanbul: Baha Matbaasi, 1963.

Turner, ed., 1996
Turner, Jane, ed. *The Dictionary of Art.* 34 vols. London: MacMillan, 1996.

Ṭūsī, 1993
Ṭūsī, Naṣīr al-Dīn Muḥammad ibn Muḥammad. *Naṣīr al-Dīn al-Ṭūsī's Memoir on Astronomy (al-Tadhkira fī 'ilm al-hay'a).* Translated and edited by F. J. Ragep. 2 vols. New York: Springer-Verlag, 1993.

al-ʿUmarī, 1968
al-ʿUmarī, Shihāb al-Dīn. *Masālik al-akbār wa mamālik al-amṣār.* Edited by Klaus Lech,

Das Mongolische Weltreich. Asiatische Forschungen, Bd. 22. Wiesbaden: Harrassowitz, 1968.

Vahram, 1869
Vahram d'Édesse. 'Chronique.' In *Recueil des historiens des Croisades: Documents arméniens*, edited by H. Omont. Paris: Imprimerie nationale, 1869.

Vardan, 1862
Vardan. *Universal History*. Venice: Mekhitarist Press, 1862.

Varjavand, 1975
Varjavand, Parviz. 'Rapport préliminaire sur les fouilles de l'observatoire de Mâraqé.' *Le monde iranien et l'Islam* 3 (1975): 119–24.

Varjavand, 1987
Varjavand, Parviz. *Kāvish-i rasadkhānah-'i Marāghah va nigāhī bih pīshīnah-'i dānish-i sitārah'shināsī dār Īrān/La découverte archéologique du complexe scientifique de l'Observatoire de Maraqé*. Tehran: Amīr Kabīr, 1987.

Velmans, 1980
Velmans, Tania. 'Maniérisme et innovations stylistiques dans la miniature cilicienne à la fin du 13e siècle.' *Revue des Études Arméniennes* N.S. 14 (1980): 415–33.

Vesel, 2001
Vesel, Z. 'Science and Scientific Instruments.' In *The Splendour of Iran*, edited by C. Parham. London: Booth-Clibborn Editions, 2001.

Victoria and Albert Museum, 1970
Victoria and Albert Museum. *Mount Trust Collection of Chinese Art*. London: Victoria and Albert Museum, 1970.

Virani, 2003
Virani, Shafique N. 'The Eagle Returns: Evidence of Continued Ismaili Activity at Alamut and in the South Caspian Region following the Mongol Conquests.' *Journal of the American Oriental Society* 123, no. 2 (2003): 351–70.

Voegelin, 1940–41
Voegelin, Eric. 'The Mongol Orders of Submission to European Powers, 1245–1255.' *Byzantion* 15 (1940–41): 378–413.

Waḥīd Qazwīnī, 1951
Waḥīd Qazwīnī, Muḥammad Ṭāhir. *'Abbās-nāma*. Edited by Ibrāhīm Dehgānī. Arak: Dawūdī, 1951.

Waley and Titley, 1975
Waley, P., and Norah M. Titley. 'An Illustrated Persian Text of Kalila and Dimna dated 707/1307–08.' *The British Library Journal* 1 (1975): 42–61.

Wālih Iṣfahānī, 2001
Wālih Iṣfahānī, Muḥammad Yūsuf. *Khuld-i Barīn*. Edited by Muḥammad Riḍā Nāṣirī. Vol. 2, parts 6 and 7 of section 8, *Iran under the Reign of Shah Safi and Shah Abbas*. Tehran: Anjuman-i Āsār va Mafākhir-i Farhangī, 2001.

Wang Dayuan, 1981
Wang Dayuan, 汪大淵. *Daoyi zhilüe jiaoshi* 島夷誌略校釋. Edited by Su Jiqing, *Zhongwai jiaotong shiji congkan*. Beijing: Zhonghua shuju, 1981.

Ward, 1993
Ward, Rachel. *Islamic Metalwork*. London: British Museum Press, 1993.

Ward, 1996
Ward, Rachel. 'Painted Book Illustration, c. 1250–c. 1500: Egypt and Syria.' In *The Dictionary of Art*, edited by Jane Turner. London: MacMillan, 1996.

Wardwell, 1988–89
Wardwell, Anne E. '*Panni Tartarici*: Eastern Islamic Silks Woven with Gold and Silver (13th and 14th Centuries).' *Islamic Art* 3 (1988–89): 95–173.

Waṣṣāf, 1853
Waṣṣāf, ʿAbd Allāh ibn Faḍl Allāh. *Tajziyat al-amṣār wa tazjiyat al-aʿṣār*. Edited by Muḥammad Mahdī Iṣfahānī, 1853. Reprint, Tehran: Ibn Sīnā, 1959–60.

Waṣṣāf, 1856
Waṣṣāf, ʿAbd Allāh ibn Faḍl Allāh. *Geschichte Wassaf's*. Edited and translated by Joseph Freiherr von Hammer-Purgstall. Vienna: Kaiserlich-Königliche Hof- und Staatsdruckerei, 1856.

Waṣṣāf, 1967
Waṣṣāf, ʿAbd Allāh ibn Faḍl Allāh. *Taḥrīr-i tārīkh-i Waṣṣāf*. Edited by ʿAbd al-Muḥammad Āyatī. Tehran: Bunyād-i Farhang-i Īrān, 1967.

Waṣṣāf, n.d.
Waṣṣāf, ʿAbd Allāh ibn Faḍl Allāh. *Geschichte Wassaf's*. Translated by Joseph Freiherr von Hammer-Purgstall. Unpublished typescript, n.d.

Watson, 1975
Watson, Oliver. 'The Masjid-i ʿAli, Quhrud: An Architectural and Epigraphic Survey.' *Iran* 13 (1975): 59–74.

Watson, 1979
Watson, Oliver. 'Persian Silhouette Ware and the Development of Underglaze Painting.' In *Decorative Techniques and Styles in Asian Ceramics*, edited by M. Medley. London: School of Oriental and African Studies, University of London, 1979.

Watson, 1985
Watson, Oliver. *Persian Lustre Ware*. London and Boston: Faber and Faber, 1985.

Watson, 1994
Watson, Oliver. 'Documentary Mina'i and Abu Zaid's Bowls.' In *The Art of the Saljuqs in Iran and Anatolia*, edited by Robert Hillenbrand. Costa Mesa, Calif.: Mazda, 1994.

Watson, 1999a
Watson, Oliver. 'Fritware: Fatimid Egypt or Saljuq Iran?' In *L'Égypte Fatimide: son art et son histoire*, edited by Marianne Barrucand. Paris: Université de Paris-Sorbonne, 1999.

Watson, 1999b
Watson, Oliver. 'Museums, Collecting, Art-History, Archaeology.' *Damaszener Mitteilungen* 11 (1999): 421–32.

Watson, 2004
Watson, Oliver. *Ceramics from Islamic Lands*. London: Thames and Hudson, 2004.

Watt, J. C. Y., 2002
Watt, James C. Y. 'A Note on Artistic Exchanges in the Mongol Empire.' In *The Legacy of Genghis Khan: Courtly Art and Culture in Western Asia, 1256–1353*, edited by Linda Komaroff and Stefano Carboni. New York, New Haven, and London: Metropolitan Museum of Art and Yale University Press, 2002.

Watt, J. C. Y. and Wardwell, 1997
Watt, James C. Y., and Anne E. Wardwell. *When Silk Was Gold: Central Asian and Chinese Textiles*. New York: Metropolitan Museum of Art in cooperation with the Cleveland Museum of Art, 1997.

Watt, W. M., 1971
Watt, W. Montgomery. 'God's Caliph: Qur'anic Interpretations and Umayyad Claims.' In *Iran and Islam: In Memory of the Late Vladimir Minorsky*, edited by C. E. Bosworth. Edinburgh: Edinburgh University Press, 1971.

Weatherford, 2004
Weatherford, Jack McIver. *Genghis Khan and the Making of the Modern World*. New York: Crown, 2004.

Weiers, ed., 1986
Weiers, Michael, ed. *Die Mongolen. Beiträge zu ihrer Geschichte und Kultur*. Darmstadt: Wissenschaftliche Buchgesellschaft, 1986.

Weissman, 1990
Weissman, Keith. 'Mongolian Rule in Baghdad: Evidence from the Chronicle of Ibn al-Fuwati, 656 to 700 A.H./1258 to 1301 C.E.' Ph.D. diss., University of Chicago, 1990.

Weitzmann, 1959
Weitzmann, Kurt. *Ancient Book Illumination*. Cambridge: Harvard University Press, 1959.

Weitzmann, 1970
Weitzmann, Kurt. *Illustrations in Roll and Codex: A Study of the Origin and Method of Text Illustration*. 2nd ed. Studies in Manuscript Illumination, no. 2. Princeton: Princeton University Press, 1970.

Weitzmann, 1971
Weitzmann, Kurt. *Studies in Classical and Byzantine Manuscript Illumination*. Edited by Herbert L. Kessler. Chicago: University of Chicago Press, 1971.

Weitzmann, 1977
Weitzmann, Kurt. *Late Antique and Early Christian Book Illumination*. New York: G. Braziller, 1977.

Weitzmann, ed., 1979
Weitzmann, Kurt, ed. *Age of Spirituality: Late Antique and Early Christian Art, Third to Seventh Century*. New York: Metropolitan Museum of Art, 1979.

Wessel, 1969
Wessel, Klaus. *Byzantine Enamels, from the 5th to the 13th Century*. Translated by Irene R. Gibbons. Shannon: Irish University Press, 1969.

White, 1991
White, David Gordon. *Myths of the Dog-Man*. Chicago: University of Chicago Press, 1991.

Whitehouse, 1976
Whitehouse, David. 'Kish.' *Iran* 14 (1976): 146–47.

Whitehouse, 1983
Whitehouse, David. 'Maritime Trade in the Gulf: The 11th and 12th Centuries.' *World Archaeology* 14, no. 3 (1983): 328–34.

Wickens, 1962
Wickens, G. M. 'Nasir al-Din Tusi on the Fall of Baghdad: A Further Study.' *Journal of Semitic Studies* 7 (1962): 23–35.

Wiesehöfer, Matthee, and Floor, 2001
Wiesehöfer, Josef, Rudi P. Matthee, and Willem Floor. 'Gift-Giving.' In *Encyclopaedia Iranica,* edited by Ehsan Yarshater. New York: Bibliotheca Persica, 2001.

Wiet, 1947
Wiet, Gaston. *Soieries Persanes.* Cairo: Institut français d'archéologie orientale, 1947.

Wilber, 1931
Wilber, Donald N. 'The Parthian Structures at Takht-i Sulayman.' *Antiquity* 12 (1931): 389–410.

Wilber, 1939
Wilber, Donald N. 'The Development of Mosaic Faiënce in Islamic Architecture in Iran.' *Ars Islamica* 6, no. 1 (1939): 16–47.

Wilber, 1955
Wilber, Donald N. *The Architecture of Islamic Iran: The Il Khanid Period.* Princeton: Princeton University Press, 1955. Reprint, New York: Greenwood, 1969.

Willey, 1963
Willey, Peter. *The Castles of the Assassins.* London: Harrap, 1963.

Wilson, 1954
Wilson, Arnold Talbot. *The Persian Gulf.* London: Allen & Unwin, 1954.

Wink, 1991–97
Wink, André. *Al-Hind: The Making of the Indo-Islamic World.* 2nd ed. 2 vols. Leiden and New York: Brill, 1991–97.

Wood, 1995
Wood, Frances. *Did Marco Polo Go to China?* London: Secker & Warburg, 1995.

Woods, 1990
Woods, John E. *The Timurid Dynasty.* Papers on Inner Asia, no. 14. Bloomington: Research Institute for Inner Asian Studies, Indiana University, 1990.

Woods, 1999
Woods, John E. *The Aqquyunlu: Clan, Confederation, Empire.* Rev. and expanded ed. Salt Lake City: University of Utah Press, 1999.

Wright, 1997
Wright, Elaine Julia. 'The Look of the Book: Manuscript Production in the Southern Iranian City of Shiraz from the Early-14th Century to 1452.' Ph.D. diss., Oxford University, 1997.

Yaghan, 2000
Yaghan, M. A. J. 'Decoding the Two-Dimensional Pattern found at Takht-i Sulaiman into Three-Dimensional Muqarnas Forms.' *Iran* 38 (2000): 77–95.

Yarshater, ed., 1985 continuing
Yarshater, Ehsan, ed. *Encyclopaedia Iranica*. London, Boston, New York, and Costa Mesa, Calif.: Imprint varies, 1985 continuing.

Yazdī, 1987
Yazdī, Munajjim. *Tārīkh-i Shāh 'Abbas*. Edited by Sayfallāh Waḥīdniyā. Tehran: Intishārāt-i Waḥīd, 1987.

al-Yūnīnī, 1954
al-Yūnīnī, Mūsā ibn Muḥammad. *Dhayl mir'āt al-zamān*. 4 vols. Hyderabad, India: Dā'irat al-Ma'ārif al- 'Uthmāniyya, 1954.

Zarkūb Shīrāzī, 1931–32
Zarkūb Shīrāzī, Abū al-'Abbās Aḥmad b. Abī al-Khayr. *Shīrāznāma*. Edited by Bahman Karīmī. Tehran: Maṭbā'i-yi rawshanā'ī, 1931–32.

Zerjal et al., 2003
Zerjal, Tatiana et al. 'The Genetic Legacy of the Mongols.' *American Journal of Human Genetics* 72 (2003): 717–21.

Zetterstéen, ed., 1919
Zetterstéen, K. V., ed. *Beiträge zur Geschichte der Mamlukensultane in den Jahren 690–741 der Higra, nach arabischen Handschriften*. Leiden: Brill, 1919.

Zhao Rugua, 1996
Zhao Rugua, 趙汝适. *Zhufan zhi jiaoshi* 諸蕃志校釋. Edited by Yang Bowen, *Zhongwai jiaotong shiji congkan*. Beijing: Zhonghua shuju, 1996.

Zhu Jieqin, 1984
Zhu Jieqin, 朱傑勤. *Zhongwai guanxi lunwen ji* 中外關系史論文集. Luoyang: Henan renmin chubanshe, 1984.

COLOR PLATES

1a. Installation view with tent panels. *The Legacy of Genghis Khan*, Los Angeles County Museum of Art, 2003 (exhibition designer Bernard Kester; photo © 2003 LACMA/Museum Associates)

1b. Tent panels (detail), eastern Iran or western Central Asia, late 13th–early 14th century. Lampas weave (tabby and twill), red and purple silk, gilded strips. Museum of Islamic Art, Doha (TE.40.00) (photo © 2003 LACMA/Museum Associates)

a

b

c

2a–c. Set of belt fittings (details), Golden Horde (Southern Russia) and China, 13th century. Gold sheet, engraved, stamped, chased, and punched, worked in repoussé. State Hermitage Museum, St. Petersburg (KUB-705–721)

3. Set of belt fittings, Mongol Empire, 13th century. Silver gilt. State Hermitage Museum, St. Petersburg (ZO-762)

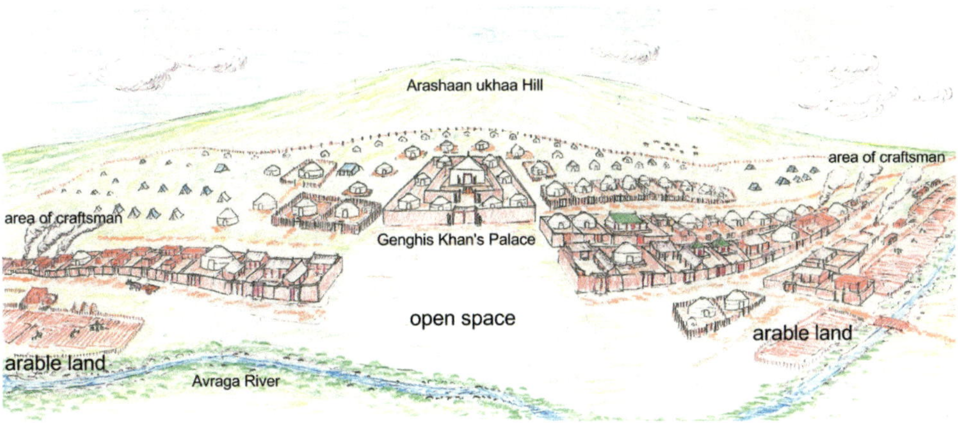

4. Reconstruction of Genghis Khan's palace (drawing by N. Shiraishi)

5. Takht-i Sulayman, view from southwest into the destroyed Ilkhanid north *īwān* with the stairs leading to the throne hall atop the Sasanian temple (photo D. Huff)

6. Takht-i Sulayman, glazed frieze tile with dragon in *lajvardina* from the Ilkhanid palace. Staatliche Museen zu Berlin-Preußischer Kulturbesitz, Museum für Islamische Kunst, Berlin (photo D. Huff)

7. *Enthronement Scene*, illustration from the Diez Albums, Iran (possibly Tabriz), early 14th century. Ink, colors, and gold on paper. Staatsbibliothek zu Berlin-Preußischer Kulturbesitz, Orientabteilung (Diez A, fol. 70, S. 22)

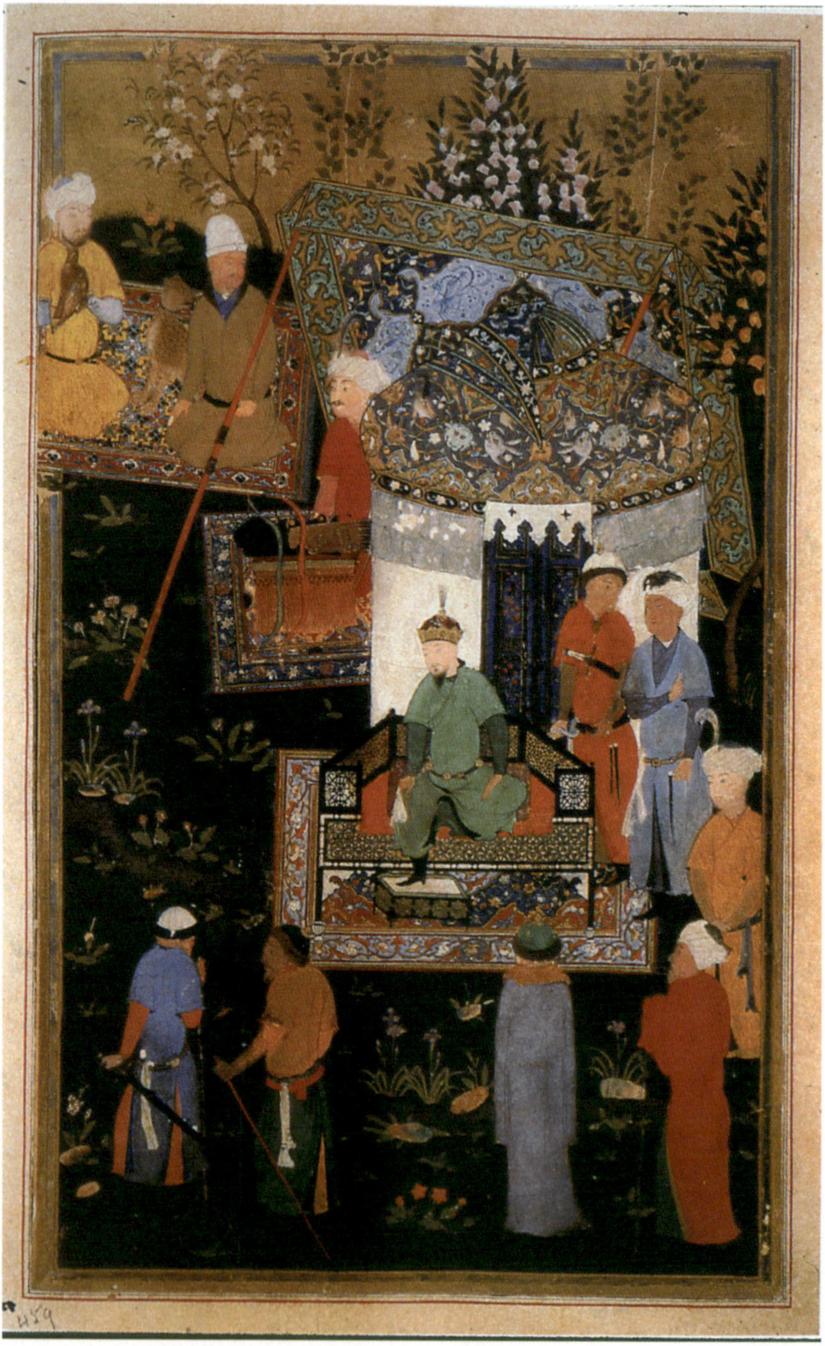

8. *Tīmūr Granting an Audience in Balkh on the Occasion of His Accession to Power in April 1370*, from a *Ẓafarnāma* of Sharaf al-Dīn ʿAlī Yazdī copied by Shīr ʿAlī for Sulṭān-Ḥusayn Mīrzā. Iran, Herat, dated 872/1467–68; paintings executed c. 1480. Opaque watercolor, ink, and gold on paper. Baltimore, Johns Hopkins University, Milton S. Eisenhower Library, John Work Garrett Collection, fol. 82b

9. Illuminated page from a copy of Rashīd al-Dīn's theological works entitled *Majmūʿa al-rashīdiyya*, copied by Muḥammad ibn Maḥmūd ibn Muḥammad, known as Amīn Zūdniwīs al-Baghdādī, at Tabriz between Shaʿbān and Ramaḍān 711/December 1311–February 1312. Museum of Islamic Art, Qatar (MA.006.98CH)

10. *Nūshirwān Writing to the Khāqān of China*, from the Great Mongol *Shāhnāma*. Iran, probably Tabriz, 1330s. Ink, colors, and gold on paper. The Trustees of the Chester Beatty Library, Dublin (Per. 111.7)

11. One leaf of double frontispiece, *Rasāʾil Ikhwān al-Ṣafāʾ*, Baghdad, Shawwāl 686/November 1287. Süleymaniye Mosque Library, Istanbul (Esad Efendi 3638, fol. 4r). After Ettinghausen (1962), 98

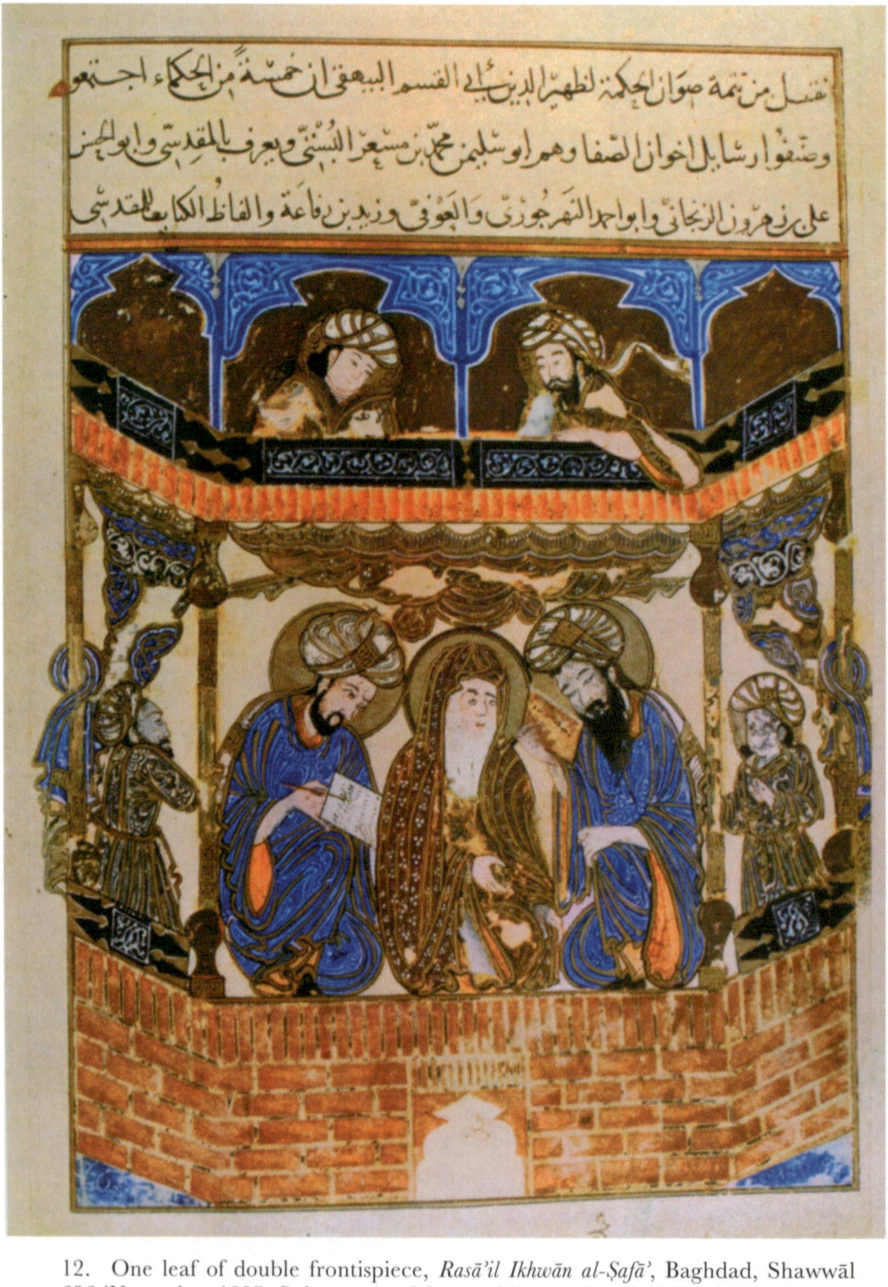

12. One leaf of double frontispiece, *Rasā'il Ikhwān al-Ṣafā'*, Baghdad, Shawwāl 686/November 1287. Süleymaniye Mosque Library, Istanbul (Esad Efendi 3638, fol. 3v). After Ettinghausen (1962), 99

13. Double frontispiece, *Ta'rīkh-i jahān-gushāy* of 'Alā' al-Dīn 'Aṭā Malik Juwaynī, probably Iraq (Baghdad), dated 4 Dhū al-ḥijja 689/8 December 1290. Bibliothèque Nationale, Paris (suppl. persan 205, fols. 1v–2r)

14. Frontispiece, Tarjama-yi taʾrīkh-i Ṭabarī of Balʿamī, attributed to the Jazira (Iraq), possibly Mosul, c. 1300. Freer Gallery of Art, Smithsonian Institution, Washington, D.C. (Purchase, F1957.16, fol. 1a)

15. Frontispiece, Kalīla wa Dimna of Abū al-Maʿālī Naṣrallāh, attributed to Iran, c. 1300. Topkapı Palace Museum Library, Istanbul (H. 363, fols. 1b–2a)

16. Frontispiece, Kalīla wa Dimna of Abū al-Maʿālī Naṣrallāh, attributed to Iran (possibly Shiraz), dated 707/1307–8. By permission of The British Library, London (Or. 13506, fols. 2b–3a)

17. Frontispiece, Shāhnāma of Firdawsī, attributed to Shiraz, dated Ṣafar 731/November 1330. Topkapı Palace Museum Library, Istanbul (H. 1479, fols. 4b–5a)

18. Frontispiece, Shāhnāma of Firdawsī, attributed to Shiraz, dated end of Ramaḍān 741/mid-March 1341. Arthur M. Sackler Gallery, Smithsonian Institution, Washington, D.C. (Smithsonian Unrestricted Trust Funds, Smithsonian Collections Acquisition Program, and Dr. Arthur M. Sackler, S1986.112a–b, S1986.113a–b, fols. 1b–2a) [as reconstructed]

19. Text-frontispiece, Qur'ān, n.d., copied for Fārs Malik Khātūn. The Nasser D. Khalili Collection of Islamic Art, London (QUR 182, fols. 26b–27a)

20. *The Dīw Akwān Throws Rustam into the Sea*, Stephens *Shāhnāma*, attributed to Shiraz, inscribed date of 753/1352–53. Arthur M. Sackler Gallery, Smithsonian Institution, Washington, D.C. (Lent by Mr. and Mrs. Farhad Ebrahimi, LTS1998.1.1.2 and 1.1.3, fol. 145v) (photo E. Wright)

21. Author's reconstruction of the pattern on a 14th-century silk lampas textile in the Cooper-Hewitt Museum, New York

22. Stucco, terracotta and tile on the interior of Öljeitü's mausoleum at Sultaniyya, completed in 713/1313–14 (photo Blair and Bloom)

23. Headpiece with Christ Emmanuel and Chinese animals, from the Lectionary of Het'um II, 1286. Erevan, Matenadaran (M979, fol. 293, detail) (photo Matenadaran)

24. Headpiece with dragon and phoenix motif (detail), from the Lectionary of Het'um II, 1286. Erevan, Matenadaran (M979, fol. 334) (photo Matenadaran)

25. Silk textile with teardrop-shaped medallions of a phoenix amid clouds, Jin Dynasty (1115–1234). Plain weave with gilded animal substrate supplementary weft patterning. Los Angeles County Museum of Art (M.2005.127.1) (Museum Associates/LACMA, Costume Council Fund; photo © 2005 Museum Associates/LACMA)

26. Albarello decorated in *lajvardina* technique (enamels and gilding over a blue glaze), 13th–14th century. H. 35.5 cm. The Metropolitan Museum of Art, New York, Henry G. Leberthon Collection, Gift of Mr. and Mrs. A. Wallace Chauncey, 1957 (57.61.12a, b). After Komaroff and Carboni, eds. (2002), fig. 241. Reproduced by permission of The Metropolitan Museum of Art

27. Tile panel, Masjid-i ʿAlī, Kashan, 1303–7 (photo B. O'Kane)

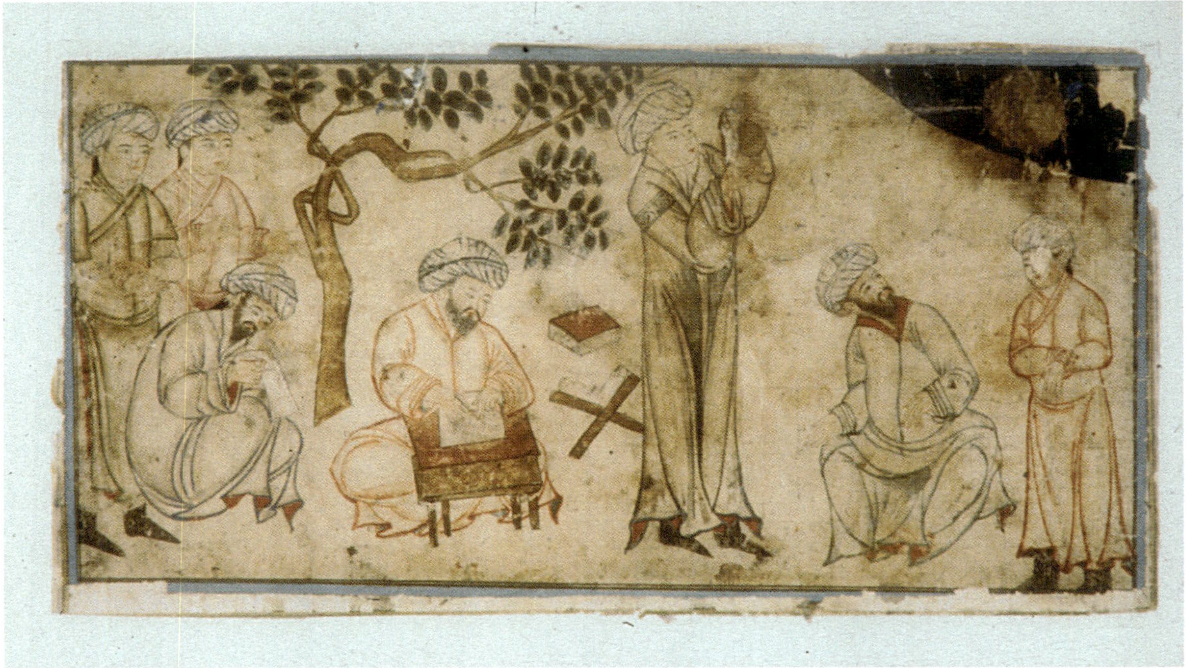

28. *Scene with an Astrologer*, illustration from the Diez Albums, Iran (possibly Tabriz), early 14th century. Ink, colors, and gold on paper. Staatsbibliothek zu Berlin-Preußischer Kulturbesitz, Orientabteilung (Diez A, fol. 72, S. 16, no. 1)

29a. Ilkhanid-period tile, fritware, overglaze luster-painted. Courtesy of the Freer Gallery of Art, Smithsonian Institution, Washington, D.C.: Purchase Fund, F1973.14

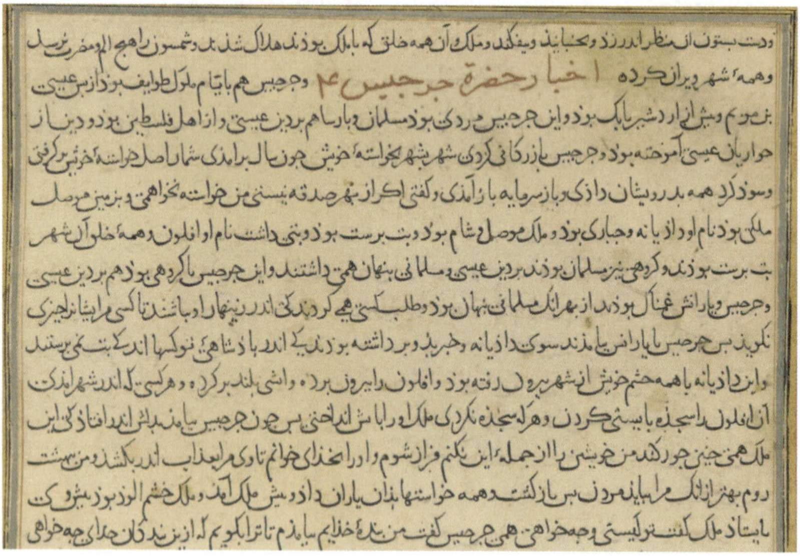

29b. Section heading for St. George, Balʿamī's *Tārīkhnāma*. Courtesy of the Freer Gallery of Art, Smithsonian Institution, Washington, D.C.: Purchase Fund, F1957.16, fol. 108b

30. *The Battle of Badr*, Balʿamī's *Tārīkhnāma*. Courtesy of the Freer Gallery of Art, Smithsonian Institution, Washington, D.C.: Purchase Fund, F1957.16, fol. 182a

BLACK AND WHITE FIGURES

1. Installation view. *The Legacy of Genghis Khan*, Los Angeles County Museum of Art, 2003 (exhibition designer Bernard Kester; photo © 2003 LACMA/Museum Associates)

2. Installation view. *The Legacy of Genghis Khan*, Los Angeles County Museum of Art, 2003 (exhibition designer Bernard Kester; photo © 2003 LACMA/ Museum Associates)

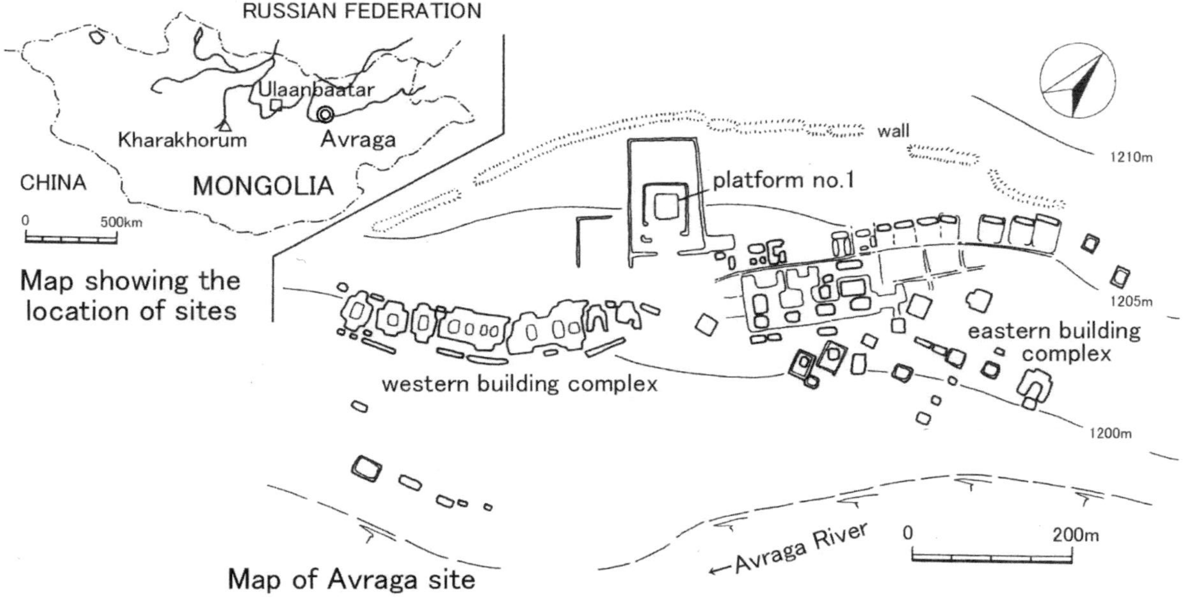

3. Topographical map of Avraga site (drawing by N. Shiraishi)

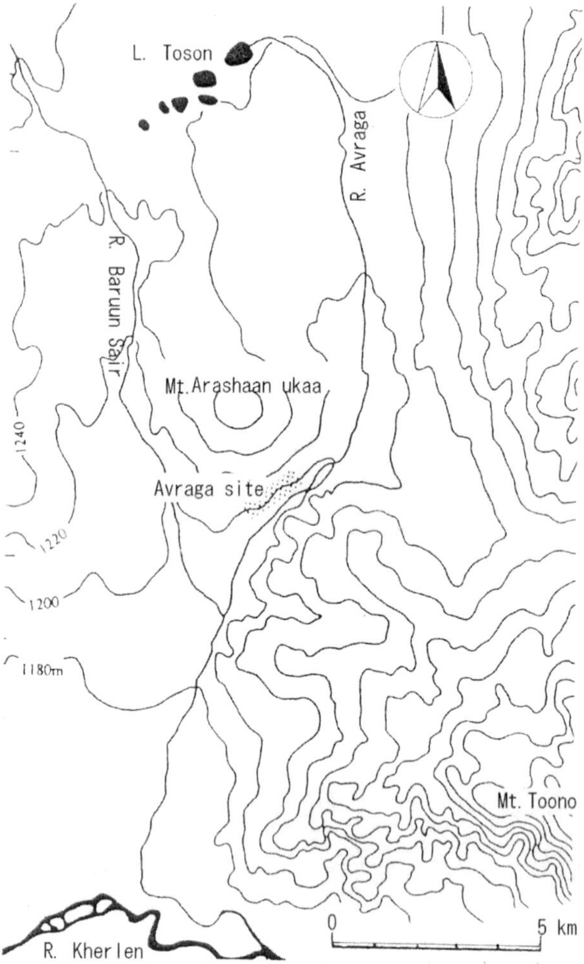

4. Location of Avraga site (drawing by N. Shiraishi)

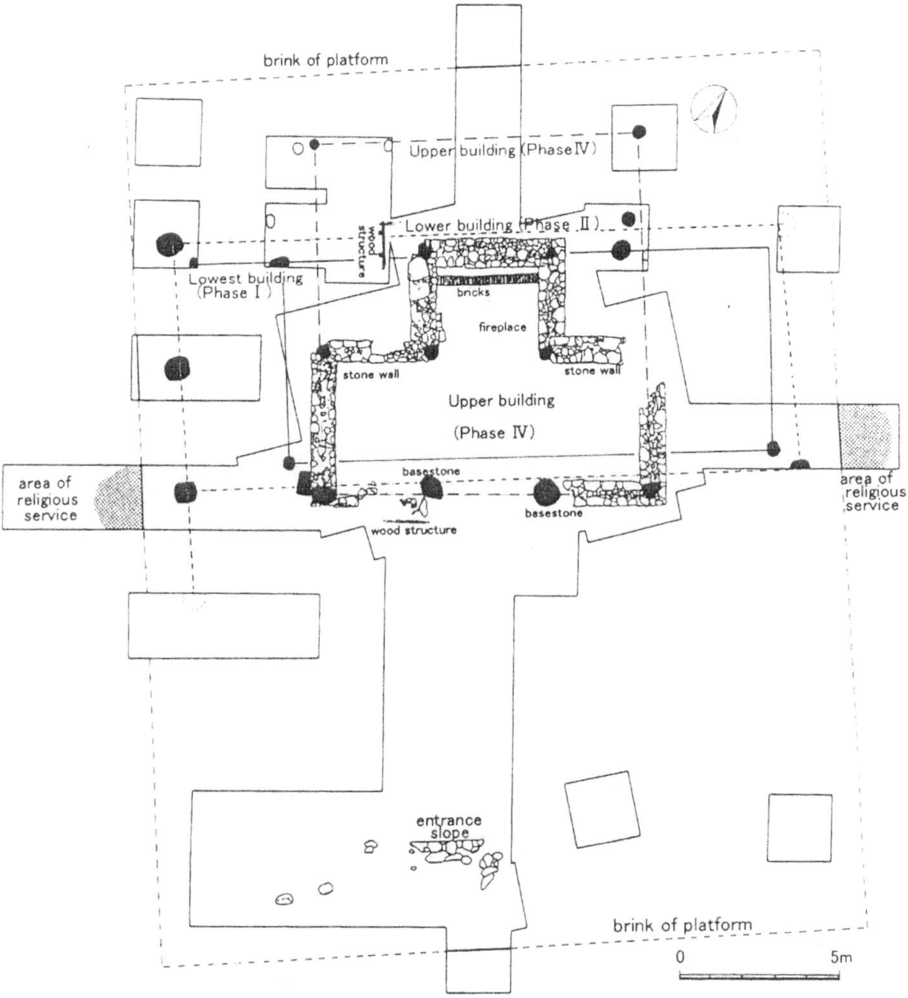

5. Column holes arrangement of building of Platform no. 1 (drawing by N. Shiraishi)

6. Aerial photograph of Platform no. 1 (photo N. Shiraishi)

7. Column hole of the tent of Genghis Khan (photo N. Shiraishi)

8. Fritware from Avraga (H. 7.6 cm) (photo N. Shiraishi)

9. Earthenware from Avraga (Diam. 8.5 cm) (photo N. Shiraishi)

10. *Ta ting t'ung pao* from Avraga (Diam. 2.5 cm) (photo N. Shiraishi)

11. Takht-i Sulayman, view from the southeast. The breach in the defense wall on the left is the Ilkhanid gate; the Sasanian gate lies in the narrow curtain next to the right. Beyond the lake is the tall ruin of the west *īwān* of the main palace. At the top left is the Zindan-i Sulayman (photo D. Huff)

12. Takht-i Sulayman, aerial view from the south (photo G. Gerster/D. Huff)

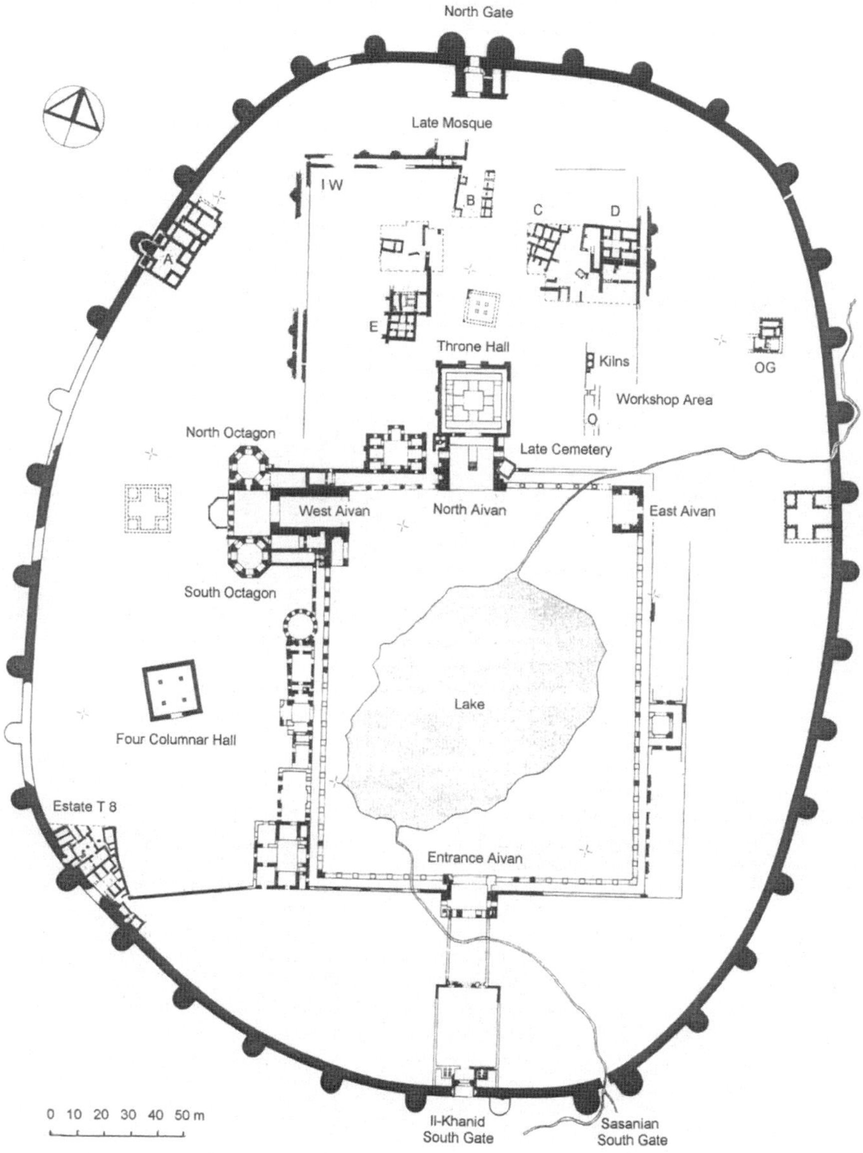

13. Takht-i Sulayman/Sughūrlūq, plan of the site in the Ilkhanid period. A: 'kiosk' A; B: bazaar; C: small houses; D: four-*īwān* ('potter's house'); E: four-*īwān* house (PC/PD); O: potter's refuse pit; IW: ruined inner wall of Sasanian sanctuary; OG: reused Sasanian house (drawing by D. Huff)

14. Takht-i Sulayman, Ilkhanid facade of the restored Sasanian west *īwān* (photo, expedition of the American Institute of Iranian Art and Archaeology, 1937)

15. Takht-i Sulayman, west *īwān* after collapse of the southern part of the facade (left) and ruin of the Ilkhanid north *īwān* with stairs to throne hall above a Sasanian fire temple (right) (photo D. Huff)

16. Takht-i Sulayman, glazed star-shaped wall tiles decorated with luster from the Ilkhanid palace. Staatliche Museen zu Berlin-Preußischer Kulturbesitz, Museum für Islamische Kunst, Berlin (photo D. Huff)

17. Takht-i Sulayman, hexagonal unglazed and underglaze-painted tile with phoenix from the Ilkhanid palace. Staatliche Museen zu Berlin-Preußischer Kulturbesitz, Museum für Islamische Kunst, Berlin (photo D. Huff)

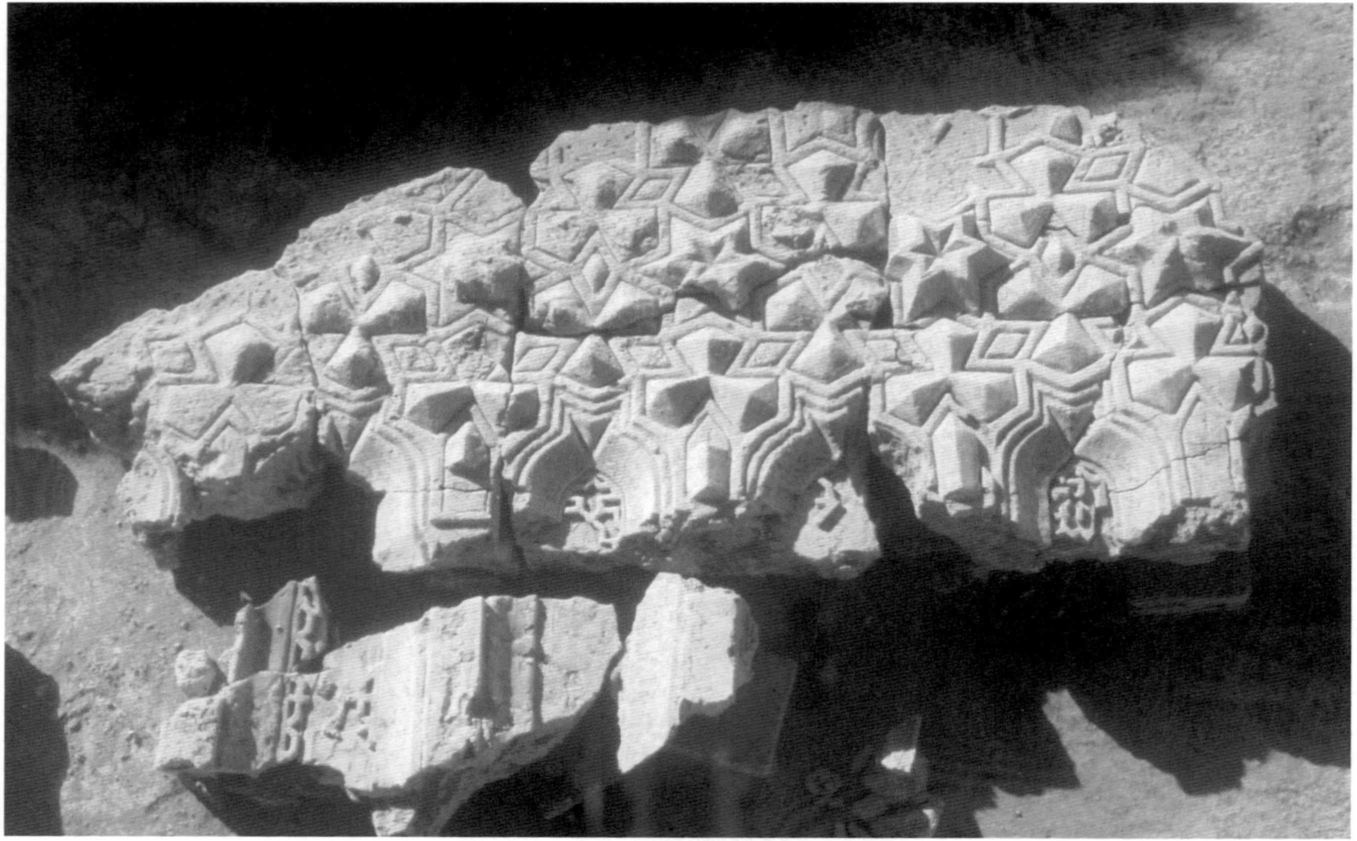

18. Takht-i Sulayman, stucco wall panel from the southern octagon of the Ilkhanid palace (reconstructed from fallen fragments by R. Naumann) (photo D. Huff)

19. Takht-i Sulayman, Ilkhanid buildings at the southwestern corner of the palace courtyard around the lake (photo D. Huff)

20. Takht-i Sulayman, impressions in the mortar bed that once anchored wall tiles in the northern octagon of the palace (photo D. Huff)

21. Takht-i Sulayman, decorated doorjamb of the four-column hall, west of the palace courtyard; in foreground, bronze cauldron from the pottery workshop area (room O) (photo D. Huff)

22. Takht-i Sulayman, four-*īwān* house D, late or post-Ilkhanid mosaic decoration, cut from reused wall tiles of the Ilkhanid phase (photo D. Huff)

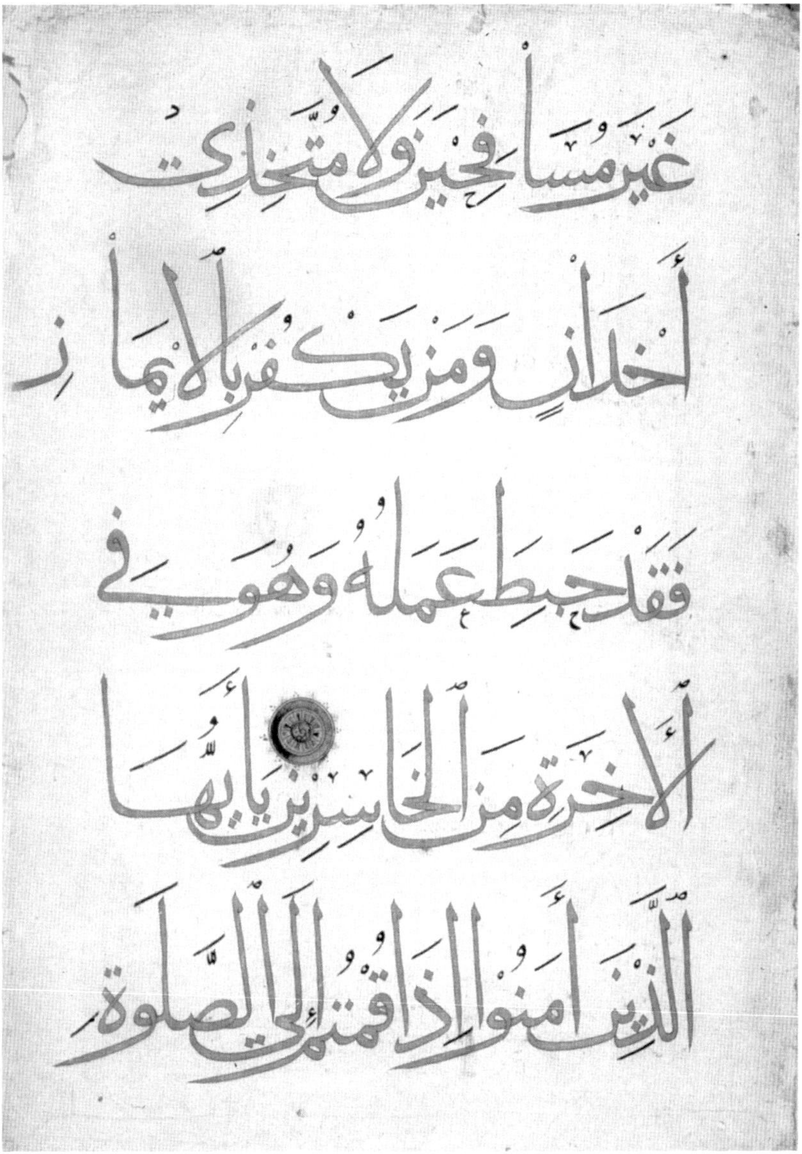

23. Folio from a manuscript of the Qurʾān copied for Sultan Öljeitü under the auspices of Rashīd al-Dīn and his co-vizier. Iraq, Mosul, 706–11/1306–12. Ink, colors, and gold on paper, with five lines of *muḥaqqaq* script to the page. The Trustees of the Chester Beatty Library, Dublin (Is. 1613.2, fol. 1v)

24. One leaf of double frontispiece, *Mukhtār al-ḥikam wa maḥāsin al-kalim* of Abū al-Wafā᾽ al-Mubashshir ibn Fātik, probably early 13th century. Topkapı Palace Museum Library, Istanbul (Ahmet III, 3206, fol. 1v)

25. One leaf of double frontispiece, *Mukhtār al-ḥikam wa maḥāsin al-kalim* of Abū al-Wafā' al-Mubashshir ibn Fātik, probably early 13th century. Topkapı Palace Museum Library, Istanbul (Ahmet III, 3206, fol. 2r)

26. One leaf of double finispiece, *Mukhtār al-ḥikam wa maḥāsin al-kalim* of Abū al-Wafā' al-Mubashshir ibn Fātik, probably early 13th century. Topkapı Palace Museum Library, Istanbul (Ahmet III, 3206, fol. 173v)

27. Detail from one leaf of double frontispiece, *Ta'rīkh-i jahān-gushāy* of 'Alā' al-Dīn 'Aṭā Malik Juwaynī, probably Iraq (Baghdad), dated 4 Dhū al-ḥijja 689/8 December 1290. Bibliothèque Nationale, Paris (suppl. persan 205, fol. 1v)

28. Detail from one leaf of double frontispiece, *Rasā'il Ikhwān al-Ṣafā'*, Baghdad, Shawwāl 686/November 1287. Süleymaniye Mosque Library, Istanbul (Esad Efendi 3638, fol. 3v). After Ettinghausen (1962), 101

29. Frontispiece, *Hayūlā ʿilāj al-ṭibb* of Dioscorides, dated 621/1224. Süleymaniye Mosque Library, Istanbul (Ayasofya 3703, fol. 2r)

30. Frontispiece, *Hayūlā ʿilāj al-ṭibb* of Dioscorides, 13th century. Süleymaniye Mosque Library, Istanbul (Ayasofya 3704, fol. 1v)

31. Frontispiece, *Kalīla wa Dimna* of Ibn al-Muqaffaʿ, 1220s. Bibliothèque Nationale, Paris (arabe 3465, fol. 34r)

32. Frontispiece, *Kitāb qawā'id al-aḥkām fī ma'rifat al-ḥalāl wa al-ḥarām* of al-Ḥillī, probably early 14th century. Private collection

33. Frontispiece, Shāhnāma of Firdawsī, attributed to Baghdad, c. 1300 or Shiraz, 1330s. Freer Gallery of Art, Smithsonian Institution, Washington, D.C. (Purchase F1929.25a-b, fol. 1a) [as reconstructed]

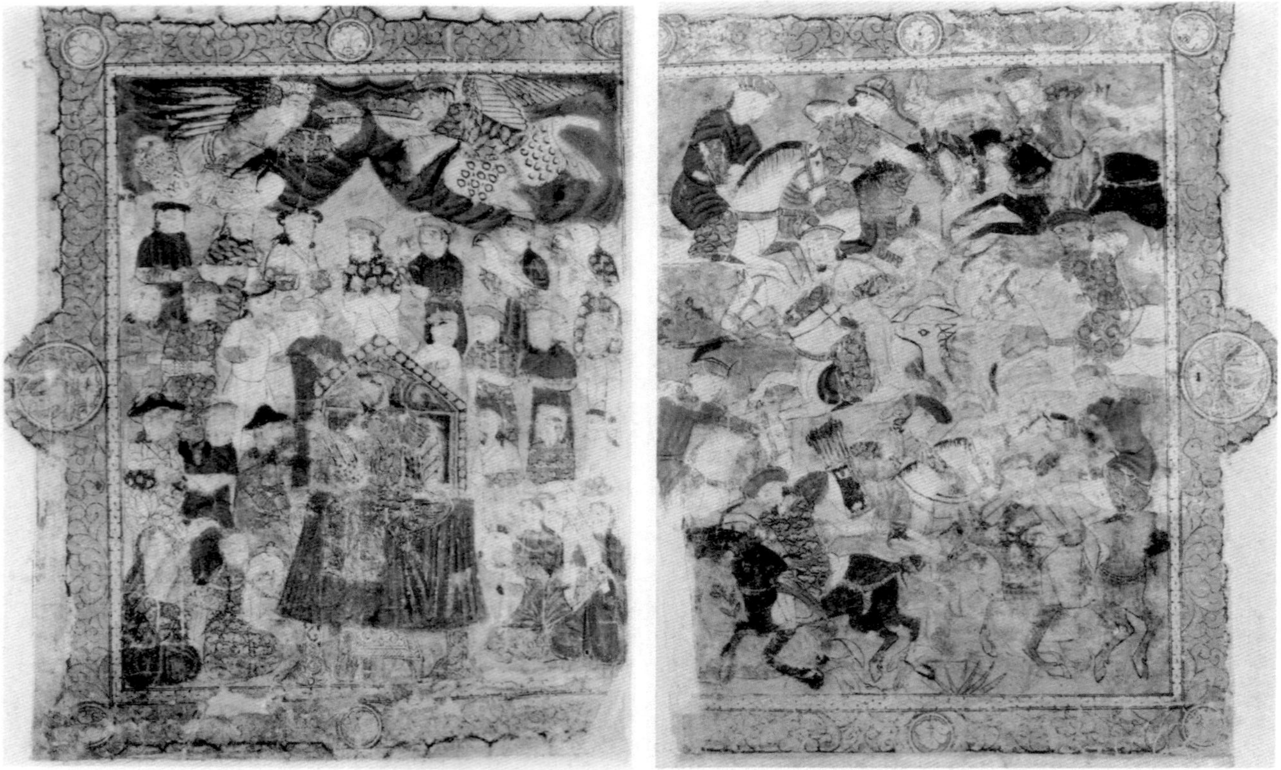

34. Frontispiece, Shāhnāma of Firdawsī, attributed to Shiraz, dated last day of Jumādā I 733/16 February 1333. National Library of Russia, St. Petersburg (Dorn 329, fols. 1b–2a) [reconstructed as fols. 4b–5a]. After Adamova and Giuzal'ian (1985), 42–43

35. Frontispiece, Mu'nis al-aḥrār fī daqā'iq al-ash'ār of Muḥammad ibn Badr al-Dīn Jājarmī, attributed to Isfahan, dated Ramaḍān 741/February–March 1341. Copyright Dar al-Athar al-Islamiyya, Kuwait National Museum, Kuwait City (LNS 9 MS, fols. 1b–2a)

36. Frontispiece, Stephens *Shāhnāma*, attributed to Shiraz, inscribed date of 753/1352–53. Arthur M. Sackler Gallery, Smithsonian Institution, Washington, D.C. (Lent by Mr. and Mrs. Farhad Ebrahimi, LTS1998.1.1.2 and 1.1.3, fols. 4b–5a) [as reconstructed]

37. Single-page *shamsa* frontispiece, *Āthār al-bilād* of Qazwīnī, 729/1329. By permission of The British Library, London (Or. 3623, fol. 2a)

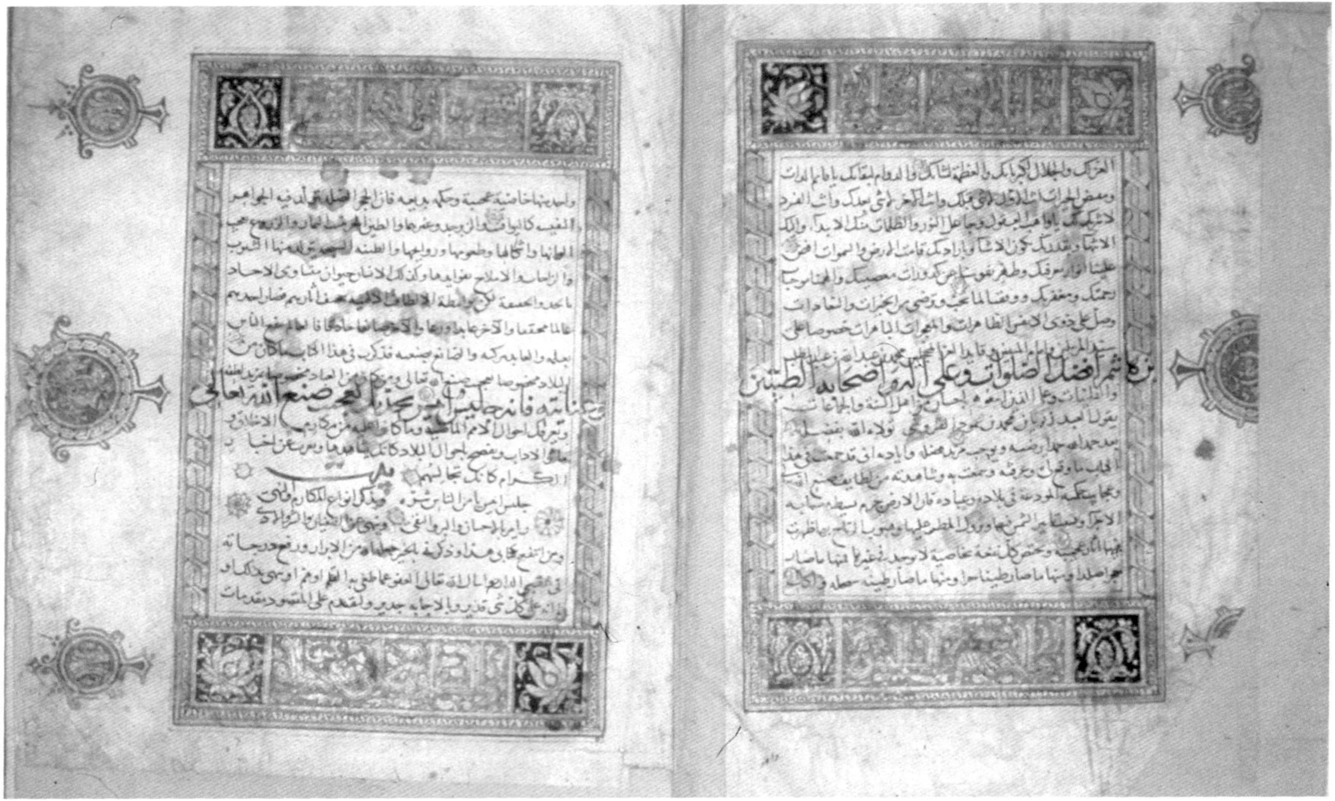

38. Text-frontispiece, *Āthār al-bilād* of Qazwīnī, 729/1329. By permission of The British Library, London (Or. 3623, fols. 2b–3a)

39. Single-page *shamsa* frontispiece, *Jawāmiʿ al-ḥikāyāt* of Muḥammad ʿAwfī, 732/1332. By permission of The British Library, London (Or. 2676, fol. 4a)

40. Text-frontispiece, *Ta'rīkh-i Ṭabarī*, 734/1334. By permission of The British Library, London (Add. 7622, fols. 1b–2a)

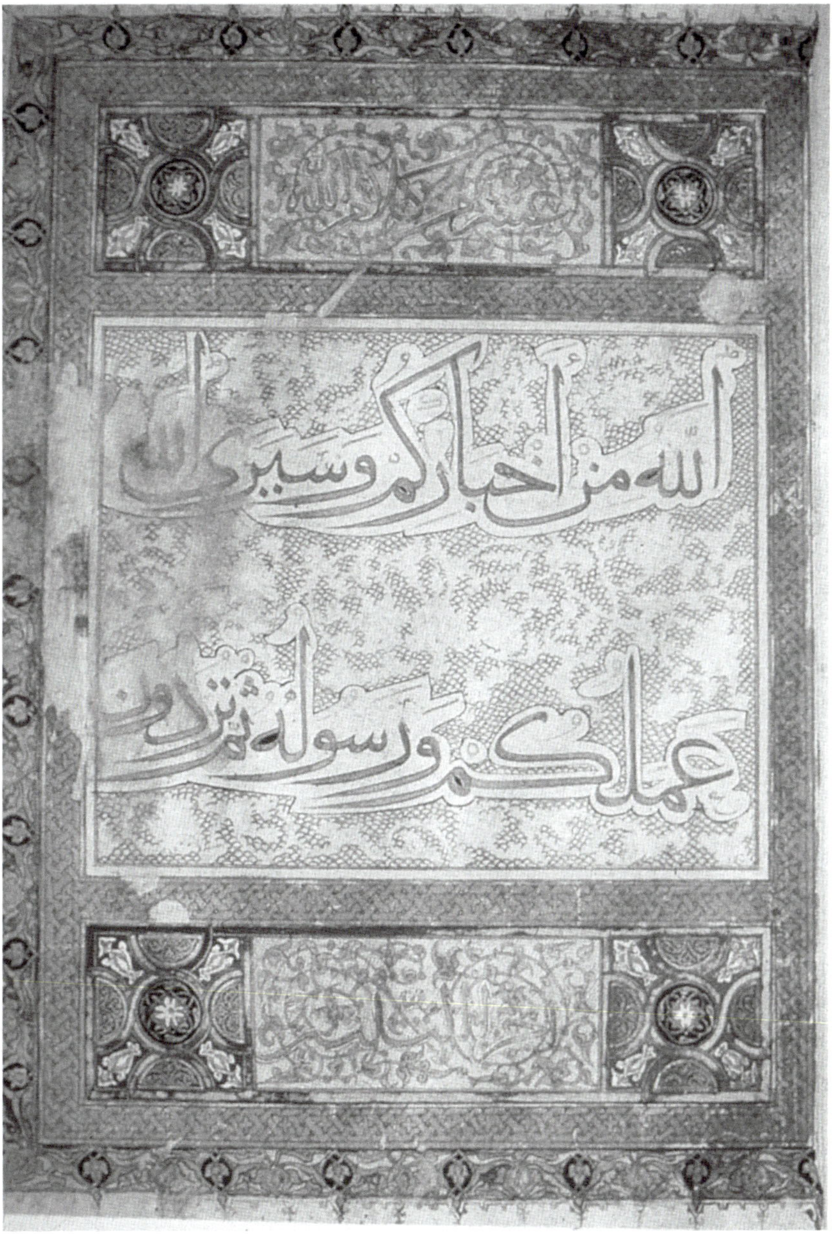

41. One half of a double-page frontispiece, Qurʾān, 745–46/1344–46, copied by Yaḥyā al-Jamālī al-Ṣūfī. Pars Museum, Shiraz (No. 456, fol. no. unknown)

42. Single-page frontispiece, Qur'ān, n.d., copied for Fārs Malik Khātūn. The Nasser D. Khalili Collection of Islamic Art, London (QUR182, fol. 26a)

43. *Kay Khusraw Attacks Gang Dizh*, Stephens *Shāhnāma*, attributed to Shiraz, inscribed date of 753/1352–53. Arthur M. Sackler Gallery, Smithsonian Institution, Washington, D.C. (Lent by Mr. and Mrs. Farhad Ebrahimi, LTS1998.1.1.2 and 1.1.3, fol. 191v) (photo E. Sims)

44. *Rustam Entertained by Kay Khusraw*, from the earliest Īnjū *Shāhnāma*, 731/1330–31. Istanbul, Topkapı Palace Museum Library (H. 1479, fol. 89v) (photo Ernst J. Grube)

45. Inlaid brass pouring vessel, Iran, early 14th century (?). Present whereabouts unknown (photo E. Sims)

46. *Rustam Shoots Isfandiyār with the Forked Arrow*, from the earliest Īnjū *Shāhnāma*, 731/1330–31. Istanbul, Topkapı Palace Museum Library (H. 1479, fol. 156v) (photo Ernst J. Grube)

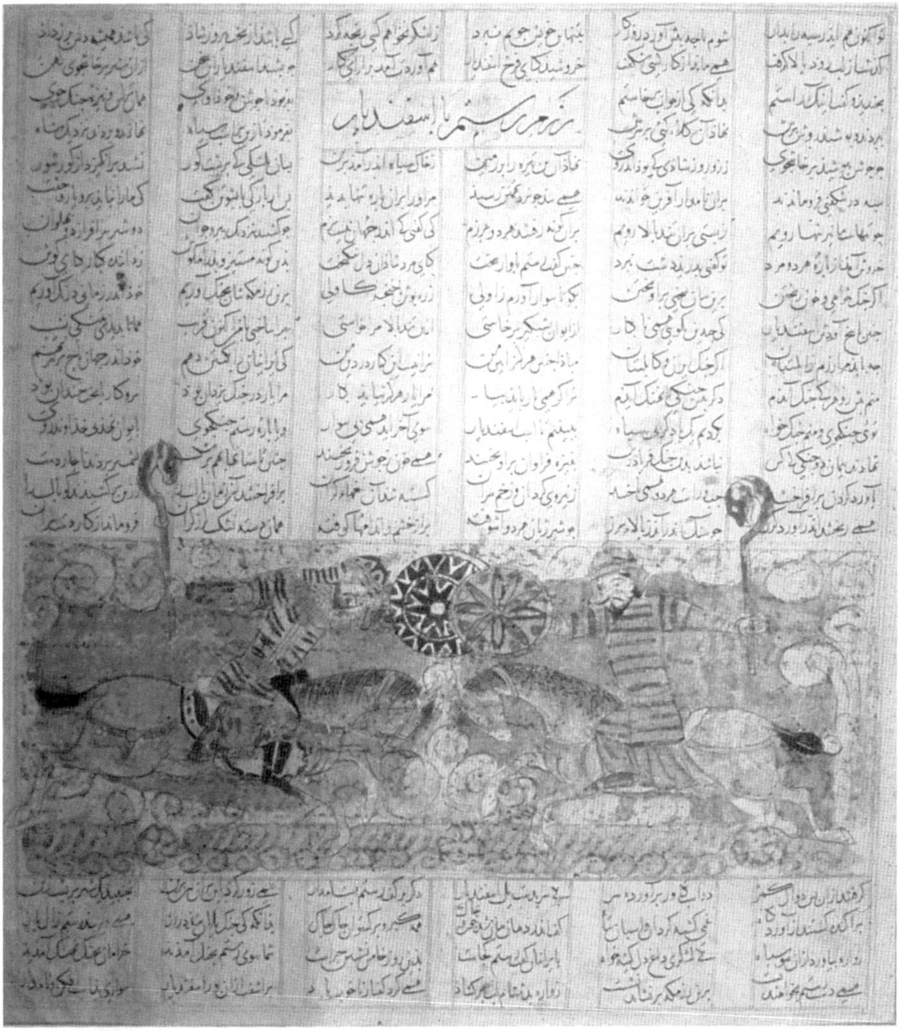

47. *Rustam and Isfandiyār Test Each Other*, fol. 191r from the dispersed *Shāhnāma*, Shiraz, 741/1341. Buffalo, Albright-Knox Gallery, 35.15.2 (photo Ernst J. Grube)

48. *Bahrām in the House of the Peasants*, from the Great Mongol *Shāhnāma*, Tabriz, probably between 1314 and 1336. Montreal, McGill University Library, on loan to the Montreal Museum of Fine Arts (photo Ernst J. Grube)

49. *Bahrām in the House of the Peasants*, fol. 237r from the dispersed *Shāhnāma*, Shiraz, 741/1341. Baltimore, Walters Art Museum, 10.677 (photo Ernst J. Grube)

50. Inscription 'signed' by the calligrapher Ḥaydar in the north īwān of the court of the Congregational Mosque at Natanz, 707/1307–8. Note how it must be read with one's back to the *qibla* (photo Blair and Bloom)

51. Detail of the plaster *miḥrāb* ‘signed’ by Ḥaydar in the winter prayer hall of the Congregational Mosque at Isfahan, dated Ṣafar 710/July 1310 (photo Blair and Bloom)

52. Detail of the plaster vaults of the outer gallery at Öljeitü's Mausoleum at Sultaniyya, completed in 713/1313–14 (photo Blair and Bloom)

53. Vault over the tomb of ʿAbd al-Ṣamad at Natanz, 707/1307–8 (photo Blair and Bloom)

54. Complete tile mosaic on interior of Öljeitü's mausoleum at Sultaniyya, completed in 713/1313–14 (photo E. Sims)

55. *Miḥrāb* 'signed' by Ḥasan b. ʿAlī at Mahallat-i Bala in 736/1335–36 (photo Blair and Bloom)

56. Medium-sized tomb cover in the shape of a *miḥrāb* from Veramin, dated 10 Muḥarram 705/3 August 1305. State Hermitage Museum, St. Petersburg (photo Blair and Bloom)

57. Luster tomb cover in the shape of a *miḥrāb* dated 710/1310. Calouste Gulbenkian Foundation, Lisbon. Courtesy of the Gulbenkian Foundation, Lisbon

58. Archbishop John, brother of King Het'um, in ordination scene, from a book of the Gospels, 1289. Erevan, Matenadaran (M197, fol. 341v) (photo Matenadaran)

59. Tunic of Archbishop John with a Chinese dragon, from a book of the Gospels, 1289. Erevan, Matenadaran (M197, fol. 341v, detail) (photo Matenadaran)

60. Silk textile with coiled dragons in roundels, Yüan Dynasty (1279–1368). Lampas weave (twill and twill), silk and gold thread. Cleveland Museum of Art, Edward I. Whittemore Fund (1995.73). After Komaroff and Carboni, eds. (2002), fig. 206

61. Frieze tile with dragon from Takht-i Sulayman, 1270s. Fritware, overglaze luster-painted. Victoria and Albert Museum, London (541.1900). After Komaroff and Carboni, eds. (2002), fig. 100

62. Star tile with phoenix, Takht-i Sulayman, 1270s. Fritware, overglaze painted (*lajvardina*). Arthur M. Sackler Gallery, Smithsonian Institution, Washington, D.C., gift of Osborne and Gratia Hauge (S1997.114). After Komaroff and Carboni, eds. (2002), fig. 101

63. Monumental dragon with *miḥrāb*, 1265–82. Viar, Iran. Courtesy of Marco Brambilla

64. *The False Prophet Baalam Riding an Uphill Path with a Crouching Lion*, from the Lectionary of Het'um II, 1286. Erevan, Matenadaran (M979, fol. 10, detail) (photo Matenadaran)

65. Incipit of St. Matthew with animals including two *qilin*, from a book of the Gospels, c. 1270s–80s. Erevan, Matenadaran (M7651, fol. 10). After Buschhausen and Buschhausen (1981), fig. 19

66. Silk mandala with imperial portraits, China, Yüan Dynasty (1271–1368). New York, Metropolitan Museum of Art, purchase, Lila Acheson Wallace Gift, (1992.54, detail). After Watt, J. C. Y. and Wardwell (1997), no. 25, 95–99

67. Portrait of Queen Keran and King Levon II with their children, from the Keran Gospels, Sis, 1272. Jerusalem, Armenian Patriarchate (J2563, fol. 380). After Der Nersessian and Agemian (1993), fig. 641

68. Bowl painted in luster, second half of 13th century. Ex-Rabenou Collection, present whereabouts unkown. After Pope and Ackerman, eds. (1938–39), pl. 774b

69. Sherd of a bowl, decorated in *lajvardina* technique (enamels and gilding over a blue glaze), 13th–14th century. Courtesy of British Museum, London (91.6-25.84)

70. Bowl, molded with a 'celadon' green glaze, 13th–14th century. Ex-Brangwyn Collection, Victoria and Albert Museum, London (C.10-1947). After Pope and Ackerman, eds. (1938–39), pl. 769a

71. Bowl, decorated with gray and white colored slips and black outlines (the 'Sultanabad' technique), 13th–14th century. Ex-Raphael Collection. After Pope and Ackerman, eds. (1938–39), pl. 779a

72. Bowl, underglaze-painted in the 'panel style,' 13th–14th century. Courtesy of Victoria and Albert Museum, London (C.8-1939)

73. Bowl, polychrome underglaze-painted in the 'wiry animal' style, 13th–14th century.
Los Angeles County Museum of Art (M.2002.1.227) (Museum Associates/LACMA, The Madina Collection of Islamic Art, gift of Camilla Chandler Frost; photo © 2005 Museum Associates/LACMA)

74. Bowl, polychrome underglaze-painted in the 'interlace' style, 13th–14th century.
Courtesy of Victoria and Albert Museum, London (978-1907)

75. Bowl, painted in black under a turquoise glaze in 'peacock-eye' style, 13th–14th century. Ex-Kelekian Collection, present whereabouts unknown. After Lane, A. (1947), pl. 93a.

76. Bowl, painted in black under a turquoise glaze in simplified version of the 'peacock eye' style, dated Rabīʿ I 676/August 1277. Courtesy of Victoria and Albert Museum, London (Circ. 350-1929)

77. Bowl with painting in blue and black and pierced rim, 13th–14th century. Ex-Kelekian Collection, present whereabouts unknown. After Pope and Ackerman, eds. (1938–39), pl. 781b

78. Large jar with molded decoration under a blue glaze, 13th–14th century. After Riefstahl (1922), frontis.

79. Bowl, black, blue, and white and gray slips (in 'Sultanabad' technique), 14th century, from Sarai Berke. State Hermitage Museum, St. Petersburg. After Lane, A. (1957), pl. 5a

80. Tile panel, *khānqāh* of Pīr-i Ḥusayn near Baku, 1284–86. State Hermitage Museum, St. Petersburg (IR-233-287). After Piotrovsky and Vrieze, eds. (1999), cat. no. 190

81. Tile panel, probably from the Imāmzāda Ja'far, Damghan, 1266–67. Museum für Islamische Kunst, Berlin

82. Cup, bronze inlaid with silver, 14th century. National Museum, Tehran

83. *Caravansaray*, north of Marand, 14th century, detail of kufic inscription on portal (photo B. O'Kane)

84. Mosque, Asnaq, dated 733/1333, detail of inscription over window (photo B. O'Kane)

85. Buqʿa-yi Khiḍr, Hamadan, 14th century, interior (photo B. O'Kane)

86. Frontispiece, Balʿamī's *Tārīkhnāma*. Freer Gallery of Art, Smithsonian Institution, Washington, D.C.: Purchase Fund, F1957.16, fol. 1a (drawing by T. Fitzherbert)

87. Frontispiece, Balʿamī's *Tārīkhnāma*. Freer Gallery of Art, Smithsonian Institution, Washington, D.C.: Purchase Fund, F1957.16, fol. 1a, detail of inscription (drawing by T. Fitzherbert)

88. Frontispiece, *Kitāb al-aghānī*, vol. 17. Courtesy of the Süleymaniye Mosque Library, Istanbul, Feyzullah Efendi 1566, fol. 1a

89. Stone inscription panel, Ince Minareli Medresesi, Konya. Courtesy of Scott Redford

90. Portal of Governor's House, Amadiya, N. Iraq. Courtesy of A. F. Kersting

91. *Ibrāhīm is Thrown into the Fire by Namrūd*, Balʿamī's *Tārīkhnāma*. Courtesy of the Freer Gallery of Art, Smithsonian Institution, Washington, D.C.: Purchase Fund, F1957.16, fol. 24b (detail)

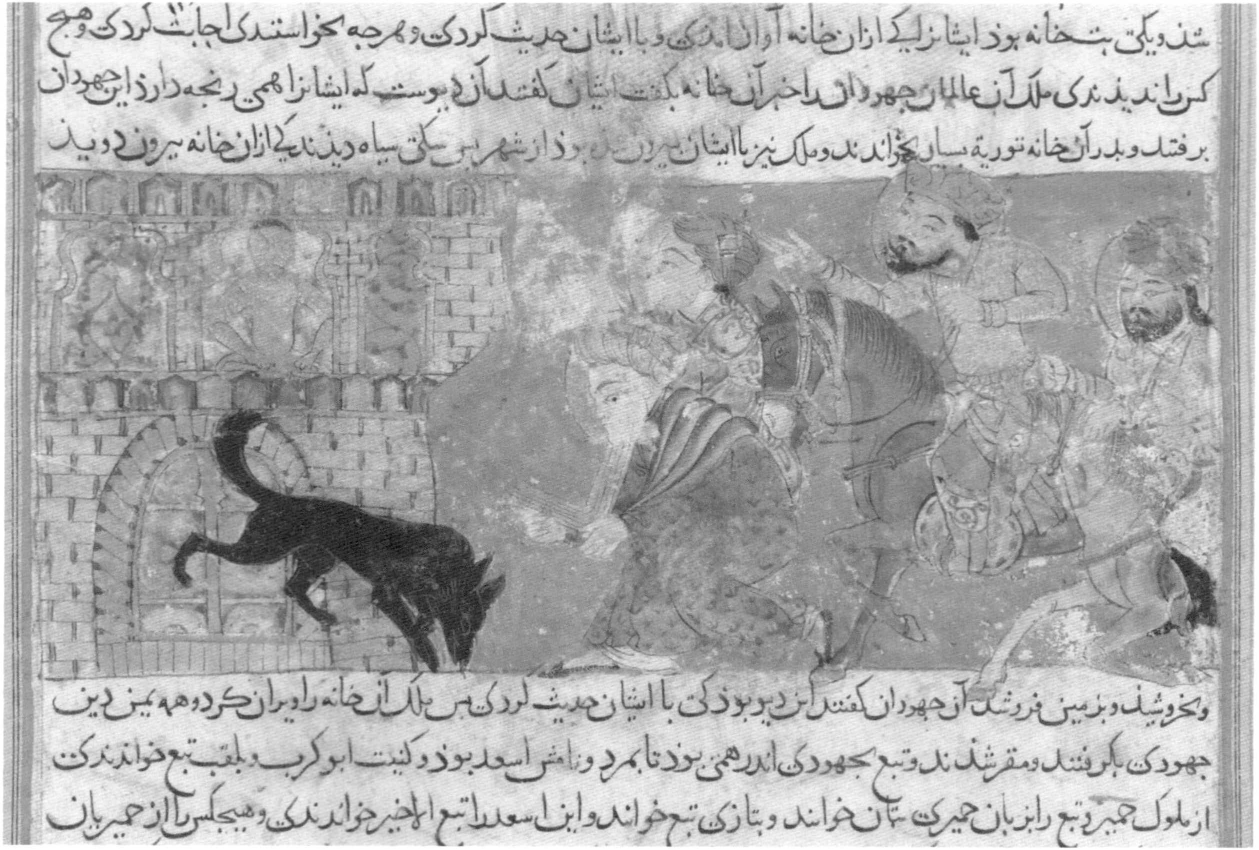

92. *Jewish Doctors Exorcise Evil Spirit from Heathen Temple*, Balʿamī's *Tārīkhnāma*.
Courtesy of the Freer Gallery of Art, Smithsonian Institution, Washington, D.C.: Purchase Fund, F1957.16, fol. 126a

93. *Cleansing of the Prophet's Heart by Three Divine Messengers*, Balʿamī's *Tārīkhnāma*.
Courtesy of the Freer Gallery of Art, Smithsonian Institution, Washington, D.C.: Purchase Fund, F1957.16, fol. 138a

94. Frontispiece, *Kitāb al-aghānī*, vol. 20. Courtesy of the David Collection, Copenhagen, Det kongelige Bibliotek, Cod. Arab. CLXVIII, fol. 1a

95. Stucco relief of royal hunter from Kubadabad Palace. Ince Minareli Medresesi, Konya (photo T. Fitzherbert)

96. *St. George and the Dragon*, wallpainting, datable to 1282–1304, Kırk Dam Altı Kilise, Belisirama, eastern Cappadocia. After Restle (1967), ill. 515

97. *St. George flanked by Thamar and the Emir and Consul Basil*, datable to 1282–1304, Kırk Dam Altı Kilise, Belisirama, eastern Cappadocia. After Restle (1967), ill. 516

98. *The Afshīn Ḥaydar Parleys with Bābak*, Balʿamī's *Tārīkhnāma*. Courtesy of the Freer Gallery of Art, Smithsonian Institution, Washington, D.C.: Purchase Fund, F1947.19, fol. 181b (detail)

99. *Dream of St. Simeon*, Syrian Orthodox lectionary, dated 1260 AD/1571 Seleucid era, from the Monastery of Mar Mataï near Mosul. Courtesy of the Biblioteca Apostolica Vaticana, Siriaco 559, fol. 48a

100. *Entry of Christ into Jerusalem*, Syrian Orthodox lectionary, dated 1260 AD/1571 Seleucid era, from the Monastery of Mar Mataï near Mosul. Courtesy of the Biblioteca Apostolica Vaticana, Siriaco 559, fol. 105a

101. Walls of Nineveh and Shrine of Nabī Yūnus, Mosul. Courtesy of A. F. Kersting

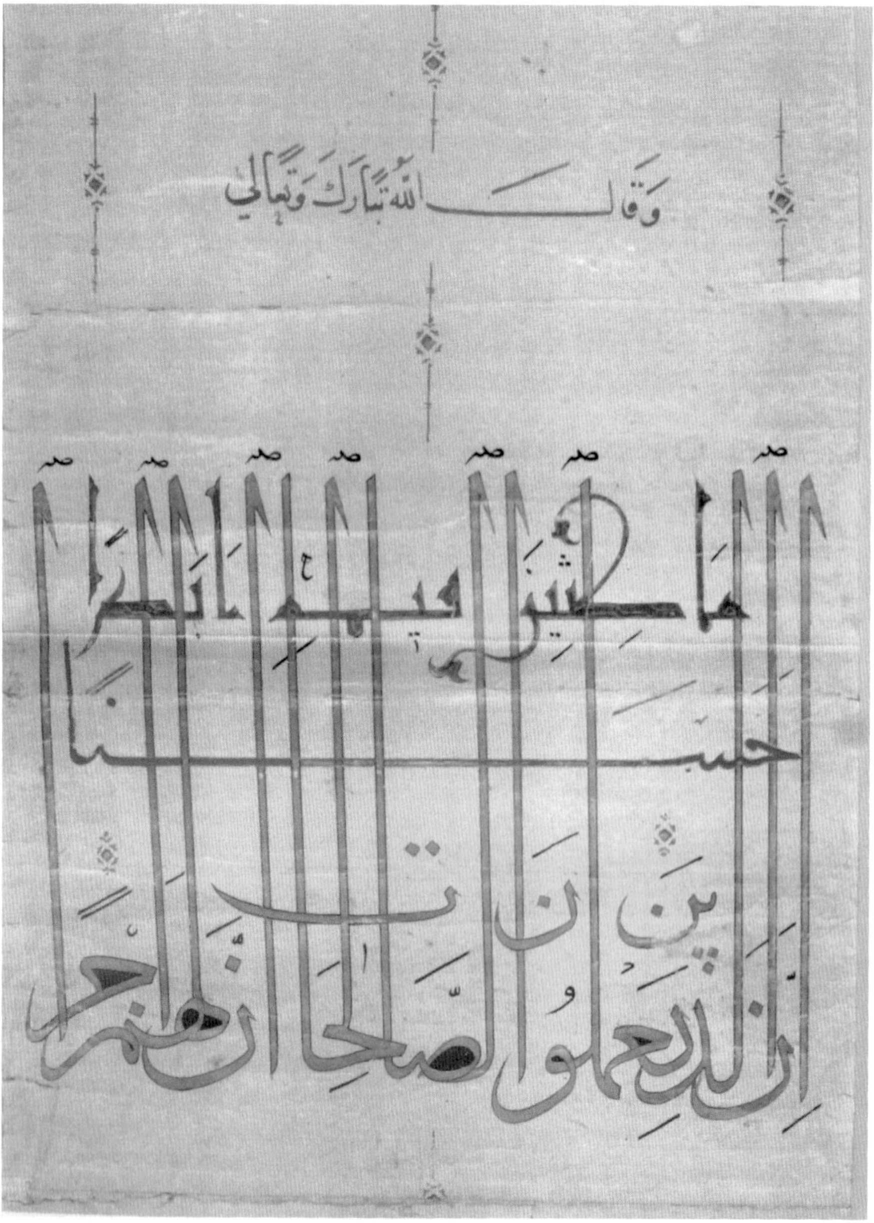

102. *Farmān* of Uzun Ḥasan, section 1. Private collection

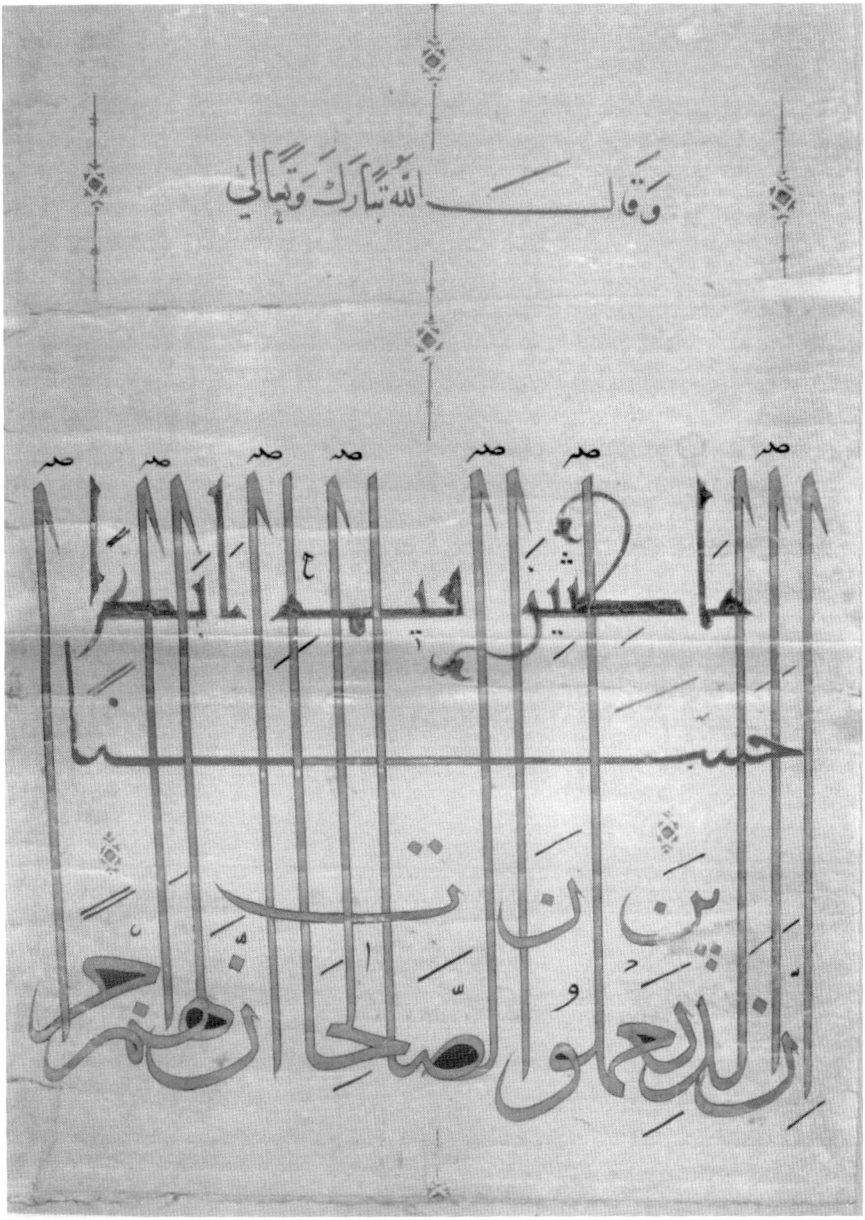

103. *Farmān* of Uzun Ḥasan, section 2. Private collection

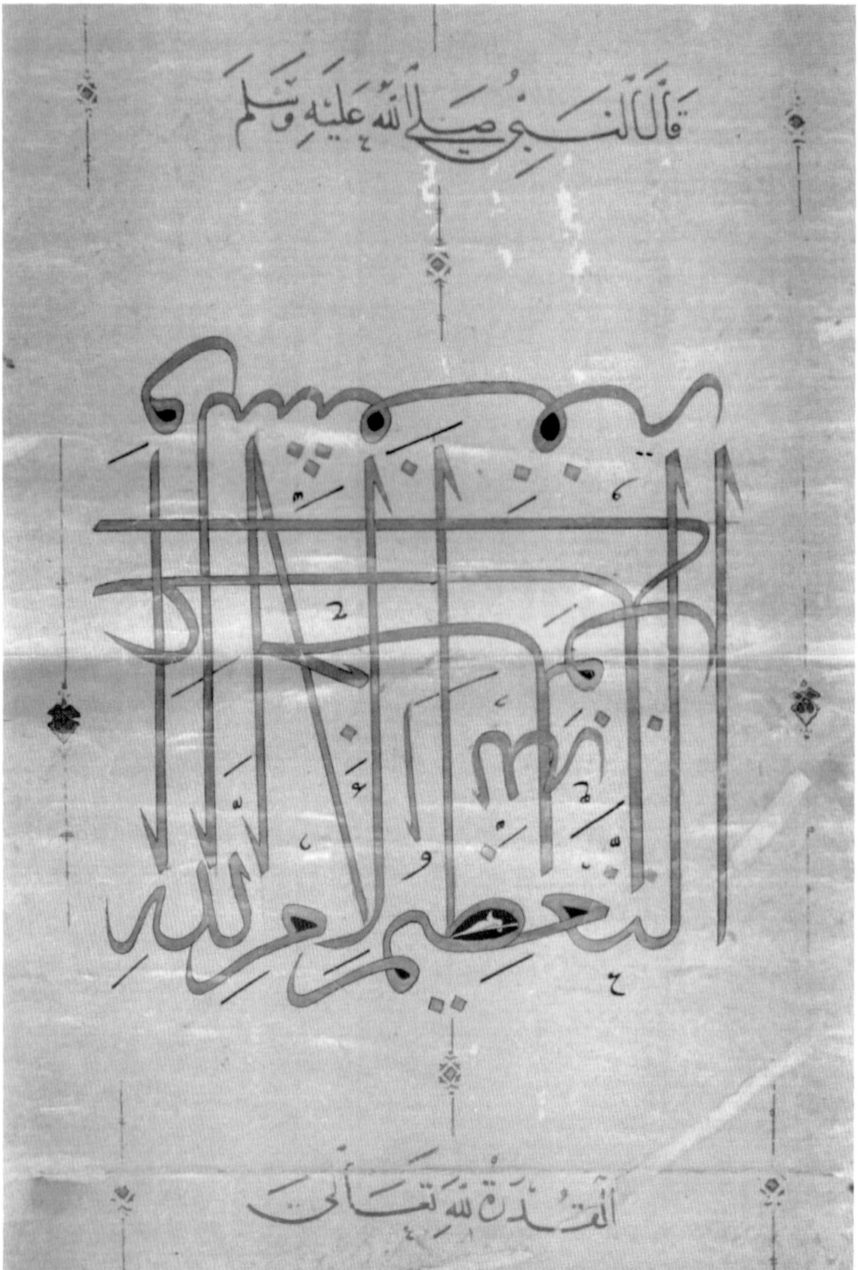

104. *Farmān* of Uzun Ḥasan, sections 3–4. Private collection

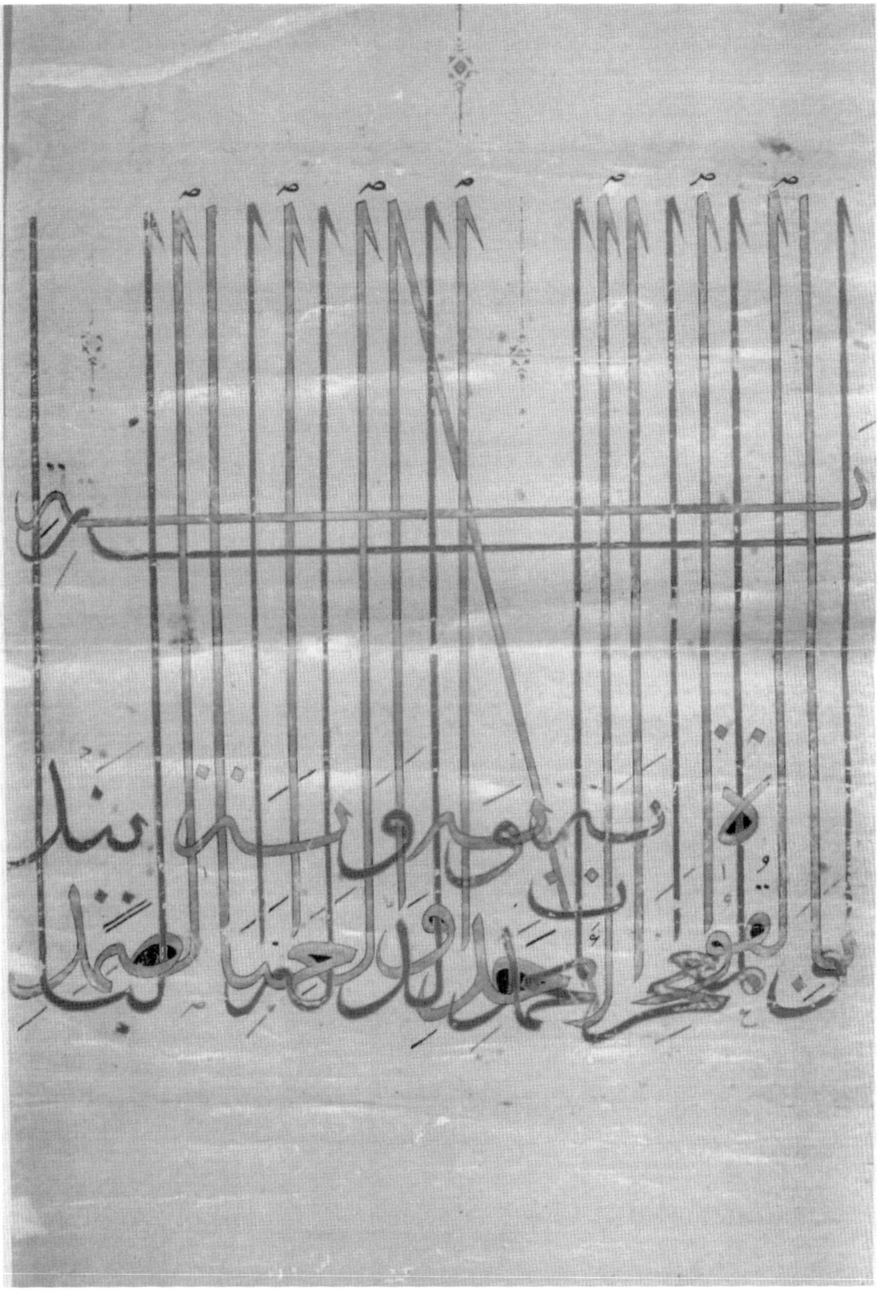

105. *Farmān* of Uzun Ḥasan, section 5. Private collection

106. *Farmān* of Uzun Ḥasan, section 6. Private collection

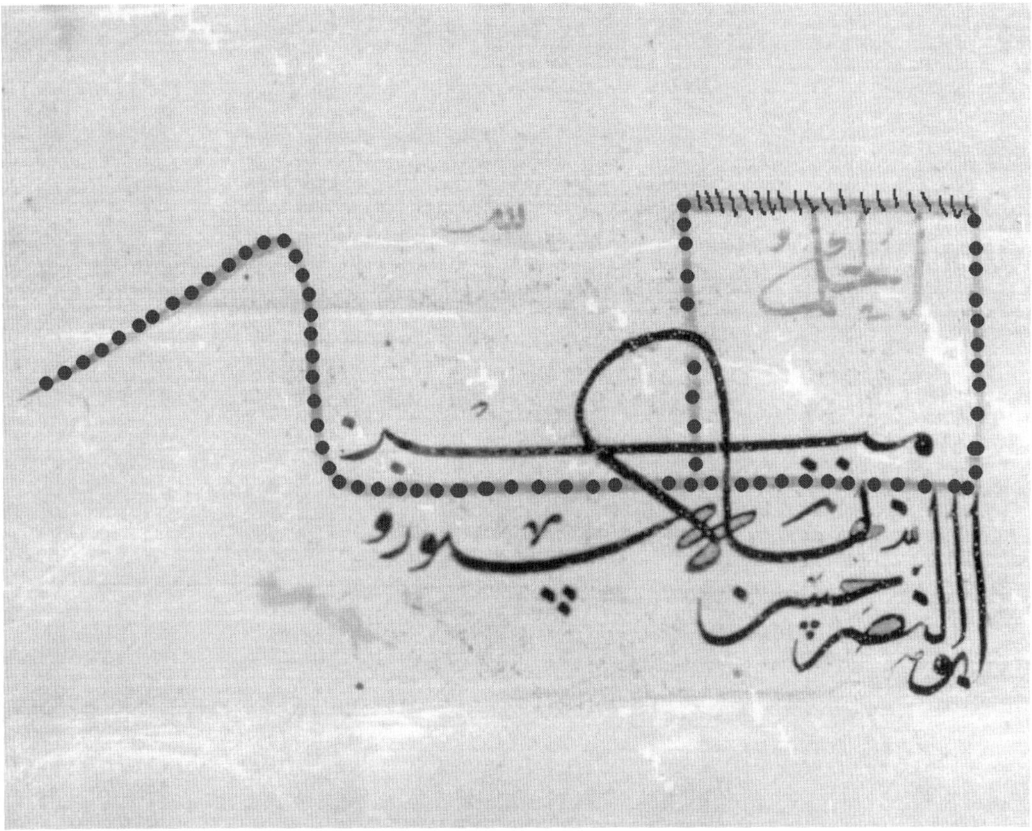

107. *Farmān* of Uzun Ḥasan, section 6 (detail). Private collection

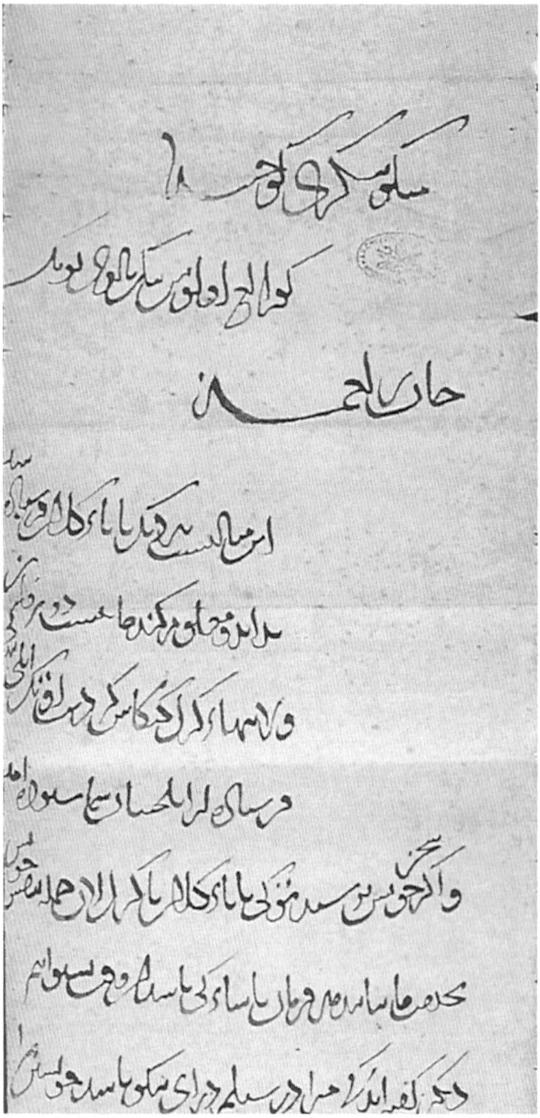

108. Letter of Güyüg Khan (detail). Vatican Archives (AA, Arm. I–XVIII, 1802 [3]). After Natalini et al., eds. (1991), 68

109. *Farmān* of Muḥammad b. ʿUthmān, detail. Ardabil Shrine documents. After Herrmann (1994), 299

110. *Farmān* of Geikhatu (detail). Art and History Trust, no. 9

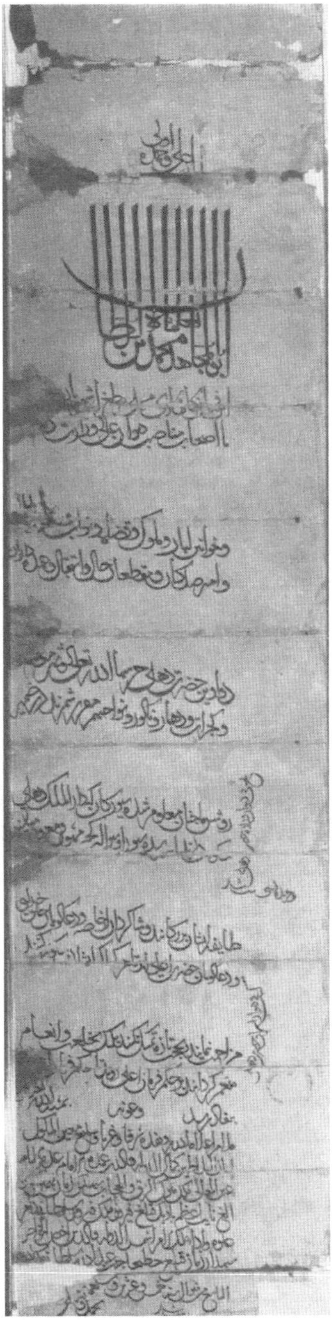

111. *Farmān* of Muḥammad b. Tughlugh (detail). Keir Collection, Surrey. After Robinson (1976), pl. 150

112. *Dīnār* issued in the name of Ṭughril by the Kākūyid Abū Manṣūr Farāmurz. Isfahan, 435/1043. Private collection

INDEX